Driving With Care

D1608708

DEDICATION

To our families and friends,

to the providers of impaired driving
education and therapy programs who gave consultation
and knowledge to the authors

and

to clients who complete this program.

Driving With Care:
Education and Treatment of the Impaired Driving Offender

Strategies for Responsible Living and Change

The Provider's Guide

Kenneth W. Wanberg
Center for Addictions Research and Evaluation, Denver, Colorado

Harvey B. Milkman
Metropolitan State College of Denver

David S. Timken
Timken & Associates

SAGE Publications
Thousand Oaks ▪ London ▪ New Delhi

Preparation and development of the *Driving With CARE Level I Education, Level II Education,* and *Level II Therapy Workbooks* and the *Provider's Guide* were supported by the Colorado Alcohol and Drug Abuse Division through the Persistent Drunk Driver Cash Fund under contract number OE IHM NC 000000010, $10,000; OE IHM NC 010000010, $15,000; OE IHM NC 010000013, $25,000.

The copyright holders grant, and the State of Colorado, Alcohol and Drug Abuse Division reserves the rights to reproduce, publish, translate or otherwise use within the State of Colorado all or any of the copyrighted material contained in this publication.

Opinions are those of the authors or cited sources and do not necessarily reflect those of the Colorado Department of Human Services, Alcohol and Drug Abuse Division, State of Colorado.

For information:

Sage Publications, Inc.
2455 Teller Road
Thousand Oaks, California 91320
E-mail: order@sagepub.com

Sage Publications Ltd.
1 Oliver's Yard
55 City Road
London EC1Y 1SP
United Kingdom

Sage Publications India Pvt. Ltd.
B-42 Panchsheel Enclave
Post Box 4109
New Delhi 110017
India

Printed in the United States of America

Library of Congress Cataloging-in-Publication Data

Wanberg, Kenneth W.
Driving with Care: Education and treatment of the impaired driving offender — strategies for responsible living and change: The provider's guide/Kenneth W. Wanberg, Harvey B. Milkman, David S. Timken.
p. cm.
Includes bibiographical references and index.
ISBN 1-4129-0596-6 (pbk.)
1. Drunk driving. 2. Drugged driving. I. Milkman, Harvey B. II. Timken, David S. III. Title.
HE5620.D7W36 2005
364.6—dc22

2004019885

ISBN 1-4129-0596-6

Direct correspondence should be sent to:
The Center for Interdisciplinary Studies
899 Logan Street, Suite 207
Denver, CO 80203
303-830-8500
www.drivingwithcare.com

04 05 06 07 10 9 8 7 6 5 4 3 2 1

Kenneth W. Wanberg, Th.D., Ph.D., is a private practice psychologist and the Director of the Center for Addictions Research and Evaluation (CARE), Arvada, CO. Harvey Milkman, Ph.D., is Professor of Psychology at Metropolitan State College of Denver. David S. Timken, Ph.D., is a consultant to the Colorado Alcohol and Drug Abuse Division and Director of Timken and Associates, Boulder, CO.

Acquisitions Editor: Arthur Pomponio
Editorial Assistant: Veronica Novak
Graphic Design and Layout: Karyn Sader

ACKNOWLEDGEMENTS

THE AUTHORS HAVE drawn upon numerous resources, documents and publications in developing the *Participant's Workbooks* and the *Provider's Guide* for this work, *Driving With CARE: Education and Treatment of the Impaired Driving Offender.* A number of experts in the field were interviewed in order to receive input around what should be the content and process of effective intervention programs for impaired drivers. A formal questionnaire was sent to a large group of providers in the State of Colorado to solicit input as to what content should be included in driving while impaired (DWI) intervention programs and how these programs should be structured and delivered. They also provided input on what has worked best and what has not worked in the DWI education and treatment programs currently being delivered in the State of Colorado.

A three hour focus group was conducted comprised of providers representing over 50 agencies within the DWI delivery system in Colorado. The input and discussion of this group provided a valuable basis upon which to proceed in developing the education and treatment protocols of this work. Valuable input was also received from this project's advisory group.

A number of DWI education manuals and programs were reviewed, including several programs used by providers in the Colorado DWI delivery system. The program content, concepts and process described in these manuals were helpful in developing the current work. As well, the results of a review of the DWI research, theoretical and intervention literature provided a sound basis upon which to develop the Driving With CARE education and treatment platform and curriculum. The results of these reviews are presented in Section I of this Provider's Guide.

The clinical, research and academic experience of the authors provided a substantive basis for the development of the DWI education and treatment platform and curriculum. Kenneth Wanberg, Th.D., Ph.D., has 40 years experience in the evaluation, treatment and research of DWI offenders and alcohol and other drug use and abuse problems both within public and private agencies and in private practice. Harvey Milkman, Ph.D., has 30 years of experience in research, development and evaluation of DWI education programs. David Timken, Ph.D., has over 30 years of experience in research, development and evaluation of DWI education and treatment programs. He is considered one of the experts in the field of AOD impaired driving. The combined skills of the authors provided a substantial basis for the development of the content, skill practice and exercises of the treatment curriculum.

The authors are especially appreciative of the consultation and support of personnel from the Alcohol and Drug Abuse Division (ADAD) of the State of Colorado, and particularly the support and wise consultation received from Lance Musselman, the ADAD coordinator of this project. Karyn Sader is highly commended for her skill and artistry in the layout and design of the four books developed with this project.

TABLE OF CONTENTS

EXTENDED DWC THERAPY SESSIONS: REFLECTION AND REVIEW AND THE
THERAPY PROJECTS 347

LIST OF FIGURES

SECTIONS I AND II

SECTION III

LIST OF TABLES

SECTION I AND II

PREFACE

No man is an island entire of itself; any man's death diminishes me, because I am involved in mankind, and therefore never send to know for whom the bell tolls; it tolls for thee.

JOHN DONNE, 1572-1631

AS THE 20TH century dawned, medicine was confronted with a new type of malady. It was functional or psychologically based. The condition was called "neurosis." Freudian thinking and psychoanalysis defined both the cause and response to this new "illness." Freudian theory concluded that the basis of neurosis was the dominant conscience or superego that repressed freedom of expression and desires (Mowrer, 1963, p. 160).

The Freudian response to this new illness set the stage for a 100 years of psychotherapy that was self-oriented and directed at relieving the psychological pain of guilt, depression and anxiety. At the time, this was a therapy that people needed. It was a therapy that saw the "cure" as being free of the constraints and repression of a strong conscience and guilt - of the superego. But it did not provide us with the answer to the problem of moral responsibility towards others and the community and the problem of freedom of choice. Freudian theory was just as deterministic as were the voices of moral suasion, philosophy and theology of the past (Mowrer, 1963).

O. H. Mowrer observed that as the 19th century came to a close, Western society was left with two major dilemmas: the failure of the voices of moral suasion, philosophy and theology to provide us with a reasonable answer to the problem of guilt and moral responsibility and the issue of freedom of choice (1963, 1964). Freudian psychology gave us insight and a therapy that helped to address the problem of neurosis. What was lacking was a clear approach to responsibility towards and caring about others and the issue of freedom of choice. As Mowrer observed, "....to be 'free' in the sense of embracing the doctrine of....irresponsibility is not to be free at all, humanly speaking, but lost" (1963, p. 161).

Behaviorism was a response to the Freudian doctrine. It repudiated the idea that things internal, personal or subjective, had anything to do with the outcome of behavior. The stimulus-response model was all that was needed to explain behavior. Yet, behaviorism was just as deterministic as Freudian doctrine. Accountability and choice were removed. As Mowrer (1963) noted, behaviorism ended up "obliterating the whole notion of freedom, choice, responsibility by reducing behavior, absolutely and completely, to S-R connections and reflexes" (p. 163).

At the mid-point of the 20th century, psychotherapy and psychology were still left with the solution to the two major dilemmas:

▶ a need for a theory that was not deterministic, but one that could give the individual the freedom to choose right and wrong, to develop what we might call *moral freedom*; and

▶ a need to develop a therapeutic method that places the responsibility of behavior on conscious choice; and to challenge individuals to be responsible in their choices.

As a response to the determinism of psychoanalysis and behaviorism, new approaches began to emerge that clearly addressed the dilemma of freedom of choice - or that the disturbances in behavior were not determined by factors and conditions beyond individual choice.

Mowrer's work, *The New Group Therapy* (1964), provided us with some guidelines with respect to resolving the issue of moral freedom and responsibility. He saw some hope in existential psychology, particularly in its firm stand against the determinism of behaviorism and psychoanalysis. He noted the change in behavior theory as it moved away from the simplistic ideas of behaviorism, and began to give credence to the concept of choice and deciding as determinants of behavioral outcomes.

He also noted that the emphasis on the unconscious, even within the psychoanalytic school, was giving way to a focus on "ego psychology," "ego strength" and "ego weakness," and a renewed interest in the superego or conscience. He saw psychology moving towards a greater awareness of man being a social creature that needs to be connected, united and that "current therapeutic effort is in the direction of trying to help such individuals recover their sociality, relatedness, community, identity" (1963, p. 166).

Other schools emerged that began to provide some solutions to these issues. Humanistic approaches, and more specifically, the client-centered models of Rogers gave clear guidelines with respect to freedom of choice and self-responsibility. Within this framework, each individual has the capacity to make choices, and to make decisions about his or her own destiny.

The integration of cognitive approaches with behavioral therapy provided greater strides in rendering a model as to how individuals can be responsible for their own behavior. The cognitive behavioral paradigm that the individual can be in control of the thoughts that produce feelings and behavioral outcomes provided an even clearer resolution of moral freedom and the resolution of the guilt problem.

Yet, all of the new therapies developed within the humanistic, existential and cognitive-behavioral schools were still self-directed or self-focused. These therapies were primarily concerned with alleviating the pain of the client, whether this pain be depression, anxiety, disturbed thinking or substance abuse. The issues of sociality, relatedness and responsibility to others and the community were still to be addressed by mainstream psychotherapy.

The philosophical roots of mainstream psychotherapy are based on the world view of modernity which sees man as egocentric, puts the individual as supraordinate to social role obligations, and focuses on individualism, freedom and individual expression (O'Hara, 1997). This world view idealizes and codifies the individual and projects the individual outward. Thus, mainstream psychotherapy is essentially egocentric. O'Hara (1997) sees a need to move beyond the egocentric therapy of Western civilization to a sociocentric, more holistic framework. This is moving towards a connected consciousness and builds on the gains of egocentric psychology. Sociocentric therapy focuses on prosociality, relational awareness and moral responsibility to others and the community.

There was some clear movement in this direction in the last one-third of the 20th century as social systems theory and family therapy impacted on the helping-psychology movement. The effect of the "system" on the individual, relationship building and maintenance and interpersonal theory became important focuses. Success in marriage, in relationships and in the work place became strong focuses in psychology. The family and interpersonal movements introduced the element of responsibility towards others. Yet, boiled down, the ultimate focus of therapy was still on responsibility to the self, personal growth and change, and the mitigation of psychological pain. The new therapies that emerged to address the determinism of psychoanalysis and behaviorism remained egocentric and still did not fully address the issue of moral responsibility towards others, the community and society.

At the close of the 20th century, we were again faced with a another malady, one that became recognized in the last half of the 20th century, one that inundates human service treatment centers and clinics and the helping professions. It is an even more serious malady than that of neurosis since it has a profound effect on society and culture. It is called sociopathy or character pathology. Whereas a strong and restrictive superego and conscience and a repressed id may have been a valid explanation of psychopathology and an important focus in therapy in Freud's day and even during much of the 20th century, it failed to address an epidemic psychopathology - sociopathy. The focus on responsibility to the self, the mitigation of personal psychological pain, personal growth, unbounded self-expression in therapeutic approaches and treatment and in pop psychology may have been at the expense of ignoring the importance of moral development, character building and responsibility towards others and society. This may be what Paul Tillich meant by "the psychic disintegration of the masses" in modern times (from Mowrer, 1964).

In a lecture delivered at a theological seminary in the early 1960's, O. H. Mowrer pointed out that psychology and psychiatry failed to firmly address moral responsibility (Wanberg, 2004). In that lecture, Mowrer, somewhat explicitly, predicted that in the latter part of the 20th century we would see an increase in antisocial behaviors, criminal conduct and the violation of the rights of others including an increase in violence in American society.

Indeed, in the last quarter of the 20th Century, we saw prisons fill faster than we could build them. At the turn of the 21st century, close to two million Americans were incarcerated and almost 10 million juveniles and adults were under some kind of criminal justice supervision. Yet, the offender element represents only one component of the new psychopathology. Antisocial behavior, character pathology and violence became major and dominant character expressions and themes in movie and television productions. In the last 20 years of the 20th century, traffic accidents, mostly caused by carelessness and irresponsibility, resulted in an annual average of over 50,000 deaths, hundreds of thousands of injuries and billions of dollars in cost. This lack of moral responsibility can be found at all levels of society.

In the last decade of the 20th century, a large percent of the clients in mental health and addiction treatment centers were found to have characterological and antisocial problems. These problems are prominent features among mental health and substance abuse client populations, and in many treatment centers they are found in the majority of the treatment population. Leukefield and Tims (1992) stated: "...the criminal justice system is awash with drug users." The opposite is just as true. "The mental health and substance abuse treatment system is awash with offenders and clients with characterological and antisocial problems." We acknowledge this. But this is not the main issue.

The main issue is that we have not significantly developed our approaches to psychotherapy in order to address sociopathy. We continue using therapeutic interventions based on the old model of focusing mainly on individual growth and change, enhancing responsibility to the self and easing psychological pain. For a long time, we refused to even offer psychotherapeutic and mental health services to individuals who were labeled "antisocial."

During the 1970's up through the early 1990's, there was a resistance on the part of adolescent mental health treatment facilities to admit juvenile offenders. Often such requests were met with downright refusal even when a mental health problem was apparent with the offender (Wanberg, 2004). The stock response was, "he's antisocial." Up until the 1990s, psychiatry and psychology often judged individuals with antisocial personality problems or a history of criminal conduct as untreatable.

Even as late as 1999, treatment of the antisocial personality disorder was left out of a text that addressed the treatment of personality disorders (Sperry, 1999). In that work, it was concluded that antisocial personality disorders are not considered as treatable and are less commonly seen in outpatient settings (p. xvii).

Beck et al (2004) did include a chapter on the treatment of the antisocial personality disorders (ASPD) in their book *Cognitive Therapy of the Personality Disorders.* Acknowledging that therapists view this group of clients as "especially difficult," they clearly state that cognitive therapy of ASPD can "be conceptualized as improving moral and social behavior through enhancement of cognitive functioning" (p. 168). Such cognitive growth would involve "fostering a transition from concrete operations and self-determination towards more abstract thinking and interpersonal consideration. Moral functioning is regarded as a dimension within the broader context of epistemology, or ways of thinking and knowing" (p. 169).

Today, a large percent of clients in adolescent and adult mental health and substance abuse outpatient and inpatient programs have significant if not serious antisocial problems. In fact, juvenile offenders make up a large proportion of many of these treatment settings across America. But have the mental health and substance abuse treatment institutions risen to the challenge of delivering a sociocentric therapy of moral responsibility and caring towards others and the community?

We are beginning to acknowledge the importance of sociocentric therapies and bringing together the therapeutic and the correctional approaches. Our first work in this field, *Criminal Conduct and Substance Abuse Treatment: Strategies for Self-*

Improvement and Change, made this the key focus in developing an approach in treating the substance abusing offender (Wanberg & Milkman, 1998). In our review of the literature it was apparent that we are at the beginning stages of this effort.

Suffice it to say, if psychotherapy is to be effective in treating offenders, the therapeutic goal of helping clients resolve their psychological problems and pain must be integrated with the correctional goal of helping the client develop thinking and behaviors that demonstrate moral responsibility towards others and towards society. Even more important, if we are to effectively address the "new" psychopathology of sociopathy found in many clients who are not offenders, then we must shift the egocentric therapeutic paradigm to a sociocentric one that includes a psychology of caring and social responsibility towards others and the community.

A number of disciplines during the last half of the 20th century did acknowledge the importance of addressing moral and character development, going beyond responsibility to the self and the treatment of personal pain and problems, and focusing on responsible living and responsibility to society. Piaget's work on moral judgment in childhood (1932), Erikson's work on the developmental stages and integrity (1959, 1968, 1975), Kohlberg and Colby's work on moral development and judgement (Colby & Kohlberg, 1987; Kohlberg, 1964), Bandura's (1977a) work on social learning theory, Hare's work on psychopathy (1970, 1980), Ross and his colleagues' (Ross, Fabiano & Ross, 1986) work on reasoning and rehabilitation and Hoffman's (1984, 1987) studies on the relationship of empathy to prosocial behavior and moral judgement are but a few that should be acknowledged. As well, the emergence of community psychology during the 1960s addresses the importance of the individual's relationship to the community and the society at large.

Alan Wolfe (2001) noted that the 19th century was about gaining economic freedom and the 20th century was about gaining political freedom. He suggests that the 21st century will be about deciding what is moral and what is not moral - or gaining moral freedom. Choosing to live unbounded by moral rules is not a viable option. The higher consciousness of the 21st century will enable us to live with a clear sense of responsibility, not only to oneself, but to others and the community. Wolfe concludes from his interviews that "Americans make a clear distinction between moral choice and unboundedness. The former, they usually insist, is something worth having. The latter, most of them feel, is something worth avoiding" (p. 51).

The underlying assumption of this *Provider's Guide* and the three *Participant Workbooks* is that effective intervention and prevention of alcohol or other drug (AOD) impaired driving must include an education and therapeutic model that is sociocentric and centered around responsibility to others and the community. Our current work is premised on the concept that it is essential that we go beyond the more traditional egocentric therapeutic approaches of self-caring and responsibility to the self and make caring about and responsibility to the community and society of equal importance.

There is no other area as important in doing this as in the education and treatment of the impaired driving offender. *Driving With Care* is our metaphor for responsibility towards others. CAREFUL driving demonstrates our sense of caring for other people and for our community. It is a prima facia demonstration of responsible living. We hope to provide the participant with strategies that will prevent problematic AOD use and subsequently prevent impaired driving. However, as conveyed by our subtitle, *Strategies for Responsible Living,* we feel that the education and therapy the client receives in these programs will enhance responsible living in many other facets of life.

INTRODUCTION: CORE STRATEGIES AND ASSUMPTIONS

OVERVIEW

THE EDUCATION and treatment of the driving while impaired offender (DWIO) has its roots in the effort of state and federal agencies during the 1970s to develop a viable answer to the serious health and safety threat of alcohol and other drug related impaired driving. Since that time, a vast corpus of research literature and education and treatment approaches have been developed to address the problem. This work, *Driving With Care: Education and Treatment of the Impaired Driving Offender,* and its three education and treatment protocols makes an effort to build on this large body of literature.

This work goes beyond the literature that specifically addresses the impaired driving problem. It builds on and utilizes the vast work and literature found in the general treatment of alcohol and other drug (AOD) problems. It also builds on and utilizes recent developments in the area of mental health, psychology, assessment and psychotherapy.

A review of this literature and the review of a large number of education and treatment programs for the impaired driving offender clearly indicated that there are some essential elements and strategies upon which the education and treatment programs for addressing the impaired driver must be built. This review also indicated some very important elements and strategies that were simply lacking in impaired driving education and treatment programs. From this review the authors developed a set of core strategies and assumptions utilized in developing the three *Driving With Care* service protocols and the provider guidelines for delivering these protocols. This introduction will summarize these essential elements and strategies. The organization of this *Provider's Guide* will then be outlined.

SERVICE DELIVERY STRATEGIES AND ASSUMPTIONS

This work is based on ten core strategies that are essential in delivering services to the impaired driving offender. In essence, these represent the basic assumptions of this work. These will be briefly reviewed. Subsequent chapters in this *Provider's Guide* will discuss many of these strategies in more detail.

1. Impaired offender intervention must focus on moral responsibility towards others and the community

Our first strategy and underlying assumption is that impaired driving offender treatment must focus on the client's moral responsibility to others and the community. This is best summed up in the statement: "When you drink, it is your business, when you drive and drink, it is everybody's business." The basic assumption of this program is that impaired driving is irresponsible behavior that jeopardizes the safety and welfare of others. It goes against society and in that sense, it is antisocial. Thus, strategies for building moral responsibility towards others and the community are important elements in DWIO education and treatment.

Moral responsibility represents a set of ethical and principled thoughts, attitudes and behaviors directed at respecting the rights of others, being accountable to laws and rules of our community and society, having positive regard for and caring about the welfare and safety of others, and contributing to the ongoing good of the community. In essence, it means engaging in responsible thinking and actions towards others and society.

As discussed in the Preface to this *Provider's Guide*, moral responsibility has not been a salient focus in traditional egocentric psychotherapeutic and AOD treatment. It is not only appropriate to integrate this into impaired driving education and treatment - it is essential.

2. Cognitive-behavioral approach as a basic platform for implementing learning and change

Another assumption and strategy of *Driving With Care: Education and Treatment of the Impaired Driving Offender* is that the concepts and methods of cognitive behavior therapy provide the basis for impaired driving intervention. One of the most significant advances in treating individuals with (AOD) use problems and/or criminal conduct has been in the field of cognitive-behavioral psychology. An underlying strategy of *Driving With Care* is to bring together effective cognitive-behavioral approaches for the education and treatment of individuals who have a history of impaired driving.

The term "cognitive behavioral therapy" or "cognitive behavioral treatment" (CBT) is used quite broadly to refer to approaches that focus on the interplay between thought, emotion and action in human functioning and in psychopathology (Freeman, Pretzer, Fleming & Simon, 1990). Although there are varying forms of CBT, most would agree with Hollen & Beck (1986) who define cognitive behavioral therapies as "those approaches that attempt to modify existing or anticipated disorders by virtue of altering cognitive processes" (p. 443).

This work has taken the basic principles and processes of cognitive-behavioral treatment and applied them to the education and treatment of persons convicted of impaired driving. This is an essential platform for the three service protocols. These protocols are built around the two traditional cognitive-behavioral (CB) approaches: cognitive or thought restructuring or helping clients learn the skills of changing thoughts so as to modify or change behavior; and social and interpersonal skill building. However, a third approach has been added to this work that utilizes the basic methods and concept of CBT: community responsibility skill building.

3. Relapse and recidivism prevention as core focuses in impaired driving education and treatment

The core content focus of *Driving With Care* is relapse and recidivism prevention. Our literature review indicated that relapse prevention was an integral part of most DWIO (driving while impaired offender) interventions (we will use the term intervention to refer to both DWIO education and treatment methods). However, this review indicated very few programs had a clear and distinct conceptual framework and strategy for addressing recidivism prevention - which is the most important objective of DWIO intervention.

The principles of relapse prevention as defined by Marlatt and Gordon (1985) and adapted by Wanberg and Milkman (1998) were applied to both relapse and recidivism prevention in the DWIO

education and treatment protocols in this work. Any effective DWIO intervention must have separate though linked models for addressing relapse and recidivism and relapse and recidivism prevention. These protocols need to include the concept of *zero tolerance-zero risk* as the preferred recidivism prevention goal and the concept that the goal of preventing legal recidivism (driving while legally impaired) is the expectation and goal of society.

4. Flexible AOD education and treatment outcome goals

Outcome goals for DWIO intervention must be broader than the traditional AOD treatment goal of abstinence. Research indicates that a large percent of DWIOs do not have diagnosable AOD problems, e.g., substance abuse or substance dependence, as defined by the *Diagnostic and Statistical Manual of Mental Disorders IV* (American Psychiatric Association, 1994). Thus, from a professional assessment perspective, let alone from the client's personal perspective, an AOD outcome goal of abstinence would not be appropriate for many DWIOs. An important strategy for DWIO intervention programs would be to help clients gain a clear perspective of the nature and level of their own AOD problems and then to help them make choices as to their AOD outcome goals. The protocols described in this *Provider's Guide* indicate two broad relapse prevention goals: preventing involvement in AOD problem outcome use and patterns; and total abstinence from AOD use.

5. Integrating the therapeutic and the correctional

Effective DWIO intervention must integrate the principles of therapeutic and correctional intervention and treatment models. Past impaired driving education and treatment programs have been based mainly on the former. The outcome research of DWIOs indicate that effective interventions are those that integrate sanctions with the education and treatment approaches. DWIO providers become partners with the judicial system in helping to administer the judicial sentence. Treatment providers must be willing to assume both the correction **and** therapeutic roles when working with impaired driving offenders.

6. Applying the three steps of therapeutic change

Effective DWIO intervention involves applying and utilizing the three steps and methods of therapeutic communication and change: 1) getting the client to openly share by developing a climate of rapport and trust; 2) provide the client feedback as to the areas that need change, utilizing both correctional and therapeutic feedback and confrontation; and 3) strengthen client change through the methods of therapeutic reinforcement.

Developing a therapeutic alliance provides the basis for the motivation to change. Gaining the client's cooperation and preventing program dropout are vital to successful outcomes. Clients with greater character problems and antisocial histories are most likely to drop out of treatment. Once a therapeutic alliance is forged, self regulating skills may then be learned through motivational counseling, therapeutic confrontation and reinforcement of responsible and positive behaviors.

7. DWIO intervention based on stages of change

This program is built on the assumption that change takes place in stages. Research has shown that people go though a series of stages as they make changes in their lives (Connors, Donovan & DiClemente, 2001; DiClemente, 2003; Prochaska and DiClemente, 1986, 1992; Prochaska, DiClemente and Norcross, 1992). This concept holds for the driving while impaired offender (DWIO). DWIO intervention strategies for achieving increased self-regulation for preventing AOD use problem outcomes and impaired driving must fit the individual's level of awareness, cognitive development and determination to change patterns of thoughts and behaviors. Effective treatment will use the right strategies at particular stages of each client's process of change.

The *Driving With Care* protocols are based on three stages of change (Wanberg & Milkman, 1998, 2005). The first is the **challenge to change.** Most clients experience this challenge through the judicial system when initially arrested and convicted of DWI (driving while impaired). The provider integrates this judicial and sanctioning process into the intervention process and continues to challenge clients. The second stage is **commitment to change.** Through both intervention and correctional approaches, clients come to commit themselves to change and to prevent recidivism. Finally, many clients go beyond the expectations of society and others and live up to their relapse and recidivism prevention goals because they want to do it for themselves and their community - they take **ownership of their change.**

8. DWIO program provider roles are broader than the role of the traditional therapist

The role and tasks of DWIO intervention providers go beyond the traditional AOD therapist. An underlying assumption of this program is that DWIO intervention specialists are educators, teachers, skill trainers, coaches and consultants rather than traditional treatment providers as narrowly defined by the disciplines of psychiatry, psychology, social work and substance abuse counseling.

9. Engaging significant others

Effective DWIO intervention will engage the client's significant others, the client's primary social unit and the viable community resources in helping clients to achieve their relapse and recidivism prevention goals. The support, understanding and the reinforcement of the family and significant others are powerful elements in implementing responsible living and change.

10. Screening and assessment are based on a convergent validation model and a multidimensional approach

Effective screening and assessment of the DWIO will use self-report and other report in order to converge on the best estimate of the client's willingness to self-disclose, past and current AOD use patterns and problems, past and current life-adjustment problems, and motivation and strengths for responsible living and change. Assessment is most effective when it is based on the idea that the origins, expressions and continuation of DWI conduct are multidimensional in nature (Wanberg & Horn, 1987, 2005). Individuals will vary according to how they fit the different causes and patterns of substance use and DWI conduct and different patterns of life-adjustment problems. Effective DWIO intervention is based on a comprehensive and accurate assessment of the problems, vulnerabilities and resiliency factors that exist for each client.

HOW THIS PROVIDER'S GUIDE IS ORGANIZED

BUILDING ON these assumptions, we have organized this *Guide* into three sections.

Section I

Section I provides a historical perspective and theoretical foundation of the issues relevant to the development of this program: *Driving With Care: Education and Treatment of the Impaired Driving Offender.* It provides an overview of the scope and nature of the problem of impaired driving, history of DWI (Driving While Impaired) legislation, causative factors, special populations of impaired drivers and intervention approaches that have been used in AOD abuse and DWIO intervention and treatment.

Because the cognitive-behavioral (CB) approach is a core component of DWC intervention strategies, the historical roots, the underlying principles and the key focuses of cognitive-behavioral (CB) approaches to education and change are presented. General perspectives on assessment with particular focus on DWIO evaluation are discussed. Understanding the impact of culture, ethnicity, life-span and life-experiences on DWIO intervention are also covered.

Section II

Section II of this *Provider's Guide* presents the conceptual framework and key elements of the education and treatment platform for *Driving With Care: Education and Treatment of the Impaired Driving Offender.* These include therapeutic alliance and motivational enhancement, relapse and recidivism prevention, stages of change, the integration of the correctional and therapeutic and the CB conceptual framework that underlay this work. The traits and characteristics of the effective SAO service delivery provider are also discussed.

Multifactorial assessment, conducted in an atmosphere of empathy and concern, provides a basis upon which clients can plan for change. The rationale, methods and approaches for screening clients into DWI education and treatment and for doing the in-depth differential assessment

of the client are provided. The in-depth assessment provides the basis upon which the client's Master Assessment Plan (MAP) is developed. The MAP is then used to develop the client's Individual Treatment Plan (ITP) which is used as a guide for the client's intervention and treatment.

Section II also outlines the operational procedures and methods for the DWI intervention protocols. It provides guidelines for group facilitation and recommended ground rules and guidelines to be used with clients. It also discusses issues pertaining to client admission, consent for treatment, counselor full disclosure and client confidentiality.

Section III

Section III provides the guidelines for delivering the two DWC education curriculums and the DWC treatment curriculum. The education protocols are broken into discrete lessons and the treatment protocol is separated into discrete sessions. *The Participant's Workbooks* provide the detailed content to be covered in each of the lessons and sessions. For each lesson or session, an overview and rationale, summary of the content and specific presentation guidelines are provided.

The education protocol represents the **challenge to change** component of *Driving With Care.* It involves the client in a reflective-contemplative process, building a working relationship with clients, helping clients develop the motivation to change and providing information on how people learn and change thinking and behavior. It helps clients develop self-awareness through self-disclosure and receiving feedback. It provides clients with important information about impaired driving and AOD use and abuse and challenges clients to look at their own AOD use and impaired driving patterns. It also gives them opportunity to discern what kind of AOD use and impaired driving problems they have.

There are two DWC education protocols. *DWC Level I Education* is a six lesson, 12 hour program that focuses on the most basic issues of impaired driving, AOD use and misuse, relapse and recidivism prevention and the cognitive and behavioral change processes that lead to self-control and positive outcomes. *DWC Level I Education* is designed for first time offenders who have lower levels of BAC at arrest and indicate no discernable evidence of AOD use problems.

DWC Level II Education is a 12 lesson, 24 hour program that explores in greater depth the issues related to AOD misuse, impaired driving, and the factors related to relapse and recidivism. Level II Education is designed for impaired driving offenders who have higher levels of BAC at arrest and who indicate at least some problems related to AOD use. *Level II Education* is a prerequisite to the DWC therapy program.

The treatment protocol, *DWC Level II Therapy,* represents the commitment to change and the ownership of change components of *Driving With Care.* This protocol involves clients in an active demonstration of implementing and practicing change. Clients undergo an in-depth assessment of their AOD use and impaired driving patterns and their life-situation problems. Targets for change are identified. A core treatment curriculum of 21 two-hour sessions focuses on AOD use problem outcomes, relapse and recidivism, skills in cognitive self-control, building social and relationship skills and developing community responsibility skills. Clients are confronted with their AOD use and impaired driving patterns. They are given specific methods and procedures to make life-changes so as to prevent relapse and recidivism.

The *Extended DWC Treatment* protocol goes beyond the core 21 session program and provides a substantive basis upon which clients can take ownership of their change. This protocol involves treatment experiences designed to reinforce and strengthen established changes. Depending on the length of stay in this protocol, clients are asked to complete a number of therapy projects that build on the themes and content of the core 21 session treatment program.

Most of the *Extended DWC Treatment* protocol is built around the in-depth assessment findings and the individualized treatment plan (ITP). It devotes more effort to addressing individual treatment needs using a number of provider resources. These may include involvement in therapy support groups and individual, family, relationship and marital counseling. These resources may also

include the use of urine and breath analyses in monitoring the client's goals of maintaining drug-free behavior. Pharmacologic treatments may also be available, depending on the resources of the service provider. These may include antabuse, blocking AOD effects (naltrexone), treating abstinence syndromes, and the use of adjunct pharmacologic treatment for anxiety, mood or thought disorders.

The DWC treatment protocol is identified as *DWC Therapy* in this *Provider's Guide. Level II Education* should be completed before starting *DWC Therapy.*

THE PARTICIPANT WORKBOOKS

A SEPARATE participant's workbook for each protocol provides detailed content of the lesson or session theme or topic. It includes in-session skill development exercises and homework assignments carefully designed to complement each lesson or session plan. The workbooks, which have Spanish translations, have been carefully reviewed to ensure cultural appropriateness, sensitivity and optimal responsibility. The *Participant's Workbooks* were written to accommodate a seventh to eighth grade reading level. Clients with reading levels below grade seven may need assistance in understanding some portions of the workbooks. Reading skills can be checked by asking the client to read and explain portions of the workbook text at the time the client is introduced to DWC.

DRIVING WHILE IMPAIRED - DWI

In this *Provider's Guide* and the education and treatment protocols, we will use the term DWI (Driving While Impaired) to refer to various descriptions used to label impaired driving conduct. These would include Driving While Ability Impaired (DWAI), Driving Under the Influence (DUI) and Operating While Impaired (OWI).

SECTION I
historical perspective and theoretical foundations

We are not moved by things, but the view which we take of them.
-Epictetus, First Century A.D.

The purpose of this section of the *Provider's Guide* is to provide an historical perspective and a theoretical foundation of *Driving With CARE: Education and Treatment of the Impaired Driving Offender - Strategies for Responsible Living and Change*. *Chapter 1* defines the scope of the problem, the factors that determine impaired driving and some societal and legal approaches that have been used to reduce the impact of driving while impaired (DWI) conduct on society. *Chapter 2* focuses on the history, evolution and impact of the enforcement of DWI legislation. *Chapter 3* outlines the causative and interactive factors of DWI conduct and *Chapter 4* describes the characteristics and patterns of driving while impaired offenders (DWIO). *Chapters 5 and 6* focus on two DWI special populations: adolescent impaired drivers and the repeat hard-core offenders. *Chapter 7* outlines some perspectives

regarding assessment and introduces the provider to the convergent validation model for screening and evaluating the DWIO. *Chapter 8* reviews the education and treatment approaches that have been used for DWIOs and some outcome results of these approaches. *Chapter 9* provides an historical perspective and overview of the cognitive-behavioral approach to treatment and change. *Chapter 10* discusses some of the cultural and diversity issues related to impaired driving and provider competency relating to and integrating these issues into the education and treatment of the DWIO. The material covered in Section I provides the foundation for developing *Driving With CARE:* education and treatment platform and curriculum protocols.

CHAPTER ONE: SCOPE OF THE PROBLEM

DEFINITION AND SCOPE OF THE PROBLEM

IMPAIRED DRIVING occurs when people operate a vehicle while having a blood-alcohol concentration of .01 or greater, or being under the influence of some other psychoactive substance. Measurable impairment of performance begins as low as .01 on some cognitive and psychomotor tasks (International Council on Alcohol, Drugs and Traffic Safety, 2001).

Each year about 3 million people are victims of alcohol related traffic accidents resulting in about 17,400 deaths or about 41 percent of the total annual traffic fatalities (National Highway Traffic Safety Administration, NHTSA, 2003a). Someone dies in an alcohol-related crash about every 33 minutes (NHTSA, 2003a). Fatal alcohol-related crashes are determined by whether a driver or non-occupant, such as a pedestrian, has a BAC equal to or greater than .01 in a police-reported traffic crash.

In 1998, drivers with BACs of greater than .09 were involved in about 999,000 alcohol-related accidents, resulting in 12,530 deaths and 719,000 injuries. Drivers with BACs of .08 - .09 were involved in around 17,000 alcohol-related crashes, resulting in 993 deaths and 32,000 injuries. Those drivers with BACs of less than .08 were involved in around 33,700 alcohol-related crashes, resulting in 2,412 deaths and 70,000 injuries (NHTSA, 1999a).

Of all fatal crashes, about 41% are related to alcohol. In 1998, these alcohol-related crashes cost more than $110 billion with over $40 billion in damages and $70 billion in quality of life costs. It is estimated that in 1998, those not involved in alcohol-related crashes paid $51 billion of this $110 billion. On the average, the cost of one alcohol-related death is 3.5 million dollars in damages and $2 million in quality of life costs. The average cost of one injured survivor is $99,000 in damages and $43,000 in quality of life costs. Of the $127 billion in auto insurance payments, 16% are for alcohol-related crashes (NHTSA, 2003a).

According to the National Highway Traffic Safety Administration (NHTSA, 2003a) there are about 1.5 million DWI citations annually. About one-third of these are repeat offenders (NHTSA, 2003a). In 1986 the Fatal Accident Reporting System (NHTSA, 1986)

estimated that since 1900 there had been more than 2.6 million automobile fatalities in the U.S. (our current estimate is over three million) and more than half were alcohol related.

Every year, one percent of drivers in the United States is arrested for drunk driving. This is down from two percent in the 1970's (Voas and Lacey, 1999). Seventy-eight percent of fatally injured drivers who were impaired by alcohol have a blood-alcohol concentration of .10 or greater. Young adults between the ages of 21 and 34 account for the highest rate (49.8 percent) of drunken-driving fatalities (Peters et al., 1998).

FACTORS INVOLVED IN IMPAIRED DRIVING

THERE ARE A NUMBER of variables that interact with impaired driving. These include the effect of alcohol and other drugs on driving ability, the effect of blood alcohol concentration, the nature and characteristics of the driving while impaired offender (DWIO), law enforcement techniques, and geographic density. We briefly review the impact of psychoactive substances on driving ability and the issue of BAC as it relates to DWI behavior. Characteristics and patterns of the DWIO population are presented in Chapter 3 of this Guide.

Impact of Alcohol and Other Drugs (AOD) on Driving Ability

The most obvious variable that provides us with an understanding of impaired driving is the impact of alcohol and other drugs on driving ability. These drugs are classified into two categories:

▶ system suppressors such as alcohol, sedatives (sleeping medicines, tranquilizers), opiates (morphine, codeine, heroin) and marijuana; and

▶ system enhancers such as cocaine, amphetamines or hallucinogens.

These drugs have both direct and indirect effects on the system. With respect to impaired driving, we usually focus on the direct effects of the drug. We are very aware that alcohol impairs judgment, impairs muscle coordination, impairs vision, reduces reaction time and causes drowsiness - all causing severe impact on driving ability.

However, we often fail to acknowledge that the indirect or withdrawal effects of alcohol also impact on driving ability - hyperactive, over-reactive, impaired vision, risk taking, stimulation, aggressive actions, etc. The curriculum portion of this work, *Driving With Care: The Education and Treatment of the Impaired Driving Offender,* emphasizes helping the DWIO understand the impact of all of these drugs on driving ability.

Blood Alcohol Concentration (BAC)

The basis for testing for intoxication is the work done by Widmark (1932) in Sweden who developed the relationship between amount of alcohol consumed and the elimination of blood alcohol concentration (BAC). This becomes the primary determinant of an impaired driving event and represents the amount of alcohol found in the body.

In the field of traffic safety, BAC is typically expressed as the percentage of alcohol in deciliters of blood. A 160-pound man, who consumes two 12-ounce bottles of beer, will have a BAC of .04 one hour after drinking on an empty stomach. A social drinker will show visible and debilitated characteristics of being intoxicated at a BAC of 0.10.

BAC increases with the absorption of alcohol into the gastrointestinal tract. First a small percent of alcohol is absorbed in the stomach. The rate of this absorption is dependent on the concentration of the alcohol. A weak drink will be absorbed slower (Goldstein, 1992). If there is food in the stomach, alcohol is digested with the food, which takes longer to digest than liquid. Food holds alcohol in the stomach and consequently a small amount of alcohol may be absorbed into the stomach walls. Most of the alcohol is absorbed in the intestines. Again, the rate of absorption depends on the amount of food being digested along with the alcohol. While in the intestines, it is absorbed into the gastrointestinal tract, enters the blood stream, and then arrives at the brain, thus causing changes in behavior.

From a legal standpoint, the time it takes for alcohol to leave the body is very important. Fisher, Simpson, and Kapur (1987) showed that it takes more time for alcohol to leave a woman's body than to leave a man's body. On average it takes 1 hour for a standard drink (12 oz of beer, 5 oz of wine, or 1.5 oz. of hard liquor) to leave the human body. Alcohol has a stronger effect on behavior in women because females have lower amounts of body water and a higher percent of body fat per body weight than men. The more the body fat, the longer the alcohol stays in the system and the slower it is catabolized. Menstruation is unrelated to changes in BAC (Lammers, Mainzer & Breteler, 1995).

An important content component of the curriculum portion of this work is on helping the DWIO understand the relationship of BAC to impaired driving. The simplest way to understand BAC is that it is the ratio of drops of pure alcohol to drops of blood at different levels of BAC (NHTSA, 1989; Harold Wells, Colorado Department of Health, 2003, personal communication).

▶ a BAC of .05 means that there are five drops of pure alcohol for 10,000 drops of blood;

▶ a BAC of .10 means that there are 10 drops of pure alcohol for every 10,000 drops of blood; and

▶ and a BAC of .20 means that there are 20 drops of pure alcohol for every 10,000 drops of blood.

Simple as this may be, BAC is a complex phenomenon and is related to many factors. The direct variables that determine BAC are:

▶ the person's weight;

▶ amount of alcohol consumed;

▶ hours over which the alcohol was consumed;

▶ time over which it takes for the body to reach a zero BAC; and

▶ gender.

Although there is some evidence that BAC at time of arrest is not a good predictor of recidivism, or returning to impaired driving behavior, it is the principal variable upon which impaired driving arrests and convictions are based.

APPROACHES TO REDUCING IMPACT OF DWI CONDUCT

THE STATISTICS PROVIDED in this chapter point out the enormous scope of the DWI behavior in American society. Table 1 provides a summary of these statistics. What are some of the answers to this problem?

Below are NHTSA (1999a) suggestions for reducing costs and increasing accountability for the relatively small population of AOD abusers who are directly responsible for this fiscal burden. In addition to fatalities, injuries and property damage, these costs also include treatment, incarceration and judicial processing.

▶ Enforcing the *Serving Intoxicated Patrons Law* would reduce alcohol-related fatalities by an estimated 11% and would save $30 for every licensed driver.

▶ Using *administrative license revocation* policies would reduce alcohol-related fatalities by 6.5% and would save $44,000 for every driver who encounters this policy of license revocation.

▶ Lowering the *legal BAC to .08* would reduce alcohol-related fatalities by eight percent and save $2 for every licensed driver.

▶ *Graduated Licensing* that restricts driving for new drivers would reduce alcohol-related fatalities by 5-8% and would save $600 per new driver.

▶ *Ignition Interlocks* would reduce alcohol-related fatalities by seven to 12 percent and would save $10,200 per vehicle equipped with this device.

▶ *Sobriety Checkpoints* would enforce drunk driving laws thereby reducing alcohol-related fatalities by 15% and would save $50,700 per checkpoint.

▶ *Primary Belt Laws* permit officers to stop and ticket drivers for not wearing safety belts and as a result would reduce alcohol-related fatalities by 10% and would save $2,000 per driver.

Another essential approach is that of preventing recidivism through programs of education and treatment. As noted above, about 35 percent of those convicted of impaired driving will become repeat offenders. As we will see later, the cost of repeat offenders with respect to accidents and fatalities is significant. Thus, education and treatment of the DWIO is a major component of dealing with the problem of impaired driving. The education and treatment protocols in this work are directed specifically at doing just this - preventing recidivism.

Is offering education and treatment to those who have been convicted of impaired driving enough? As we will see in Chapter 8, education and treatment are effective in preventing recidivism. Certainly, the recommendations of NHTSA outlined above can have significant impact on the problem of impaired driving in our society. Yet, the fact is that first offenders contribute to the major impact of impaired driving. If education and treatment are effective in preventing recidivism, then it would logically follow that offering at least DWI education protocols to all drivers who are high risk for engaging in impaired driving behavior would contribute in a major way to reducing the problem in our society.

One approach would be to simply require a short-course in preventing impaired driving to all licensed drivers - one similar to the six session, *Driving With CARE Level I (DWC)* educational protocol in this work. Another approach would be to identify those drivers who are at high risk for engaging in impaired driving and encourage them to take part in a *Driving with CARE* education protocol. Certainly, this recommendation has considerable problems of logistics, not the least of these being that of identifying those who fit this high-risk group. Yet, these kinds of proposals need to be explored, and if possible, implemented, if we are to have a long-range impact on the problem of impaired driving.

Statistical summary indicating scope of the DWI problem

DESCRIPTION OF STATISTIC	STATISTIC
Annual victims of alcohol related accidents	3,000,000
Number of annual traffic fatalities	42,800
Annual alcohol related traffic fatalities	17,400
An alcohol related traffic fatality occurs every	33 min.
Annual crashes involving BACs greater than .09	999,000
Annual injuries involving BACs greater than .09	719,000
Annual fatalities involving BACs greater than .09	12,530
Annual crashes involving BACs of .08 - .09	17,000
Annual injuries involving BACs of .08 - .09	32,000
Annual fatalities involving BACs of .08 - .09	993
Annual crashes involving BACs less than .08	33,700
Annual injuries involving BACs less than .08	70,000
Annual fatalities involving BACs less than .08	2,412
Annual cost of alcohol related crashes in dollars	110 billion
On average, cost of one alcohol related death	3.5 million
Average cost of one injured survivor in dollars	79,000
Number of annual DWI citations	1.5 million
Percent of annual citations that are repeats	35.0 %
Estimated number of alcohol related deaths in 20th century	1.5 million
Percent fatalities with BAC > than .10	78.0 %
Percent DWI fatalities in age range 21 - 34	49.8 %
A 160 lb male 1 hour after drinking 2 beers has a	.04 BAC
5 drops of pure alcohol in 10,000 drops of blood	.05 BAC
10 drops of pure alcohol in 10,000 drops of blood	.10 BAC
20 drops of pure alcohol in 10,000 drops of blood	.20 BAC

CHAPTER TWO: HISTORY OF DWI COUNTERMEASURES AND LEGISLATION

INITIAL STRATEGY: PUNISHMENT

DRUNK DRIVING was first seen as a problem in 1904, five years after the first alcohol-related automobile fatality in the United States. In 1910, the state of New York instituted the first legal sanctions against drunk drivers. California soon followed. In 1924, Connecticut arrested 254 drivers for drunk driving (Voas, 1982). In the 1930s, chemical tests were introduced to determine driver intoxication and in 1939, Indiana became the first state to require chemical tests. Maine, New York and Oregon soon followed. The stage was set for establishing the legal system for the social control of impaired driving behavior.

Up until the 1970s, the legal system and punishment was the primary effort to control the DWI problem premised on the idea that punishment would deter DWI conduct. This punishment response approach (Cavaiola & Wuth, 2002; Robbins, 1988), which began in the 1930s, did show that "significantly increasing the threat of punishment for drinking and driving did reduce alcohol-related crashes. However, over time, drinking-driving problems would return to previous levels" (Cavaiola & Wuth, 2002, p. 5). Thus, the legal system and its punishment codes were not achieving their expected outcomes with respect to preventing DWI behavior. One problem was that the laws established to intervene in DWI conduct did not adhere to the principles of effective threat or deterrence which are certainty, severity and swiftness of punishment (Ross, 1982).

Strengthened by, 1) the modification of the deterrence model (increasing speed and certainty of arrest, conviction and punishment), 2) the utilization of BAC as the basis of presumption of intoxication, and 3) the utilization of the Scandinavian Model of two levels of BAC and different levels of severity, legal means as a DWI countermeasure became more effective (Cavaiola & Wurth, 2002). These combinations and the laws related to them are the cornerstones of legal DWI intervention and prevention today.

REHABILITATION AND TREATMENT

ALTHOUGH SANCTIONING IS the key component and cornerstone of the judicial system for DWI prevention, rehabilitation, education and treatment were introduced as important components in the countermeasures effort in the 1970s. The foundation for the emergence of DWI education and treatment in the countermeasures movement occurred through the coalescing of the European and Scandinavian models, establishment of the relationship between BAC levels and car crashes (Borkenstein et al., 1964), and the awareness that there were different kinds of impaired drivers, many of whom were social drinkers, some were problem drinkers and some were alcoholic. Momentous to this movement was the establishment in the 1970s of the National Highway Safety Bureau, later designated as the National Highway Traffic Safety Administration (NHTSA) within the Department of Transportation.

Following the lead of the Scandinavian model and the Phoenix Program (Cavaiola & Wuth, 2002), NHTSA created 35 programs called Alcohol Safety Action Projects (ASAP). ASAP was a broad band program attempting to impact the community and the rehabilitation of the DWIO. At the community level, funding was enhanced for police, court and public safety programs to reduce alcohol-related crashes. Efforts were made to increase the effectiveness, certainty and swiftness of arrest and administration of offense penalties (Levy et al., 1977). Law enforcement training for detecting impaired driving and conducting field sobriety testing was enhanced. These tests gave the officer the ability to more accurately estimate the driver's BACs (Tharp, Burns & Moskowitz, 1981). Special police patrols were deployed on weekends with significant increases in DWI arrests. Most important, the ASAP programs focused on the education and treatment of the DWIO with greater attention given to the DWIO problem drinker (Nichols et al., 1978; Levy et al., 1977).

Although the ASAP programs were terminated after three years of federal funding, NHTSA concluded that the ASAP program had a positive effect on increasing the focus on and knowledge about the rehabilitation and treatment of the DWIO.

However, evaluation results were mixed. There was not a lot of evidence to indicate that the ASAP programs decrease DWI arrests or alcohol-related crashes (Jones & Joscelyn, 1978). Most evaluations did indicate that ASAP had a positive effect on first-time, but not repeat offenders, particularly those with more serious alcohol-related problems (Ellingstad and Springer, 1976).

What ASAP did was to bring screening, evaluation, education and treatment intervention within the purview of the adult judicial system. This was the beginning of the development of a partnership between the treatment community and the judicial system. The judicial system not only began mandating screening and assessment but also education and treatment. The assessment process was enhanced with two identifiable stages: Screening and in-depth. Formalized screening and in-depth assessment instruments began to emerge. Independent agencies began offering education and treatment for the court-referred client.

The major problem in this stage of countermeasures development was that the programs available for court-mandated referrals were based on traditional alcoholism and drug abuse treatment models. Many if not most DWIOs did not fit the traditional alcohol dependent mold. Most programs directed their treatment efforts towards this kind of client, and focused mainly on abstinence and relapse, and not on DWI recidivism, with the belief if you prevent relapse, you prevent recidivism. As well, these programs were used to treating "voluntary" patients, and not court mandated clients (Cavaiola & Wuth, 2002).

Because of this initial lack of sync between the judicial and treatment systems, there was a phase in DWIO countermeasure efforts where treatment programs functioned relatively independent of the judicial system. In this phase, the partnership between the treatment community and judicial system was, at best, loose. In the last decade of the 20th century, we began to see a strengthening of this partnership. It was clear that to enhance the DWI intervention and countermeasures effectiveness, there had to be a strong tie between the correctional-judicial system and the DWI education-treatment community. The current work, *Driving With Care: Education and Treatment of the Impaired*

Driving Offender, considers the integration of the judicial-correctional system and the treatment-rehabilitation system an essential component of an effective DWI countermeasures strategy. No longer can the DWI treatment community operate independently of the judicial countermeasures effort. Treatment programs must work with and integrate the correctional methods, goals and objectives and focus on the primary purpose of intervention: recidivism prevention. Likewise, it is essential that the judicial system work with objectives and methods of treatment providers. Within this framework, the education-treatment community becomes a partner with the judicial community in administering the judicial sentence of the DWIO.

DEFINING DWI: THE BAC LEVEL

Since the 1930s, when Widmark (1932) identified the relationship between alcohol consumption and BAC, there has emerged a large corpus of research that supports the relationship between level of BAC and the risk of involvement in highway crashes (Cavaiola & Wuth, 2002). For example, one study showed that the BAC of 80 percent of impaired drivers who were fatally injured had a BAC greater than .10 and that 64 percent had a BAC greater than .15 (Simpson & Mayhew, 1991).

Although the fatal crash is considered alcohol-related if the BAC is .01 or greater, most judicial jurisdictions base the legal definitions of impairment at .02 or higher. For drivers age 21 or older, all states use the BAC threshold range for impaired driving as .05 to .10. Some states have a two tier model for defining impaired driving. Colorado uses .05 to indicate Driving While Ability Impaired and .08 for Driving Under the Influence. Almost all states have the presumptive BAC standard of .08. All 50 states have zero-tolerance laws for drivers under age 21 with the impairment BAC of .02 or less.

The BAC is the standard in all states for determining legal sanctioning. Many states use the BAC as one of the primary factors in determining the level of education and treatment for individual DWIOs. For example, for first offenses, Colorado requires 24 hours of education if the BAC is .15 or greater and 12 hours of education if the BAC is less than .15. That model increases the number of treatment sessions and hours as the arrest BAC increases.

Even though the benchmark for determining sanctioning levels and level of intervention is the BAC, some studies have indicated that BAC levels do not necessarily predict alcoholism diagnosis or problems (Wieczorek, Miller, and Nochajski, 1992) or that BAC levels do not differentiate between first-time and repeat offenders (Cavaiola, Wolf, & Lavender, 1999). Wanberg and Timken (2005a), however, found a statistically significant positive correlation between level of BAC and: prior DWI arrests, prior DWI treatment and self-reported alcohol involvement.

Although all states define a BAC range of above .05 as legally impaired, the National Safety Council Committee on Alcohol and Drugs takes the position that DWI legislation should not assume that the driver is not impaired if the BAC is under .05. As noted in Chapter 1, measurable impairment of driving performance begins as low as .01 and epidemiological studies, including case control studies of traffic crashes, are consistent with laboratory evidence of the impairment effects of low-level BACs.

Over the years, states have adopted different legal terms to refer to impaired driving. These include driving while ability impaired, driving under the influence, operating while impaired, etc. In the literature, driving while impaired (DWI) has become the standard reference, and will be used in this text to refer to all levels of alcohol and other drug (AOD) impaired driving conduct.

PER SE LEGISLATION AND BAC

PER SE LAWS require courts to enforce a mandatory license revocation and make it a criminal offense to drive with a BAC at or above a specific level (Voas and Lacey, 1990). The verified level of BAC is the basis of guilt. For many years, a BAC of .10 was considered to be the per se standard. However, as of 2004, 48 of the 50 states have established .08 as the per se standard.

Most states with the .08 per se BAC level have measured significant declines in alcohol–related automobile fatalities. For example, Kansas recorded a drop from 40.2 percent in 1996 to 29.5 percent in 1997. Some policymakers argue that the law should be even more stringent and advocate for lowering the BAC level to .02 as is the case in South Carolina. Hingson, Hereen, and Winter (1996) have shown that "fatal crashes involving drivers with recorded prior DWI convictions" declined by 25 percent following passage of the Maine .05 DWI law, while the proportion rose in the rest of New England during the same year. Before the change, Maine had a .10 BAC law.

PRECEDENT CASE FOR CHEMICAL TESTING

AN IMPORTANT LEGAL test was needed to establish the authority to administer chemical tests. This precedence was established in the case of *Schmerber vs. California* in 1966. The Supreme Court decided that drivers are required to take chemical tests under limited circumstances (Voas and Lacey, 1990). The court found no violation of the 5th Amendment because there was no verbal, only physical, testimony. The court also found that there was no violation of the 4th Amendment (against unreasonable searches and seizures) because there was evidence to support probable cause that the driver had been intoxicated.

The following describes the scenario in the Legal case of *Schmerber vs. California.*

▶ A serious accident occurred. A police officer at the scene recognized the smell of alcohol on one of the drivers. The officer then proceeded to draw a blood sample from the man, which tested positive for alcohol. So the man was then convicted.

▶ Was taking the blood sample from the man against his 4th and 5th Amendment rights? The court ruled that "Physical evidence, since it is silent, does not incriminate a witness against himself." So his 5th Amendment rights were not infringed upon. The court also ruled that the objective inference of the police officer constituted a reasonable search (blood sample), so the evidence was valid.

The Schmerber case set directives for courts to follow regarding testing which include the following.

- Physical evidence (blood, breath, hair, and urine) taken directly from a witness does not come under protection against self-incrimination;

- Any medical test is a 4th Amendment search, subject to constitutional limitations.

With this court decision, states were free to require chemical tests. However the state could not physically force a driver to withstand these tests. This led to legislation passed by states asserting that drivers had given *implied consent* when they chose to drive their vehicles on state highways. If a driver refuses a BAC test, a state's motor vehicle administration has the right to suspend the driver's permit for a decided period of time. All states now use the *implied consent* or *expressed consent term.*

This system gives a great deal of discretion to police officers who have the right to decide which cars to stop and how to proceed once the car is stopped. Studies of officers' attitudes about this enforcement system reveal that many have suspected intoxication but did not continue with the investigations because of the length of time and paperwork involved with the process of arresting and prosecuting the DWI offender (Oates, 1974; Meyers, Heeren, & Hingson, 1987). Officers were also found to not make arrests in certain areas where penalties are severe and where the driver appears to be only marginally intoxicated. There are also accounts of officers not making arrests but instead letting a passenger drive. In other anecdotal reports, police sometimes do not make arrests when the driver is underage but instead have driven teenagers home (Oates, 1974).

EFFECTS OF CITIZEN ACTIVIST GROUPS ON ENFORCEMENT

IN 1980 THE beginning of citizen activist organizations like M.A.D.D. (Mothers Against Drunk Driving) and R.I.D. (Remove Intoxicated Drivers) altered the system of enforcement. These organizations called attention to drunk driving and were successful at pushing for tougher legislation. They put pressure on the courts and police officers to improve upon evidence to the court. Citizen activist groups also made significant contributions to passage of more strident DWI legislation in all states. These include:

- Raising the minimum legal drinking age to 21;

- Zero tolerance laws for youth;

- Laws lowering blood alcohol concentration (BAC) limits for adult drivers to .08.

It seems that the most important effect of these organizations is that they reminded police departments and courts that they supported the enforcement of DWI legislation, and thus turned the spotlight on public support for the work that was being done to enforce these laws (Voas and Lacey, 1990).

STRATEGIES FOR ENFORCING DWI LEGISLATION

THE SYSTEM THAT the United States uses to enforce DWI laws is based on the behavioral enforcement model. There are four steps to this approach to enforcement.

- The first is to **identify** cars that seem to have impaired drivers. This is done when there is a crash or when an officer observes strange driving behavior.

- The second step is after the car has been stopped. The officer **interviews** the driver to decide if the driver is intoxicated.

- The third step is to invite the driver out of the car and **perform a series of tests** to tell if the driver is indeed intoxicated. All of this consists of evidence if it is necessary for the officer to support a DWI charge.

- The fourth step derives from **evidence obtained after the roadside screen.** Finding that the driver is intoxicated, the officer will charge, arrest and take the driver to the police station to administer the chemical test, e.g., breath test, which is most widely used.

EFFECTS OF DWI ENFORCEMENT

EVEN THOUGH THE incidence of alcohol related accidents and fatalities is alarmingly high, considerable progress has been made in reducing the harm associated with impaired driving since 1975 when DWI record keeping began. Beginning in the early 1980s, largely due to the influence of citizen activist groups, the American society became increasingly sensitized to the high number of AOD related automobile fatalities. The total number of traffic deaths in 1980 was over 50,000 but by 1983 the number dropped to about 40,000 where it seems to have stabilized. Based on coroners' measurement of blood alcohol levels of fatally injured drivers, estimates are derived for the number of alcohol related crash fatalities.

Figure 2.1 shows the downward trend in the percentage of all traffic fatalities that are considered to be alcohol related. From a peak of over 57 percent in 1982, the percentage declined to 40 percent by 1998 (NHTSA, 2003a). However, studies in 2003 indicated that the proportionate number of DWI related fatalities increased some in 2000 to 2002.

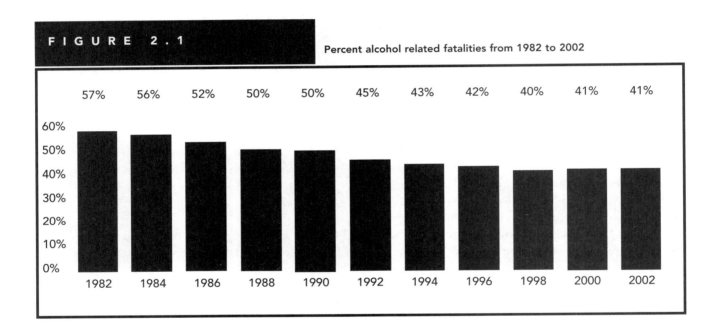

FIGURE 2.1 — Percent alcohol related fatalities from 1982 to 2002

CHAPTER THREE: CAUSATIVE AND INTERACTIVE FACTORS OF IMPAIRED DRIVING

OVERVIEW

CONSIDERABLE RESEARCH effort has gone into explaining the causative factors leading to impaired driving behavior and describing the driving while impaired offender. This summary is designed to help providers better understand the phenomenon of impaired driving and more effectively address the education and treatment needs of DWI offenders.

CAUSATIVE THEORIES

A NUMBER OF causative factors of impaired driving have been identified in the literature. Some will be briefly discussed.

Life History and Environmental Factors

Hawkins et al. (1985) identified a number of life history and environmental factors that contribute to impaired driving.

▶ Family - history of problem behavior, problems with discipline from parents, parents approving of use, or use of drugs and alcohol by the parents.

▶ School - little commitment or success in school.

▶ Peers - friends who use drugs and alcohol.

▶ Attitudes, beliefs, personality traits, e.g., rebellion and alienation from society.

Early Age Drinking Onset

The earlier the age of drinking onset, the greater the likelihood of being involved in a motor vehicle crash because of drinking (NHTSA, 2001a). Several factors may contribute to this relationship.

First, those who engage in deviant or illegal behaviors at an early age are probably more likely to engage in these behaviors later in life. Early onset of AOD use is predictive of use and abuse in adulthood. This has been a robust finding in AOD research for the past thirty-five years (e.g., Grant, 1998; Wanberg & Horn, 1970). Since AOD use and abuse are directly related to impaired driving, early onset of AOD use and abuse is predictive of adult impaired driving (Hingson et al., 2002).

Second, people who start drinking at an early age frequently drink more heavily than those who start drinking later in life, even if they are not alcohol dependent (Hingson et al., 2000; Horn & Wanberg, 1969; Wanberg, 1992). This increases the probability of impaired driving behavior.

Third, those who begin drinking at an early age may be less likely to believe that driving after drinking increases the risk of accidents or injury. They may believe that driving while under the influence is dangerous only for people who are visibly intoxicated.

Finally, heavy consumption of alcohol may result in greater impairment of judgement for those who start drinking at an earlier age. For example, after drinking they may be less likely to appreciate their increased crash risk than when sober (NHTSA, 2001a).

Personality Factors as Causative

A number of studies have focused on personality factors to address the question of, "Why do people drink and drive?" Donovan et al.(1983) found certain aspects of personality related to automobile accidents - *anxiety, frustration, depression, low self-esteem, and feeling out of control.*

McMillan et al. (1992) found that some people who are risk takers get cues from alcohol that they should take bigger risks than they normally would. Some individuals who thought they had alcohol in their system (who were given non-alcoholic drinks without their knowing it), drove more impaired and took more risks on the road than those with alcohol in their systems (they were using simulators, not real cars, to study driving skills).

Zuckerman (2000) examined the question of whether multiple forms of **risk taking** activities - smoking, drinking, drugs, sexual behavior, gambling and reckless driving - are related to a generalized risk-taking tendency. He found that smoking, drinking, sex and drugs were found to work in tandem with each other. However, reckless driving was related to only one other area of risk - drinking!

Some high risk drivers may derive pleasure or an increased sense of self-importance by taking chances behind the wheel (Wanberg & Timken, 1991). People who drink and drive are more likely to speed and less likely to wear seat belts (NHTSA, 2001a).

Problem Behavior Theory (PBT)

PBT (Jessor 1987a) defines the structures and elements of three systems. The **behavior system** includes a problem behavior structure that manifests problem behavior and a conventional behavior structure that exemplifies conventional behavior. Problem behavior is defined as behavior that departs from the social and legal norms of the larger society. DWI conduct fits this definition.

The **personality system** includes the *motivational-instigation structure,* determined by value placed on achievement and independence; the *personal belief structure,* related to a person's concept of self relative to society; and *personal control structure,* which gives a person reasons to not participate in problem behavior.

The **perceived environment** system includes two structures: *distal,* inclusive of a person's support network, and *proximal,* which deals with a person's environment in relationship to available models of behavior.

Problem behavior can emerge when there is a conflict between the personality and the perceived environment. From a PBT perspective, individuals who are at high risk for becoming involved in impaired driving behavior may fit this pattern:

▶ a predominate behavior structure featuring normalized images of drinking and driving;

▶ low value placed on achievement and success;

▶ a poorly developed personal control structure; and

▶ a perceived environment steeped in role models and opportunities (e.g., work environment, friends drink at bars, living situation) that support drinking and driving.

PBT is illustrated mainly to indicate that problem behavior such as impaired driving, must be viewed within the complex system of behavior, personality and the perceived environment. Attempts to develop intervention strategies for the DWIO must address all of these systems. By treating all behaviors (not just drinking behavior), non-alcohol related accidents and problems might decrease as well. The specific lessons and sessions in the education and treatment protocols of this work attempt to do just this: to address the DWIO's behavioral, personality and perceived environment systems.

Cognitive Model

The Cognitive Model (Reinecke & Freeman, 2003; Clark & Steer, 1996) provides another perspective in understanding the etiology of impaired driving. Although application of the cognitive approach is dealt with later in this *Provider's Guide,* a brief summary of how The Cognitive Model relates to impaired driving will be given at this point.

The Cognitive Model holds that basic cognitive structures and processes can operate in such a manner to prevent responsible behavior towards self, others and the community. DWI behavior is a consequence of an individual's cognitive organization and cognitive processes through which these structures are expressed. We begin education and treatment by modifying and changing the proximal structures or short-term structures which we call thought habits - expectancies, appraisals, attributions and decisions - and then move to words working on changing the distal or long-term structures - beliefs, attitudes and perception of self-efficacy.

The cognitive change process in preventing recidivism and relapse in the impaired driving offender is:

▶ helping the offender to identify the thought habits that lead to behaviors resulting in bad or negative outcomes;

▶ changing these thought habits or the proximal structures resulting in behaviors that lead to positive and adaptive outcomes;

▶ through understanding and changing the proximal structures or thought habits, helping clients identify the ingrained beliefs and assumptions that underlie these structures;

- challenging these old views and helping clients replace these beliefs and assumptions and transform their assumptions and world view into a more adaptive belief system; and

- having the client continue to practice these changes so that both the behavior changes and the cognitive changes are reinforced and self-efficacy is enhanced.

Stress as a Causative Factor in Impaired Driving

Stress and its emotional syndromes of anger, guilt and depression are powerful determinants of AOD use behavior and are related to negative outcomes of AOD use such as DWI behavior. One of the major triggers of AOD relapse identified in the literature is unpleasant emotions such as sadness, depression and anger (Wanberg & Milkman, 1998). Beck (1993) sees these as stress syndromes. Stress is the systems response to situations that exceed coping abilities and the demands made on the system by those situations (Bloom, 1985; Fried, 1993; Meichenbaum, 1993a). It becomes manifested in specific syndromes of depression, anger and guilt.

People use alcohol to cope with or relieve stress and the emotional states associated with stress (e.g., Lightsey and Sweeney, 1985; Powers and Kutash, 1985). There are a number of theories that have been used to explain the coping model including Social Learning Theory (Abrams & Niaura, 1987), Expectancy Theory (Goldman, Brown & Christiansen, 1987), Opponent Process Theory (Shipley, 1987), Tension Reduction Theory (Cappell & Greeley, 1987), the Self-awareness Model (Hull, 1987), and the Stress Reduction Dampening theory (Sher, 1987).

Stress is a double-edged sword with respect to DWI behavior. First, it can be an important part of the equation that interacts with other variables resulting in impaired driving. Second, a DWI arrest can lead to stress.

Impaired driving is often the consequence of using alcohol or other drugs to manage stress. Brenner and Selzer (1969) found that people who perceive that they are under stress (e.g., relationship problems, death of a loved one, financial, job problems) are five times as likely to be involved in an accident. Add drinking to that equation and the probability of an accident increases significantly.

Veneziano et al. (1994) studied stress-related factors associated with impaired driving among 498 DWI offenders arrested in four Missouri judicial districts. Most were in the age range of 20 to 30 years, 87% were male and 95% Anglo-White American. Their study examined the types of stress that DWI offenders were under during the year before they were arrested. These offenders admitted to experiencing financial stress, new job pressures, job loss or unemployment, problems at home, death or illness of a loved one, marriage problems and having been in a car accident. Those who were seen as alcohol dependent indicated that they had even higher levels of stress. The various types of stress identified by this study were seen as important causal factors leading to impaired driving behavior.

The Veneziano et al. (1994) study also pointed out the other edge of the stress sword - that a DWI arrest can also lead to high levels of stress. When DWI offenders were asked to rate stressful problems from the last year, 92.2% listed their DWI arrest as the most stressful event, followed by job loss and unemployment (40%), financial troubles (38%), marriage problems (35.5%), death or illness of a loved one (35.5%).

Thus, stress is often a precursor to and a result of impaired driving behavior. The management of stress and its related emotional syndromes must be a component of an effective DWI intervention and treatment program. Stress is an important component of the mental-behavioral impaired control cycle (ICC), another factor that provides causative explanation of DWI behavior.

Mental Behavioral Impaired Control Cycle

The mental-behavioral impaired control cycle (ICC) (Wanberg, 1974, 1990; Wanberg & Milkman, 1998) is an important model in understanding the causative and interactive factors of AOD use and impaired driving behavior. The ICC is based on both a positive and negative reinforcement model.

When a behavior is used to enhance positive feelings or to manage or eliminate negative and stress events, that behavior and the cognitions leading to that behavior are learned and reinforced.

Many DWI offenders begin to depend on using alcohol (or other drugs) to manage life's negative events and the stress associated with those events. When alcohol use results in negative life events and stress, the most likely response will be to use alcohol to manage the stress resulting from its use. When this happens, the user enters into the impaired control cycle. Drinking becomes an important factor in managing, not only the normal stresses of life, but the problems and stress resulting from using alcohol. This increases the risk of engaging in impaired driving, since the importance of drinking to handle stress can often override the necessary judgement that leads to responsible behavior, i.e., not driving when drinking. When a DWI arrest and conviction becomes one of the negative consequences, then the offender is at risk of drinking to handle the stress resulting from this negative consequence. With many DWIOs, this increases the risk of reoffending.

Most DWIOs will fit some point of the impaired control cycle (ICC). All fit the point where a problem results from drinking, e.g., getting arrested for DWI. Others become entrenched in the cycle where drinking to handle the negative consequences and symptoms of drinking become a way of life. The Veneziano et al. (1994) study points out that about half of the DWI offenders drank more than they had planned, 44 percent experienced objections to their behavior by family members, one-third admitted having blackouts, over 26 percent neglected responsibilities when drinking, 25 percent were rebuked by their physician, over 23 percent had a car accident due to impaired driving, almost 20 percent reported being violent when drinking, 20 percent reported relationship problems and more than 40 percent had a previous DWI arrest.

The ICC is an important model in the *Driving With CARE* education and treatment protocols. It is used to help clients understand how problems result from drinking, and how drinking is used to handle these problems. It is also used to help clients understand the nature of their own AOD use patterns. It will be more fully discussed in Section III of this *Provider's Guide* and in the *Participant's Workbooks*.

SUMMARY: AN INTERACTION MODEL TO EXPLAIN IMPAIRED DRIVING BEHAVIOR

A NUMBER OF theories and concepts have been described in this Chapter to provide some insights into the etiology of impaired driving. There is no simple cause and effect model that can explain, let alone predict, impaired driving conduct. Thus, it is best to view the above described theories and concepts from an interactive perspective. There are many factors - early age drinking, environmental events, problem behavior, personality characteristics, stress and the emotional syndromes of stress, cognitive and behavioral reinforcement and the impaired control - that interact with drinking and driving to result in impaired driving behavior. An important objective of impaired driving education and treatment is to help clients understand the interactions of various factors in their lives that led to their involvement in this behavior.

Following is a summary of the most salient findings outlined in this Chapter.

- A number of life-history factors increase the risk of involvement in DWI conduct including family, school failure, negative peer involvement and rebellious behavior during development and early age drinking onset.

- A number of personality and emotional factors are associated with impaired driving including stress, frustration, depression, low self-esteem, feeling out of control and risk taking.

- DWI conduct must be viewed within the complex system of behavior, personality and the perceived environment. Attempts to develop intervention strategies for the DWIO must address all of these systems and not just drinking and driving behavior.

- Cognitive theory provides a basis for understanding and preventing impaired driving and a basis upon which to identify and change basic cognitive structures and processes that operate in such a manner that prevent responsible behavior towards self, others and the community.

CHAPTER FOUR: CHARACTERISTICS OF THE DRIVING WHILE IMPAIRED OFFENDER

OVERVIEW

USING DATA FROM SELF-REPORT, traffic fatality reports, driving records and BACs, collected at crash sites, random roadside sobriety check points and from DWIOs who were evaluated for intervention services, a number of studies have characterized the drinking driver population. We first look at the demographic descriptions of the DWIO population. Then we review the other variables that are significantly related to DWI conduct and behavior.

DEMOGRAPHIC DESCRIPTIONS

SUMMARIZING ACROSS a number of studies, the following general demographic and descriptive charactristics seem to characterize the DWIO population (Cavaiola & Wuth, 2002; Jonah, 1990; Jonah & Wilson, 1986; McCord, 1984; Moskowitz, Walker, & Gomberg, 1979; Timken, 2002; Wanberg & Timken, 2005a).

▶ Predominately male - from 70 to 80 percent.

▶ A high representation in the age range of 20 to 30 with most falling in the 20 to 45 year old range; in 1997 the highest arrest rates were in the 21 to 24 year age group (1,695 per 100,000) while those over 65 had the lowest arrest rates (78 per 100,000).

▶ Majority are Anglo-White males.

▶ Non-White and non-Asian subgroups are over-represented when compared with the general population (Jones and Lacey, 1998; Liu, et al., 1997; Lund and Wolf, 1991; Townsend et al., 1998).

▶ From 65% to 75% fall in the marital status categories of single, separate or divorced with about half being unmarried or never-married.

▶ Most are employed, however, a significantly greater percent, when compared to the general population, are unemployed.

▶ The majority have no college education, although most have at least eight years of education.

A study by Wanberg and Timken (2005a) of a sample of 2,554 DWIOs being processed through the Colorado judicial system lends support to the above findings with respect to the demographic and DWI related characteristics of this population. Table 4.1 provides a summary of these findings.

Gender differences.

The most notable gender difference is percent of arrests and convictions. A 1991 report indicated that about 11 percent of the DWIOs were female (Maguire & Flanagan, 1991) and that there was a trend upward with respect to female DWIOs (Cavaiola & Wuth, 2002). However, in Colorado, the 18 to 20 percent DWIO female distribution has remained stable for over 20 years. In 1991, Wanberg and Timken (1991) found 18.5 percent female in a representative sample in Colorado and in 2002, they found 19.3 of the DWIO convictions were female (Wanberg & Timken, 2005a).

Some reports have indicated that women are at higher risks for alcohol-related crashes and crash fatalities when their BACs are .10 or higher (Cavaiola & Wuth, 2002; Jones & Lacey, 1998). However, the Fatality Analysis Reporting System (FARS: NHTSA, 2004) indicates that the percent of female drivers involved in fatal crashes with BACs of .01 or higher has remained stable from 1995 through 2002 (15 to 16 percent); and percent of female drivers involved in fatal crashes with BACs of .08 or greater has remained stable, fluctuating between 12 and 13 percent since 1995. Chapter 10 provides a more detailed study of gender comparisons, using the sample in Table 4.1.

Ethnic differences

Studies of ethnic differences among DWIOs have been sparse and mixed. Some studies indicate African Americans and Hispanic Americans are overrepresented (Ross et al., 1991) and that Anglo-White American males between the ages of 21 and 34 represent the largest percentage of DWIOs involved in alcohol-related fatal crashes (Jones & Lacey, 1998). Wanberg & Timken (2005a: Table 4.1) reported that Hispanic Americans are overrepresented and Anglo-White Americans are underrepresented. This is congruent with the literature. Chapter 10 provides a more detailed study of ethnic differences using the sample in Table 4.1.

TABLE 4.1

Summary of Demographic Information for 2,554 DWIOs Convicted of Impaired Driving and Processed through the Colorado Judicial System.

DESCRIPTION OF VARIABLES	PERCENT
Gender: Males	80.7
Ethnicity: Anglo-White American	60.9
Hispanic American	29.4
African American	4.2
Native American	4.0
Marital Status: Never Married	49.7
Married	24.4
Divorced	19.0
Separated	5.5
Age at Arrest: Age 15 through 20	11.0
Age 21 through 30	37.8
Age 31 through 40	26.2
Age 41 through 50	17.6
Over age 50	7.4
Education: Six or less years of education	4.7
Seven to nine years education completed	6.8
10 to 12 years education completed	53.5
13 to 15 years completed	21.3
16 years or more education	13.6
Employment: Employed full time	71.6
Employed part time	10.2
Unemployed	18.2
Income: Income Less than 800 dollars a month	15.9
Income 800 to 1,199 dollars a month	22.1
Income 1,200 to 1,500 dollars a month	21.3
Income 1,600 to 1,999 dollars a month	10.4
Income 2,000 to 2,999 dollars a month	16.6
Income 3,000 dollars a month or more	13.7

Marital

The literature indicates that divorce and marital separation are overrepresented in DWIO samples (Jonah & Wilson, 1986; Selzer et al., 1977; Yoder & Moore, 1973). Table 4.1 points out that 75 percent are not currently married. Not being in a marital situation or in an unstable marriage increases the probability of engaging in impaired driving behavior, and is congruent with Jonah's (1990) argument that relationship problems and issues are strong covariates with DWI conduct.

Age

The literature shows that a large percent of DWIOs are in the younger age range, with close to 50 percent being under age 30. Table 4.1 is congruent with this finding. DWIOs are generally younger than the general driving population (Donelson, 1985; Mercer, 1986).

Income, employment and education

DWIOs tend to fall in the lower-to-middle income status (Donovan et al., 1985) and are typically employed. Although data in Table 4.1 indicate income levels may be somewhat higher than reported in the literature, most of the reports on income date back to the 1980s. Although the majority of DWIOs are employed, the unemployment rate among DWIOs, as reported in the literature and in Table 4.1 (18 percent), is 3 to 4 times the general population. Results in Table 4.1 with respect to years of education are fairly congruent with that found in the literature.

DWI RELATED VARIABLES

THE WANBERG and Timken (2005a) study also looked at variables directly related to DWI behavior such as BAC levels at arrest, prior arrests, prior interventions, and accident involvement. Table 4.2 provides a summary of these findings.

One percent of the DWIOs in this sample had a BAC less than .05. Whereas about 20 percent fell in the .05 to .099 range, over 60 percent fell in the .10 to .199 range. About seven percent had a BAC of .25 or higher, and the highest recorded BAC was .46. These BAC statistics seem to be close to that

reported in the literature.

The prior DWI arrests of around 35 percent and prior intervention/treatment of around 30 percent are statistics compatible with other research reports.

About 14 percent of the sample in Table 4.2 were involved in an accident at the time of arrest. About 3.7 percent involved injury (including fatality) and .5 percent (or 5 out of a thousand) involved a fatality.

PERSONALITY TRAITS AND PATTERNS

A NUMBER OF studies and reports have identified personality characteristics of the DWIOs (Cavaiola & Wuth, 2002; Donovan et al., 1983; Donovan et al., 1985; Jonah, 1990; Jones & Lacey, 1998; Lund & Wolf, 1991; Nochajski et al., 1991; Perrine et al., 1989; Selzer, Vinokur, & Wilson, 1977; Sutker, Brantley, & Allain, 1980; Wilson, 1992). Following are the most salient personality variables that are associated with DWI conduct.

- Agitation, irritability, resentment, aggression, overt and covert hostility.

- Thrill and sensation seeking.

- Low levels of assertiveness, low self-esteem and feelings of inadequacy and sensitive to criticism and rejection.

- Helplessness, depression and emotional stress.

- Impulsiveness.

- External locus of control.

- Social deviance and nonconformity, anti-authoritarian attitudes.

One salient marker is sensation-seeking. Zukerman (1990, 2000) defines sensation-seeking as a demand to find varied, intense and novel experiences with the willingness to take risks to seek these experiences. Related to DWI conduct, sensation-seeking contributes to a multiple-location drinking pattern (Wieczorek, Miller & Nochajski, 1990)

TABLE 4.2	Summary of Driving While Impaired Information for 2,554 DWIOs Convicted of Impaired Driving and Processed Through the Colorado Judicial System.

DRIVING WHILE IMPAIRED VARIABLES	PERCENT
BAC less than .05	1.1
BAC between .05 and .099	19.5
BAC between .10 and .149	33.4
BAC between .15 and .199	26.9
BAC .20 or higher	20.1
Accident, Injury, property damage: No accident	86.6
Accident and property damage and no injury	9.8
Injury	.7
Property damage and injury	2.5
Property damage and fatality	.4
Fatality	.1
Prior Treatment Episodes: None	70.3
One prior treatment episode	20.5
Two or more prior treatment episodes	9.2
Prior DWI arrests: No prior arrests	65.1
One prior arrest	21.3
Two or more prior arrests	13.6
Arrest Charge: First offense DUI or DWAI	66.3

Aggression and hostility contribute to DWI behavior in that it is associated with interpersonal conflict and rejection. When this happens, the DWIO tends not to care, is more risk-taking, less careful, is apt to be agitated, and may engage in multiple-location drinking patterns.

Several studies have found little differences between high-risk drivers and DWIOs across several personality traits, including sensation-seeking and hostility (Donovan, Umlauf, & Salzberg, 1990; Perrine, 1970; Zelhart, Schurr, & Brown, 1975). This suggests that risk-taking contributes significant variance to DWI involvement.

As well, most studies have failed to find significant personality differences between first-time and repeat offenders (Cavaiola & Wuth, 2002) suggesting first offenders are really repeat offenders who have only been caught once.

Some suggest that the personality influences and alcohol use are not only interactive, but synergistic with respect to increasing the risk of DWI behavior particularly when combined with certain situational factors. This concept is in concert with Problem Behavioral Theory (PTB: Jessor, 1987a).

Miller and Windle (1990) suggest that personality and mental health symptoms can interact with and influence drinking and driving in several ways.

- Some personality characteristics such as sensation seeking, poor impulse control, rebellious or deviant behavior leads to unsafe driving in general.

- Specific drinking patterns such as location and time of drinking are influenced by some personality traits such as sensation seeking or being lonely.

- Driving behavior is indirectly influenced by the direct effect that some personality traits have on drinking behavior, such as impulsivity.

- Excessive drinking or drinking and driving can result from personality characteristics that increase probability of interpersonal conflicts such as an angry attitude, aggressiveness, hostility.

Several studies have identified personality sub-types (Donovan & Marlatt, 1983; Donovan et al., 1986; Wilson, 1991). Here are some.

- Driving-related aggression, including competitive speed, sensation seeking, assaultive and hostility.

- Depression, resentment, low levels of assertiveness and internal locus of control.

- Deviant, antisocial and irresponsible.

ANTISOCIAL AND CRIMINAL HISTORY

STUDIES HAVE indicated a significant prevalence of antisocial and criminal conduct among DWIOs (Chang & Lapham, 1996; Jessor, 1987b; Moskowitz, Walker, & Gomberg, 1979; Irgens-Jensen, 1975; Elliot, 1987; McCord, 1984; Perrine, 1990; Wilson & Jonah, 1985; Donovan, 1980, 1993; Donovan, et al., 1985; Vingilis, 1983). The following is a summary of these findings.

- Higher degree of involvement in antisocial and criminal behavior.

- Higher involvement in the criminal justice system other than impaired driving.

- Less involvement in socially acceptable behavior and report more disturbed psychosocial problems.

- Reluctance to comply with court mandates and frequent under-reporting of past criminal conduct.

- Higher rates of traffic violations than the average population.

A large proportion of DWIO's have criminal records. One study of Massachusetts DWIOs (Argeriou, et al., 1986) found that more than half had prior criminal records for offenses other than DWI. Among repeat DWI offenders the number grew to more than two-thirds. Using a scale of criminal careers to rate the criminal records of males in Louisiana, Gould and Gould (1992) found that 4.3% of first time DWI offenders scored within the "career criminal" range, while 30% of the multiple DWI cases scored in this range.

RESISTIVE AND DEFENSIVE

It is generally recognized that DWIOs are more defensive and resistive to self-disclosure and treatment than the "typical" AOD client. For example, DWIOs score much higher on a defensive scale than do non-DWI offenders in the criminal justice system (Wanberg & Timken, 1998). Miller and Rollnick (2002) see this defensiveness and resistance to treatment related to the stages of change theory and the failure to effectively utilize motivational enhancement skills in working with DWIO resistance. The fact that the DWIO is a court-mandated referral certainly adds to the resistance.

The utilization of motivational enhancement skills to manage resistance is one answer to this robust characteristic of the DWIO. Resistance is most apparent at the initial screening and assessment level. As Cavaiola and Wuth (2002) note, "...most DWI offenders are not willing participants in the evaluation process; therefore, the task of coming up with accurate assessment of their status with regard to drinking behavior, drinking and driving behavior and psychological status is very difficult to say the least" (2002, p. 65). Utilization of the convergent validation model of assessment (Wanberg, 1997), discussed in Chapter 7, provides resolution to the concern around client resistance and defensiveness.

DRINKING PATTERNS AND BEHAVIORS

A NUMBER OF studies have focused on DWIO drinking behavior and patterns (Chang, Lapham & Wanberg, 2001; Vingilis, 1983; Donovan, et al., 1985; Jonah & Wilson, 1986; Perrine, 1990; Selzer & Barton, 1977; Zelhart et al., 1975; Donovan & Marlatt, 1982; Horn, Wanberg & Foster, 1990; Wanberg & Timken, 2001).

▶ DWI offenders drank more frequently and more alcohol per occasion than the average drinker.

▶ DWIOs were more likely to indicate alcoholic-type patterns and more alcohol-related problems.

▶ Predominant pattern of gregarious and convivial drinking.

▶ Multiple-location drinking pattern.

▶ Drink to manage personal and emotional problems.

COMPARING DWIOS AND DIAGNOSED ALCOHOLICS

THE DIFFERENCES between diagnosed alcoholics in treatment and DWIOs are marked. Diagnosed alcoholics reflect much greater disruptions in the areas of economics and employment, family and marital problems and emotional adjustment than do DWIOs (Cavaiola & Wuth, 2002). The levels of alcohol-related disruption and symptoms were much higher among diagnosed alcoholic clients than among DWIOs (e.g., Moskowitz, Walker, & Gomberg, 1979; Packard, 1987; Horn, Wanberg, & Foster, 1990; Wanberg & Horn, 2005).

The main problem is that the estimates of the extent of problem drinking and alcoholism among DWIOs are conflictive and broad ranged. Cavaiola and Wuth's summary of these studies illustrates this problem (2002, pp. 61-62).

▶ Two to 10 percent of DWI offenders are problem drinkers (Filkins et al., 1973);

▶ The incidence of alcoholism was 20 percent of DWIOs (Kelleher, 1971);

▶ Around 39 percent of one sample tested on the MAST scored 6 or more in the alcoholism range whereas 99 percent in the alcoholic group scored six or more (Selzer et al., 1977);

▶ From 50 to 80 percent were determined to be problem drinkers (Filkins et al., 1973);

▶ About 50 percent can be considered alcoholic (Vingilis, 1983);

▶ Around 51 percent of a sample of DWI offenders referred for an alcoholism evaluation were alcohol dependent based on the DSM-III-R (Wieczorek et al., 1989);

▶ Around 62 percent of first-time DWIOs were alcohol abusers and 84 percent of repeat offenders were alcohol dependent (Wieczorek et al., 1990);

▶ From 54 to 74 percent tested on the Michigan Alcoholism Screening Test (MAST) had scores in the alcoholism range (Selzer, 1971);

▶ Using the MAST, 68 percent scored in the alcoholism range (Selzer & Barton, 1977);

▶ There is a substantial overlap between incarcerated DWI populations and criminal and clinical alcoholic populations.

DRUG USE AMONG DWI OFFENDERS

WE HAVE NOTED that DWIOs are defensive with respect to self-disclosure. We would expect this defensiveness to be more prominent in the area of self-disclosure around drug use. Wanberg and Timken (2005a) found this not to be the case. When comparing the magnitude of correlations between the DEFENSIVE scale and other scales in the Adult Substance Use and Driving Survey (ASUDS), DWIOs were much more defensive when disclosing alcohol involvement, driving risk and AOD disruptive symptoms than when disclosing the use of drugs other than alcohol.

It is a general finding that multiple-drug users have more severe AOD and psychosocial problems. Nochajski et al. (1997) found that recidivism rates were higher for a drug-treatment group than for an alcohol-only treatment group.

Distributions across nine drug categories were studied in the sample described in Tables 4.1 and 4.2. The percent reporting having used drugs in the following categories were: marijuana, 49.4; cocaine, 16.7; amphetamines, 11.9; hallucinogens, 11.8; inhalants, 2.6; heroin, 1.5; other opiates, 4.8; barbiturates and other sedatives, 2.9; and tranquilizers, 3.1.

Because of the defensive nature of the DWIO at screening and initial assessment, it is most likely that the above self-reported data are an underdetermination of the "true" drug use history of these clients. Yet, what seems to be the case is that around 11 to 12 percent of these clients are multiple-drug users who report significant involvement in drugs other than alcohol and marijuana. It is noteworthy that close to 50 percent report a history of marijuana use.

DRIVING PATTERNS AMONG DWIOS

MOST OF THE studies of the DWI offender have focused on drinking behavior, deviant and antisocial behavior and psychosocial and personality variables (Jonah, 1990). There are only a small number of studies that have focused on the driving behavior and attitudes of the DWIO. These are briefly reviewed.

The DWIOs did not differ from the general population with respect to driving attitude measures (Donovan, et al., 1985). DWI offenders are less apt to use seat belts, had more traffic violations, and had more auto accidents than non-drinking or the moderate-drinking drivers (Donovan, et al., 1990; Wilson & Jonah, 1985). Donovan and Marlatt, (1982b) attempted to include driving attitudes and behavior measures in their effort to define personality subtypes among the DWI group. They used five *a prior* defined subscales, drawing from the work of Goldstein and Mosel (1958) and Parry (1968), to define a cluster of measures which they saw as a subtype characterized by driving-related aggression, competitive speed, sensation seeking, assaultiveness, irritability, and indirect and verbal hostility.

There has been the suggestion that the tendency to drive while impaired may represent but a single manifestation of a broader constellation of irresponsible and high risk drivers (Cameron, 1982;

Clay, 1974; Donovan, Marlatt & Salzberg, 1983).

High risk drivers (HRD) are indicated to have four characteristics: emotional lability, impulsiveness and thrill seeking, expressions of hostility and depression, and lack of personal worth (Donovan et al., 1983). These are also common personality features of DWIOs. Comparison of DWIs and HRDs indicated that DWIs scored higher on drinking related variables (Donovan et al., 1985). As noted above, there has been a failure to find significant personality differences across the two groups.

Although there has been some effort to define different patterns within the DWI populations, such as personality subtypes (e.g., Mulligan, Steer, & Fine, 1978; Sutker, Brantley, & Allain, 1980; Donovan & Marlatt, 1982b), there has been little effort to define independent dimensions of driving behaviors and attitudes among the DWIOs. Wanberg and Timken addressed this issue using the Driving Assessment Survey (DAS: 1991; 1997, 2005b). The guiding assumption of this study was that there are distinct differences among the DWI offenders with respect to driving attitudes and behaviors, and that these differences can be operationally defined through independent dimensions or factors derived from a large set of variables measuring driving attitudes and behaviors.

The study of the DAS identified seven reliable patterns (factors) in several large samples of DWIOs.

▶ POWER: measures the extent to which the respondent reports feeling power when driving a motor vehicle.

▶ HAZARD: indicates the degree to which an individual takes part in hazardous or high-risk driving behavior.

▶ IMPULSE: indicates impulsive and temperamental driving behaviors and attitudes.

▶ STRESS: indicates the person feels irritability, stress and anger when driving.

▶ RELAX: indicates that driving is used as a means to relax and calm down.

▶ REBEL: measures rebellion toward authority and rules.

- CONVIVIAL: measures convivial and gregarious drinking.

The DAS study also identified a general risk factor that measures overall driving risk and hazard among DWIOs.

Wanberg and Timken (1997) compared a sample of average drivers renewing their driver's licenses with a sample of DWIOs across the seven DAS primary factor scales and the general risk scale. The following statistically significant differences were observed.

- DWIOs scored higher on POWER, HAZARD, REBEL and CONVIVIAL than average drivers. This indicated that DWIOs were more antisocially oriented and more apt to drink in convivial and gregarious settings. It also indicated that DWIOs were more apt to experience a sense of power when driving a motor vehicle.

- Most noteworthy was that the two groups did not differ across the IMPULSE scale.

- Average drivers scored significantly higher on RELAX than DWIOs indicating that the former group is more apt to use driving as a means to relax and calm down than the DWIO drivers.

These findings would suggest that DWI offenders present a greater risk than the average driver and are more involved in drinking involving gregarious and convivial environments, such as parties and bars. These findings seem to agree with Perrine's (1990) findings that DWIOs are more likely to acknowledge driving aggressively and competitively.

SUMMARY

THIS CHAPTER has attempted to give the provider some understanding and insight into the characteristics of DWI offenders. Following is a summary of the most salient findings and some suggestions that may help the provider to be more effective in working with this intervention group.

- There are consistent and predictable demographic, descriptive and personality characteristics that help to identify persons who are at high-risk for involvement in impaired driving behavior.

- DWI offenders are identified as having more anti-social characteristics which must be addressed in the education and treatment of the impaired driver.

- DWIOs are defensive to self-disclosure and resistive to involvement in DWI education and treatment.

- There is a marked difference between DWIOs and diagnosed alcoholics as to AOD symptoms and disruption.

- There are distinct patterns of driving attitudes and behaviors found among impaired drivers, and educational and treatment programs should address these patterns.

- Common drinking patterns have been identified in the DWIO population, and these patterns must be addressed in intervention. For example, an effective intervention program must address the fact that most DWIO clients engage in a gregarious and convivial drinking pattern, and that the needs associated with these patterns are very powerful determinants of DWI conduct.

Cavaiola and Wuth (2002) stress that DWIOs referred to treatment may represent a skewed representation of impaired drivers. The data we use to describe DWIOs are based on those who have been apprehended and convicted of DWI conduct. He uses Perrine's (1990) distinctions between

- "the Quick" or those who have escaped arrest,

- "the Caught" or those apprehended and convicted, and

- "the Dead" or those fatally injured with positive BACs.

Most of our information is on "the Caught," some on "the Dead" and little on "the Quick." It is the latter on which we need more information to round out our knowledge and understanding of impaired driving offenders.

CHAPTER FIVE: UNDERAGED IMPAIRED DRIVERS

OVERVIEW

THE LITERATURE has identified two important special populations of DWIOs that warrant special consideration with respect to developing effective education and intervention programs. These are: underaged (under age 21) impaired drivers and the hard core impaired driver. This Chapter will look at underage driving offenders.

THE SCOPE OF THE PROBLEM OF ADOLESCENT DRINKING AND DRIVING

DESPITE THE FACT that all states have a minimum legal drinking age of 21, the prevalence of alcohol consumption among youth is high. Results from the *Monitoring the Future Surveys* revealed that 77 percent of adolescents have consumed alcohol by their senior year in high school and that over 50 percent are doing so by the eighth grade (Johnston, et. al. 2004). More than 48 percent of 12th graders reported drinking alcohol during the 30 days prior to being surveyed (Johnston, et al. 2000, 2004).

Binge drinking, defined as drinking three or more times in a 2-week period, has increased in the latter 1990s among high school and college students (Wechsler, Lee, Kuo, & Lee, 2000). In addition, heavy-episode drinking, defined as having four or more drinks in one sitting for females and five or more drinks in one sitting for males, is widespread (Johnston, et al., 2000, refers to this phenomenon in adolescence as binge drinking). Adult binge drinking, in contrast, is defined as heavy drinking for several days in a row followed by a period of abstinence (Horn & Wanberg, 1969; Wanberg & Horn, 1987). These two phenomena often begin about age 13, tend to increase during adolescence, peak between the ages of 18 and 22, and then gradually decrease (NIAAA, 1997). Binge drinking at least once in the two weeks before the survey was reported by more than 30 percent of 12th graders (Johnston, et al., 2004).

Drinking among college students is also prevalent and has increased in the late 1990s. Up to 81 percent of college students report using alcohol at least once in the past year (Wechsler, et al., 2000) and from 39 to 44 percent of college students are

classified as heavy drinkers (Johnston, O'Malley, & Bachman, 1997). College students who engage in binge or heavy-episode drinking are at greater risk of experiencing a variety of negative consequences including problems with the police, damaging property, getting injured, engaging in unplanned or unprotected sex and driving after drinking (Wechsler et al., 2000).

The prevalence of alcohol use among adolescents and young adults makes this population of drivers the most at-risk group for impaired driving. Not only is drinking prevalent among youth, many of those who drink also drive after drinking. Fifteen percent of students in grades 9-12 (ages 15-18) reported driving after drinking during the month before being surveyed; more than one-third reported riding with a driver who had been drinking at least once during the two weeks before being surveyed; and about 19 percent reported frequent binge drinking, i.e., drinking three or more times during the 2 weeks prior to the survey (Centers for Disease Control, 1996).

Drinking and driving during the 30 days before the survey was reported by more than 60 percent of the males and by almost 50 percent of the females who were frequent binge drinkers. By comparison, only 20 percent of the males and 13 percent of the females who were non-binge drinkers reported having been involved in situations in which drinking and driving occurred (Johnston, et al., 2004).

The estimated crash risk for male drivers ages 16-20 is at least three times higher than the risk for male drivers age 25 and older at all BAC levels (Zador, 1991). More than 33 percent of all fatalities for 15 through 20-year olds result from motor vehicle crashes, and of these, more than 35 percent are alcohol related. Alcohol-related automobile accidents are the number one cause of death for people 15-24 (Snow & Cunningham, 1985; Burnet, 1986). In 1998, 14 percent of underage drivers involved in fatal crashes tested positive for alcohol.

Young impaired drivers are involved in fatal crashes at approximately twice the rate of drivers aged 21 and over. In 1996, for every 100,000 licensed drivers, sixty-six 15- to 20- year-old drivers were involved in fatal crashes compared with 28 adult drivers (NHTSA, 1998). Young people aged 15 - 20 consisted of 36.6 percent of all alcohol-related fatalities, and most had BACs greater than .10 (NHTSA 1997a). Of 15-19 year olds involved in an accident, 60% have been drinking before the accident and 43% of those had BACs over the legal limit for their state (Williams, 1989).

For all drivers, each .02 increase in BAC nearly doubles the risk of being involved in a fatal crash. For drivers ages 16 - 20, the risk of a fatal crash increases even more with each .02 percent rise in BAC (Mayhew et al., 1986; Zador, 1991; NIAAA, 1996).

Paradoxically, young impaired drivers are less likely to be detained and arrested than their adult counterparts (NHTSA, 1999a). This may be that adolescents experience less sedation and motor skill disruption, albeit greater cognitive impairment than their adult counterparts of equal BAC levels (White, 2003).

Prevalence of use of other drugs also are of concern, particularly as such use relates to DWI conduct. *Table 5.1* provides a summary of AOD use from the 2003 Monitoring the Future Survey (Johnston et al., 2004). All drugs in that table have a profound effect on driving ability except cigarettes. The latter is not as benign as one might conclude since the use of tobacco is highly correlated with the use of other drugs.

Most noteworthy is that 21 percent of high school seniors used marijuana and almost 48 percent used alcohol during the 30 days prior to the survey. Combine this with the fact that a sizable proportion of 12 graders also drive motor vehicles, the seriousness and impact of teen AOD drug use on the problem of impaired driving in our society is clear.

The impact is not just from teens driving while engaging in AOD use. The literature is replete with findings that adolescent AOD use is the best predictor of adult use. Thus, with the alarming rate of the prevalence of AOD use in adolescents continuing to remain stable over the past two decades, we are continuing to produce a sizable "crop" of adult impaired drivers.

RISK AND CAUSATIVE FACTORS ASSOCIATED WITH ADOLESCENT SUBSTANCE USE AND ABUSE

SINCE THE PREVALENCE of alcohol and other drug (AOD) use and abuse in adolescence is directly related to adolescent impaired driving, it is important to understand the risk factors that are associated with adolescent and young adult AOD use and abuse. During the 1980s and 1990s, these risk factors became a salient focus in the adolescent AOD use and abuse literature. The following is a summary of the most salient risk factors identified in the literature (Brown et al., 1988; Botvin, 1983, 1986; Clayton, 1992; Hawkins, Lishner & Catalano, 1985; Hawkins, Catalano, & Miller, 1992; Jessor, 1984; Jessor & Jessor, 1977; Kandel, Kessler & Margulies, 1978; Kandel, Simcha-Fagan & Davies, 1986; Newcomb & Bentler, 1989; Newcomb, Maddahian & Bentler, 1986; Oetting & Beauvais, 1987; Wanberg, 1992, Winters, 2001).

▶ Parent and family factors including poor parental monitoring, parental alcoholism, parent role-modeling of alcohol use, parental and family conflicts and parental neglect and abuse.

▶ Deviant behavior factors, including antisocial attitudes and behaviors, early involvement in deviant behavior and criminal conduct, association with peers who are involved in criminal conduct and antisocial attitudes and behaviors including aggression, risk-taking behaviors, driving while intoxicated and rejection of prosocial activities.

▶ Peer influence factors including associations with deviant peers, peers who use substances and rejection by normative peers.

▶ Early substance use and abuse including early drunkenness and early use of illicit drugs.

▶ Current patterns of substance use disruption, including social, physical and behavioral loss of control.

▶ Availability and access to substances.

▶ Acceptable and favorable attitudes towards the use of alcohol and other drugs.

Psychological factors such as stress, anxiety, depression and mood adjustment problems.

Educational adjustment factors, including school failure, poor attitude and lack of commitment towards education.

Other factors such as biological, genetic, cultural, social and community-environmental are important contributors to the risk of substance abuse and thus, impaired driving, in adolescence. Kilpatrick et al. (2000) found that adolescents who had been physically and/or sexually assaulted and who had witnessed violence had increased risk for current substance abuse or dependence. They also found that posttraumatic stress disorder independently increased risk of marijuana and hard drug abuse and dependence.

Although these risk factors are important in understanding and predicting substance abuse among adolescents and young adults, no specific risk factor or specific groupings of risk factors necessarily leads to a substance use or abuse outcome in an individual adolescent (Bukstein, 1995). Predictive studies indicate that the number of risk factors will predict adolescent substance abuse better than any particular set of risk factors (Bry, 1983). As well, all of the risk factors operate within the three systems of psychological and social influence, as defined by *problem-behavior theory:* the perceived environment system, the personality system, and the behavior system (Jessor, 1987a).

TABLE 5.1	Monitoring the Future Study 2003: Prevalence of Drug Use for 12th Graders	
CATEGORY OF DRUG(S)	**PERCENT LIFETIME**	**PERCENT 30-DAY USE**
Any illicit drug	51.1	24.1
Cigarettes	57.3	24.1
Smokeless tobacco	17.0	6.7
Alcohol*	76.6	47.5
Marijuana**	46.1	21.2
Inhalants	11.2	--
Ecstasy (MDMD)	8.3	1.3
Hallucinogens	10.6	2.1
Cocaine	7.7	2.1
Crack cocaine	3.6	0.9
Heroin	1.5	.04
Steroids	3.5	1.3
Tranquilizers	11.4	2.8
Amphetamines	14.4	--
Methamphetamines	6.2	--

*Daily use of alcohol was 3.2%

** Daily use of marijuana was 6.0%

Source: Johnston, L.D., O'Malley, P.M., Bachman, J.G., and Schulberg, J.E. (2004). Monitoring the Future national results on adolescent drug use: Overview of key findings, 2003. Bethesda MD; National Institute on Drug Abuse. Website: www.monitoringthefuture.org.

ADOLESCENT IMPAIRED DRIVING RISK AND CAUSATIVE FACTORS

IN VARIOUS COMBINATIONS and patterns, the above identified factors can increase the risk of adolescents and young adults becoming involved in substance use and abuse. As a consequence, these factors are risks for adolescent involvement in impaired driving. However, there are more specific factors that can combine with the above factors to enhance the risk of involvement in impaired driving.

Adolescent Cultural Factors and Norms

First, substance use dependence in adolescents is different from that in adults (Monti, Colby, & O'Leary, 2001). Adolescence is a time of great change. There is a shift in associations and allegiances from families to peers — along with a corresponding movement toward the norms and values of the peer culture. Drinking alcohol is a commonly accepted norm in our society. Likewise, driving an automobile is an ingrained component of our culture. Both are positively accepted and cherished by our society - and they are both introduced during adolescence (Klepp & Perry, 1990). According to Klepp and Perry (1990) youth, often in contrast to adults, think that impaired driving is not a problem but just something that occurs in their communities. The repercussions of getting caught do not outweigh their reasons for drinking or for drinking and driving.

As with driving, alcohol use is well embedded in our culture (Klepp & Perry, 1990). Drinking is associated with attractive and positive events such as parties, sport events and leisure-time activities. It is little wonder that drinking is attractive to youth.

Binge or episodic drinking also becomes part of the adolescent drinking culture or norms. Adolescents tend to consume all that is available at the time. This happens because they do not often have a place to store alcohol since possession is illegal. Most underage drinkers drink at parties, in cars and in parking lots where they can easily hide the alcohol (Little & Clontz, 1994).

There is also a psychological norm and expectations in adolescence that is met through AOD use. Thrill and sensation seeking, looking cool, not being stressed, problem coping are important in youth culture. AOD use for these purposes increases the probability of impaired driving. Little and Clontz (1994) found that young DWI offenders are more apt to use alcohol to cope with problems or to satisfy needs for risk-taking.

Early Drinking Onset

As discussed in Chapter 3, the younger people were when starting drinking, the more likely they were to drive after drinking too much and of being in motor vehicle crashes (Hingson et al., 2002; NHTSA, 2000). Thus, those who begin drinking at an early age are much more likely to drive impaired during adolescence.

Problem Behavior Theory (PBT)

PBT holds that when the personality system and perceived environment system clash, behavioral problems become manifest (Jessor, 1987a). The core features of the adolescent personality - impulsivity, risk-taking, personal invulnerability or "it can't happen to me," struggling to find personal identity, errors in thinking due to being locked into peer culture ("everybody does it"), risk-taking, rebellion towards authority - coupled with disturbances in psychosocial adjustment clash with the norms and expectations of the culture and society (drive sober) resulting in problem behavior (impaired driving). We can develop effective interventions when we see impaired driving as part of the behavior system that interacts with the personality and environment.

A large research project conducted by Klepp and Perry (1990), using PBT, found that perceived environmental, personality, and behavioral factors were able to account for a large proportion of the observed variance in impaired driving as well as in the prediction of the onset of impaired driving. This study identified five factors most predictive of DWI conduct and which are important foundations for underage DWI prevention and intervention.

- Intentions to drink and drive.

- Experiences riding with a drinking driver.

- Having decided not to drive because of having had too much to drink.

- Marijuana use.

- Having experienced problems with parents, friends or school because of drinking.

Cognitive Errors and Deficits

Cognitive factors also contribute to impaired driving in young people. These factors are described as errors in thinking (Farrow, 1989) or cognitive deficits (Jessor, 1998). Here are some of the most salient of these factors.

- Failure to realize how intoxicated they are and not knowing that they will be impaired while driving (Hingson & Winter, 2003).

- Attribution of responsibility and the failure to see the seriousness of DWI behavior as dangerous and criminal behavior.

- Threat to perceived self-confidence that comes from society injunctions - "you can't tell me I can't drive." This cognitive deficit or error prevents young DWIOs from effective involvement in DWI intervention (Shore & Compton, 1998).

- Lack of information about alcohol and failure to understand different effects of different amounts and kinds of alcohol.

- Because they have driven after drinking before (without being caught), they think they can do it again.

- Risky cognitions (Arnett, 1990) and sensation seeking. DWI conduct is correlated with scores on both the Sensation Seeking Scale (SSS) and the Thrill and Adventure Seeking - Disinhibition and Boredom Susceptibility Subscales (Arnett, 1990).

- Expecting positive outcomes from driving while intoxicated or impaired such as social status, fun or thrills, breaking free of social rules and norms, and becoming more desirable in the eyes of their peers (Jessor, 1998).

- Not grasping the potentially dangerous or lethal

outcomes such as arrest, injury or death (Agostinelli & Miller, 1994; Arnett, 1990). "It can't happen to me."

- Use of DWI conduct and the streets and communities as a venue for a "rite of passage." This would include speeding, drag-racing, and "road rage." This cognitive-behavioral factor ties in with sensation seeking and risk-taking.

- Cognitive intention to drink and drive is a strong predictor (Beck, 1981; Klepp & Perry, 1990).

- Not aware or informed of the laws related to impaired driving. Over 56 percent of youth ages 16-20 surveyed did not know that driving after any drinking is illegal (Royal, 2000).

CHARACTERISTICS OF YOUTH DWI OFFENDERS

FARROW (1985; 1989) finds that young impaired drivers are most often male, doing (or did) poorly in school, hold many jobs and drive late at night. A recurrent finding is that young drivers more frequently crash at lower blood-alcohol concentrations (BACs) than do older drivers, attributable probably to driver immaturity, less experience with decision-making skills and inexperience with drinking, driving or both (Preusser & Preusser, 1992; Preusser & Williams, 1992).

Adolescent males typically drive impaired more frequently than females and more males get DWIs. However, the number of females driving impaired, being arrested for DWI and being involved in alcohol-related crashes is increasing (Popkin et al., 1988).

Wanberg and Timken (2005a) studied 281 underage impaired driving offenders using the Adult Substance Use and Driving Survey (ASUDS: Wanberg & Timken, 1998, 2001) and a personal data form. The results showed that 97.5 percent were single, 68 percent were employed part-time or full-time, 80 percent were male, 59 percent were Anglo-White, two percent African American and 35 percent were Hispanic-American. Slightly over 29 percent had BACs of less than .10, slightly over 41 percent had BACs from .10 up to .15, and 29.5 percent had BACs of .15 or greater. Only 12 percent had prior AOD treatment, 9.4 percent had a prior DWI conviction and only 14.4 percent were involved in an accident at the time of arrest. Over half were placed in only a DWI education intervention protocol.

The underage group was compared with three other age groupings: Age 21 to 30, 31 to 40 and over age 40. Following is a summary of these findings.

▶ The underage group scored lower in involvement in drugs, alcohol involvement, disruption from drug use and drug involvement, and AOD use and disruption in the six months prior to completing the DWI assessment battery.

▶ The underage group scored higher on the driving risk scale.

▶ The underage group scored higher on a scale measuring both static and dynamic antisocial attitudes and behaviors.

▶ The underage group did not differ from other groups on a scale that measured defensiveness and disclosure willingness indicating the findings were valid.

▶ The underage group had significantly fewer prior DWI convictions, fewer prior AOD treatment, were assigned to less intensive interventions and had significantly lower arrest BACs. The latter finding is at variance with reports that underage impaired drivers have higher BACs at the time of arrest.

▶ The mean younger offenders score on the ASUDS Global Adjustment scale did not differ from the other three offender age groups.

▶ Underage offenders scored significantly higher on motivation to change and willingness to be involved in intervention, a finding contrary to some reports in the literature.

The upshot of these findings is that underage drinkers report lower levels of alcohol and other drug involvement, lower levels of disruption from AOD use yet higher levels of driving risk and antisocial attitudes and behavior. These findings provide some explanation as to why the crash and fatality rates are higher among underage impaired drivers. They engage in higher risk driving behaviors, indicate significantly higher levels of antisocial thinking and behaving and act impulsively. These findings support Preusser & Preusser's (1992) conclusion that younger driving offenders are more immature and less experienced with decision-making skills and inexperienced with drinking, driving or both.

MEASURES TO MEDIATE IMPAIRED DRIVING AMONG YOUTH

A NUMBER OF approaches have been used to reduce the incidence of impaired driving among youth and to reduce the number of crashes involving impaired adolescent drivers. These are reviewed.

Strengthening Educational Approaches

Using the results from their study, Klepp and Perry (1990) suggest several ways to strengthen the educational approach to preventing underage impaired driving and DWI related crashes (pp. 62-63).

▶ Target the entire adolescent population.

▶ Tailor traffic safety and AOD abuse prevention programs to students before they reach legal driving age.

▶ Target changes in attitudes and personality attributes that are most predictive of DWI conduct including: perceived ability to drive after drinking; tolerance of impaired driving; lack of self-efficacy with respect to avoiding impaired driving situations.

▶ Focus on skills training that helps adolescents identify and avoid DWI situations both as a driver and passenger.

▶ Target the opportunities for and barriers to impaired driving in society at large. This means focusing on transportation, alcohol availability and access to appropriate places for youth to socialize and not drink. This would involve helping youth to become aware of these factors as well as developing strategies to change environmental factors that support involvement in impaired driving.

Psychosocial Approaches

A number of psychosocial approaches have been identified in the literature to mediate adolescent AOD use and abuse and subsequently impact on reducing impaired driving among adolescents (Milkman & Wanberg, 2005a).

- **Building social competence skills.** There is good evidence (e.g., Griffin, et al., 2001) to indicate that social competence provides a protective function against AOD involvement. Social competencies include assertiveness, communication and problem solving skills. Underdeveloped refusal assertiveness predicts greater drinking involvement (Epstein, Griffin & Botvin, 2001). Building social competence is more than learning to "just say no." Although initially seemingly efficacious when first ushered in the 1980s, over the long haul, the "just say no" approach, in and of itself, did not prove effective. These simple skills must be part of the overall construct of social skills training.

- **Life skills training** is effective in preventing AOD use and abuse in adolescence (Botivin & Griffin, 2002).

- **Cognitive self-management techniques and skills** (Griffin et al., 2001).

- **Building self-esteem** comes from building social competence and cognitive self-management. Low self-esteem is positively correlated with adolescent alcohol use and vulnerability to AOD abuse and impaired driving (Scheier et al., 2000).

- **Alternatives to AOD use** to achieve positive outcome expectancies. Positive AOD outcome expectancies are powerful reinforcers of AOD use in adolescents (Griffin, Botvin, Epstein, Doyle & Diaz, 2000).

- **Positive family influences.** Family activities that revolve around alcohol use justify, promote and strengthen AOD use in adolescents (Costa, Jessor & Turbin, 1999). Enhancing family activities that do not involve alcohol use will provide a strong mediating factor against AOD use in adolescents.

- **Positive social and peer influences.** The role of social and peer influence and deviant peer associations in the etiology of adolescent AOD use and abuse has been identified as central (e.g., Fergusson et al., 2002; Griffin et al., 2000).

- **Promote perceived life changes and sense of life purpose.** Jessor (1998) found a positive relationship between adolescent health behaviors in general and perception of life opportunities.

- **Building health knowledge and skills.** Understanding the risk and dangers around AOD use, impaired driving and impact on mental and physical health is positively correlated with lower levels of AOD use (Agostinelli & Miller, 1994; Scheier & Botvin, 1997).

Intensifying law enforcement efforts

Well-publicized, intensive law enforcement efforts appear to have been effective in reducing the number of alcohol-related fatalities. General deterrence models that demonstrate a plausible risk of being apprehended, followed by significant sanctions, positively influence young drivers not to drive after consuming alcohol (Ross, 1992; Nichols, 1990).

Some evidence that intensity of deterrence models does work is reflected in the fact that states with large populations of young drivers and lenient drinking and driving policies are likely to have higher rates of alcohol-related motor vehicle fatalities (IIHS, 1997). In 1996, states with the highest percentages of youth traffic fatalities involving alcohol were Vermont (68 percent), North Dakota (62 percent) and Hawaii (52 percent). The lowest percentages were found in Utah (10.7 percent) Virginia (24.9 percent), and Georgia (25.2 percent), states with less lenient impaired driving laws.

Age 21 laws

Federal legislation enacted by President Reagan in 1984 mandated that states implement age 21 drinking laws or forfeit large portions of highway safety and improvement funds. All 50 states complied with the 21 minimum drinking age within four years. This legislation makes it illegal for any person who is less than 21 years old to purchase, possess, consume alcoholic beverages or to misrepresent their age to obtain such beverages.

Exact prohibitions in each state's law vary greatly. For example, some states do not prohibit the consumption of alcoholic beverages by persons under age 21. Some states allow persons under age 21 to possess alcoholic beverages in connection with employment activities. Most states allow persons under age 21 to possess and consume alcoholic beverages for religious purposes and at home.

A number of strategies have been used to enforce the age 21 drinking law. These include decoy or sting programs, responsible beverage service training and the development of driver's licenses that are more difficult to alter or counterfeit.

The National Clearinghouse for Alcohol and Drug Information (1999) cites a noticeable drop in alcohol-related traffic fatalities between 1989 and 1998 due mainly to the age 21 laws. The National Highway Traffic Safety Administration (1999b) reported that the minimum-age drinking laws have saved an estimated 18,220 lives since their inception in 1975.

Although implementation of minimum age purchasing laws resulted in a decline of monthly use of alcohol among high school students in the late 1980s, alcohol abuse among youth, however, showed an increase in the late 1990s. Johnston et al's. (2000) finding that within any two-week period, approximately 30 percent of high school seniors engaged in heavy-episode or binge drinking, represents a 30 percent increase since 1995 levels. Increased binge drinking may be directly related to youths' opposition to age 21 legislation. Under age 21 drinking has become more clandestine and fervent.

Age 21 laws have not been vigorously enforced. In 1997, 75 percent of 8th graders and 89 percent of 10th graders reported that alcohol is "fairly easy" or "easy" to obtain (Johnston et al., 1997). Preusser and Williams (1992) report that 18-20-year-old males successfully bought beer in retail outlets in 97 percent of attempts in Washington, DC, and 80 percent of attempts in a county in New York State. Further, the rate at which juveniles are arrested for liquor law violations is quite low. In 1996, law enforcement agencies made only 518 liquor law violation arrests for every 100,000 persons 10 to 17 years old in the resident population (Snyder, 1997).

Failure by retail stores to check identification is one of the main reasons underage drinkers access alcohol. Two other main sources of access are through friends over age 21 and from their own homes. As a result, the general deterrence model has spread beyond the offenders themselves. Penalties for violating such laws can include fines, jail time and license revocation for individuals who knowingly sell alcohol to youths under the age of 21 and civil liabilities for those who knowingly serve alcoholic beverages to minors.

Zero-tolerance laws and approaches

Studies have shown that teenage drivers increase their risk of crashes after only one or two drinks. More 18-19-year-olds die in low BAC alcohol-related crashes than any other group. Beginning with Maine in 1983, most states have now adopted zero tolerance laws, which set certain BAC levels as offenses for which licenses can be revoked. These laws are often a combination of illegal per se and administrative per se laws and prohibit persons under 21 years of age from operating a motor vehicle if they have any measurable amount of alcohol in the blood or breath.

While BAC levels for underage drivers vary from state to state (.00 to .02), as of the year 2000, 34 states allow the driver-licensing agency to suspend or revoke the driver's license if the driver is found to have an alcohol concentration of .02 or above. This is equal to approximately one drink for the average person. Because of the high value young people place on driving, the threat of losing a driver's license deters many youths from attempting to drink and drive (NHTSA, 1996). Zero tolerance can be seen as a form of leverage so that youths will decide against drinking at all.

It is argued that over-the-counter medications and some food preparations might register as BACs between 0.00 and 0.01. However, as of the year 2000, ten states and the District of Columbia have adopted the 0.00 percent level and two states, 0.01 percent. States that set levels lower than the adult level, yet higher than .02 percent are not considered to have zero tolerance impaired driving laws. As of November 1997, only four states did not have some form of lower BAC limit for young drivers (IIHS, 1997).

Zero tolerance laws appear to be effective. The utilization of this approach has reduced alcohol-related crashes in the 15 to 20 year old age groups by as much as 50 percent in some states and between 17 and 22 percent consistently. The effects of the laws increase when they are combined with public awareness campaigns (IIHS, 1997).

Graduated licensing laws

Sixteen-year-old drivers have very high crash rates in proportion to the number of miles they drive. One study showed that 16 year olds had 43 crashes per million miles driven, compared with 30, 15, 10 and 5 crashes for ages 17, 18 to 19, 20 to 24 and 25 or older, respectively (Research Triangle Institute, 1991). When young people drink and drive, they experience far more trouble than older drivers do - with less alcohol.

Graduated licensing is a process whereby learning drivers can be gradually granted driving privileges. Reductions in traffic crashes, both alcohol related and not alcohol related, have been measured as a result of nighttime driving curfews, increased age of licensure and graduated driving privileges (in which a variety of driving restrictions are gradually lifted as the driver gains experience and maturity). Most European countries do not license drivers until they are 18; some license at 17; and only one, Estonia, licenses 16-year-olds. This contrasts dramatically to the United States, where most states license at age 16 and some license at age 15.

Maryland implemented a graduated licensing system with a night driving restriction in 1979. Research on youth driving problem episodes in Maryland shows a 5 percent reduction in the number of teen drivers involved in crashes and a 10 percent reduction in traffic law violations and convictions for 16 and 17-year-old drivers (McKnight, Hyle and Albricht, 1983). Upstate New York and Pennsylvania have had a night driving restriction for 16-year-olds and some 17-year-olds for several years.

Connecticut and Delaware, which licensed 16-year-olds at the time of the study but did not have graduated systems, were compared with New Jersey and Long Island, which did not license until age 17. The results indicated that New Jersey and Long Island with no licensing until age 17 had a huge advantage over Delaware and Connecticut (Ferguson, Leaf, Williams, and Preusser, 1996).

Graduated licensing, which phases in privileges as drivers gain experience, consists of three distinct steps.

▶ **Learning** - practice driving under the supervision of an experienced licensed driver.

▶ **Restricted** - allows people to drive unsupervised under certain conditions including restrictions on night driving which reduces the likelihood that the driver might use psychoactive substances, passenger limitations, and limitations on what type of vehicles can be driven.

▶ **Full** - allows full privileges without restrictions.

State laws vary on minimum learning and licensing ages. For example, Colorado has three types of learner's permits. From age 15 to 15 1/2, a student is eligible for a *Driver Education Permit,* and may drive only with an instructor. At 15 1/2, a student is eligible for a *Driver Awareness Permit* if enrolled in a driver awareness program run by the State Patrol; and they may drive with any licensed driver 21 years or older. From 16 to 18 years of age, a person may obtain a *Minor Instruction Permit* that they must hold for at least 12 months before they may apply for a minor's driver's license. Those who are 18 to 21 years old have to have an instructor permit but there is no time requirement before they may apply for a minor's license issued to people in this age category (Colorado Department of Revenue, 2004).

Coordinated efforts to mediate underage impaired driving

Although implementation of the above laws and approaches resulted in a decrease of impaired driving among underage drivers, by the mid-1990s, the number of youth traffic deaths due to alcohol was again on the rise. In 1996, the number of alcohol-related crashes involving youth between 15 and 20 years of age increased by almost 5 percent compared with the previous year. More than 3,900 youth age 21 or younger died in alcohol-related crashes in 2002 (NHTSA, 2003b).

Klepp and Perry (1990) suggest that instead of

Stoduto et al. 1993) found 62% of drivers being treated in the emergency room for major traumas had BAC levels of over .15. In South Australia, Holubowycz et al. (1994) found similar numbers. Simpson (1995) finds that the hard core drinking driver makes up 15-20% of drivers in alcohol-related accidents with injuries.

Poor Driving Skills and Records

Most hard core drinking drivers have a history of traffic problems. Recidivists have more driving problems than one-time offenders (Peck, Arstein-Kerslake & Helander, et al., 1994).

Repeat DWI Offenders

The repeat offender (offenders with multiple DWI convictions), is an important subset of HC drinking drivers. Extensive research indicates that although this group constitutes a small percent of the driving population, they represent a very significant proportion of the DWI problem and represent the most manifest of the HC impaired driver (Caviola & Wuth, 2002; Caviola, Wolf & Lavender, 1999; Fell, 1993, 1994; Jones & Lacey, 2000; McGuire, 1980; Nichols & Ross, 1989; NHTSA, 1998; Peck, Arstein-Kerslake and Helander, 1994; Simpson, 1995; Transportation Research Board and National Research Council, 1995; Vingilis et al., 1994; Wilson, 1991; Yu & Williford, 1991). From 35 to 40 percent of fatally injured drivers had a prior DWI arrest and around 35 percent of impaired drivers involved in alcohol-related fatal crashes had a prior conviction. Thus, about 30 to 35 percent of the first offender group will become repeat offenders. Around 31 percent of the 1.5 million annual DWI arrests, were repeat offenders.

Summarizing from the various sources cited above, the following characteristics provide a profile of repeat offenders.

- Predominantly male, typically over 90 percent.

- About 75 percent are under 40.

- Predominantly Anglo-White American.

- In the low income categories; less than high school education.

- Unmarried.

- Not white collar workers.

- Average arrest BAC of .18 and higher where fatal crashes are involved.

- Multiple DWI arrests and convictions.

- Higher number of prior traffic and criminal offenses.

- More severe alcohol, personality and health problems. One study showed that a majority of repeat offenders had high cognitive impairments (Glass, Chan & Rentz, 2000).

- Less flexible, less expressive emotionally, more introverted and low psychological need for affiliation.

- Drink mainly at bars or at parties at home and when out drinking, the final destination is home.

- Often plan to drive after drinking.

- Beverage of choice is beer, but often distilled spirits.

- About 10 percent per year recidivate and this increases with the number of prior DWIs. More than 50 percent refuse blood or breath tests at arrest.

- Strong perception of being capable of driving while impaired although recognizing that there is a possibility of being arrested for DWI.

- Typically given traditional DWI sanctions including jail, fines and license suspension, and are often required to attend alcoholism treatment programs.

- Some studies showed repeat offender did not differ from first time offenders as to arrest BAC (Caviola & Wuth, 2002); other studies indicate the repeat offenders had higher arrest BACs (Wanberg & Timken, 2005a).

- It is generally agreed that the "hard core" and the repeat offenders do not respond to the traditional mainstream education and treatment methods (Caviola & Wuth, 2002).

STUDY OF REPEAT OFFENDERS

IN A STUDY OF 2554 DWI offenders in Colorado, mean scores of three groups of offenders were compared across demographic, alcohol and other drug use, driving risk, mood adjustment, circumstances at time of arrest and BAC variables (Wanberg & Timken, 2005a). The groups were: first time offenders, 65.1 percent; one prior offense, 21.3 percent; and two or more priors, 13.6 percent.

The demographic and descriptive characteristics of the repeat offender sample (groups two and three) were: about 25 percent were married; about 87 percent were male; almost 58, 5.2 and 30.1 percent were Anglo-White, African American and Hispanic respectively; over 70 percent were employed full time and about 10 percent part-time; about 14 percent were in an accident at the time of arrest; and just over 76 percent had prior treatment.

Comparing the three groups across the demographic variables indicated essential agreement with previous repeat-offender reports in the literature with respect to age and gender: there was a statistically significant increase of males and age when moving from the first time through one prior to two or more prior DWIs.

Also in agreement with previous reports was the statistically significant increase in BAC levels across the three samples: BAC for first time offenders was .144; one prior DWI, .158; and two or more prior DWIs, a mean BAC of .177.

The three groups did not significantly differ with respect to: an accident at the time of arrest; being unemployed; and not married. Repeat offenders were more apt to be Anglo-White.

Most revealing were the findings comparing the three groups across the Adult Substance Use and Driving Survey (ASUDS: Wanberg & Timken, 1998) scales. These findings are summarized.

▶ There was a statistically significant increase in involvement in drugs, degree of disruption from drug use and degree of involvement in and disruption from alcohol use across the three groups. The AOD problems just get worse with increasing number of DWI convictions.

▶ There is a statistically significant increase in anti-social attitudes and behavior across the three samples. With increased number of DWIs, clients are increasingly antisocial.

▶ Disruption in mood and psychological adjustment is greater for the group with two or more prior DWIs. The first offender group did not differ from the one prior DWI offender group.

▶ Motivation for change and treatment increases across three offender groups showing that the group with one prior DWI is more motivated than the first time offenders, but the offenders with two or more prior DWIs indicate even more motivation for change and treatment than the other two groups.

▶ The group with two or more priors is less defensive and more self-disclosing than the other two groups.

▶ The overall ASUDS Global score significantly increased across the three groups supporting the conclusions of this study and prior studies that repeat offenders simply are more disrupted in the areas of AOD use, mood and antisocial behavior.

The one good news about repeat offenders is that, even though they have greater levels of psychosocial and substance use problems, they are more motivated for services and less defensive.

IDENTIFICATION AND INTERVENTION

EFFORTS TO REDUCE the problem of the HC impaired driver have been somewhat fruitful. In California, there was a decrease from 10 to seven percent in the one-year recidivism rate from 1989 to 1995 (NHTSA, 1998). Identification and intervention are the two critical areas in developing effective countermeasures for the HC and repeat offender.

Identification

The above identified characteristics and the use of reliable self-report instruments provide the technology for identifying which first-time offenders are HC and have high probability of becoming repeat offenders. First offenders who fit most if not all of the following markers are high risk for continuing DWI conduct.

- Gregarious and convivial drinking pattern, yet indicating and introvertive type personality pattern.

- Higher BACs at arrest.

- Higher levels of AOD involvement and disruption.

- A history of antisocial behaviors and attitudes.

- More mood and psychological disruptions.

- Past DWI behavior and convictions.

- Poor driving records.

- Accidents and injuries associated with past DWI behavior.

Countermeasures and Interventions

Identification is only part of the answer. Developing strategies to prevent recidivism and repeat DWI behavior is the primary goal. There are three major thrusts to this prevention effort: Changes in statutes and laws; sanctioning and correctional approaches; and education and treatment. We will look at the sanctioning-correctional and rehabilitative countermeasures efforts, including the HC and repeat offender, in Chapter 8. However, there are several important statutory changes that have occurred in recent years that have been directed at the HC and repeat offender.

- Lowering the BAC for legal intoxication for drivers with prior DWI convictions has contributed to the reduction of fatal crashes involving drivers with priors, particularly with drivers with a BAC .15 or greater (Hingson et al., 1998).

- Driver licensing sanctions have reduced recidivism and in some states, license revocation has reduced alcohol-related fatalities between six and nine percent (NHTSA, 2000).

- Mandating treatment has reduced reoffender rates.

- Instituting Section 164 of the Transportation Equity Act for the 21st Century Restoration Act that requires all states to institute certain repeat intoxicated driver laws by October, 2001 or have their Federal-aid highway construction funds redirected into other state safety activities (NHTSA, 2000). Section 164 was a response to research conducted on the HC and repeat offender as summarized in this chapter. Under this program, a repeat intoxicated driver is defined as one convicted of driving while intoxicated or under the influence more than once in any five-year period. This now required that states keep DWI convictions on record for at least five years. To comply with Section 164, each state must have laws regarding second and subsequent DWI convictions based on the following guidelines.

- Require a minimum of one-year license suspension for repeat offenders.

- Require repeat offender motor vehicles be impounded or immobilized for a period of time during license suspension, or require installation of an ignition interlock system for a period of time after the end of the suspension.

- Require mandatory assessment of repeat offender's degree of alcohol abuse and referral to appropriate treatment.

- Establish a mandatory sentence for repeat offenders: not less than five days of imprisonment or 30 days of community service for the second offense; and not less than 10 days of imprisonment or 60 days for the third or subsequent offense.

SUMMARY

Repeat offenders present an enormous challenge to law enforcement agencies, the correctional system and the treatment community. Repeat offenders need different kinds and levels of sanctioning and treatment services. Enforcement strategies that deter most law-abiding citizens are not as effective with repeat offenders. As a result, despite having histories of convictions and/or crashes, a majority of repeat offenders continue to drive while impaired. Yet, even if hard core and repeat offenders are eliminated from the picture, we would still be left with a large proportion of the problem of drunk driving and its enormous consequences.

CHAPTER SEVEN: PERSPECTIVES ON A PROCESS AND CONVERGENT VALIDATION MODEL FOR THE ASSESSMENT OF IMPAIRED DRIVING OFFENDERS

OVERVIEW

IT IS COMMON PRACTICE of most judicial agencies to use some form of screening to evaluate DWI offenders in order to determine appropriate countermeasures needs, education and treatment placement and the need for further assessment. It is also common practice for intervention and treatment agencies to do further in-depth assessment in order to determine the more specific needs of the client and to develop an individualized treatment plan (ITP).

Much of the information gathered in these assessment efforts relies on information and reports received from the DWI offender. Yet, it is common belief, particularly among correctional workers and many evaluators and clinicians that these self-reports are not reliable and are often not to be trusted. Some studies have pointed out that DWI offenders underreport their AOD use and impaired driving histories and that, among first-time offenders, there is a high percent of "false" self-reporting (Chang & Lapham, 1996).

However, most would agree that assessment, particularly initial screening is essential in the process of developing an effective countermeasures and intervention plan for the DWIO. Thus, how do we approach assessment so as to resolve the dilemma between this importance and the problem of report veridicality?

The purpose of this Chapter is to provide a theoretical framework and model that resolves the dilemma between the importance of establishing a valid information base for placement and intervention planning and the problem of report veridicality. This Chapter will discuss the assessment concepts and constructs that guide the evaluation of the DWI offender. It will provide guidelines as to the type of instrumentation and measurements that can be used in this process. Chapter 13 will provide a specific operational approach to DWI offender assessment and evaluation based on the *Differential Screening Assessment and Placement (DSAP) Model* (Timken & Wanberg, 2001).

PROCESS OF ASSESSMENT

THE ASSESSMENT OF DWIOs is a process that begins with screening and continues through the assessment of the outcome of intervention and treatment. There are four main components to this process.

- **Screening,** which could be: simple screening for the level of DWI involvement and extent of involvement in and disruption from drug use; or differential screening which goes beyond these two areas and includes screening for mental health issues, driving risk, antisocial patterns, motivation for treatment and level of defensiveness. The goal of screening is to determine the appropriate countermeasures, education and treatment services.

- **Comprehensive or in-depth assessment** focuses on distinct conditions or multiple-factors associated with DWI conduct, AOD use and life-adjustment problems. The goal of comprehensive assessment is to identify the extent and severity of problems and strengths of the DWIO and to match the problems with appropriate intervention and treatment services. It provides an in-depth understanding of the client in order to formulate a treatment plan and determine specific treatment needs and services. This is a multiple-factor or multidimensional based assessment (Donovan, 2003; Wanberg, Horn & Foster, 1977; Wanberg & Horn, 1987; Wanberg & Milkman, 1998; Winters, 1999). Comprehensive assessment is usually done with DWIO clients referred or mandated to treatment.

- **Progress and change assessment** focuses on the changes the client is making while progressing through intervention and treatment. The main areas of focus are on willingness to self-disclose, motivation to engage services, and changes in cognitions and behaviors associated with impaired driving and AOD use problems. The bottom line measurement variables are recidivism and relapse.

- **Outcome assessment,** which includes immediate, short-term or long-term assessment. Immediate outcome assessment occurs at the end of intervention and treatment; short-term usually refers to three to six month post-discharge outcome assessment; and long term refers to a minimum of six months post-discharge.

This chapter will focus mainly on the screening and comprehensive aspects of assessment. Some attention will given to the assessment of treatment process and outcome.

OBJECTIVES OF ASSESSMENT

THE GOALS OF SCREENING, comprehensive, change and outcome assessment have several specific common objectives.

▶ **To provide opportunity to disclose information.** This objective begins with screening but continues throughout treatment and follow-up. Self-disclosure defines how clients see themselves at any point of assessment and provides a baseline of the client's willingness to self-disclose and defensiveness along the points of assessment.

▶ **To gather information from other individuals associated with the client or other sources of information about the client.** "Other individuals" include probation supervisors, case managers or family members. "Other sources" include BAC reports, UA screens, official records, records of prior treatment.

▶ **To discern the level of openness or defensiveness of the client** along all points of assessment, but particularly at screening. The level of openness to disclose will have a direct bearing on the client's motivation to engage in change.

▶ **To use self-report and other-report to estimate the "true" condition of the client.** We never know how veridical or valid the information is with respect to this "true" condition. We only estimate this condition. Our estimate at screening will not be as veridical as our estimate at in-depth assessment. This estimate is ongoing and converging.

▶ **To make summary statements of the client's condition** or situation along all points of assessment. These summaries provide intervention decision guidelines, the degree and level of problems in the various domains of assessment, a diagnosis and a summary of the client's intervention progress.

▶ **To make referral and disposition decisions.** These decisions are continuous and ongoing. At screening, the decision might be to refer the client to DWI education or DWI treatment or referral for more comprehensive assessment. At the comprehensive level, the task is to match presenting problems with appropriate treatment resources. During correctional supervision, it might mean extending sanctions because of failure to comply with the judicial mandates.

DATA SOURCES FOR ASSESSMENT AND REPORT SUBJECTIVITY

THERE ARE TWO types of data that are used in screening and in-depth or multiple-factor assessment: other-report; and self-report.

Other Report Data

Other report data represent information that is collateral to the self-report of the client. These data include reports from probation officers, family members, evaluation and treatment specialists, laboratory results and official records. They are sorted into two categories: reports from individual third parties who have some familiarity with the client; and official documentation such as laboratory reports or legal records.

Individual third party other-report data can be narrative or structured into rating scales. These are always subjective data. In fact, these data are double-subjective. Information given to the evaluator by the client or collaterals is subjective. The evaluator's interpretation of the information is subjective making the evaluator's final impressions or ratings double-subjective.

In addition to being double-subjective, there are other problems with other-report data. Different evaluators often do not agree about the presence or absence of a certain condition. The same evaluator on different occasions can reach different conclusions. The evaluator may not always be consistent in asking the same questions or may be biased and make a judgment on the basis of only a few items or symptoms. Rater or other-report data can be made more objective when standardized criteria are used to rate information provided by the client or collaterals.

Official documentation data include urine analysis results, arrest BAC level and records of past offenses and treatment. These data are also subject to error, distortion, underrepresentation and misreporting. The official driving record may not fully disclose the extent or nature of the client's driving history. A final charge or conviction may be different from the original charge following plea-bargaining. The official record rarely reflects the extent of involvement in criminal activity. Documentation of one DWI will not reveal the number of times a client has driven while intoxicated. Using the same specimen, laboratory reports will differ as to BAC results or level of drug metabolites. In spite of these problems, this source of data is essential when assessing a client's condition and treatment needs.

Self-Report Data

There are two types of self-report data: Interview (narrative) and psychometric test data. These data are also subjective.

Interview self-report provides a good basis for understanding the client, particularly when recorded in a verbatim fashion. However, when the interviewer makes an assessment statement around these data, or restructures the narrative summary into ratings, then the final report by the evaluator (narrative or rating) becomes other-report data and is double-subjective.

Self-report data become most meaningful and more objective when they are based on the principles of psychological measurement. This approach reduces the subjectivity of self-report data and makes them more reliable and veridical (valid).

Self-report data are made more objective when the information is collected in a standardized format. Every subject is asked the same questions and is provided with the same response options under a consistent and standardized structure.

Self-report data become more objective when several questions are used to measure a single construct. This is called multiple variable measurement. This measurement sums across all of the questions. One area is measured by several questions reducing the risk of error being made by asking only one question. The more valid aspects of a variety of questions more accurately measure the particular area of evaluation. This is the basis of most psychological measurement (Horn, Wanberg & Foster, 1990).

Subjectivity of self-report is reduced when a client's peers are used as the normative basis upon which to interpret the client's results or scores. Thus, when comparing a defensive client's self-report with his or her peers also thought to be defensive in self-disclosure, we gain a better understanding of the meaning of the client's score rankings in relationship to his or her peers.

The subjectivity of self-report can also be reduced when trust and rapport are developed with that client. This enhances the veridicality (the hypothetical valid or true picture) of the client's self-disclosure.

VALUING CLIENT SELF-DISCLOSURE WHEN DISCERNING VERIDICALITY

The Process and Content of Assessment

Self-report information should be viewed from two perspectives: the specific content of the data that we use in estimating the client's "true" condition; and the changes of this condition as it is reported over time. The content of the data gathered at any particular point in time is relevant only as it is viewed within the process of change. The results of any one point of testing should never be taken as a fixed and final description of the client. Any point in testing only provides us with an estimate of the client's condition and gives us guidelines for treatment needs at that point in time. From this perspective, the process of assessment is just as important as the content of assessment.

As noted earlier, AOD evaluators and workers tend to distrust the "so-called" validity of client self-report, particularly those of DWI offenders. Evaluators are quick to conclude that clients are "lying" or "into denial" when they think that clients are not reporting their "true" condition. However, when we see assessment as a process, we view all self-report as a valid representation of where the client is at a particular point in time. If we feel the client is not accurately reporting his or her "real condition," we should view this within the framework of self-defensiveness, rather than denial.

Within this perspective, self-report data is viewed as a baseline measure of the client's willingness to disclose his or her problems or conditions at the time of testing. The value of self-report is that it tells us the degree of openness to self-disclosure and where the client is at testing. The discernment of the validity or veridicality of the report revolves around this baseline self-reported perception and the level of defensiveness related to reporting this perception. What we are discerning, first and foremost, is the client's level of defensiveness and then the veridicality of the client's self-report as to the "true" condition of the client. This discernment is part of the overall task of the evaluator.

Discerning veridicality

Other-report is important in discerning the veridicality - the true or valid condition - of the self-report. Both self-report and other-report data are essential in providing us with an estimate of the "true" condition of the client. We can hypothesize about this condition. Our data then can test that hypothesis.

Most important, self-report is essential in the assessment process in that it represents the client's current willingness to report what he or she perceives to be going on. This **self-perception is where the change process begins** - with the client's self-perception, or the willingness to disclose information around that self-perception.

The opportunity for self-disclosure through self-report is essential and necessary in any assessment process. This is where **intervention and treatment begins** - with the client's report of her or his perception of what is going on. If self-report in the initial assessment is not veridical with what is going on in the client's life, and if treatment is working, later self-reports will reflect a change in the reporting of this self-perception. The first indication of treatment efficacy is found in the client's increase of self-disclosure and openness in treatment. Retesting should reveal any change occurring in this self-disclosure.

Within this model of assessment, every client self-report is valid. Even a "slap-dash" responding to test items is valid - valid, not in terms of content, but in terms of the client's defensiveness and response-state at the time of testing. If we view all self-reports as the client's willingness to disclose his or her perception about the conditions being evaluated at the time of testing, then we conclude that this is a valid representation of that perception. If we have evidence that the self-report is not veridical with collateral information, and the client is highly defensive around self-disclosure, then the report is valid in the sense that we have an estimate of the discrepancy between what the client says is going on and what the other-reports indicate. We may then conclude that our estimate of defensiveness and discrepancy is valid. This discrepancy then becomes the basis for where we start treatment.

THE CONVERGENT VALIDATION AND PROCESS MODEL OF ASSESSMENT

THE CONVERGENT VALIDATION assessment model (Wanberg & Horn, 1987; Wanberg, 1992, 1998, 2000; Wanberg & Horn, 2005) utilizes self-report and other-report as valid representations of where the client is at the time of assessment. It is based on the Campbell and Fiske's classic multi-trait-multimethod matrix approach (1959). They found that using several methods of assessment was more effective than any single method alone, e.g., interview only. The convergent validation model uses all sources of information to converge on the most valid "estimate" of the client's condition in key areas of assessment. From this perspective, all sources of information are considered to be a valid representation of that "estimate" at any particular point of assessment. Report invalidity must be interpreted as indicating the discrepancy between sources of data, level of defensiveness, and the client's willingness to self-disclose and engage in intervention and treatment services.

Figure 7.1 provides a graphic representation of this model. The vertical vector (A) represents the "true" or veridical condition of the client's alcohol use problem. Vector B represents the other-report source of data for a particular client and vector C the self-report source of data for that client. The magnitude of the angle between vectors B and C (B-C) is the theoretical estimate of the level of defensiveness or the willingness of the client to self-disclose. The magnitude of the angle between vector A and the mid-point between vectors B-C represents the veridicality of the estimate of the "true" condition in the area of the client's alcohol use problem. The B-C set of vectors would indicate a client who is relatively open to self-disclosure, whose self-report is discerned to be congruent with other-report data and both sources of data are good estimates of the client's "true" condition (vector A). The D-E set of vectors represents a more defensive client whose self-report is quite discriminate from the other report, but the other-report is also discerned to be not a good estimate of the client's "true" condition.

The convergent validation approach prevents getting caught up in the question of whether the client

is "lying," "under-reporting," "denying," or "falsifying." The initial goals are to discern the client's level of willingness to disclose, the discrepancy between self-report and other-report, and a valid representation of the problems and conditions the client is willing to report at the time of evaluation. This current condition of disclosure can then be used as a baseline for comparing problem-disclosure in ongoing assessment.

FIGURE 7.1

The Convergent Validation Model: Vector representation of the client's "true" condition (A), the other-report (B), and self-report (C) for client B-C; and Vector representation of the client's "true" condition (A), the other-report (D), and self-report (E) for client D-E.

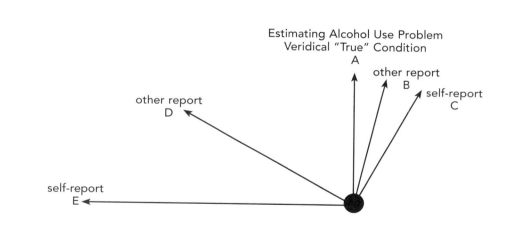

The B-C angle is the discrepancy between self-report and other-report and represents a measure of defensiveness. For this client, there is low discrepancy and low defensiveness.

The angle between A and the B-C average represents the estimate of A or "true condition" of alcohol use problems. For this client, it is a good estimate of the "true condition."

The D-E angle represents another client. Discrepancy is high and defensiveness is high.

The magnitude of the angle between A and the D-E average is large, and for this client it is a poor estimate of the client's alcohol use problem.

SUPPORT FOR THE CONVERGENT VALIDATION APPROACH

SUPPORT FOR THE convergent validation and process model of assessment is found in a study by Stinchfield (1997) which compared intake data with retest data at treatment completion. Both testings asked respondents to base their self-report on the year prior to treatment. Retest mean scores were significantly higher than those at intake indicating that respondents had a greater willingness to disclose and were less defensive following treatment.

Rather than interpreting the Stinchfield findings as indicating that the retest was more valid, compared to the intake testing, it is more logical to conclude that treatment had the effect of enhancing self-disclosure. From the convergent validation and process assessment perspective, the intake testing was no less valid than the retesting. The difference score was a measure of the change in willingness to disclose; it is a measure of treatment effect.

An unpublished study of two large samples of DWIOs tested at different times in the evaluation process provides further support for the convergent validation model (Wanberg & Timken, 2004). Using the *Adult Substance Use and Driving Survey* (ASUDS: Wanberg & Timken, 1998), one sample was tested before judicial disposition - thus, clients did not know what the sentencing or intervention requirements would be. The second was tested after judicial disposition. The second group of clients scored significantly higher across all of the ASUDS' scales and significantly lower on the defensive scale. The effect coefficients were large.

Self-report is always subject to the psychosocial posture of the respondent at the time of testing. We would expect these reports to change, even with non-clinical samples. Respondents will vary their self-reports around the age of first use (Bailey, Flewelling & Rachal, 1992) and frequency-duration patterns (Single, Kandel & Johnson, 1975). Again, rather than view these differences within the context of invalidity, we should view these within the context of self-perception and that the willingness to disclose is dynamic, ever shifting and process determined.

Winters (2001) calls this the "intake-discharge" effect and the dampening effect of initial data gathering. Although he does not conclude that the "intake" data are a valid representation, as would the **convergent validation model,** he does acknowledge that this effect is relevant to using motivational enhancement in treatment to move clients to a more realistic reporting of their so called "true condition."

Further support for the convergent validation and process approach to assessment is found in studies of the congruency between the client's self-report and parent other-report. Whereas one study reported a 17 percent agreement validity (Weissman et al., 1987), another study reported a 63 percent agreement (Edelbrook, et al., 1986) and still another reported a 78 percent validity agreement (Winters et al., 2000).

These findings merely point out that validity of self-report and other report must be viewed from the perspective of where the client and collaterals are at the time of testing with respect to willingness to self-disclose. For example, parents who have difficulty accepting substance abuse problems of their child or spouses who are having difficulty accepting their mate's alcohol addiction will initially be defensive around disclosing information that supports these conditions.

As collaterals also progress through the process of self-disclosure and self-awareness, they will provide a more veridical estimate of the client's (and their own) "true condition." The process and convergent validation model of assessment will hold that collateral disclosure at any particular point of the assessment-change process is a valid representation of that individual's view of the client, or a representation of that collateral's willingness to disclose that view.

SELF-REPORT DATA AS A VALID ESTIMATE OF THE CLIENT'S TRUE CONDITION

EVEN THOUGH THE convergent validation approach would hold that all self-report is valid, the issue of how well any self-report at any given time of assessment represents a good estimate of the client's true condition has been a focus of much debate (Babor, Stephens & Marlatt, 1987; Chang & Lapham, 1996; Watson, et al., 1984; Winters, 2001).

In general clinical populations, including adolescents, self-report is an effective way to estimate the client's "true" condition. Winters (2001) and Sobell and Sobell (2003) cite a number of sources supporting the validity of self-report in giving a good estimate of the client's "true" condition (Brown et al., 1998; Maisto, Connors & Allen, 1995; Shafer et al., 1996; Winters et al., 1991). These sources indicate that there is general consistency of self-disclosure over time, large portions of clinical samples disclose the use of illegal drugs, generally, there is a low rate of "faking bad" among self-report samples, clinical samples tend to report a much higher prevalence of use and abuse than do normal samples, and there is good convergence between self-reports and other-reports.

The DWIO group is seen by many as an exception to these findings. DWIOs are viewed as resistant to engaging in the evaluation process and engaging intervention services and underreport their AOD use and impaired driving histories (e.g., Cavaiola & Wuth, 2002; Chang & Lapham, 1996; Fine, Scoles & Mulligan, 1975). Since there is evidence that DWIOs are defensive and resistive to disclosing their impaired driving and AOD use histories (e.g., Chang & Lapham, 1996), it is all the more important that we:

▶ view assessment as a process;

▶ see any given self-report is an estimate of the client's "true" condition at that time;

▶ understand that a part of that "true" condition is the level of defensiveness and openness of the client at the time of assessment; and

▶ enhance the validity of the data to give us an accurate picture of the client when we use a convergent validation or multimethod approach to assessment.

Within this framework, our initial goal of assessment is to discern the level of defensiveness and resistance.

In response to the common view that self-reports of AOD clients in general, and DWIOs in particular are not to be trusted, some tests have used the "subtle" or "oblique" approach to determine report veridicality. This "flies in the face" of the convergent validation model and the process concept of assessment. If an important goal is to discern the level of resistance and defensiveness, then the test items need to be face-valid or the meaning of the questions should be clear and up-front. We want items that are obvious if we are to determine the client's level of defensiveness and openness, and determine how self-disclosure changes over time - the most obvious sign that treatment is working.

Our goal is to measure where the client is at the current time, to have a good assessment of the level of resistance and defensiveness so as to provide the provider with guidelines as to where to start intervention and treatment. If we conclude that all DWIOs are defensive and resistive, then DWIO treatment programs must have built in motivational enhancement and strong therapeutic alliance-building approaches.

INTERPRETING FINDINGS AND ERROR RISK

THE TYPE OF ERROR RISK must be considered when making judgments about findings. This is of particular concern with DWIOs because of their highly defensive nature. There are two kinds of errors that we define when interpreting clinical data.

The first is a *false negative* which is made when it is concluded that there is no problem when in fact there is. This error risk is reduced when our instruments are *test-sensitive* or the test will identify a certain condition that is attempting to measure in individuals who indeed have that condition. This error can also be reduced by making the criteria for inclusion less stringent. When using a psychometric scale, we lower the inclusion cutoff score so that we will include more individuals who show symptoms. The false negative is a critical error, since it may cause us to fail to provide assessment or treatment services for those who need it.

When we reduce the false negative risk, we increase the risk of the *false positive error*. This is concluding that there is a problem when there is not. This error can be reduced when our instruments have *test-specificity* or when the test designed to measure a certain condition is able to sort out those who do not have that condition. This error can also be reduced when we set more stringent inclusion criteria. This may mean that we require more symptoms, or a higher cutoff value for inclusion.

Determining the level of risk we will assume may be based on economic consideration, practice liability, client welfare or inconvenience. In medicine, reducing a false negative risk may mean that more patients may receive an expensive diagnostic procedure. Raising the false negative risk may increase medical liability in that patients who have the disorder will not receive the necessary procedure to confirm diagnosis.

Most medical patients (versus insurance carriers) are willing to decrease the false negative risk, even though it means additional testing and expensive diagnostic procedures when it is not necessary. In behavioral health assessment, where the disorder is most often not life-threatening, this imposition may be unacceptable. DWIOs who have a false-positive diagnosis of alcohol dependence may be mandated to a treatment for a condition they do not have.

One resolution to this dilemma is to have two levels of screening: preliminary and differential. We set criteria that will decrease the risk of a false negative at the level of preliminary screening, and increase the criteria at differential screening where referral decisions are usually made. The "net" is initially large where the cost of assessment is less. At the differential screening, the criteria can be made more stringent, since the risk of false negatives was decreased at the initial screening.

Use of the multimethod or convergent validation approach will reduce these error risks. We avoid depending on the sensitivity and specificity of a particular method of assessment, but allow all methods to formulate conclusions.

Most important, the final assessment or diagnosis is done by the evaluator or clinician and not a specific method. An instrument should never determine final assessment or diagnosis. The interpretative computer summaries must always state "there is indication," or "the results suggest," rather than have the summary provide a firm diagnostic statement.

GUIDELINES FOR USING ASSESSMENT INSTRUMENTS

There are important guidelines that should be followed when using self-report and interview-based psychometric instruments.

Psychometric, self-report methods

Here are the important guidelines that need to be followed when using psychometrically based self-report instruments.

1. Psychometric instruments should demonstrate **construct validity** which "refers to all the evidence, and sound theory derived from evidence, that can be brought to bear in interpretation of the measurements of a scale" (Horn, Wanberg & Foster, 1990; Wanberg, 1997). Construct validity includes **test sensitivity and test specificity,** and all forms of **test reliability.** It is important to distinguish between the **validity of a test** and **the validity of the results of the testing of an individual subject.** The latter is valid representation of the client at the time of testing, based on the level of defensiveness, and an estimate of the client's "true" condition.

2. The **test's norms** should be appropriate for the group of clients being evaluated. It is helpful to have a set of norms representing the client's peers (e.g., DWIOs) and another representing a group involved in services for which the client is being evaluated. For DWI clients, it is helpful for the test to be normed on DWIOs; and a clinical sample with which to assess the client's scores regarding need for treatment.

3. **Test instructions** should be read to the client. The most basic instructions are: "answer each question as honestly as possible"; "answer questions as to how you see yourself"; "give only one answer to each question unless otherwise specified"; "answer all questions"; "the results will be treated within the guidelines of the state and federal confidentiality laws"; "the results will be used to help

develop services and treatments most appropriate for you"; and "the results of your testing will be shared with you."

4. The methods of **test administration** should be standardized. For interview methods, the question and response choices should be read exactly as they are in the test booklet; the client should have a copy of the test booklet and read each question along with the evaluator.

5. The **reading level** of clients should be evaluated by asking them to read the first three or four questions.

6. The evaluator should **understand what the test measures** and whether it fits in with the evaluator's goals. A simple screening instrument should only be used to determine need for differential screening. Screening for treatment referral should be done with a differential screening instrument. A screening instrument should not be used for comprehensive assessment.

7. The evaluator should **have knowledge of the test itself,** and not just what a computerized report says about a client. Computerized scoring gives a standardized interpretion of the test, but will not provide the more idiosyncratic nuances of each individual client.

8. Clients should **receive feedback** as to how they compare with their peers, their level of defensiveness and how their results compare with the evaluator's estimate of the client's "true" condition. This feedback is an essential part of the treatment process (Winters, 2001) and supports the partnership model of treatment (Wanberg & Milkman, 1998; 2005).

Interview Based Assessment Instruments

The clinical interview is an essential component of the assessment process (Juhnke, 2002). Some structured interview instruments follow a strict protocol and then use scales to rate the client across various areas of assessment, using a normative basis for interpretation.

Semi-structured approaches without instrumentation require higher clinical skill level and training

(Winters, 2001), since their query method is not standardized or structured. Structured interview based instruments may not require as skilled of administrator, but require the same level of evaluation expertise in interpreting the findings.

DWI SCREENING APPROACHES

THE DIFFERENCE BETWEEN traditional AOD screening and DWI screening is that the latter is linked with mandatory involvement. Most jurisdictions require the offender to undergo a screening process. It is usually not a matter of deciding whether an offender will be referred to intervention services. It is a matter of what kind of services.

Screening involves determining past involvement in DWI behavior, level of intoxication at arrest and past and current involvement in AOD problems. These areas along with specific assessment approaches are reviewed.

Prior DWI Involvement

A critical set of information in determining intervention services is past involvement in DWI behavior and past AOD education and treatment services. The former information is usually in the official records, at least for the state in which the client was arrested.

Past intervention services may be recorded in the official record, particularly if the services were court ordered. However, the evaluator must mainly rely on self-report for a full picture of past DWI conduct and intervention services. Most generally, persons with history of DWI arrests and past intervention services will be referred to increased intervention intensity.

Prior DWI convictions and treatment are good predictors of AOD involvement and problems at the time of evaluation (Wanberg & Timken, 2005a; Wieczorek, Miller & Nochajski, 1992). Significant correlations (.001 level of confidence) were found between prior treatment and prior DWI and involvement in alcohol and other drug use, disruption from AOD use, antisocial behavior and attitudes and overall global disruption (Wanberg and Timken, 2005a).

BAC at Time of Arrest

BAC at the time of arrest is almost always seen as an important criteria for determining the need for evaluation and/or the need for intervention services. Some studies, however, have concluded that BAC may not be a good predictor of self-reported AOD use involvement or problems, AOD diagnoses and of impaired driving recidivism (Nochajski & Wieczorek, 1997; Wieczorek, Miller & Nochajski, 1992).

Using a revised cutoff BAC rate of .18 (versus .20) as indicative of high BAC, Nochajski and Wieczorek (1997) did a follow-up study of DWI offenders referred for clinical evaluation, based on high BAC levels. In their sample, they found that offenders with high BAC levels (.18 or higher) had a recidivism rate of 8.9 percent where those with an arrest BAC of less than .18 had a recidivism rate of 14.7 percent. They concluded that low BAC is a better predictor of recidivism than high BAC. Nochajski and Wieczorek (1997) conclude that whereas "BAC provides an excellent indicator of driving impairment,....this does not mean that using BAC is appropriate to screen for problem drinking" (pp. 19).

The Wanberg and Timken (2005a) study does not support the above noted findings regarding the relationship of BAC to assessment variables and prior DWI arrests. This study indicated that BAC has significant positive correlations with scales measuring alcohol involvement and problems, AOD use symptoms, prior DWI and prior treatment. As well, those with higher BACs scored higher on a motivation scale that measures the acknowledgement of having an alcohol or other drug use problem and willingness to be involved in treatment. Although the correlations are of lower magnitude (correlations are in the .10 to .18 range), all are significant at the .001 level of confidence. They indicate that those with higher BAC at time of arrest do have significant and noteworthy higher levels of AOD involvement and symptoms and higher levels of motivation. Thus, arrest BAC is a significant predictor of degree of involvement in and disruption from AOD use and abuse.

This study also evaluated the relationship of BAC at the time of arrest with prior DWI convictions. First, from the perspective of BAC level, of those offenders with an arrest BAC less than .18, the records indicated that 28.7 percent had at least one prior DWI arrest; and, of those offenders with a BAC of .18 or higher, the records indicated that 41.4 percent had one or more prior DWIs.

From the perspective of prior DWI arrests, of those offenders with no prior arrests, 24.1 percent had an arrest BAC of .18 or greater; and of those offenders with one or more arrests, 35.7 percent had a BAC of .18 or greater.

Although these data do not relate an arrest BAC to future DWI arrests, as in the Nochajski and Wieczorek (1997) study, they do indicate that arrest BAC is a significant predictor of past DWI arrests; and past DWI arrests is a significant predictor of current arrest BAC. In essence, past DWI arrests predict higher BACs; and higher current BACs predict whether there has been a prior arrest. It is important to remember that Nochajski and Wieczorek (1997) studied DWI clients referred for clinical evaluation based on high BACs whereas the Wanberg and Timken study represented a sample of convicted offenders referred for screening independent of BAC level or other clinical variables.

The Nochajski and Wieczorek (1997) findings are not too surprising. Clients with high BACs usually receive more intensive services, more severe sanctions and more structured supervision and thus, would be expected to have lower recidivism rates. This is also evidence that intervention services do work. The findings clearly indicate that BAC should not be the only determinant of level of intervention and sanctioning intensity. As Wieczorek, et al. (1992) point out, BAC is a single point measurement, it does not tell us about the pattern of AOD use and it is not always at peak at arrest.

However, for all offenders being processed through the system, the Wanberg and Timken data indicate that BAC level data should be used **along with AOD involvemen**t as the primary determinants of placement, since arrest BAC is significantly correlated with prior DWI arrests, prior treatment and past levels of AOD involvement and disruption (Wanberg & Timken, 2005a). This is the basis of the *DSAP* Model (Timken & Wanberg, 2001).

Minimum Symptom Criteria

The minimal symptom criteria approach involves defining AOD problems in terms of a set of diagnostic criteria and requiring that a certain number of these criteria be met for inclusion into the category of AOD problems, abuse or dependence. The evaluator rates the client across specified inclusion or diagnostic criteria. These ratings are considered to be other-report data.

Minimum symptom criteria are other-report or rater data and are double-subjective. The most commonly used minimum symptom criteria is the *Statistical Manual of Mental Disorders IV - DSM-IV* (American Psychiatric Association, 1994). *Table 7.1* provides the criteria for Substance Abuse and *Table 7.2* provides the DSM-IV criteria for Substance Dependence. (See Juhnke, 2002, for an excellent summary of DSM-IV diagnoses related to substance abuse.)

TABLE 7.1 Diagnostic and Statistical Manual IV Criteria for Substance Abuse

CRITERIA FOR SUBSTANCE ABUSE

A. A maladaptive pattern of substance use leading to clinically significant impairment or distress, as manifested by one (or more) of the following, occurring within a 12 month period:

  ▶ recurrent substance use resulting in a failure to fulfill major role obligations at work, school, or home (e.g., repeated absences or poor work performance related to substance use; substance-related absences, suspensions, or expulsions from school; neglect of children or household)

  ▶ recurrent substance use in situations in which it is physically hazardous (e.g., driving an automobile or operating a machine when impaired by substance use)

  ▶ recurrent substance use despite legal problems (e.g., arrests for substance-related disorderly conduct)

  ▶ continued substance use despite having persistent or recurrent social or interpersonal problems caused or exacerbated by the effects of the substance (e.g., arguments with spouse about consequences of intoxication, physical fights)

B. The symptoms have never met the criteria for Substance Dependence for this class of substance

---

TABLE 7.2 Diagnostic and Statistical Manual IV Criteria for Substance Dependence

CRITERIA FOR SUBSTANCE DEPENDENCE

A maladaptive pattern of substance use, leading to clinically significant impairment or distress, as manifested by three (or more) of the following, occurring at any time in the same 12-month period.

1. Tolerance, as defined by either of the following:
  ▶ a need for markedly increased amounts of the substance to achieve intoxication or desired effect
  ▶ markedly diminished effect with continued use of the same amount of the substance

2. withdrawal, as manifested by either of the following:
  ▶ the characteristic withdrawal syndrome for the substance
  ▶ the same (or a closely related) substance is taken to relieve or avoid withdrawal symptoms

3. the substance is often taken in larger amounts or over a longer period than was intended

4. there is a persistent desire or unsuccessful efforts to cut down or control substance use

5. a great deal of time is spent in activities necessary to obtain the substance, or use the substance

6. important social, occupational, or recreational activities are given up or reduced because of substance use

7. the substance use is continued despite knowledge of having a persistent or recurrent physical or psychological problem that is likely to have been caused or exacerbated by the substance

Specify if:

With Physiological Dependence: evidence of tolerance or withdrawal (either item 1 or 2 is present)
Without Physiological Dependence: no evidence of tolerance or withdrawal (neither item 1 nor 2 is present)

Reports in the literature vary from as low as 20 percent to as high as 50 percent as to what percent of DWI offenders fit either the DSM abuse or dependence categories. Nochajski et al. (1994) reported 28 percent of first time DWI arrests and 45 percent of repeat DWI arrests met DSM criteria for alcohol dependence. This means that the DSM-IV criteria may not be appropriate for as many as 80 percent of the DWI offenders in terms of identifying whether an offender has a problem with AOD use. Using DSM criteria will result in a high percent of false negatives with respect to AOD use problems. Nochajski and Wieczorek (1997) conclude that the rate of problem drinking (not necessarily Abuse or Dependence a la DSM) is greater than 50 percent (p. 19). A Colorado study (Colorado Department of Human Services, 1998) showed that 80 percent of DWI offenders could be classified problem drinkers. Thus, criteria other than those for abuse and dependence in the DSM are needed to determine what constitutes an AOD problem for many DWI offenders.

The Impaired-Control Cycle:

The concept of impaired control and the impaired-control cycle (ICC) can be useful in resolving this problem and in identifying the presence of an AOD problem (Wanberg, 1974, 1990; Wanberg & Horn, 1987; Wanberg & Milkman, 2005a). Impaired control occurs when notable negative consequences result from drug use (loss of job, physical problems, relationship, marital problems, etc.). The cycle begins when drugs are used to solve problems that result from their use and continues when the individual continues to use drugs to solve the problems that come from drug use.

In this approach, a person who develops significant negative consequences from alcohol use would be considered to have had an alcohol problem. All DWI offenders would fit this category, since we would consider a DWI to be a problem resulting from AOD use. An individual who uses alcohol to manage problems coming from alcohol use would be identified as a problem drinker. The clinical judgment of whether a person fits the impaired controlled cycle is considered to be other-report data. However, if an individual is knowledgeable about this cycle and considers himself to fit this cycle, this would then be considered to be self-report data.

Self-selection

Self-selection is another approach for concluding that the individual has an AOD problem. Those who openly self-select into an AOD problem category will also be up-front with respect to their AOD use involvement and problems. Low scores on ASUDS' DEFENSIVE Scale have robust correlations with scales measuring alcohol and other drug use involvement and disruption (Wanberg & Timken, 1998). DWI offenders with this configuration self-select into the AOD problem category, are usually aware of having problems related to AOD use and usually acknowledge that awareness and the need for treatment.

Self-selection is enhanced when the individual experiences some emotional concern about the disruptive quality of drug use. For treatment to be effective, DWI offenders must move towards some degree of self-selection and acceptance of treatment.

Self-report - Standardized Psychometric Approaches

There are a variety of screening devices that have been used with DWI offenders to determine whether an individual falls into the category of AOD use problems. These screening devices have been catalogued in several comprehensive summaries (Allen & Columbus, 1995; Cavaiola & Wuth, 2002; Connors & Voke, 2003; Inciardi, 1994; Timken, 2001a; Winters and Zenilman, 1994). In addition to the validity studies done by the authors of the various instruments, several independent validity studies have been implemented on many of these instruments (Lacey, Jones and Wiliszowski 1997; Peters, et al., 2001).

Simple Screening Instruments provide a very brief look at AOD use and abuse and are usually comprised of a set of items that provide a single measure that ranks the individual in relationship to a normative group. These single-scale measures vary from five to 50 items and provide cut-off values that indicate AOD problems with normative distributions. Examples of these instruments are: the *Michigan Alcoholism Screening Test* (MAST: Selzer, 1971); *Mortimer-Filkins* (Mortimer, et al., 1971); *Research Institute on Addictions Self*

Inventory, (RIASI: Nochajski and Miller, 1995); *Self Assessment Survey* (SAS: Wanberg, 1999) and the *Simple Screening Inventory* (SSI: CSAT, 1994). *Appendix A, Table A.1* provides a list of simple screening inventories with their description and author source.

Differential Screening Instruments go beyond the single task of AOD problem screening and measure other conditions relevant to offender intervention service needs. This is a multidimensional approach to screening. For example, within the domain of AOD assessment, differential screening will measure the extent to which individuals are involved in various kinds of drugs and the extent of negative consequences or symptoms resulting from this involvement and driving risk. Other domains include mental health, treatment motivation and level of defensiveness. These are the most important areas of evaluation at the screening level.

The Lovelace Comprehensive Screening Instrument (LCSI: Lapham, Wanberg, Timken & Barton, 1996), the *Adult Substance Use and Driving Survey* (ASUDS: Wanberg & Timken, 1998), and the *Driving Risk Inventory* (DRI: Lindeman, 1987) are three instruments that are more specific to and normed on DWI offenders and provide a broader base measurement of life-adjustment problems. *The Substance Abuse Subtle Screening Inventory* (SASSI: Miller, G.A., 1994) is a differential screening instrument design for a broader screening of substance use and abuse problems and is normed on a general substance abuse sample. The *ASUDS* is the psychometric screening instrument utilized in the *DSAP Model* (Timken & Wanberg, 2001). This instrument will be discussed in more detail in Chapter 13 of Section II of this Guide. *Table A.2* of *Appendix A* provides a list and description of differential screening instruments that can be used with DWI offenders.

Two-Factor Model for AOD Problem Inclusion

Research suggests that there are two relatively independent, though correlated factors, around substance use and abuse.

- The degree of AOD involvement, in terms of frequency, amount and drug type.

- The extent of negative consequences.

Examples of psychometric tests that use the two factor model for screening are the Adult Substance Use Survey (ASUS: Wanberg, 1997) and the Adult Substance Use and Driving Survey (ASUDS: Wanberg & Timken, 1998). This model provides greater specificity for screening. The User's Guides for these instruments specify combined score ranges on these two scales to provide guidelines in determining levels of AOD problems and making intervention referral decisions.

Multiple Criteria Approach

Screening of DWIOs involves determining level and type of countermeasures and intervention services based on the two areas of

- impaired driving behavior, and

- level of AOD use problems.

Although these two areas have some degree of independence, they are sufficiently correlated that high risk in one area suggests high risk in the other. The following five assessment criteria can be used to make decisions around the type and level of impaired driving education and treatment.

- High arrest BAC.

- Prior DWI convictions or arrests.

- Prior DWI education and treatment.

- Fits the DSM-IV criteria of AOD abuse or dependence.

- Fits the impaired control cycle - AOD use has led to problems that are dealt with by further AOD use.

- Meets threshold criteria on a standardized self-report and/or other-report instrument suggesting AOD problems, using either a single or a multiple-factor model.

Assessment specificity is increased when a client meets several of these criteria. Yet, a high arrest BAC alone, e.g., .15 or greater, would place the

DWIO in a high DWI risk category but also suggests inclusion into the AOD problem category. Chapter 13 will provide an illustration of utilizing the multiple criteria model for determining inclusion into DWI and AOD intervention services based on other-report and self-report data.

IN-DEPTH MULTIPLE-FACTOR ASSESSMENT

The most widely accepted model for the second level of evaluation is the multidimensional multiple-factor approach. This model holds that there are independent and separate factors, patterns and outcomes associated with AOD use and abuse. These patterns require different treatments. In order to have an in-depth understanding of offenders screened into the AOD problem category, assessment across these multiple-factors is necessary.

There is strong support in the literature for a multiple-factor assessment of clients entering AOD treatment (Caddy, 1978; Connors, Donovan & DiClemente, 2001; Donovan, 2003; Horn & Wanberg, 1969; Hart & Stueland, 1979; Hyman, 1976; Miller, Westerberg & Waldron, 1995; Pattison & Kaufman, 1982; Pattison, Sobell & Sobell, 1977; Wanberg & Horn, 1983, 1987) It is recommended that DWI offenders who are referred to treatment receive an in-depth, multiple factor assessment (Timken, 2001b). An in-depth, multiple-factor approach includes the assessment of the following major life-concerns and life-functioning domains.

- Self-disclosure versus perceptual defensiveness.

- AOD use patterns versus AOD problems and disruptions.

- Society obligations versus antisocial patterns and behaviors.

- Living adjustments versus situation and psychosocial life-functioning problems.

- Cognitive-behavioral structures.

- Motivation and readiness for change and treatment.

- Strengths and assets.

A summary of these major domains of assessment is found in *Table 7.3*. Significant problems in these domains represent multiple risk factors that interact with or contribute to the development and maintenance of AOD problems and to impaired driving behavior.

There are a number of instruments that provide measurement across these various factors, including AOD use and abuse, that are relevant to comprehensive and in-depth evaluation of DWIOs. These include the *Addictions Severity Index* (ASI: McClellan, et al., 1985, 1996) and the *Adult Clinical Assessment Profile* (ACAP: Wanberg, 1998).

There are also a number of other instruments that provide assessment within the specific areas outlined below. *Table A.3* in *Appendix A* provides a summary of some of these instruments including the specific areas of measurement.

More detailed summaries of multiple-construct and in-depth AOD assessment instruments are found in Allen & Columbus (1995), Allen and Wilson (2003), Miller et al. (1995), Inciardi (1994) and Timken (2001a). The multiple factors to be evaluated in an in-depth assessment of DWI offenders referred to treatment are reviewed along with examples of instruments used to reliably measure these factors. We will discuss the major domains outlined in *Figure 7.3*.

Self-disclosure versus Perceptual Defensiveness

Discerning the degree of defensiveness and willingness to disclose is one of the first and most important parts of screening and comprehensive assessment. The level of defensiveness, the client's approach to assessment (e.g., cooperative, hostile), congruency between self and other-report and scores on defensiveness and on scales measuring problems in the various assessment domains are dynamic and will change from the point of screening to the point of in-depth assessment. An important component of assessment is to determine changes in defensiveness and openness from screening to entering intervention services.

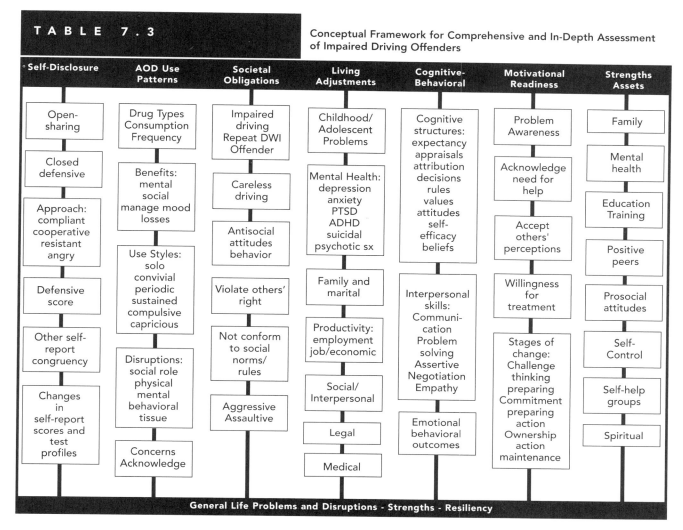

TABLE 7.3   Conceptual Framework for Comprehensive and In-Depth Assessment of Impaired Driving Offenders

Self-Disclosure	AOD Use Patterns	Societal Obligations	Living Adjustments	Cognitive-Behavioral	Motivational Readiness	Strengths Assets
Open-sharing	Drug Types Consumption Frequency	Impaired driving Repeat DWI Offender	Childhood/ Adolescent Problems	Cognitive structures: expectancy appraisals attribution decisions rules values attitudes self-efficacy beliefs	Problem Awareness	Family
Closed defensive	Benefits: mental social manage mood losses	Careless driving	Mental Health: depression anxiety PTSD ADHD suicidal psychotic sx		Acknowledge need for help	Mental health
Approach: compliant cooperative resistant angry		Antisocial attitudes behavior			Accept others' perceptions	Education Training
Defensive score	Use Styles: solo convivial periodic sustained compulsive capricious	Violate others' right	Family and marital	Interpersonal skills: Communi-cation Problem solving Assertive Negotiation Empathy	Willingness for treatment	Positive peers
Other self-report congruency		Not conform to social norms/ rules	Productivity: employment job/economic		Stages of change: Challenge thinking preparing Commitment preparing action Ownership action maintenance	Prosocial attitudes
	Disruptions: social role physical mental behavioral tissue		Social/ Interpersonal			Self-Control
Changes in self-report scores and test profiles		Aggressive Assaultive	Legal	Emotional behavioral outcomes		Self-help groups
	Concerns Acknowledge		Medical			Spiritual

General Life Problems and Disruptions - Strengths - Resiliency

Differential Assessment of AOD Use and Problem Patterns

The multiple-factor approach to AOD use assessment provides a basis for developing a treatment plan specific to the patterns of AOD use problems. These are summarized in *Table 7.3* in the AOD Use Patterns column. A conceptual framework for a comprehensive assessment of AOD use and abuse multiple factors is provided in *Table 7.4* (Wanberg & Horn, 1987). Five broad dimensions are outlined along with specific factors within these dimensions. From these broad and specific factors, four AOD types are defined at the bottom of *Table 7.4*.

There are several instruments that measure the multiple factors of alcohol or other drug use. The *Alcohol Use Inventory* (AUI: Horn, Wanberg & Foster, 1990) is one of the most commonly used for determining multiple factors associated with alcohol use. "The AUI is one of the few assessments available in the substance abuse area that take direct steps toward being treatment prescriptive" (Connors, Donovan & DiClemente, 2001, p. 63) and to identify profiles of alcohol abusing clients (Rychtarik, Koutsky, & Miller, 1998, 1999).

The *Drug Use Self-Report* (DUSR: Wanberg & Horn, 1991) provides a multidimensional assessment of different drug use and drug use patterns. The *Comprehensive Drinker Profile* (CDP: Miller & Marlatt, 1984) also provides a differential view of patterns of alcohol use. *Table A.3* in *Appendix A* provides a list of commonly used AOD differential assessment instruments.

There are two specific areas of AOD assessment that are relevant for DWIOs who have a substantial history of alcohol use problems. One is consumption or drinking measures. Sobell and Sobell (2003) identify five different consumption measures, classified into the two areas of quantity-frequency and daily drinking. An example is the Alcohol Timeline Followback (TLFB: Sobell & Sobell, 2000, 2003) which is a daily drinking estimation measure and provides a detailed picture of a person's drinking over a specific period of time.

The second is biomarkers of heavy drinking (Allen, et al., 2003). These are laboratory tests that can screen individuals for heavy drinking and alcohol use problems. Although Allen et al. acknowledge that self-report procedures will provide more accurate results (p. 47), biomarker testing is valuable in cases of trauma where the patient is unable to present an accurate drinking history or where the patient is resistant or reluctant to acknowledge level of consumption. They can provide a valuable tool in estimating the client's extent of alcohol use or problem.

Societal Obligations: Assessment of Antisocial Features of DWI Offenders

Driving while impaired is considered to be antisocial conduct. Yet, beyond DWI behavior, many DWIOs have a history of anti-legal and antisocial behavior. Important in DWIO differential assessment is discerning the degree to which offenders fit the antisocial Pattern. The key areas for this assessment are found in Table 7.3, under the *Societal Obligations* column.

Antisocial personality pattern: The antisocial personality disorder is represented by a pattern of behavior involving "disregard for, and violation of, the rights of others." "By definition, a personality disorder is an enduring pattern of thinking, feeling, and behaving that is relatively stable over time" (American Psychiatric Association, 1994, p. 632). The features of an antisocial pattern, often referred to as *character pathology,* are outlined in Table 7.5 (American Psychiatric Association, 1994; Sarason & Sarason, 1995). There are varying patterns within the antisocial domain. Not all of the antisocial features described in Table 7.5 are found in all individuals with antisocial disorders. For example, not all people with an antisocial pattern have engaged in criminal behavior.

The *ASUDS* (Wanberg & Timken, 1998) has a narrow but reliable measure of deviancy and antisocial behavior. The Psychopathy Checklist (PCL) developed by Hare (1980, 1986, 2003) has many of the items found in Table 7.5 which provides the characteristics of an antisocial personality pattern. There is a theory that the psychopath represents a discrete personality type and that psychopaths are different from other criminals (Hare, 1980, 1986; Harris, Rice & Quinsey, 1992). The PCL may be appropriate for only a small proportion of DWIOs.

Assessment of Driving Risk: Impaired driving offenders have poor driving records. They appear to be driving risks independent of AOD use. Although the measurement of driving risk is important at the front end of intervention, it is also an important component of ongoing assessment. It is included in one of the education intervention lessons of this work. Both the *Driving Risk Inventory* (Lindeman, 1987) and the *Driving Assessment Survey* (DAS: Wanberg & Timken, 1991) are effective tools for assessment in this area.

Living Adjustments: Assessment of Life-Situation Problems

As illustrated in *Table 7.3,* there are a number of life-adjustment factors that can contribute to AOD use and abuse and to impaired driving behavior. There are several instruments that provide measurement across these multiple life-adjustment factors. These include the *Addictions Severity Index* (ASI: McClellan, et. al., 1985, 1996) and the *Adult Clinical Assessment Profile* (ACAP: Wanberg, 1998). Following is a summary of these life adjustment domains that are important to assess in a multiple-factor assessment of DWIOs referred to treatment.

Problems of childhood and adolescents. Problems of childhood and adolescents are good predictors of problems in adulthood. With most individuals, problems of development are child-adolescent limited (Milkman & Wanberg, 2005). With some, they are life-persistent. Since the extent of problems in development may contribute to problems in adults, including DWI conduct, this area needs to be part of comprehensive and in-depth assessment. Problems of development include substance abuse, family disruption, physical and sexual abuse, emotional difficulties, neighborhood environment, learning and education problems, deviancy and physical health. Assessment may also

TABLE 7.4		Conceptual Framework for Describing Multidimensional Drug Use Patterns and Conditions		
BENEFITS	**STYLES**	**CONSEQUENCES**	**CONCERNS**	**ACKNOWLEDGEMENT**
Social	Gregarious	Behavioral control loss	Guilt	Acknowledgement
Mental	Solo	Social role maladaptation		Awareness of problem
Manage depression and stress	Periodic	Psychophysical withdrawal	Prior help to stop	
	Sustained			
Coping with losses	Compulsive	Psychoperceptual withdrawal		Acknowledgement of problems
Coping with relationships	Capricious	Relationship disruption	Concern by significant other	Willingness and readiness to seek help
	Drug of choice	Emotional disruption		
	Quantity of Use	Tissue and organ damage		
Self enhancement from use	Involvement in Use	Disruption from use	Anxiety from use	Motivation to change use pattern
	Psychosocial dependence-commitment to drug use	Physical dependence with impaired control	Anxious impaired control with disruption	Anxious awareness-commitment not to use

CHARACTERISTICS OF ANTISOCIAL PATTERNS

▶ Repeatedly performing acts that do not conform to social norms with respect to obeying the law and that are grounds for being arrested;

▶ Impulsivity and failure to plan ahead;

▶ Patterns of deceit, lying, conning others for personal gain or pleasure;

▶ Inability to handle anger in adaptive ways;

▶ Low frustration tolerance and irritability;

▶ Ineffective problem solving in relationships;

▶ Irresponsibility in finances, relationships, and societal obligations;

▶ Reckless disregard for the safety of others and of self;

▶ Inability or unwillingness to delay gratification;

▶ Aggressive and even assaultive behavior;

▶ Denial of personal responsibility and blaming others;

▶ Associating with friends who are antisocial and engage in illegal conduct and devious behavior;

▶ Manipulating and exploiting relationships;

▶ Lack of empathy for others;

▶ Lack of remorse, guilt or shame for past misdeeds;

▶ Aggrandizement of self and inflated view of self.

reveal that these are unresolved issues that need to be addressed in treatment.

Mental health and psychological-emotional adjustment. This area includes the assessment of depression, anxiety and phobias, mood fluctuations, anger, levels of self-esteem, distrust of others and unusual, suicidal thinking, post-traumatic stress, attending deficits, hyperactivity, and disturbed (psychotic-like) thinking. Mental health problems interact with other areas of life-adjustment problems. Several instruments can be used for a more in-depth assessment of psychological and mood adjustment problems. These include the *Minnesota Multiphasic Personality Inventory II* (Butcher, et al., 1989) and the *Symptom Checklist 90* (SCL-90: Derogatis, 2001) and the *Millon Clinical Multiaxial Inventory III* (Millon, 1997).

Marital, family and relationship adjustment involves marital conflict, family problems, lack of family support, problems in close and intimate relationships and problems in parenting.

Social-interpersonal adjustment involves problems in establishing supportive social relationships, getting along with people, social isolation, restricted interests and lack of social and residential stability.

Current legal problems is broader than but includes those related to antisocial behavior and criminal conduct. All DWIOs have legal problems by nature of their DWI offense. DWIOs may have other legal problems involving misdemeanor and felony acts, divorce proceedings, financial debt, civil proceedings, etc., that contribute to the risk of relapse or recidivism and that need attention in treatment.

Productivity adjustment. This involves the assessment of job adjustment problems, inadequate vocational and occupational skills, economic difficulties and income and economic problems. For some DWIOs, it will also involve school adjustment problems.

Health adjustment includes both physical and self-reported medical and physical problems. The client's self-report in the area of health and medical problems is of particular value in this assessment (McClellan et al., 1996).

Assessment of Cognitive-Behavioral Processes

The rationale behind cognitive-behavioral therapy is that emotions and actions are determined by the individual's cognitive structures and processes. One assessment task is to understand the way the individual structures his or her world through various cognitions (McDermott & Wright, 1992). This involves "the identification and measurement of a broad spectrum of relevant factors that are necessary to ensure the best possible alteration of a particular individual's maladaptive behavior" (Goldfried, 1995, p. 21).

Whereas the traditional personality assessment involves "the assessment of personality constructs that, in turn, are used to predict overt behavior..." (Goldfried, 1995, p. 49) the CBT approach involves assessment "of the individual's response to various life situations" (Goldfried, 1995, p. 32). Greater emphasis is placed on what a person does or how an individual responds to various situations or the environment. The selection of behavioral test responses is based on the situation most relevant to target behaviors or cognitions.

As outlined in *Table 7.3*, CBT assessment involves: 1) the identification of the cognitive structures (e.g., thoughts, attitudes, self-efficacy, beliefs) and processes that respond to the person's internal and external world; 2) interpersonal skills such as problem solving, communication, critical reasoning; and 3) the affective and behavioral outcomes

resulting from the cognitive events (see cognitive-behavioral column, *Figure 7.3*). Cognitive assessment is premised on the idea that we engage in information processing by selecting and using internal and external information in constructing our view of reality (Gardner, 1985).

Goldfried (1995) stresses that although the primary targets for change in CBT are thoughts and emotions, CB assessment must also include the behavioral responses resulting from our thoughts and emotions. Freeman et al. (1990) remind us that "cognition, emotion and behavior are the three aspects of human functioning that are of prime importance in cognitive therapy and that are the targets of assessment of ongoing therapy" (p. 32). CBT focuses on these three areas.

An important cognitive construct in CBT is self-efficacy (SE), defined as perceived performance competency in specific situations (Bandura, 1977b), 1981, 1982). The level of self-efficacy is often a determinant of relapse or recidivism (Donovan, 1999, 2003; Marlatt, 1985a; Marlatt et al., 1995). SE is usually viewed as situation-specific and cannot be measured like a general personality construct such as self-esteem (Marlatt, 1985b). Yet, it is a major cognitive factor to be assessed (Donovon, 1999, 2003) in the AOD evaluation process. Connors & Volk, (2003) indicate that the *Inventory of Drinking Situations* (IDS: Annis, Graham, & Davis, 1987) is valuable in determining cue strength for drinking in certain situations.

The *Situational Confidence Questionnaire* (SCQ: Annis & Davis, 1988) is specifically directed at the individual's SE in coping with different situations without drinking or without drinking heavily. Both the IDS and SCQ provide good assessment of SE related to drinking situations. Donovan (2003) provides a more comprehensive list of instruments designed to measure SE in relationship to alcohol use.

An important component of cognitive-behavioral assessment is the evolution of cognitive structures and behaviors that lead to DWI behavior. What are the thoughts, beliefs and attitudes that lead to DWI conduct?

Utilizing a variety of sources (e.g., Goldfried, 1995; Blankenstein & Segal, 2001; Freeman et al., 1990;

Glass & Arnkoff, 1997), the following cognitive-behavioral assessment model has been developed for use with DWI offenders. It is congruent with the basic cognitive-behavioral approach described in Chapters 9 and 11 and used in client's workbook.

▶ Performing a situational analysis in which relevant internal and external events are identified that are part of problematic behavioral outcomes, e.g., impaired driving behavior and AOD problems.

▶ Identifying the individual's cognitive structures and responses (thoughts, values, rules, attitudes and beliefs) to these situations, particularly those that lead to DWI conduct and AOD problems

▶ Identify the emotional and behavioral outcomes resulting from the use of these structures and responses and evaluate whether they lead to positive outcomes (e.g., lead to prosocial behavior) or to negative outcomes (e.g., lead to antisocial behavior).

▶ Selecting and utilizing cognitive skills (thought restructuring, relaxation exercises) to replace, change or manage maladaptive cognitive structures and responses with those that are more likely to produce good outcomes (e.g., never drive impaired, no AOD use problems) and then developing a pool of effective cognitive responses to sustained positive outcomes.

▶ Identifying and selecting different interpersonal coping and community responsibility skills congruent with the improved or changed cognitive responses that can lead to positive outcomes.

▶ Continuing to evaluate the effectiveness of the new cognitive responses and the new interpersonal coping and responsible behavior skills to determine their efficacy in producing positive outcomes.

This CB assessment model is applied during the formal assessment process but also throughout education and treatment.

Assessment of Motivation and Readiness for Treatment

The work on stages of change (DiClemente &

Valesquez, 2002; Donovan, 2003; Prochaska & DiClemente, 1986; Prochaska, DiClemente & Norcross, 1992; Connors, Donovan & DiClemente, 2001; Wanberg & Milkman, 1998) has demonstrated that an essential task in assessment is determining the client's motivation and readiness for treatment. The area of treatment motivation and readiness is not only assessed in the intake interview but is ongoing during intervention and treatment. The most salient areas are listed in Table 7.3 under the Motivation-readiness column.

The stage of change model used in this work, *Driving With Care: Education and Treatment of the Impaired Driving Offender,* incorporates the traditional stages developed by Prochaska & DiClemente (1992), and is based on three stages: the **challenge** stage involving awareness, recognition and preparing for change; **commitment** stage involving preparing and taking action; and the **ownership** stage, involving a pattern of stable change and attributing change to self (Wanberg & Milkman, 1998).

There are a number of measures and scales that can be used in this area. High scores on the acknowledgement of a need for help (AWARENES) and the receptiveness to treatment (RECEPTIV) scales of the *Alcohol Use Inventory* (Horn, Wanberg & Foster, 1990) indicate treatment motivation and readiness. The *Stages of Change Readiness and Treatment Eagerness Scale* (SOCRATES: Miller, 1994, Miller & Tonigan, 1996) provides a measure of the five areas of change: precontemplation; contemplation; determination; action; and maintenance. The *Adult Self Assessment Questionnaire* (ASAQ: (Wanberg & Milkman, 1993, 2002) provides six specific and two broad measures of readiness and change. Donovan (2003) provides a detailed discussion and summary of measurement instruments of motivation and readiness for change.

Assessment of Strengths

Those concerned about resiliency and strength assessment might conclude that the above multiple-factors do not consider the client's strengths. Inherent in the above identified problem factors are strengths. Persons who score low on job and economic problems indicate strengths in these areas. So is the case across all of the assessment factors. However, the direct measurement of strengths is also important. Thus, assessment needs to include a factor that measures the client's strength, from both a self-report and other-report perspective. The *Adult Clinical Assessment Profile - ACAP* (Wanberg, 1998) provides both a self-report and other-report client strengths measure.

ASSESSMENT OF CHANGE AND OUTCOME

THE FINAL TWO components of assessment are the evaluation of changes in and the outcome of treatment.

Change and Progress in Treatment

There are a number of dimensions of change and progress that can be evaluated in the DWIO progressing through DWI education and treatment. These are often called proximal outcome measures (Rosen & Proctor, 1981). Donovan provides an excellent discussion on assessing treatment and treatment processes and measures that can be used in this area (Donovan, 2003). These assessments can be done at various points along the treatment progress and at discharge from treatment.

Changes in self-disclosure. If we assume that self-disclosure leads to self-awareness and self-awareness leads to change, then assessment in the change in willingness to disclose is important. As rapport and trust are developed and a therapeutic alliance is established, clients become more open and self-disclosing. There are two ways to assess this change (Milkman & Wanberg, 2005).

▶ Retesting on parts or all of the differential screening or intake instruments (e.g., those in *Appendix A, Table A-2*). DWI clients who were very defensive initially will indicate higher scores on scales measuring AOD use and disruption, DWI behavior and other areas of life adjustment. Clients who are very self-disclosing in screening and intake will not show significant increases in their scores. In fact, these clients will often show some decrease in their scores.

▶ Retest on scales designed to measure defensiveness will also provide a measure of change in willingness to self-disclose. Those low on defensiveness at intake will often show some increase in their defensiveness scores.

Changes in problem awareness and acknowledgement. The specific areas most noted as defensiveness decreases is greater awareness and acknowledgement of problem behavior. This is noted when:

▶ initial low scores on scales measuring problem behavior increase at retesting, a sign of a decrease in defensiveness, but also an increase in problem awareness and acknowledgement;

▶ increase in scales that directly measure acknowledgement of having AOD and impaired driving problems.

Changes in motivation and readiness for treatment can be noted by retesting clients on instruments designed to assess these areas, e.g., SOCRATES, ASAQ. Clients who have completed a substantial portion of DWI education and treatment may actually score lower on scales measuring the need for and willingness to engage in treatment. Their need decreases because they have had a large component of their treatment needs met.

Changes in problem thinking and problem behavior. Several methods can be used to assess changes in this area.

▶ Test-retest method, the most common being to measure the individual's involvement in problem behavior in the six months prior to entering treatment, and then at six month intervals following treatment admission and at treatment discharge.

▶ Daily or weekly monitoring of thinking and behaviors related to AOD use and impaired driving.

▶ Repeated (viz., monthly) self-report and rating assessments of the client's thinking and behaviors in the target areas of change.

Changes in therapeutic alliance. As we will see in a later chapter, therapeutic alliance has a major influence on the outcome of psychosocial therapies. Since there are no specific measures in this area for alcohol treatment (Finney, 2003), and for DWI intervention, the provider must assess this area through clinical observation.

Outcome Assessment

Donovan (2003) refers to these as *ultimate outcome* assessment. They are also referred to as short-term, involving assessment at six-month post discharge from treatment; and long-term, more than six months post-discharge.

For DWIOs, the ultimate outcome measure is recidivism, or returning to any impaired driving. Certainly, the other critical measure is relapse. As discussed previously, clients can relapse and not recidivate - return to impaired driving conduct. Tonigan (2003) argues that, with respect to evaluating AOD use outcomes, "....the effectiveness of a treatment ought not be judged on the basis of a single measure of drinking collected at an arbitrary point after...treatment" (p. 232). Yet, with respect to DWI, outcome assessment is based on recidivism, and more specifically, on the single, big-face valid measure of getting rearrested and convicted for DWI conduct.

SUMMARY: MAXIMIZING VERIDICALITY - INTEGRATING SELF-REPORT AND OTHER-REPORT

This chapter presented perspectives on a process and convergent validation model for impaired driving offenders. This model views self-report as essential in getting the baseline perception of the client and represents the starting point in intervention and treatment. All self-report data are seen as a valid representation of the client's ability and willingness to disclose self-perception and is a valid representation of where the client is at any point in the assessment and intervention process. The integration of self-report and other-report provides the basis upon which to estimate the client's defensiveness and "true" condition. Both sources of data are used in evaluating changes in intervention and treatment.

The primary tasks of the DWIO evaluator in screening and assessment is to discern the client's level of defensiveness, determine the veridicality of the client's self-report in relationship to the other-report, understand that data gathered at any one point are relevant as they are viewed within the process and stages of change, take this information as an estimate of the client condition and then develop intervention recommendations that address these conditions.

This Chapter also provides guidelines for effective use of psychometric instruments in assessment. Approaches to screening DWI offenders for intervention services are discussed. The criteria for substance abuse and substance dependence diagnosis are provided. A conceptual framework for in-depth, comprehensive assessment is outlined, along with a discussion of the various constructs that make up this assessment. The various components of the assessment of change and progress in treatment are presented. Instrumentation resources are described for each of the various levels of DWI offender assessment.

CHAPTER EIGHT: COUNTERMEASURES, INTERVENTIONS AND TREATMENT APPROACHES AND OUTCOMES

OVERVIEW

IN THE LAST decade of the 20th century, there was strong support in the literature to integrate the sanctioning and punishment systems with the treatment and therapeutic systems for all offenders, including DWIOs (e.g., Cavaiola & Wuth, 2002; Edwards et al., 1994; DeYoung, 1997; Nichols, 1990; Wanberg & Milkman, 1998). There is considerable evidence that exclusive punishment and sanctioning alone - for offenders in general and DWI offenders in specific - will not effectively reduce recidivism. On the contrary, averaged across all sanctioning disposition, punishment may contribute to a slight increase in recidivism (see Andrews & Bonta, 1998, 2003; Wanberg & Milkman, 1998; and other references cited in the discussion below). Likewise, treatment without the sanctioning system will not have significant impact (Andrews & Bonta, 2003; Andrews, 1995). DeYoung (1997) points out that combining sanctioning with treatment is probably the most effective approach for preventing DWI recidivism.

In practice, achieving this integration is only in the beginning stages. The observations of the authors of this work indicate that the two systems, although recognizing the benefit of each other, most often operate independently and without a strong integrated cooperative effort. The correctional community, although putatively seeing the value of education and treatment services, has avoided developing a solid and functional association with the treatment community. Likewise, the treatment community, while seeing the value of the sanctioning process, tends to "stay at a distance" with the correctional and sanctioning community, often viewing the latter with some distrust and suspicion.

A fundamental premise of this work, *Driving With CARE: Educational and Treatment of the Impaired Driving Offender,* is that any effective DWIO intervention program must not only engage the efforts of the sanctioning community, but must also become part of the sanctioning process itself. The importance of this approach will become more apparent as the efficacy of "sanctioning only" is discussed below.

This Chapter examines the various intervention and treatment approaches that have been used with DWIOs. Essentially, these intervention approaches fall into three categories: correctional and sanctioning interventions; DWI education programs; and treatment and therapeutic services. As these approaches are presented, outcome findings related to their use will be presented when available.

SANCTIONING AND CORRECTIONAL APPROACHES

EARLY EFFORTS OF DWI intervention focused solely on sanctioning and punishment and it was not until the 1970s that education and treatment approaches became part of this effort (Timken, 2002). There are three main objectives of DWI sanctions:

▶ protect the driving and non-driving public;

▶ hold the offender accountable for his or her actions; and

▶ provide education and/or treatment to the DWI offender combined with the various sanctioning strategies of retribution, deterrence, incapacitation and restorative justice.

This work, *Driving With CARE*, defines recidivism as engaging in any driving with a BAC that exceeds legal limits or while impaired by a mind-altering drug. Most studies of recidivism are based on rearrest and/or conviction of another DWI charge. This does not give a true picture of the extent to which offenders return to impaired driving behavior. For example, in 1996, an estimated 46.5 million people drove after drinking and many of these individuals drove more than once after drinking during that year (Townsend, et al. 1998). Yet, only 1.5 million DWI arrests were made in 1996. The estimated odds of being arrested for each incident of impaired driving are one in 1,100 (Transportation Research Board, 1995). Yet, the primary research method to determine program efficacy is rearrest and/or conviction of another DWI charge.

In most states, sanctions and punishment are imposed on offenders by two jurisdictional entities: the courts; and state motor vehicle departments. There are two primary categories of DWI sanctions: driver-based; and vehicle-based. The most salient of these are reviewed along with, when available, studies regarding their efficacy in preventing recidivism.

Driver-Based Sanctions

License Restraints - Suspension and **Revocations:** State departments of motor vehicle (DMV) can suspend and deny a driver's license and vehicle registration and monitor the records to determine eligibility for reinstatement. The optimum suspension appears to be from 12 to 18 months (NHTSA 1996; NIAAA, 1996).

Although the main purpose of license restraint is to protect the public, it does serve as a punitive, deterrent and sanctioning action. Typically, a DWI arrest results in two kinds of license actions: *administrative license revocation* (ALR), a civil action imposed by the motor vehicle administration; and judicial post-conviction action ordered by the court (Tashima and Helander, 1995).

ALR is the suspension or revocation of the driver's license at arrest (Lacey, et al., 1991). The officer confiscates the license and issues a notice of ALR which may serve as a temporary license for a period of time during which the driver may request an administrative hearing for license reinstatement. A hardship license may be issued while the suspension remains in effect (NHTSA, 1993). Regardless of the hearing outcome, the offender is still subject to a separate criminal process that may lead to additional penalties, including judicial license actions (Williams, Weinberg & Fields, 1991).

License suspension has been effective in reducing DWI recidivism and the ensuing risk of AOD related crashes (Bloomberg et al., 1987; Klein, 1989; Nichols and Ross, 1989). As mentioned above, suspension periods between 12 and 18 months appear to be optimal for reducing DWI recidivism (Homel, 1981; NHTSA, 1993). Suspensions of less than 3 months seem ineffective (Paulsrude & Klingberg, 1975; Peck, Wilson, et al., 1994). Although more than 50 percent of offenders continue to drive under suspension, they drive less frequently and

more cautiously to avoid apprehension (Ross & Gonzales, 1992; Nichols & Ross, 1990; Simpson & Mayhew, 1991). ALR reduced alcohol-related accidents five to nine percent in New Mexico, four percent in Minnesota, and three to 14 percent in Delaware (Ross, 1992). Mann et al. (2002) found ALR laws contributed to a 13-19 percent reduction in adult drivers in fatal crashes. Approximately five percent of drivers in California have suspended licenses (Voas, et al., 1996).

Probation: Probation conditions vary widely across cases, courts and the diverse array of criminal offenses. For DWI offenders probation may require: abstinence from AOD use; random breath or urine testing; sanctions for driving under suspension or without insurance; court-ordered treatment; home detention; license or vehicle restrictions; or other options.

Probation in general seems to slightly reduce recidivism among low-risk DWI offenders (Wells-Parker, et al., 1995), but, alone, does not measurably reduce recidivism among those at high risk (Jones & Lacey, 1991). There are a number of different probation options and adjuncts. Some of these approaches are more effective than others. These will be briefly summarized.

▶ *Intensive probation,* an alternative to incarceration for less dangerous offenders, involves high density probation contacts and may require job placement and the completion of education and/or treatment (Harding, et al., 1989; Transportation Research Board, 1995). Noncompliance often results in incarceration. This approach has shown consistent effectiveness in preventing recidivism (Green and Phillips 1990; Jones, et al., 1996; Latessa and Travis 1988).

▶ *Home detention* recognizes the offender's need to drive in order to work or attend court-ordered treatment. Its purpose is to keep potentially intoxicated drivers off the road during evening and nighttime hours when most DWI offenses occur. Electronic monitoring is mainly used to enforce home detention (discussed below) with non-compliance resulting in jail (Jacobs, 1990).

- *Electronic monitoring (ELMO)* is an alternative to jail or a post-jail step-wise programmed for persistent offenders needing close scrutiny and control. It verifies offender location through radio frequency and programmed contacts (Harding, et al., 1989) and can be combined with a breath test, video surveillance and standard and adjunct therapies for higher risk offenders with a history of treatment failure and non-compliance. DWI offenders do better on ELMO than comparisons groups (Baumer & Mendelsohn, 1992). One study indicated recidivism rates as 3.5 percent less than for comparison groups resulting in a savings of up to one million dollars when compared with jailed offenders (Jones, Lacey & Fell, 1996). Lilly, et al. (1993) found recidivism to be less than three percent in an ELMO monitored DWI sample over a two month probation period; however, recidivism increased when monitoring was terminated. Courtright et al. (1997) reported a 98 percent success rate in keeping ELMO offenders from drinking and driving, and a Minnesota study (Minneapolis Department of Corrections, 2002) reports only one to two percent were rearrests for a new DUI while on ELMO.

- *Random urine analysis (UA)* testing is used when drugs other than alcohol are involved or for offenders switching drugs during supervision. When used to assess drug use problems, it should be administered randomly over a period of one to two months. Compliance testing should be utilized for an extended period, or for the full length of supervision. Testing frequency may be decreased if the offender remains "clean" for six months or longer. The NIDA-5 protocol is effective in testing for cocaine, opioids, THC, amphetamines and PCP metabolites. It has more validity than single-drug screening based on an offender's suspected drug choice. UAs are not effective in monitoring alcohol use since it is water soluble and its metabolites do not store in body tissue (Timken, 2002).

- *Breath testing* is effective in monitoring alcohol abstinence or even for offenders who are required to not drink to impairment. It may be used when disulfiram (antabuse) is medically contraindicated or if drinking is suspected during an antabuse regimen. Various testing schedules or methods can be used, depending on the type of offender, e.g., high risk non-compliant offenders. Treatment or law enforcement agencies may be utilized to perform the breath testing.

Jail and Incarceration: Although providing a public safety benefit, the findings regarding the efficacy of incarceration are mixed. Incarceration may have a short-term deterrent effect on first-time DWI offenders, but it does not appear to have long-term impact (Hingson, 1996). The use of incarceration alone may even increase recidivism (Mann, et al., 1991). Other studies suggest that jail as a deterrent is no more effective in preventing DWI recidivism among first-time or repeat offenders than other forms of sanctions (Hagen, 1978; Homel, 1981; Jones, et al., 1988; Mann, et al., 1991; Martin, et al., 1993; Ross, et al., 1990; Salzberg and Paulsrude, 1984).

Lengthier sentences have not been found to result in lower rates of recidivism (Weinrath & Gartrell, 2001; Brooker, 2002). Conversely, they are associated with higher crash and recidivism rates (Friedman, et al., 1995; Homel, 1988; Joksch, 1988; Martin et al., 1993; Mann, et al., 1991; Nichols and Ross, 1989; Ross and Klette, 1995). Since many convicted impaired drivers, e.g., repeat offenders, have severe life-stress problems and may be alcohol dependent, long jail terms are unlikely to resolve their problems and may even exacerbate them (Homel, 1981).

There are studies that report findings contrary to those cited above. For example, the use of 2-day jail sentences has a general deterrent effect for first-time offenders (Falkowski, 1984; Jones, et al., 1988; Zador, 1991). It has been suggested that a weekend in jail may be useful for first-time offenders for whom a "taste of punishment" may be an effective deterrent (Jones et al. 1988; Simpson & Mayhew 1991). A Tennessee study indicated that mandatory jail time for first-time offenders resulted in a 40% decrease in recidivism. Other studies produced similar findings (Compton, 1986; Falkowski, 1984; Grube and Kearney, 1983).

Researchers have also noted that mandatory jail sentences tend to negatively affect court operations and the correctional process by increasing the demand for jury trials, plea-bargaining, and jail crowding (NHTSA, 1986; Voas & Lacey, 1990). While 16 states in the US have mandatory jail time for first-time offenders, almost every state has jail time for the repeat offender.

Because the findings regarding short-term jail time for DWI offenders are mixed and long-term jail time appears to be costly and ineffective, DWI rehabilitation programs tend to avoid incarceration or combine time spent in jail with other forms of punishment and treatment. DWIO dedicated detention facilities, as an alternative to traditional incarceration, have eased overcrowding in correctional facilities. Review of five of those programs found recidivism reduction rates ranging from four to 16 percent compared with 35 percent for non-participating DWIs (Century Council, 2003). These findings point toward the use of probation in combination with sanctions imposed by the department of motor vehicles (DMV) as means to achieve improved outcomes. For the persistent hard core DWI offender, incarceration is the most frequently imposed sanction (NHTSA, 1996; NIAAA, 1996).

Other Sanctioning Approaches: Other sanctioning approaches are used as correctional interventions in preventing DWI recidivism.

▶ *Financial sanctions* include fines, court costs, and the cost of public services responding to an offender involved crash. Fines may be fixed in amount or based on a percentage of the offender's income. In some jurisdictions, fines are suspended and applied to court-ordered counseling in court approved treatment venues. Fines probably have little deterrent value unless they are more immediate and costly, as in Europe where they are often one and a half month's salary (Brooker, 2002).

▶ *Community service programs* is one way for offenders to pay restitution. The few studies of this form of sanctioning have failed to show positive effects (Popkin & Wells-Parker, 1994).

▶ *Publishing offenders names in newspapers* is rarely applied and has the effect of social stigma. To date this has not been studied (Fazzalaro, 2001; Popkin and Wells-Parker 1994).

▶ *Victim Impact Panels (VIP),* founded by *Mothers Against Drunk Driving (MADD),* are groups comprised of victims and offenders who describe the impact of DWI on their lives. Offenders are sentenced to victim impact panels and are required to attend a session on a one-time basis. Shinar and Compton's (1995) review of the literature found little measurable and consistent impact of VIP on recidivism. One study indicated that 12-month follow-up arrest rates were lower for a VIP versus a comparison group (Fors & Rojek, 1999). Anglo-White males, 26-35, with only one prior arrest and lower levels of severity did better in the VIP group. Other studies have indicated that VIPs have a negative impact on repeat offenders (C'de Baca et al., 2000; Woodall et al., 2000). Probably a single episode exposure to a VIP is of little value without follow-up and therapeutic processing.

▶ *Victim restitution programs* direct the offender to pay financial and service benefits to victims or their family. They are rarely invoked and their efficacy has not been evaluated.

▶ *Court-ordered visits to emergency departments or service at chronic physical rehabilitation facilities.* These sanctions have been proposed for their specific deterrent effects and as a form of community service by the offender (Transportation Research Board, 1995). To date, their effectiveness has not been documented.

Vehicle-based Sanctions and Interventions

Vehicle based sanctions have become more common for offenders whose licenses are suspended or restricted since many offenders drive with revoked licenses (Donovan et al., 1990). Vehicle-based sanctions: *restrict the conditions in which the car can be driven and the driver can drive; or immobilize or render the vehicle inaccessible to the offender.*

Autotimers restrict the car from being driven during certain periods of time and records the times in which the car is driven. It monitors offender compliance with mandatory driving regulations. It neither prevents offenders from driving nor detects impairment.

Fuel Locks are placed on the motor of the car and makes it impossible to start the car during specific times. Like the autotimer, fuel locks do not prevent drunk driving.

Breath alcohol ignition interlocks prevent vehicle operation if the driver's BAC is above a predetermined level (Compton, 1988; Baker and Beck, 1991). Interlocks are effective in preventing recidivism (Coben & Larking, 1999; Bierness, 2004; Simon, 2004). Positive BAC's detected during interlock installation are very good predictors of future recidivism (Marques et al., 2003). This method is compromised if the interlock is not installed as ordered or if the offender finds a way to circumvent the device or simply uses a different car (EMT Group, 1990; Baker and Beck 1991; Popkin et al. 1992). Interlocks do not seem to alter overall behavior patterns and recidivism rates may rise after interlocks are removed (Morse and Elliot, 1992; Popkin, et al., 1992). It is recommended that interlocks are used as a condition of license reinstatement after a period of suspension, rather than as a substitute for license sanctions (Transportation Research Board, 1995). Also, keeping interlocks installed after treatment for a period of time and coupling the extended use with brief "booster" counseling may make this approach more effective.

The electronic driver's license card is required to start the car. The card can also be connected to a computer to allow the car to start only during set hours.

Vehicle restriction, impoundment and forfeiture procedures involve immobilizing the vehicle through "club" or "boot" or impoundment. Some jurisdictions require that the offender sell the vehicle (Lapham, 1999). Impoundment and forfeiture are used in most states and require statutory authority. These methods are used with repeat offenders or those caught while driving under suspension. This approach works best when applied administratively by police, without the need for a criminal conviction (Voas, 1992). A study by Voas, et al. (1996) combining immobilization (e.g., a "boot") with impoundment showed a 50 percent reduction in recidivism rates that were maintained beyond the expiration of the penalty. Forfeiture is the strongest and least applied sanction but the results are similar to impoundment (Century Council, 2003; Crosby, 1995; NTSB, 2000; Peck & Voas, 2002).

Special plates or stickers. When arresting a motorist for driving during license suspension, officers can place a zebra sticker over a portion of the license plate. This allows officers to check whether these vehicles are being driven by persons with a suspended license or who are impaired. After implemented in Oregon and Washington State, there was a 33 percent reduction in moving violations and a 23 percent reduction in crashes for drivers whose licenses were suspended (Voas and Tippits, 1994). In Minnesota, there was a 50 percent decrease in recidivism over a two-year period (Jones & Lacey, 2000; Voas & DeYoung, 2002). The above cites indicate license plate seizure laws are poorly enforced.

The major problem with the above countermeasures is enforcement. Overburdened law officers, crowded courts, prolonged adjudications, minimal judicial supervision all tend to mitigate the enforcement of these sanctions.

EDUCATION AND TREATMENT INTERVENTION

MOST OF THE above countermeasures and sanctioning methods have a dual purpose: making the offender accountable for impaired driving behavior, viz., punishment; and intervention-rehabilitative purposes - viz., changing thinking and behavioral patterns to preventing relapse and recidivism. Although the distinction is being made between sanctioning and intervention in this text, most courts consider the latter as part off the sanctioning process.

Many jurisdictions separate DWI intervention into education and treatment programs. Education programs tend to blend in with treatment programs for DWIOs and the distinctions between the two are somewhat blurred. For this review, the two will be separated.

Early DWI Education and Treatment Protocols

Education and treatment programs for DWI offenders started in Phoenix in the early 1970's (Stewart & Malfetti, 1970) and initial results were interpreted as positive. With the establishment of 35 Alcohol Safety Action Projects (ASAPs) by the *National Highway Traffic Administration* (NHTSA, 1972; 1979), DWI rehabilitation programs were implemented throughout the U.S. (Voas & Lacey, 1990). A rash of evaluation studies followed, generally showing that brief (2-6 session) education programs, sometimes supplemented with group counseling or other treatment modalities, had the positive effect of reducing subsequent DWI arrests, but had little effect on reducing subsequent traffic crashes (Timken, 2002). The positive effects of these short-term programs seemed to diminish as the number of prior offenses increased (Nichols, 1990).

In 1975 NHTSA funded eight ASAPs that used *Power Motivation Therapy (PMT),* a standardized, short-term education and counseling protocol. Whereas initial ASAP rehabilitation efforts were idiosyncratic to the treatment philosophies and preferred service models of providers and their agencies, great lengths were taken to ensure fidelity to the PMT model. The results, however, were discouraging. There were no data to show that PMT reduced crash or arrest recidivism, increased abstinence, or diminished alcohol consumption. Some evidence indicated that PMT might actually result in worse outcomes (Stewart & Ellingstad, 1989).

Efficacy of Mandated Education and Treatment

Almost all, if not all, DWI intervention (education and treatment) is based on court mandated participation. However, there was the common belief that clients coerced into substance abuse treatment would not be motivated, would show non-compliance and poorer outcomes.

The literature does not support this view. Few differences were found between persons mandated to treatment and "volunteers," regarding treatment compliance and positive program outcomes (Brecht, et al., 1993; DeLeon, 1988; Stitzer and McCaul, 1987). When differences were found they **often favored the court mandated client** who had greater probability of undergoing a traumatic loss such as a job, marriage or driver's license (Mark, 1988).

DWI Education

DWI education is usually designated for first time offenders who clearly do not show an AOD problem and where there is little if any evidence of disruptive use of substances other than disruption resulting from impaired driving. Traditional DWI education programs are structured, media based, didactic, non-interactive and concentrate on imparting knowledge and information to clients. Clients are often in the passive-participant role, although there is an emphasis on facilitating group discussion. Clients are typically not expected to apply program content to their specific situation through interactive curriculum material. Clients are often expected to disclose their history around substance use and their DWI experiences. However, they are typically not expected to engage in a concentrated and continual self-assessment, self-awareness and self-change process as the program progresses. The goal is one of learning and there is little expectation of DWI education clients to change thinking or behaviors other than preventing engagement in impaired driving conduct.

A review of the DWI literature by the authors indicated that the content of DWI education programs focuses mainly on AOD education and the relationship of AOD use to impaired driving. The disease model is often the basis for AOD education. Although most education programs focus on relapse and relapse prevention, few programs made recidivism (returning to any impaired driving) a primary focus. Most education programs invariably tie recidivism to relapse. DWI educational protocols are most often manual-guided. The dominant form of DWI intervention is the educational group (Wells-Parker, 1994).

Effects of Education Protocols

These programs are based on the idea that offenders have insufficient knowledge about drugs, how AOD use affects their social, economic and health functions or about drunk driving laws. It is believed that enhanced knowledge in these areas will prevent DWI recidivism. However, offenders do seem to be relatively informed about these areas (Sheppard and Stoveken, 1993).

A review of studies by NHTSA indicated that didactic education programs reduced recidivism by approximately 10% for the **non-problem offender.** However, research indicated that **only therapeutically oriented programs had impact on offenders with some degree of AOD problems** (NHTSA, 1996; Mann, et al., 1988; Nichols, et al., 1978). Increased knowledge about the hazardous effects of alcohol is more effective with offenders who do not have serious drinking problems.

Considering that the majority of studies in the 70's and 80's primarily measured the effects of traditional DWI education programs in the absence of license and criminal sanctions, the average recidivism reduction of **seven to nine percent** shown by Wells Parker, et al. (1995) might seriously underestimate the power of current approaches. During the 1990s, there was a strong move towards seeing licensing and criminal sanctioning as an important part of education and treatment intervention. There is growing evidence to suggest that the combination of sanctioning with education **and** treatment provide the most leverage for deterring repeat DWI offenses. DWI education programs developed in the late 1990s began emphasizing client-content interactive models, learner versus information centered approaches, consistent and more intense self-disclosure and self-assessment and change in thinking and beliefs, particularly as these are related to impaired driving.

The effort to integrate the correctional with the education and treatment and the newer DWI educational approaches will hopefully reduce recidivism. Thus, even the modest reduction in recidivism rate of seven to nine percent over the large population of impaired drivers who received traditional DWI education (Wells-Parker et al., 1995) not only translates into an important reduction in DWI incidents, arrests, crashes and fatalities but hopefully will be enhanced with the newer approaches.

Definition of DWI Treatment

Offenders referred to treatment indicate higher risk with respect to levels of BAC at arrest and repetitive DWI conduct. Such offenders are also identified as having evidence of an alcohol use problem if not diagnosed as having patterns of alcohol abuse or dependence. DWI education alone is considered to be insufficient in addressing this increased risk.

The general goal of AOD treatment is to change psychological perceptions and behavior so as to reduce or eliminate the use of alcohol and other drugs as a contributing factor to physical, psychological, and social dysfunction and to arrest, attenuate or reverse progress of associated problems (Institute of Medicine, 1990). Although this general goal may fit the needs of some DWI clients (estimates are in the 20 percent range), this goal does not fit the majority of DWI offenders.

The specific goal of DWI treatment is the same as with DWI education: to prevent impaired driving recidivism. The separating of drinking behavior from driving behavior by an abstinence or drinking below legal limits goal will also reduce AOD related crashes. Treatment approaches and objectives must focus on this specific DWI treatment goal - recidivism prevention. There is the expressed need to change patterns of thinking, psychological perceptions and behavior. The assumptions of DWI treatment are that offenders need to make significant cognitive, affective, behavioral and life adjustment and AOD use changes in order to achieve the goal of preventing recidivism. DWIO treatment involves a range of primary and supportive services including identification, brief intervention, assessment, diagnosis, counseling, medical services, psychological services, and follow-up provided for persons with alcohol and other drug problems.

There are numerous approaches to the treatment of DWI offenders. No one approach has emerged as most effective (Wells-Parker, et al., 1995). Although some treatment strategies have been identified as being helpful with DWIO's (Cavaiola & Wuth, 2002), DWI research does not identify specific models for effective treatment. However, there has been much progress in the delineation of efficacious approaches to treating substance abuse and criminal conduct. The most effective approaches to AOD problems are assessment driven, involving cognitive-behavioral, motivational enhancement, relapse prevention and stages of change models of intervention and treatment (Connors et al., 2001; Marlatt and Barrett, 1994; Miller and Rollnick, 2002; Prochaska and DiClemente, 1992; Wanberg and Milkman, 1998). Similarly, efficacious treatment for criminal conduct and judicial clients rests on the foundations of humanistic models of client-therapist interactions utilizing cognitive-behavioral strategies to enhance self-improvement and change (Andrews, 1995; Andrews & Bonta, 2003; Izzo & Ross, 1990; Lipsey, 1989; Lipsey, 1992; Lipsey & Wilson, 1993; Lipton, 1994; McGuire & Priestley, 1995; Van Voorhis, 1987; Wanberg & Milkman, 1998).

Characteristics of Traditional DWI Treatment Approaches

A review of the literature and numerous education and treatment protocols indicates some rather distinct characteristics of traditional DWI treatment. *First,* whereas DWI education is more topic-focused, DWI treatment is traditionally client centered, focuses on self-disclosure and self-awareness and the client's personal material.

Second, traditional DWI treatment most often involves unstructured therapy groups that are not topic or theme-focused and are not manual-guided. When a topic or theme-focused approach is used, it is usually client-centered and will center on the client's personal material and self-disclosure to achieve change rather than facilitate the therapeutic interaction between the client and a specific topic or session theme to bring about change.

Third, traditional DWI treatment focuses on AOD addiction, often based on the disease model. Timken (2002) notes that treatment for DWI offenders, in general, has been based on a disease orientation which determines treatment needs through symptom-assessment and emphasizes total abstinence as the treatment goal (Timken, et al., 1995). This approach usually limits assessment to symptom-focus at the expense of other psychosocial and driving behavior determinants. Considerable time is spent on life-long AOD abstinence rather than critical issues such as specific skills to prevent recidivism. Programs that emphasize only the disease model may fail to attend to other crucial variables that predict recidivism. This approach also views alcohol problems as present or absent and results is a one-size-fits-all treatment plan. This enhances the probability of program dropout. Many DWI offenders reject the disease model

and do not accept abstinence as a lifestyle goal (Timken, 2002).

Fourth, an assumption of traditional DWI treatment is that the pathway to preventing recidivism is to prevent relapse. Most (but not all) education and treatment protocols focused on relapse. Most fail to clearly focus on recidivism and none of the programs reviewed (education and treatment) provided a distinct model for recidivism and recidivism prevention separate from relapse models. Although the pathways to and the skills of preventing relapse are similar to those of recidivism, the two must be seen as separate even though they are interactive. This has been a major weakness of most DWI education and treatment protocols reviewed.

Fifth, although traditional treatment has acknowledged the importance of deterrence and sanctioning procedures for offenders, most program providers do not see themselves as part of the process of administering these sanctions. Effective interventions will include the treatment provider as a partner with the criminal justice system in administering the judicial sentence.

The literature suggests that there is a need to change these more traditional approaches. This involves developing structured protocols or manual-guided approaches that are therapy directed and client centered and integrate topic-focused therapy with unstructured process discussion. There is a need to build therapeutic models that focus on preventing recidivism as well as relapse. There is a need to broaden the traditional focus on AOD abuse and addiction and the disease model to include a social learning and cognitive-behavioral understanding of impaired driving behavior. There is a need to expand beyond an abstinence-based relapse prevention model to one that also includes preventing relapse into patterns of disruption and abuse.

Summary of DWI Education and Treatment Outcome Studies

Timken's (2002) comprehensive review of DWI education and treatment outcome studies, Cavaiola and Wuth's (2002) summary of DWI treatment strategies and Wells-Parker et al's. (1995) meta-analytic study of DWI outcome studies along with other resources provide a basis for summarizing what does and does not work in DWI interventions. Below is a summary of some of these findings.

Since early DWI education programs were lecture-didactic in nature, studies were conducted to determine the efficacy of this approach. A study by Landrum et al. (1982), comparing a lecture-didactic oriented DWI education program with a no-treatment group, indicated no differences in recidivism rates between the two groups. Lecture-oriented programs in large classroom settings may in fact be counterproductive for problem drinkers (Nichols et al., 1978).

In a study reported by (Reis, 1982), *first time offenders* were randomly assigned to one of three groups: no intervention control; four session driver education program; a home study educational program. *Repeat offenders* were assigned to one of four groups: no intervention; active intervention counseling group; therapeutic counseling plus antabuse; bi-weekly contacts without counseling or antabuse. First time offenders showed **small reductions** in DWI recidivism for both educational programs. Multiple offenders showed **20 – 30 % reduction** in recidivism in the **bi-weekly contacts and group counseling** group. None of the reduced recidivism rates were significant when controlling for driving record or other driver characteristics. The control groups had no license restrictions while the intervention groups did. **Therefore any reduction in recidivism was influenced by this sanction.**

Popkin et al. (1983) report on a study comparing the effect of education and sanctions. A group of first offenders was given an alcohol and drug education program in lieu of license sanctions. **The education group had higher recidivism rates than the sanctions group.** A later study showed that **combining education with license suspension led to lower recidivism rates than suspension alone** (Popkin, et al., 1988).

Tashima & Peck (1986) report on the effects of alternative sanctions for first and repeat DWI offenders involving outcomes for over 29,000 first time offenders differentially sentenced to: jail; license suspension or license restriction; and license restriction with mandated rehabilitation.

The **mandated rehabilitation group had the lowest rates of minor traffic offenses and the lowest rates of total convictions.** The findings are confounded because those sentenced to jail had worse driving records than those in other groups.

Siegel (1987) compared the effectiveness of the 72 hour Weekend Intervention Program (WIP) with jail or suspended sentence. **Repeat offenders in WIP had almost 20% fewer subsequent DWI offenses than offenders sentenced to jail and almost 30% fewer offenses than those offenders who received a suspended sentence.** First offenders assigned to the WIP showed lower recidivism rates than other first time offenders (9.2 versus 12.7 percent), however the difference was not statistically significant.

Wells-Parker, et al. (1995) conducted a meta-analysis of 215 independent outcome studies of DWI offender intervention programs identified through a comprehensive literature review. **The magnitude of positive program effects on both DWI recidivism and alcohol–related crashes, was in the range of a seven to nine percent reduction.** While the temporal parameter variables (e.g., total hours, duration in weeks, etc.) didn't reveal differences in treatment effects, programs in which participants received combinations of treatment modalities (including education, psychotherapy/ counseling) and follow-up meetings such as contact probation, showed better recidivism outcomes than contact probation alone. The use of Alcoholics Anonymous (AA) as the primary intervention showed negative results on DWI recidivism. The authors note, however, that AA tended to be assigned to offenders in the highest level of problem risk and that results for mandatory attendance at AA should not be interpreted as comparable to the results of AA attendance in programs that are not court mandated. Future study is indicated to understand the effects of AA as an element of programs that involve AA in combination with other educational, therapeutic and aftercare components.

Summarizing across both the sanctioning and intervention studies, it appears that certain types of sanctioning are effective in reducing the negative impact of impaired driving, e.g., reducing recidivism, AOD related crashes and fatalities.

Incarceration alone seems to have little long term, if not short term, impact. License restrictions and revocations and monitoring use and restriction of vehicle access (impoundment, interlocks, selling vehicle) all contribute to a reduction in recidivism. Morse and Elliot (1992) indicate that these approaches are promising yet the effectiveness of the long term deterrence of these methods has been questioned.

Sanctioning is most effective when it is tied into loss of and regaining driving and vehicle access privilege. These judicial actions, which Jones and Lacey (2000) classify as "alternative sanctions", appear especially effective, "offering potential reductions in recidivism in the 15% to 90% range." Thus, during the 1990s, considerable effort was directed at such interventions and deterrence (Lapham et al., 1997; Peck et al., 1994; McMillen, 1992; Wieczorek et al., 1992; Nichols and Ross, 1990; Perrine et al., 1989). Such deterrence strategies most often involve both correctional (sanctioning) and therapeutic efforts. Incarceration that is not tied into these deterrence and treatment approaches seems to have little impact and may even increase recidivism.

Taken as a whole, the findings also suggest that education and treatment approaches are more effective in reducing recidivism than punishment or deterrence intervention approaches alone. License revocation combined with treatment is effective, with the potential for reducing recidivism by as much as 50 percent (NHSTA, 1999b). Thus, during the later part of the 1990s, there has been a strong push to integrate the correctional-deterrence strategies with the education-therapeutic interventions, particularly with higher risk and repeat offenders.

Measuring Treatment Efficacy

The most obvious and simplest, and the one always used, to measure intervention efficacy is recidivism as measured by rearrest and/or AOD related crashes or fatalities. Yet, as Cavaiola and Wuth (2002) contend, "the value of treatment cannot be measured in the reduced crashes and recidivism alone" (p. 149). Treatment efficacy is also measured in terms of improving self-control, improving the DWIO's relationship to family, others and the community, reducing problems related to AOD use and overall improvement of the quality of life.

Some even argue that recidivism may not be a valid measurement of treatment outcome (McCarty & Argeriou, 1986).

One major problem is that recidivism is typically based on rearrest records. What about those who do not get rearrested? Do they continue driving impaired? Or, do they just learn to "drive smart?"

Another problem in using recidivism as the only evidence of intervention efficacy is that it does not tell us about the process of treatment and what components of treatment are and are not working (Cavaiola & Wuth, 2002, pp. 179-180). Treatment efficacy determined by the recidivism variable alone does not control for other sources of variance that can contribute to the reduction of arrest recidivism or AOD related crashes and fatalities, such as changes in laws or changes in enforcement methods and goals.

The single measure of recidivism fails to identify what type of clients do and do not recidivate nor does it identify the different types of recidivism patterns. The outcome measure of recidivism will take on more meaning when we relate DWIO types identified at pre-intervention to different types of recidivism patterns, e.g., multiple criterion and multiple predictors (canonical correlations). If impaired drivers and the behavior of impaired driving are as diverse and multidimensional as the literature suggests, then the results from intervention will also be multidimensional and diverse. Using a single outcome measure will not capture the multiple patterns of outcome. This diversity can be discerned if multivariate theory is used adroitly. Thus, multivariate measurement at initial evaluation, in the treatment process, and with outcome assessment should become the primary method in determining DWI intervention efficacy.

Summary of Intervention Approaches that Impact Outcome

In addition to the traditional DWI treatment approaches described above, the above outcome studies, and other summaries in the literature suggest a number of components of DWI intervention that can enhance positive outcomes. Some of these will be presented.

Matching DWI client dimensions and types with appropriate services. Different AOD use, personality and behavioral dimensions and types have been identified in impaired driving samples (Donovan & Marlatt, 1982; Gurnak, 1989; Packard, 1987; Prochaska, 1999; Steer et al., 1979; Wanberg & Timken, 1991, 1998; Wells-Parker et al., 1990). Matching these types with different amounts and types of interventions increases overall effectiveness in the system (Gurnak, 1989; Simpson, et al., 1996). This matching has been an important innovation in DWI intervention (Timken & Wanberg, 1999; Wells-Parker et al., 1995; Wieczorek, 1993). Deyle (1997) found that DWIOs classified as problem drinkers and sent to a didactic, brief education program, rather than interactive education and protracted treatment, recidivated at a rate of 20 percent compared to seven percent for those properly matched. Placement of DWIOs in inappropriate treatment modalities will produce an increase in dropout rates. The DSAP Model is based on matching intervention with weighted scores that discriminates types, e.g., low BAC, low AOD disruption, no prior arrests versus high BAC, moderate AOD disruption, prior arrests and interventions (Timken & Wanberg, 2001).

Matching stages of change with appropriate placement. DWIOs differ as to their stage of change when entering intervention services. There is evidence that failure to match stage of change with kinds of intervention will decrease the probability of positive outcome. Placing DWIOs who are in the challenge (Wanberg & Milkman, 1998) stage of change into a program based on commitment or ownership of change will decrease positive outcomes. Or, using the traditional, transtheoretical model (DiClemente, 2003), "we simply cannot treat people with a precontemplation profile as if they were ready for action interventions and expect them to stay with us (Prochaska, 1999).

Enhancing motivation and readiness and using the principles of motivational interviewing have shown positive effects as to compliance and outcome for DWIOs (Miller & Hester, 1986; Miller & Rollnick, 2002; Stein & Lebeau-Craven, 2002; Timken et al., 1995). Building client rapport, trust and a therapeutic alliance are essential in DWI treatment. Strong confrontational approaches tend to be counter-productive to positive outcomes

for DWI offenders (Miller & Rollnick, 1991, 2002). Using motivational and client-oriented skills builds a therapeutic alliance that increases the probability of the client completing the intervention program and overall positive outcomes. Nochajski, et al. (1993) found that the recidivism rate for high risk drivers over a 24 month follow-up phase was 34 percent for dropouts versus 14 percent for those completing the program. Several other studies support this finding (e.g., Deyle, 1997; Darbey, 1993).

Multimodal programs that use a variety of approaches, education, counseling, UA monitoring, manual-guided protocols, etc., are more effective than single-mode programs, e.g., education only (Wells-Parker, 1994). Education is one component of a multimodal program. The countermeasures and sanctioning options must also be varied and multimodal. This includes weekend, short-term and long-term incarceration and alternative sentencing appropriately determined based on offender type and level of risk. Success of the DWI judicial system is based on imposing appropriate sanctioning (Jones et al., 1998).

Protracted length of treatment with a continuing care component may reduce recidivism and improve outcomes if treatment for the problem drinker is in the range of nine to twelve months or even longer (NHTSA, 1996; Timken et al., 1995). The more serious the problems of both AOD misuse and impaired driving, the more comprehensive the intervention should be in terms of length and intensity.

Protracted and close judicial supervision and monitoring with frequent contacts increases probability of positive outcomes. During supervision, there should be a quick implementation of sanctions for those who violate the terms of their judicial sentence.

Development of an individual treatment plan (ITP), within a multimodal structure, gives the provider and client a guide for individualized treatment. The ITP also determines the extent to which protocol-guided or structured programs are meeting the individual needs of the client and which individual services are needed beyond the structured program.

Client responsibility for program cost appears to impact treatment outcome. DWI offenders who pay for all or part of any intervention have better outcomes (NHTSA, 1979, 1983; Timken, 2002).

Social learning theory and the cognitive-behavioral model for change (see Chapter 9) is an effective platform for AOD and DWI education and treatment. It provides the client with concrete ways to learn skills to restructure thinking, interpersonal, and societal relationships for more positive outcomes. The efficacy of cognitive-behavioral approaches in offender treatment has been well established (see Wanberg & Milkman, 1998; and Chapter 9).

Relapse prevention models unique to DWI conduct. As noted above, abstinence-oriented relapse prevention models utilized in traditional AOD treatment have been imported into DWI intervention programs. These models are not appropriate for many DWIOs and need to be modified for effective use.

Recidivism prevention focus. At the expense of the high focus on relapse prevention in DWI programs, the development of effective models for recidivism prevention has been lacking. Although linked, they are separate in their pathways to occurrence and prevention (Wanberg & Milkman, 1998). Recidivism has its own high risk exposures different from relapse. Recidivism should take on a separate and unique focus in DWI intervention programs.

Manual guided or protocol treatment models have become a major innovation in psychosocial and correctional therapies over the past 10 years. For DWIOs, these programs were initially structured education groups; however, they have become core components of DWI treatment. To be effective, these programs will use interactive, multimedia and experienced-based approaches, including role playing, tying program content to the real-life experiences of the client, using session work sheets and continued skill practice in applying the concepts of change. One of the first comprehensive approaches to this method was Project Match (1993, 1997) in which treatment was structured around three different theoretical approaches: motivational interviewing, cognitive-behavioral approaches, and the 12-step model. All approaches had comparable outcomes. Research on provider satisfaction of protocol-guided approaches indicates a variety of results: very positive (Najavits, et al., 2000); positive but tends to ignore unique provider contributions (Addis & Krasnow, 2000); positive and allows therapist to address the unique needs of clients (Godley, et al., 2001); and very positive, need time to feel comfortable with delivery, and supervision important along with the manual in implementation (Najavits, et al., 2004). These programs are most effective when they are the core component of a multimodal DWI intervention framework.

Focus on community responsibility skills and empathy building. Few DWI intervention programs have a strong approach to skill development in the area of community and moral responsibility. These are empathy-based skills that increase prosocial thinking, attitudes and conduct. They help DWIOs put themselves in the place of others, have empathy for persons they have or could injure through their DWI conduct, and help DWIOs engage in productive and positive interactions with the community. This is an important component of the *Driving With Care* education and treatment protocols.

Integration of correctional and educational/ therapeutic strategies. As summarized above, sanctioning is effective in reducing recidivism, particularly license revocations and education and therapeutic interventions are effective in reducing recidivism across all offenders and treatment types. The more recent evidence is that combining sanctioning with treatment interventions is more effective than either of the two approaches alone (e.g., Cavaiola & Wuth, 2002; Hagen, 1978; Nichols & Ross, 1989; Nichols et al., 1978; Popkin et al., 1983; Sadler & Perrine, 1984; Tashima & Peck, 1986). Sanctioning and treatment should be complimentary, not competing (Wieczorek, 1993). Effective intervention programs will include both deterrence (correctional) and education-therapeutic approaches. DWI intervention is society and client centered. The provider is an advocate of the client **and** society. DWI education and treatment is part of the judicial sentence. *The provider is a partner with the court in administering that sentence.*

SPECIAL CONSIDERATIONS IN EDUCATION AND TREATMENT

Family and Significant Other (Collateral) Involvement

Cavaiola and Wuth (2002) note the very significant discrepancy between the emphasis on family involvement in traditional AOD treatment programs and the lack of this emphasis in DWI education and treatment. "When it comes to treating the DWI offender...there are only a handful of articles written and even fewer empirical studies that advocate for family involvement" (p. 200: Note, see Cavaiola & Wuth, Chapter 10, for an excellent discussion of issues around involvement of significant collaterals in intervention).

Even though a large percent of DWIOs are not in a marriage situation, most if not all have family connections and involvement, many have gone through divorce or separation, and most are in "significant other" (SO) relationships. These involvements are important factors in both DWI conduct and prevention. Family members and SO collaterals are also impacted by the DWIO's impaired driving history and legal consequences. They need information about the program, basic knowledge about AOD use and DWI conduct, the change process, and available support resources. The overall goal is to enhance the reinforcement potential of collaterals in strengthening the change process and preventing recidivism.

It has been the experience of the authors of this work that engaging collaterals, viz., family members and SOs, in the intervention process is difficult. There are several reasons for this. First, the response of collaterals to the DWIO's legal problems and expense becomes a barrier. The response is often shock and surprise, anger, blame, "I told you so," and even relief (Cavaiola & Wuth, 2002). Second, collaterals become defensive and resistive much in the same manner as the DWIO. Third, the authors of this work have found that many DWIOs what to "go it alone" in resolving the legal and intervention requirements of their DWI conviction. Many simply don't want their significant collaterals to be involved. This is due in part to the DWIO's characteristics: young, male and not in a marriage

situation. It is also due to the embarrassment and guilt that many DWIOs experience. Yet, many DWIOs do want their family and SOs involved.

Here are some guidelines regarding enhancing involvement of significant collaterals.

- Involvement at intake as part of assessment. This would include a session with the DWIO and significant collaterals. It could also include a brief questionnaire for family members to document their needs, concerns and questions.

- Have two intervention track opportunities: one with family involvement; another with only DWIO involvement. This may be impractical for many agencies.

- Provide a collateral support group that meets at least monthly, if not weekly, in order to include SOs in the ongoing intervention process.

- In structured or protocol-guided programs, have at least one if not two sessions for collaterals to attend, and in which family relationships and building intimacy and closeness are the main focus topics.

- Make available ongoing family and marital counseling resources that the DWIO and collaterals can use to resolve conflicts and strengthen relationships.

- Have significant collaterals involved in closure sessions.

Many significant collaterals do want to be involved in the DWIO's intervention. Family members and SOs often see themselves as having complicity in the DWIO's impaired driving history and the arrest event. There is some reality to this perception in that Yoder (1975) reports that 75 percent of DWI arrests could have been prevented had significant collaterals (friends and relatives) taken a proactive role in dissuading the DWIO from drinking and driving (p. 1575).

Addressing Resistance and Defensiveness

DWI offenders display high levels of defensiveness and resistance to involvement in assessment, education and treatment (Cavaiola, 1984; Cavaiola & Wuth, 2002). This often contributes to difficulty in establishing a positive and working relationship with DWI offenders. Yet, the levels of defensiveness vary among DWI clients. Some are very defensive; some are very open and self-disclosing. Defensiveness is also dynamic, and varies at different points in the assessment process. As noted, pre-sentenced clients are much more defensive than post-sentenced clients (Wanberg & Timken, 2004).

We tend to see resistance as anti-treatment or anti-intervention or indicating a person who is "not motivated." It is helpful to view resistance within the framework of defensiveness. It is a manifestation of a strong defense system working against a realistic assessment and recognition on the part of DWI offenders of their involvement in AOD use and in DWI conduct. It is the utilization of a complex of errors in thinking, errors that the client has used in many areas of life, and not just around DWI conduct. It is a defense of the self, similar to any average person who is strongly invested in the phenomenological view of self and goes to any length to defend that view, particularly when it is threatened by outside forces or there are high expectations to change that view. It may be part-and-parcel of the personality pattern that leads individuals to engage in antisocial and irresponsible behavior towards society. As Lazarus and Fay (1982) note, defensive or resistive clients are persons for whom self-disclosure, self-awareness and change are psychologically painful and threatening.

We can also view defensiveness and resistance from the perspective of the stages that people go through when making changes (DiClemente, 2003). Resistance and defensiveness are different at different stages and around different areas of change.

Resistance is also a response to confronting forces in the outside world. A number of studies have indicated that confrontation involving countering, correcting or arguing against the client's resistance to acceptance and awareness of problem behavior only increases resistance and defensiveness (Miller & Rollnick, 1991, 2002; Wells-Parker et al., 2000). This seems to be particularly true when countering and confrontation are used in the client's early involvement in intervention.

Cavaiola and Wuth (2002) outline what they have observed to be stages of resistance in the DWI offender. The **initial stage** is anger, particularly towards the provider, who is the most amenable target for anger building up through systemic experiences. The **testing stage** is more cognitive, and clients even make an effort to bargain their way through the process, trying "to get off." The **compliance stage,** is "giving in" or "agreeing to go along" and "get it over with." There is considerable manipulation and maneuvering to this stage. The **anger stage (part 2)** is anger resulting from being *challenged* (e.g., Wanberg & Milkman's challenge stage) to look at AOD use and DWI conduct. The **self-depreciation stage** involves clients turning anger and blame towards themselves. "It's my fault," "dumb of me to do this." Finally, in the **acceptance stage,** clients begin to become committed to treatment and take *ownership* of their change (Wanberg & Milkman, 1998).

Given that defensiveness is elevated among DWIOs, that it varies from client to client and across different points of assessment, methods and approaches need to be built into the education and treatment protocols that manage resistance in an ongoing and on an individual basis. Here are some approaches that can be effective in managing DWIO resistance and defensiveness.

▶ Continual assessment of the level of defensiveness to provide a guide as to what kind of clinical skills should be used with a particular level of resistance. The most important initial component of assessment is discerning the client's level of openness and resistance.

▶ Help the client see that assessment is ongoing, seeing all client self-report as a valid representation of the willingness to disclose, and communicate that the client's self-reports are valued.

▶ Focus on topics that are external and neutral in initial phases of intervention. Give clients information which will have direct implications for their unique situation.

- In the early phases of intervention, do not confront resistance, but use strong reflective acceptance skills that "rolls with the resistance" (Miller & Rollnick, 2002). Also, use feedback clarification rather than feedback confrontation. Feedback clarification will help the clients see their thinking errors.

- Build a partnership of change early on (Wanberg & Milkman, 1998).

- Work together to establish a shared individual treatment plan. This involves common goals, mutual contracts, win-win agreements.

- Make the initial feedback confrontation based on past behaviors that are "the facts" or "part of the record." "Here is what is documented about your DWI arrest."

- Have others share their view of the client in a safe and non-threatening environment. This is difficult for the DWIO, who wants to "go it alone," and not want family and significant others involved.

- Objectify the education and treatment experience through work sheets and other activities that all persons in the group do.

- Give constant feedback on what the client is doing, with high therapeutic reinforcement schedules. Always look for windows of reinforcement opportunity. When a client finishes his or her first work sheet, praise and reinforcement is essential.

- Capitalize on the client's vulnerabilities or what Cavaiola and Wuth (2002) call "the weak spots." Defenses are lowered and there is openness to being supported and reinforced during these critical and vulnerable moments. It is helpful to always remember that all DWIOs have experienced considerable embarrassment, hurt, anxiety, stress and even depression because of their DWI

arrest. Capitalizing on the affective dimensions of this experience will give the provider a segue into developing a therapeutic alliance that increases self-disclosure, self-awareness and change.

- Use therapeutic confrontation and correctional confrontation adroitly and after rapport and trust have been established with the client. Therapeutic confrontation is client-centered and confronts discrepancies between the client's goals and the client's behavior. It confronts the client with the client. Correctional confrontation confronts the client with the goals of society and impact of the client's behavior on society. It is society-centered.

Intervention of the Hard Core Offender

Chapter 6 defined hard core (HC) drivers as repeat offenders or first DWI offenders with a high arrest BAC. Colorado refers to this group as the *persistent drunk driver,* and places the arrest BAC at .20 (BBC Research & Consulting, 2003). Chapter 6 also summarized some of the legal and statutory approaches that are used to address hard core (HC) offenders. These approaches have been effective, particularly those that focus on vehicle and licensing sanctioning and close monitoring of alcohol-related behaviors (NHTSA, 2000). However, with respect to treatment, Cavaiola and Wuth note that the HC offender "...does not respond to current mainstream treatment methods" (2002, p. 160). It is clear that intervention programs need to be more tailored to address the HC offender. Some of the intervention issues that are relevant for HC and repeat offenders are summarized.

More extensive assessment to discern co-occurring problems. Repeat offenders have higher levels of mental health and AOD use problems (Wanberg & Timken, 2005a). Treatment programs need to meet the treatment needs of these problems. It is logical (though not empirically determined) that these co-occurring problems contribute to the establishment and reinforcement of the HC offender pattern.

Protracted or extended treatment and supervision services. The HC offender needs multimodal services that go beyond core or standard manual-guided programs. This may be due, in part, to the finding that repeat offenders have higher degrees of cognitive impairment. Glass, Chan & Rentz (2000) found cognitive impairment in repeat DWI offenders as "extremely high." This impairment may require more time for the learning and change process. They may just "not catch it" as soon or as easily as first offenders. This supports Argeriou and Manohar's (1977) finding that less severe AOD clients require less time to complete therapeutic programs and tasks than more severely impacted AOD clients.

Enhanced cognitive-behavioral focus. The HC offender needs enhanced and more intense focus on cognitive-behavioral change with repeated practice of the cognitive, interpersonal and community restructuring skills (see Chapter 11).

Intensive integration of correctional-deterrence with education-therapeutic services. NHTSA (1999b) stresses that strong enforcement and strict penalties in coordination with treatment are necessary to curb repeat DWI behavior.

An approach congruent with the NHTSA advice has been implemented in Multnomah County's (Portland, Oregon) *Intensive Supervision Program (DISP) for repeat offenders,* implemented in 1998 (Lapham, 1999).

This comprehensive three year program includes a combination of sanctioning, intensive supervision and treatment. The program integrates a combination of honesty, zero tolerance of alcohol and drug use, zero tolerance of driving, education and treatment programs and monetary obligation payments. The specific strategies and approaches are offender-funded electronic monitoring with a bracelet and phone-communication breath testing, polygraph testing, a patch or urine drug testing, sale of the offender's vehicle on the open market, full time employment, attendance of a victim's impact panel and involvement in education and treatment. These approaches are in addition to other sanctions imposed by the court such as incarceration and fines. All offenders receive the same intensive supervision program. Failure to comply with the program components will lead to further sanctioning and incarceration.

Initial studies of the impact of this program indicated that .5 percent of third time DWIOs were rearrested after one year compared to a much higher rearrest rate for non-participating repeat offenders. A comprehensive research protocol was implemented in 2000 to study the effectiveness of various combinations of the program components (Lapham, 1999).

Social marketing strategies. In efforts to reduce the problem of the HC offender, the *BBC Research and Consulting* (2003) group developed a social marketing strategy to target the persistent drunk driver. The goal was to change behavior in their target audiences, not just inform the public. From a focus-group research project, involving 64 persistent drunk drivers, and using hypothetical vignettes of persistent drunk drivers, a behavior change model was developed that can be used in multiple marketing channels, e.g., T.V., radio, etc. Targeting change in the persistent drunk driving population will use marketing strategies that revolve around core elements of this behavioral change model: awareness, trust, desire, ability, optimism and success.

SUMMARY OF FOCUS TOPICS OF DIFFERENT EDUCATION AND TREATMENT PROTOCOLS

In preparation for the development of the *Driving With Care* education and treatment protocols, a number of DWI education and treatment programs were reviewed. A summary of this review include the focus topics of these programs. Most of the intervention DWI manual-guided protocols reviewed by the authors were strongly education based. Of the 14 manuals reviewed, 13 were designed as education protocols. Only one was designed as a manual-guided therapy program for impaired drivers. Although some of the education protocols had some therapy-type topics that focused on cognitive, emotional and behavioral change, the 13 were primarily education in nature.

The 14 DWI education and treatment protocols that were reviewed are: *Alcohol and Drug Education Traffic Schools - ADETS* (North Carolina Division of Mental Health, 1995); *Alcohol and Other Drug Information School* (James, et al. 1998); *Assessment*

Course Treatment (ACT: Boyd Andrew *Chemical Dependency Care Center,* 1997); *Back on Track Education Program* (Centre for Addiction and Mental Health, 1999); *Driver Alcohol Education Program* (Commonwealth of Massachusetts, 1996); *Drug and Alcohol Education* (Empowerment Counseling Services, Inc., 1998); *Impaired Driving Program - Level II Education* (Island Grove Community Counseling Center, 1999a); *Impaired Driving Program - Level II Group Therapy* (Island Grove Counseling Center, 1999b); *Kentucky Alcohol and Other Drugs Education Program* (Walsh, Kaplin, et al., 1999); *Mississippi Alcohol Safety Education Program* (Snow, et al., 1995); *Multiple Offender Program* (Responsible Driving, Inc., 1996); *Offender Education Program* (Missouri Division of Alcohol and Drug Abuse, 1998); *Virginia Alcohol Safety Action Program* (Serenity Support Services, Inc., 1993); and *Weekend Intervention Program - WIP* (Fischer, Dixon & Maxwell, 1994).

The 13 DWI education protocols varied from 12 hours to 32 hours. The one DWI therapy protocol was a 42 hour program. Table 8.1 provides a summary of the different topics represented in the 13 education programs. The number of programs that used each of these topics is provided in the right hand column of Table 8.1. The one 42 hour DWI therapy program essentially expanded on the psychosocial issues related to AOD use and DWI conduct.

The review of these 13 education and the one therapy programs indicated some important gaps and deficiencies in DWI intervention.

▶ Many of these protocols did not have a clear and distinct model for defining relapse and relapse prevention, particularly pertaining to issues of high risk situations and high risk thinking.

▶ Many did not clearly define a model for recidivism and recidivism prevention, although several programs did focus on DWI avoidance and recidivism. This was certainly the weakest link in the various protocols.

▶ Of those programs that did focus on recidivism, many did not clearly distinguish between recidivism as returning to any DWI conduct and rearrest.

Recidivism was often referred to as getting rearrested.

▶ Although implicit in most of the program content, only a very few programs explicitly stated that the primary goal of the program was preventing recidivism.

▶ Most programs focused on AOD use and abuse and AOD relapse prevention rather than recidivism prevention. Most programs linked relapse to recidivism and did not deal with these two issues as separate problems and phenomena.

▶ Only a few programs provided a clear model for defining AOD use problems beyond DSM diagnosis of abuse and dependence or beyond the traditional disease and addiction models. Essentially, this provides the majority of DWI offenders with no clear handle of defining their own AOD use and misuse pattern.

▶ Most programs did not define clear alternatives to abstinence, e.g., preventing relapse into an AOD abuse pattern; avoiding AOD use negative outcomes, etc.

▶ Programs varied as to the degree of client-content interaction. Most programs had interactive exercises and work sheets.

SUMMARY AND CONCLUSIONS

The results from the above review indicate some important conclusions. *First,* recidivism must be measured by involvement in impaired driving and not by rearrest. Although rearrest data are much more accessible to the researcher, they fail to indicate the extent of recidivism among those who have received sanctioning and intervention (education and treatment). More rigorous research protocols need to be established to clearly determine the extent of post-intervention impaired driving behavior among DWI clients.

Second, sanctioning in general, particularly without formal intervention services, is not effective, and with some methods, has been found to be associated with an increase in recidivism. However, some specific sanctioning methods have been shown to be effective, particularly when certain methods are combined and are associated with close monitoring. These are intensive supervision, electronic monitoring, loss of driving privileges through license revocation, vehicle use monitoring and restriction and vehicle forfeiture. The use of incarceration has little long-term effect, mainly because those who are incarcerated usually have more severe expressions of AOD problems and incarceration does not treat the underlying substance abuse or psychosocial problems.

Third, in general, education and treatment approaches are more effective in reducing recidivism than deterrence methods or sanctioning alone. Didactic education approaches seem to reduce recidivism to some extent for offenders who do not have AOD problems. However, only therapeutically oriented programs seem to have impact on offenders with clear AOD problems.

Intervention (education and treatment protocols) approaches have primarily focused on AOD abuse and addiction and relapse. Yet, few programs have used a formal relapse prevention model. As well, most of the DWI programs did not treat recidivism prevention as the core and primary program component and emphasis. Few programs provided a sound and clear model for describing the pathways to recidivism and recidivism prevention. There are specific therapeutic approaches that seem to be more effective than others. These have been summarized in this chapter.

Fourth, considerable progress has been made in DWI education and treatment interventions since the initiation of the ASAP programs in the 1970s. What has become most clear is that these interventions combined with sanctioning and punishment seem to provide the best outcomes with respect to preventing recidivism. Yet, effective models of integrating the correctional-sanctioning approaches with the therapeutic-treatment approaches are still in the infancy stage.

Finally, as mentioned in the Preface to this work, DWI education and treatment must make a major paradigm shift that involves the incorporation of sociocentric treatment. Traditional AOD and DWI treatment is based on egocentric approaches that focus primarily on the treatment needs of the individual. When working with DWIOs, we need to incorporate a sociocentric, more holistic approach that also focuses on the treatment needs of the community. This involves moving towards a treatment of connected consciousness and builds on the principles and gains of egocentric treatment. Sociocentric therapy helps clients build cognitive structures and learn and reinforce behaviors that are prosocial and relational with the goal of engaging in moral and social responsibility in the community and society at large.

TABLE 8.1

Frequency of DWI topics and content across 13 DWI education protocols

SUMMARY DESCRIPTION OF TOPICS	FREQ
General orientation and introduction to program	12
Learning to listen and share in group	7
Clients share their DWI arrest experience, cost, burden	10
Providing different goals: abstinence versus other	6
Monitoring daily use of alcohol or other drugs	4
DWI related statistics: accidents, crashes, number DWI drivers	10
BAC information and relationship to impaired driving	13
AOD effects on body, brain, physical effects and damage	13
AOD effects on driving ability	8
Different drugs, types, tolerance, interactions, mood effects	13
AOD use patterns, problems, symptoms, consequences, types	13
Addiction, abuse and chemical dependency	11
Focus on disease concepts	6
Focus on denial and relationship to addiction	3
Focus on defining AOD problem outside of DSM Diagnoses	2
Introduction to 12-Step Program of AA	5
Focus on feelings, emotions, stress, anger, related to AOD use	8
AOD use/abuse and family relationships, roles, co-dependency	10
DWI laws, penalties, drivers license regulation	10
Focus on changing thinking, attitudes, beliefs, values	5
Anger and anger management	3
How people change and stages of change	3
Problem solving, decision making and critical reasoning skills	4
Family roles	5
Model for relapse	2
Model for recidivism (involvement in impaired driving)	2
Having clients develop personal change/relapse prevention plan	5
Clients develop plan to avoid DWI contact and recidivism	6
High risk behavior topics such as HIV, FAS, birth defects	7
AOD use and social relationships	2
Focus on safe driving skill/attitudes, driving risk/hazards	2
Stress management and relaxation skills training	3
Emphasis/exercises on client self-evaluation	8
Victim awareness and empathy training	4
AOD refusal and assertiveness skills training	3
Relationship of AOD use to non-DWI criminal conduct	3
Focus on job, employment and relationship to AOD use	2
Peer relationships and drinking	2
Diet and health issues both AOD and non-AOD related	5
Relationship of thinking errors to DWI conduct	2
Use of thinking reports	2
Interactive exercise, work sheets, homework	10
Communication skills training	2
Cognitive restructuring training and skills	1
Focus on life-style balance	1
Differential and in-depth assessment	1
Pre-post testing on program content	5
Grief and loss	1
Self-esteem	2

CHAPTER NINE: OVERVIEW OF COGNITIVE-BEHAVIORAL THEORY

HISTORICAL ROOTS OF COGNITIVE-BEHAVIORAL THERAPY

Since *Driving With Care: Education and Treatment of the Impaired Driving Offender* is based on the theory and practice of cognitive-behavioral approaches, it is important that the reader understand the historical roots of this approach and how the two paths of behavior therapy and cognitive therapy joined.

The development of behavioral therapies of the late 1950s and 1960s provided the evolutionary foundation of the behavior component of cognitive-behavioral therapy. Franks and Wilson (1973) note that behavioral therapy has a long past but a short history. This long past is found in the work of the behaviorists and learning theorists in the first half of this century (Glass and Arnkoff, 1992). Pavlov's work in classical conditioning (1927), the behaviorism of Watson (1913) and the operant conditioning models of Skinner (1938) in the early part of this century provided the empirical and theoretical foundations of behavioral therapy.

During this same period, the work of Thorndike (1931), Guthrie (1935), Hull (1943) and Mowrer (1947) in the psychology of learning also added to the theoretical grounding of behavioral therapy. As these theories emerged, so did a number of efforts to apply them clinically (Glass and Arnkoff, 1992). Most noteworthy was Dunlap's (1932) use of "negative practice" involving the repetition of undesirable behavior such as tics, Mowrers' (Mowrer & Mower, 1938) "bell and pad" method of treating bed wetting, Jacobson's (1938) method of progressive relaxation and Salter's (1949) method of directly practicing a behavior in a particular situation.

Emerging methods such as systematic desensitization (Wolpe, 1958) to manage anxiety and the applications of contingency reinforcement (Skinner, 1953) in behavioral management spelled the beginning of modern behavioral therapy in the 1950s and 1960s. Eysenck (1960) was the first to use the term "behavioral therapy" in a book title and he along with Rachman founded the *Journal Behavioral Research and Therapy*. Behavioral therapy gained a strong foothold in psychology with the introduction of the concepts and applications of modeling (Bandura, 1969), anxiety management through flooding, behavioral self-control and self monitoring (Goldiamond, 1965; Kanfer, 1970, 1975) and social skills training (Lange & Jakubowski, 1976) which is an important component of contemporary cognitive-behavioral therapy.

The historical roots of the cognitive component of cognitive-behavioral therapy (CBT) are found in the literature of philosophy and psychology and in the studies on self-change (Arnkoff & Glass, 1992). The concept that our view of the world shapes the reality that we experience is found in Greek thinking and in Plato's concept of the ideal forms (Leahy, 1996). Plato saw these forms as existing within the mind and representing what is real in the world. Seventeenth and 18th century philosophers built their view of the world around the idea that the mind determines reality. This is particularly found in Descartes' concept that "I think, therefore I am," and Kant's idea that the mind makes nature (Collingwood, 1949).

Arnkoff and Glass (1992) note that there is a differing of opinions as to whether cognitive therapy evolved within modern behavioral therapy or whether it emerged as a new and independent movement. Whichever the case, it seems fair to conclude that the cognitive approach was a reaction to the more narrow view of behavioral psychology which did not attend to, and even rejected, the importance of internal mediating cognitive responses and processes, e.g., attribution, problem solving, expectancy, etc. Bandura's classic work *Principles of Behavioral Modification* (1969) challenged the traditional view of non-mediational behavioral psychology. Bandura (1969, 1977a) stressed the importance of internal mental processes in the regulation and modification of behavior.

Arnkoff and Glass (1992) see modern cognitive restructuring therapies as emerging in the mid-1950s with the work of Ellis (Ellis & Harper, 1961) and his development of rational-emotive therapy (RET) which he presented in the book *Guide to Rational Living* (1961). The work of Ellis is seen as an important precursor to the work of Beck (1963, 1964) who is commonly seen as the founder and developer of cognitive therapy emerging out of his work with depression at the University of Pennsylvania in the early 1960s (Arnkoff and Glass, 1992; J. Beck, 1995; Leahy, 1996). Leahy (1996) attributes Kelly (1955) in his development of cognitive constructs as "the early founder of cognitive therapy" (p. 11). Beck (1996) made it clear that he borrowed from Kelly's cognitive constructs when he first applied "the concept of negative cognitive schemas to explain the 'thinking disorder' of depression...." (p. 1). The work of Kelly and Piaget (1954) in his study of the structure of thinking provided a firm foundation for the development of the cognitive restructuring therapies.

Following the work of Beck (1963, 1970, 1976) in applying the cognitive model to the treatment of depression, other cognitive restructuring therapies began to emerge. These different forms of cognitive therapy began to blend the elements of behavioral therapy with cognitive-restructuring therapy.

Thus, as Dobson and Dozois (2001) note, the earliest of the CBTs emerged in the early 1960s (e.g., Ellis, 1962). The first major texts on cognitive-behavioral modification did not appear until the 1970s (Kendall & Hollon, 1979; Mahoney, 1974; Meichenbaum, 1977).

Meichenbaum (1975, 1977) was instrumental in developing self-instructional training, stress inoculation and coping skills training. This approach had a strong behavioral therapy flavor. Goldfried et al. (1974) implemented systematic rational restructuring which teaches the individual to modify internal sentences (thoughts) and then to practice the rational reanalysis of these thoughts through role playing and behavioral rehearsal. Cautela (1966, 1990) conceived covert sensitization (1966) as a method for cognitive-behavioral change. Problem solving therapies and training became prominent features of cognitive behavioral treatment (Shure & Spivack, 1978; Spivack & Shure, 1974; D'Zurilla & Goldfried, 1971). The coping skills and stress inoculation training approaches were developed to help clients deal with problem and stressful situations (Meichenbaum, 1977, 1985). The stress inoculation method involves teaching the individual coping skills and then practicing these skills when deliberately exposed to a stressful situation.

Although behavioral therapies and cognitive restructuring approaches seemed to develop in parallel paths, over time, the two approaches merged into what we now call cognitive-behavioral therapy. As Arnkoff and Glass (1992) note, "the line distinguishing behavior therapy from cognitive therapy has become blurred, to the point that cognitive-behavioral is a widely accepted term" (p. 667). The behavioral component is of crucial importance particularly in the treatment of children (Arnkoff and Glass, 1992) but also in the treatment of alcohol and other drug abuse problems and of criminal conduct. Alan Marlatt has noted (personal communication, 1995) that cognitive therapy a la Ellis and Beck has over the years become progressively more behavioral and that behavioral therapy a la Bandura, Goldfried, Kanfer, Mahoney, Meichenbaum, etc., has over the years become progressively more cognitive - together creating contemporary CBT.

THE INTEGRATION OF COGNITIVE AND BEHAVIORAL PRINCIPLES AND APPROACHES

BEHAVIOR THERAPY PLACES the focus on current determinants of behavior with an emphasis on overt behavior change guided by specific treatment objectives (Kazdin, 1978). It involves the application of principles that come from learning theory, social and experimental psychology. It involves environmental change and social interaction using approaches that enhance self-control (Franks & Wilson, 1975). It is further characterized by a focus on client responsibility and the therapeutic relationship (Franks & Barbrack, 1983). The common intervention approaches used in behavioral therapy are coping and social skills training, problem solving training, contingency management, modeling, exposure-based treatment, anxiety reduction and relaxation methods, self-management methods, and behavioral rehearsal (Antony & Roemer, 2003; Glass & Arnkoff, 1992).

The underlying principle of cognitive therapy is that disturbances in behaviors, emotions and thought can be modified or changed by altering the cognitive processes (Dobson & Dozois, 2001; Hollen & Beck, 1986; Reinecke & Freeman, 2003). In simplistic terms, "cognitive therapy is based on the simple idea that your thoughts and attitudes — and not external events — create your moods

(Burns, 1989, p. xiii). The fundamental idea of the cognitive model of emotion as outlined by Beck (1976) is that "....emotions are experienced as a result of the way in which events are interpreted or appraised. It is the meaning of the event that triggers emotions rather than the events themselves" (Salkovskis, 1996a, p. 48).

The role of the cognitive therapist is to help the individual see the alternative ways of thinking about and appraising a situation, to check the relative merits and accuracy of the alternatives against past, present, and future experiences, and then help the individual "identify any obstacles to thinking and acting in this new, more helpful way" (Salkovskis, 1996a, p. 49). The goal is not to convince the individual that his or her view of the situation is wrong, right, negative, irrational; but rather to help the person discover other ways of looking at the situation.

Yet, this does not necessarily mean a straightforward cause and effect (thinking being the cause, and emotions and action the results). Cognitive psychology assumes an interplay between thought, emotion and action. As Freeman and colleagues (1990) note, "the cognitive model is not simply that 'thoughts cause feelings and actions' " (p. 6). Emotions and moods can change cognitive processes. Actions can have an influence on how one sees a particular situation. Emotions can arouse behaviors. There are a number of studies to indicate how moods and emotions influence cognition, e.g., memory, perception (Freeman, et al., 1990).

The common intervention approaches used in cognitive therapy are restructuring cognitive distortions found in negative schemas, maladaptive assumptions and automatic thoughts (Leahy, 1996), self-instructional training, problem solving, coping skills, relaxation therapy, modeling strategies, thought stopping and covert conditioning (Kendall & Bemis, 1983; Arnkoff & Glass, 1992, Leahy, 1996; Reinecke & Freeman, 2003).

Contemporary CBT, then, is an integration of the key components of behavioral and cognitive therapy. Even though prominent recent publications have titles designated as "Cognitive Therapy," (e.g., Judy Beck, 1995; Leahy, 1996; Leahy & Doud, 2002; Salkovskis, 1996b), the descriptions of the

methods and approaches of cognitive therapy in these texts clearly integrate the behavioral therapy counterpart (Reinecke & Freeman, 2003). In 1983, Kendall and Bemis argued that behavioral influences were predominant in the practice of cognitive therapy. Even though there appears to have been an evolutionary merging of the two approaches over the past 20 to 25 years, there has been some resistance to integration, particularly from behavior therapists (Arnkoff & Glass, 1992). However, during the 1990s, there was a strong movement towards the integration of all forms of contemporary psychotherapy (Arnkoff & Glass, 1992; Goldfried, 1995).

The underlying principle of *Driving With CARE* is that both cognitive and behavioral approaches bring combined strengths to the implementation of effective education and treatment for the impaired driving offender. Alan Marlatt (personal communication, 1995) states "I believe the strength of CBT is in its combined emphasis on aspects of both cognitive and behavioral approaches to change."

Sometimes the distinction is made between cognitive-behavioral modification (CBM) and cognitive behavioral treatment (CBT). Dobson and Dozois (2001) see the underlying assumption of the two as similar if not identical. If there is a distinction, they see it as in the area of outcome. Based on Kazdin (1978) and Mahoney (1974), CBM views overt behavior change as the primary outcome or result. However, CBT focuses on the change in cognition (e.g., beliefs) as the outcome and behavioral change will follow in due course (Ellis, 1962; Dryden & Ellis, 2001). Dobson and Dozois (2001) conclude that CBT is a broader term than CBM and that CBM is subsumed within CBT (p. 4).

Our review of the literature leads us to conclude that the combining element of cognitive and behavioral approaches is found in the principle of **self-reinforcement.** This concept simply states that cognitive and behavioral changes reinforce each other. When cognitive change leads to changes in action and behavior, there occurs a sense of well being which strengthens the change in thought structures that led to changes in action. In turn, the changes in thinking reinforced by the changes in behavior further strengthen those behavioral changes. It is not just the reinforcement of the behavior that strengthens the behavior; it is the reinforcement of the thought structures leading to the behavior that strengthens the behavior. This self-reinforcing feedback process is a key principle which becomes the basis for helping clients understand the process and maintenance of change and is the basis for the cognitive-behavioral approach to change in this work - *Driving With CARE.*

UNDERLYING PRINCIPLES OF COGNITIVE-BEHAVIORAL THERAPY

There are many forms and variations of CBT. Mahoney and Lyddon (1988) note that CBT is a generic term that refers to more than 20 approaches within this tradition. Yet, there are some basic or fundamental core principles shared across many of these variations in CBT (Antony & Roemer, 2003: Arnkoff & Glass, 1982; Beck, 1976, 1996; Beck, Freeman & Davis, 2004; J. Beck, 1995; Clark & Steer, 1996; Dobson & Block, 1988; Dobson & Dozois, 2001; Dryden & Ellis, 2001; Ellis, 1962; 1975; Freeman, et al., 1990; Kendall & Bemis, 1983; Kendall & Hollon, 1979; Mahoney & Arnkoff, 1978; Reinecke & Freeman, 2003; Schuyler, 2003; Wanberg & Milkman, 1998). Some of these principles are premised on behavior therapy, others on cognitive therapy. All are important in the understanding and effective implementation of CBT.

Cognitive structures and processes mediate learning and behavior

Cognitive structures, activities and processes affect and mediate learning and behavior. This mediation concept is at the core of CBT (Mahoney, 1974; Dobson & Dozois, 2001) and applies to affective and behavioral disturbances. Disturbance in behavior and emotion are a result of disturbances in mental activities - thinking, perceiving, feeling. Thus, behavioral outcomes are a direct result of these cognitive activities.

People respond to their mental interpretation of the environment

People respond to their mental interpretations of the environment - or external events - rather than the environment itself. CBT approaches examine the idiosyncratic meaning and interpretations the individual assigns to these external events or the

environment in order to understand the resulting emotional and behavioral responses to these events (Neenan & Dryden, 2001). Individuals are actively involved in the construction of their realities and the role of the therapist is to "see" the world through the eyes of the client (Neenan & Dryden, 2001). Beck (1976) calls this tapping into the client's internal communications or self-talk.

Underlying cognitive therapy, then, are constructivist and phenomenological approaches. More recently, these views have led to the emergence of constructivist cognitive therapies (Arnkoff & Glass, 1992) as found in the works of Guidano (1987), Guidano and Liotti (1983) and Mahoney (1990, 1993). The underpinnings of this aspect of CBT are found in constructivist philosophy as expressed in the works of Kuhn (1970), Hanson (1958), Toulmin (1972) but are also found in Cicourel's (1974) cognitive sociology, Schultz's (1967) phenomenological social theories, the personal construct theory of Kelly (1955), Husserl's phenomenological theories of knowledge (1960) and certainly the work of Beck (1976). Constructivism and phenomenology hold that individuals construct and create their own realities. Thus, the therapist cannot necessarily assume to know what is going on with the client only through logical observation. This model has increased CBT therapists' awareness of the importance of understanding how the client constructs his or her perceived reality and how that reality brings about disturbed thinking and actions.

This principle tends to move cognitive therapy away from the modernist worldview and embraces the postmodern worldview (Lyddon & Weill, 2002; Neimeyer & Bridges, 2003). The modernist worldview holds that "there is a belief in a singular, stable and knowable reality" (Lyddon & Weill, 2002). In contrast, the postmodernist view assumes that there is no "true" reality, and that realities are constructed by individuals and cultures across time (Neimeyer, 1993). People respond to their mental interpretation of the environment. In the strict view of the postmondernist-constructivist, there is no objective datum (Lyddon & Weill, 2002).

This does not mean that CBT theorists are "empirical nihilists" (Leahy, 1996). CBT approaches maintain that there are consistent patterns of thinking, feeling and behaving that can be measured and tested, both across people and within individuals. Leahy (1996) notes that "we see ourselves as structural empiricists. This implies that the structures of knowledge - the patient's schemas - may be tested in the real world" (p. 12). CBT theorists and practitioners use both standardized assessments as well as cognitive and affective processing and situational analysis in evaluating and understanding the clients substance use patterns, current life problems, personality traits, motivation for change and cognitive schemas (e.g., Freeman et al., 1990; Goldfried, 1995; Leahy, 1996).

Individuals can monitor and control their cognitive structures and activities

Individuals can know about, get in touch with, monitor and control their cognitive structures and activities. As Dobson and Dozois (2001) state, "…. clients are architects of their own misfortune, and that they therefore have control over their thoughts and actions" (p. 28).

Many CB theorists see self-monitoring and control as premised on the construct of self-efficacy. Since Bandura's introduction of this concept in social learning theory (Bandura, 1977b), this has become a prominent emphasis with many CB therapists and will be explored later in this Chapter. As noted below, this construct is not seen as salient by some CBT practitioners and theorists but is seen by many in the field as an important focus in the application of CB approaches in the treatment of substance abusing clients.

An important corollary to this proposition is that an *accurate assessment* of these cognitive structures and activities *is an essential step* to changing thinking in order to change behavior. Cognitive-behavioral theories often categorize these structures into short and long-term mental elements. One category of short-term elements is expectations. These are referred to as automatic thoughts. For example, we take a drink because we expect the drink to relax us. When it does, not only is the behavior of drinking reinforced, the expectancy (cognitive structure) is also reinforced. Attitudes, beliefs and values are considered to be long-term, more underlying cognitive elements. Both self-assessment and professional assessment are possible in this monitoring process. Part of this

assessment involves the identification of underlying functional and dysfunctional beliefs.

Individuals can alter or change their cognitive world which leads to changes in behavior

Individuals can alter or change their mental or cognitive world. We not only can change our thoughts, we can alter our underlying beliefs. This was an early proposition of CBT in the work of Ellis. This proposition implies that specific methods and techniques can be used to change thinking and beliefs. The methods fall under the rubric of cognitive restructuring. An elaborate cataloging of such methods is found in the work of McMullin (2000). Self-control is increased when the individual discovers that thinking can be changed, and this thinking can lead to positive outcomes. Most important, as a result of changes in cognition, changes in behavior follow.

Thoughts that lead to behavioral outcomes are strengthened

Changes in behavior are reinforced through the strengthening of thoughts that lead to those behaviors. Regardless of the outcomes of certain actions or behaviors, the thoughts and underlying beliefs that lead to those behaviors may be strengthened. This self-reinforcement process is an essential determinant of maintaining maladaptive behaviors or maintaining changes in behavior.

A traditional view of behavioral reinforcement holds that if a behavioral outcome is negative, the behavior should have less probability of repeating itself. However, common experience often belies this axiom. Why do people repeat behaviors that lead to negative outcomes, e.g., punishment, pain? One main reason is that the outcomes strengthen the thoughts and underlying beliefs that lead to those behaviors.

For example, an argument with a spouse may produce thoughts of "not being understood, not being treated fairly" *(appraisals)*. The *core belief* leading to these thoughts might be that "no one has really cared about me." This may lead to feelings of anger and going to the bar to have a few drinks with "those who do care about me." On the way home, the person is arrested for impaired driving and jailed overnight. This event leads to further thoughts that "it isn't fair," and "no one really cares" *(appraisals),* reinforcing the *underlying belief* that "no one has really ever cared." Unless efforts are made to change these automatic thoughts of "life isn't fair," and the underlying core beliefs related to these thoughts, then the person will continue to engage in behaviors that lead to negative outcomes and the thoughts leading to those outcomes continue to get strenghtened.

Outcomes can be improved by learning skills and behaviors that lead to positive outcomes.

Behaviors are strengthened or reinforced when they result in certain consequences or outcomes. This is the basis for the social-interpersonal skills component of cognitive-behavioral therapy and change. Self-control can be enhanced through learning and practicing skills that lead to better problem solving, more positive communication with others, resolving conflicts in a more positive manner. Thus, when these behaviors lead to positive outcomes, they are strengthened. Behaviors get reinforced not only when they result in positive outcomes but when they are efficacious in avoiding negative outcomes. Positive and negative reinforcement are the underlying principles of behavioral therapy.

Distortions in thinking and beliefs lead to disturbances in emotions and behavior

This is a commonly held view among most CB theorists and practitioners and is an important focus in cognitive therapy. Using an information-processing model, Beck (1976) holds that information-processing errors or distortions occur when individuals experience or encounter stressful events. During these stressful and threatening situations, our thinking can become rigid and distorted (Weishaar, 1996). Our information-processing skills and abilities become faulty resulting in errors or distortions in thinking (Neenan & Dryden, 2001). Identifying and changing thinking errors or distortions have become salient components of cognitive therapy (e.g., Beck, 1976; Burns, 1980; DeRubeis, Tang & Beck, 2001; Ellis, 1984; Freeman, et al., 1990; Wanberg & Milkman, 1998). These sources provide long lists of thinking errors that include catastrophizing, all or nothing thinking, magnifying, blaming, procrastinating, jumping to conclusions, etc.

Identification of the cognitive structures underlying maladaptive feelings and behaviors is ongoing

Self-assessment is the process of identifying thoughts that lead to certain behaviors and outcomes and attitudes and beliefs that underlie those thoughts. This is an integral component of learning and change and does not stop at intake. It is ongoing and continuous. Assessment is mainly for the benefit of the client. The provider is continually providing feedback to the client with respect to findings and interpretation of this ongoing assessment.

CBT is problem and solution (goal) oriented

In the CBT approach, clients are asked to identify specific problems that bring them into treatment. Intervention and treatment are then focused on solving those problems. The basis of these problems and the solutions sought are built around identifying the cognitive structures that generate the problems and then to change those structures so as to provide favorable and adaptive outcomes and solutions. Although all therapeutic approaches attempt to identify the referring and focal problem(s) of the client, CBT makes a specific effort to see the cause and solutions to these problems at the cognitive as well as behavioral levels.

CBT is a structured and usually time-limited therapy

Sessions are most always structured, with this structure determined by the focal problems and focal solutions. During sessions, clients review homework, do work sheets, exercises, role playing and practice the various skills that are used in managing cognitive and behavioral problems. However, time is also provided for unstructured sharing and self-disclosing to allow for the expression of thoughts and emotions or to share experiences the client had between sessions. Yet, material emerging from these unstructured periods are used as "grist for the mill" in the CBT process.

Sessions are usually time-limited (J. Beck, 1995; Dobson & Dozois, 2001). This is a clear distinction from the more traditional unstructured therapies such as client-centered, psychoanalytic or psychodynamic approaches. Guidelines for the number of therapy sessions usually fall in the five to 15 session range. For clients who have more ingrained thinking and behavioral problems, e.g., character pathologies, substance abuse, it is recommended that treatment be protracted for as long as one year (see Wanberg & Milkman, 1998 for more complete discussion around length of treatment for substance abuse clients and offenders).

CB Providers go beyond the traditional role of counselor and therapist

Counselors and treatment providers fulfill the roles of evaluator, educator, teacher, consultant coach, as well as traditional therapist, in understanding disturbed and maladaptive thought processes and in developing, with the client, life-response changes. CBT approaches "...are by nature explicitly or implicitly educative" (Dobson & Dozois, 2001, p. 28). For example, clients are taught the CBT change model and a rationale is usually provided for the specific CBT interventions that are used.

The provider and client work as partners in solving client problems

An important component of CBT approaches is that the counselors or treatment providers and the client work together in a partnership or team in evaluating, assessing and developing solutions to problems. Beck et al. (1979) call this collaborative empiricism which involves the process of "reality-testing clients' thoughts, assumptions and beliefs" (Neenan & Dryden, 2001, p. 11). These cognitions are viewed as hypotheses that clients develop about reality.

Therapy involves the process of the client collecting information to test these hypotheses. For example, a client's cognitive response (thoughts) to an interaction with mother is that "she is nosey." However, through cognitive restructuring, this thought is changed to "maybe she is just concerned." This hypothesis is tested through the application of effective communication skills (social skills building), and the client discovers that mother's responses are based on concern and caring. Thus, rather than experiencing anger the next time that mother offers advice, he acts on the underlying assumption that "mother cares and she may

have some good advice" and this anger is replaced with reciprocal feelings of love and warmth.

The development of therapeutic alliance

Through the implementation of the partnership model and the application of collaborative empiricism, a therapeutic alliance between the therapist and client is forged. Most CB (cognitive-behavioral) therapists construct that alliance through the application of the Rogerian (1951, 1959, 1980) principles of empathy, genuineness, respect, warmth and unconditional positive regard.

Early approaches to CBT saw therapeutic alliance and the therapeutic relationship as vehicles through which the CBT approach was applied. Now, most CBT theorists view the therapeutic relationship as a method for change in and of itself (Blackburn & Twaddle, 1996) and as an important and essential part of CBT (Beck et al., 1979, 2004; Arnkoff & Glass, 1992). Thus, building rapport and trust with the client, applying motivational methods and techniques in the therapeutic process and building an environment to maximize self-disclosure have become important factors in the evolution of CBT (Miller & Rollnick, 1991, 2002; Beck, et. al., 1993).

Between session application

One of the most important components of CBT is to practice the skills learned in therapy between sessions. Informal and formal homework is an ongoing ingredient of CBT. Many therapists use formal and structured work sheets as part of the homework. An important CBT homework construct is the thinking report and the rethinking report (see Wanberg & Milkman, 1998; 2005). The specific elements of the thinking report are discussed in Section III of this work.

There is a reciprocal interaction of thoughts, emotions and behaviors

An individual's thoughts, emotions and behaviors interact and affect each other. Neenan and Dryden (2001) note that the CBT model is not based just on the linear process whereby thinking leads to emotions and actions. Emotions and moods can lead to certain thoughts. Actions can influence how one thinks or feels. Emotions can lead to certain actions. Yet, the change model as utilized in most CBT approaches and the one used in this work is premised on the idea that we start with identifying the thinking, and the underlying beliefs, that lead to certain emotional and behavioral outcomes. In order to prevent dysfunctional emotional and behavior outcomes, we then make efforts to change the thinking and the underlying beliefs so as to increase the probability of more favorable and functional emotional and behavioral outcomes.

Greenberger and Padesky (1995) suggest that the environment and the individual's physiological responses are equally important components in this reciprocal or interactive process. External (or internal) events are important in bringing on certain thoughts based on the individual's beliefs and attitudes (Wanberg & Milkman, 1998). As well, initial physiological responses (e.g., rapid heart beat, urges or cravings) to these events or to thoughts, emotions and behaviors are also important focuses in the change processes. Greenberger and Padesky conclude that change in any one of the five components - the environment, thoughts, attitudes/beliefs, emotions and behavior - can have impact on the other four.

CBT initially places emphasis on the here and now

CBT focuses on thoughts and underlying beliefs that emerge out of here and now events in the client's life. It is problem and solution focused and self-improvement and change are based on the client's existential experiences. It is recognized that the thought habits and underlying beliefs have their roots in past experiences. Yet, the restructuring of these thoughts, the changing of these beliefs and the efforts to help clients build effective skills in managing interpersonal relationships are based on current life experiences. Past experiences and memories are dealt with as they are relevant in understanding and changing current dysfunctional thoughts, emotions and actions.

Enhancing client therapeutic independence

Most CB therapists and theorists agree that the ultimate goal of therapy is to build self-direction and therapeutic independence in the client. In essence, this means that the client becomes a self-therapist (Neenan & Dryden, 2001). "Cognitive therapy...aims to teach the patient to be her own therapist.." (Judy Beck, 1995, p. 7). As clients increase self control through inculcating the skills of cognitive restructuring and effective interpersonal management, the client becomes more and more his or her own therapist. Clients not only solve problems in therapy, they learn the process of problem solving and establishing self control. The ultimate goal of the CBT therapist is based on the "teaching to fish" metaphor: give a person a fish, and you can feed him for a day; teach the person to fish and you will feed him for a lifetime."

KEY FOCUSES OF CBT

CBT USES TWO basic approaches in bringing about change: restructuring of cognitive events so as to bring about adaptive and positive outcomes; social and interpersonal skills training to enhance adaptive interactions and positive outcomes. These two approaches are built on the two pathways of reinforcement: strengthening of the thoughts that lead to that behavior; strengthening behavior due to the consequence (reinforcement) or outcome of that behavior. The former has it roots in cognitive therapy; the latter has it roots in behavioral therapy. Together, they form the essential platform of cognitive-behavioral therapy.

The cognitive focus of CBT: Cognitive elements and structures

Very early cognitive therapy (CT) theorists and practitioners focused on some key cognitive elements or structures and processes (e.g., Beck, 1976; Beck et al., 1979; Burns, 1989; Ellis & Harper, 1975). These are:

▶ Automatic thoughts and automatic thinking;

▶ Underlying assumptions; and

▶ Underlying core beliefs.

These basic cognitive events are the key focuses of cognitive therapy (Neenan & Dryden, 2001). These early theorists also identified the important **automatic thoughts** that the cognitive therapist should focus on - expectations and appraisals. These reinforced thoughts are traditionally called automatic thoughts (e.g., Beck, 1976, 1996; J. Beck, 1995; Freeman et al., 1990) because they seem to occur "without thought," or "automatically" as a response to external events. Wanberg and Milkman (1998; 2005) call these **thought habits** in order to help clients understand that thinking habits, which become the focus of change, are similar to our behavioral habits which also become the focus of change.

Underlying assumptions and core beliefs are often seen as schemas that structure our thinking. In fact Beck (1996) sees the "basic systems of personality - cognitive (or information processing), affective, behavioral, and motivational - as composed of structures 'labeled schemas' " (p. 4). Schema-focused therapy (McGinn & Young, 1996; Young, 1994) has been part of the "new paradigms for treating patients with character pathology" (p. 182). It is "designed to extend Beck's original model of cognitive therapy and to specifically address the needs of patients with long-standing character disorders" (p. 182). It integrates cognitive, behavioral, experimental and interpersonal techniques, using a "schema" as the unifying element.

Seligman, Walker and Rosenhan (2001) categorize the mental or cognitive processes that are the main focus of cognitive therapy into **short-term** and **long-term processes.** They identify the short-term cognitive processes which become the focus of treatment as expectations, appraisals and attributions. The long term processes are beliefs. Although Seligman et al., refer to these as processes, they are also referred to in the literature as schemas, constructs, concepts, cognitive events and structures.

Expectations, appraisals and attributions are mental events (automatic thoughts) that often come quickly and without deliberate thought and are the short-term processes in the Seligman et al. scheme. **Expectancies** are mental expectations that certain behaviors will bring certain outcomes, e.g., pleasure. Bandura (1977a, 1981) distinguishes between outcome expectations and efficacy expectations. **Outcome expectancies** represent the individual's judgement about whether the performance of a particular behavior will produce a particular outcome. Or, it is knowledge of what

to do and what will be obtained. If that behavior does fulfill the expectation, then the behavior is reinforced.

Efficacy expectancy refers to the individual's assessment of his or her ability to successfully execute a particular behavior. Bandura sees this as a person's belief that he or she can carry out a certain course of action to get a certain outcome. If a person believes that he or she can perform a particular behavior, than most likely that individual will engage in that behavior. If the behavior is performed successfully, this reinforces the efficacy expectation.

An important part of expectancy theory is self-efficacy. Bandura (1977b) calls these "efficacy expectations." This concept is of particular importance in the treatment of the substance abuser. Helping the client develop the skill of coping with anxiety in ways other than AOD use will build the efficacy expectation that conditions which produce stress can in fact be handled in ways other than drinking. Self-efficacy will be further discussed below.

Appraisals represent cognitive events that lead to action and feelings (Clark, 2004; Rosenhan & Seligman, 1995; Seligman et al., 2001). This is the cognitive process that continually evaluates the value and meaning of what we are experiencing and our responses to those experiences. Often, these cognitive appraisals become distorted and result in thinking errors. Identifying and changing thinking errors or distortions have become salient components of cognitive therapy. For example, an appraisal of the depressed person who experiences rejection might be "I'm no good." This would also be classified as a thinking error or an error in logic. Beck (1996) holds that such appraisals, or automatic thoughts, usually precede and cause emotions. The appraisal that "he's taking advantage of me" usually leads to the emotion of anger.

Attributions are the individual's explanation of why things happen or the explanation of outcomes of certain behaviors. An important part of attribution theory is where the individual sees the source of his or her life problems or successes or one's locus of control (Rotter, 1966). This locus of control might be internalized ("I'm responsible for the accident") or externalized ("If they would have locked their car doors, I wouldn't have ripped off their stereo"). Attributions can be global or specific (Abramson, Seligman, & Teasdale, 1978). "I got drunk because life is just not fair" is a global attribution whereas a specific attribution would be, "I got drunk because my wife yelled at me."

The long-term cognitive processes (Seligman et al., 2001) are less available to our consciousness. These mental processes are more durable and stable and they help determine the short-term mental processes that are in our conscious state. "One of these long-term cognitive processes is belief" (Seligman, et al., p. 114).

Beliefs are ideas that we use to judge or evaluate external situations or events. A belief is embodied with the event or person. It bonds us to the outside event. Changing underlying core beliefs is a primary focus of cognitive therapy. For example, it is one of the primary target areas in Rational Emotive Therapy (Ellis, 1962, 1984). Irrational beliefs underlie and form our short-term cognitive events - expectations, attributions and appraisals (Seligman et al., 2001).

J. Beck's (1995) cognitive model introduces an intermediary layer of cognitive constructs which she calls intermediate beliefs distinguished from core beliefs. She labels the intermediate beliefs as rules, attitudes and assumptions. The core and intermediate beliefs are constructs that people use to make sense of their environment and organize their experience in a coherent way in order to function adaptively (J. Beck, 1995, p 16; Rosen, 1988).

Freeman and his colleagues (1990) suggest that cognitive therapy will focus on four major areas which are seen as basic to bringing about change in maladaptive and dysfunctional cognition and behavior. These are:

▶ automatic thoughts;
▶ underlying assumptions and beliefs;
▶ cognitive distortions; and
▶ the influence of emotions and mood on cognition.

Most cognitive approaches see the process of treatment as starting with helping the client to identify automatic thoughts and cognitive distortions; and then addressing the long-term underlying assump-

tions, intermediate and core beliefs that are associated with the automatic thoughts and which lead to dysfunctional emotional and behavioral responses and outcomes (e.g., J Beck, 1995; Dobson, Dozois, 2001; Freeman, et al., 1990; Leahy, 1997).

Cognitive restructuring (CR) is the main method and technique used to change the above described short-term and long-term cognitive processes and structures that become maladaptive. Self-talk is seen as a generic CR method and includes thought stopping, planting positive thoughts, countering, shifting the view, exaggerating the thought, etc. (see McMullin, 2000, for a resource in CR techniques). Other examples of cognitive restructuring approaches are: relaxation training (Jacobson, 1938), stress inoculation training (Meichenbaum, 1985, 1993b), self-instructional training (Meichenbaum, 1975), problem solving skills (D'Zurilla & Goldfried, 1971; D'Zurilla & Nezu, 2001) and mood-management training (Beck, 1976; Monti et al., 1995), critical reasoning (Ross et al., 1986) and managing and changing negative thoughts (Beck, 1976; Wanberg & Milkman, 1998; 2005).

Reinecke and Freeman (2003) provide some very specific CR Techniques: Questioning the evidence, rational responding, decatastrophisizing, exaggeration or paradox, scaling emotions and examining options (pp. 245-248).

There are also a number of specific cognitive restructuring focuses that are relevant in treating substance abusing clients. These include managing cravings and urges, critical reasoning and managing high risk thinking in preventing relapse (Wanberg & Milkman, 1998, 2005).

The behavioral focus of CBT: Interpersonal and social skills training

Coping and social skills training (CSST) evolved over the last two decades of the 20th century to become an essential component of cognitive-behavioral therapy (Monti, et al., 1995). It emerged out of social learning theory (Bandura, 1977a) and has a solid empirical support from outcome research (Monti et al., 1989, 1995). Its premise is that clients with maladaptive thinking and behavioral patterns do not have adequate skills for facing daily living issues and problems.

There are a number of specific areas in which interpersonal and social skills building focus (see Wanberg & Milkman, 1998 for a comprehensive summary of these approaches). These include communication skills, assertiveness training, interpersonal problem solving skills, skills in building and maintaining intimate relationships, conflict resolution and managing aggression and violence and activity structuring.

SELF-EFFICACY: A FOCAL COGNITIVE CONSTRUCT IN SUBSTANCE ABUSE TREATMENT

The importance of self-efficacy (SE) in CBT is stressed by most authorities in the field. Bandura (1977b) sees SE as the unifying construct of the social-cognitive framework of therapy and SE has a primary role in his conceptual scheme. Self-efficacy is a cognitive construct that relates to and strengthens self-control (Bandura, 1978).

Wilson and O'Leary, in their Principles of Behavioral Therapy (1980) identified SE as a key concept in the overall theory of behavioral change and "efficacy expectations play a major part in the initiation, generalization, and maintenance of coping behavior" (p. 269). Goldfried (1995) sees the facilitation of SE and the client's perceived sense of self-mastery and competence as a key focus in treatment and devotes an entire chapter to this focus. Thus, the importance of this cognitive construct in CBT and self-management therapies is well established (e.g., above references; Freeman, et al., 1990; Maisto, Carey & Bradizza, 1999; Rokke & Rehm, 2001, etc.). Yet, it is of note that several recent major works in cognitive therapy did not address self-efficacy or efficacy expectations as a salient focus in cognitive therapy (e.g., J. Beck, 1995; Leahy, 1996, 1997; Lyddon & Jones, 2001; Safran, 1998). Authors who focused on social learning theory and both cognitive and behavioral change were more apt to see SE as a critical construct in CBT.

Within the area of the intervention and treatment of substance use problems, SE is seen as a major focal construct. Marlatt sees four cognitive constructs as most salient in the intervention and treatment of individuals who have alcohol or other drug use problems. These are: **self-efficacy, outcome expectancies, attributions and decisions**

(Marlatt, 1985b). Self-efficacy is a critical link in his relapse prevention model. Self-efficacy plays a major role in determining and strengthening behaviors in many different domains, e.g., success, academic achievement, managing anxiety and stress. It is considered to be one of the most important determinants of self-control over substance abuse problems and preventing relapse (Marlatt, Baer & Quigley, 1995).

Self-efficacy is defined as "a perception or judgement of one's capability to execute a particular course of action required to deal effectively with an impending situation" (Abrams & Niaura, 1987, p. 134). It is "perceived control." It refers to the belief that one is able to execute successfully the behavior required to produce a particular outcome and "refers to the strength of our convictions about our personal effectiveness" (Sarason & Sarason, 1995, p. 76). Efficacy expectations have a major effect on whether a person initiates a coping behavior and how much effort will be put towards that implementing that behavior (Bandura, 1982). SE is reinforced if the person copes successfully over time (Dimeff & Marlatt, 1995).

Bandura sees SE as perceived performance competency in specific situations and differs from the constructs of self-esteem and self-concept, the latter of which refers more to global constructs of self-image (Bandura 1977b, 1981, 1982). Marlatt also concludes (1985c) that SE is not a global, cross-situational construct like self-esteem or locus of control. It refers to expectations or judgments people make about their capacity to cope with situation- specific events. Marlatt sees it as a state measure and not a trait measure such as self-esteem (Marlatt, 1985c).

Bandura argues that perceived self-efficacy is a major determinant of whether a person initiates a certain action or behavior and whether that person is motivated to extend that behavior. He holds that any effective psychosocial intervention is successful because it alters a person's expectation of self-efficacy (Bandura, 1977b).

Connors, Donovan & Diclemente (2001) indicate that helping clients increase their sense of self-efficacy is of particular importance during the action stage of change. Increasing the client's perceived

SE involves focusing on the clients' successes, strengthening positive decisions and helping clients make intrinsic attributions as to their source of change.

There is strong empirical evidence to support the hypothesis that individuals with low self-efficacy in a particular situation are more likely to engage in frequent self-appraisals of inadequacy and people with strong sense of efficacy are able to exert their skills to the demands of the situation without negative or doubtful self-appraisal (Marlatt, 1985a, p. 130). Bandura's research has demonstrated that there is a strong association between an individual's level of perceived situational self-efficacy and the level of performance accomplishments (Bandura, 1982).

A number of studies in nonclinical samples indicated that alcohol-specific SE had significant relationships to alcohol use outcomes (see Maisto, et al., 1999 for an excellent summary of studies relating SE to alcohol use outcomes). Moore, et al. (1996) found that pregnant women with high abstinence self-efficacy drank less during pregnancy than those with low abstinence self-efficacy. Young et al. (1991) found that low social pressure, opportunistic drinking and emotional relief SE predicted concurrent alcohol consumption in both college and community samples. Hays and Ellickson (1990) found that non-using adolescents with lower levels of resistance SE predicted future alcohol use. For using adolescents, lower levels of resistance SE at time one not only predicted future use, but also SE influences adolescents' expectations of future use, thus predicting future alcohol use.

Although SE has been viewed as a situational-specific expectancy structure (Bandura, 1977b; Marlatt, 1985c), Hays and Ellickson (1990) provide evidence that SE may have a "generic" quality. They found that SE generalized across drugs, e.g., marijuana, tobacco and alcohol.

In clinical samples, longer term abstainers reported higher levels of abstinence SE than either the active abusers or recently detoxed clients (Strom & Barone, 1993; Miller, et al., 1989). Although SE measured at pretreatment did not generally relate to posttreatment outcomes (Langenbucher et al., 1996), Solomon and Annis (1990) found that lower

pre-treatment SE scores predicted higher levels of average daily consumption at treatment follow-up for those clients who were drinking at follow-up.

Completing treatment for alcohol use problems enhanced SE and the mean levels of SE for controlling heavy drinking increased from pretreatment to posttreatment to follow-up (Sitharthan & Kavanagh, 1990). Sitharthan and Kavanagh also found that post-treatment SE showed to be a significant predictor of treatment outcome, even at long-term follow-up. As well, high levels of post-treatment SE predicted more percent days abstinent and fewer percent days of heavy drinking (McKay, Maisto & O'Farrell, 1993). In general, posttreatment SE measures seem to be a better predictor of outcome, mainly since treatment has a significant effect on developing SE.

In some of the research cited above, SE was defined as situational-specific, such as resistance-to-use SE, abstinence SE, emotional-relief SE. However, other studies only referred to the measurement as SE, indicating a more global and generic construct. The literature seems to treat SE from both perspectives.

Thus the question: Is self-efficacy a short-term expectancy construct or is it a long-term, underlying belief structure? As noted, Bandura (1977b) and Marlatt (1985c) identify it as an expectancy, which puts it into the category of short-term cognitive process. Yet, there must be an underlying, longer-term belief structure or process that leads to efficacy expectation.

Rokke & Rehm (2001) refer to SE as a construct that has certain characteristics. They see it as central to adequate functioning and to a sense of self-competency. Although they do not see it as a "single dimensional, overarching trait" (p. 177), they do see it as representing a system of beliefs. Each of these beliefs is specific to a particular area of functioning. They indicate that these beliefs can refer to a set of cognitive skills. These skills are founded on the basis of experience and are situational and behavior specific.

Gleaning from the above review of the literature, it appears that SE can be seen as both a belief about self and a short-term expectancy thought structure that leads to certain behaviors and outcomes (as in Seligman, Walker & Rosenhan, 2001 and Bandura, 1977b). As will be described in Chapter 11, Section II of this work, self-efficacy is defined as a belief structure about the self and efficacy expectation as a thought habit or short-term structure that leads to specific emotional and behavioral outcomes. These outcomes will strengthen or weaken the efficacy expectancy thought habits and strengthen or weaken the underlying belief construct of self-efficacy.

IMPLICATIONS FOR IMPAIRED DRIVING EDUCATION AND TREATMENT

Psychosocial oriented therapies are now into their second 100 years. It was not until well into their 50th year that the efficacy of psychosocial therapies was challenged. Hans Eysenck published a review of 24 psychotherapy outcome studies and concluded that there was no evidence to support the efficacy of psychotherapy (Eysenck, 1952). Although his data and methods have been called to question over the years, his challenge has been taken seriously.

Since that challenge, research with respect to the effectiveness and outcome of psychotherapy and psychosocial oriented therapies has indicated that there is a general positive treatment effect. Summaries of meta-analyses of outcome studies conclude "Psychotherapy is effective at helping people achieve their goals and overcome their psychopathologies at a rate that is faster and more substantial than change that results from the client's natural healing process and supportive elements in the environment" (Lambert & Bergin, 1992). For example, the meta-analysis of 475 studies by Smith, Glass and Miller (1980) provided evidence for the efficacy of psychotherapy and concluded that those who had received psychotherapy were better off than 80 percent of those who did not.

Several findings are evident in the growing body of research literature regarding the outcome of psychosocial oriented therapies. One rather robust finding is that no one clinical approach seems to be superior over another (Lambert & Bergin, 1992) and that different therapeutic approaches,

e.g., behavioral, psychodynamic, client-centered, "appear to secure comparable outcomes" (Garfield, 1992, p. 349). Differences in outcome between various forms of treatment are simply not as pronounced as might be expected (Lambert & Bergin, 1992) and that "other purportedly unique features of a system may be relatively inconsequential" (Strupp & Howard, 1992, p. 313). These findings are supported by the American Psychological Association's special issue on outcome research (VandenBos, 1986) and by the work of Nathan and associates (Nathan & Gorman, 1998; Nathan, Gorman & Salkind, 1999).

This general finding of no-difference in outcome across diverse therapies leads us to the following possible conclusions (Lambert & Bergin, 1992): 1) that different therapies can achieve similar goals through different processes; 2) different outcomes do occur but these are not detected by current research strategies; or 3) different therapies embody common factors that are curative but not emphasized by the theory of change central to a particular school.

The research literature today supports the third conclusion that the common features of psychosocial therapies may be the major contributor to the effectiveness of treatment (Frank, 1992, p. 393). This conclusion is supported by a long history of research on the efficacy and effectiveness of psychological oriented therapies. The early work of Rogers and Dymond (1954) on the efficacy of client-centered therapy supports this conclusion. The research of Truax and Carkhuff (1967) on the effectiveness of the paraprofessional in effecting change in clients certainly supports the common factors theory. The Vanderbilt study (Strupp & Hadley, 1979) which found comparable outcomes among analytically-oriented therapists, experientially-oriented therapists and college professors is but another example of support for the common factors theory. Regardless of the theoretical orientation or even the type of disorder being treated, the common features or factors findings in psychosocial therapies is robust (Arkowitz, 1992; Elkin, 1986; Garfield, 1992; Glass & Arnkoff, 1988).

But what are these common features? Two of these common features that have been identified with psychotherapy efficacy are:

- counselor personal characteristics; and

- the counselor/therapist-client relationship.

These two features will be further explored in Chapter 12 of this work. Most relevant to the topic of this chapter, other common factors have been identified across the various therapies (Lambert & Bergin, 1992). These elements are grounded in cognitive-behavioral approaches, and include the teaching and training of intrapersonal and interpersonal skills in treatment, the development of self-efficacy through training in self-help skills and overall skill development. Cognitive and cognitive-behavioral therapy are often seen as a basis for psychotherapy integration (Alford & Norcross, 1991; Arkowitz, 1992; Beck, 1991; Goldfried, 1995).

Another trend that has emerged out of the efforts to evaluate the efficacy of psychosocial therapies in the last part of the 20th century has been the development of empirically designed research to discern the efficacy of specific therapeutic interventions for specific kinds of psychosocial disorders (Lyddon & Jones, 2001). Particularly relevant to this work, *Driving With Care,* is the development of a cadre of literature that supports cognitive behavioral treatment for those with a history of substance use problems and a history of criminal conduct and character pathology.

Support for the use of CBT with individuals with a substance abuse history is robust (e.g., see Beck, et. al., 1993; Nathan, Gorman & Salkind, 1999; Wanberg & Milkman, 2005). "One of the most promising types of psychological therapies available for alcohol substance disorder is cognitive-behavioral therapy" which includes enhancing the individual's cognitive and interpersonal skills in coping with everyday life circumstances (Nathan et al., 1999, p. 80).

There is also robust support for the use of CBT approaches to effect change with individuals with personality disorders (Beck et al., 2004; Cottraux & Blackburn, 2001), character pathology (McGinn & Young, 1996; Young, 1994)) and a history of criminal conduct (Andrews and Bonta, 2003; Wanberg & Milkman, 2005). The combination of these two bodies of literature provide the basis for using cognitive-behavioral approaches in the education

and intervention of individuals with a history of impaired driving.

SUMMARY

SINCE THE MID-POINT of the 20th century, behavioral and cognitive approaches to treatment have merged into a robust cadre of approaches that we call cognitive-behavioral therapy. These approaches have established a major role in psychosocial therapies and led the way for the test of *empirically supported treatments* (Gurman and Messer, 2003). The core concepts of CBT have been summarized in this chapter. Most important of these concepts is that cognitive structures and processes mediate learning and change and that behaviors are strengthened when they lead to positive outcomes or when they reduce or eliminate negative or unpleasant experiences (negative reinforcement). CB approaches are directed at helping clients learn skills that change the short-term and surface cognitive structures, or automatic thoughts, and the longer-term and deeper structures, such as attitudes and beliefs that support the automatic thought structures and processes. CB approaches also help clients learn behavioral skills that lead to positive adjustment and then to reinforce those skills so that they become part of the behavioral patterns of the client's daily living.

CBT, then, has taken two primary approaches to enhancing change: cognitive restructuring; and social or interpersonal skills training. The former is the cognitive component of CBT and the latter is the behavioral component. Both of these approaches are directed at helping individuals overcome psychological stress, improve personal adjustment, and establish a healthier and more meaningful life. Both are directed at improving the individual's relationship with self and with others.

However, this Chapter's review reveals that if the CB model is to be effective and appropriately used with impaired driving offenders and with individuals with antisocial attitudes and patterns, an enhancement of the CB model is needed. More poignantly, a paradigm shift for the application of CB theory and methods is necessary.

As noted in the preface of this work, O'Hara (1997) sees psychotherapy as shaped by the world view of modernity, which views man as egocentric, puts the individual supraordinate to any social role or obligation, focuses on individualism, individual freedom and individual expression, idealizes and codifies the individual, and projects the individual outward. She states that Western psychology and particularly 20th century psychotherapy has not only reinforced this view, but its theory and methods **are** egocentric.

As noted in Chapter 7, in order to provide an effective basis for the treatment of the impaired driving offender, traditional egocentric psychotherapy theory and methods must incorporate sociocentric approaches. A sociocentric therapy incorporates a more holistic framework and moves towards a "connected consciousness" (O'Hara, 1997). It helps offenders, and more specifically, DWIOs, develop sociocentric empathy as "contextual awareness," and as "relational" (O'Hara, 1997), giving them a way to know, understand, and participate with the community and society in a prosocial and morally responsible manner.

Most if not all impaired driving offenders have antisocial features, certainly in varying degrees. **DWI conduct** does not conform to social norms with respect to obeying the law, violates the rights of others, is a reckless disregard for the safety of others, positions people to deny personal responsibility and displays a lack of empathy for others. All of these are key descriptions of antisocial behavior. To be effective, DWI education and treatment must address the antisocial attitudes and behaviors of the impaired driving offender.

The egocentric orientation of 20th century psychotherapies has placed significant barriers in the treatment of the antisocial personality pattern and disorder. Sperry (1999), in his book *Cognitive Behavior Therapy of DSM-IV Personality Disorders,* includes antisocial personality disorders in the group of "not considered as treatable and less commonly seen in outpatient settings" (p. xvii). Thus, he did not include them in his manual for CB treatment. They are classified as in the *low-amenability of treatability* (p. 11). This response is the result of the failure of 20th century psychotherapy to incorporate strong and meaningful sociocentric theory and methods. In addition, it ignores the fact that a large percent of individuals in mental health and substance treatment settings have significant if not serious antisocial features. A substantial percent of these populations are involved in adolescent and adult judicial systems.

As noted in the *Preface* of this work, Beck et al. (2004) include a chapter on the treatment of the antisocial personality disorder (ASPD) in their book, *Cognitive Therapy of the Personality Disorders.* They contend that cognitive therapy of the ASPD can "be conceptualized as improving moral and social behavior through enhancement of cognitive functioning" (p. 168) and that "...moral functioning is regarded as a dimension within the broader context of epistemology, or ways of thinking and knowing" (p. 169).

Therefore, as with our previous work, *Criminal Conduct and Substance Abuse Treatment* (Wanberg & Milkman, 1998), we include in this work a third focus of CB treatment: helping clients restructure their relationship with the community and society. It includes cognitive and behavioral skills and approaches that will help DWIO clients become morally and socially responsible to the community and society in which they live.

CHAPTER TEN: ISSUES OF CULTURE AND DIVERSITY RELATED TO IMPAIRED DRIVING AND ITS INTERVENTION: ENHANCING PROVIDER CULTURAL COMPETENCE

INTRODUCTION

THE TERM *CULTURE* refers to common characteristics, styles of expression and identifiable influences that exist among a subgroup of the population — including beliefs, values, behaviors, communication patterns, language, and religion. Though culture is generally associated with ethnicity and race, many other subgroups of the population may be described as having a certain cultural identity (Harper, 2003). In this list, we can include age groupings, gender identification, socioeconomic standing, and even the culture of the tavern or bar (Milkman & Sunderwirth, 1998). For example among certain adolescent subgroups regarding AOD-related behavior — drinking, driving, as well as drinking-and-driving may all serve as rites of passage for individuals participating within the norms of these groups.

In this chapter culture refers to any identifiable group in the community or society that directly or indirectly impacts on or influences conditions or circumstances related to impaired driving behavior and its intervention. Thus, in addition to focusing on the referenced groups of African American, Hispanic, Anglo-White American, Native American and Asian, traditionally seen as cultures, this chapter focuses on a broad range of cultural identities that impact on impaired driving conduct.

Since the early eighties, cultural and diversity awareness, in general, has grown from a deficit-based perspective into a strength-based perspective. This strength-based perspective (Banks, 1991) seeks to build upon the values and behaviors inherent in each culture to create skills and beliefs that maximize positive outcomes regarding DWI recidivism. The use of this strength-based intervention requires that providers move through a "transformational process of cultural competence" (Guajardo-Lucero, 2000), which involves movement from cultural awareness through cultural sensitivity to cultural valuing.

Diversity in this chapter refers to the real and perceived differences that occur among various cultural subgroupings in our society. For example, there is a distinct group of people who do not and would not drink; and there is a group where alcohol use is an integral part of its members' life-style. Within drinking cultures, we find distinct differences such as the social drinking environment and the bar or pub drinking environment.

Of particular importance to DWI education and treatment is building self-efficacy. Dimeff & Marlatt (1995) ask, "How do the internalized effects of race, class, and/or gender prejudice and discrimination interact with efforts to establish and maintain self efficacy?" (p.178). While the primary intervention goal of DWI treatment is to heighten clients' sense of competence for maintaining a responsible life free of AOD related problems and impaired driving, societal portrayal of certain groups (ethnic minorities, teenagers, women, gays, working class) as being unacceptable, "low achievers," or impaired often work against this very goal (Wallace, 1991).

DWI intervention providers are challenged to help DWI offenders to counter these portrayals, particularly when they are internalized and subsequently contribute to negative self-views and a sense of failure. Often, clients are predisposed to expect failure and low achievement, which may imply tacit acceptance of relapse and recidivism. Racism, injustice or financial need, as well as anger, frustration or depression around these portrayals may serve as triggers for recidivism and relapse.

The main purpose of this chapter is to improve *Driving With CARE* education and treatment outcomes by first, increasing the awareness of diversity of DWI offenders; second, enhancing cultural competence of providers; and third, identify special intervention needs of certain groups. Improved cultural competence among counselors should result in more relevant experiences for clients, engendering greater cooperation, reducing dropout rates and thereby enhancing intervention outcomes.

This chapter begins with a discussion of macro cultures that impact on impaired driving. We then look at the relationship between different groups with cultural identities and impaired drivers. We then provide a philosophical framework for approaching issues of diversity and enhancing provider cultural competence among diverse groups.

Differences and similarities in cultural beliefs and values are explored, with specific reference to their impact within the therapeutic environment. The question of racial or cultural profiling is examined, in terms of the disproportionate prosecution in DWI offenses. Cultural strengths inherent in all cultures are emphasized as we examine critical components of understanding diversity and achieving cultural competence. Finally, we explore some specific issues that pertain to major societal groupings of ethnicity, gender, social class, broad brush cultures and the culture of the pub or bar.

BROAD CULTURAL IDENTITIES THAT IMPACT ON DWI CONDUCT/ INTERVENTION

There are two broad culture identities in Western society that have major impact on the prevalence, understandings and intervention of DWI conduct. These are: the culture of drinking; and the culture of driving. Although having their diverse expressions, they operate in a universal way across all cultural groups in society. We will briefly address the various nuances of these two cultures that often meet in a head-on collision in our society.

The Culture of Drinking Alcoholic Beverages

Drinking has been part of the American society since the 1700s when the per capita consumption of alcoholic beverages was much greater than current levels (Ray & Ksir, 2002). There are two distinct cultures in American society relative to drinking: those who use alcohol; and those who do not. About one-third of Americans abstain from use of alcohol (Ray & Ksir, 2002) and about 66 percent of adults 18 years or older are lifetime drinkers. The 66 percent of drinking Americans consume at least 12 alcoholic drinks during any one year of their lives (Grant et al., 1994). Per capita annual consumption is about 25 gallons of beer, about two gallons of wine and about 1.5 gallons of distilled spirits (Ray & Ksir, 2002). The two-thirds that do drink, consume, on the average, about three drinks per day.

Among those who do drink, we also find two rather distinct groups: those who drink infrequently or ceremonially; and those whose drinking is a part of their life-style. A large percent of Americans who

do drink take one to two drinks per day. What is most important is that half of the alcohol consumed is done by about 10 percent of the drinkers.

Finally, within the group for whom drinking is part of their life style, we can identify a group of what we would call heavy drinkers. If we use the criteria of two drinks per day as the threshold for heavy drinking (Williams & Debakey, 1992), almost one fourth (23.4 percent) of U.S. adults would exceed that threshold and many of these would be classified as heavy drinkers (Grant & Dawson, 1999). Grant & Dawson (1999) conclude that about one third of all lifetime drinkers could be classified as heavy drinkers at some point in their drinking histories.

The definition of the culture of drinking goes beyond the concept of consumption. Drinking has been the basis of various movements and impacts on different components of our society. These include the Temperance Movement, the era of prohibition, extensive efforts and costs related to government regulation and taxation. The advertisement of alcoholic beverages impacts all levels of American culture including physical strength, intimacy, romance, sex, sports, camaraderie, good health, having fun, relaxing, "time-out," college life, etc.

The culture of drinking has its own common characteristics, values, styles of expression and identifiable influence. It exerts a strong message that to be accepted in society or to be part of the American culture, one must join that culture - one must drink. It is identified as social, convivial and gregarious.

The culture of drinking is also identified as personal. It is defined by its location - pub, bar, parties, social gatherings, home. It is perceived to be part of most social activities and gatherings. It is identified as an integral part of culinary activities and the culture of eating. It is portrayed as the basic element of camaraderie.

The power and influence of the culture of drinking is an important basis of the problems that emerge from alcohol use itself, particularly DWI conduct. It is not so much the consumption of alcohol but the power and influence of the culture of drinking that determines DWI conduct. Any effective impaired driving intervention program must address the power and influence of this culture.

The Culture of Driving

The possession of a motor vehicle and driving represent an entrenched culture in American society and, synonymous with freedom. It is hard to sort out the culture of driving from American culture. It probably depicts American culture better than any one single fact about American (and most Western) society.

There are an average of 1.8 vehicles per each U.S. household. People in the average U.S. household drive an average of 21,100 miles per year (Household Vehicles Energy Consumption, 1994). Since 85 million households have vehicles, this amounts to almost 1.8 trillion miles a year.

Households whose primary drivers are in the age range of 18 through 29 drive more than any other age range. This helps explain why this age range accounts for almost 38 percent of DWI offenders in Colorado (Wanberg & Timken, 2005a). Households with teenagers drive more; and households with higher incomes drive more. For example, households with incomes of $50,000 or higher coupled with the presence of teenagers of driving age increased their average from the 21,100 miles to 40,200 miles per year. These statistics clearly indicate America is a driving culture.

What are the characteristics, values, influences and styles of expression of the culture of driving? First, there is a strong value of independence and freedom represented by going where you want, when you want and being in charge of your destination. Second, it is an expression of control and dominance. When driving, one is dominant over passengers, and often, there is an attitude of dominance over others on the road. One is in charge. This is one of the bases of road rage. Third, there is the influence of expediency - of going from one place to another without interference and quickly. Finally, driving is an expression of necessity. The culture of driving is defined by necessity.

Putting these elements of the culture of driving together, we see why persons drive when knowing they have had too much to drink. The characteristics, expressions, values and influences of driving override good judgment and decision making.

CULTURAL COMPARISONS WITHIN DWI OFFENDER GROUPS

TWO GENERAL STATISTICAL questions are important when understanding the relationship between different cultural groupings and DWI behavior. First, how do cultural sub-groups differ with respect to disclosing involvement in DWI conduct? Second, what is the cultural description of DWI offenders? Third, what are the ethnic and gender differences across the variables of substance use and abuse, psychosocial problems, recidivism, past treatment, DWI risk and treatment recommendations?

Comparing DWAI Self-Report of DWI Conduct Across Ethnicity

There are some clear differences across ethnic groups with respect to reporting involvement in DWI conduct. In a national survey (*Office of Research & Traffic Records,* 1998) a sample of 10,453 persons ages 16-64 (7,955 Anglo-White Americans, 1026 African Americans, 274 Asian Americans, 197 Native Americans, and 743 Hispanic Americans) were asked if they had driven within two hours of drinking within the last month. Across five ethnic groups, 28 percent Anglo-White Americans, 21 percent Native Americans, 17 percent Hispanics/ Latinos, 16 percent African Americans and 13 percent Asian Americans reported "yes." Young Anglo-White Americans were more likely to admit to drinking and driving than other cultural groups.

With respect to gender, males were two to three times more likely than females to report DWI behaviors. This was consistent across all cultural groups.

In that same study it was found that, while Anglo-Whites made up 77 percent of the total population, they account for 84 percent of the DWI trips, compared to African-Americans who make up 9 percent of the population, but account for 5 percent of the DWI trips (*Office of Research & Traffic Records,* 1998). However, a Fatality Analysis Reporting System report showed that about 50 percent of

African American drivers, passengers, pedestrians and cyclists killed in motor vehicle crashes had been drinking. *The National Roadside Surveys between 1973-1996* (Office of research & Traffic Records, 1998) found that African Americans were more likely than whites to have blood alcohol levels above .05 and .10. However, between 1973-1996 the rate of drinking and driving declined more sharply among African Americans than they did among Anglo-Whites (SAMHSA, 1998).

Ethnic and Gender Description of DWI Offenders

Chapter 5 of this *Provider's Guide* gave a descriptive summary of a large sample of DWI offenders in Colorado that was considered to be representative of the DWI population in general. Only those relevant to cultural differences will be summarized.

About 61%, 29.4%, 4.2% and 4.0% were Anglo-White American, Hispanic American, African American and Native American respectively. Anglo-Whites were under-represented and Hispanic-Americans were over-represented when compared with the general population. The age group of 21 through 30 was clearly over-represented, accounting for almost 38 percent of DWI offenders. Females represent about 20 percent of the group.

The mean age of the four groups was 33.2, 36.6, 31.3 and 35.1 for Anglo-White, African American, Hispanic-American and Native American, respectively. African Americans are older than Hispanics and Anglos; Hispanics are younger than the other three groups.

As to income, Anglos have higher average incomes than the other three groups which have comparable income levels. The percent females was 20.5, 23.2, 15.1 and 30.1 for Anglos, African Americans, Hispanics and Native Americans, respectively. Hispanics have a significantly lower percent of females and Native Americans have a higher percent of females in the DWI offender group. There is no difference between African Americans and Anglos.

Mean number of years of schooling are 13.1, 13.1, 10.5 and 11.0 for Anglo-White, African American, Hispanic and Native American, respec-

tively. Hispanics have significantly less years of education than Anglo-Whites, Native Americans or African American; and Native Americans have less education than African-Americans and Anglos.

Differences across Ethnic Groups within DWI Group

Table 10.1 provides the results of a study of 2,554 DWI offenders referred to education and treatment in the Colorado adult justice system. General results of this study indicate that, on the average, Anglo-White and Native Americans score higher on the scales measuring alcohol or other drugs (AOD) involvement and disruption. Hispanics are more defensive around self-disclosure; the level of defensiveness does not differ among African Americans, Anglos and Native Americans. Anglos indicate more mood adjustment problems than Hispanics, however, the levels of mood adjustment are the same for Anglos, Native Americans and African Americans. Anglos indicate levels of driving risk independent of AOD use.

Most significant is that the four groups do not differ on the measure of global AOD and psychosocial disruption. As well, there is no difference across the four groups as to prior intervention and treatment services and prior DWI arrests. African Americans have higher levels of BAC at arrest than the other three groups, with no arrest BAC differences among these three groups.

UNDERSTANDING AND ENHANCING CULTURAL COMPETENCE

American society is one of the most diverse of all societies. Yet its strength is found in that diversity. Ethnic minorities have grown from 11 percent of the U.S. population in 1960, to 28 percent in 2000 (Guajardo-Lucero, 2000).

However, this very diversity has led to limitations and restrictions on the rights and freedoms of numerous cultures, particularly minority groups. For example, minority ethnic groups have experienced limited access to economic and political power in American society and, for the most part, have been hindered from influencing the structures that plan and administer therapeutic programs.

T A B L E   1 0 . 1

Study of ethnic groups across ASUDS scales and DWI measures: Significant differences are noted as greater than (>) or less than (<) under ethnic comparisons and for gender; M indicates males score higher and F indicates females score higher and NSD means no significant difference; Anglo-White =A; African American=AA; Hispanic American=H; and Native American=N; Male=M, Female=F.

MEASURES	ETHNIC COMPARISON	GENDER
ASUDS Alcohol	H<AA, N; A=AA=N	M
ASUDS Driving	A>H; N>H, AA; A=N; A=AA	NSD
ASUDS Disrupt	A>H, AA; N>H, AA; A=N; N=AA	NSD
ASUDS Antisocial	A>H; A=AA=N; AA=H=N	M
ASUDS Mood	A=AA=H=N	F
ASUDS Defensive	H>AA, A, N; A=AA=N	M
ASUDS Motivation	A<AA. H, N;AA=H=N	M
ASUDS Global	A=AA=H=N	NS
Prior DWI	A=AA=H=NA	M
Prior Intervention	A=AA=H=N	M
BAC at Arrest	AA>H, A, N; H=A=N	NSD
Recommended Service Level	N>A; A=AA=H; N=AA=H	M
DWI Risk Level	A>H; N>H, AA; A=N; A=AA	M

Counseling professionals have begun to recognize that culturally responsive treatment strategies are essential to successful outcome. This has produced a growing interest in diversity, as well as increased training and policy efforts to develop cultural competence among providers.

The approach presented here affirms diversity awareness as central to effective service delivery. Diversity awareness involves an enhanced understanding of the real and perceived differences among the many subgroups in our society. Such awareness reaches far beyond the therapeutic context. Appreciating real differences that exist among people is the essence of the **democratic attitude.** Developing viable programs to ensure equal opportunity regardless of those differences is the essence of a **democratic agenda.** Attenuating and eliminating stereotypes and prejudicial attitudes based on perceived differences is the essence of the **democratic process.**

The cultural competence model with regards to DWI education and treatment defines a set of congruent behaviors, attitudes and policies that come together in a system, agency or amongst professionals and enables them to work effectively in cross-cultural situations to reduce DWAI recidivism. Becoming culturally competent is a developmental process, which unfolds with much commitment and over a considerable period of time. We now look at some of the concepts and methods that help in enhancing cultural competence.

The Continuum of Cultural Competence

Cultural competence may be viewed as a goal towards which individuals, professionals, agencies, and systems can strive. Cross, et al., (1989) provide a framework for a continuum of cultural competence with six possibilities.

- Cultural Destructiveness - discriminatory or exclusionary.

- Cultural Incapacity - paternalistic/negative attitudes.

- Cultural Blindness - culture viewed as neutral or irrelevant.

- Cultural Pre-Competence - sensitivity to cultural inadequacies in the organization.

- Cultural Competence - recognition of dynamics of cross-cultural interactions and presence of culturally-preferred service models.

- Cultural Proficiency - celebration of diversity, ongoing cultural self-assessment and knowledge building.

Essential Elements of a Culturally Competent Care System

The culturally competent system of care is made up of institutions, agencies and professionals, which collectively demonstrate the following five elements (Cross, et al., 1989).

- Values diversity.

- Has the capacity for cultural self assessment.

- Is conscious of the dynamics inherent when cultures interact.

- Has institutionalized cultural knowledge.

- Has developed adaptations to diversity.

In order to be effective, DWI programs must be aimed to fit the client's profile of AOD involvement and disruption as well as other lifestyle issues and problem areas. Likewise, they must directly address a client's cognitive patterns and motivation to change. These are often defined within the context of an individual's cultural experience. Awareness of inter-cultural dynamics allows providers to identify specific vulnerability factors for relapse and recidivism in their ethnic minority clients. Guajardo-Lucero (2000) describes this growth process as part of a "Cultural Competence Spiral", one that moves through the following five stages.

- *Pre Engagement* - where there is no awareness of culture or ethnicity.

- *Beginning Engagement* - intentional focus of program and staffing that values and integrates culture.

- *Continuing Engagement* - greater commitment to diversity and cultural competence, using a strength-based cultural perspective.

- *Advanced Engagement* - policies reflect commitment to and integration of diverse world views.

- *Full Engagement* - all areas of the organization value and integrate diverse perspectives as a strength.

Critical Considerations in Developing Cultural Competence

Issacs and Benjamin (1991) define a number of concepts and basic approaches that are important in developing effectiveness in cross-cultural situations. These are briefly discussed.

1. Recognizing universal ethnocentricity

Humans and groups of humans tend to center on their own culture or group. We tend to value our own group above others. Cultural competent service providers balance their own cultural identity and simultaneously recognize, and work toward enhancing, the strengths and values of other cultures. This balance helps us to live harmoniously in a pluralistic, multicultural society.

2. Developing non-judgmental acceptance

Providers who accept their own cultural identities as well as their clients' without judgment are more apt to utilize effective interventions that enhance cultural strengths while at the same time helping clients change their thinking and beliefs and thus change drinking behavior. It is not necessary to learn all about the numerous cultural groups and customs in this country in order to do this. What is key is a non-judgmental recognition that we all operate from an ethnocentric frame of reference.

3. Separating ethnicity from socioeconomic conditions

In our society, ethnic cultures are often confused with socioeconomic conditions. Some equate minority ethnic groups with poverty. Culturally competent providers distinguish culture from economic conditions, and understand that it is the cultural strengths and values within many ethnic groups that have allowed them to survive and grow in the midst of impoverished and hostile environments. Culturally competent providers are fully aware that socioeconomic conditions are not "cultures" in and of themselves, but often represent a struggle to adapt to restrictive and often degrading interactions with the dominant society. It is important to recognize and understand the cultural factors that have provided strength and sustenance to ethnic minority groups, and to incorporate these strengths into DWAI intervention program designs.

4. Avoiding stereotype substitutions

In attempts to become more sensitive to other cultures, it is important not to substitute one set of stereotypes for another. For example, American society shifted from viewing Asian Americans as the "yellow peril" during World War II to the "model minority," particularly in terms of academic achievement today. The latter stereotype has placed undue pressure on many Asian Americans, often at the expense of good mental health. Any stereotype or over-generalization, whether positive or negative, can reflect cultural insensitivity.

5. Acknowledging resistance to change

Although some of these reactions stem from the generalized response to any change, many are related to historical interactions, hostilities, and fears that have often marked relationships between ethnic minority groups and the dominant society. Such resistance to change, whether having a cultural basis or not, must be dealt with through reflective listening and acceptance. Ongoing and open communication and dialogue are essential. Opportunities for such dialogue must be built into the therapeutic process and the structure of the agency or organization seeking to become more culturally competent.

6. Cultural competence is a developmental process

Cultural competence is dynamic and on-going and takes a long-term and consistent commitment to achieve. It is not something that comes to the individual or agency quickly, nor at a fixed point in time. The process is cumulative and continuous.

7. Cultural competence is multidimensional and multifactorial

The degree of cultural competence that may be achieved is not dependent on any one factor. Attitudes, structures, policies and behavior are the major arenas where development occurs. Attitudes change to become less ethnocentric, patronizing or biased. Policies change to become more flexible and culturally impartial. Practices become more relevant to the culture of the client, from initial contact through discharge. Organizational structures support and enhance the growth of cultural competence among DWAI providers and clients alike.

Necessary Ingredients for Culturally Competent DWI Programs

There are a number of institutional and individual factors that enhance cultural competency in DWI education and treatment providers and programs. The following are some of these.

1. Flexible programming

There must be a real commitment to developing DWI services that are strongly based on meeting the needs and enhancing the strengths of diverse clients. For example, are the group sessions scheduled so as to meet the work and family schedules of the client population being served?

2. Ongoing process and outcome evaluation within the community

Needs assessment and planning are important when determining whether services are meeting the needs of both the community and the judicial system. How are clients from different ethnic groups responding to program services? Is the retention or dropout rate correlated with any particular group in the community, ethnic, age, gender? Agency staff need to interact with community agencies that are advocates for particular groups. Ethnic minority communities are dynamic and ever-changing, which means that this assessment and planning process is ongoing. Providers should strive to understand and meet the unique intervention and social needs of the various diverse groups being serviced. Agency staff participation in the activities of different cultural groups in the community will help to build trust between these groups and the intervention agency.

3. Diversity involvement at all levels of service delivery

Agencies must strive to hire professionals reflecting the diversity within the intervention population, including age, gender, sexual identity and ethnicity. Agencies should strive to offer the necessary training and skills development to make these professionals effective with various diverse groups. Just hiring professionals with diverse backgrounds is not enough. On-going cultural training for all staff must be a critical component of the service program.

The Culture of Counseling versus Traditional Cultures

Psychotherapy and counseling have developed a set of values and an underlying philosophy that often are different from and at odds with mainstream values (Wanberg & Milkman, 1998).

Some of the characteristics of the culture of counseling include verbal emotional expressiveness, individual orientation, openness and intimacy and a somewhat linear cause-effect orientation (Sue, 1990, 1997; Sue and Sue, 1999). Other characteristics of the culture of counseling include placing responsibility on the shoulders of the client, having the client take the lead in counseling, and equality of roles in relationships and self-disclosure (Wanberg & Milkman, 1998). Dana (1993, 1998) also identifies a number of values that operate within the orientation of psychotherapy of Western society. These include action orientation, individualism and competition, hierarchical power, controlled communication, the Protestant ethic, Western notions of progress and history, family structure, religion and aesthetics, and a scientific orientation towards problem solving.

The values of the culture of counseling may run counter to diverse and even mainstream values. These values may confuse or frustrate a client with a different cultural orientation (Dana, 1993, 1998). For example, individualism and the scientific method are not highly valued by a number of cultural groups, Asians and American Indians being examples. In American Indian, Hispanic, and Asian cultures, a person's identity is generally more communal in nature (less individualized). Often, the thrust of intervention and treatment is to enhance individuality. For a client coming from a tradition where identity is more communal, the goals of intervention and treatment may be at variance with this identity. Within some cultures, self-disclosure to strangers is not acceptable.

The culture of counseling can also be at variance with the dominant American culture. For example, American culture is egocentric, based on rugged individualism, which connotes independence - solving your own problems. A dominant value of the American family and American rural culture has been to "keep one's problems to oneself," i.e., "don't hang your dirty linen in public," "keep your cards close to your chest." An important philosophical orientation of counseling and psychotherapy is to share your problems, "hang out your dirty linen," at least in the counseling setting.

Problem solving in American culture has been based on an adversarial model, which involves blaming someone else for one's problems - proving one party right and the other wrong (a win-lose, or zero-sum model of solution). One value of the culture of counseling is to resolve conflicts in a win-win rather than adversarial manner.

The culture of counseling can run counter to the dominant idea of "don't be selfish." Counseling places a premium of talking about the self and using "I" in communicating with others.

These differences between the traditional American culture and the culture of counseling are some of the reasons why rapport building and trust-development in psychotherapy are often hard to accomplish. Counselors should consider all of these issues when attempting to meet the needs of clients whose cultural orientations are in contrast to the culture of counseling and psychotherapy. Culturally competent providers are sensitive to these issues and show flexibility in the counseling process in order to facilitate the therapeutic interaction while not compromising the values and culture of counseling. A comprehension of the client's cultural background facilitates this process.

Communication with a Diversity Focus and Sensitivity

The major elements of diversity in DWI education and treatment populations are gender, age, ethnicity, geographic origin and language. Language and cultural differences between clients and treatment providers, lack of training in cultural sensitivity, and supervisory failure to confront and challenge bias attitudes may be some of the reasons why counseling minority ethnic groups may not be as successful as desired (Atkinson, et al., 1993, p. 49). Cross-cultural counseling may not be as successful when participants misinterpret each others' statements, when language differences support negative and prejudicial attitudes and when different styles of communication are not experienced as positive expressions of a client's identity (Scott and Bordovsky, 1990, p. 167). Improving ethnic focus and sensitivity in DWI programs in order to maximize relapse and recidivism prevention involves several factors related to communication and language (Wanberg & Milkman, 1998).

1. Verbal skills

Not all clients, especially those with less education, have the verbal skills to profit from extensive "talk" therapy. The use of complicated or abstract concepts to facilitate change should be monitored to suit the abilities of particular clients. At the same time, the language used in intervention - either informal or in manual-guided programs - should always challenge clients to reach above their levels of comprehension and language skills. When new and more difficult terminology are used, time should be taken to help the client learn these terms.

2. Importance of primary language

When possible, counseling must be done in the language of the client, especially if English is not the primary language. When this is not possible, time should be taken to be sure that clients understand the meaning of the words being used. Because of the significant number of clients for whom Spanish is their first or only language, the *DWC Level II Education and Treatment Participant's Workbooks* have been translated into Spanish.

3. Accent and dialect

Time and patience should be used when clients speak with an accent or dialect and do not use standard grammar. Deliberate efforts should be made by the provider to understand and respect the client's accent or dialect. These dialects or accents may be due to learning English as a second language, or dialects due to different cultures or ethnic groups, e.g., Ebonics-based linguistic expression (a combination of the words ebony and phonics) found in African American culture.

4. Use of psychological terminology

Some terms are unique to the culture of counseling and psychology that are essential in helping clients learn certain change concepts. For example, *self-concept* and *self-efficacy* are important terms in enhancing cognitive and behavioral change. A list of important "change" terms can assist clients in learning terminology and putting to practice the concepts in everyday life.

5. Use of appropriate normative language by the provider

A sincere but common error in thinking among service providers is to attempt to "be like the client" in order to "be liked by the client." This may cause providers to mimic the client's jargon, talking or communication style in an attempt to establish rapport. Clients often experience this behavior as patronizing. It may cause ambiguity and misinterpretation, and it is not in line with the therapeutic purpose. One of the main goals of DWI intervention and treatment is to help clients become prosocial and to fit into the normative culture, e.g., follow the law, fit into society. We should understand and accept the client's jargon if it is not at variance with the goal of developing prosocial behavior and a sense of moral responsibility to the community. Therapeutic alliance is built on maintaining empathy and feedback, not on attempting to merge with a client's cultural identity. In sum, providers should "dig the jive, but not talk it."

6. Use of profanity

The use of profanity by the provider may work against positive outcomes. This is a common occurrence, particularly within the language of therapeutic confrontation (Ellis, 1990, Live Demonstration of Rational-Emotive Therapy). Sometimes it is effective when used appropriately. However, within some subcultures of religious or moral suasion, swear words may be offensive and damaging to therapeutic alliance and treatment outcome. It is important to remember that maintaining a professional demeanor is at all times appropriate.

7. Body language

Lack of familiarity with body language that has cultural roots may result in misinterpretation of a client's postures, gestures, or inflections (Sue, 1990, 1997; Sue & Sue, 1999). Anglo-White Americans tend to look away when speaking to another more often than do African Americans. However, when listening, African Americans are more likely to avoid eye contact while Anglo-White Americans make eye contact. This may lead the provider to conclude that African American participants are not paying attention during counseling interactions or during didactic presentations. It has been reported that teachers or counselors may perceive African Americans as angry, because of what is interpreted as an "intense stare" when speaking (Sue, 1990; Sue and Sue, 1999).

The Counselor's Personal Beliefs and Cultural Bias

Counselors have their own set of beliefs related to the problem faced by their client. They may have first-hand acquaintance with the tragedies often involved in DWI contexts. They have a culture of their own which may dictate their personal view of the world. Cultural schemas influence one's perception of and interaction with others, and, ultimately, how change may occur. Culturally sensitive counselors are aware of their own cultural biases, values, assumptions, and stereotypes (Sue and Sue, 1999).

Understanding the Client's Cultural Identity

A crucial element of therapeutic effectiveness involves understanding the nuances of a particular client's self-defined cultural identity. Bernal and Knight (1995) outline three components of such identity, which are helpful in enhancing a provider's cultural competence.

- **Self identification,** or the extent to which an individual perceives him or herself as a member of any given ethnic or racial group.

- **Group identification,** or the degree to which clients understand the values, customs and traditions of their group.

- **Unique perceptions,** or the client's unique perceptions and feelings about his or her group.

The issue of self-identification is related to acculturation. To what extent does this client identify with a particular ethnic group? For example, a client may have a Spanish surname but not perceive himself as Chicano. This lack of identification might result from acculturation-assimilation into and thus identification with the dominant culture - or from a general lack of information regarding his/her own ethnicity. Even when the client does self-identify as a member of a particular ethnic or racial group, to what extent does the client have knowledge of and adhere to his or her own culture's traditions? Guajardo-Lucero (2000) offers two views of acculturation that may be useful.

- The linear view which places people on a continuum from entirely ethnic-identified, or not acculturated, to total assimilation into mainstream culture (acculturation).

- The 3-dimensional view recognizes that people can vary in identification with all of the cultures with which they participate. Thus, a person can be high in both ethnic-traditional and mainstream identifications, low in both, or high in one at the exclusion of the other.

Dana (1993, 1998) gives a step-wise typology for assessing the identities of multicultural clients. He suggests that there are four levels of cultural orientation.

- *Nontraditional clients* are acculturated to the dominant culture. There is little association with their traditional culture. Some argue that this orientation may result in negative psychological consequences related to denying elements of themselves, but this assumption is controversial.

- *Bicultural clients* are able to function well in both their traditional culture and in the dominant culture, allowing two cultural identities to exist independently within the person. The person can be placed across a continuum of being high, medium or low in each of the two cultures.

- *Marginal clients* are low in both cultural orientations with little connection to either. They are disconnected from all of their societies and in a state of "anomie" or isolation from cultural involvement or identity. There is some suggestion that these individuals are more susceptible to psychological and other problem behaviors.

- *Traditional clients* primarily associate with their traditional culture. They might experience trans-cultural difficulties (or culture shock) as they attempt to establish themselves in majority culture and still retain their culture of origin.

Understanding a particular client with respect to this continuum will allow the provider to adapt the therapeutic encounter to the specific world view and identity of each client. Avoiding assumptions and over-generalizations and letting clients speak their own identity are essential to building rapport, and increasing the likelihood of positive outcomes when working with people of various cultural and ethnic backgrounds.

Ethnic Differences Between Counselors and Clients

Many clients prefer a counselor with a shared ethnic background. Recruitment and training of ethnically diverse DWI service providers have not been proportionate to ethnic group representation in the DWI client population. Both addiction counselor certification and DWI intervention programs should be more proactive in their recruitment of counselors from different cultural and ethnic backgrounds.

TREATMENT CONSIDERATIONS FOR SPECIAL POPULATIONS

WE NOW FOCUS on some specific dynamics operating within traditional cultural groupings within American society. The main purpose of this section is to enhance counselor communication and empathy in working with specific cultural groups including the major ethnic cultures, gender and other factors that are important in developing cultural competence within the client and provider.

Generic diversity issues that pertain to each group will be presented. There is considerable information in the literature around how these issues relate to AOD use and abuse and to criminal conduct not related to impaired driving. Some of these issues will be discussed. However, there is a dearth of information in the literature as to how these issues relate to DWI conduct and recidivism. An effort will be made to relate issues pertaining to these special populations to DWI conduct and intervention. This effort is based mainly on the experience of the authors. There is some information around racial profiling as this pertains to motor vehicle drivers.

African Americans

African Americans represent a community of about 34 million people or around 12.3 percent of the total U.S. population, U.S. Bureau of Census, 2001a). African Americans are projected to constitute 15 percent (58 million) of the U.S. population by 2050 (U.S. Bureau of Census, 2000). Currently, over half are located in the southeastern United States.

1. Substance use among African Americans

Findings with respect to the prevalence of AOD use among African Americans, when compared with other ethnic groups, are not clear. There is some evidence that African Americans are less likely to drink than Anglo-Whites (Ray & Ksir, 2002), may be more apt to use cocaine than either Anglo-Whites or Hispanics (National Institute on Drug Abuse, 1983) and are more likely (along with Hispanics) to be in treatment for substance abuse than Anglo-

Whites (National Institute on Drug Abuse, 1983). Within non-DWI treatment populations, however, African Americans do not manifest more severity of alcohol abuse problems than Anglo-Whites or Hispanic/Latino Americans (Horn, Wanberg & Foster, 1990; Wanberg, Lewis & Foster, 1978).

2. The criminal justice system

African Americans appear more likely to commit crimes than are Anglo-Whites with about 45% of those arrested for serious crimes being African American. However, there appear to be many more unfounded arrests of African Americans, with a greater likelihood of African Americans being jailed before trial, paying on average twice as much bail as Anglos, and receiving heavier sentences for the same crime (*The Economist,* June 8, 1996, p. 25). Although African Americans make up 12% of the American population, with 13% saying they used drugs in the past month, they account for 35% of arrests for drug possession, 55% of convictions, and 74% of prison sentences.

Many point to racial profiling as a contributing factor in these statistics. This refers to "police-initiated action that relies on race, ethnicity, or national origin rather than the behavior of an individual or information that lead police to a particular individual who has been identified as being, or having been, engaged in criminal activity" (Ramirez, McDevitt, & Farrell, 2000). Observers conclude that racial profiling has become so common that it has been labeled DWB - "driving while black" or "driving while brown" within communities of color (Bartol, 2002). Seventy two percent of black men between the ages of eighteen and thirty-four believed they had been stopped by police because of their race, compared to only 6% of Anglo-White men (1999 Gallop Poll reported in Bartol, 2002).

Racial profiling rests on the assumption that persons of color are involved in drug trafficking or carrying contraband more than Anglos. Empirical research, however, does not support this assumption (Bartol, 2002). A study conducted by the ACLU on traffic stops along I-95 in Maryland revealed "dramatic and highly statistically significant disparities" which show "without question a racially discriminatory impact on blacks and other minority motorists from state police behavior"

(Harris, 1999, p.24).

In 1985, the Florida Department of Highway Safety and Motor Vehicles set guidelines for law enforcement which urged officers to "be suspicious of drivers whose status does not 'fit the vehicle,' and drivers who represent *'ethnic groups associated with the drug trade' "*. In 1986, a similar system was issued by the Drug Enforcement Administration to law enforcement agencies across the nation (Harris, 1999). In 1999, a survey in San Diego found that Hispanic/Latino and African-American drivers were far more likely to be stopped and searched than others (Dvorak, 2002). Similar results have been found in New York, New Jersey, and other states (Ramirez et al., 2000).

Empirical data, anecdotal evidence and surveys all confirm the conclusion that racial profiling is clearly racially biased. There is also very little research to support a valid profile based strictly on race (Bartol, 2002, p.251). Profiling has yet to be affirmed as accurate or appropriate. "Much profiling is guesswork based on hunches and anecdotal information accumulated through years of experience, and it is full of error and misinterpretation" (Bartol, 2002, p. 252).

Some states have outlawed the use of racial profiling. A number of detection cues have been advanced that law enforcement officers can use to identify impaired drivers, such as driving well below the speed limit, being too meticulous about signaling, etc. These criteria, if put into general use, would shift attention away from race as a criteria of profiling, towards characteristics of the impaired driver. *The National Black Alcoholism and Addictions Counsel* (NBAC) has worked with NHTSA to inform African Americans about the importance of DWI prevention.

3. African Americans and impaired driving

A number of findings from the study summarized in Table 10.1 provide us with important insights into impaired driving among African Americans. First, this group is not different from other groups as to prior DUI arrests, prior DWI intervention services and overall global disruption related to AOD use and psychosocial problems. Even more important, African Americans score lower than

Anglos on AOD disruption and have the same post-assessment level of recommended intervention. It is important to note that African Americans in this study do have statistically significantly higher levels of BAC at arrest than the other three ethnic groups. Yet, they are just as open to self-disclosure as Anglo-Whites and are more motivated for DWI intervention than Anglo-Whites.

What the above findings indicate is that DWI African Americans, on the average, do not have any more AOD or psychosocial problems than do other ethnic groups, and in fact, may, on the average, have fewer AOD problems. This group has a lower risk than Anglos and Native Americans with respect to recidivism. Within non-DWI treatment samples, African Americans apparently do not differ from other ethnic groups with regard to the consequences and symptoms of use (Wanberg & Horn, 1987; Horn, Wanberg & Foster, 1990; Wanberg, Lewis & Foster, 1978).

The good news in these findings is the evidence that, at least within the Colorado DWI adult justice system, there does not seem to be the disproportionate and discrepant sanctioning that seems to be found in the non-DWI criminal justice system. This may be due, in part, to the clear criteria that the Colorado model has for sanctioning and referral.

4. DWI intervention and treatment issues for African Americans

The history and culture of African Americans provide unifying experiences that may aid in the design and implementation of more effective treatment programs. African Americans have developed a world view that combines historical experiences with present-day striving, along with shared language, values and symbols. As defined by Karenga (1980) the Black Value System, the Nguzo Saba consists of seven principles, which guide "functioning in an Afrocentric frame of reference" (Butler, J.P., 1992, p 29). These principles, recognized in the African American holiday of Kwanzaa, include: *unity, self-determination, collective work and responsibility, cooperative economics, purpose, creativity, and faith.* The core elements of African American culture define the group's individual and collective reality, including self-identity, knowl-

edge, emotions and behavior.

By definition, African Americans are group members; each individual's identity is tied to the group. African Americans have been described as highly cohesive and emotionally expressive, often responding spontaneously in a "...sense of oneness with life and of harmony with nature" (Butler, 1992, p.32). As life proceeds, individuals become more aware of the group's origins, its interrelationships and interdependence on past and present generations. Knowledge comes from a combination of symbols, language and rituals transmitted from elders to the next generation. "Life experiences are given depth and meaning through the realization of their inter-relatedness and significance in the life and existence of the group" (Butler, 1992, p.32). This identity as group members may enhance the effectiveness of group work with those of African American heritage.

Bell and Evans (1981) posit that, because of trans-generational discrimination in the United States, African Americans must be understood through a double-consciousness model (p. 28). The model examines two critical racial perspectives, coexistent in African American consciousness.

▶ *How I see myself as a Black person* — acculturated, bicultural, traditional, culturally immersed? Do other Black people see me in the same way as I view myself?

▶ *How I see Anglos* — racist, covert racist, culturally ignorant, culturally liberated, color blind? In relationship to Anglos, Do I see myself as inferior, superior, equal, powerful or powerless? How do Anglo people see me in relationship to power and acculturation?

Not all African American DWI client will identify with the above cultural values and heritage. Yet, for many African Americans in DWI programs, these values and identities can be of value when developing the individualized treatment plan (ITP) and can have potential impact on the outcome of intervention.

For example, the strong African American identity factor can become a major strength in DWI intervention. Change may be strengthened and reinforced when preventing problems of AOD use or preventing DWI recidivism is associated with a strong sense of cultural pride and group identity.

For more information about treatment efficacy with AOD clients, see *Blacks Against Drunk Driving: A Culture-based Handbook to Promote Traffic Safety Awareness* (NHTSA, 2001b). This handbook utilizes a combination of spiritual and cultural perspectives that have been shown to be effective with African Americans. Copies can be obtained by contacting the *Office of Communications and Outreach* at 202-366-2726 or fax 202-493-2062.

Hispanic/Latino Americans

1. Terminology

The term "Hispanic" is used in the U.S. Bureau of Census (1980) to designate individuals living in the United States whose cultural origins are in Mexico, Puerto Rico, Cuba, Central America and other Latin American countries. This term, however, was not used as an ethnic label until late 1970s and is not universally accepted by those to whom it refers. Among Hispanics with ties to Mexico, for example, one may find self-references such as Mexicano, Mexican American, Chicano, Latino or Spanish American.

Hispanics/Latinos (we will use the term, Hispanic, henceforth, to designate all residents who have ancestral ties to Spanish speaking countries) represent the largest ethnic/racial minority population in the United States, with a total population of 35 million (U. S. Bureau of the Census, 2001b). By the year 2050, the Hispanic population is expected to grow to 98.2 million or 24.3 percent of the total population (U.S. Bureau of Census, 2000). Around 60 percent are of Mexican ancestry, 12 percent Puerto Ricans, five percent Cuban and 23 percent account for all other Hispanic-Americans.

Most people of Mexican ancestry reside primarily in the Southwest and Western regions. In contrast to the widespread perception that Hispanics are agricultural workers, approximately 90 percent live in large urban centers.

2. Substance abuse among Hispanics

Within adult clinical groups, Hispanics/Latinos do not differ from Anglos and African Americans with respect to the disruption and negative consequences from alcohol or substance abuse (Horn, Wanberg & Foster, 1990; Wanberg, 1990; Wanberg, Lewis & Foster, 1978). Despite the findings in clinical samples, Hispanic drinkers measured in the general population are more likely than others to be considered problem drinkers (*Office of Research & Traffic Records*, 1998).

Some findings show an inverse relationship between ties to Hispanic culture and illicit drug use. "Of Hispanics born in the United States, 53% reported using some illicit drugs during their lifetime, compared to only 25% of those born in Puerto Rico and 11% of Hispanics born in other Hispanic countries" (Ruiz & Longrod, 1997, p. 706). A parallel finding is that 45% of Hispanics who speak English had used illicit drugs during their lifetime, compared to only 8% who speak mostly Spanish. Values and responsibilities incumbent within some Hispanic cultures may be utilized toward the prevention of DWI recidivism.

3. Comparison of Hispanic impaired drivers with other ethnic groups

Hispanic drinkers are more likely than others to have "higher traffic fatality and impaired driving rates" (NHTSA, 2001c). Rates of death from alcohol-related causes are higher among Hispanics than among whites and African Americans. The 1996 *Roadside Survey* shows Hispanics are more likely than African Americans to drink and drive, and more likely than whites to drive with blood alcohol levels over .05 (Sacramento Department of Health and Human Services, 2001). Moreover, differences in behavior exist among Hispanic subgroups, e.g., rates of impaired driving differ widely between Mexican Americans and Cuban Americans (NHTSA, *Hispanic Outreach - How-to--Manual,* 2001c).

Somewhat contrary to the above findings, the Wanberg and Timken (2005a) study found that Hispanic-American clients had lower levels of involvement in and disruption from AOD use than Anglo-Whites and Native Americans. In this sample, Hispanics had the same BAC arrest level as Anglos and Native Americans.

In the Wanberg and Timken (2005a) study, 750 of the 2554 subjects were Hispanic. Of this group, 212 spoke mainly Spanish and the ASUDS' Spanish version was administered to this group. A comparison of mean scores between these two Hispanic samples - English speaking and Spanish speaking - was done across the ASUDS scales and the DWI assessment variables in Table 10.1.

The English speaking Hispanics indicated higher levels of: alcohol and other drug involvement; disruption from drugs; antisocial attitudes and conduct; prior DWI interventions, prior DWI arrests; overall risk for recidivism; and overall Global disruption related to AOD and psychosocial adjustment. There was no difference between the two groups as to driving risk behavior, mood adjustment problems and BAC at arrest. Spanish speaking clients were more defensive, yet more motivated for services. English speaking clients were recommended for higher and more intensive levels of intervention services. It is of note that the mean age and monthly income between the two groups did not differ. Yet, what is most important is that 20.8 percent of the English speaking Hispanics were female whereas less than one percent of the Spanish speaking Hispanics were female.

These findings tend to support some of the findings of previous studies where it was found that Spanish speaking Hispanics reported lower levels of AOD use and abuse. There may be some inoculation factors that exist among Hispanics who are more proximal to their cultural origin versus Hispanics who have become more of a part of mainstream American society.

4. DWI intervention issues for Hispanic Americans

An important factor that sets the Hispanic cultures apart from other ethnic groups in the education and treatment samples is the fact that this group has experienced two types of mobility: foreign and domestic migration; and upward or downward stress-producing moves on the economic ladder. Geographic mobility and migration often works against intervention and treatment efforts. It can lead to breakdown of the family network, leaving family members, without these bonds, more vulnerable to deviant associates and escape-oriented activities. These mobility factors provoke continuous and cumulative stress.

The use of substances may be one major way for Hispanics to escape from the stress of these two mobility factors (Ruiz & Langrod, 1997, p. 708). These mobility factors need to be considered when developing intervention plans for Hispanic DWI clients. For example, disenfranchised clients may be encouraged to visit their native country and correspond with distant, yet cherished, family members. Group discussions with a skillful focus on historical or patriotic themes may improve participant self-esteem and treatment alliance.

An important intervention issue is the lack of bilingual staff members in AOD treatment programs in general and in DWI programs in specific. Sometimes non-Spanish speaking staff have difficulty relating to the specific problems confronted by the Spanish speaking Hispanic client. Treatment regulations are sometimes at odds with the cultural schema of the Spanish speaking DWI client.

UA testing can also be a problem with Hispanic clients, particularly when this testing is not part of the formal intervention and treatment program. UAs can connote that the client is not to be trusted and may offend the Hispanic's sense of dignity (Ruiz & Langrod, 1992). When urine analysis testing is hooked entirely into criminal justice monitoring, and not into treatment, it will only serve to increase distrust and suspicion. UA testing has its greatest advantage when rapport and trust are established with the client, and when the client understands that such testing may serve to strengthen trust between client and counselor and lead to positive outcomes for the client. Certainly, the conveyance of distrust inherent in UA testing is not unique to Hispanic clients.

It is widely recognized that family, *"la familia"*, is of central importance to Hispanic culture. Most research points to the value of involving the strong networking systems of Hispanic families in the treatment process (Ruiz & Langrod; 1997). Rapport and trust are secured as providers display respect for and comprehension of the individual roles of family members. Traditionally, each member of the Hispanic family has a special role: grandparents for their wisdom; fathers, for their authority; mothers for their commitment; children for their promise in the future; and godparents for their availability and support during times of crisis. It is important to utilize these resources when providing education and treatment services to Hispanic American clients (Ruiz & Langrod, 1997, p. 707).

Key Hispanic cultural values such as dignity, respect and love (*dignidad, respeto y carino*) can all be beneficial in the intervention and therapy process. Valuing a client's religious affiliations or non-institutional spiritual beliefs and practices, including Spiritism, Santeria, Brujeria, and Curanderism, may play a positive role in increasing client comfort and the sense of belonging and stability which may prevent return to disruptive AOD use patterns and impaired driving.

More information about treatment efficacy with DWAI clients may be found in the *Hispanic Outreach 'How-to' Manual,* which has been created in a joint collaboration between Mothers Against Drunk Drivers (MADD) and NHTSA (2001c) - *National Highway Traffic Safety Administration Office of Communications and Outreach,* Phone: 202-366-2726; Public Affairs Office 202-366-9550.

Native Americans

1. Demographics and history

There are over 2 million Native Americans (American Indians, Alaskan Natives, and Aleuts) residing in the US (U.S. Bureau of Census, 2000) with a unique history of alcohol and other drug use in our society. Prior to the introduction of alcohol in the late 1700's by frontiersmen, methods of obtaining altered states of consciousness to communicate with the Great Spirit and the spirits of nature were achieved mainly through dancing, fasting, drumming and isolation (Westermeyer, 1992, 1997). As the concept of Manifest Destiny promoted colonization of the West, alcohol became the most important item exchanged for furs. In the spirit of good business practice, many Native Americans accepted spirits as a gesture of friendship from "white skinned" traders. With little history to guide alcohol use, many tribes came to believe that alcohol had magical powers.

2. Substance use problems among Native Americans

Although there is much inter-tribal variation, alcohol abuse ranks high among social and medical problems in many Native American populations (Price, 1975; Snake et al., 1977; Weibel-Orlando, 1989; Westermeyer, 1997). Death from alcohol-related causes among this group is more than three times that of other groups, and accounts for a third of all Native American deaths (*National Center for Health Statistics,* 2000). Some risk factors associated with substance use among Native Americans are peer pressure, coping with tension, general alienation and grief (Fisher & Harrison, 2000) and depression (Zeiner et al., 1976).

There is a common stereotype that Native Americans are more prone to the effects of alcohol and to alcohol addiction, and that the typical Native American pattern is to drink rapidly seeking long periods of intoxification (Lurie, 1971; Weisner, Weibel-Orlando & Long, 1984). Yet, studies have failed to show a significant difference in alcohol metabolism among Native Americans (Bennion, 1976; Farris & Jones, 1978; Westermeyer, 1997; Zeiner et al., 1976). Westermeyer (1997), citing several sources, notes "...the Native American norm for alcohol is abstention, rather than use" (page 712).

Research does indicate that Native American clients in treatment do show more severe alcohol-related disruptions and symptom patterns. Studies by Wanberg and associates (Wanberg et al., 1978; Horn, Wanberg & Foster, 1990) compared randomly selected samples of Anglo-White, Native, African and Hispanic Americans from a large population of alcoholism patients. Mean scores on education, marital status, income, unemployment, drinking-related social role disruption, quantity of alcohol use and alcohol-related deterioration or disruption were compared across the four groups. In all measures except one, the Native American group scored in the direction of being more socially, economically and vocationally disrupted. Native Americans/Indians ranked third (and Hispanic Americans fourth) for fewest years of education. As well, Native Americans scored higher than the other three groups on gregarious drinking.

The fallacy of stereotypical views of Native Americans is most clearly exposed by the high degree of variance found within the population. Native Americans differ across tribal groups, socioeconomic strata, age and living environments (Westermeyer, 1997). For example, in a study comparing a sample of Native Americans in an urban treatment setting with one in a reservation treatment setting, using the scales of the AUI, it was found that the rural Native Americans showed significantly less alcohol-related problems and disruption (Horn, Wanberg & Foster, 1990). Thus, it is more helpful to identify Native Americans as a multiple-variable group and not as a single target population; thus, over-generalizations should be cautiously avoided.

3. Comparisons within DWI group

Results from the Wanberg and Timken (2005a) study and summarized in Table 10.1 provide further insight into the nature of the Native American DWI offender. Compared with African Americans and Hispanics, Native Americans report higher levels of alcohol use and abuse, involvement in and disruption from drugs and overall higher risk for DWI recidivism. Across all of these factors, Native Americans are similar to Anglo-Whites. Thus, these findings are similar to those found in studies of AOD clinical samples except, in the DWI sample, Anglo-Whites are just as AOD involved and disrupted as Native Americans.

4. Treatment issues for Native Americans

Outcome studies of non-DWI alcoholism treatment have indicated low rates of success among Native American clients (Weibel-Orlando, 1987). This may be, in part, because clients in this population generally come to treatment more severely disrupted, unemployed, having lost family support, and with fewer job skills (Westermeyer, 1992, 1997). Another reason may be that the traditional Western-American culture of counseling has not met the needs of the Native American client (Weibel-Orlando, 1987; Westermeyer, 1992).

For example, a counselor's preference for confrontation in the therapeutic setting may lead to more directive strategies. This may run counter to a

Native American's value of harmony and "noninterference", especially with regards to raising children, whose inner spirits are trusted and respected. If such clients withdraw from this confrontational counselor, this may be misinterpreted as a "lack of cooperation" (Fisher & Harrison, 2000). Such frequent incongruity between the practices of counseling and traditional Native American values has led treatment experts to call for more indigenous healing methods (Weibel-Orlando, 1987, 1989; Westermeyer, 1992, 1997).

Another intervention consideration is that because AOD involvement and disruption levels of Native Americans tend to be high, this would indicate that these clients will be placed in longer-term and more intensive DWI services. This would suggest that more Native American clients will need an individualized treatment plan at the front end of intervention. It would also mean that this group would need, along with Anglo-Whites, more preparation for longer term services.

Another consideration is the issue of time. With many Native American Cultures, particularly those in rural settings or who are more proximal to traditional values, time is cyclical (not linear). Time is viewed in terms of personal rhythms (somewhat like biorhythms) that take place within seasonal cycles (months and years). Calendars and watches are external to these rhythms (Fisher & Harrison, 2000). Though many of the original connections to nature that underlie these rhythms have been disrupted, these differences in the sense of time may result in tardiness or missed appointments.

A counselor may do well to integrate a cyclical component into the treatment process, to imbue regular meeting times with a sense of ritual purpose. Further, counselors should be sensitive to the fact that thoughts of historic time may be disturbing, or inspiring, for a Native American client, that the past may be measured in just a few generations, or in eons, and that the future, no longer tied to predictable roles and the seasons, may seem frightening and unpredictable, or a formidable challenge (Attneave, 1985). These may all impact on AOD treatment outcomes.

Several other treatment emphases are indicated from studies comparing Native Americans with other ethnic groups. Drinking patterns of Native Americans are more gregarious which support the use of self-help and 12 step groups, peer mentoring and role modeling. Because of the higher levels of alcohol involvement and problems in this population, there is need for more structured programs, transitional living resources and high impact job and vocational counseling programs. Given these impressions and findings, the social-role learning and community reinforcement components of CBT should be strongly emphasized.

Anglo-White Americans

It is commonly found that when ethnic groups are discussed in the AOD descriptive and intervention literature, the Anglo-White American group is often omitted. This is often the case because Anglo-Whites are not seen as a minority ethnic group. Yet, in California, Anglo-Whites now represent a minority (less than 50 percent of the population) when compared with all other ethnic groups. The Wanberg and Timken (2005a) study indicates that, as a group, Anglo-Whites have patterns that are different from the other three ethnic groups. As well, there are distinct differences among subgroups within the Anglo-White population. Only a few of these issues will be discussed.

1. Criminal justice system

Evidence cited above would suggest that Anglo-Whites may be treated differently by the criminal justice system compared to the other ethnic groups. That difference seems to be that Anglo-Whites are not profiled and may, on the average be allowed to "get by" without being sanctioned or with lesser sanctioning. The ultimate result of this phenomenon would be that antisocial behaviors actually get reinforced, and there may be a "get by mentality" that operates. Thus, rather than "nipping the problem in the bud," it is allowed to evolve untreated and unsanctioned.

With respect to DWI clients, the above interpretation may not in fact hold true. For example, all four ethnic groups do not differ with respect to prior DWI arrests and prior DWI intervention (Wanberg & Timken, 2005a). As well, the recommended level of DWI intervention service is essentially the same for Anglos, African Americans and Hispanics.

2. Cultural differences within Anglo-White samples

Within the Anglo-White group, there have been some traditional differences. Both Irish and Russian cultures are associated with heavy drinking, particularly distilled spirits (Ray & Ksir, 2002). Irish-Americans have been found to have high rates of alcohol-related problems, do not model responsible drinking for their children and adolescents, accept heavy drinking in adult males, value spirits and promote drinking in bars and away from family influences (Vaillant, 1986). This is contrasted with Italian-Americans who allow their children to drink wine at home but disapprove of intoxication in children and adults. These are only a few of the many other differences that exist across various subgroups of Anglo-Whites.

3. Comparison of DWI Anglo-Whites with other DWI ethnic groups

The Wanberg and Timken (2005a) study clearly showed that Anglo-Whites report more involvement in and symptoms from the use of alcohol when compared with Hispanic and African American groups. As well, this group reports higher levels of driving risk behavior and attitudes. Anglo-Whites, however, indicate lower levels of motivation for services and willingness to change. Anglo-Whites indicate higher risk for recidivism than Hispanics but comparable to Native Americans and African Americans in the DWI sample.

4. Treatment issues

The fact that there are diverse subgroups among Anglo-White clients in the DWI system, it is important that the unique cultural background be considered as intervention services are developed. Clients with cultural histories that portend more severe alcohol problems may need special kinds of information, education, or even therapeutic approaches.

Based on the above findings, on the average, Anglo-White clients will present with higher levels of alcohol problems and higher levels of AOD disruption than Hispanics or African Americans. Although intervention services must be based on the individual needs of clients, it may be that Anglo-Whites will need higher and more intense levels of intervention services.

Issues of Gender Related to DWI Conduct and Intervention

The prevalence of lifetime alcohol use among women is significantly less than among men: 54.7 percent for women and 78.3 percent for men (Grant & Dawson, 1999). However, differences between men's and women's alcohol and other drug use go well beyond the use prevalence rates. The purpose of this section is to look at some of these gender differences, summarize some of the demographics and prevalence rates among women and then look at intervention issues related to women.

1. Demographics and Gender Prevalence Rates

Treatment of women with substance abuse problems has received more concern and attention in light of a growing body of research identifying male-female differences in the way AOD problems develop and in treatment needs (Straussner & Zeulin, 1997; Blume, 1998). This is in part due to the trend of an increased number of women with substance abuse problems and the equalization of the impact of AOD use on women as compared with men.

According to 1993 estimates by the *National Institute of Drug Abuse* (in Straussner & Zeulin, 1997) men are almost three times as likely to drink alcohol or to smoke marijuana on a weekly basis than women. In other surveys, men report greater than average alcohol consumption and more alcohol-related problems than women (Wilsnack & Wilsnack 1991).

Kaufman (1994) summarized that men use more alcohol, marijuana, heroin, cocaine, hallucinogens and inhalants and women use more legal, mostly prescribed drugs. Women also tend to use stimulants or illegal drugs such as cocaine and amphetamines to lose weight or overcome depression. There has been a trend in the increase of illicit drug use by women, as this pattern has become more ego-syntonic with being female (p.30).

In the Horn & Wanberg studies in the early 1970s comparing male and female alcoholism patients,

women scored lower on a factor measuring classical alcoholism - physiological symptoms and long binge drinking (Wanberg & Horn, 1970; Horn & Wanberg, 1973). Using samples from the same treatment center almost a decade later, this difference all but vanished (Horn et al., 1990).

Although the prevalence rate of alcohol and other drug use among women is much lower than among men, what has been the ratio with respect to treatment populations? Historically, women represent from 20 to 25 percent of treatment program patients (McCaul & Svikis, 1999; Connors et al., 2001), and that percent range has remained rather stable (NIDA/NIAAA, 1993). However, there is some evidence that women are entering treatment facilities for AOD abuse at higher rates than before (Blume, 1997).

Blume (1997), using DSM IV criteria, estimated that, in any 12-month period, there were 2,068,000 women (age 18 and above) who could be diagnosed as having alcohol abuse and 1,950,000 women (18 and older) who could be diagnosed as having alcohol dependence for a combined total of 4,018,000 women affected. This is a male/female ratio of over 2:1; the total of over 4 million women compared with more than 11 million males who could be classified as either alcohol abuse or dependence (Blume, 1997). Demographic risk factors for alcohol problems in women have been found to be age dependent (Wilsnack & Cheloha, 1987). Women ages 21-34 reported the highest problem rates, with those at highest risk those who were never married, childless, and unemployed. Regarding male influence, several researchers have documented the role of male "significant others" on the substance abuse patterns of women. Males are likely to introduce drugs to women and to supply drugs to their female partners (Amaro & Hardy-Fosta, 1995).

Regarding drugs other than alcohol, 4.1% of American women admitted some illicit drug use during the past month (Blume, 1997). Among women of child bearing age (18-34) the prevalence was higher: 8.1% for ages 18 to 25 and 5.9% for 26 to 34 year olds. Regular use of marijuana (once a week or more) was reported at 2.6% for women between the ages of 18 and 25. The National Household Survey, by definition, excludes women not living in households (e.g., military, college dormitories, homeless), therefore, these prevalence rates must be considered very conservative estimates (Blume, 1997).

2. Gender differences in substance use and abuse

There are noticeable gender differences between men and women with respect to AOD use and abuse patterns and consequences. Although alcoholic women enter treatment about the same age as males, with about the same degree of alcohol dependence, they begin heavy drinking at a later age and their age of first drunk is significantly later than men (Connors et al., 2001; Gomberg, 1986; Schmidt, Klee & Ames, 1990; Wanberg & Knapp, 1969; Wanberg & Horn, 1970). This suggests a more rapid development of the problem in women (Connors et al., 2001; Smith & Cloninger, 1981). While women with alcohol problems drink less than their male counterparts, they are more likely to use other sedative drugs (e.g., Valium or Xanex) in tandem with alcohol.

Several studies suggest three distinct patterns that differentiate men from women. First, women tend to fit the solo, isolative pattern of use more than men (Gomberg, 1986; Horn & Wanberg, 1973; Horn, Wanberg & Foster, 1990; Schmidt et al., 1990). However, this difference has clearly attenuated over the past 20 years, and the prevalence of gregarious, convivial drinking is a common pattern now found among women. Second, women tend to use alcohol and other drugs to manage moods and psychological distress more than men do, and score higher on emotional and psychological disruption from AOD use (Blume, 1997; Gomberg, 1999; Horn & Wanberg, 1973; Horn et al., 1990; Wanberg & Timken, 2005a). This same finding was found among adolescent females with AOD problems. Girls scored significantly higher on the psychological problems scale than boys (Wanberg, 1992). Finally, women tend to indicate less social role disruption due to AOD use (Horn, Wanberg & Foster, 1990). This is certainly congruent with the fact of fewer women in the criminal justice system.

Utilizing the above cited references, the following is a summary of ways in which women tend to differ from men.

‣ Later onset of alcohol and drug use.

‣ Seek treatment earlier in the course of alcohol problem development suggesting less time for problem onset.

‣ Greater prevalence of spousal heavy drinking/substance abuse.

‣ Drink significantly less.

‣ Higher rates of co-morbid mental health disorders, particularly clinical depression and suicide atempts.

‣ Drinking more linked to depression - about one third of women with problem drinking patterns experience depression prior to onset of problem drinking (Turnbull, 1988).

‣ Drink alone and at home more often; however, this difference has decreased over the years (Horn et al., 1990).

‣ Higher rates of co-morbid prescription drug use and dependence.

‣ More likely to have a history of physical and sexual abuse.

‣ More often date the onset of pathological AOD use to a specific stressful event.

‣ Higher reported marital problems and disruption.

‣ More vulnerable to physical and medical problems due to drinking and other drug use.

‣ Greater financial instability and deprivation and more disparity with respect to lack of specific vocational skills.

3. Gender differences within DWI offender population

The above discussion presents differences between

men and women with respect to the general population and within treatment samples. However, what about difference within DWI samples? The Wanberg and Timken (2005a) study compared men and women within the large sample of DWI offenders. Table 10.1 provides the results from this analysis. The following represents a summary of these findings, all based on results that are statistically significant.

▶ Men indicate higher levels of involvement in drugs in general and alcohol in specific.

▶ Women report the same level of disruptive symptoms as men.

▶ Men indicate higher levels of antisocial attitudes/conduct.

▶ Women indicate higher levels of psychological symptoms and mood problems.

▶ Men are more defensive, yet indicate higher levels of treatment motivation and readiness to change.

▶ Global disruption - both AOD and psychosocial - is the same across genders.

▶ The records indicate men have more prior DWI offenses and more prior involvement in intervention services. Yet, BAC arrest levels are the same.

▶ Women have lower levels of risk for DWI recidivism.

▶ The mean age at admission to intervention services is the same (33.0 for men and 32.7 for women).

These findings are similar to gender similarities and differences found in non-DWI treatment samples. These findings indicate that women are just as disrupted from AOD use and abuse as men, more willing to self-disclose, yet more resistant to involvement in treatment and to change. The finding that men are more antisocial and women are more psychological disrupted is robust across both DWI and traditional treatment samples.

4. Comparing Women DWI offenders with other judicial offenders

Do women in non-DWI criminal justice systems differ from those in the DWI adult justice system? The Wanberg and Timken (2005a) study compared females from two non-DWI offender samples with females from the DWI Colorado sample. Across the board, the DWI female offenders reported much less severity relative to non-DWI offenders. For example, the Global Disruption scale for female DWI offenders was 18.64 versus 55.90 and 49.44 for the North Carolina and Arizona non-DWI samples, respectively.

What is most interesting is that the percent of females across the three samples did not differ. The DWI sample had 19 percent and the Arizona and North Carolina groups had 24 and 20 percent respectively. These statistics are similar to the percent of females found in most traditional AOD treatment programs.

Findings in this and the above two sections lead to the conclusion that DWI offenders, males and females, cannot be seen as comparable to non-DWI offenders nor can they be seen as comparable to clients in traditional clinical AOD treatment programs. DWI offenders are more defensive, less motivated for services and change and see themselves (and are seen by evaluators), on the average, as having low profiles with respect to AOD involvement and problems and psychosocial problems.

Furthermore, DWIO females, compared with male DWIOs are less defensive, less motivated for help, less involved in AOD use (though comparable to males as to AOD symptoms), show more psychological distress, and lower levels of antisocial attitudes and behaviors. It is important to keep these findings in mind when we discuss treatment issues for women in the next section of this Chapter.

5. Treatment Issues for Men

The literature has neglected this topic to a great extent. This is primarily because the assumption is made that treatment programs have been developed mainly for men, and women had to fit into these programs. This, however, may not be the case. For example, treatment programs tend to want to mitigate the client's guilt around past actions related to AOD use. This is probably a good approach for women who tend to have excessive shame and guilt around their past AOD conduct and tend to be ego-dystonic and have negative views of themselves.

However, this may not address the fact that male clients tend to be more antisocial, less prosocial, and may in fact benefit from a strengthening of conscience and moral responsibility. Thus, one important treatment issue for male DWI clients is to help them to have appropriate guilt around their past AOD use and their impaired driving conduct.

Male clients, particularly those in DWI programs, also are much more defensive than women. Thus, there is a need for more intense use of motivational enhancement and interviewing skills with male clients.

Clinical experience of the authors also indicates that men have poor social and interpersonal skills and are not as acculturated as women with respect to handling household finances. Men, on the average are poorer spellers, and their sense of self-efficacy, on the average, is much lower in these areas. For example, men often lack the skills to write checks, keep household books, negotiate services needed to manage and maintain household operations, particularly if this involves interpersonal and social interfacing. These daily management skills should be part of intervention programs for males.

6. Treatment Issues for Women

Because historically, AOD treatment and DWI intervention programs have predominantly served men, these programs tend to be male-oriented in content and delivery format (Gomberg, 1999; McCaul & Svikis, 1999). Although studies comparing men and women alcohol patients go back to the late 1960s (see Horn & Wanberg, 1973; Wanberg & Horn, 1970; Wanberg & Knapp, 1969), it has been only in recent years that specialized programs have been designed to address gender-specific treatment needs (McCaul & Svikis, 1999). Blume (1992, 1997) concludes that female AOD abusers in the criminal justice system are often overlooked, although their need for gender specific treatment is high.

There is little evidence that individual versus group treatment is more efficacious for women (Blume, 1992; Gomberg, 1999; Vannicelli, 1986). As well, there is no consensus regarding the efficacy of female-specific versus mixed sex groups (Blume, 1992, Gomberg, 1999). Yet, there is consensus that it is important that women clients have adequate opportunity to explore issues that may be hard to discuss with male patients present (Blume, 1997, p. 650). Sensitive topics may be more thoroughly and appropriately discussed within individual counseling or an all-female group.

Connors et al. (2001) identify a number of barriers to treatment seeking for women: fear of being stigmatized, defensiveness around admitting to problem behavior, lack of social support for treatment, seeing treatment facilities as male-oriented, lack of child-care facilities, and fear of losing custody of children.

Based on the identified differences between men and women reviewed above, and based on a review of treatment program literature, it appears that a large proportion of traditional AOD treatment approaches and DWI intervention services meet the needs of both men and women. However, there are a number of special needs considerations for women AOD and correctional clients that intervention and treatment programs must address. These are based on some of the salient differences outlined above between men and women AOD and judicial clients. Some of these special needs should be addressed at the programmatic level. However, most must be addressed at the individual treatment plan level.

This discussion focuses mainly on treatment issues for women in more traditional treatment and correctional settings. Thus, some of the concepts need to be modified when applying to women in DWI intervention programs. The following is a summary of these individual treatment needs taken from several sources (Blume, 1992, 1997; Connors et al., 2001; Gomberg, 1999; McCaul & Svikis, 1999).

▶ Focusing on an empowerment model of competency building which has indicated to be more effective than a medical model which attempts to cure client pathology.

- Addressing the higher rates of traumas and abuse in the family and the years of development, including sexual, physical abuse and exposure to violence (see McCaul & Svikis, 1999).

- Addressing vocational and legal problems that are unique and often more prevalent for women (McCaul & Svikis, 1999).

- Using the cognitive-behavioral approach of DWC which is a "good fit" with the empirical findings of "what works" for female DWI clients.

- Addressing issues related to pregnancy - either current or future - particularly the negative impact of AOD use on pregnancy.

- Need for child care services as part of outpatient treatment.

- Mental health assessment and treatment of comorbid states and conditions that include psychotropic medications assessment.

- More intense training in coping skills and assertiveness in interpersonal relationships, particularly with males.

- Mixed gender programs should provide gender-specific support groups that focus mainly on women's issues.

- Attention to past history and present risk of physical and sexual abuse and assaults which correlate with AOD dependency in women. These topics should be approached gently due to the deep feelings of shame and rage that may be associated with such experiences.

- Medical-physical assessment resources since women tend to have more medical problems associated with AOD use and abuse.

- Specific classes on parent-effectiveness that also address single-parenting skills and needs.

- Involvement of family members in AOD dynamics (partly because women are more likely to have spouses with AOD problems, and children who suffer fetal alcohol or drug effects).

- Need for parenting education and information about fetal AOD effects, AIDS prevention, and other STDs.

- Female role models, including women staff who have overcome AOD problems and antisocial behavioral patterns.

- Experiences of sexism (e.g., unequal social roles, under-valuation of her contributions, etc.).

- Awareness that dependence on therapy may reinforce social stereotypes and a self-fulfilling prophecy that women can't make it on their own.

- Attention to special populations of women, such as lesbian women who appear to have a higher rate of AOD dependency, and who may profit from gay or lesbian self-help groups.

- Assessment and treatment of sexual dysfunction.

- Attention to guilt, shame and self-esteem issues.

- Vocational education opportunities for women in treatment should transcend stereotypic job categories.

Some reports indicate that 34% of female offenders (in the general criminal justice population) have been diagnosed with post-traumatic stress disorder as a result of a rape or other abuse experience (GAINS Center, 1997). This may be just the "tip of the iceberg" of negative and destructive experiences that women offenders, including DWI clients, have experienced. With specific regard to women's emotion and evaluation of self worth, Bem (1996) has asserted that development of the gender schema in women often becomes so internalized that it develops primacy, and the "self becomes its hostage." Negative self-evaluation, low self esteem and feelings of powerlessness and desperation are often the result.

Unfortunately, these self-evaluations are seemingly validated by realistic life experiences within a sexist environment, the reactions of others who hold unrealistic expectations about obligations as a woman, and her own counter-productive thinking. The complex feedback loop between experience, thought, feeling and behavior becomes a self-perpetuating cycle of self-destructive behavior and worsening life circumstance.

The methods of cognitive behavioral treatment can be effective in helping women to overcome these difficulties in their lives. But essential to this effectiveness is ensuring that treatment is directly related to and placed within contexts that are relevant to a woman's sociocultural experience. The constructivist approach advocated by Arnkoff & Glass (1992), Mahoney (1990) and many others necessitates that treatment be directed toward the subjective reality of the client. It is imperative that we understand the life conditions experienced by the DWI female offender, in order to appreciate how that reality has undermined the development of constructive thought and behavior.

7. Relevancy of women's issues for DWI offenders

The above special focuses for women in treatment apply mainly **to those who have AOD abuse and dependent problems.** We have presented research findings, however, that clearly indicate women DWI offenders are significantly different from women in traditional clinical programs and in non-DWI offender treatment programs and different from men DWIOs. The most robust finding is that DWI women offenders are low profile (by self-report and by collateral information) with respect to AOD involvement but their disruptions from AOD use are the same as male DWIOs. Although they may indicate much lower levels of antisocial attitudes and behavior, they have greater levels of mental health and mood adjustment problems. Consequently, there will be higher levels of medical problems and greater incidence of co-occurring disorders.

What these findings mean is that these needs should be assessed and adjustments made at individual treatment plan level and, to some extent, at the programmatic level. Certainly, programs should have capabilities to assess these needs and

resources available to meet them when detected. There are some **basic programmatic elements** that should be considered for **women DWI offenders** and that should be built into DWI programs. These are:

- Empowerment model of competency building and greater focus on treatment and change motivation;

- The cognitive-behavioral approach;

- Child care services;

- Careful screening for mental health needs;

- More intense assertiveness skills training;

- Female-only support and process groups;

- Screening for medical-physical problems;

- Female staff role models;

- Staff training and ongoing supervision should be geared toward maintaining a non-sexist attitude in the treatment of women with AOD abuse problems.

The Culture of Ceremony and the Bar

The majority of DWI offenders fit the gregarious, convivial drinking pattern (Horn, Wanberg & Foster, 1990). Certainly, there is a group of DWI offenders who drink solo (often in a bar setting), yet even individuals in this group often venture into social or gregarious settings to drink. Thus, the culture of ceremony and the pub are powerful determinants of DWI conduct.

Ritualized use of alcohol is widely practiced. Making friends, maintaining old friendships, business arrangements, weddings, births, funerals, secular and religious ceremonies - all are occasions for liberal use and often abuse of alcohol. Although substance use may be heavy at ceremonial events, even involving intoxication, the usual social control over dosage and demeanor has a dampening effect on hazards associated with prolonged or chronic abuse.

Problems can develop, however, when the group's reason for existence is to experience the effects of intoxication. This is often the case in the culture of the cocktail lounge, neighborhood or ethnic bars, and street drinking groups. In these instances, group norms for alcohol or drug use may foster substance abuse, rather than prevent it (Westermeyer, 1998).

The ubiquity of drinking establishments in Western culture serves as a bastion of male — increasingly female — camaraderie, diversion and psychosocial support. Without doubt, the bar serves an important function as a center for relaxation, interpersonal encounters and casual business negotiations. However, the role of the pub as an informal "clinic," that serves a sizeable population of clients with multiple social and personal needs and problems, including alcohol abuse, loneliness, isolation, remains largely understated (Milkman & Sunderwirth, 1998).

The hospitable personnel in pubs not only provide episodes of human relatedness but also administer a powerful sedative drug - alcohol. Clients can satisfy some of their needs for affiliation, belonging, stress management, and anxiety reduction by frequenting establishments that cater to like clientele, e.g., sex bars, sports bars, singles clubs, etc. (Milkman & Sunderwirth, 1998). Most DWI offenders who drink in bars are "addicted" as much to the lifestyle "benefits" of bar culture as to the reinforcing qualities of the drug, i.e., feeling good or simply feeling "not bad."

The Community Reinforcement Approach (CRA: Sisson & Azrins, 1989; Smith & Meyers, 1995), advises AOD treatment providers to discuss the relationship between the client's AOD consumption and his or her recreational or social life. It is important for clients to recognize that the friends and activities, which are often associated with heavy drinking, are not supportive of their relapse and recidivism goals. Because some clients have been so involved in the bar culture, the CRA usually includes substitute gregarious and convivial environments where clients can go, either alone or with their families, to enjoy a festive social atmosphere without the risks associated with alcohol consumption.

Caring communities are challenged to develop alternative means for gratifying the needs previously met through tavern life. Atmospheres must be created where surrogate family networks promote constructive measures for coping with internal conflict and social stress. The sense of adventure, spontaneity, relaxation, and human relatedness, all within reach at the pub must somehow be preserved, without the unwanted consequences of repetitive intoxication and the enormous risk of driving while ability is impaired.

SUMMARY

CULTURE IS A powerful force that can determine the use and abuse of substances and whether an individual engages in impaired driving. Culturally competent counselors will appreciate how treatment outcomes are affected by cultural factors in the client, counselor, agency and broader community. As effective counselors, we understand our own cultural values and how these may differ from those of other cultures and of their clients. We are conscious of the dynamics of cultural interaction, and are actively committed to self-assessment and to developing the skills necessary to utilize cultural strengths - in ourselves and in our clients - to improve treatment effects.

As DWI providers, we become more effective when we create a balance of respect for our own cultural values and the values of others. Only when recognizing the critical importance of valuing diversity are we able to help clients explore and optimize their own cultural values and priorities, which help to prevent relapse and recidivism.

Cultural competence emerges when the specific treatment needs of DWI offenders are clearly understood within the context and *strengths of diversity* - strengths in beliefs, styles of learning, spiritual experiences, verbal and non-verbal skills and orientations to family and community. As DWI providers, we become culturally competent, and thereby improve AOD outcomes, when we capitalize on the commitment of Hispanic Americans to *honor, word, dignity and family,* when we capitalize on African Americans' alliance with the *power and strength of ancestry and a shared sense of cultural identity* and heritage, when we integrate Native Americans' *spirituality and reverence for nature, rural values and the artistic* and when we strengthen an Asian American's dedication to *family honor and tradition.*

We honor the strengths of diversity when we convey to the historically disenfranchised groups of our American society - African Americans, Hispanics, Native Americans - that they have demonstrated profound internal strength to survive and maintain continuous growth and change in the face of the obstacles of prejudice and discrimination. We employ cultural competence when we recognize the different needs that stem from gender and experiences with poverty, and can build on the strengths, which have helped these groups manage oppression, discrimination and adversity. We enhance cultural competence when we emphasize the concept of renaissance - renewal - rooted in European culture, and help Anglo-Americans share this cultural value with all cultural groups.

Finally, we secure cultural competence when we recognize variability among members within any particular culture, with care not to substitute one set of stereotypes for another. We inquire into the self-defined identity of our clients, with attention to issues of acculturation and personal choice, so that our clients experience themselves being respected, listened to and heard. A crucial factor to remember is this: Do not make assumptions; let clients speak their own needs and identities to you. This is central to a positive therapeutic outcome, and thus to prevention of DWI recidivism.

Cultural competence and sensitivity also seek and embrace common bonds across cultures. One common bond is found in alcohol and drug use. Alcohol and other drugs have a leveling effect on people of all cultures. Drugs are not biased; they do not discriminate. With respect to the impact of alcohol and other drugs on individuals, there are more similarities than differences. Any differences found across groups are also found within groups. For example, although women may be more apt to drink alone, there is also a clear pattern of convivial and gregarious drinking among women. Substance use can cause mental, emotional, social and physical impairment and dysfunction in all people. There is a commonality that binds together the diversity of cultures in AOD and DWI intervention which unite us in one common treatment goal - to help DWI clients to break out of the bonds of thinking and behavioral patterns that contribute to AOD problems and impaired driving.

A sense of common purpose comes as we seek common values and search for what is important.

Ultimately, we must heed the voice of Henry James. When asked by his nephew what he thought he ought to do in life, James replied: *"Three things in human life are important. The first is to be kind. The second is to be kind. The third is to be kind."*

SECTION II
the education and treatment platform

I have found it enriching to open channels whereby others can communicate their feelings, their private perceptual worlds.

-Carl Rogers

The purpose of *Section II* of this *Provider's Guide* is to delineate the conceptual and operational guidelines of the education and treatment platform for *Driving With CARE: Education and Treatment of the Impaired Driving Offender.* Chapter 11 defines the conceptual framework and the core elements of the *Driving With CARE* (DWC) education and therapy protocols. The process of growth and change will be presented within a framework of a three-stage model of change. The core strategies that define the education and treatment structure are described. Chapter 12 discusses the characteristics of the effective DWI provider (counselor) and the provider (counselor)-client relationship. The DWI change triad is discussed - interaction among the counselor, client and community. Chapter 13 focuses on the specific issues involved in screening and in-depth assessment of the DWIO. Specific instruments and an evaluation model are discussed. Tools and methods used in the in-depth and differential assessment are presented. This will include the presentation of the *Client Self-assessment Profile* and the *Client Master Assessment Plan* (MAP). Chapter 14 provides the essential basic program operational guidelines to be used in presenting the DWC education and treatment protocols.

Driving With CARE: Education and Treatment of the Impaired Driving Offender is comprised of two education and one therapy protocols. *Level I Education* is designed for first DWI offenders whose evaluation revealed no evidence of AOD problems and who had lower arrest BACs. It covers basic AOD and impaired driving education, the basic cognitive-behavioral principles and methods to change thoughts and behavior, and the basic principles of relapse and recidivism prevention. Level II Education is more extensive, covering all of the topics of *DWC Level I Education,* but expands into intrapersonal, interpersonal, social responsibility and marital/family adjustment areas. It provides a comprehensive treatment of relapse and recidivism prevention and an in-depth coverage of the principles and methods of cognitive-behavioral change. *DWC Level II Education* provides the foundation and preparation for *DWC Therapy,* which is referred to as *Level II Therapy* since we see it as a continuation of *Level II Education.* *DWC Therapy* assumes the client has learned the basic concepts of cognitive and behavioral change conveyed in *Level II Education.* Throughout the text, *DWC Education* refers to *Level I* and *Level II Education* and *DWC Therapy* refers to *Level II Therapy.*

CHAPTER ELEVEN: CONCEPTUAL FRAMEWORK FOR THE EDUCATION AND TREATMENT OF THE IMPAIRED DRIVING OFFENDER

OVERVIEW

This chapter defines the conceptual framework and the core elements of the *Driving With CARE* (DWC) education and therapy protocols. Since DWC is based on both an education and therapy approach to intervention, we first define these two approaches and see how they fit together in the DWC protocols. The core strategies that define the education and treatment structure will then be described. Finally, a conceptual framework will be presented which provides an integration of the process and structure of the education and treatment skills utilized in implementing the DWC program.

DEFINING AND INTEGRATING THE EDUCATION AND THERAPY APPROACHES

The DWC protocols are based on both an education and therapy approach. Even though, "the terms intervention and psychotherapy have been use interchangeable" (Trull & Phares, 2001, p. 294), both education and therapy or treatment are described in this work as impaired driving interventions. Yet, education is viewed as a different kind and level of intervention than treatment or therapy. As well, in this work, we view treatment and therapy as synonymous and based on the traditional meaning of psychotherapy and counseling. Thus, we first look at the meaning of psychotherapy and counseling, discuss the differences between these approaches and education and then provide a model for integrating these two approaches for DWC.

Defining Psychotherapy and Counseling

Psychotherapy is defined simply as "a situation where two people interact and try to come to an understanding of one another, with the specific goal of accomplishing something beneficial for the complaining person" (Bruch, 1981, p. 86), "achieving personal change and growth" (Rogers, 1951, 1980) or changing "....the patient's image of himself from a person who is overwhelmed by his symptoms and problems to one who can master them" (Frank, 1971, p. 357). Even more simply, it can be defined in terms of its goal: either symptom relief or cure - the prevention of recurrence (Seligman et al. 2001, p. 11).

Patterson, in his seminal work, *Theories of Counseling and Psychotherapy* (1966), defines counseling and psychotherapy as "processes involving a special kind of relationship between a person who asks for help with a psychological problem and a person who is trained to provide that help" (p. 1). Over 30 years later, Patterson and Hidore, (1997) gave a similar definition as a psychological relationship between a person (client), whose progress in self-actualization has been blocked or impeded by the absence of good interpersonal relationships and a person (therapist) who provides that relationship (p. xiii).

Lang (1990) also sees psychotherapy as "a relationship and interaction between an individual with an emotionally founded problem who is seeking help....and an expert who is capable of assisting him or her in effecting its resolution.... " (p. 3). He defines the core dimension of psychotherapy as the object relationship between the patient and therapist and the interpersonal interaction that unfolds on the basis of this relatedness (p. 219). Bateman, Brown & Pedder (2000) see psychotherapy as "a conversation that involves listening to and talking with those in trouble with the aim of helping them understand and resolve their predicament" (p. xiii).

Jerome Frank, who provided some of the earlier definitions of psychotherapy, considers the core of all psychotherapy approaches as a process through which a socially sanctioned healer works to help individuals to overcome psychological stress and disability through a method or procedure that is based on a theory of the sufferer's difficulties and a theory of the methods to alleviate them. Thus, he sees five features common to all forms of psychotherapy (Frank, 1963, 1974): 1) a trusting and emotionally charged relationship between client and therapist; 2) the therapist is genuinely concerned about the sufferer's welfare and is committed to bring about some kind of change that is seen as desirable; 3) a conceptual framework that explains what has happened and what will happen; 4) a procedure or method that the therapist and patient follow for the purpose of bringing about changing and/or restoring health; and 5) the theory, approaches and outcome are linked to the dominant world view of the client's culture.

All of these definitions have several factors in common. There is a trusting and working relationship, a provider who has concern and empathy for the client's pain and welfare, a theory of psychological and behavioral problems, a method of how to approach those problems, a client who presents with a unique set of problems, and an expectation of change found within the context of a set of cultural and societal values.

In this work, psychotherapy (therapist) and counseling (counselor) have similar meanings and, essentially, are used synonymously. However, there has been a long standing discussion about whether psychotherapy and counseling are synonymous. The term *psychotherapy* was first used in the late 1880s (Efran & Clarfield, 1992) when at the time, psychological problems came to the forefront in medicine ("psyche" meaning mind, and "therapeia" meaning treatment). Carl Rogers began using *counseling* in the 1930s in order to "sidestep" the legal restriction that only medical doctors were allowed legally to practice psychotherapy (Dryden & Mytton, 1999).

Most experts in the field see the two as having the same or similar processes and methods. Dryden & Mytton (1999) view the two as having the same meaning. Both refer to helping individuals with personal or relationship problems directed at effecting personal and emotional changes so as to improve personal functioning. Both definitions refer to a process of bringing about self-improvement and change.

Patterson (1966) made an effort to look at their differences and similarities and concluded that there is no essential difference between the two in terms of the process, methods or techniques, the goals or expected outcomes, the relationship between the client and therapist or the clients involved. The one distinction he indicates that can be made is that counseling sometimes refers to work with less disturbed clients or clients with special change

needs and psychotherapy may refer to work with the more seriously disturbed persons. Ivey and Sienek-Downing (1980) also saw this as a noteworthy distinction: counseling directed at assisting "normal people" to achieve their goals or to function more effectively and psychotherapy as a longer term process concerned with the implementation of personality change.

George and Cristiani (1981) concluded from their literature review that the distinction is more on a continuum, with counseling directed more at aiding growth, focusing on the present, aimed at helping individuals function adequately in appropriate roles, more supportive, situational, problem-solving and short term; whereas psychotherapy is more reconstructive, analytical, focuses on past and present, directed at more severe emotional problems and at change in basic character and personality (p. 8).

How Education Differs from Psychotherapy/ Counseling

Given that the differences between psychotherapy and counseling seem to lie on a continuum, we will treat the two as synonymous in this work. We will use the term *therapy* to refer to the counseling-psychotherapy continuum, and, as noted above, synonymous with treatment. However, how does therapy differ from education? More specifically, what is the primary distinction between *DWC Education* and *DWC Therapy* in this work?

There is little discussion in the literature as to the differences between these two approaches. Patterson (1966), however, does make a distinction between counseling or psychotherapy and education. He states that most in the field would agree that counseling and psychotherapy "deal with the conative or affective realm - attitudes, feelings, and emotions, and not simply ideals" (p.3). He sees teaching or education as being concerned only with the rational, non-ego-involved, solution of problems. "Where there are no affective elements involved, then the process is not counseling, but is probably teaching, information giving, or an intellectual discussion" (p. 3). More specifically, Patterson (1966) clearly states that counseling and psychotherapy are not just giving of information, advice, suggestions or recommendations, although counseling may involve these activities. He sees them as influencing and facilitating voluntary behavior change.

The DWC education protocols involve helping the client understand and learn about how change takes place, about substance use and impaired driving patterns and the psychosocial factors that lead to those patterns and the client's legal relationship to the community relative to the DWI conviction. The protocols are based on a learning centered rather than an information-centered model of adult education (Hart, 1991) with the goal of giving personal meaning to the content of the lessons. The protocols create a learning environment whereby clients interact with the curriculum content so as to disclose personal information for the purpose of self-assessment and to identify personal problems. The protocols encourage clients to make changes where these changes will help prevent relapse and recidivism. The specific skills and approaches to this model of learning are discussed in more detail in Chapter 12.

The two education protocols are designed to help the client learn certain lessons so as to prevent further problems related to alcohol and other drugs. These protocols give information without the expectation that an individual will change attitudes, feelings, emotions or behaviors. Yet, DWI Education sets the groundwork for this kind of change and is seen as the prerequisite to *DWC Therapy* where the sessions are clearly directed at implementing changes at the cognitive, affective and behavioral levels.

The education protocols do not assume that the client has significant psychosocial and substance problems that need to be changed, but rather has the goal of enlightening the client as to those possible problems. As the client progresses through DWC Education, there is the goal of increased self-awareness through self-disclosure. Where that self-awareness suggests change, efforts are made to enhance motivation to make change. Thus, the transition from education to therapy does take place within the DWC Education protocol, and more specifically, *DWC Level II Education.*

The therapy protocol of DWC *(Level II Therapy)* moves the client beyond the level of self-aware-ness to a level of cognitive, affective and behavioral change. *DWC Therapy* deals with the realms of thoughts, feelings, attitudes and behavior at a more intense and deeper level. The client is more involved in the affective elements of change and there is greater focus on helping the client have more intense personal identification with the therapeutic themes and content. To use Patterson's term, it is clearly more "conative" in nature - that is, it directs mental processes (thought and feeling) and behavior towards action and change. For example, *DWC Therapy* goes beyond challenging clients with information and ideas around relapse and recidivism. It moves the client to a commitment and ownership level of change.

Integrating Education and Therapy - The Therapeutic Educator

As described above, the DWC curricula provide a basis upon which impaired driving education and therapy are integrated. The two interventions are seen on a continuum, with the education protocols laying the groundwork for and being a prerequisite to the therapy protocol and the therapy protocol focusing on the process of cognitive, affective and behavioral change.

A second basis upon which education and therapy are integrated in DWC is in the role of the provider. The DWC provider is both educator and therapist - or to use DeMuro's concept - a therapeutic educator (DeMuro, 1997). DeMuro sees the DWIO interventionist as being both an adult educator and therapist. He draws from both the education and therapy literature to provide the basis for this integration. He points out the difference between *pedagogy,* or the art and science of helping children learn and *andragogy* which is the process of adult learning and education (Knowles, 1980). The distinction is important. In pedagogy, the learner is viewed as underdeveloped and dependent upon the teacher. In andragogy, it is assumed that the learners are diverse and have reached certain levels of physical, intellectual and emotional maturity with greater collaboration between educator and learner in the process of learning.

DeMuro (1997) in developing the concept of the therapeutic educator, points to Knowles's (1980) ideas that the adult educator is a teacher, facilitator and mentor who has six main functions: to help adults **identify** (diagnose) their needs for learning; to **plan** their learning experiences; to **motivate** the learner; to provide a **method** and **resources** for learning; and to **evaluate** the learning process. The therapeutic educator integrates these adult educator functions with those of the therapist resulting in a role that helps individuals interpret their life experiences in order to change their behaviors (DeMuro, 1997, p. 65). This integrated role is essential in the effective implementation of the education and treatment of the DWIO and an important component of the DWC education and treatment platform. The more specific aspects of this role are discussed in Chapter 12. In this work we use the term *provider* to refer to therapeutic education or counselor.

THE CORE STRATEGIES AND ELEMENTS OF THE EDUCATION AND TREATMENT PLATFORM

IN THE INTRODUCTION to this *Provider's Guide,* the underlying assumptions of DWC were defined. Section I provided an historical review and theoretical concepts of impaired driving and its intervention. From this information, eight core strategies have been defined which form the basis of the DWC education and treatment platform and structure. We now describe these core stategies and see how they help define the DWC treatment platform and structure.

Screening and Assessment are Multidimensional and Based on Convergent Validation

The first core strategy for the DWC education and treatment platform is that client screening and assessment are based on a convergent validation model and lead to a multidimensional assessment of the clients' condition. *Chapter 7* provided the basic concepts of the convergent validation model for differential screening and in-depth assessment. The specific methods for DWC screening and assessment will be covered in *Chapter 13* of this *Provider's Guide.*

Facilitating the process and structure of Learning, Growth and Change

The second core strategy for DWC is facilitating the process of learning, growth and change. This process and structure will be explained.

Most approaches to therapy identify the process of treatment as one of personal growth and change. Building on the concepts of learning and change found in Lewin's steps of learning (Ham, 1957; Lewin, 1935, 1936, 1951) and Werner's Orthogenetic Principle (1957), a process and structure for change in treatment was developed by Wanberg (1974, 1983, 1990; Wanberg & Milkman, 1998). This process of growth and change model is seen as an essential foundation of the DWC education and treatment platform.

Kurt Lewin conceptualized the process of learning, growth and change as involving three response phases: undifferentiated or global; differentiation; and integration. The initial phase of growth and learning is a **global or undifferentiated** response to a set of stimuli or a situation that expects change and growth. This response can be observed in all living organisms. It occurs in a rapid, undifferentiated multiplication of cells in the first stages of a new organism; it can be observed in an infant child whose whole body responds to a stimulus. Resistance and tension are also identified in this stage of growth.

The second response phase of growth occurs when the individual units of the organism begin to **differentiate** among each other. Different sizes and shapes of cells begin to emerge; now the infant can reach out with his arms without the rest of the body moving. Lewin describes this stage as the differentiated phase of growth and change. "Ambivalence" about existence is resolved and organism identity is defined.

The third response phase of growth occurs when the various units begin to show purpose and functional **integration.** Now the elongated cells of the plant carry water and minerals to the flat leaf cells responsible for photosynthesis. The infant's reach now is for food which she successfully places in her mouth.

Werner, in his *Orthogenetic Principle,* conceptualizes growth taking place in a very similar manner. "Wherever development occurs it proceeds from a state of relative globality and lack of differentiation to a state of increased differentiation, articulation, and hierarchic integration" (Werner, 1957, p. 126). The constructivism school of philosophy views the Orthogenetic Principle (and thus, the concepts of growth and learning developed by Lewin) as the manner in which the cognitive system develops and sustains itself (Delia, O'Keefe & O'Keefe, 1982).

The constructivists view mental constructs as the most basic units of cognitive organization. The most general units of cognitive organization are called "interpretive schemes" (Delia et al., 1982), similar to Kelley's causal schemes constructs (1971) and Heider's balance schemes (1958). The "interpretive scheme" is simply a concept or classification method that people use to make sense of the world.

The "interpretive scheme" becomes one of the main units of focus in cognitive therapy (J. Beck, 1995). The focus is also on the emotional and behavior units that interact with the mental or cognitive units or interpretive schemes used to make sense of the world (Delia, et al., 1982). These cognitive constructs are continually developing and become the basis through which the individuals make their adjustment to the world. Their development is in accord with the process of change and growth described above by Lewin and Werner. Thus, we can use the Orthogenetic Principle in both understanding how individuals develop and change their specific units of cognitive responding and behavior. Or, we can use this principle in understanding how people respond in general to education and treatment processes.

Utilizing the concepts of the process of growth and change provided by Lewin and Werner's Orthogenetic Principle, Wanberg (1983, 1990; Wanberg & Milkman, 1998) developed a cyclical or spiral model to explain the process of therapeutic change and a counseling skill structure to facilitate change. This is illustrated in *Figure 11.1*. The value of this model for growth and change is that it occurs over the course of learning and treatment; or it occurs within any one segment of learning and change. It is not a linear model that describes change in a stepwise fashion. Rather, it describes change as spiral in nature, and the model is applied to each individual growth experience.

Within the framework of DWI education and treatment, we see this process taking place for the client. First, there is the global, undifferentiated phases of unpacking. The client globally responds to the DWI arrest with undifferentiated response. Or, when going to education or treatment, clients begin hearing information and share their stories. There is always a global, undifferentiated, and even confused response to all of the new events at certain points of dealing with the DWI episode.

Second, there is the sorting out phase. With the arrest event, the client understands the charges, gets detoxed, calls a lawyer, makes decisions about contacting a family member, and begins to sort out various responses that can be made. As clients experience education and treatment, they hear specific information about AOD use, about impaired driving behavior, receive feedback about their own story, and begin to label and identify thoughts, feelings and behaviors.

Third, there is the acting on the story and integrating the events. With respect to the arrest event, the client hires an attorney, the responses of family members are accepted and life is pulled back together with certain decision responses. The client enters education and treatment (new event that takes him or her through the three phases again). Now, as a consequence of getting feedback, understanding and learning cognitive and relationship coping skills, these skills are applied, impaired driving behavior is prevented, driving privileges are restored, and irresponsible thinking and errors in logic are replaced so as to lead to more positive outcomes.

Thus, the phasic-spiral learning and change process occurs with both micro and macro life events. It is a process that occurs within the client's education and treatment experiences. These phases of unpacking (client receives information or client telling story), sorting out (client hearing story) and integrating (client acting on his or her story) may: 1) occur around one topic or issue in a session; 2) occur several times in the course of one session; 3) occur over several sessions around one theme, problem or topic; or 4) be descriptive of the client's total treatment experience, e.g., over the entire CBT (cognitive-behavioral treatment) program.

The spiral concept illustrates that the client never returns to the same place, but each cycle moves the client further away from the baseline conditions that brought him or her into treatment.

Thus, the client may relapse, but if therapeutic intervention and change are effective, the relapse does not take the client back to the pre-treatment level of adjustment.

FIGURE 11.1

The Cyclical Process and Change in Treatment

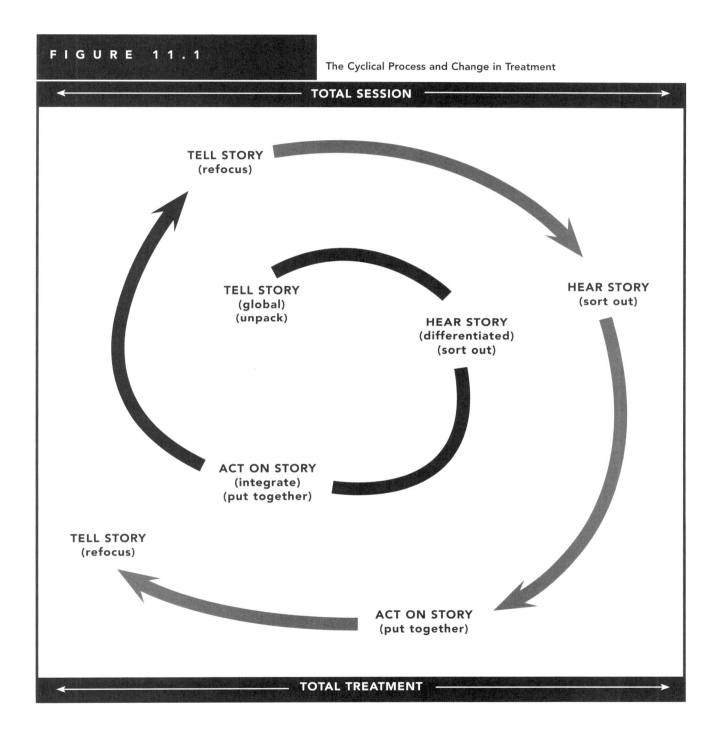

Facilitating the Client Through Stages of Change

The **third core strategy** of DWC is when clients experience the process of learning and change, they go through specific stages of change. In our model, we identify three stages of change: *Challenge to Change, Commitment to Change, and Ownership of Change.* These stages integrate the more traditional stages developed by Prochaska and associates (Connors, Donovan & DiClemente, 2001; Prochaska & DiClemente, 1992; Prochaska, DiClemente & Norcross, 1992). The six stages of this transtheoretical model of how people change addictive lifestyles will be briefly reviewed.

At the **precontemplative stage,** clients are resistive, do not process information about their problems, and give little or no thought or energy to self-evaluation or serious change in their behavior. Clients in the **contemplative** stage give some thought to change, but take little action to change. Clients are ambivalent about change but **are** more open to consciousness-raising techniques such as information feedback and interpretations and are more likely to respond to educational procedures. There is an increased self-evaluation, awareness of problems and a greater openness as to how these problems impacted others. If the ambivalence about change is resolved, this stage becomes a turning point for the client.

As clients move into the **determination or preparation** for change (or treatment) stage they continue to increase the use of cognitive, affective and valuative processes of change. In this stage, clients begin to take steps towards using specific techniques to reduce their use of substances and to control their unique situations with methods other than using substances.

In the **action** stage, a sense of self-direction and self-liberation begins to develop. There is greater internalization of self-determination and self-regulation and more openness to using reinforcement tools and techniques to change behavior. There is an increased reliance on support and understanding from significant others and helping relationships. The development of alternative responses to substance use is an important part of this stage.

The maintenance stage involves the prevention of relapse through the development and reinforcement of alternative responses. Strategies to reinforce established changes and stimulus control (e.g., urge to drink when with friends) are used. There is a commitment to therapy and receiving support from significant others and a continued practice of established skills to manage potential relapse are all a part of this phase. Self takes on a greater value and change supporters are an important part of this process.

Prochaska and Diclemente (1992) have postulated **relapse** as a sixth stage where the individual begins to engage in behaviors and thinking that indicate a process of relapse or where the individual relapses into the full pattern of use. In this model, relapse is recognized as normal in the recovery process, i.e., "each slip brings you closer to recovery." Rather than inviting clients to relapse, the aforementioned phrase may simply prevent patients and staff from demoralization when unsteadiness or backsliding occurs.

The Wanberg and Milkman (1998) three stage model integrates many of the concepts of the Prochaska & DiClemente model. These three stages are integrated into the process and structure of therapeutic growth and change as described above. These three stages will be discussed within the framework of the DWC impaired driving education and treatment protocols.

1. The Global and Undifferentiated Response - Challenge to Change

The initial phase of growth and change finds the client in a global and undifferentiated response. At the global phase of learning, clients are presented with material and specific skills are used that facilitate self-disclosure - to get clients to tell their story or at least facilitate the clients' awareness of their story - what is going on with them. Both information given to clients and their self-disclosure should be at their level of cognitive organization.

Clients differ with respect to the degree of global, undifferentiated states they are in when entering DWI intervention. In this phase of learning and change some clients are defensive and resist self-disclosing and sharing. Individuals in a highly defensive state or who are experiencing considerable anxiety or stress are often unable to get thoughts and feelings into organized mental and verbal components. Although this is often interpreted as resistance to change or ambivalence about changing, it is best viewed as a phase in the learning process and an essential step that people go through when making changes. Other clients may do just the opposite and openly share and there may even be a spurting forth of material that, at the most severe level of dysfunction, may be disconnected and uncontrolled.

DWC education is the **Challenge to Change** phase of DWI intervention. It helps clients work through the global, undifferentiated phase of intervention, and challenges them to listen to information relevant to their AOD use and impaired driving. It also challenges them to disclose their own AOD use and impaired driving history. Although the education component of DWC represents this challenge phase, as the client moves through DWC education, education and therapy become integrated, and the therapeutic experience of *self-disclosing* begins to lead the client to a greater awareness of the need to change.

The overall goal of the *Challenge* phase is to help clients develop a basic trust in and rapport with the purpose of DWC and in the provider delivering the program so as to effectively motivate clients to begin engaging in the learning and change process. The objectives of this phase are:

▶ to build rapport and trust so as to allow clients to openly share inner feelings and thoughts and to tell their stories;

▶ to help clients develop a core knowledge base in the areas of impaired driving, AOD abuse, the process of change and, the cognitive-behavioral basis of change;

▶ to help clients set their goals of relapse and recidivism prevention;

▶ to help clients develop an awareness of their own cognitive sets and overt behaviors in the areas of DWI and AOD abuse and then motivating them to

commit to making changes and shifts in these cognitive sets and in DWI and AOD behavior emerging from these sets;

▶ to provide clients with the cognitive and behavioral concepts and tools of relapse and recidivism prevention;

▶ to help clients, through a climate of trust, to disclose critical information about self including their impaired driving conduct and their AOD use and abuse patterns; and

▶ to prepare clients for a commitment to change.

An underlying premise of the Challenge phase is that the first step in change is self-disclosure which leads to self-awareness. Self-disclosure is enhanced through the use of motivational enhancement and client-centered skills to be discussed below.

The counseling skills used to facilitate the Challenge phase of intervention and change are based on the skill categories of giving information through interactive learning approaches, attending to and inviting clients to share, and through the completion of work sheets that challenge them to self-disclose and to share. These skills facilitate change in the undifferentiated, global phase of growth. Utilization of these skills helps clients to effectively share and express concerns and problems, lower defenses, and experience a release of cognitive and affective material. This provides the basis for the next phase of growth, differentiation of feelings, thoughts and behaviors. It is a necessary step to cognitive-behavioral change.

The **Challenge** phase begins with the screening and assessment process which challenges clients to self-disclose through formal, psychometric methods and through structured interviews. Yet, assessment of clients occurs in each session as clients explore and share their past AOD abuse and impaired driving history and their current thoughts, beliefs, attitudes and emotions in areas other than AOD use and impaired driving.

From the Prochaska and DiClemente model, the global, undifferentiated and "unpacking" phase of growth and the challenge stage represents the precontemplative and contemplative stages of change.

The education protocols (e.g., *Level II Education*) represent the challenge to change phase of DWC, particularly in the early lessons of these protocols.

2. The Differentiation Response - Commitment to Change

Once clients have been exposed to some key concepts of AOD use, impaired driving and how people change and once they begin to "unpack" the thoughts and feelings related to the treatment focus, the differentiation process can unfold. This is a sorting out and labeling process. Thoughts, core beliefs and feelings are identified and issues and concerns are then explored in greater depth. The feedback loop is the critical experience for the client in this phase and is the key process through which the clients hear their story and their dilemmas. Through the feedback loop, clients also begin to "hear and see" their problems, dysfunctions and pathological responses to the world. The defensive system begins to open up and allow increased self-awareness and self-understanding, critical to the growth and change process.

There are several methods in DWC that facilitate this feedback loop. Clients receive feedback from the provider, from peers and from the work sheets and exercises they complete in the program.

DWC Therapy is designed to move the client through the differentiation phase of learning and change and reinforces commitment to change. Thus, we call this the **commitment phase** of intervention. The awareness of needed growth and change occurs during this phase; but more than this, this phase is designed to motivate clients to make specific and clear changes. Although this commitment begins in the education protocols of DWC, the commitment to change is bound up in the *DWC Therapy* protocol. In this phase, both therapeutic and correctional confrontation are used (see the discussion on integrating correctional and therapeutic confrontation below).

In the *Commitment to Change* stage, clients take action in making cognitive and behavioral changes. This stage is facilitated through an in-depth assessment to enhance the clients' awareness of their life-situation problems, of their AOD use

patterns, of their cognitive schemes and behavioral patterns associated with DWI and AOD use and to identify their unique cognitive and behavioral patterns. Clients then engage in specific coping and responsibility skills training experiences (e.g., intrapersonal, interpersonal and community responsibility skill development) to bring about shifts in cognitive schemes and actual behaviors associated with impaired driving and AOD abuse. This phase is devoted to testing out and practicing cognitive and behavioral changes. The principles and methods of preventing relapse and recidivism are continually practiced throughout this phase of intervention.

The overall goal is to strengthen the client's commitment to change through strengthening and enhancing the basic skills essential for changing patterns of AOD use and impaired driving. The treatment process also focuses on other psychosocial problems and changes. The following are the more specific objectives of this phase of intervention and stage of change.

 ▶ Clients develop, through self-disclosure and intensive feedback, an awareness, understanding and clear recognition of their **patterns of thinking and behavior** in the areas of impaired driving, AOD use and abuse, high risk exposures that trigger relapse and recidivism, and how unique patterns of thinking, feeling and perceiving lead to involvement in impaired driving and AOD abuse.

 ▶ Clients learn and demonstrate skills in cognitive self-control, managing and coping with relationships and community responsibility.

 ▶ As a result of developing an in-depth awareness of their impaired driving and AOD use patterns and through coping and social skills training, the client commits to engaging in specific patterns of change so as to enhance self-efficacy in preventing relapse and recidivism and commit to changes that strengthen prosocial behaviors and AOD problem-free living.

The skill structure for the **Commitment** phase includes the skill categories of feedback skills (reflection, paraphrasing, summarization, change clarification) and confrontation skills (therapeutic and correctional). Through feedback clarification, the clients begin to hear their own story, sort out the feelings, thoughts and behaviors involved in dysfunctional and pathological responding and begin to develop a clear perspective of needed growth and change. This process increases self-awareness and self-understanding.

Therapeutic and correctional confrontational skills are used in this phase. Herein lies the difference between correctional and therapeutic treatment. DWC is designed to blend these two approaches in the treatment of the DWI client. The differences between these two skills and the blending process (an important component of SAO treatment) is discussed below.

Assessment in this phase of treatment is more in-depth and differential. The results of assessment are used in the feedback process to help clients sort out their own patterns of DWI behavior, AOD use, feelings, thoughts and emotions.

From the Prochaska et al. (1992) model, this phase represents the determination and the action stage of change. Clients resolve the ambivalence to committing to change and some changes have been made.

The core 21 Session *DWC Therapy* program represents the commitment phase of DWC. Yet, there are elements of the therapy part of DWC intervention in *DWC Education,* and there is a blending of the education and therapy in both *DWC Education* and *DWC Therapy.*

3. The Integration Response - Ownership of Change

The **integration** and **Ownership** phase of intervention represents the strengthening and maintenance of the changes that have been made. Clients now put together the meaning of the intervention experience and demonstrate consistency in changes they have made. Although the change goals may still be those of some external system - the court, family, marriage, the motor vehicle authority, criminal justice system - what is important is that there is not only consistent demonstration of change, but clients internalize the change and claim it to be theirs.

Data for these changes come from client self-reports in the lessons and sessions. These include reports of commitment and ownership of never driving while impaired, of having not had problems related to alcohol use for several months, of improved communication with spouse, increased ability to handle stress, etc. Data around these changes are observed during the core 21 session *DWC Therapy* program, and during *DWC Education.* The difference between commitment and ownership is that clients talk about "owning" changes and the desire for these change independent of expectations from external systems.

The Ownership phase of intervention is the integrative phase of growth and change. Clients integrate what they have learned in such a manner that there is consistent involvement in self-control and positive outcomes. There is also a demonstration of self-efficacy or self-mastery over thoughts and situations that are high risk for recidivism and relapse.

In this **Ownership** phase, intervention builds on the client's increased self-awareness and the coping and change skills the client has learned and practiced in DWC. The provider (used synonymously with the term therapeutic educator or counselor) helps clients tie together various feelings, thoughts and behaviors that have emerged in the overall treatment experience. The provider then reinforces and strengthens improvement and change in specific areas. Relapse and recidivism prevention training is continued in this phase. Clients are taught to utilize community resources and self-help groups in maintaining change. The following are the more specific objectives of this phase.

▶ Help clients take ownership of these changes and demonstrate maintenance of these changes over time.

▶ Help clients develop a sense of confidence about not engaging in impaired driving behavior and have ownership of their recidivism prevention goals.

- Help clients prevent cognitive recidivism and relapse from manifesting into overt conduct and behavior.

- Help clients utilize community support and reinforcement resources to maintain change.

- Clients will, as a result of the commitment to and ownership of change, provide role modeling for other clients who are engaged in the process of change.

The counselor skill categories used to help the client to achieve change ownership are change clarification, change confrontation and change reinforcement. Clients are confronted with the discrepancies between behaviors, feelings and thoughts (i.e., "you say you don't want to drink, but you keep spending time in the bars with your friends!"). Changes that can be made are clarified, and when change is noted, then this change is reinforced through the use of change reinforcement skills.

Important in this phase of intervention is the concept of **attribution.** The ideal model for change is one that facilitates change from within the individual. The most effective changes occur when clients attribute change to themselves, or when the changes are attributed to an inner motivation by the client (Kanfer, 1970. 1975, 1986). This means taking ownership for the changes that do occur. The internalization of change is most apt to occur when the feedback reinforcement skills are utilized in such a manner that clients feel that changes are due to their own efforts.

In this phase of treatment, the client experiences consistent cognitive, affective and behavioral changes, and begins to feel the strength of the maintenance of these changes. The extended therapy program of *DWC Therapy* (Tracks B through D) is the core of the ownership phase of DWC intervention.

The **Ownership** phase begins in the education component of DWC intervention and continues throughout the DWC protocols. The essence of the **Ownership** Phase of DWC is found in the *therapy projects,* in doing homework willingly for both the therapy projects and for the core *DWC Therapy*

sessions, for voluntary engagement in community reinforcement resources and in modeling and mentoring others who are going through the same DWI intervention experiences.

Within the context of the Prochaska et al. (1992) model, this phase of treatment represents both the action and maintenance stages of change.

Building a Knowledge Base

The fourth core strategy is helping the client build a knowledge base through a learner-centered model of education.

An important strategy in the DWC intervention program is providing a working knowledge base for clients. This is an important role of the therapeutic educator (provider, counselor, therapist). However, as alluded to above, this is not a role found in the tradition of pedagogy, which, in its literal translation, is the art and science of helping children learn (Knowles, 1980). As DeMuro (1997) points out, adult education is far different from childhood education, and this difference is very important in the education component of DWI intervention programs.

At the turn of the last century, many educators began deviating from the traditional approaches of pedagogy and began to develop approaches that led to the founding of the adult education movement (DeMuro,1997) and to the concept of andragogy, a term coined in the mid 1960s by European adult educators (Knowles, 1980). This distinction became necessary, as DeMuro points out, in that an adult "enters a learning situation with his or her own complete set of values, beliefs, attitudes, needs, life experiences, self-concept, and perceptions of life" (1997, p. 59). This is no less true for the DWIO who enters the DWC education and therapy programs. The DWIO is an adult learner.

Thus, when creating the learning environment for the DWIO, it is important to acknowledge that the learner is an adult with vast experiences and background and cognitive sets that have been operating for some time. Learning must be interactive, experiential and clients must have a sense of personal identification with the material being learned.

Developing the Intervention Relationship: Motivational Enhancement and Building Therapeutic Alliance

The **fifth** core strategy of DWC is building a relationship of trust and rapport with clients - or the therapeutic alliance.

As noted several times, most DWI clients initially present with a considerable degree of defensiveness and resistance to involvement with DWI intervention. Developing a working relationship with DWI clients requires adroit utilization of the skills of motivational enhancement and therapeutic alliance building. There is a great deal of research evidence supporting the efficacy of motivational enhancement as an important component in building the therapist-client relationship and implementing treatment readiness and change in alcohol abuse clients (e.g., Miller & Rollnick, 1991, 2002; Project Match Group, 1997).

The necessity for the use of motivational enhancement methods is found in client resistance and ambivalence. Most individuals with AOD problems display an ambivalence about changing their lives or at least, changing the behavior patterns that lead to AOD use problems (Miller & Rollnick, 2002) such as impaired driving. Resolving ambivalence and resistance to these patterns, and helping clients to develop an internal sense of readiness, openness and responsiveness to treatment are primary objectives of the early phases of any intervention program. Some of the important elements of building the intervention relationship and enhancing motivation for involvement in education and therapy are explored.

1. Therapeutic Stance

The provider's therapeutic stance exerts large effects on the outcome of treatment (Gurmon & Messer, 2003). The therapeutic stance underlies the intervention relationship and motivates clients to change. It is based on the core elements of the client-centered therapeutic relationship: warmth, empathy, genuineness and positive regard (Rogers, 1951, 1957). There is a long research history supporting the finding that the degree of empathy shown by counselors during treatment is a significant predictor of treatment efficacy. Style of relating becomes apparent early in the intervention encounter and can impact retention, even in one introductory session. With respect to AOD clients, Miller and Rollnick (1991, 2002) show that successful therapy is predicated upon counselors providing clients with three critical conditions: accurate empathy, non-possessive warmth; and genuineness. These effective counselor features are discussed in more detail in chapter 12.

2. The Therapeutic Alliance

Therapeutic alliance builds on but goes beyond the core elements of the therapeutic stance that underlie motivation enhancement. Therapeutic alliance involves a collaborative relationship, affective bonding, rapport building, and a mutual understanding and sharing of the intervention goals between the client and the provider (Bordin, 1979; Conners et al., 1997; Raue, Goldfried & Barkham, 1997).

As will be discussed in Chapter 12, one of the robust predictors of treatment retention and outcome is the relationship between the client and the provider, regardless of the therapeutic orientation or treatment approach (Bachelor, 1991, 1995; Barber, et al., 2001; Connors, et al., 1997; Gaston, 1990; Hartley & Strupp, 1983; Horvath & Symonds, 1991; Krupnick et al., 1996; Martin, Garske & Davis, 2000; Raue & Goldfried, 1994; Raue et al., 1997; Zuroff et al., 2000). Results from these various studies also indicate that client ratings of therapeutic alliance are more predictive of outcome than therapist ratings; therapeutic alliance scores tend to be higher for cognitive-behavioral sessions than for sessions conducted under a psychodynamic-interpersonal orientation; that the efficacy of therapeutic alliance is found across various therapeutic approaches and modalities; and that the positive therapeutic alliance from the early part of treatment predicts positive outcome in psychotherapy.

Conners et al.'s (1997) examination of the therapeutic alliance data gathered in Project MATCH (Project MATCH Research Group, 1993, 1997) revealed a consistent positive relationship between therapeutic alliance and treatment participation and positive drinking-related outcomes, regardless of whether the rating was based on client self-report or on therapist-report. This finding was consistent across treatment approaches, modalities and different nosological groupings and clearly indicates the crucial importance of this component in the treatment process.

The importance - even necessity - of developing rapport and trust in the therapeutic relationship and therapeutic alliance was established very early in psychosocial therapies. Freud made it clear that treatment should proceed when the therapist has effectively established rapport with the client (Freud, 1913). Such rapport is established when the therapist shows interest in the psychological condition of the patient but also shows personal concern for the patient (Freud, 1893-1895, p. 265). He notes that the initial phase of treatment will go well when the therapist demonstrates concern and interest and "sympathetic understanding" (Freud, 1913, pp. 139-140).

3. The use of Reflective Confrontation in Managing Resistance and Ambivalence

Developing a positive intervention relationship and building rapport and trust with the client depends on how client resistance, defensiveness and ambivalence are managed. This management is of particular importance in the early stages of intervention.

We distinguish reflective therapeutic confrontation from the traditional methods of confrontational therapy and cohersive intervention in managing resistance and "denial." The traditional methods were previously touted as the treatment choice for substance abuse, often resulting in increasing client resistance and defensiveness. Bill Wilson, one of the co-founders of Alcoholic Anonymous, held that intervention works best on the basis of attraction and support. Wilson advocated that alcoholics be treated with an approach that "would contain no basis for contention or argument ... Most of us sense that real tolerance of other people's shortcoming and viewpoints, and a respect for their opinions are attitudes which make us more helpful to others" (Alcoholics Anonymous, 1976, p. 19-20). These words are of particular relevance to the DWIO.

According to Miller and Rollnick (1991, 2002) research does not support the common belief that people with AOD problems display pathological lying or an abnormal level of self-deception. Nor does self-labelling promote more effective recovery. In fact Sovereign and Miller (1987) found that problem drinkers randomly assigned to confrontational counseling showed a far greater incidence of arguing, denying or changing the topic than those given a client-oriented motivational enhancement approach.

The most effective way to manage client resistance, defensiveness and ambivalence is to **first** encourage the client to share thoughts and feelings of resistance and defensiveness and **second,** to use reflective-acceptance skills to help clients hear their resistance. These are the two basic steps of the therapeutic change process as described above, and represent the elements of reflective or therapeutic confrontation (Wanberg, 1974, 1983, 1990; Wanberg & Milkman, 1998). These are the key components in Miller and Rollnick's motivational interviewing model (Miller & Rollnick, 1991, 2002). This involves providing the environment of acceptance for clients to share their thoughts and feelings and then reflecting the client's specific statements of anger, resistance and ambivalence. Miller and Rollnick's (2002) clinical principles of *avoid argumentation, develop discrepancy and roll with resistance* underlie the reflective-confrontation approach in dealing with client resistance and defensiveness.

4. Enhancing Interest in Change

Motivational strategies are based on the compensatory attribution model of treatment (Brickman et al., 1982) which sees the client as having the power to influence change and focuses on building client self-efficacy and responsibility in the change process. Motivation is a state of readiness and openness or eagerness to participate in a change process. Miller, Zweben, et al. (1994, p. 2) have summarized the research to date on what motivates problem drinkers to change. Their work on *Motivational Enhancement Therapy* (MET) highlights the effectiveness of relatively brief treatment for problem drinkers. The elements that the authors consider necessary to induce change are summarized by the acronym FRAMES:

▶ FEEDBACK of personal risk impairment;

▶ Emphasis on personal RESPONSIBILITY for change;

- ADVICE;
- A MENU of alternative change options;
- Therapist EMPATHY;
- Facilitation of client SELF-EFFICACY or optimism.

Therapeutic interventions containing some or all of these motivational elements have been demonstrated to be effective in "initiating treatment and in reducing long-term alcohol use, alcohol-related problems, and health consequences of drinking," (Miller, Zweben, et al., 1994, p. 2).

An important focus in enhancing motivation and interest for change in the DWI clients is that of developing "a more enlightened view of their self-interest and recognize that it is in their own best interest to anticipate the long-term consequences of their actions...." (Freeman et al., 1990, p 229). This model is designed to help the DWIO to control impulsivity long enough to perceive the consequences of drinking and driving as not as rewarding as the long term consequences of prosocial behavior. In essence, motivation is enhanced by helping the DWIOs take a long-term view of their self interest. This can only be done when the counselor takes a *collaborative approach to treatment* (a key component of CBT) and a trust-based working relationship has been developed. These two objectives of treatment - *building a collaborative relationship and helping the client take a long-term view of self-interest* - are primary focuses in the DWC education lessons and the treatment sessions.

The Cognitive-Behavioral Model for Change: Underlying Assumptions and the Process of Change in Impaired Driving Cognitive-Behavioral Intervention

The **sixth core strategy** of DWC, and the platform for implementing growth and change, is the **Cognitive-behavioral** (CB) approach. *Chapter 9* provided a review of the historical development and the main principles of the CB approach. From that review, a CB model for the education and treatment of the driving while impaired offender (DWIO) was developed. This model is a core strategy of the DWC education and treatment protocols.

1. CB assumptions for explaining impaired driving conduct and its intervention

The CB assumptions underlying AOD misuse and impaired driving behavior is that cognitive structures and processes operate in such a manner so as to prevent self-control over the use of substances and responsible behavior in the community. AOD abuse and impaired driving conduct are consequences of the individual's cognitive organization and cognitive processes through which these structures are expressed.

The CB approach to education and treatment is to modify and change the *proximal* or short-term structures which we call thought habits or automatic thoughts, e.g., outcome expectancies, that lead to the loss of control of AOD use and irresponsible behavior (e.g., impaired driving) in the community, and then moves to working on changing the *distal* or long-term structures, e.g., beliefs. This change process involves:

- identifying the thought habits or automatic thoughts that lead to substance abuse outcomes and impaired driving;

- changing thought habits or proximal structures to those that lead to self-control and adaptive prosocial outcomes;

- helping the client, through changing the proximal structures, identify the more distal and ingrained structures of rules, values, attitudes and beliefs that reinforce the thought habits or proximal structures that led to substance use problems and impaired driving outcomes;

- challenging old beliefs and transforming and replacing these beliefs and assumptions into a belief system that generates and strengthens the thought habits or proximal structures that lead to self-control and prosocial outcomes; and

- having the client practice these changes so that both the behaviors and cognitive changes are reinforced.

2. Cognitive Structures and Processes that are the Focus of CB Change

The CB model developed for the DWC education and treatment protocol is built upon three levels of cognitive structures. This model utilizes a combination of the work of Seligman et al. (2001), J. Beck (1995), Beck (1976, 1996) and Bandura (1977a). These structures have been discussed in Chapter 9, but will be reiterated as the essential focuses in DWI intervention.

Level 1: Proximal structures. In the DWC model, these are referred to as thought habits and in the literature as automatic thoughts. Seligman et al. (2001) refer to these as short-term, more surface cognitive processes. We take these structures and draw upon Bandura's work (1977a) to expand them to five essential proximal structures.

> **Outcome expectancies** are the individual's judgment about whether the performance of a particular behavior will lead to a certain outcome. It is the knowledge of what to do and what will result. If the behavior, and the outcome expectancy thoughts are fulfilled, both the thoughts and behavior are reinforced. Example: "If I take a drink, I'll relax."

> **Efficacy expectations** refer to the individual's assessment of his or her ability to successfully execute a particular behavior. This is the belief that one can carry out a certain course of action to get a certain outcome. If there is the belief that one can perform a particular behavior, then most likely one will engage in that behavior. If the behavior is performed successfully, this reinforces the efficacy expectation. Example: "If I hold my cool, I won't get into an argument with my boss - and I can hold my cool."

> **Appraisals** are proximal structures that evaluate the value and meaning of what we are experiencing and our responses to those experiences. These can become distorted resulting in thinking errors. Examples: "I feel better because she respects my opinion." "I must be a failure because I can't hold a job."

> **Attributions** are explanations of why things happen or the explanations of outcomes. They might be internalized, "I'm responsible for the accident," or externalized, "The reason I got the DUI is the cops were after me."

> **Decisions** are structures that actually lead to the behavior that can result in good or bad outcomes. This is an important component of Marlatt's (1985b) relapse prevention model, and represents the individual's conscious choice to think in a certain way to take a certain action. It provides the basis of the underlying philosophy of freedom of choice in change and in self-determination and self-control.

Level II: Intermediary or mediating structures. J. Beck (1995) refers to these as intermediate beliefs. We will refer to these as go-between structures or mediating structures. They mediate between the underlying core beliefs and the thought habits or automatic thoughts. They orient us with our inside world or the outside world. Some important intermediary structures noted in the literature are attitudes, values and rules. We focus on these in DWC education and treatment.

> **Attitudes** position us for or against a situation or person. Attitudes cause us to orient ourselves in a certain way to something or someone outside ourselves or for or against ourselves. They are usually emotionally charged and we often see them as good or bad. Examples: "I hate myself." "The world is a crappy place to live in."

> **Values** are what are important or worthwhile in our relationship with ourselves or the outside world. Our values determine what we invest in or relate to and determine the strength of that investment. If we value family, then we will invest ourselves in family. If we value work, then we will invest ourselves in a positive way in certain jobs or tasks.

> **Rules** direct or control our behaviors in relationship to ourselves and the outside world. If we have an internal rule that "I will not steal," that rule will determine how we associate ourselves with people and with systems. The person who has a strict rule

of "never cheating," will point out to the waiter that the dessert was left off of the bill. Rules are important in mediating core beliefs into thought habits or proximal structures. For example, a core belief that "I am an honest person," will translate into a rule of "I will never cheat someone," leading to the automatic thought "I need to tell the waiter" the dessert was left off of the bill.

Level III: Core beliefs and assumptions. Although some put assumptions as the intermediary structure (J. Beck, 1995), assumptions and core beliefs are used synonymously in this model. Core beliefs are concepts that are used to judge or evaluate ourselves, situations, people, the world. Beliefs bond us to ourselves or to the outside world. We see these as the "truth," or a "conviction." Core beliefs are usually 100 percent and they are deeply ingrained. There are two kinds of core beliefs or assumptions that become the focus in CB treatment of impaired driving offenders.

▶ **Beliefs about self** bond us to our sense of self. They include the core belief of self-efficacy, self-importance and self-value. Self-efficacy is an important focus in treating substance abuse and antisocial behavior (e.g., impaired driving). Examples of these beliefs about self are: "I'm a good person," "I feel I can handle life's problems," "I've made a contribution," "I can't handle life," and "I'm worthless."

▶ **Beliefs about the world** bond us to the outside world. They involve a basic assumption about how we see and perceive the world. The core beliefs of "the sacredness of life," "right to make choices," "people are created equal," "all persons should live in a government that is for the people, by the people, of the people." These beliefs are mediated by attitudes, rules and values and surface into automatic thoughts.

Figure 11.2 provides a schematic design for these three levels of cognitive structures. For example, a core belief that one should "treat fellow humans with respect," may be mediated by the rule of being "courteous," and an automatic thought of "I'm sorry when one makes a mistake or offends

someone. Note that in *Figure 11.2*, the base of the pyramid is represented by the core beliefs about self and the world, which are mediated by the intermediary structures to surface in thought habits and automatic thoughts.

3. **Cognitive Processes that Underlie the expression of cognitive structures**

There are important cognitive processes that operate in such a manner as to allow the expression and manifestation of cognitive structures. **Automatic thinking** produces a thinking pattern or thought habit that leads to the mental reactions already formed inside our heads (proximal structures). This is a response to the events that we experience. Automatic thinking lead us to form an opinion about an appraisal and outcome expectancy: "I need a drink and a drink will relax me." **Decision making** is a cognitive process that allows the expression of the decision structure.

Cognitive distorting is a process where our reaction to the outside world leads to thought habits that are errors in judgment about what we are experiencing. "I can't handle things," is an appraisal that may be an error in thinking and needs changing to "I'll try to handle things."

Another cognitive process related to the above structures is **underlying assuming.** This is the operational process through which attitudes, rules, values and core beliefs get expressed. Thought habits or automatic thoughts are manifestations of the process of underlying assuming.

Another cognitive process is the **interaction of thoughts, emotion and behaviors.** Thoughts can lead to emotions and behaviors. However, emotions can lead to behaviors and thoughts; and behaviors can lead to thoughts and emotions. Our starting point in change is with our thoughts. However, we may have to label the emotion first in order to work back to the thought habit that leads to the feelings and outcome behaviors.

The five cognitive processes that underlie the expression of the core cognitive structures are noted in the three-dimensional pyramid of *Figure 11.2.* They are positioned in such a manner to indicate that they provide an essential support to

FIGURE 11.2   Model of Cognitive Structures and Processes

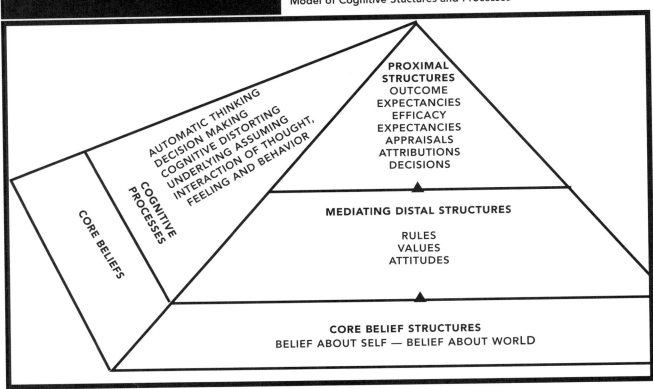

the DWC cognitive structure model.

4. Cognitive Restructuring as a method of Changing Maladaptive Cognitive Structures

As discussed in Chapter 9, there are two traditional focuses in CB learning and change: **Cognitive restructuring** and **interpersonal training.** Cognitive restructuring involves helping clients develop skills to alter the key short term and long term structures that determine feelings and actions. Sometimes we call this **intrapersonal skill** building. Some of the specific methods that are used in changing both the proximal and distal maladaptive cognitive structures are:

- self-talk;
- thought stopping;
- thought replacement;
- changing negative thinking;
- changing thinking errors;
- relaxation skills;
- managing depression; and
- managing guilt, anger, stress.

5. Interpersonal Restructuring

The second focus involved in CB learning and change is on interpersonal and social skills that enhance self-efficacy and lead to positive outcomes. This is the interpersonal restructuring component of CB treatment. This approach focuses on enhancing self-efficacy in interpersonal and social interactions. The specific focus areas of interpersonal or social skills training are:

- communication skills;
- problem solving skills;
- conflict resolution skills; and
- building life-style balances.

The cognitive-behavioral (CB) assumption underlying AOD misuse and impaired driving behavior is that cognitive structures and processes operate in such a manner so as to prevent self-control over the use of substances and responsible behavior in the community. AOD abuse and impaired driving conduct are a consequence of the individual's cognitive organization and cognitive processes through which these structures are expressed.

6. Community and Societal Relationship Restructuring

For impaired driving intervention, the traditional CB focuses of developing self-control through cognitive restructuring and social and interpersonal skill development are not sufficient. In the education and treatment of impaired driving offenders, a third focus is essential: developing skills to enhance prosocial behavior and moral and social responsibility to the community. This is the sociocentric focus in the treatment of the DWIO, discussed in the Summary of Chapter 9.

The issue of moral responsibility and prosocial behavior was an important component of our work, *Criminal Conduct and Substance Abuse Treatment* (Wanberg & Milkman, 1998). Our review of the literature indicates a paucity of material addressing this issue for DWI education and treatment. Up to this date, it is essentially absent in the overall treatment and psychosocial therapies literature, as noted in our Preface and Chapter 9. This is one of the key foundations of impaired driving treatment.

Snortrum and Berger (1989) early on indicated that the variables of "personal morality," which they define as the extent to which a person feels that drinking and driving is morally wrong and "social morality," which they define as the extent to which one's personal friends believe that drinking and driving is morally wrong, are important variables in DWI deterrence.

Mauck and Zagummy (2000) address this issue from a drinking and driving intervention (DDI) research perspective. They state that the one element that has been conspicuously absent from the DDI research has been the role that moral/social obligation plays in the decision to intervene in a potential drunk-driving situation. They found that the level and sense of moral/social obligation on the part of a peer to intervene in drunk driving behavior significantly predicted DDI effort and the subsequent success of DDI.

This approach is based on the idea that cognitive processes and structures are organized and operate in such a manner as to prevent prosocial and morally responsible behavior in the community. This approach involves the restructuring of clients'

relationship with society and the community. Here are some specific CB approaches that address moral responsibility.

- ▶ Managing aggression and preventing violence.
- ▶ Moral development and reasoning.
- ▶ Understanding and practicing empathy.
- ▶ Critical reasoning.
- ▶ Focusing on prosocial activities and behaviors.
- ▶ Role modeling and mentoring.

7. The affective component of the CB approach

Most CB models assume that our thinking can lead to certain emotions that result in certain behavioral outcomes. Some theorists see emotions and feelings as the consequence or outcome that precede the behavior. The basic model in the DWC protocols is that thinking leads to emotions, and these emotions are representations of self-control or lack of self-control. Thus, the automatic thought, "He's cheating me," leads to feelings of "I'm damn mad about that." The next logical consequence is a behavioral response. The CB model identifies a number of core emotions that result from thought habits coming out of intermediary and core beliefs. These are usually anger, guilt, depression or sadness.

8. The CB Model for Change that is the Core of DWC Education and Treatment

The **first assumption of the CB change model** is that patterns of AOD misuse and patterns of impaired driving are determined by the individual's cognitive structures and processes that lead to emotions and feelings and result in overt AOD misuse and impaired driving. Thus, DWC education and treatment is directed at changing the thinking and underlying beliefs resulting in a change in feeling and subsequently bringing about change in behavior.

The **second assumption** is that external events or inside memories and feelings lead to automatic thoughts that are based on core beliefs about self and about the world. A primary focus is to help the client recognize those automatic thoughts and the errors and distortions in thinking associated with those thoughts, and to change the core beliefs and intermediary attitudes, values and rules that underlie the automatic thoughts and thinking distortions. The key guiding principle of DWC education and treatment is that we can have control over our thoughts and feelings - we can change and choose our thoughts and our beliefs. **Cognitive restructuring, interpersonal skill development and community responsibility skills** training are the vehicles through which change is achieved.

The **third assumption** is that automatic thoughts, which are based on core beliefs and attitudes, lead to overt behaviors. The CBT model holds that individuals make conscious choice of their behavioral responses to external events and to their internal thoughts and feelings. Social and community responsibility skills training provide the key interventions in helping clients learn to choose adaptive behaviors to manage outside events and internal feelings.

Finally, the coping actions we choose and the outcomes of those actions reinforce internal thoughts, underlying beliefs and the mediating assumptions that lead to certain outcomes. When the outcomes are positive, they strengthen the cognitive structures leading to the outcomes and reinforce the behavior responses.

Figure 11.3 provides the basic CB model for the process of learning and change used in DWC. *Figure 11.3* also provides an explanation for the two pathways of learning and reinforcement. When certain automatic thoughts (based on underlying beliefs and mediated by attitudes, rules and values) lead to certain behaviors, those behaviors can result in positive adaptive actions or negative adaptive actions. If the action results in a positive outcome, then that behavior gets reinforced, as indicated by the return arrow from positive outcome back to adaptive positive action (upper right corner of *Figure 11.3*).

Note that there is no comparable return arrow in the lower right of *Figure 11.3,* from negative outcomes back to negative maladaptive action. There are return arrows leading back to automatic thoughts from both positive outcomes and negative outcomes. This implies that the automatic thoughts and underlying beliefs can get reinforced, whatever the outcome.

An example related to DWI behavior will illustrate this case - one that is used in the *Participant's Workbook.* A client had a fight with his spouse before going to work. On the way home he thinks (automatic thought - **expectation**), "I'll stop off and have a couple. Make me feel better." Some more automatic thoughts - **appraisals**: "She doesn't care. Nobody cares." Beneath these thoughts and feelings are the long held **beliefs** that "life isn't fair" and "not being cared about." From these beliefs there developed an underlying **attitude**: "To hell with it, the hell with everybody, screw it." This leads to a feeling of discouragement. He then has another automatic thought - **decision**: "I'll just stay here (at the bar) with my 'real' friends, where I'm cared about," (**appraisal**) and he has a couple more. Automatic thought - **expectation**: "I'm not going home now because I'll just get chewed out."

He continues to feel bad and sorry for himself and drinks. He thinks, "I shouldn't drive after having so many," but the **underlying beliefs** of "life isn't fair and not being cared about" and the **underlying attitude** of "screw it," lead to the automatic thoughts - **appraisals**: "I'm not that drunk. I can drive. And anyway, I don't care." **Expectation**: "I won't get busted." But he gets busted, is thrown in jail and charged with a DWI. This event merely strengthens or reinforces this maladaptive thought pattern and strengthens his original thought of "nobody cares." It also strengthens the attitude of "screw it," and the **underlying beliefs**, of "life isn't fair and no one has really cared about me."

Relapse and Recidivism Prevention

DWI intervention is about preventing relapse and recidivism, **the seventh core strategy** of DWC. Clients set their own relapse and recidivism goals, and these goals are continually reevaluated, and the skills of achieving these goals are continually learned and practiced, as clients proceed through the program.

The model for relapse and recidivism is based on Marlatt's model of RP (1985d). This model is dealt with in greater depth in Section III of this *Provider's Guide* and also in the *Participant's Workbook.* It will be briefly presented in this section.

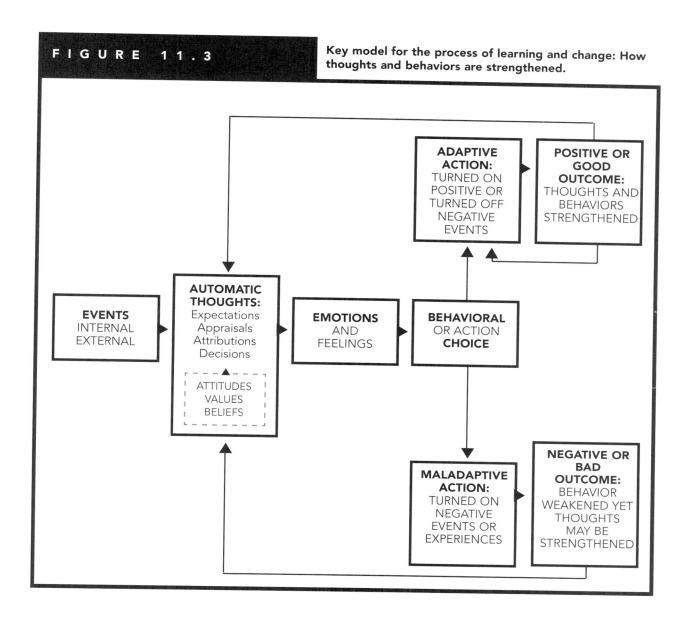

FIGURE 11.3

Key model for the process of learning and change: How thoughts and behaviors are strengthened.

1. Marlatt's Relapse Prevention Model

Relapse prevention (RP) is a CBT self-management program "that combines behavioral skill training procedures with cognitive intervention techniques to assist individuals in maintaining desired behavioral changes" (Marlatt & Barrett, 1994, p. 285). Clients are taught new coping responses (e.g., alternatives to addictive behavior); they learn to modify maladaptive beliefs and expectancies concerning their behavior; they learn to change personal habits and lifestyles. The Marlatt RP model has been used as adjuncts to treatment programs and also as a stand-alone program for the cessation and maintenance phases (Dimeff & Marlatt, 1995). A stand-alone Marlatt RP program is summarized in Dimeff & Marlatt (1995).

In the Marlatt model, presented in *Figure 11.4*, relapse is defined "as any violation of a self-imposed rule regarding a particular behavior" (Dimeff & Marlatt, 1995). The model stresses that relapse must be reframed from the traditional "all-or nothing" view to the view that it is a transitional process in which slips or lapses may or may not result in a full return to the level of the pretreatment substance use pattern. A single occurrence is different from a full-blown relapse (Dimeff & Marlatt, 1995).

As a person develops control over the behavior targeted for change, there is an increase in self-control and self-efficacy. The self-efficacy is strengthened over time. Self-control becomes challenged when the person encounters a high risk (HR) situation -

a situation where the person's sense of self-control is threatened. HR situations can be external or internal cues that can set off relapse. If the person copes effectively with the HR situation, self-control and self-efficacy increase. If coping is ineffective, self-efficacy decreases. The first step in Marlatt's RP model is to help the client identify HR situations. The second step is to help the client build coping and problem solving skills to deal with HR situations without returning to the use of substances.

Another important component of the Marlatt RP model is to help the client deal with a lapse so that it does not lead to a full blown relapse. The model uses the rule violation effect (RVE) to explain how lapses can lead to full relapse and help the client manage lapses or slips (Curry & Marlatt, 1987; Dimeff & Marlatt, 1995; Marlatt & Gordon, 1985). RVE is the result of violating the individual's rule to change target behaviors and will be discussed in more detail below. When RVE refers specifically to abstinence, then it is appropriate to use the expression abstinence violation effect (AVE), a term used earlier in the Marlatt model (personal communication with Marlatt, 1995).

Finally, the Marlatt Relapse Prevention (RP) model focuses on helping the client to deal with life-style imbalances that occur between the individual's perceived external demands or "shoulds" and perceive desires or "wants." Strong imbalances in the direction of "shoulds" may lead to strong feelings of being deprived and resulting desire to indulge (even to the point of a craving or urge). The goal is to help the client build a balanced life-style which ultimately helps the client deal with HR situations that can lead to relapse. The Marlatt RP model has developed Global Intervention procedures aimed at helping the client to build a balanced life-style. This includes developing coping skills to effectively manage factors that are precursors to high-risk situations and relapse (Dimeff & Marlatt, 1995).

2. The DWC Model for Impaired Driving Intervention

Wanberg and Milkman (1998) have presented evidence of the robust relationship between AOD use and abuse and criminal conduct. The relationship between AOD misuse and impaired driving behav-

ior is even more clear - they are always linked. Thus, applying the Marlatt model for relapse prevention to recidivism prevention is appropriate. We are extrapolating on our application of the Marlatt model to criminal conduct recidivism (Wanberg & Milkman, 1998) to its application to impaired driving recidivism. Impaired driving recidivism is engaging in driving conduct when an individual's BAC level exceeds legal limits or if the person is impaired by the presence of drugs other than alcohol.

There are a number of elements of the Marlatt model that we have enhanced so as to best explain recidivism and recidivism prevention. These are briefly reviewed and covered in more detail as we present the lessons and sessions of the *Participant's Workbook* and Section III of the *Provider's Guide*.

We want the clients to see that the relapse and recidivism (R&R) are gradual processes of erosion and that the first steps in the erosion process are to engage in **high risk (HR) exposures: HR thinking** (I'll get drunk); **high risk situations** (drinking soft drinks with friends at the bar); **high-risk feelings** (intense anger). Thoughts about AOD use that would lead to further AOD use problems and thoughts about driving while impaired are initial steps of relapse and recidivism (R&R).

Relapse begins with HR exposures which lead to use or a use pattern that leads to problem use. Recidivism begins when the individual engages in HR exposures that lead to impaired driving. Thus, relapse and recidivism (R&R) refer to lapsing back to thoughts, feelings and actions that lead to impaired driving, to AOD use problems. Thus, R&R does not simply mean that the person has engaged in impaired driving or has engaged in a pattern of AOD abuse.

It is important to distinguish between lapse and relapse as these apply to drinking and impaired driving. A lapse may be any drinking or engaging in a drinking pattern that could lead to further problem drinking. We ask clients to determine their own goal of relapse: no use or non-problem use. In the DWC model, we accept the client's lapse and relapse patterns and work with these in the education and treatment process. With impaired driving, we must interpret the initial stages of recidivism as engaging in thoughts and actions that lead to impaired driving and we apply the zero tolerance approach. We **do not need** to apply *zero tolerance* criteria to substance use. We **do need** to apply the *zero tolerance* criteria to impaired driving conduct. This is not to say that if an DWIO does reoffend, we "write him or her off." We work with changing the client's thinking and behavior leading to impaired driving. However, we are obligated to deal with the impaired driving both

therapeutically and correctionally. This approach will be discussed further below.

Another important modification of the Marlatt model is that we have expanded the concept of high risk situations to high risk exposures. Since high risk exposures lead to recidivism and relapse, it is important for DWIOs to clearly understand these high risk exposures they face in their lives.

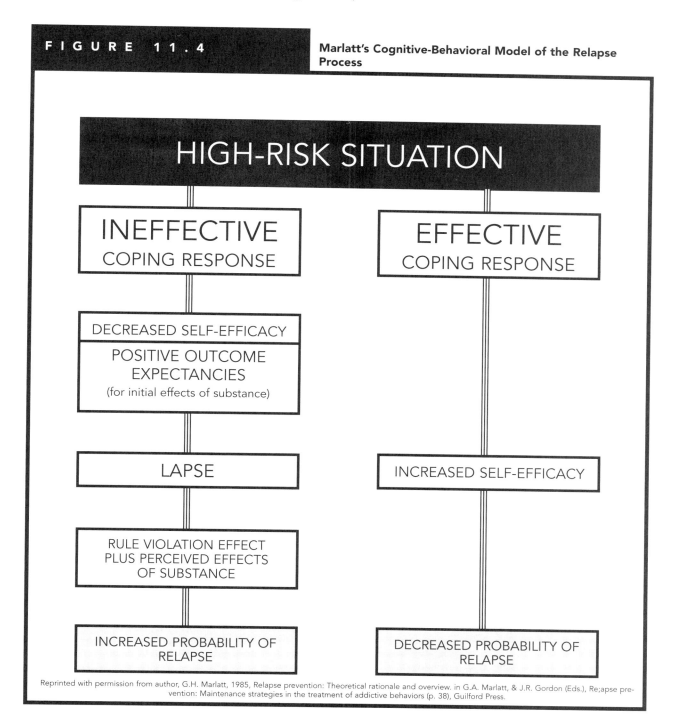

FIGURE 11.4   **Marlatt's Cognitive-Behavioral Model of the Relapse Process**

Reprinted with permission from author, G.H. Marlatt, 1985, Relapse prevention: Theoretical rationale and overview. in G.A. Marlatt, & J.R. Gordon (Eds.), Re;apse prevention: Maintenance strategies in the treatment of addictive behaviors (p. 38), Guilford Press.

Figure 11.5 provides a summary of these high risk exposures - high risk situations, thinking, feelings, attitudes and beliefs - within the framework of both relapse and recidivism. Note that the arrows that lead back and forth between the high risk exposures to relapse and recidivism indicate that these two patterns are linked or connected. Yet, they also can operate independently.

Figure 11.6 provides the pathway for relapse and recidivism and the pathway for RR prevention. It is an adaption of the Marlatt relapse model in *Figure 11.4* to fit the DWIO. Relapse and recidivism (RR) occur in steps. Individuals can be in R&R before they use a substance or before engaging in impaired driving. We will explain the key concepts in the two columns in *Figure 11.6*.

High-Risk Exposures: situations, thoughts, feelings, attitudes and beliefs that threatens the sense of control, thereby increasing the risk for RR.

Weak/Strong Coping Skills: Includes cognitive interpersonal and community responsibility skills.

Self-Efficacy or Self-Mastery is the clients' judgement about how well they are coping with the high risk exposures and whether they have succeeded or failed when exposed to similar high risk exposures. If clients have learned skills of managing the high risk exposures, they will develop strong coping responses and increased sense of self-mastery and self-efficacy. Relapse and recidivism most likely will be prevented.

Expected Outcome: these are what clients' expect the outcome to be. They may expect drinking to have a particular desired effect, e.g., makes you feel good. However, "expected effects" may be quite different from "real effects." When the prospect of AOD use is hooked in with a short-term positive outcome of AOD use, the probability of relapse and recidivism increases. Or, clients may think that impaired driving is necessary, will solve their immediate problem of getting home, or even give them a sense of feeling in control or powerful.

Rule Violation-Effect: this is the clients' reaction resulting from lapsing into a pattern where problem drinking can result. They have violated the rule of "never to drive to the bar alone to drink." Or, they take the initial risk and drive home knowing they have had too much to drink. Clients have seen themselves as not engaging in impaired driving or a problem drinking pattern. Now they have violated those rules. They experience a lot of inner conflict. To solve this conflict, they are likely to return to their old view of themselves - acceptance of driving while impaired or engaging in the old patterns of drinking. The strength of this rule violation will depend on: 1) how much conflict and guilt they experience in their R&R; 2) how much they blame their own personal weaknesses for the cause of the R&R behavior.

Self-Attribution or Self-Credit: this type of thinking is most important when clients find themselves engaging in relapse or recidivism behavior. If they believe that the initial relapse is due to *personal weakness,* then they set themselves up for continuing the relapse. This is because they believe they have lost total control or it is beyond their control. If they *credit strength* to themselves by stopping at the point of initial relapse (engaging in thinking or action which leads to drinking or actual drinking) or stopping at initial recidivism (driving to the bar alone) then it is unlikely that they will go into a full relapse/recidivism.

Figure 11.7 provides a skills map for preventing relapse and recidivism. In *Figure 11.7,* in the left column, the high-risk exposures and pathways leading to RR are reiterated. In the right column, examples of adaptive and management skill responses to these high-risk exposures are provided. Note that the *rule violation effect, decreased self-efficacy and weak coping responses* are critical to leading to full recidivism and relapse. The connecting arrows indicate that at any point in the path, the client can manage the high-risk exposures and get on the track of prevention or on the path leading to recidivism and relapse. *Figure 11.7* provides the clients with the structure for developing a personalized relapse and prevention plan.

3. Flexible and Realistic Relapse and Recidivism Prevention Goals

We have seen in our literature review that many DWIOs will not fit the traditional diagnosis of substance abuse and substance dependence. Many if not most of these DWIOs will see the relapse prevention goal of life-time abstinence as not acceptable.

FIGURE 11.5

Defining high-risk (HR) exposures that lead to relapse and recidivism

RELAPSE HR EXPOSURE		RECIDIVISM HR EXPOSURE

HIGH-RISK SITUATIONS
Relationship conflicts. Problems at work. Socialize with drinking friends. Attend drinking parties. Friends pressure you to drink.

HIGH-RISK SITUATIONS
Attend drinking parties often. Drinking at the bar after driving to the bar alone. Run out of booze at home after having a few drinks. Drink at bar with friends.

HIGH-RISK THINKING
No one really cares. Being unfairly treated. A few drinks will help. Not fair, can't drink. I don't fit in when I don't drink. A couple would feel good.

HIGH-RISK THINKING
I only had two beers when I got my DUI. I've had a couple of beers but I can drive OK. Nobody is going to drive me home. I'm not too drunk to drive.

HIGH-RISK FEELINGS
Happy over getting a raise. Feeling down and depressed. Angry at spouse and boss. I'm feeling stressed. Angry at everybody. Feeling lonely.

HIGH-RISK FEELINGS
I don't care if I get caught. I don't feel quite so down drinking here with friends. I feel more accepted and relaxed here at the bar.

ATTITUDES AND BELIEFS
To hell with everyone. Nothing works out. The world is not fair. I feel better when I drink. Drinking won't hurt me.

ATTITUDES AND BELIEFS
Screw 'em, I can drive OK. Nobody's going to tell me I can't drive. I'm not going to get caught.

RELAPSE PATTERN
Frequent drinking at bar. Daily pattern of use. The world is unfair. Into frequent/heavy use.

RECIDIVISM BEHAVIOR
Driving home after many drinks. Into pattern of driving with BAC above legal limit.

FULL RELAPSE

HARMFUL AND DISRUPTIVE RESULTS FROM DRINKING.

NEW DWI CITATION

CONVICTED OF ANOTHER DUI/DWAI

FIGURE 11.6

The process of relapse and recidivism (RR) prevention: How it works. Adaption of Marlatt's Relapse Prevention Model in Figure 11.4.

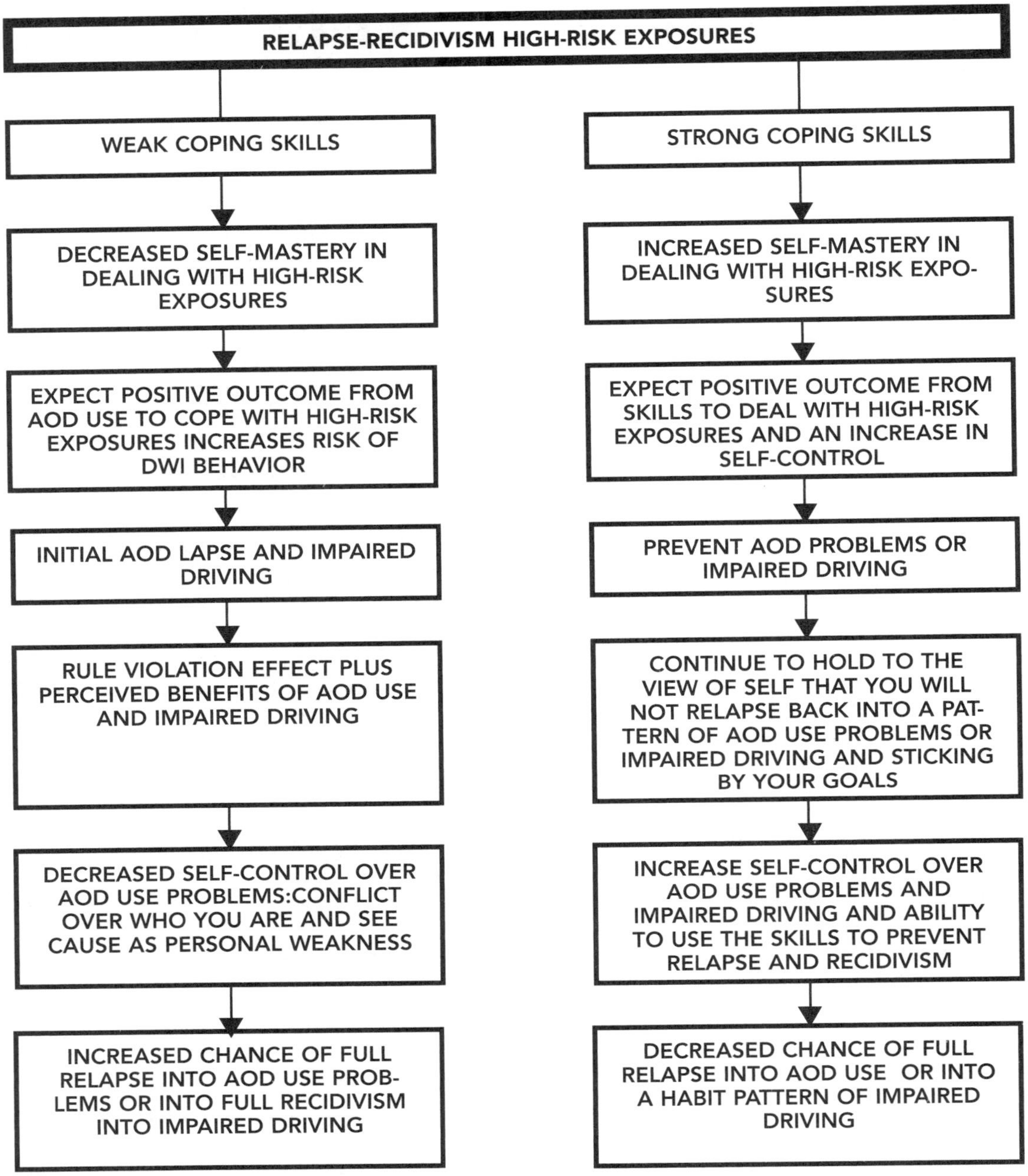

RELAPSE-RECIDIVISM HIGH-RISK EXPOSURES

WEAK COPING SKILLS	STRONG COPING SKILLS
DECREASED SELF-MASTERY IN DEALING WITH HIGH-RISK EXPOSURES	INCREASED SELF-MASTERY IN DEALING WITH HIGH-RISK EXPOSURES
EXPECT POSITIVE OUTCOME FROM AOD USE TO COPE WITH HIGH-RISK EXPOSURES INCREASES RISK OF DWI BEHAVIOR	EXPECT POSITIVE OUTCOME FROM SKILLS TO DEAL WITH HIGH-RISK EXPOSURES AND AN INCREASE IN SELF-CONTROL
INITIAL AOD LAPSE AND IMPAIRED DRIVING	PREVENT AOD PROBLEMS OR IMPAIRED DRIVING
RULE VIOLATION EFFECT PLUS PERCEIVED BENEFITS OF AOD USE AND IMPAIRED DRIVING	CONTINUE TO HOLD TO THE VIEW OF SELF THAT YOU WILL NOT RELAPSE BACK INTO A PATTERN OF AOD USE PROBLEMS OR IMPAIRED DRIVING AND STICKING BY YOUR GOALS
DECREASED SELF-CONTROL OVER AOD USE PROBLEMS:CONFLICT OVER WHO YOU ARE AND SEE CAUSE AS PERSONAL WEAKNESS	INCREASE SELF-CONTROL OVER AOD USE PROBLEMS AND IMPAIRED DRIVING AND ABILITY TO USE THE SKILLS TO PREVENT RELAPSE AND RECIDIVISM
INCREASED CHANCE OF FULL RELAPSE INTO AOD USE PROBLEMS OR INTO FULL RECIDIVISM INTO IMPAIRED DRIVING	DECREASED CHANCE OF FULL RELAPSE INTO AOD USE OR INTO A HABIT PATTERN OF IMPAIRED DRIVING

FIGURE 11.7 **Cognitive-behavioral map for relapse and recidivism prevention**

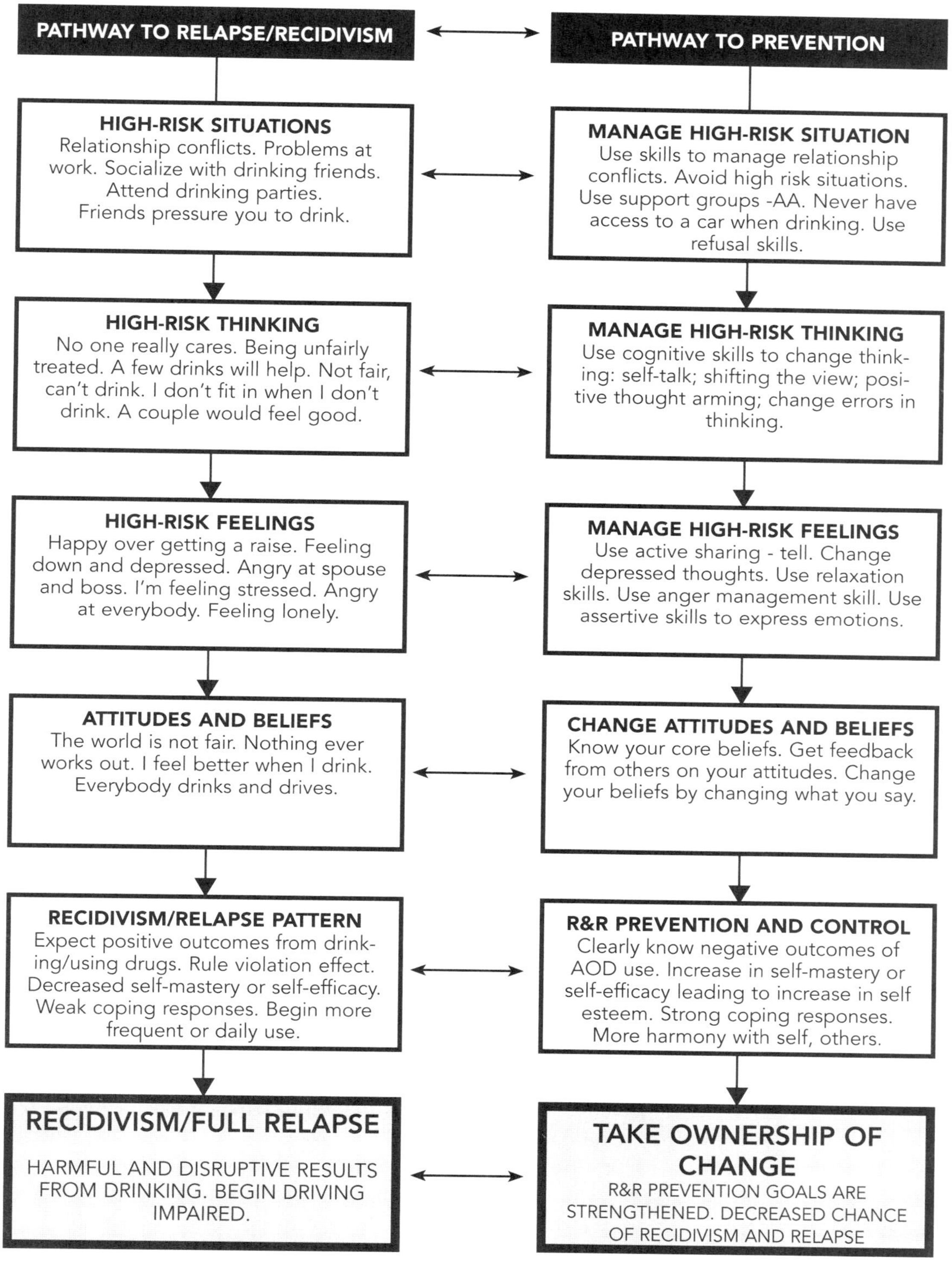

PATHWAY TO RELAPSE/RECIDIVISM ↔ PATHWAY TO PREVENTION

HIGH-RISK SITUATIONS
Relationship conflicts. Problems at work. Socialize with drinking friends. Attend drinking parties. Friends pressure you to drink.

↔

MANAGE HIGH-RISK SITUATION
Use skills to manage relationship conflicts. Avoid high risk situations. Use support groups -AA. Never have access to a car when drinking. Use refusal skills.

HIGH-RISK THINKING
No one really cares. Being unfairly treated. A few drinks will help. Not fair, can't drink. I don't fit in when I don't drink. A couple would feel good.

↔

MANAGE HIGH-RISK THINKING
Use cognitive skills to change thinking: self-talk; shifting the view; positive thought arming; change errors in thinking.

HIGH-RISK FEELINGS
Happy over getting a raise. Feeling down and depressed. Angry at spouse and boss. I'm feeling stressed. Angry at everybody. Feeling lonely.

↔

MANAGE HIGH-RISK FEELINGS
Use active sharing - tell. Change depressed thoughts. Use relaxation skills. Use anger management skill. Use assertive skills to express emotions.

ATTITUDES AND BELIEFS
The world is not fair. Nothing ever works out. I feel better when I drink. Everybody drinks and drives.

↔

CHANGE ATTITUDES AND BELIEFS
Know your core beliefs. Get feedback from others on your attitudes. Change your beliefs by changing what you say.

RECIDIVISM/RELAPSE PATTERN
Expect positive outcomes from drinking/using drugs. Rule violation effect. Decreased self-mastery or self-efficacy. Weak coping responses. Begin more frequent or daily use.

↔

R&R PREVENTION AND CONTROL
Clearly know negative outcomes of AOD use. Increase in self-mastery or self-efficacy leading to increase in self esteem. Strong coping responses. More harmony with self, others.

RECIDIVISM/FULL RELAPSE
HARMFUL AND DISRUPTIVE RESULTS FROM DRINKING. BEGIN DRIVING IMPAIRED.

↔

TAKE OWNERSHIP OF CHANGE
R&R PREVENTION GOALS ARE STRENGTHENED. DECREASED CHANCE OF RECIDIVISM AND RELAPSE

Adapted with permission from author, G.H. Marlatt, 1985, Relapse prevention: Theoretical rationale and overview. in G.A. Marlatt, & J.R. Gordon (Eds.), Relapse prevention: Maintenance strategies in the treatment of addictive behaviors (p. 38), Guilford Press.

The DWC protocols present clients with two possible goals for relapse: abstinence from use; and preventing involvement in a use pattern that portends or results in problem drinking or problem AOD use. As well, clients are presented with the two recidivism prevention goals: zero-tolerance or not engaging in driving with a BAC greater than the legal limits or when under the influence of drugs other than alcohol. Zero tolerance - zero risk is driving alcohol and drug-free. Clients are challenged to accept the zero-tolerance objective. The DWC education protocols makes clear the risks of driving after having one or two drinks.

Developing a Partnership between the Therapeutic and Correctional (Sanctioning) Approaches and Systems

Our review of the literature in this and our previous work (Wanberg & Milkman, 1998) clearly indicated that sanctioning and punishment alone are not effective methods to prevent recidivism. We also indicated that treatment and intervention alone is not as effective as when intervention is integrated with the sanctioning process. **The eighth core strategy of DWC** is that of integrating the efforts of the sanctioning and judicial system with the efforts of the education and treatment system.

There are some traditional differences between the treatment of AOD abuse and intervention and treatment of criminal conduct and impaired driving. First, alcohol abuse by adults in and of itself does not have legal implications and the treatment of AOD abuse does not necessarily involve sanctions; only certain behaviors associated with AOD use such as impaired driving.

Treatment outcomes for **AOD abuse** can tolerate relapse. Such treatment or education is usually psychotherapeutic and it **is client-centered** in that treatment starts with the client's goals, needs and expectations. The healing expectations come from the client.

The education and treatment of impaired driving offenders always involve sanctions: treatment and sanctioning are almost always integrated. The client's referral to education or treatment is considered part of the judicial sentence. There is "zero tolerance" for impaired driving recidivism - or returning to driving while impaired. Recidivism

is not tolerated and when occurring, the provider must engage the correctional and judicial process. **Treatment of impaired driving conduct is society-centered,** it is correctional and parenting with a focus on behavior that violates society. The change expectations, at least initially, come from society - from outside the offender.

Thus, when addressing DWI recidivism, the focus must be on cognitive, affective and pre-recidivism behavior with these elements being considered as leading to recidivism (thinking about driving when drinking; becoming involved in high-risk situations or high risk thinking that leads to DWI behavior).

The confrontational process is also different. The provider in the correctional role states, "I confront you with me, I represent the external world you have violated and I confront you with the values and laws of society and I expect you to change." The provider or therapist represents society in the intervention process and is the clients' "victim" as is any other member of society who is potentially impacted by impaired driving. *The provider has the clear role of helping to administer the judicial sentence.* The intervention referral and the sentence are clearly linked.

The provider in the therapeutic role states, "I confront you with you, I confront you with what you say you want and need and the contradictions in your thinking, emotions and behavior that violate your own needs and goals." The provider, in the therapeutic role, always works towards helping clients achieve their agenda and assume responsibility for their own behavior.

What is most important in this integration process is that the provider always responds to the correctional process within the framework of the therapeutic role. For example, if the client violates his terms of probation, such as driving and drinking, the provider first manages this situation from a therapeutic stance. The provider works with the client's thoughts, underlying beliefs and emotions that led to that behavior and helps the client to identify the triggers that led to that behavior. However, the provider has the final judicial obligation of engaging and informing the correctional system in sanctioning or correcting the behavior that violates the judicial status of the client.

This is done from a therapeutic perspective, and if there is a therapeutic alliance, then the client will take responsibility to engage and inform the judicial system of his or her infraction.

PROGRAM CONCEPTUAL FRAMEWORK

UTILIZING A GROWTH and change model, the multidimensional stages of change concept, and a multidimensional approach to assessment, a conceptual framework for the Driving With CARE education and treatment programs was developed. This structure involves three phases of intervention which have been described above.

A three phase learning and change model is utilized as the primary conceptual structure upon which the DWC education and therapy programs rest. This three phase structure is premised on theory regarding the process that individuals go through when experiencing self-improvement, personal growth and change. The conceptual framework of the program is outlined in **Figure 11.8.** This framework includes the following elements.

▶ Intervention phases and stages of changes.

▶ Provider delivery goals and objectives.

▶ The provider skills required to facilitate growth and change within the program phases.

▶ The assessment components which provide the necessary data base for treatment planning and client self-awareness.

▶ Client education and treatment goals which guide the change process.

▶ The basic CB intervention strategies used to bring about change which are the building stones for the education and treatment framework.

It is within this framework that the education and treatment lessons and sessions are delivered with the goal of effecting change and growth in the client.

SUMMARY

THIS CHAPTER PROVIDES the conceptual framework for delivering education and treatment services to the DWIO. Psychotherapy and counseling were defined, and their integration into an educational-therapeutic approach was discussed. The eight core strategies of DWC education and treatment were outlined.

▶ Multidimensional screening and assessment.

▶ Facilitating the process of the three phases of growth: the undifferentiated and global response; the differentiation and sorting out response; the integration and putting together responses.

▶ Facilitating the client through the stages of change: challenge to change, commitment to change, and ownership of change.

▶ Building a knowledge base in the client utilizing learner-centered, interactive, multisensory and multimodal approaches.

▶ Developing a therapeutic alliance through the use of motivational enhancement skills.

▶ Utilization of a cognitive-behavioral model to implement intrapersonal, interpersonal, and community relationship restructuring. The sociocentric model of therapy and treatment is integrated into the cognitive-behavioral approach.

▶ A relapse and recidivism (R&R) prevention strategy that provides the client with knowledge around the pathways to R&R and the skills to prevent R&R.

▶ Developing a partnership between the therapeutic and correctional approaches and systems.

A program conceptual framework is provided that integrates the intervention phases, stages of change, the change process, provider objectives and skills, assessment approaches, client education and treatment goals and the strategies for delivering DWC education and treatment.

Conceptual framework for the Education and Treatment of the Impaired Driving Offender

INTERVENTION PHASES	CHALLENGE TO CHANGE	COMMITMENT TO CHANGE	TAKING OWNERSHIP FOR CHANGE
CHANGE PROCESS	**UNDIFFERENTIATED**	**DIFFERENTIATED**	**INTEGRATIVE**
DWC PROTOCOLS	DWC Education	DWC Education and Therapy	DWC Education and Therapy/enhanced
PROCESS GOALS AND OBJECTIVES	Client tell story: → Unpack thoughts, feelings and problems Self-disclosure	Cient hear story: → Sort out and label thoughts, beleifs, emotions and behaviors Self-awareness	Act on story: change thoughts, feelings, behavior Self-change
PROVIDER BASIC EDUCATION AND THERAPY SKILLS TO FACILITATE LEARNING, SELF-IMPROVEMENT, RESPONSIBLE LIVING AND CHANGE	Facilitate open → sharing Motivational → enhancement — Learner centerd and → interactive teaching Group sharing → Multi-media presentation Interactive work sheets Rehash discussions →	Reflection of thoughts, → feelings and behavior Therapeutic → confrontation Correctional → confrontation Feedback clarification — Group therapy → Treatment plan → Referral service → Skill rehearsal →	Change rehearsal Change reinforcement skills
ASSESSMENT	**SCREENING**	**IN-DEPTH**	**CHANGE MONITORING**
CLIENT EDUCATIONAL, TREATMENT AND CORRECTIONAL GOALS AND EXPERIENCES	Develop trust Accept climate of caring Build AOD, DWI and CB knowledge base Decrease resistance Indentify areas of change Prevent R&R	Commit to changing thoughts/beliefs Develop self-control, relationship and moral responsibility skills Prevent R&R	Maintain consistent pattern of change Establish self-regulation self-direction self-determination Resolve personal problems Reinforce change Prevent R&R
BASIC EDUACATION AND TREATMENT STRATEGIES	Self-evaluation → Build knowledge → Motivation → Learn skills to change → thinking, relationships to others and society Recidivism and relapse → prevention		

CHAPTER TWELVE: CHARACTERISTICS OF THE EFFECTIVE DWI PROVIDER AND THE CLIENT-PROVIDER RELATIONSHIP

OVERVIEW

THE TWO MOST IMPORTANT components of impaired driving intervention programs are the *DWI provider* (counselor, therapeutic educator, therapist) and the *relationship* between the provider and the client. In this chapter, we will look at the factors that have been identified in the literature as accounting for most of the variance of positive education and treatment outcomes. We then look at the elements of the effective DWI counseling relationship and the three broad variables involved in therapeutic change. The variables that comprise the profile of the effective DWI provider are defined. Finally, we present a model whereby DWI counselors can evaluate their own therapeutic educator styles. The overall purpose of this chapter is to help DWI providers enhance their effectiveness in working with impaired driving offenders.

DETERMINANTS OF THERAPEUTIC AND TREATMENT OUTCOMES

Previous discussions in this work have pointed out that there is a general positive effect of psychosocial therapies. Summaries of meta-analyses of outcome studies conclude "Psychotherapy is effective at helping people achieve their goals and overcome their psychopathologies at a rate that is faster and more substantial than change that results from the client's natural healing process and supportive elements in the environment" (Lambert & Bergin, 1992, page 363). But what is responsible for this outcome? What is it in psychosocial therapies that works?

What has been established, and also previously discussed is that no one clinical approach seems to be superior over another (Lambert & Bergin, 1992) and that different therapeutic approaches, e.g., behavioral, psychodynamic, client-centered, "appear to secure comparable outcomes" (Garfield, 1992, p. 349). Differences in outcome between various forms of treatment are simply not as pronounced as might be expected (Lambert & Bergin, 1992, p. 363) and that "other purportedly unique features of a system may be relatively inconsequential" (Strupp & Howard, 1992, p. 313). Also previously discussed is that different therapies embody common factors that are curative but not emphasized by the theory of change central to a particular school (Gurman & Messer, 2003; Wampold, 2001). What has been established is that the two factors that seen to account for much of the positive outcomes of psychosocial therapies are: the provider's (counselor, therapist, therapeutic educator) *personal characteristics;* and the *counselor-client relationship.* We now look at these two robust determinants of treatment outcome.

1. Counselor Personal Characteristics

One common factor that contributes to the effectiveness of psychosocial therapies is a set of personal characteristics and features of the treatment provider. After some 50 years of studies, there has emerged what has been identified as the core dimensions and characteristics of the effective service delivery personnel of psychosocial therapies including DWI interventions (e.g., Berenson & Carkhuff, 1967; Bohart, 2003; Carkhuff, 1969; Carkhuff, 1971; Carkhuff & Berenson, 1977; Miller & Rollnick, 2002; Rogers, Gendlan, Kiesler & Truax, 1967; Truax & Carkhuff, 1967; Truax & Mitchell, 1971; Wanberg & Milkman, 2005).

Much of this research and the description of these core dimensions are based on the work of Carl Rogers and his associates. Rogers (1957) concluded that the communication of **genuine warmth** and **empathy** by the therapist alone are sufficient in producing constructive changes in clients. He was the first to clearly identify in the literature the traits of **warmth, genuineness, respect and empathy** as essential in not only establishing a therapeutic relationship with clients, but also in producing the desired change in clients. The studies of Truax (1963) and Carkhuff and Truax (1965) support this conclusion. Through the therapist's warmth and empathy, even the most severely disturbed clients can be helped (Rogers et al., 1967).

Today, although interpreted in different ways, these core characteristics of empathic understanding, genuineness or congruence, positive regard and respect, warmth, and concreteness or specificity of expression are considered basic to the effective helping relationship and are consistently emphasized in almost every text on therapy and counseling (e.g., Bohart, 2003; Bateman, Brown & Pedder, 2000; Dryden & Mytton, 1999; George & Christiani, 1981; Miller & Rollnick, 2002; Patterson & Hidore, 1997; Wallace, 1986).

More specific to our concern, George (1990) identifies the personal characteristics of the effective substance abuse counselor as genuineness, ability to form warm and caring relationships, sensitivity and understanding, sense of humor, having realistic levels of aspirations for client change and self awareness. Lazarus (1971) discovered that the most desirable characteristics that clients found in counselors were sensitivity, honesty and gentleness. As Andrews and Bonta look at the effective counselor relationship with the offender, they emphasize the core characteristics of *caring, genuineness and empathy* (Andrews and Bonta, 1994, 1998, 2003).

2. The Counselor-Client Relationship

The core worker's characteristics of warmth, empathy and positive regard are also the core elements of an effective therapeutic relationship (Lambert & Bergin, 1992). What is most prominent among the common factors identified as being the primary basis for treatment effect across all forms of therapy is the *client-counselor relationship*. Strupp and Howard (1992) state poignantly: "…..the growing research literature has strongly suggested, generic (or common) relationship factors in all forms of psychotherapy (e.g., empathic understanding, respect, caring, genuineness, warmth) carry most of the weight…" (p. 313). "Reviewers are virtually unanimous in their opinion that the therapist-patient relationship is central to therapeutic change" (Lambert & Bergin, 1992, p. 372; also documented in other references cited above).

The elements of the therapist-client relationship are central to verbal therapies which are premised on acceptance, tolerance, therapeutic alliance, working alliance and support (Bohart, 2003; Gurman & Messer, 2003; Lambert & Bergiin, 1992; Wampold, 2001). They are also seen as important elements in cognitive and behavioral therapies "as an essential means for establishing the rapport necessary to motivate clients to complete treatment" (Lambert & Bergin, 1992). These are also basic elements of developing motivation in the treatment of the sub-

stance abuser (Miller & Rollnick, 2002).

George and Christiani (1981) contend that the essential elements that promote an effective treatment relationship are *trust and acceptance of the client*. Here are some of the specific characteristics of the effective therapeutic and helping relationship (George and Christiani, 1981; Wanberg & Milkman, 1998).

▶ The relationship is affective: it explores emotions and feelings.

▶ It is intense: the relationship promotes an open sharing of perceptions and reactions between client and worker.

▶ It involves growth and change: it is dynamic, continually changing.

▶ It is private and confidential.

▶ It is supportive.

▶ It is based on honest and open and direct communication.

The more specific components or elements of the therapeutic change relationship are best illustrated as summarized by Marmor (1975).

▶ The relationship promotes a release of tension.

▶ It involves cognitive learning.

▶ It involves operant conditioning and reinforcement.

▶ The client identifies with the counselor.

▶ It involves reality testing.

Sloane, et al. (1975) indicate that successful clients in treatment identify a number of factors that are important to their change and improvement, several of which were specific relationship factors. These involve the therapist's helping them to understand their problems; receiving encouragement to practice facing the issues that bother them; being able to talk to an understanding person; and developing greater understanding from the therapeutic relationship.

ELEMENTS OF THE EFFECTIVE CORRECTIONAL COUNSELING RELATIONSHIP AND THE CORRECTIONAL-INTERVENTION PARTNERSHIP

DWI CLIENTS ARE different from other AOD abuse clients in that they are required to attend education and treatment - *they are coerced clients.* As previously discussed, this means that the provider must integrate both the therapeutic and correctional roles in delivering effective services to DWI clients. The metaphor we have used is that the DWI counselor or therapeutic educator is part and parcel to the administration of the client's judicial sentence. DWI education and treatment are part of that sentence.

What this boils down to is that the provider must be both a therapeutic and correctional specialist. Thus, it is important to understand the elements of an effective correctional counseling relationship and the correctional partnership. This relationship certainly includes the elements of the counselor-client relationship discussed above. The provider utilizes the skills and traits of warmth, genuineness, respect and empathy in developing and maintaining that relationship.

However, there are some unique characteristics of the correctional counseling relationship that serve to enhance effectiveness in working with DWI correctional clients. We review some of these elements that have been identified in the literature and some emerging out of the clinical experience of the authors and then define the correctional-intervention partnership.

1. Essential Elements of the Effective DWI Correctional Counseling Relationship

Andrews and Bonta (1994, 1998, 2003) have identified the following as some of the essential elements of the effective correctional counseling relationship which apply to the counselor-DWI offender relationship.

▶ **Establish high quality relationship with clients.**

Productive interactions between correctional counselors and clients are predicated upon staff enthusiasm and openness to the free expression of attitudes, feelings and experiences. Mutual respect and caring facilitate the meaningful disapproval of procriminal expressions. Within the limits of mutually agreed upon boundaries, counseling is offered in an atmosphere of genuineness, empathy and caring.

▶ **Model and demonstrate anticriminal expressions.** Offenders look for antisocial characteristics and behaviors in others in order to justify their own antisocial and deviant behaviors. DWI offenders are always on the edge of justifying their impaired driving behavior. The DWI provider must be consistent in holding to the view that impaired driving behavior is criminal conduct, is morally irresponsible behavior, and that it is a crime committed against society. The effective correctional counselor must be consistent and unerring in communicating prosocial and high moral values.

▶ **Approve (reinforce) the client's anticriminal expressions.** This is a vigilant process. Missing opportunities to reinforce client changes and efforts to change may make significant differences in the overall change process. A continual reinforcement of abstinence from impaired driving, recognizing that the client could, but does not drive while under license revocation, and reinforcing thinking and behaviors that prevent relapse and recidivism are absolutely essential in bringing about change in DWI offenders.

▶ **Disapprove (punish) the client's procriminal expressions.** Often, this must go beyond disapproval to actually engaging in the sanctioning process by reporting violations of probation and court sentencing conditions. As discussed earlier, such sanctioning should take place within the therapeutic process. Ultimately, the provider is obligated to be sure that the judicial system is informed of client infractions. It is not enough to disapprove of procriminal expressions, e.g., of the client driving under revocation. Effective correctional work will provide and demonstrate alternatives to antisocial and procriminal behaviors, e.g., help the client find alternative transportation to work and treatment. This approach should be part of the correctional counselor's ongoing agenda.

2. Distinguishing Between Anticriminal versus Procriminal Expressions

Most DWI offenders do not see themselves as criminals or as offenders per se. In fact, initially in the intervention process, many do not see themselves as having engaged in anti-legal or antisocial conduct.

A basic assumption of DWC is that impaired driving is antisocial and morally irresponsible behavior. We also consider it to be an expression of criminal conduct. Along with this assumption is that, for many DWI offenders, impaired driving is part of a broader antisocial and characterological pattern. Thus, an important priority in developing DWI correctional counseling acumen is helping clients distinguish between anticriminal and procriminal expressions. Thus, making the distinction between anticriminal and procriminal expressions is ongoing in the DWI intervention for clients and the provider.

Procriminal expressions include specific attitudes, values and beliefs that imply that antisocial attitudes and conduct are acceptable. Included in this category are: negative attitudes toward the law, police and courts; acceptance of rule violations and disregard of the law; endorsement of strategies for exoneration; and, most important, overlooking specific antisocial and anti-legal acts of DWI offenders. A good example of the latter is the counselor overlooking the fact that a client is driving to treatment while under license revocation.

Anticriminal expressions include: emphasizing the painful consequences of impaired driving and its impact on the community and victims; rejecting rationalizations for impaired driving; and highlighting the hazards of associating with impaired driving. Specific antisocial and criminal attitudes outside of impaired driving are therapeutically confronted, e.g., "all my buddies drive and drink," "everybody does it," "look at those guys driving home from the bar that aren't caught," etc. Effective correctional counselors actively reinforce reduced association with friends who are at risk for DWI conduct and other social environments that increase risk for recidivism.

DWI offenders are encouraged to examine their own conduct while making *self-evaluative judgements* as to whether their behavior reflects prosocial or antisocial values and beliefs. They receive support for considering the consequences of their actions and weighing the benefits of alternative ways of acting in situations that are high-risk for recidivism (returning to impaired driving conduct). Attending sessions and completing homework assignments are seen as prosocial expressions. When both staff and clients jointly reinforce positive expression by offender participants, therapeutic effects are significantly enhanced. Crucial to increased counseling efficacy is staff selection and training that stresses the value of modeling and differential reinforcement of anticriminal expressions.

3. Reinforcing Positive Thoughts and Behaviors

Rewarding positive thoughts and behavior requires the availability of a wide variety of reinforcers in the repertoire of DWI correctional counselors. Minimal visual cues such as eye contact or approving smiles may sometimes be effective while other anticriminal expressions may call forth explicit comments reflecting agreement and support. The continuation of a positive and therapeutic counseling relationship may serve as the most powerful reinforcer of prosocial attitudes and conduct.

Andrews and Bonta (1994, 2003) offer specific suggestions regarding high level reinforcement of offenders by their providers, and these are appropriate for the DWI offender.

▶ Strong, emphatic and immediate statements of approval, support and agreement with regard to expressions of prosocial attitudes and conduct by the DWI offender, e.g., nonverbal expression, eye contact, smiles, shared experiences.

▶ Elaboration of the reason why agreement, approval and reinforcement are being offered, i.e., identifying specific attitudes and behaviors being approved.

- Expressions of support should be sufficiently intense and have affective components.

- The providers should at least match the client's statement in emotional intensity (i.e., be empathic) and his or her elaboration of the reason for support may involve some self-disclosure (i.e., openness).

4. Sanctioning within the therapeutic context

Sanctioning and punishment around administering the DWI's judicial sentence should occur within a *therapeutic context*. Andrews and Bonta (1994, 1998, 2003) indicate that effective sanctioning and punishment occur within the context of a caring, genuine and empathic relationship. Providers should not let the fear of client retribution or termination prevent appropriate confrontation of antisocial and even procriminal (driving while impaired, driving under revocation) attitudes or conduct.

Expressed disapproval is more effective in an atmosphere of trust and mutual caring. Yet, supportive statements should outnumber disapproving ones, e.g., a ratio of 4-1. The expression of disapproval should stand in contrast to the levels of interest, concern and warmth previously offered. The lev-

els of disapproval should be immediately reduced and approval introduced when the client expresses morally responsible and prosocial attitudes and behavior.

5. Interactive partners of the DWI Correctional System

The DWI correctional and intervention system involves three partners: *the community, the client and the provider*. The success of the DWI correction-intervention system - preventing recidivism - depends on the development of a collaborative relationship among these three partners. Initially, clients do not see themselves as being part of this partnership. If intervention is successful, clients - mainly in the *Commitment* and *Ownership* phases of intervention - see themselves as a part of the partnership.

Figure 12.1 describes this collaborate partnership and the parts that each play in fulfilling the terms of the partnership. The payoff for the community is fulfillment of the law, safety, victim satisfaction and reduced cost to the community. For the client, the payoff is fulfilling his or her obligation to the community, being morally responsible in the community, freedom from further correctional involvement, contributing to the good of the community and responsible living.

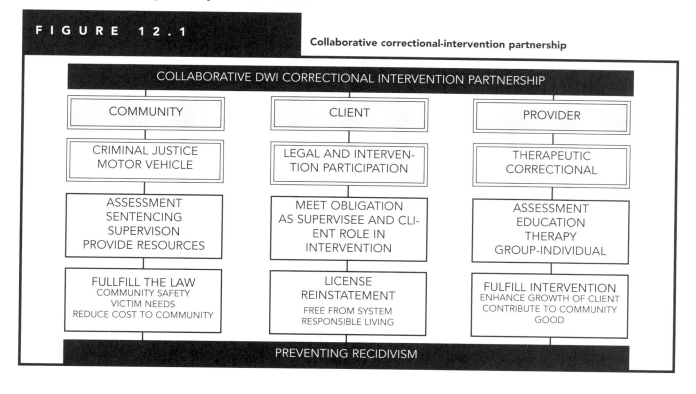

FIGURE 12.1 Collaborative correctional-intervention partnership

The payoff of the provider is fulfilling the provider's therapeutic and correctional role and obligation, enhancing growth of the client, contributing to the safety and good of the community, and generating models for the prevention of impaired driving.

THREE BROAD VARIABLES INVOLVED IN THE EDUCATION AND CHANGE PROCESS

CONSIDERING COMMON, specific and client type factors involved in the education and treatment of impaired driving offenders, there are *three broad variables* that interact in the intervention process to bring about change in the client. These are: *the counselor as person, the counselor-client relationship and the client as person.* These are depicted in *Figure 12.2*. Each of these broad variables are sources of variance that impact the outcome of intervention. Effective treatment providers utilize these variables in the change process.

PROFILE OF THE EFFECTIVE DWI THERAPEUTIC EDUCATOR

There are three broad dimensions that define the primary characteristics of the effective DWI offender specialist: the counselor's personal characteristics and traits; technical development; and philosophical perspectives. *Figure 12.3* provides an outline of these three dimensions.

1.   The Personal Dimension

The *personal dimension* is defined by the core counselor traits of warmth, genuineness, empathy and respect. Whether these traits can be learned or whether they are natural to the individual is certainly debatable. However, each of these traits is observable, measurable, and thus trainable. Other personal characteristics that impact on effective DWI intervention counseling are the counselor's values, beliefs, personal experiences, social role orientation and unresolved personal conflicts.

Biases with respect to orientation towards social and cultural roles, representative groups within the society, and orientation towards job productivity can all influence the provider's (therapeutic educator's) response to the client and the correctional system. Each counselor has a set of unique personal experiences, personal values, attitudes and beliefs that can impact on treatment. Counselors with unresolved personal issues might find these issues getting in the way of being client-oriented and objective.

Effective counselors have full awareness of their own values, beliefs, attitudes, personal experiences and biases and will understand how these personal characteristics can contribute to or hinder the delivery of effective counseling to the driving while impaired offender (DWIO). *Self-disclosure* is the primary skill through which these personal values, beliefs and experiences can be effectively utilized in treatment (Wanberg & Milkman, 1998).

Self-disclosure by the treatment provider is the sharing of personal, emotional and experiential feelings and experiences that are unique to the counselor. It *can enhance* the opening up process and increase treatment communication between the counselor and client or among clients. It can help the client feel more at ease knowing that the counselor has had very real and human feelings and experiences.

There is evidence that self-disclosure is working when: 1) the client continues to share at a deeper and more personal level; 2) the client begins to utilize some of the personal approaches that the counselor has used in his or her own problem-solving and conflict resolutions; and 3) the client expresses greater acceptance of his own inner feelings and problems.

Self-disclosure can present major barriers in treatment (Wanberg, 1990; Wanberg & Milkman, 1998). It can *slow down* or even stop the opening up and sharing process. If the counselor indicates having been through such and such an experience, the client may internally reflect that "there is no reason to go on; the counselor already knows what I've been through."

Self-disclosure may cause the client to lose confidence in the counselor, a finding that is born out in the research literature. As a consequence of self-disclosure, the client may move away from self-focus and focus more on the counselor's issues. Finally, self-disclosure may cause the counselor to lose concentration and attention on the content and affect flow of the client.

Interactive components of the DWI education and treatment process.

COUNSELOR AS PERSON	COUNSELOR-CLIENT RELATIONSHIP	CLIENT AS PERSON
COUNSELOR TRAITS - VALUES	THERAPEUTIC CLIMATE HAS: Empathy and warmth Honesty and respect Genuineness Caring	DEVELOPMENTAL HISTORY
MODELS PROSOCIAL BEHAVIOR		CURRENT STATUS PROBLEMS
COUNSELOR BELIEFS		MENTAL STATUS
EDUCATION-THERAPY PLATFORM SKILLS	CORRECTIONAL RELATIONSHIP Expects compliance Builds moral responsibility Helps administer judicial sentence	PERSONALITY TRAITS
CB CHANGE SKILLS		PATTERNS OF DWI CONDUCT
CASE MANAGEMENT SKILLS		PATTERNS OF SUBSTANCE USE
THEORETICAL ORIENTATION	THERAPEUTIC RELATIONSHIP Promotes growth and change Builds coping skills Is supportive Based on trust Conveys acceptance Clear Boundaries	RISK FACTORS
PERSONAL EXPERIENCES		THOUGHT PROCESS
DWI PROVIDER STYLE		STAGE OF CHANGE

CHANGE IN CLIENT'S THOUGHT, EMOTIONS AND ACTIONS

Profile of the DWI Counselor or Therapeutic Educator

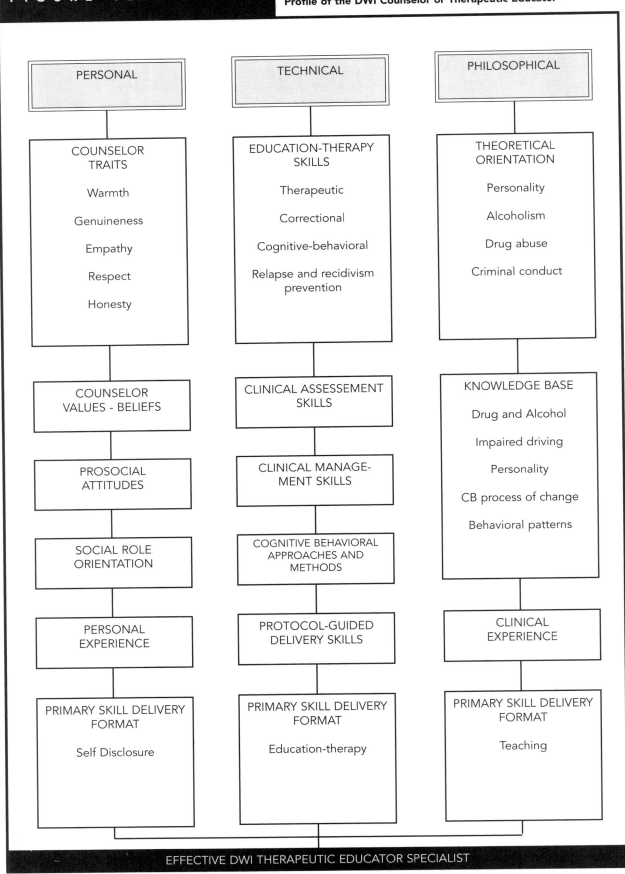

In summary, self-disclosure by the treatment provider becomes effective when, following its use, clients think they are *better understood and more deeply supported* and then continue to share personal material at a deeper level. It should be *used with caution.* It is a complex factor in the treatment process. It does not necessarily enhance, and may inhibit, the client seeing the counselor as empathic, trustworthy or competent. It could reinforce anti-social behavior.

2. The Technical Dimension

The second dimension that defines the effective DWI therapeutic educator is the area of technical training and development. This involves the development of the education and therapy skills necessary to deliver a manual-guided and individual-based intervention program. This also involves the skills of *assessment* and of *client management.* These skills form an important component of the conceptual framework of the treatment platform discussed in the last chapter.

A standard for the application of the technical dimension is found in the practice of surgery in medicine. During a surgical procedure, a physician's knowledge, skills and ethical behaviors are continually operating. At any given moment in the surgical process, the surgeon knows what skills are needed for successful surgery. The surgeon knows the process for each surgical procedure. The skills, tools and instruments are precisely labeled and identified, and the surgeon knows under what conditions the application of the skills and the use of the instruments are needed. You would not only expect, but require that of a surgeon operating on you. Imagine being operated on, and you wake up and hear the surgeon say: "Gee, that's an interesting instrument. Don't know what it is, but I'll try it." Needless to say, you would be in shock.

Let us apply the same standard to counseling and psychosocial treatment. We ought to have an awareness of the process of education and therapy and therapeutic change. We should be able to label our education and therapy skills and tools, and then we should know when in the intervention and change process we apply those skills and tools. We should also have a fairly decent idea of the outcome of the application of the process and skills. We would expect no less of our surgeon; our clients will

expect no less of us.

In psychosocial treatment, we may not always have the definitive knowledge of the process and the skills, as in medicine. Yet we should be grounded in a process that we feel works for us and we should be able to label the skills we use to implement that process of therapeutic and correctional change. A model for the process, skills and strategies of the education and treatment of the DWI offender was presented in Chapter 11. This model provides a guideline for your own adaptation of psychosocial and correctional treatment.

3. Philosophical Perspectives

Finally, the dimension of philosophical perspective provides counselors with a theoretical orientation and knowledge structure within which they practice the delivery of services to DWI offenders. It is important that the counselor or therapeutic educator have some theory of human personality, a theoretical view of education and teaching (e.g., learner-centered model), of counseling and treatment (cognitive-behavioral), some theories or at least some ideas around drug abuse and alcoholism and some perspective on the nature, etiology and development of impaired driving conduct. Teaching and imparting knowledge is the primary skill through which counselors bring to bear their knowledge and theoretical orientation on the DWI education and treatment process. **Sections I and II** of this manual have been devoted to helping you become grounded in a theoretical and philosophical perspective in the treatment of the impaired driving offender.

THERAPEUTIC EDUCATOR STYLES AND APPROACHES

THE ABOVE DISCUSSION indicates that there are many different kinds of counselor styles, traits and characteristics and there are different kinds of counselor-client relationships. The literature, however, has little to offer with respect to empirically defining these different styles and approaches. This led DeMuro (1997) to address empirically what these different styles and approaches might be. Drawing from outside of the DWI counseling literature, he hypothesized that DWI therapeutic educators would differ along the lines of approach, orientation and techniques. To address the measurement of these differences, he constructed the *Therapeutic Educator Countermeasures Inventory* (TECI: DeMuro, 1997; DeMuro & Wanberg, 1998). Results from multivariate analyses indicated six reliable primary order factors (scales) and two broad second order factors (see DeMuro, 1997 for methods and procedures used in the development of these scales).

The scales of the TECI can be used to help individual providers (therapeutic educators - TEs) understand their own unique styles, approaches and techniques when working with DWI offenders. Following is a brief description of the TECI scales.

▶ COURT ORIENTED TEs focus on the client's criminal justice issues and stress the court's influence on the client's motivation and emphasize this perspective throughout the intervention process.

▶ DISEASE ORIENTED TEs focus on and connect the DWIO drinking and driving offense with some aspect of the disease model of alcoholism and drug abuse.

▶ FORMAL APPROACH TEs would most likely be autocratic in their approach to clients and believe in extrinsic motivation and present themselves as the expert on DWI subjects and topics.

▶ PARTICIPANT ORIENTED TEs see the offender as a unique person and presume the offender has specific reasons for being involved in DWI conduct and will make an effort to develop an individualized treatment plan.

▶ INFORMAL APPROACH TEs put more emphasis on class discussion and client interaction than on presenting material, are more likely to use reflective listening skills and stimulate group discussions, and evoke students' insights and perspectives.

▶ EMPATHY ORIENTED TEs assume a positive, supportive and reinforcing role with offenders and stress the importance of offenders taking responsibility for their own behavior and change. This TE style gives offenders room to express themselves and evaluate their own progress.

▶ The broad scale PROCESS ORIENTED, is comprised of the primary scales of EMPATHY, PARTICIPANT ORIENTED and INFORMAL APPROACH. This scale describes a provider who focuses on the individual personal growth and development of clients and the interactions between the educator and the clients. It focuses on the relationship aspects of DWI therapeutic education.

▶ The broad scale TASK ORIENTED is comprised of the primary scales of FORMAL APPROACH, DISEASED-ORIENTED, and COURT-ORIENTED. It describes a style where the TE focuses on the education content, stressing the importance of the course material and curriculum and stresses the importance of court compliance. It describes a TE who is more formal and structured.

The above scales certainly address both the *therapeutic and correctional issues* in DWI intervention. The **correctional dimension** of DWI intervention is best represented by the COURT, DISEASE, FORMAL primary scale and the broad TASK SCALE. The **therapeutic dimension** of DWI intervention is represented by the INFORMAL, EMPATHY and PARTICIPANT primary scales and the broad PROCESS scale.

DeMuro found that TEs who scored high on the PROCESS scale (focus on group interaction, client growth, empathy, relationship building) tend to score lower on the TASK (formal, disease, education oriented) scale and vise versa. However, in line with the philosophy of DWC, it would be important that providers *practice both of these approaches*, particularly with respect to manual-guided programs. The most desirable description would be a therapeutic educator who scores moderate-high on both dimensions, indicating the TE is focusing on both the therapeutic and the correctional.

The TECI is found in *Appendix B* which also includes the TECI profile. It is suggested that you take the TECI and follow the scoring instructions on the instrument in order to generate a profile. Where do you score? If you are low on PROCESS and high on TASK, you might need to work on the skills and approaches that are more client-focused, motivational oriented, rapport building, and group focused. If you are high on the PROCESS scale and low on TASK, you might be neglecting the community responsibility or sociocentric element of DWI intervention and neglecting the correctional role of DWI education and treatment.

Discuss your findings with your colleagues. Ask them how they see you. Does that feedback fit with your TECI profile?

SUMMARY

A robust finding in the research and theory literature on counseling and psychotherapy is that two dimensions contribute major variance to positive treatment outcome: the personal characteristics of the provider (counselor or therapist); and the provider-client relationship. The salient aspects of these two dimensions were discussed in this Chapter.

The essential characteristics of the provider and of the provider-client relationship identified in the literature that contribute to effective treatment outcomes are also discussed. However, to be effective with DWI and other correctional clients, additional features and characteristics of providers and the provider-client relationship need to be considered. These include:

▶ a collaborative partnership between the provider and the correctional system;

▶ the provider using correctional confrontation; strong emphasis on modeling prosocial and anti-criminal values and behaviors; and

▶ utilizing disapproval and sanctioning reinforcement approaches along with positive reinforcement approaches.

The interactive components of the DWI education and treatment process are presented, which include: the counselor as person, counselor-client relationship; and the client as person. A profile of the effective DWI counselor or provider is presented, which includes the personal, technical and philosophical dimensions.

The chapter ends with an opportunity for DWI

providers to view a profile of their own provider style, using the scales of the *Therapeutic Educator Countermeasures Inventory* (TECI). The TECI, along with its profile and scoring guide, is in the *Appendix B* of this Provider's Guide. Providers are able to view where they fall on the correctional and therapeutic dimensions in their work with DWI offenders.

CHAPTER THIRTEEN: ASSESSMENT OF THE DRIVING WHILE IMPAIRED OFFENDER

OVERVIEW

CHAPTER 7 OF THIS *Provider's Guide* outlines a conceptual framework for the evaluation and assessment of impaired driving offenders. The two assessment components of differential screening and in-depth differential assessment are described within the framework of a convergent validation model. This conceptual framework provides a rationale for the necessity of using both *self-report* and *other-report* information to determine the level of willingness of the client to self-disclose and to converge on the best estimate of a valid description of the client's past and current conditions related to AOD use and major life-concerns and life-functioning. DSM IV criteria for both substance abuse and substance dependence are summarized. The purpose of this chapter is to illustrate an approach based on the assessment framework provided in *Chapter 7* by describing a specific *differential screening* and *multiple-factor assessment* approach that can be used in the evaluation of the DWIO.

DIFFERENTIAL SCREENING AND PLACEMENT ASSESSMENT MODEL

THE DIFFERENTIAL SCREENING, assessment and placement (DSAP) model illustrated in this chapter is utilized in the assessment and placement of DWIOs in Colorado and is similar to that used in many states and jurisdictions. These states have statutory requirements that individuals convicted of or receiving a deferred sentence for impaired driving must be evaluated. The evaluation determines whether an AOD and impaired driving problems exist, the severity of such problems, amenability to treatment, the setting, length and intensity of any needed care, adjuncts such as Antabuse, self-help group, and recommendation and/or actual referral to a specific program.

The *DWI DSAP Model* also recommends that an in-depth, differential assessment be completed on all clients who are referred for impaired driving treatment (*DWC Therapy*). This chapter will spell out the essential specific domains of in-depth assessment and will provide an example of a psychometric multiple-factor assessment of these domains based on self-report and other report.

Differential Screening

The *DSAP Model* is based on the convergent validation assessment approach described in Chapter 7: *Perspectives on Assessment.* It uses the following three sources of data:

▶ a validated, self-report psychometric differential screening instrument designed for and normed on DWI offenders;

▶ collateral, other report data which include the BAC level, prior arrest and convictions and treatment history; and

▶ motivationally based interview (other report data) conducted with each DWIO.

Data obtained from these three sources are utilized in conjunction with a standardized placement criteria in a decision making process. Each of these three sources of data will be discussed.

1. Adult Substance Use and Driving Survey - ASUDS

The validated psychometric instrument utilized in the *DSAP Model* is the *Adult Substance Use and Driving Survey* (ASUDS: Wanberg & Timken, 1998). It is available in Spanish as well as English. A *User's Guide for the ASUDS* provides instructions for the administration and scoring the ASUDS, a description of the scales, the use of the scales in making placement recommendations, psychometric and validation information regarding the scales.[1]

The ASUDS provides a psychometric approach to screening individuals charged with or convicted of driving while impaired. It is a self-report survey comprised of 89 standardized self-report questions appropriate for use with DWI offenders 16 years or older. All questions have multiple response choices so as to maximize response variance (versus a yes

---

1. For further information and qualifications in the use of ASUDS, contact the Center for Addictions Research and Evaluation, 5460 Ward Road, Suite 140, Arvada, CO, 80002.

or no response choice). It is presented in a four page test booklet.

The ASUDS has 12 scales that measure involvement of alcohol and other drugs, driving risk, disruption related to AOD use, antisocial behavior, mental health issues, defensiveness, level of motivation and a global measure comprised of the sum of the AOD involvement, disruption, antisocial and motivation scales. The first 10 scales of the ASUDS are normed on a large sample of impaired driving offenders being processed through the judicial system. The ASUDS was administered during the process of differential screening and used in determining appropriate intervention services.

The AOD involvement and disruption scales are also normed on a clinical sample *(Involvement2 and Disruption2)*. This allows the *Alcohol and Drug Evaluator* (ADE) to compare a client's scores on these two scales with the client's peers (other DWI offenders) and with a sample of clients referred to intensive AOD outpatient or AOD inpatient treatment. *Figure 13.1* provides the ASUDS profile.

It is recommended that the DWI provider utilize the ASUDS profile in developing the individualized treatment plan for clients. For example, clients with high defensive scores and low motivation scores, yet who have significant AOD use problems may need motivational enhancement services beyond those that are built into the DWC protocols. Clients with high DISRUPTION scores may need more specialized AOD interventions.

SCALE 1: INVOLVEMENT1, provides a measure of the lifetime involvement in drugs from 10 different drug categories. A high score on this scale could mean that the individual is endorsing high use of a few drugs or minimal to moderate use of many drugs. This scale provides insight into whether the client is a monodrug or a polydrug user and the degree of involvement in the use of multiple substances.

SCALE 2: ALCOHOL INVOLVEMENT, is a general alcohol influence scale designed to measure individuals with a history of alcohol use, but not necessarily, alcohol abuse. The scale measures a low level of alcohol use patterns and problems. Many items in this scale can be endorsed by the average drinker with no alcohol use problems. The value

of this scale is that even the average drinker will have raw scores in the one to 10 range. It is difficult for clients to not provide low-range affirmative responses to many of the items. Clients with scores in the first and second decile range are most likely defensive and resisting self-disclosure.

SCALE 3: DRIVING RISK, measures driving attitudes and behaviors using questions ranging from low-risk to high-risk driving behaviors. Drivers with raw scores in the six to nine raw range fall in the moderate range of risk, and those with scores higher than nine will fall in the higher risk range. DWI clients are quite defensive on this scale since they will perceive the endorsement of too many of these items as a threat to their driving privilege. The client is retested on this scale in *Lesson 9* of the *DWC Level II Education.*

SCALE 4: DISRUPTION1 represents a broad measure of problems and negative consequences due to AOD use. The focus of the measurement of these disruptive signs and symptoms is how the individual sees these occurring in relationship to drugs in general, and not any specific drug or drug category. Moderate to high scores on this scale indicate that drugs cause loss of control over behavior, disruption of psychological and physiological functioning, and cause problems at home, work, and at school.

SCALE 5: ANTISOCIAL measures rebellious and antisocial behavior and attitudes, both in history and in the present. Although this cannot be construed as a measure of an antisocial personality disorder per se, the antisocial pattern is certainly represented in this scale. Individuals with high scores on this scale may be resistive to treatment, and indicating character disorder problems that may mitigate against productive involvement in therapy. However, individuals who do score moderate to high on this scale are self-disclosing, and probably represent a group of individuals who are more apt to respond in a positive way to treatment than individuals with strong antisocial patterns who score low on this scale - and who will score high on the DEFENSIVE scale. Thus, we can construe a moderate or higher score on this scale as being positive in that the first step towards constructive involvement in treatment is a willingness to self-disclose.

FIGURE 13.1   Adult Substance Use and Driving Survey (ASUDS) Profile

ADULT SUBSTANCE USE AND DRIVING SURVEY—ASUDS
DUI/DWAI OFFENDER PROFILE
(ASUDS SUMMARY PROFILE)

SCALE NAME	RAW SCORE	Low			Low-medium		High-medium			High			NUMBER IN NORM SAMPLE*
		1	2	3	4	5 (DECILE RANK)	6	7	8	9	10		
1. INVOLVEMENT1		0		1		2		3	4 5	6 7	8 10 40		2286*
2. ALCOHOL INVOLV		0 1	2	3	4 5	6	7	8 9	10 11	12 14 16	17 21 37		2282*
3. DRIVING RISK			0	1	2	3		4	5	6 7	8 10 34		2280*
4. DISRUPTION1			0	1		2	3	4 5	6 7	8 10 12	13 21 80		2170*
5. ANTISOCIAL		0 1	2	3	4	5	6	7	8 9	10 11	12 14 26		2191*
6. MOOD ADJUSTMT			0		1	2	3	4	5 6	7 8	9 11 29		2190*
7. DEFENSIVE		0 1 5 9	10 11	12	13	14	15	16	17	18 19	20 21 24		2232*
8. MOTIVATION		0	1 2	3 4	5	6	7 8	9 10	11 12	13 14 15	16 18 21		2017*
9. SIX MONTHS			0		1		2	3	4 5 6	7 9 54			2312*
10. GLOBAL		0 3 4 5	6 7 8	9 10	11 12	13 14 15	16 17 18	19 20 22	23 25 27	28 32 37	38 159		1920*
11. INVOLVEMENT2		0 1 2 3	4 5	6 7 8 9	10 11 12	13 15 16	17 18 19	20 22 23	24 25 26	27 30 32	33 36 40		668**
12. DISRUPTION2		0 1 3 5	6 11 15	16 21 26	27 30 34	35 38 41	42 45 47	48 50 53	54 57 59	60 63 65	66 70 80		635**

| 1 | 10 | 20 | 30 | 40 | 50 | 60 | 70 | 80 | 90 | 99 |
PERCENTILE   *DUI GROUP   **Public Hospital and IOP

ASUDS WEIGHTED SCORE: _____   **BAC:** _____   **Evaluator Name:** _____

#PRIOR AOD OFFENSES: _____   **# PRIOR AOD ED/TX:** _____

RECOMMENDATIONS: _____

TX TRACK (Circle): A   B   C   D   None   TX ADJUNCTS: _____

Table for Assessing Severity Level and Treatment Needs

Variable or Scale Description and Raw Scores Values for Determining Weighted Score	Score
Involvement 1 raw score: 0-1 Score = 0; 2-5 = 1; 6-10 = 2; 11 or more = 3	
Alcohol involve raw score: 0-2 = 0; 3-7 = 1; 8-14 = 2; 15-39 = 3	
Driving Risk raw score: 0-2 = 0; 3-6 = 1; 7-13 = 2; 14-36 = 3	
Disruption 1 raw score: 0-1 = 0; 2-7 = 1; 8-15 = 2; 16 or higher = 3	
Prior DUI/DWAI offenses: 0 = 0; 1 prior = 1; 2 priors = 2; 3 or more priors = 3	
Blood Alcohol Concentration: 0 = 0; refuse or<.10 = 1; .10-.149 = 2; .15-.199 = 3; .20 or greater = 4	
Drug use: Positive for other drugs for current offense = 2	
Prior AOD education episodes: 0 = 0; 1 prior = 1; 2 or more episodes = 2	
Prior treatment episodes: 0 = 0; 1 prior TX episode = 1; 2 or more TX episodes = 2	
Total Weight Score (Recommended Level of Service for Weight Ranges provided below)	

Circle Recommended Level of Services

Level of Service Description		Override Rationale & Enhancement TX Description
1. Level I Education	1 - 2	
2. Level II Education	3 - 4	
3. Level II Ed and Weekly OP	5 - 9	
4. Level II Ed, Weekly OP and enhanced TX	10 - 25	
No Treatment recommended (explain)		

SCALE 6: MOOD DISRUPTION, measures a single dimension of psychological and emotional disruption. A high score indicates that the individual is experiencing depression, worry, anxiety, irritability, anger and possibly feelings of not wanting to live. There may be problems in emotional control and acting out behavior.

SCALE 7: DEFENSIVE, provides a measure of the degree to which the client is able to divulge personal and sensitive information on the ASUDS. It is comprised of statements to which almost all individuals can give a yes answer, even though it may be at a "Hardly at all" level of response. Almost every individual has gotten angry, felt unhappy, not told the truth, felt frustrated about the job and not told others what he or she was feeling inside. It is of note that about five percent of the DUI sample answered no to all of these questions.

SCALE 8: MOTIVATION, provides a reliable measure of the degree to which the client is motivated to seek help to make life changes, to seek help for AOD problems and to stop or to continue to not use alcohol or other drugs. Persons with low scores (decile ranges of one or two) on the ASUDS profile indicate little desire for help or to stop AOD use. A high DEFENSIVE score (ninth and 10th decile ranges) and a low MOTIVATION score would suggest considerable resistance to treatment or AOD intervention services. A low score on MOTIVATION, DEFENSIVE and DISRUPTIVE may simply indicate the client's AOD use and problems are truly in the low range and that a high level of treatment services are not needed. This kind of profile should be corroborated with collateral or other-report data.

SCALE 9: SIX MONTHS, provides a measure of the client's willingness to report AOD use and problems from use that have occurred in the past six months. The "last six months" measures apply to the 10 drug categories and to the 20 symptoms in DISRUPTION. This scale provides a picture of recent use. Clients complete the items based on the most recent six month period of AOD use, typically prior to their DWI arrest. Often, clients will stop using once they are charged with a DWI. Over 40 percent of the DWI normative group disclose no AOD use in the six month period.

SCALE 10: GLOBAL DISRUPTION is the sum of the four scales of INVOLVEMENT, DISRUPTION, SOCIAL, and MOOD. This scale provides a global measure of the degree to which the client is indicating life-functioning problems in the areas of substance use, mood adjustment and community compliance.

SCALES 11 AND 12: INVOLVEMENT2 AND DISRUPTION2 use the same items as INVOLVEMENT1 and DISRUPTION1. However, the normative samples for INVOLVEMENT2 and DISRUPTION2 are based on clients treated in public intensive outpatient or residential care facilities for alcohol and other drug abuse. This provides the evaluator with an option of comparing the client's raw score on these two scales with both a DWI normative and an AOD clinical group with a severe history of substance abuse. It is important to see where a client, with raw scores in the eighth or above decile range on INVOLVEMENT1 and DISRUPTION1, falls on the INVOLVEMENT2 and DISRUPTION2 scales, particularly for a client whose INVOLVEMENT raw score is greater than 10 and whose DISRUPTION raw score is greater than 21.

2. Collateral data

Five collateral variables are used in making referral decisions into the four service levels in *Figure 13.1*. These are:

- number of prior DWI offenses;
- BAC at arrest;
- drug use: positive for other drugs for current offense;
- prior AOD education episodes; and
- prior AOD treatment episodes.

These data are factored in with the results of the ASUDS and interview data when making decisions around education or treatment referral.

3. Interview Data

The interview enables the *Alcohol Drug Evaluator* (ADE) to gather information about the DWI offender's past and present use of alcohol and other drugs, and whether there is a problem that needs some degree of attention. The interview also discerns whether there are inconsistencies in the DWIO's reporting and allows the ADE to identify individuals who have difficulty in understanding and answering test questions. The interview should be based on the motivational interviewing approach (Miller & Rollnick, 1991, 2002) and the utilization of basic counseling skills. These are non-confrontational approaches that identify client defensiveness. The result is a more accurate screening leading to a better referral and probability of a better outcome. These approaches have been summarized in *Chapters 11 and 12*.

Guidelines for Referral Decisions

A weighted scoring system is utilized in assessing preliminary severity and treatment needs. ASUDS raw scores along with the collateral information are used to generate the weighted score. *Figure 13.1* provides the *Table for Assessing Severity Level and Treatment Needs*. This table generates a weighted score that is then use to help the evaluator make decisions around recommended levels of service.

The total weighted score is utilized to determine the *Recommended Level of Service* outlined in the table at the bottom of *Figure 13.1*. Before a final recommendation is made, a review of the standardized placement criteria is done to determine whether the ASUDS, the collateral data, and the obtained weighted score are congruent with the placement criteria.

Placement Criteria

The placement criteria utilized in the DSAP model is the *Alcohol Drug Driving Safety (ADDS) Program Placement Criteria - Revised* (PPC-R: Timken, 2001b). It is based on the *American Society of Addiction Medicine Patient Placement Criteria-2-Revised* (ASAM PPC-2-R: ASAM, 2001). The *ADDS Placement Criteria-Revised* uses five dimensions:

1) biomedical conditions and complications;

2) emotional behavioral or cognitive conditions and complications;

3) readiness to change (motivation, treatment compliance and resistance);

4) relapse, continued use or continued problem potential; and,

5) recovery and living environment.

All dimensions are evaluated in making appropriate placement. Placement in intensive residential treatment and hospital settings requires problems in the biomedical and/or behavioral or cognitive areas.

Interactions among the five dimensions are important when considering placement. For example, significant problems with *readiness to change* (Dimension 3) coupled with a poor *recovery environment* (Dimension 5) or moderate problems with *relapse or continued use* (Dimension 4) may increase the risk of recidivism or relapse. Another commonly seen combination involves problems in Dimension 1, such as chronic pain that is distracting, coupled with problems in Dimensions 3, 4 and/or 5.

The converse may also be true. For example, problems with *relapse potential* (Dimension 4) may be offset by a high degree of *readiness to change* (Dimension 3) or a very supportive *recovery environment* (Dimension 5). The interaction of these factors may result in a lower level of severity, and in turn, level of care that is seen in any one dimension.

Assessments are most accurate when they take into account all of the factors (Dimensions) that affect each DWIO's receptivity and ability to engage in education and/or treatment at a particular point in time. People must be treated where they are, not where we want them to be.

The more intense the problems, the more intense level of care is recommended. No one source of information is utilized in making referral recommendations. For example, this decision is never made solely on the basis of the ASUDS scores. Using all sources of information, the evaluator converges on estimating the "true" condition of the client and then converges on the final referral recommendation decision.

Placement Menu and Service Options

Although four categories define the recommended level of services, as outlined at the bottom of *Figure 13.1,* there are 11 options regarding education and treatment for DWIOs. Ten of these specify level and intensity of education and/or treatment and one option is that of "no recommended treatment." In the latter case, a referral is mader for an in-depth evaluation concerning psychological and/or cognitive status.

An *Assessing Severity Level and Treatment Needs* weighted score of 10 or more (Middle Table in *Figure 13.1*) means that serious consideration is given to placing the client in enhanced services or more than just *Level II Education* and weekly outpatient care. Included in enhanced treatment services are intensive outpatient, day care and various types of residential care, including therapeutic community.

The following are the 11 service options that define the placement menu.

▶ Level I Education.

▶ Level II Education.

▶ Level II Education and Weekly Outpatient Treatment.

▶ Level II Education, Intensive Outpatient and Weekly Outpatient.

▶ Level II Education, Day Treatment and Weekly Outpatient Treatment.

▶ Level II Education, Half-Way House, Intensive Outpatient and/or Weekly Outpatient Treatment.

▶ Level II Education, Transitional Treatment, Intensive Outpatient and/or Weekly Outpatient Treatment.

▶ Level II Education, Intensive Residential Treatment, Intensive Outpatient and/or Weekly Outpatient Treatment.

▶ Level II Education, Hospital, Intensive Outpatient and/or Weekly Outpatient Treatment.

▶ Level II Education and Therapeutic Community.

▶ No treatment due to extreme severity, mental illness, or cognitive problems - refer for in-depth psychological assessment.

Summary Description of Level of Services for the DSAP Model

Table 13.1 provides a summary of recommendations for DWI offenders based on the weighted scores derived from the variables in the Table for *Assessing Severity Level and Treatment Needs* in *Figure 13.1*.

Driving with CARE (DWC) specifies three kinds of DWI services: *Level I Education, Level II Education* and *Level II Therapy. Level II Therapy* is essentially a sequel to *Level II Education*. Clients entering *Level II Therapy* should have completed the *Level II Education* curriculum. *Level II Therapy* can include from 42 to 86 hours of outpatient therapy plus, when determined necessary, enhanced services as described in the above options.

Summary of DWC Treatment Tracks

DWC is structured into four treatment tracks based on the Colorado Placement Model. These four tracks are based on different levels of BAC and offense history. They are summarized in Table 13.2 below.

Summary of Screening Criteria Recommendation for the Three Service Protocols

Admission criteria recommendations for *Level I Education* are a low level profile on the ASUDS; BAC less than .15; no history of prior diagnosis of substance abuse or dependence; no prior impaired driving offenses and no evidence of a history of AOD misuse. However, it is quite likely that, as clients progress through *Level I Education,* some will discover, or be willing to more openly disclose, that they do have substance abuse problems in their history. One of the goals of *Level I Education* will be to help clients to have a clear picture of the extent to which they have been involved in problem AOD use and to discern if they do, in fact, need treatment services.

Admission criteria for *Level II Education* requires evidence of a history of problems related to AOD use beyond DWI conduct. Clients must have a BAC level of .15 to .199 and/or there are at least minimal indicators of AOD problems.

TABLE 13.1

**DSAP AOD Treatment Level and Enhanced Services Summary
Description: Level of Treatment based on the weighted scores in
Severity Level Table in Figure 13.1.**

DESCRIPTION OF FOUR LEVELS OF AOD IMPAIRED DRIVING SERVICES	
LEVEL	DESCRIPTION OF LEVEL OF TREATMENT SERVICE
1	**Level I Education:** 12 hours of AOD education; this is a stand-alone service and is used for DWI offenders who have no AOD problem.
2	**Level II Education:** 24 hours of AOD and impaired driving education over period of 12 weeks.
3	**Level II Education and Level II Therapy:** Includes the 24 hours of Level II Education, a core 42 hour Level II Therapy plus possible additional 44 hours of therapy (Tracks A through D in Table 13.2 below). Thus, this level could include outpatient therapy from 42 to 86 hours and from six to 11 months, depending on AOD severity level.
4	**Level II Education, Level II Therapy (42 to 86 hours) plus enhanced services that could include:** Intensive Outpatient, Half-Way House, Intensive Residential Treatment, Hospital Care.

TABLE 13.2

**Colorado Model: Four different treatment tracks that are based on
different levels of BAC and offense history**

TRACKS	CRITERIA		LENGTH OF LEVEL II ED HOURS/WEEKS	LENGTH OF TREATMENT HOURS/WEEKS	COMBINED LEVEL II ED AND TREATMENT HOURS/MONTHS
	BAC	PRIORS			
A	.150 - .199	NONE	24 HOURS 8-12 WEEKS	42 HOURS 21 WEEKS	66 HOURS 7-8 MONTHS
B	= OR > .20	NONE	24 HOURS 8-12 WEEKS	52 HOURS 26 WEEKS	76 HOURS 8-9 MONTHS
C	< .20	1 OR MORE	24 HOURS 8-12 WEEKS	68 HOURS 34 WEEKS	92 HOURS 10-11 MONTHS
D	= OR > .20	1 OR MORE	24 HOURS 8-12 WEEKS	86 HOURS 43 WEEKS	110 HOURS 12-13 MONTHS

Criteria for admission to *Level II Therapy* include more substantive evidence of a history of AOD problems, generally a BAC of .15 or higher, and evidence of substance abuse or dependence. AOD problems may range from mild to severe. There may be evidence of problems in areas of mental health, family and job and productivity.

DIFFERENTIAL, IN-DEPTH ASSESSMENT FOR TREATMENT SERVICES

IT IS RECOMMENDED that the convergent validation model also be used in doing the differential and in-depth assessment for clients who are referred for DWI treatment (e.g. DWC Therapy). This means that an assessment model be used that combines both an *in-depth psychometric self-report* and a *psychometric rater-report* based on a psychosocial history.

In *Chapter 7,* the broad domains and their specific areas of assessment are outlined in *Table 7.2.* In the present chapter, the focus will be on the specific assessment areas that are critical to the evaluation of the DWIO, and which represent the broad domains of *Table 7.2.* Then, a psychometric instrumentation model for self-report and other-report will be presented to illustrate an effective approach to meeting the expectations of an in-depth, differential assessment for DWI treatment clients.

Areas and Domains of Assessment

In the broadest sense, DWI treatment assessment takes in all of the areas of the person's life that contribute to or represent maladaptive or problem thinking and behavior and that represent triggers to relapse and recidivism.

One area discussed in *Chapter 7,* but often overlooked in DWI assessment, is *childhood adjustment problems.* The areas of childhood assessment would include: AOD use and abuse; parental and family conflict; physical and sexual abuse; school adjustment problems; deviancy and legal problems; emotional problems such as depression or anxiety; and physical and medical problems.

The following is a summary of the specific domains of assessment that need to be addressed in DWC

differential and in-depth assessment and which represent the domains in *Table 7.2.*

- Problems in childhood and adolescence.
- Adult family and marital problems.
- Interpersonal conflicts and isolation.
- Mood adjustment and psychological problems.
- Work, job and school adjustment problems.
- Legal and antisocial problems.
- Drug use and abuse patterns.
- Assessment of driving risk.
- Health and medical problems.
- Motivation and treatment readiness.
- Defensiveness in self-disclosure.
- Assessment of strengths.

Chapter 7 also identified cognitive-behavioral constructs as an important part of the assessment process. Assessment of this area is an ongoing process in DWC. For example, every session challenges clients to evaluate their patterns of automatic thinking, attitudes and underlying beliefs in relationship to specific and existential events occurring in their lives. A number of work sheets focus on this kind of ongoing assessment.

Psychometric Instrumentation for In-depth, Differential Assessment

All sources of information are used in completing the in-depth assessment of DWI treatment clients. These include:

- the ASUDS profile;

- the five collateral data elements of BAC at arrest, prior DWI offenses, prior education and treatment intervention and drugs other than alcohol involved in the DWI;

- interview data; and

- results from an in-depth, multi-dimensional psychometric instrument using both self-report and other-report data.

There are a number of instruments that can be used for the in-depth assessment process. These are summarized in *Table A.3* of *Appendix A* along with information to access their use. Instruments that focus more specifically on the patterns of AOD use include the *Alcohol Use Inventory* (Horn, Wanberg & Foster, 1990), *The Drug Use Self-Report* (DUSR: Wanberg & Horn, 1991) and the *Comprehensive Drinking Profile* (CDP: Miller & Marlatt, 1984). Two instruments that provide a broader assessment of the various life-functioning domains described above are: *The Addictions Severity Index* (ASI: McClellan, et al., 1996) and the *Adult Clinical Assessment Profiles* (ACAP: Wanberg, 1998).

Illustration of an In-depth Psychometric Assessment Model: The Adult Clinical Assessment Profile

The ACAP will be used as a model to illustrate a convergent validation approach to an in-depth, multiple-construct psychometric assessment using both self-report and other-report data. The ACAP is comprised of two psychometric instruments: The *Adult Self-Assessment Profile* (ADSAP) and the *Rating Adult Problems Scale* (RAPS). Each of these will be briefly discussed.

The *Adult Self-Assessment Profile* (ADSAP) is a self-report instrument comprised of 126 items and a 24 treatment needs checklist. It is comprised of 14 life-time measurement scales, one needs checklist scale, a strength-based assessment scale and six scales measuring AOD use and life-adjustment problems in the past six months. It measures all of the essential assessment domains described above and is normed on a sample of adult criminal justice clients referred for treatment. A significant proportion of this sample is comprised of impaired driving offenders referred to treatment (not education) services. All scales have demonstrated optimal reliabilities and construct validity. An example of the ADSAP profile for particular client is found in *Figure 13.2.*

The *Rating Adult Problems Scale* (RAPS) provides a psychometric-based measurement of information emerging from a structured psychosocial interview format. It provides a psychometric summary of seven scales measuring major life-adjustment. It also has a strength based scale. The RAPS represents ACAP's other-report component of convergent

validation approach. The RAPS profile is found in *Figure 13.2.*

A comprehensive assessment data base for DWI clients is established when using the ASUDS in conjunction with instruments in the genre of the ACAP or ASI instruments. In this manner, all of the assessment domains are accounted for, including a measure of defensiveness at screening.

The ACAP model is presented only to illustrate a comprehensive, psychometric-based in-depth approach to the assessment of clients entering DWI treatment services.[2] The other differential screening and in-depth instruments listed in Tables A.2 and A.3 in *Appendix A* are also recommended as reliable resources that can be used in completing initial differential screening and in-depth differential assessment of DWI offenders. Sources for the acquisition of these instruments are also provided.

Case presentation: *Figure 13.2* represents a 35 year old employed male, who is divorced and has a high school education. He is a successful salesman with a large company. He was arrested for DWI on the way home from the bar. He claims to have "never gotten over" his divorce. He has had recent conflicts with his girlfriend that contribute to his current depression. He lives by himself in an apartment. He has one child who lives with the client's ex-wife in another state. This is his second DWI in his current state of residence. However, he has had four DWI convictions since age 16. His arrest BAC was .23. Based on the ASUDS, he was required to take a 24 hour education program followed by 86 hours of therapy. He has a high-bound profile on the ADSAP with severe problems in the areas of AOD use, anxiety and depression, history of marital and family problems, job stress and vocation dissatisfaction and a history of legal problems coming mainly from his DWI history. He has been experiencing depression and anxiety related to his divorce and recent conflicts with his girlfriend. He rates himself low on strengths, though his evaluator rates him somewhat higher. Overall, he openly admits to having multiple problems that need to be addressed in treatment. His self-report is congruent with the evaluator's RAPS profile. He is self-disclosing and motivated. A portion of his MAP is found in *Figure 13.4.*

THE CLIENT MASTER PROFILE (MP) AND MASTER ASSESSMENT PLAN (MAP)

AS PART OF THE DWI treatment program, clients referred to *DWC Therapy* are asked to generate their own differential assessment and a treatment plan to guide their involvement in DWC. They are asked to complete the MP and MAP at the closure of *DWC Education*. The MP and MAP are then reviewed and finalized in *Session 2* of the *Orientation to DWC Therapy*.

The Master Profile (MP)

Figure 13.3 provides the *Master Profile* which is *Work Sheet 4* of *Session 2* of *DWC Therapy*. The methods and procedures for implementing the completion of the MP is found in Section III of this Guide and in Session 2 of the client's *DWC Therapy Participant's Workbook*. The provider and client use all sources of information when completing the MP and the MAP.

The in-depth assessment and the MP are completed in partnership with the provider and the client and the client's treatment group. It is recommended that the provider and client complete the MP independently and then compare ratings. The group can also provide feedback as to their perceptions of the client.

The Master Assessment Plan - MAP

The MAP is developed from the *Master Profile*. It becomes the guide for the work that the client will do in DWC therapy. As additional information becomes available through client self-disclosure and feedback, both the MP and the MAP can be revised and updated. *Figure 13.4* provides a portion of the MAP for the client whose profile is illustrated in Figure 13.2.

SUMMARY

BUILDING ON THE concepts and perspectives presented in Chapter 7, this chapter provides an operational framework for the differential screening and in-depth assessment of the impaired driving offender. The *DSAP* Model was used to illustrate DWI assessment and criteria for placing clients in appropriate services. Although the specific criteria

for placement in the DSAP Model may not fit other jurisdictions, the differential screening instrument (ASUDS) and the in-depth ACAP assessment instruments (ADSAP and RAPS) can be effectively used as psychometric tools to help evaluators determine treatment needs and recommendations.

This chapter also presents an approach which facilitates helping clients take responsibility for self-assessment and treatment planning. The Master Profile (MP) and the Master Assessment Plan (MAP) are completed by the client, in consultation with the provider. The MP provides clients with a profile that helps them identify their major problem areas. These problem areas become the basis for completing the MAP. This approach is congruent with DWC's underlying philosophy of DWI treatment being a partnership process that maximizes interaction between the client and provider. This approach is also part of helping clients move into the ownership stage of change.

---

2. For information in the use of the *Adult Clinical Assessment Profile (Adult Self-Assessment Profile - AdSAP,* and the *Rating Adult Problems Scale - RAPS)* contact the Center for Addictions Research and Evaluation, 5460 Ward Road, Suite 140, Arvada, CO, 80002.

FIGURE 13.2

SCALE NAME	RAW SCORE	Low			Low-medium		High-medium		High		
		1	2	3	4	5	6	7	8	9	10
1. CHILDHOOD	11								12 13┊14 15 17┊18 20 32		
2. FAMILY-MARITAL	13										21
3. INTERPERSONAL	4							5	┊6 7 8┊9 10 21		
4. MENTAL HEALTH	18										19 31
5. WORK-JOB	6						┊7 8┊ 9 10┊11 14 21				
6. LEGAL	14					┊15 16 ┊17 18 19┊20 21 22┊23 25 34					
7. DRUGS LIFETIME	4		┊5 ┊6 7 ┊8 9 10 11┊12 13 ┊14 16 18┊19 22 40								
8. AOD SUSTAINED	13										15
9. AOD BENEFITS	17								18┊19 23 33		
10. AOD DISRUPT	23									24 36	
11. PRIOR AOD HELP	2			┊3 ┊4 5 ┊6 7 8┊9 11 16						
12. AODLIFE GLOBAL	56									64 92	
13. HEALTH	7								┊8 10 18		
14. MOTIVATION	9									10 18	
15. HELP NEEDS	5								6 7┊8 10 23		
16. STRENGTHS	9	11 12┊13 14 15┊16 ┊17 18 ┊19 20 ┊21 ┊22 23 24┊25 26 27┊28 30 33									
17. FAM-IN 6 MONTH	6						7 8┊9 11 13┊14 17 39				
18. MENTAL 6 MONTH	10								11┊12 16 33		
19. WORK 6 MONTH	2			┊3 ┊4 ┊5 ┊6 7 8┊9 12 21						
20. LEGAL 6 MONTH	3			┊4 ┊5 ┊6 7┊8 ┊9 13 29						
21 DRUGS 6 MONTH	0			┊1 ┊2 ┊3 ┊4 5 6┊7 9 27						
22. AOD 6MO GLOBAL	10						11 13┊14 17 21┊22 29 76				

PERCENTILE: 1 10 20 30 40 50 60 70 80 90 99

Norms based on 700 adult probation clients

RATING ADULT PROBLEMS SCALE PROFILE - RAPS

SCALE NAME	RAW SCORE	Low			Low-medium		High-medium		High		
		1	2	3	4	5	6	7	8	9	10
1. CHILDHOOD	19								┊20 21 28		
2. FAMILY-INTER.	16										17 24
3. MENTAL HEALTH	7				┊8 9 ┊ 10 ┊11 12 ┊13 14 15┊16 18 30						
4. WORK-JOB	9						┊10 11 ┊12 13 15┊16 17 24				
5. LEGAL	12					┊13 14┊15 16 ┊17 18 ┊19 21 31					
6. AOD GLOBAL	17						18 ┊19 20 21┊22 24 31				
7. HEALTH	5						6┊7 8 9 ┊10 12 20				
8. STRENGTHS	26				┊27 28 ┊29 30 ┊31 32 33┊34 35 37┊38 40 44						

PERCENTILE: 1 10 20 30 40 50 60 70 80 90 99

Norms based on 700 ratings of adult probation clients

FIGURE 13.3 YOUR MASTER PROFILE (MP)

I. ALCOHOL AND OTHER DRUG USE ASSESSMENT

	LEVEL OF INVOLVEMENT IN DRUG		
YOUR QUANTITY/FREQUENCY OF USE	**NONE OR LOW**	**MODERATE**	**HIGH**
Alcohol Involvement	1 2 3	4 5 6 7	8 9 10
Marijuana Involvement	1 2 3	4 5 6 7	8 9 10
Cocaine Involvement	1 2 3	4 5 6 7	8 9 10
Amphetamine Involvement	1 2 3	4 5 6 7	8 9 10
Other Drugs	1 2 3	4 5 6 7	8 9 10
STYLE OF ALCOHOL/OTHER DRUG USE	**NONE OR LOW**	**MODERATE**	**HIGH**
Convival or Gregarious Use	1 2 3	4 5 6 7	8 9 10
Solo or Use by Yourself	1 2 3	4 5 6 7	8 9 10
Sustained or Continuous Use	1 2 3	4 5 6 7	8 9 10
BENEFITS OF AOD USE	**NONE OR LOW**	**MODERATE**	**HIGH**
Cope with Social Discomfort	1 2 3	4 5 6 7	8 9 10
Cope with Emotional Discomfort	1 2 3	4 5 6 7	8 9 10
Cope with Relationships	1 2 3	4 5 6 7	8 9 10
Cope with Physical Distress	1 2 3	4 5 6 7	8 9 10
NEGATIVE CONSEQUENCES OF USE	**NONE OR LOW**	**MODERATE**	**HIGH**
Behavioral Disruption from Use	1 2 3	4 5 6 7	8 9 10
Emotional Disruption from Use	1 2 3	4 5 6 7	8 9 10
Physical Disruption from Use	1 2 3	4 5 6 7	8 9 10
Social Irresponsibility	1 2 3	4 5 6 7	8 9 10
Overall Negative Consequences	1 2 3	4 5 6 7	8 9 10
CATEGORIES OF AOD USE PROBLEMS	**NONE OR LOW**	**MODERATE**	**HIGH**
Drinking/Drug Use Problem	1 2 3	4 5 6 7	8 9 10
Problem Drinker or Drug Use	1 2 3	4 5 6 7	8 9 10
Alcohol/Other Drug Abuse	1 2 3	4 5 6 7	8 9 10
Alcohol/Other Drug Dependent	1 2 3	4 5 6 7	8 9 10

FIGURE 13.3 **CONTINUED**

II. IMPAIRED DRIVING ASSESSMENT

AREAS OF IMPAIRED DRIVING PROBLEMS AND RISK	LEVEL OF PROBLEM SEVERITY									
	LOW			MODERATE				HIGH		
BAC Level at Time of Arrest	1	2	3	4	5	6	7	8	9	10
Disruption to Your Lifestyle	1	2	3	4	5	6	7	8	9	10
Bodily Injury to Yourself	1	2	3	4	5	6	7	8	9	10
Bodily Injury to Others	1	2	3	4	5	6	7	8	9	10
Property Damage Including Car	1	2	3	4	5	6	7	8	9	10
Overall Problems From DWI	1	2	3	4	5	6	7	8	9	10
Overall Driving Risk	1	2	3	4	5	6	7	8	9	10

III. ASSESSMENT OF THINKING, FEELING AND ATTITUDE PATTERNS

THINKING, FEELINGS, TRIGGERS AND ATTITUDE PATTERNS THAT CAN LEAD TO DUI/DWAI BEHAVIOR/CONDUCT	LEVEL OF PROBLEM SEVERITY									
	LOW			MODERATE				HIGH		
Blame Others for Problems	1	2	3	4	5	6	7	8	9	10
Victim Stance	1	2	3	4	5	6	7	8	9	10
Care-less: Don't Care	1	2	3	4	5	6	7	8	9	10
Think: Better Than Others	1	2	3	4	5	6	7	8	9	10
Irresponsible Thinking	1	2	3	4	5	6	7	8	9	10
Act Without Thinking	1	2	3	4	5	6	7	8	9	10
Angry and Aggressive Thinking	1	2	3	4	5	6	7	8	9	10
Feeling Depressed and Sad	1	2	3	4	5	6	7	8	9	10
Rebellious/Against Authority	1	2	3	4	5	6	7	8	9	10
Time with Drinking Friends	1	2	3	4	5	6	7	8	9	10
Friends Angry at Laws/Society	1	2	3	4	5	6	7	8	9	10
Conflict with Spouse/Family	1	2	3	4	5	6	7	8	9	10
Second Home at Bar	1	2	3	4	5	6	7	8	9	10
Having Bad/Unpleasant Feelings	1	2	3	4	5	6	7	8	9	10
Loss of Self-Importance	1	2	3	4	5	6	7	8	9	10
Loss of Someone Important	1	2	3	4	5	6	7	8	9	10

FIGURE 13.3 CONTINUED

IV. BACKGROUND: PROBLEMS OF CHILDHOOD/ADOLESCENCE

PROBLEMS IN CHILDHOOD AND TEENAGE YEARS	LEVEL OF PROBLEM SEVERITY									
	LOW			MODERATE				HIGH		
Teenage Alcohol/Drug Use	1	2	3	4	5	6	7	8	9	10
Problems with Law During Teens	1	2	3	4	5	6	7	8	9	10
Problems with Parents/Family	1	2	3	4	5	6	7	8	9	10
Emotional-Psychological	1	2	3	4	5	6	7	8	9	10
School Adjustment Problems	1	2	3	4	5	6	7	8	9	10
Physical Illness in Childhood	1	2	3	4	5	6	7	8	9	10

V. CURRENT LIFE SITUATION PROBLEMS

AREAS OF ADULT PROBLEMS	LEVEL OF PROBLEM SEVERITY									
	LOW			MODERATE				HIGH		
Job and Employment Problems	1	2	3	4	5	6	7	8	9	10
Financial and Money Problems	1	2	3	4	5	6	7	8	9	10
Unstable Living Situation	1	2	3	4	5	6	7	8	9	10
Social-Relationship Problems	1	2	3	4	5	6	7	8	9	10
Marital-Family Problems	1	2	3	4	5	6	7	8	9	10
Emotional-Psychological	1	2	3	4	5	6	7	8	9	10
Problems with the Law	1	2	3	4	5	6	7	8	9	10
Physical Health Problems	1	2	3	4	5	6	7	8	9	10

VI. MOTIVATION AND READINESS FOR TREATMENT

AREAS OF ASSESSMENT	LOW			MODERATE				HIGH		
Awareness of AOD Problem	1	2	3	4	5	6	7	8	9	10
Awareness of DWI Problem	1	2	3	4	5	6	7	8	9	10
Acknowledge Need for Help	1	2	3	4	5	6	7	8	9	10
Willingness to Accept Help	1	2	3	4	5	6	7	8	9	10
Willingness for DWI Therapy	1	2	3	4	5	6	7	8	9	10
Have Taken Action to Change	1	2	3	4	5	6	7	8	9	10

FIGURE 13.4   Master Assessment Plan (MAP)

I. ALCOHOL AND OTHER DRUG USE PROBLEM AREAS

PROBLEM AREA AND DESCRIPTION	CHANGES NEED IN THOUGHT AND ACTION	RESOURCES TO BE USED TO MAKE CHANGES
Have continual thoughts and desire to go out and drink with friends	Replace thoughts about going out with non-drinking friends and engage non-drinking friends in social activities	*Social Skills:* Learning assertiveness and refusal skills

II. IMPAIRED DRIVING PROBLEMS

PROBLEM AREA AND DESCRIPTION	CHANGES NEED IN THOUGHT AND ACTION	RESOURCES TO BE USED TO MAKE CHANGES
Live alone, and social life at the bar and always stop off after work and no one to drive me home	Change thoughts that "must drive self home" and seek other outlets for social life	Use *cognitive restructuring* to change thoughts; develop awareness of harm to others when drink and drive

III. THINKING, FEELING, TRIGGERS AND ATTITUDE PATTERNS THAT LEAD TO DUI/DWAI BEHAVIOR AND CONDUCT

PROBLEM AREA AND DESCRIPTION	CHANGES NEED IN THOUGHT AND ACTION	RESOURCES TO BE USED TO MAKE CHANGES
Get depressed because live alone and have hopeless thoughts about ever having a trusting relationship with a woman	Change depressed thoughts; identify underlying beliefs that lead to hopeless thoughts about having trusting relationship	Cognitive restructuring; develop social skills to help meet people and get involved in social groups

IV. CURRENT LIFE SITUATION PROBLEMS

PROBLEM AREA AND DESCRIPTION	CHANGES NEED IN THOUGHT AND ACTION	RESOURCES TO BE USED TO MAKE CHANGES
Conflicts with girlfriend that are upsetting and lead to thoughts "she doesn't care," that lead to depression and going to the bar and drink	Develop communication skills to improve relationship with girlfriend; identify underlying beliefs that lead to "she doesn't care"	Interpersonal skills training; restructuring thoughts; couples counseling

CHAPTER FOURTEEN: OPERATIONAL GUIDELINES AND PROCEDURES FOR DRIVING WITH CARE EDUCATION AND TREATMENT PROTOCOLS

OVERVIEW

THE PURPOSE OF this chapter is to introduce the provider to some of the basic guidelines and procedures for the delivery of the DWC education and treatment protocols. The structure and process of the three protocols are briefly outlined. General guidelines for the admission and intake of clients are described including the forms recommended for each of the three protocols. Program agreements and guidelines for clients are described. As well, role expectations of providers who present the DWC protocols are also outlined. The techniques and methods for facilitating a therapeutic education program are also outlined. Some guidelines regarding effective group facilitation and management are also provided. Finally, methods for the evaluation of DWC lessons and sessions are recommended.

Section III of this Guide provides a detailed description of the guidelines and procedures for the delivery of each of the three DWC protocols.

SUMMARY OF STRUCTURE AND PROCESS OF DWC PROTOCOLS

THE *Driving with CARE* (DWC) curricula has two broad components: education and treatment. The education component has two levels: *Level I Education* and *Level II Education.* The treatment component is a sequel to the *Level II Education* component. These three levels of services and their delivery will be briefly reviewed. Section III provides detailed information and guidelines for the implementation and delivery of these three protocols.

Level I Education is comprised of six two-hour lessons designed to service first time DWI offenders who present no detectible evidence of AOD problems and who had lower BAC levels. It is recommended that *Level I Education* lessons are delivered in sequence in six two-hour sessions once a week in a closed group. This gives the provider opportunity to work with the client over a six week period and allows the client time to assimilate the material. Although not recommended, *Level I Education* can be delivered in two six hour time blocks or three four hour time blocks.

Level II Education, comprised of 12 two-hour lessons delivered over 12 weeks, is for persons who present marginal AOD problems and whose BAC levels were somewhat higher. People with moderate to severe AOD problems and/or high arrest BACs should take *Level II Education* and *Level II Therapy,* *Level II Education* being completed first.

Level II Education may be presented in a closed or open group. If a closed group is used, then the same group proceeds from *Lesson 1* and continues through *Lesson 12* with a closing exercise in *Lesson 12.* If an open group is used, then *Lesson 1* is used as an orientation to *Level II Education* and all clients must have *Lesson 1* before proceeding into the *Level II Education* protocol. Agencies using an open group model for *Level II Education* will have periodic orientation sessions for new clients. When using the open group format, providers must not schedule clients to enter a lesson where the prior lesson was a prequisite. The lesson no-entry points, along with other open group procedures are fully described in Section III.

DWC Therapy, which ranges from 42 hours to 86 hours of treatment, is organized into four tracks. These tracks are outlined in Table 13.2 of Chapter 13. This protocol is designed for individuals who show fairly definite signs of AOD misuse and problems and/or who had BAC levels of .15 or higher. Tracks B through D are designed for clients who need, or are required, to take additional therapy. The additional therapy needs are usually based on the client's arrest BAC level, offense history, and level of AOD use and psychosocial problems.

Track A of *DWC Therapy* is the core curriculum for the treatment protocol and is comprised of 21, two hour manual-guided therapy sessions. Track B clients complete an additional five two-hour *DWC Therapy* group sessions and two manual guided *therapy projects.* Track C clients complete an additional 13 two-hour *DWC Therapy* group sessions and four manual guided *therapy projects.* Track D clients complete an additional 22 two hour group sessions and eight manual guided therapy projects. The two hour education and therapy sessions do not include break time.

The core 21 *DWC Therapy* sessions may be presented in a closed or open group format. When an open group format is used, *Sessions 1 and 2* are used as an orientation to the program. Agencies using open groups will have periodic orientation groups that take clients through *Sessions 1 and 2*. Orientation can be done in individual sessions. As with *Level II Education,* because two sessions may be sequential, there are specific sessions for which clients do not enter. These are clearly outlined in Section III.

The *Level I and Level II Education* are presented in discrete learning experiences called lessons, indicating that the protocol is educational rather than therapeutic. For the three protocols, the *Participant's Workbook* will include a full descripiton of the lesson and session content. Thus, only a summary of this content will be given in the *Provider's Guide*. An intake protocol for each of the two educational protocols will be outlined and discussed.

The core 21 session *DWC Therapy* protocol is presented in discrete sessions. These sessions will have specific structured experiences followed by a period of therapeutic processing. The *Provider's Guide* provides supportive information for each lesson and session, and will also enhance the content of some sessions.

GENERAL INTAKE AND ADMISSION GUIDELINES

THE FOLLOWING DISCUSSION provides a recommended protocol and guidelines for intake and admission into DWI education and treatment programs. However, it is recognized that most agencies or jurisdictions will have their own intake and admission procedure and forms. More specific guidelines will be provided for each of the three DWC program protocols.

Referral Information and Data

It is recommended that each client undergoes a *differential screening assessment* which includes an interview, review of all collateral data and the administration of the ASUDS (or similar screening device). From this evaluation, recommendations are made by the court and the judicial sentences is ordered which, for most clients, includes referral to education and/or treatment. That report, which

includes past DWI arrests and convictions, past DWI education and treatment, arrest BAC and the ASUDS profile, should be sent to the education and treatment service provider.

Intake and admission forms

Clients entering all three protocols should complete the following or comparable forms.

▶ Personal Data Questionnaire.

▶ Consent for Program Involvement.

▶ Consent for Release of Information.

▶ Client Rights and Responsibility Statement.

▶ Federal Requirement for Confidentiality.

▶ Counselor Full Disclosure Statement.

Although most agencies have their own forms, examples of these forms are found in *Appendix C.* Agencies will also want to have a statement outlining the agency fees and collection procedures.

Intake and Admission Interview and Individual Treatment Plan

Most agencies will not require an intake interview for *Level I Education.* Clients should complete an intake form and then proceed into the first Lesson. It is recommended that the intake and admission procedures for *Level II Education* clients include a short interview following which the basic intake forms can be completed. It is recommended that clients taking both Level II Education and DWC Therapy complete all intake forms.

A formal interview and an in-depth differential assessment should be done on all *DWC Therapy* clients. This assessment includes the completion of a comprehensive assessment instrument. This procedure was discussed in Chapter 13 and a list of recommended instruments is found in Table A.3 of *Appendix A.*

From this interview, the initial *Individual Treatment Plan* (ITP) is developed. For the *DWC Education* clients that the provider knows will proceed into *DWC Therapy,* the ITP could be started at *DWC*

Education intake. However, it is best that the ITP is not completed until the client has completed *DWC Education.*

Completing the Driving With Care Inventory - DWCI

The DWCI is a pre-post test for clients in both *Level I and Level II Education.* Clients may complete the DWCI either at intake or during the orientation sessions. For *Level I Education,* clients will complete this in their first lesson. Clients are then readministered the DWCI during the last lesson of these protocols. A copy of the DWCI is found in *Appendix B.*

PROGRAM AGREEMENTS AND GROUND RULES: EXPECTATIONS OF CLIENTS

The orientation lessons and sessions for all three protocols include what are called "Program Agreements and Guidelines." These are also provided in Section III of this Guide. We now briefly present a generic set of client expectations and agreements that are recommended for all three protocols. Each individual agency or provider will have its own unique program agreements and expectations.

1. Abstinence from Substance Use

DWC presents clients with two different options with respect to relapse prevention goals: the goal of maintaining total abstinence from alcohol or other drugs; and the goal of preventing involvement in AOD disruptive use patterns. Even though clients are presented with these two goals, *we want them to set the goal of abstaining from all AOD use while in the DWC program.*

There are several important issues regarding this abstinence-during-program expectation. **First,** for some clients, the terms of probation may not require abstinence. As well, some judicial jurisdictions do not require this as part of probation. Those clients will show considerable resistance, at least initially, when entering a program that expects abstinence during the period of program involvement. With these clients, motivational and client-centered approaches should be used along with confronting the fact that a DWI clearly indicates that the client had a problem with AOD use

and that if the client is unable to commit to abstinence during the program, this may mean that there are some addictive-related issues with that individual's AOD use. The inability or refusal to maintain abstinence during the program may portend a problem in and of itself.

Clients in *Level II Education* most generally do not have problems with AOD abstinence since it is only for a period of six to 12 weeks. Clients referred to *DWC Therapy* may have more difficulty with this expectation. However, these clients are referred to *DWC Therapy* because there is evidence of greater levels of AOD use problems.

Second, some clients will lapse into use from time to time. In the cases where this is a violation of the terms of probation, the use episodes need to be dealt with both therapeutically and from a correctional perspective. That is, the provider may need to put on the "correctional hat" and fulfill the agreement that probation is informed of the infraction. This should be therapeutically dealt with, and every effort should be made to have the client be responsible for disclosing the "lapse" to probation.

Third, for those clients who do experience a "lapse" or relapse, it should be made clear that members are asked to not come to a session under the influence of alcohol or drugs. Such clients are unable to participate fully in the group and this would disrupt other group members' efforts to maintain abstinence during the program. Participants are informed that the group leader may require an alcohol or drug test at any time if there is a question of a participant's sobriety. If the test is positive, then the client should not be allowed to be in the group session. If the client is a threat to the safety of others because of intoxication, then appropriate measures must be made to protect the community (e.g., police called, client taken to detoxification treatment, etc.).

A client with a positive breath alcohol reading or drug screen should be staffed to determine disposition. The client might be suspended from the program temporarily, be referred to a detoxification center, or be expelled from the program. These kinds of decisions need to be made on a case-by-case basis. Providers should have the appropriate releases on all clients so that proper notification of supervisory personnel (parole or probation worker) can be made.

Note: As noted above, some agencies and/or jurisdictions do not require alcohol abstinence during program attendance. Although an expectation of the DWC protocol is that clients will maintain abstinance during program attendance, this decision is really up to each agency. All agencies, however, should require clients to be alcohol and drug free when attending sessions.

2. Attendance and Promptness

Meeting places and schedules should be clear to the client. Consistent attendance is required. Clients are expected to make up missed lessons or sessions. This could mean that a client has to wait until that particular lesson or session comes around in the curriculum cycle. If the client is unable to wait, then the session can be administered on an individual basis. Providers may hold separate "make up" groups where certain sessions and lessons are conducted for several clients who may have missed particular sessions. All clients are expected to be on time for each session. Required program lesson and session hours (e.g., 24 hours of *Level II Education*) should not include breaks.

3. Active Positive Participation

Active participation in group exercises, role-playing demonstrations, completion of all work sheets and timely completion of homework assignments are required aspects of the DWC protocols. Clients also agree to having a positive attitude towards the group leader and peers.

4. Confidentiality

Confidentiality is essential for the success of the group. Members commit to not discuss group conversations with outsiders. The group leader explains that confidentiality can be maintained to the extent that clients' behavior do not reflect imminent danger to themselves or others or where the provider has a duty to report as in the case of child abuse.

Leaders do not make a commitment to keep secrets about anything the sponsoring agency or supervisory personnel need to know. Assurance is provided that client participation and treatment

details will be used appropriately and in context. Individual *Thinking Reports* or self-disclosing statements should **not** become a part of the general correctional record without client permission. Clients should expect that *summary progress reports* are submitted to the supervising agencies, including both court and motor vehicle. Releases for such reports are required.

5. Removal of Client From Group and Program Termination

Each agency will have its own policy for the removal of a client from group or for terminating the client from the program. Such circumstances should be dealt with therapeutically as well as correctionally. The basic guideline is that therapeutic skills and approaches should always be the basis for dealing with adverse and disruptive client behavior, both within the group and individual context. Even when taking a correctional role when dealing with fractious and infractious behaviors, that role should be implemented within the framework of therapeutic skills and communication.

EXPECTATIONS OF PROVIDERS AND GROUP LEADERS

EXPECTATIONS AND ground rules also apply to providers. The most basic guideline is that the provider maintains a high level of ethical and professional standards in all contacts with clients. Providers will want to maintain appropriate dress and appearance and model normative and prosocial behavior. Providers will be thoroughly prepared and ready to present each lesson or session.

THERAPEUTIC EDUCATION PRINCIPLES UNDERLYING DWC

There are some core therapeutic education principles that underlie the implementation and delivery of the three DWC manual-guided protocols. These will be reviewed.

Learner-Centered Versus Information-Centered

The DWC program is based on a learner-centered approach where the goal is to have the client assume ownership of learning, self-improvement and change. Hart (1991) identifies some specific characteristics of learner-centered instruction and education. These are:

- the goal is to improve and change performance, not to just get information across;

- the learner is a source of expertise as well as the provider;

- learners are actively involved and express their thoughts, views, beliefs versus being in a passive, "soaking up" role;

- feedback from learners is for the purpose of determining whether ideas and concepts are being applied rather than whether the learner just retains and understands information;

- risk-taking and exploration are reinforced versus control through reward and punishment; and

- learning is experiential.

Lesson Based Education and Therapy

Although we learn from experience, experience is not a good teacher because - *experience gives us the test before the lesson.* Effective teaching and learning will give the learner the lesson first, and then the test. DWI clients have failed many life-tests because of not having learned important lessons of living. The overarching goal of DWC is to give clients important lessons so as to prevent relapse and recidivism. DWC is lesson-based. It is structured around specific lesson and therapy themes that are the basis of interactive participation.

Skill Development Based

DWC skill development is built around three broad therapeutic education themes: 1) developing cognitive skills for self-control; 2) developing skills to enhance positive relationship outcomes; and 3) developing skills to enhance responsible behaviors and actions in the community and society. All of these skills are specifically directed at preventing relapse and recidivism and developing strategies for responsible living and change.

Interacting with and Personalizing Curriculum Content and Themes

The DWC model makes an effort to maximize the client's interaction with the curriculum material. Every effort possible should be made to have clients personalize and identify with the content and themes of DWC. Even when presenting material in a didactic format, the presenter should make an effort to have clients share their personal experiences that illustrate the concepts and ideas being presented. The work sheets and thinking reports in the various lessons and sessions are designed to maximize the client's interaction with the material and to apply the material to their own experiences.

The use of reflective-interactive approaches can help to enhance personal identification with the material. For example, to a client's comment, "all my friends drink," the reflective-interactive response might be "how is that an error in thinking? Are all your friends drinkers? What about some friends in this group who don't drink?"

Maximizing Interactive Participation

An underlying principle of DWC delivery is that of maximizing interactive participation within the group and among group members around the lesson and session themes and concepts. There are a number of techniques that can be used to maximize interactive participation including some of the following.

- Role playing and role reversal.

- The round robin technique of having every group member share thoughts and ideals.

- Group members give and receive feedback.

- Using reflective-interactive skills when presenting material.

- Facilitating client elaboration around ideas and themes.

- Using the exercises identified in the guidelines provided for each lesson and session in Section III.

▶ Using the focused activities approach.

Multi-Media and Multi-Sensory Formats

Using various media to help clients interact with the curriculum material and with each other will enhance interactive participation. These include visual aids such as posters, overhead transparencies, charts and work sheets. It is helpful for the provider to develop a wall poster illustrating the basic cognitive-behavioral change schemata (*Figure 11.3* in Chapter 11). Media approaches should also be multisensory involving seeing, listening, talking and kinesthetic approaches.

Seating Arrangements

The ideal seating arrangement is to arrange tables in a square so that clients can face each other and yet have a table on which to work in the *Participant's Workbook*. Some may argue that this arrangement prevents full interaction among group members; however, this has not been the experience of the authors. DWC is based on the model of clients interacting with group members, with the curriculum material and the provider.

PROVIDER SKILL REQUIRED TO DELIVER DWC PROTOCOLS

In Section III, various skills are identified that are needed in delivering the various DWC protocols. These are briefly summarized.

▶ Skills in differential screening.

▶ Skills in differential and in-depth assessment, mainly for *DWC Therapy*.

▶ Counseling skills that facilitate individual and group sharing, to get clients to hear their story through feedback clarification and confrontation, and to get clients to act on their story through thought and action challenge and reinforcement.

▶ Motivational enhancement skills which include basic counseling skills along with being non-confrontational around resistance, avoiding argumentation, maximizing sharing, expressing empathy, rolling with the resistance and reinforcing changes in attitudes and behavior.

▶ Skills in effective group management and leadership discussed below.

▶ Skills in cognitive-behavioral approaches in helping clients change their thoughts and behaviors.

▶ Understand and operationally integrate the correctional and the therapeutic approaches.

▶ Use of the community reinforcement model, referral resources in the community and effective referral to aftercare services.

PRINCIPLES OF EFFECTIVE GROUP MANAGEMENT AND LEADERSHIP

THE EFFECTIVE management of the DWC group is essential in the successful delivery of the DWC protocols. Some of the basic guidelines and principles for effective group facilitation and management are summarized.

1. Methods of Group Facilitation

There are three approaches to group facilitation that are important in the delivery of the DWC protocols (Glassman, 1983; Wanberg & Milkman, 1998). These will be briefly reviewed.

The first is called *facilitation **in** the group.* This approach focuses on individuals in the group and is actually doing *individual counseling* within a group setting. The vehicle for change in this approach is the personal experiences of individual group members.

The second approach is to facilitate the interaction among individuals in the group. This is called *facilitation **with** the group.* The group leader tries to get people to interact and uses the *interpersonal interactions* to help individual clients to disclose themselves and work on their problems and issues. The vehicle for change is the interaction the client experiences in the group.

The third approach involves seeing the group as an individual. Glassman (1983) calls this *facilitation **of** the group.* In this approach, the treatment of the client occurs through the treatment **of** the group.

The group "is the client," and the group becomes the vehicle for change and growth in the individual based on the idea that a *healthy group produces healthy members*. The skills that the counselor uses to facilitate the expression and change in individual counseling are used with the group. The counselor invites the group to share, disclose and tell its story. The counselor reflects the group's feelings, thoughts, actions, gets the group to change and then reinforces that change. The development of group cohesion and trust become primary focuses. The group becomes a powerful initiator and reinforcer of the changes in its members. The group leader will look after the group to nurture it, to protect it, and to facilitate its growth.

2. Depersonalizing the Leadership Authority

DWI groups tend to see the authority for controlling and sanctioning behavior as centered in the group leader or counselor. An effective approach is to allow the structure, rules and guidelines of the program to manage the group and the individual behaviors of group members. This centers the authority on the program rules and guidelines.

Bush and Bilodeau (1993) identify this as *depersonalizing the use of leader authority* while maintaining control of the process and upholding the rules. The group leader makes it clear that the process will proceed as it has been defined, not because of leader power, but because this is a change process that works, i.e., "it's nothing personal." Managing disruptive behavior is part of the group leadership role. The leader should communicate to the DWI group, within the context of therapeutic skills, that: 1) the behavior disrupts the task at hand; 2) the client has the choice whether or not to participate; and 3) there are consequences related to not fully participating in the group. With regard to rules, leaders will communicate that the intent is not to force clients to comply, but rather helping them to succeed.

3. Center the Authority Within the Group

Centering the authority for group management with the group is congruent with the "leadership **of** the group" model. The leader facilitates group responsibility in developing positive behavioral responses. This is not always possible, and the center of authority may, at times, fall back on the group leader. In most cases, control and management of individual behavior in groups can be effectively done through the group itself. This will not work if the group leader is unwilling to relinquish the power and control, or gets caught up in a power struggle with the group.

4. Center the Authority in Group Members

Another method for effective group management is to place the authority and responsibility with the individual offender on questions of appropriate behavior. The goal of DWC is to empower the DWIO by enhancing self-control through skill development. The therapeutic and correctional confrontation strategy of DWC stresses that the *locus of control is always internal* and the decision to change or not to change is always within the power of the client.

5. Keep the Focus on the DWC Themes and Concepts

Group process and interaction are an important focus of manual-guided programs. However, providers can get caught up with process and interaction at the expense of not focusing on helping the client interact with the curriculum content and theme. Strong process-oriented providers will have to shift their therapeutic education paradigm in order to effectively deliver manual-guided programs. Clients, however, do need time to process, both the experiences with the group and the content. This is built into the *DWC Therapy* sessions.

6. Keep the Focus on the Steps of Cognitive-Behavioral Change

Each group session should focus on underlying cognitive-behavioral patterns. The group is continually reminded that the purpose is *preventing relapse and recidivism* and to focus on the CB processes of change that achieves this purpose. Participants should have a clear understanding of how the session content, exercises and work sheets assist in the process of self-directed change.

7. Collaborative Relationship Between Provider and Group Members

Group management is always directed at achieving cooperation between group members and the provider (Bush and Bilodeau, 1993). The initial DWIO posture of "us or them" must eventually be worked through to achieve this collaborative relationship. Patterns of hostility and social conflict need to be replaced with patterns of prosocial cooperation between participants and provider. When angry and hostile attitudes block channels of communication, these attitudes may be *exposed as disruptive* and challenged according to the established guideline for program participation. Member's resentment of the leader's authority may indicate a need to allow clients more freedom to express their views.

8. Maximize Individual Involvement in the Group Process

Effective group leadership is directed at maximizing the participation of group members. At the same time, the leader needs to be keenly aware that individuals differ with respect to group comfort, feeling at ease in a group and ability to be open and to share. As group cohesion and trust build, even the most "threat sensitive" group member will begin to feel a greater degree of comfort in sharing with the group.

Providers will use skills to attend to all group members while at the same time attend to the group itself. This will involve helping each member to be actively involved in the discussions. Although the group leader may work with a single group member on a given exercise, all participants should be actively contemplating the lessons involved. Leaders may "check in" with the group to be sure that everyone is following what is going on. The group may be asked to assist the leader in actively engaging its members.

THE MANY HATS

The DWI provider wears many "hats" when working with impaired driving offenders. These "many hats" have been discussed in *Chapter 11*. The provider wears the personal "hat" in expressing empathy, warmth, genuineness and respect. There is the therapeutic "hat" where the provider utilizes all the skills of effective counseling. The philosophical "hat" gets expressed through the teaching of a theoretical view of alcoholism, drug abuse, criminal conduct or a particular approach to counseling. The provider will need to wear the correctional "hat" when holding the client responsible for violating the terms of probation or the law.

The provider is always in the process of *effectively integrating these various roles* when working with the impaired driving offender.

PROVIDER AND CLIENT RESPONSE EVALUATION

It is recommended that providers build into their program methods to evaluate their work. *The Provider Evaluation Summary* (PES) allows opportunity for providers to rate their effectiveness in program delivery and impressions of how delivery is working. The *Client Evaluation Summary* (CES) provides opportunity for clients to give feedback to providers around program helpfulness. These forms are found in *Appendix C.*

SUMMARY

In Section 1, the scope, history of legislation, and causative and interactive factors of impaired driving were discussed. Issues related to the underage and hardcore DWIO were presented. Various methods of the assessment of DWIOs were reviewed including a special focus on the multimodal and convergent validation assessment model. Countermeasure approaches were reviewed with a summary of those that are most effective in preventing recidivism. Since the CB approach is an important component of DWC, the history of CB therapy along with the critical constructs that define this approach were presented. Issues of culture and diversity related to impaired driving were presented, with a focus on how to enhance competence in working with diverse cultural groups.

Section II focused on the delivery of the DWC education and treatment programs. A DWI serviced delivery framework was presented that integrated into a single service delivery model the phases of growth, stages of change, specific provider skills and goals and objectives of impaired driving education and treatment. Characteristics of an effective DWI therapeutic educator were defined. A specific DWIO assessment model was illustrated and operational guidelines for the deliver of the DWC protocols were described. We now present the three DWC protocols and provide guidelines for the delivery of the DWC lessons and sessions.

SECTION III
the education and treatment curriculums

What a man thinks of himeself, that is what detrmines or rather indicates his fate.
-Henry David Thoreau

The purpose of *Section III* of this *Provider's Guide* is to describe the methods and approaches for the delivery of the three *Driving With Care* protocols: *Alcohol, Other Drugs and Driving Safety Education - Level I Education; Alcohol, Other Drugs and Driving Safety Education - Level II Education;* and *Impaired Driving Offender Treatment - Level II Therapy.*

For each of the three protocols, the specific goals and objectives are defined, content presentation and delivery strategies are outlined, completion requirements and expectations of clients are summarized, and intake, assessment and orientation guidelines are provided. For *Level II Education* and *Level II Therapy,* different protocol delivery options are suggested. As well, provider service delivery skills needed to deliver each of the protocols are outlined. The latter is of particular importance since different skill levels are required for each protocol. For example, delivery of the therapy protocol requires more clinical skills and expertise than does the delivery of the education protocols.

Service delivery guidelines for each of the specific lessons and sessions in the three protocols are outlined in some detail. For the *DWC Level I and Level II Education* protocols, a rationale and overview, a summary of the content, and presentation process and guidelines are provided for each lesson.

For each *DWC Therapy* session, a rationale and overview are provided and session content and presentation sequence are outlined. Guidelines for processing and closing each therapy session are also summarized. The rationale and overview for each lesson and session in the three protocols provide literature and research support for the education and therapy concepts being delivered.

The provider should carefully read the guidelines for each lesson and session before delivery. Since the essential lesson and session content is included in the *Participant's Workbooks,* this content is briefly summarized in the *Provider's Guide.* For some lessons and sessions, there are additional exercises included in the *Provider's Guide* that are not in the *Participant's Workbooks.*

Brief guidelines are also provided in this section for the 10 Therapy Projects in the *DWC Therapy Participant's Workbook.* A rationale and overview of each therapy project is provided along with brief guidelines for project implementation. The provider will want to give the client as much assistance as possible in doing the therapy projects.

INTRODUCTION TO THE EDUCATION AND TREATMENT SERVICE PROTOCOLS

_____

_____

_____

_____

_____

_____

Section I of this manual discussed the impact of impaired driving on society and reviewed education and treatment services traditionally used in treating the impaired driver. It summarized the historical development of cognitive-behavioral treatment and outlined the important principles of cognitive-behavioral approaches to self-control and change. Section I also provided a basis upon which to select the most relevant concepts, principles and approaches in the treatment of the *Driving While Impaired Offender* (DWIO).

The main conclusion from our review is that education and intervention services for the DWIO have relied mainly on the standard approaches to the intervention and treatment of alcohol and other drug (AOD) abuse problems. Evidence to date is that little variation from these approaches has been used in the education and treatment of the driving while impaired offender (DWIO). The one variation is that education and intervention services have focused on the area of responsible driving in relationship to alcohol and other drug use. This is the most unique component of intervening and treating DWI behavior.

From our review of the literature and from our other work (Wanberg & Milkman, 2005) it is apparent that there are some essential components in the intervention and treatment of AOD abusing clients. We will briefly summarize these since they are essential foundations of the education and treatment curriculum set forth in this work.

First, it was clear that building a strong *therapeutic alliance* is essential when working with the DWIO. This alliance is achieved through the use of *motivational enhancement* skills and building treatment readiness. **Second,** education and treatment needs to be structured around the process and *stages of change*. **Third,** *self-disclosure* and building self-awareness are necessary to open doors for the DWIO to change thinking and behavior to prevent further impaired driving behavior. **Fourth,** *cognitive-behavioral therapy principles* and methods are effective in bringing about change in individuals with substance abuse problems. **Fifth,** *relapse prevention* should be an integral component of AOD education and treatment. **Sixth,** *initial screening* and *differential assessment* are seen as integral parts of treatment services. **Finally,** changes that occur in treatment can be strengthened and sustained through *involvement in community programs* that promote and reward AOD problem free living and prosocial activities.

Our review indicated some major weaknesses in utilizing only the more standard and more traditional approaches to AOD education and treatment of the DWIO. **First,** there was a clear *lack of focus on the responsibility* of the DWIO to the community and to society. This issue has been an important part of our discussion in Section I. Focus on the self or egocentric therapy approaches, e.g., handling emotions, anger, stress, and on interpersonal relationships, e.g., family, seemed to be standard. Using sociocentric treatment approaches that focus on prosocial thinking and behavior, moral responsibility to the community, and building empathy and concern for the welfare of others were often missing, or weakly represented.

A **second** area of weakness was that intervention and treatment of the DWIO was primarily therapeutically based. As we saw earlier in this work, evidence is clear, that when working with driving while impaired and other offenders, the intervention process must *integrate the therapeutic with the correctional* and that sanctioning is seen as an essential component of education and treatment when promoting responsibility and change. The curricula in this manual make responsibility and caring about others and the community a major focus. Thus, our subtitle: *Strategies for Responsible Living and Change.*

Third, a strong focus and *emphasis on recidivism* was often missing or weakly represented. Recidivism should be the primary goal of DWIO intervention. The primary, and often only, emphasis on relapse (into AOD abuse) is only part of the story. If the philosophical position is taken that abstinence is the only way to prevent recidivism, then relapse may be the only focus. But outcome literature clearly indicates that around two-thirds of DWIO clients return to some drinking or other drug use. In these cases, a relapse-only focus clearly misses the mark. In this work, we are taking the position that *recidivism prevention is the primary objective.* The focus on AOD issues and problems, at least in the education phase of DWIO services is to help clients discern whether they have an AOD problem and then determine what is the best approach in addressing that problem.

In Section II, we provided the important components of the platform upon which this program is built. A conceptual frame for a cognitive-behavioral treatment program for the DWIO was provided. We also identified the key characteristics of the provider and the relationship between the provider and the client. An assessment protocol was described that provided guidelines for referral into the three education and treatment protocols. Specific operational guidelines were outlined, and a format for client assessment and treatment planning was presented.

This section (III) of the *Provider's Guide* presents the **three curricula** that address the education and treatment of the DWIO. From the results of our literature and curricula review, input from DWIO educators and treatment specialists, the authors' previous works and clinical experience, we constructed intervention protocols with specific education and treatment courses. We included the standard approaches of DWIO intervention identified in the curricula reviewed. These included the basic themes of AOD education and addiction, relapse prevention, legal obligations and issues, safe driving, and the interaction of AOD issues and problems with psychological, social and family issues and concerns. Our primary theme is *Driving With CARE.* Our overarching theme is *Strategies for Responsible Living and Change.* The primary goal was to make the lesson and session process and content interactive and multisensory and always relevant to the participant's situation and circumstances.

The primary focus of the education components of the curriculum (*Level I and II Education*) was the prevention of recidivism - involvement in DWI behavior and conduct. The criteria for referral into both *Level II Education and Therapy* programs are directed at selecting clients with more pathognomonic signs of AOD problems. This requires that we shift our focus for *Level II Therapy.* As described in Section II of this *Provider's Guide,* we saw *Level I and II Education* curricula as representing the essential and necessary components for addressing DWI conduct and behavior.

The treatment component of this curricula (*DWC Therapy*), continues our focus on

Driving With CARE and on the treatment of AOD problems. However, we expand our focus on developing strategies and skills to enhance cognitive self-control, manage and improve social and interpersonal relationships and increase responsible behavior in the community. *DWC Therapy* is more intensive and more therapeutically based. The emphasis on community responsibility and the correctional approach are seen as just as important. Again, the primary objectives are *preventing recidivism and relapse with the overarching goal of developing strategies for responsible living and change.*

STRUCTURE OF THE CURRICULUM GUIDE - SECTION III

The Driving with CARE (DWC) curricula have two broad components: education and treatment. The education component has two levels and the treatment component is a sequel to the *Level II Education* component. These three levels of services will be briefly reviewed.

DWC Level I Education is comprised of six two-hour lessons designed to service first time DWI offenders who presented no evidence, at evaluation, of AOD problems, and they had lower BAC levels. These lessons are designed so as to be delivered in different time blocks, depending on how the providing agency (provider) structures its services. The recommended method of delivering the *Level I Education* is six two-hour sessions, one time per week for six weeks. This allows the provider to work with the client over a more protracted period of time and gives the client time to assimilate the material.

DWC Level II Education is comprised of 12 two-hour lessons and is designed for persons who may present marginal AOD problems and whose BAC levels were somewhat higher. It is to be delivered over a period of twelve weeks. For agencies using an open group format and a rolling admission policy for *Level II Education, Lesson 1* should be used as the orientation session and *Lessons 2 through 12* are done sequentially with clients entering after they complete orientation. In this curriculum, clients should complete *DWC Level II Education* before entering DWC Therapy.

> We expand our focus on developing means to enhance cognitive self-control, manage and improve social and interpersonal relationships and increase community responsibility. The primary objectives are preventing recidivism and relapse with the overarching goal of developing strategies for responsible living and change.

The *DWC Therapy* program ranges from 42 hours to 86 hours of treatment. The four tracks of Level II have been described in the Chapter on *Program Operational Guidelines and Procedures* of Section II. This protocol is designed for individuals who show fairly definite signs of AOD misuse and problems and/or who have higher arrest BAC levels (e.g., .15 or higher).

The *DWC Level I and Level II Education* protocols are presented in discrete learning experiences called lessons. Lesson is used to indicate that the protocol is educational rather than therapeutic. For the two education protocols, the *Participant's Workbook* will include a full description of the lesson content. Thus, only a summary of this content will be given in the *Provider's Guide*. An intake protocol for each of the two educational protocols will be outlined and discussed.

The *DWC Therapy* protocol is presented in discrete sessions. These sessions have specific structured experiences followed by a period of group discussion and therapeutic processing. A full description of the content of each session is provided in the *Participant's Workbook.* The *Provider's Guide* provides supportive information for each session, and also enhances the content of some sessions.

For the *DWC Level I Education* protocol, the presentation of the lessons in this *Provider's Guide* is divided into four parts.

- Rationale and overview of the lesson to include general purpose of the lesson and provider support material to enhance presentation skills and knowledge.

- Summary of lesson content and process to include exercise descriptions not included in the Participant's Workbook.

- Presentation process and guidelines including instructions for effective presentation and methods to best utilize the lesson work sheets.

- Lesson closure.

For the *DWC Level II Education* protocol, the summary of lesson content and the presentation process and guidelines are merged into one section. The lesson content for the education protocols is complete and detailed in the *Participant's Workbook*.

For the *DWC Therapy* protocol, this *Provider's Guide* will have the following structure.

- Rationale and overview of the session to include objectives and purpose of the session and provider support material to enhance presentation skills and knowledge.

- Summary of session content and presentation sequence, process and guidelines.

- Session closure which includes guidelines for therapeutic processing.

The rationale for certain lessons in the *DWC Level I Education* protocol may be the same as for those in the *DWC Level II Education* and *Therapy* protocols. For example, the rationale and guidelines for developing a working relationship will be similar for each of the three protocols. The tables and figures that are relevant for more than one service protocol will not be repeated once they are introduced in a particular protocol and reference will be made to their location in the *Provider's Guide*. The tables, figures and work sheets in the *Participant's Workbook* will not be repeated in the *Provider's Guide*, except for a couple of key tables and figures.

SCREENING OF DWIO CLIENTS INTO THE THREE LEVELS OF SERVICES

In the assessment chapter, the criteria for selecting clients into the three levels of services were outlined. These are briefly reviewed.

Recommended client admission criteria for *DWC Level I Education* is based on a *low level profile* on the ASUDS. The BAC is less than .15, there is no history of prior diagnosis of substance abuse or dependence, no prior impaired driving offenses and no evidence of a history of AOD misuse. Some clients progressing through DWI education will discover that they do have substance abuse problems in their history. One of the goals of DWI education is to help clients have a clear picture of the extent to which they have been involved in problem AOD use and to discern if they do, in fact, need treatment services.

Recommended admission to *DWC Level II Education* is based on evidence of a history of problems related to AOD use beyond DWI conduct. Clients have higher arrest BAC levels (e.g., .15 or higher) and have at least minimal indicators of AOD problems.

Recommended criteria for admission to *DWC Therapy* include more substantive evidence of a history of AOD problems, a BAC of .15 or higher, and evidence of substance abuse or dependence. AOD problems may range from mild to severe. There may be evidence of problems in areas of mental health, family and job and productivity.

INTRODUCING THE PARTICIPANT'S WORKBOOK

A separate *Participant's Workbook* is provided for each service protocol. Each lesson and session in the three workbooks include an introduction with lesson/session purpose and objectives. Session content for each protocol is complete and detailed and includes all of the material necessary to present the lesson or session. The *workbooks* also include classroom and homework assignments in the form of written exercises and work sheets. Thinking reports are included in the treatment protocol workbook. Tables and figures are used in order to illustrate the relevant content of each session.

As outlined above, the *Provider's Guide* gives a rationale and overview, a brief summary of the content and guidelines for presentation and closure for each lesson or session. Support material for each session is included, and documentation of sources used in the sessions, where relevant, is included. Source documentation for the same topics across the three protocols is not repeated once it has been cited. Additional exercises are also included in the *Provider's Guide* for various lessons and sessions. Some of the key figures are included in the *Provider's Guide*, but the guide does not include the work sheets. Clients should be required to bring their workbooks to each group meeting.

The *Participant's Workbooks*, for the most part, are written in such a manner that the material addresses the client in the second person. This helps to personalize the instructional material and also allows the provider to teach directly from the curriculum content in the workbook. Sometimes the content is presented in a factual manner without personalizing it in the second person. Exercises are also included in the content part of each session.

The *Participant's Workbook* is given to the client at the initial intake session and interview. **The entire workbook is given to them so as to enhance their sense of ownership of the program.** Have clients put their name in the front of the workbook. Encourage the client to read the upcoming lesson or session before coming to group. It is suggested that the provider introduce the client to the purpose and structure of *Participant's Workbook* during the intake and initial interview. The *Workbook* should be presented as representing the client's handbook for successful completion of the program.

THE THEMES OF THE EDUCATION AND TREATMENT CURRICULUM

Building on the findings of our historical and theoretical review, the *DWC Education and Therapy* curricula are built around key themes for driving with CARE and responsible living. These themes are not necessarily presented in sequence, but are imbued in the curriculum content and process.

▶ Building trust and rapport with the client.

▶ Enhancing motivation and readiness for treatment involvement.

▶ Developing knowledge about the cognitive-behavioral models for learning and change.

▶ Gaining a general knowledge about AOD use and abuse patterns.

▶ Clients identifying their own use and abuse patterns and seeing how these are related to DUI/DWAI behavior.

▶ Understanding the process of relapse and its prevention.

▶ Understanding the process of recidivism and its prevention.

▶ Developing skills to change thinking, attitudes and beliefs and to manage intrapersonal emotions and stress.

▶ Developing skills to manage interpersonal problems and stress.

▶ Developing skills to increase prosocial behavior and responsibility to others and the community.

▶ Developing a balanced lifestyle.

DEVELOPING A WORKING RELATIONSHIP WITH CLIENTS

In Section II of this *Provider's Guide,* we discussed the issues of therapeutic alliance and building a working relationship with clients. The initial task of the DWIO provider will be to develop trust and rapport and a working relationship with clients at all three levels of intervention services.

The attitude and response of clients in the first lesson of *Level I Education* and the orientation sessions of *Level II Education and Therapy* set the tone for the client's involvement throughout the program. Client ambivalence, resistance and even anger will need to be addressed. Highly resistive clients may need individual attention.

As also discussed in Section II, the provider is not only an advocate of the client, but of the court and society as well. The provider takes on both a correctional and therapeutic-educational role. Clients, up front give consent to the provider to send periodical reports around their response and participation in the program to their judicial supervisor. Providers become agents of the court and the legal system. As one provider stated, "when we agree to accept a DWI client in our program, we agree to participate in administering the judicial sentence." Both the educational-clinical system and the criminal justice system share a common goal: to prevent recidivism. Thus, *a balance must to be established between the provider's correctional and therapeutic roles.* Even when the correctional role is exercised, it will be most effectively done within the context of a therapeutic environment using effective therapeutic skills.

> Clients will be anxious and even confused as to what is to happen in the program. The first sessions are geared toward establishing group comfort and trust while clearly explaining the rationale, goals and procedures of the program and group.

The outcome of the client's experience, therefore, is significantly dependent on building a therapeutic alliance with the client and with the group. This alliance and trust building are given special focus in the first lessons and sessions and will continue to be an important focus throughout all three levels of service. These goals are achieved through the use of the focal counseling skills of responding attentiveness, encourages to share, feedback clarification and confrontation and reinforcement of changes in thinking and behavior.

The first lessons and sessions will be some of the most important, yet most difficult, to lead. Clients will be anxious and even confused as to what is to happen in the program. The first sessions are geared toward establishing group comfort and trust while clearly explaining the rationale, goals and procedures of the program and group. After a brief introduction of the staff to present the program - including counseling and educational background - the counselor states that the introductory lessons and sessions will include an overview of the purpose of cognitive-behavioral approach for DWIOs, the ground rules of the program and some exercises for getting to know one another.

RESOURCES FOR THE DEVELOPMENT OF THE THREE SERVICE PROTOCOLS

Many resources were utilized in developing the three service protocols. Input was received from DWI education and treatment service providers. The *Colorado DUI/DWAI Alcohol Education Programs Standardized Curricula and Format* (Revision III) (Alcohol Drug Abuse Division, 1998), which provides guidelines for the assessment, education and treatment of DWI offenders, was used as a resource in developing the DWC curriculums.

The work of Wanberg & Milkman (1998) was reviewed and utilized as a guideline in developing the elements of the education and treatment protocols. A number of DWI education and treatment manuals were reviewed in order to gain an understanding of the key focuses of DWI education and treatment. These are listed at the end of Chapter 8. Resources used in supporting the development of various lessons and sessions are cited and referenced.

The clinical, research and academic experience of the authors provided the most substantive basis for the development of the treatment curriculum. Kenneth Wanberg, Th.D., Ph.D., has over 40 years experience in the evaluation, treatment and research of substance abuse problems and criminal conduct, both within public and private agencies and in private practice. Harvey Milkman, Ph.D., has over 30 years of experience in developing multidisciplinary perspectives on the causes, consequences and solutions for addictive behaviors. David S. Timken, Ph.D., has over 30 years of experience as a researcher, consultant and practitioner in the field of traffic safety and impaired driving. His work is recognized internationally. The combined skills of the authors provided a substantial basis for the development of the content, skill practice and exercises of the treatment curriculum.

ALCOHOL, OTHER DRUGS AND DRIVING SAFETY EDUCATION: LEVEL I EDUCATION

OVERVIEW AND INTRODUCTION TO LEVEL 1 EDUCATION

This is a 12-hour education program for persons who have been convicted of driving while their blood alcohol level went beyond legal limits or while they were under the influence of a drug other than alcohol. More specifically, it is for first time offenders who, when evaluated, showed no problems, other than impaired driving, associated with AOD use, who had no prior offenses, no prior diagnosis of *Substance Abuse or Substance Dependence*, and no other problems related to AOD use or misuse.

The main purpose of this *Driving with CARE Level I Education* program is to help clients prevent future driving while impaired by alcohol or other drugs - **to prevent recidivism.** Also important is the purpose of helping clients avoid a future pattern of alcohol or other drug use that has caused past problems and discomfort in the past and led to impaired driving - **to prevent relapse.**

Participants will take an active part in each of the six lessons. Each lesson has exercises and work sheets that help clients apply the topics and material to their own situation. Clients are asked to take an active role in the group through sharing what they have learned in the exercises and work sheets.

An important component of *DWC Education* is to help clients understand that change is made in behavior by changing our thoughts, attitudes and beliefs. We want clients to acquire a good view of their own patterns of drug use and possible abuse and make decisions about how to change those patterns to prevent AOD problems and returning to DWI behavior.

> **Level I Education** is for first time offenders who, when evaluated, showed no problems, other than impaired driving associated with AOD use, who had no prior offenses, no prior diagnosis of *Substance Abuse or Substance Dependence*, and no other problems related to AOD use or misuse.

We want participants to understand that *Driving With CARE* means caring about themselves and caring about others. We want CARE to be an important part of their driving and CARING to be an important part of their lives. Our overall goal is to help clients to be responsible to themselves, to others and to their community. And so, what this program is really about, is helping clients to develop approaches and *strategies for responsible living and change.*

SPECIFIC GOAL AND OBJECTIVES OF LEVEL 1 EDUCATION

The specific goal of *Driving With CARE: Alcohol, Other Drugs and Driving Safety Education - Level I Education*, is to help clients develop knowledge and learn skills that will help them to engage in CAREFUL and responsible thinking and behavior about alcohol or other drug (AOD) use and to prevent involvement in impaired driving. Here are the objectives of this program.

▶ **Prevent recidivism** or returning to driving a motor vehicle while exceeding the legal BAC limits or while having ingested any other mind-altering drugs that impair driving behavior.

- **Prevent relapse** or returning to a pattern of alcohol and other drug use that is harmful and disruptive to normal living including impaired driving.

- Help clients to become aware of their past history of driving while impaired and to help them understand their current DUI/DWAI charge and conviction.

- Help clients learn how to change thoughts, beliefs and attitudes that control their behavior and that, in the past, led to driving while involved in AOD use.

- Help clients understand how alcohol or other drug use and abuse affect and influence their mind, body, social behaviors, relationship with others, and their responsibilities towards the community.

- Help clients understand how the patterns of alcohol and other drug use and misuse fit them and learn approaches and strategies that will help them avoid future problems of use and misuse.

- Help clients understand the laws of their state around impaired driving and to be clear about their obligation to the court and to the Motor Vehicle Division.

- Encourage clients to commit to a goal of **zero tolerance-zero risk** - never driving while having alcohol or any other mind-behavior altering drug in their system.

- **TO HAVE CLIENTS COMMIT TO DRIVING WITH CARE.**

CONTENT PRESENTATION AND DELIVERY STRATEGIES

Two hours are needed to present each of the lessons in Level I. It is recommended that it be presented in a closed group with lessons presented in the sequence they are found in the *Participant's Workbook*. Most work sheets can be done in class. Clients should be encouraged to share their work sheet and exercise material in group.

Providers of DWC are asked to present the lesson content and material as spelled out in the *Participant's Workbook*. If providers feel that critical material should be added to the presentation, this material should be integrated into and complement the objectives and content of the lesson. Infusion of new material should not detract from the purpose and content of the lesson.

Lesson 2 presents a generic description of the legal factors and state laws related to DWI convictions. The specifics of these laws change periodically. The provider will need to periodically update *Lesson 2* with handouts that cover the most recent changes in the law.

It is essential and expected that clients be given the complete workbook at the beginning of the program or, preferably, at intake. The Provider should encourage clients to read the lesson material before sessions.

It is recommended that the following approaches be used in presenting material.

▶ Present the lesson content in an interactive-teaching manner.

▶ Use overheads, media posters, charts and flip charts for presentation.

▶ Have clients read portions of the material to the group.

As mentioned previously, keep a good balance between a lecture-didactic format of presentation and having the group members interact around the lesson content and material.

PROVIDER SKILLS AND SERVICE STRATEGIES NEEDED FOR LEVEL I

Significant proportions of the content of this protocol need to be presented within a teaching format. This does not mean only lecture. Material should be presented so as to maximize the participants interaction with the material, the provider and members of the group. Providers should have the skills to: facilitate individual and group sharing; facilitate self-disclosure; utilize feedback clarification; enhance client participation; motivate positive involvement in the program; and reinforce clients for positive program participation. Providers should be knowledgeable in patterns of AOD use and abuse and relapse and recidivism prevention.

COMPLETION REQUIREMENTS AND EXPECTATIONS OF CLIENTS

The following are the comprehension and skill development expectations of clients.

▶ Develop a good understanding of the facts and details of their DWI conviction.

▶ Develop a basic understanding of the patterns of AOD use and abuse and have an understanding of how their use fits these patterns.

▶ Have a basic understanding of the cognitive-behavioral principle that our thoughts, attitudes and beliefs, not the events outside of ourselves, lead to our feelings and behavior choices that determine good or bad outcomes.

▶ Have a basic understanding of the principles of relapse and recidivism prevention.

▶ Develop a basic relapse and recidivism plan.

The following are the participation expectations of clients.

▶ Complete all of the exercise and work sheets.

▶ Attend and be on time for all sessions.

▶ Be involved in structured sharing exercises in the group.

- Keep all information learned about group members in trust and confidence, and not discuss it with other people.

- Come to all sessions free of alcohol or other drugs.

- Remain free of problems from alcohol use and remain free of use of all other drugs while in the program.

DRIVING WITH CARE INVENTORY (DWCI)

The Driving With Care Inventory is administered to clients during the orientation session and then readministered in the last session that the client attends. The re-testing can take place before the client's last group or as part of the closure lesson with the client. The DWCI is found in the appendix of this *Provider's Guide*.

Make it clear to clients in the initial administration of the DWCI that they are not expected to know many of the answers to the test questions. They are asked to do their best. At re-testing, clients should be expected to get at least 80 percent correct. The results should be reviewed with each client, and wrong answers are discussed in light of the correct answer. The DWCI, along with an answer sheet and scoring guide is found in *Appendix B.*

INTAKE, ASSESSMENT AND ORIENTATION

If possible, the provider should meet individually with the client for the intake session. This would first involve completing the basic intake procedures that should include the following information.

- Consent to treatment and follow-up.

- Consent for release of information to court, probation department or other agencies and persons as requested by the client.

- Confidentiality advisement and client rights and responsibilities.

- Fees and collection procedures.

- Advisement of credentials and full disclosure statement.

It is also recommended that a brief personal data form be completed by the client to include name, address, gender, and other information that is needed for the agency to meet its policy, and procedure requirements.

Although an in-depth assessment is not necessary for *DWC Level I Education* clients, the provider should review the referral information from the evaluator, including the results of any screening instruments administered during the evaluation process. This will help the provider understand the level of defensiveness of the client as well as the level of AOD involvement and disruption disclosed by the client.

Level I Education is comprised of the following six discrete lessons.

1. Program orientation: Developing a working relationship.

2. Alcohol and other drug impaired driving: The laws and beyond the law.

3. Changing our thoughts, beliefs and actions: Learning self-control and driving with care.

4. Alcohol and other drugs: How do the facts and ideas about alcohol and other drugs fit you?

5. Understanding alcohol and other drug (AOD) use and misuse patterns: How do they fit you?

6. Preventing recidivism and relapse.

The content of these six lessons is provided in detail in the *Participant's Workbook*. Guidelines for presenting these lessons are now discussed including a lesson rationale and overview including lesson purpose and objectives, a summary of the lesson content, presentation process and guidelines and suggestions for lesson closure.

LESSON 1: DEVELOPING A WORKING RELATIONSHIP

RATIONALE AND OVERVIEW OF LESSON

Most clients entering this level of DWI education and driving safety will come with the primary goal of meeting their obligation to the court. Most will not perceive themselves as having an AOD use problem. Many will not even see that getting a DWI is indicative of such a problem. Resistance will be high. There will be reluctance to openly share and participate in discussion. Clients would be content maintaining a passive role in the process, having the provider lecture and show films, and avoiding interacting with the material or sharing in the group. DWC is designed to do just the opposite and maximize participation and interaction. Yet, this is accomplished within the context of a non-confrontational, motivation enhancing and a client-centered facilitation model. Client resistance is not confronted but accepted and reflected. Parenting and correctional approaches are kept at a minimum. **Motivation to change is not as important as motivation to interact and participate in group discussion and lesson exercises.**

> The clear mission of the provider and the primary change focus is that of helping clients alter their thinking and behavior patterns so as to prevent future DUI/DWAI behavior and conduct (recidivism). The desired spin-off of Driving with CARE is responsible living and change.

It is important that the provider convey that the focus is on AOD and driving safety education. The clear mission of the provider and the primary change focus is that of helping clients alter their thinking and behavior patterns so as to prevent future DWI behavior and **prevent recidivism**. The focus on changing AOD use patterns is to the extent that this helps prevent recidivism, and to help clients see that they have had at least one problem related to AOD use: impaired driving. There is no intent to make the client see that they need to make major changes in other areas of their life outside of this primary change focus. There is no intent to convince these clients that they have alcohol or drug use problems other than related to impaired driving.

Driving With CARE is the major theme. Yet, underlying this theme and the desired spinoff would be responsible living and change, which is the subtitle of this program. *Driving With CARE*, not engaging in DWI conduct and behavior and changing life direction enough to avoid future AOD related problems represent a demonstration of responsible living.

The primary objectives of *Lesson 1* are to: outline the objectives and goals of the program; introduce clients to the key program concepts and ideas that will be the focus of the program; have clients become acquainted with each other; share their own DWI arrest event and circumstances; and outline the expectations of clients and program agreements and guidelines.

SUMMARY OF LESSON CONTENT

The essential material and content to be presented in all of the *DWC Level I Education* lessons are spelled out in detail in the *Participant's Workbook*. Only the most salient components of this content will be summarized in this *Provider's Guide*. .

There are three important concepts that are introduced that clients are asked to discuss and interact around: *recidivism; relapse; and that our actions and behaviors are determined by our thoughts, our attitudes and our beliefs.* These themes are at the core of *DWC Education.*

First, clients are provided with the basic concept of legal recidivism - returning to the behavior of driving with a blood alcohol concentration (BAC) at .05 or higher, or, for those under age 21, when the BAC is .02 or higher and to not drive under the influence of any mind-behavior altering drug. Society's expectation of the client is to prevent legal recidivism. However, this lesson asks clients to consider the personal recidivism prevention goal of being drug and alcohol free every time they operate a motor vehicle. This is the **zero tolerance-zero risk** recidivism goal. This lesson challenges clients to commit to this goal and provides some cogent arguments for this goal.

▶ Stress that recidivism does not only mean getting rearrested.

▶ Recidivism involves any episode or event where the client drives with a BAC that exceeds legal limits or when impaired by any mind altering drug.

Second, relapse is defined and the link between recidivism and relapse is discussed. Most clients in **Level I Education** have no intention to stop using alcohol, let alone other drugs they have been using. Thus, to take an abstinence approach for this group may only serve to increase resistance. The provider needs to strike a delicate balance between acknowledging that one can use alcohol and not go into recidivism - drinking and driving - while at the same time conveying the concept that alcohol use and misuse certainly increase the risk of future DWI behavior.

A working definition of relapse and variations of that definition is provided and discussed.

▶ **Pattern or pathway to relapse:** This involves the process of thinking about AOD use or putting oneself in situations that could cause involvement in or return to a harmful pattern of alcohol or other drug use.

▶ **A lapse:** Any pattern of AOD use that could lead to harming self or others after having made a commitment to a non-harmful pattern of use or to no use at all.

▶ **Relapse:** Going to the point where the person has further problems from alcohol or other drug (AOD) use or to the point that the person is into a harmful pattern of AOD use - which may or may not involve DWI recidivism.

At this point, help clients see their choices around AOD use and preventing relapse.

▶ **The client's legal and moral community commitment.** This is the same as the legal community commitment around recidivism: *to not drive when the presence of alcohol in your body has gone beyond the legal BAC limits and to not drive when you are impaired by the presence of other drugs.*

- **The client's personal commitments or goals around AOD use:** At this point, help clients see that, beyond legal and moral commitment to the community with respect to AOD use and driving, there are clear choices around AOD use and that these choices can provide the basis for the client setting a relapse prevention goal. Here are three choices for clients to consider.

    - **To use alcohol or other drugs with no goal of harmful outcome prevention.** This is letting the "cards fall as may." It is important to help clients see the consequences of this goal.

    - **To not use alcohol or other drugs to the extent that they cause harmful effects to oneself, to others, or to the community.** Remind clients that they are in the program because they lost self-control and that use of alcohol or other drugs led to harmful or potentially harmful effects on others and the community — impaired driving.

    - **To live an alcohol and drug-free life or abstaining from the use of alcohol and all mind-behavior altering drugs unless prescribed by a medical specialist.** Because the **Level I** admission criteria rules out clients with even minimal indication of AOD use problems, this personal goal will not be acceptable to most clients.

Third, the cognitive-behavioral approach to self-control and change. Spend some time presenting and discussing these concepts.

- We develop self-control and make changes in our actions by changing how we think, what we believe about ourselves and the world and how we feel. Change and improvement begin first in our mind.

- It is our thoughts and our beliefs and our attitudes - not what happens around us or to us - that cause us to feel and act in a certain way or cause us to do certain things. It was the client's thinking that led to DWI behavior.

- Changing our mental world gives us more control over our life and prevents repeating the behavior or action of driving while using alcohol or other drugs. This will involve learning:

    - how thinking, attitudes and beliefs control our actions and behaviors, and

    - how actions or behaviors become habits that can result in a positive or negative response to the world.

- At this point, define the three skills that clients will learn in the program:

    - mental restructuring or thought changing skills to enhance self-control over actions and prevent future DWI conduct;

    - social and relationship skills that enhance self-control over our relationship with others and prevent driving and AOD use; and

    - community responsibility skills that increase reliable and responsible actions in the community.

PRESENTATION PROCESS AND GUIDELINES

It is important that providers develop a balance between the didactic presentation and facilitating interaction around the lesson content. Utilizing the group facilitation approaches of encouraging group sharing and openness though the invitation to share skills, reflecting back what the group and clients are saying, and reinforcing positive group sharing and involvement are the basic group counseling skills to use in this and subsequent lessons.

- Be non-confrontational and avoid argumentation.

- Express empathy.

- Roll with the resistance.

- Reinforce positive involvement and sharing.

The following presentation process and sequence is recommended.

- Welcome the group, spell out the theme of the program, *Driving With Care* and define how the sessions will be structured.

- Administer the DWCI (pre-test).

- Introduce the group to the concepts of recidivism and relapse and have group members define their initial goals in this area.

- Present the partnership of caring triad — client, community and provider.

- Go over the CPR — Client Progress Report. Clients are asked to complete this at the end of Lesson 6 and give it to their judicial supervisor or have the provider send it to the supervisor (probation officer).

- Go over the objectives of the program.

- Spell out the expectations of clients and define the program agreements and guidelines.

- Introduce the group to the cognitive-behavioral approach to self-control and change.

- **Exercise:** Have group members briefly introduce themselves and share their DWI arrest and conviction story. Make this brief - only a couple of minutes per person.

- Have clients complete *Work Sheet 1* and then give clients further opportunity to share some content of that work sheet.

- Introduce the *AOD Use Thinking and Action Patterns (TAP) Charting* forms at the end the *Participant's Workbook*.

Most clients will resist being open and self-disclosing on the TAP work sheet. Take time to explain how to to complete the work sheet as described in the client's *Participant's Workbook*. When the two six-hour session format is used for *Level I Education*, this only gives clients a one-time chance to do the TAP. Thus, opportunity to enhance openness and facilitate self-disclosure on the TAP is minimal. When sessions are protracted over time, clients become more open and self-disclosing on the TAP work sheet. It is suggested that the following guidelines be used when introducing TAP.

▶ Encourage clients to be as honest as they can in completing the TAP.

▶ Explain it is for their benefit - that they do not have to share what they put on the TAP.

▶ Help them to see how TAP charting can reveal thinking patterns around alcohol use that could help prevent recidivism.

LESSON CLOSURE GUIDELINES

Structure a round-robin feed-in exercise by having clients briefly share what they got out of the program thus far. For agencies who do two six-hour sessions, this would be at the end of *Lesson 3*.

LESSON 2: ALCOHOL AND OTHER DRUG IMPAIRED DRIVING: THE LAWS AND BEYOND THE LAW

RATIONALE AND OVERVIEW OF LESSON

This lesson will provide clients with legal information related to DWI penalties, sanctions (punishments) and loss and reinstatement of driving privileges. The purpose of presenting this material is to prevent recidivism. Clients will also look at the skills, attitudes and behaviors that may contribute to safe and CAREFUL driving and at what makes people driving risks and hazards. Clients will take a more in-depth look at their own DWI situation. One goal of this lesson is to have clients see the impact of their DWI arrest on their own lives and on those who have become victims of their DWI behavior. On whom has their DWI impacted? Who were their victims? This is the **responsibility to the community focus** of this program. Help clients keep this major theme of the program continually in mind: **Responsible living involves *Driving With CARE.***

This lesson gets clients to more clearly identify their current court and legal obligations and to define where they are in fulfilling those obligations. The primary rationale of this lesson is that the greater the personal identification with the laws and statutes and the more clients clarify their own involvement in DWI legal issues and obligations, the higher the probability of preventing recidivism. When this identification reaches affective levels, the impact may be even greater. The specific objectives of this *Lesson* are provided in the *Participant's Workbook.*

LESSON CONTENT

The major content of this lesson is the summary of the DWI laws and statutes that almost all states have in common. Each provider will give clients a handout on the most updated laws in their state. It is very important that clients understand the following regarding these laws:

▶ categories of offenses;

▶ outcomes of charges and convictions;

▶ an understanding of the two separate legal agencies or authorities that impose sanctions (punishments) and AOD education or treatment for charges related to DWI;

▶ how driver's licenses are revoked or suspended and how they are reinstated; and

▶ understand the specific laws and conditions related to DWI convictions such as the *Expressed Consent Law, Habitual Offender Law, the Persistent Drunk Driver Law, Ignition Interlocks, and penalties for DWI offenses.*

The *Driving Risk Survey (DRS)* is administered in order to give clients feedback as to their own level of risk and hazard.

PRESENTATION PROCESS AND GUIDELINES

Getting clients to identify with the lesson content is a major goal of all lessons in *DWC Education*. Presenting the legal issues can be boring and tedious. However, when the provider gets clients to apply the material to their own situation, the material takes on a personal and emotional quality. Have clients identify which of the three categories of offenses and the possible outcomes of these offenses apply to them and help them determine that if they get another DWI arrest, which sanctions and outcomes would then apply to them. At various points in the presentation, ask the question "how does this one apply to you?" Select different people to interact with the material.

The following presentation process and sequence is recommended for this lesson.

▶ **Exercise:** Have a few group members share their specific DWI offense; have others share their specific sanction; have others share their BAC at arrest.

▶ Present the generic information on DWI laws in the *Workbook*.

▶ Present the DWI laws, convictions and penalties specific to the clients' state.

▶ Have clients complete exercises for Tables 1 and 2.

▶ Present the statistics related to driving a motor vehicle.

▶ Present the skills and attitudes that determine safe and CAREFUL driving.

▶ **Exercise:** Do *Work Sheet 2*, the DRS and discuss the results.

▶ **Exercise:** Do *Work Sheet 3* that describes their driving habits, attitudes and skills and the habits and attitudes they feel they need to improve or change.

▶ **Exercise:** Have clients write down their arrest BAC.

▶ **Exercise:** Complete *Work Sheet 4*, the obligations that clients still have to meet.

▶ Present the victim material and DWI related statistics.

▶ **Exercise:** Have clients mark in *Figure 1* as instructed in the *Participant's Workbook*. Have them circle those in *Figure 1* that they see as victims of their DWI. Then, have them list who might have been affected by their DWI.

LESSON CLOSURE

Exercise: Have clients briefly share what they got out of the session. Give the group feedback as to how it did and reinforce positive group responding. Remind clients to complete the *TAP — Thinking and Action Patterns Charting* for the week.

LESSON 3: CHANGING OUR THOUGHTS, BELIEFS AND ACTIONS: LEARNING SELF-CONTROL AND DRIVING WITH CARE

RATIONALE AND OVERVIEW OF LESSON

If we believe that the cognitive-behavioral (CB) approach is an effective way to bring about self-control and change, then it is important that the client have an understanding of the CB processes that lead to both maladaptive and adaptive thinking and acting. An important component of self-control and change is enhancing clients' belief that they have the skills and confidence to develop self-control and to avoid thinking and behaviors that cause bad outcomes. Resources used to develop this lesson include: Beck et al. (1993), Burns (1989) Bush and Bilodeau (1993), Clark (2004), Dobson & Dozois (2001), Freeman et al. (1990), McMullin (2000), Reinecke & Freeman (2003), Sperry (1999), Wanberg & Milkman (1998, 2005) and the clinical experiences of the authors.

The research literature clearly supports the efficacy of cognitive-behavioral (CB) approaches to intervene in AOD misuse. The main purpose of this lesson is to apply the principles of CB learning and change to preventing DWI recidivism and AOD relapse.

There are two pathways to developing self-control and positive and adaptive behaviors: *through reinforcing thoughts that lead to positive outcomes and behavior; and by reinforcing the behaviors that produce positive outcomes or events.* The traditional behavioral therapy model focused mainly on the idea that when behavior leads to favorable outcomes, that behavior is reinforced. The cognitive component adds another link to that reinforcement path: that favorable and unfavorable outcomes often strengthen the thoughts that lead to them. This explains why behaviors from negative outcomes often do not become weakened or extinguished. No matter how unfavorable the outcomes, if the outcomes reinforce the thoughts that lead to the behaviors, then those behaviors are likely to occur again. This model is particularly relevant to DWI behavior and conduct. The specific objectives of this *Lesson* are provided in the *Participant's Workbook*.

> Steps are outlined for changing thoughts and behaviors. Specific thought changing and behavioral changing tools and skills are also practiced.

LESSON CONTENT

The first part of this lesson explores how our thoughts, attitudes and beliefs lead to our actions and behaviors and to driving while impaired. Five rules of thinking are presented to help the client see how this happens. The first rule has to do with the idea that automatic thoughts or thought habits are responses to outside events and that these precipitate feelings and actions. Underlying these thought habits are attitudes and beliefs. Other rules of thinking that are discussed are: we resist making changes; we have choices over our thoughts; we develop thinking errors that lead to disturbed thoughts and emotions and to bad outcomes; and that we can train ourselves to use the thought "what is best for me in the long-term" before responding to events that happen to us. A map is provided for developing self-controlled thinking and different automatic thoughts or thought habits are presented which include expectations, appraisals, attributions and decisions.

Clients gain confidence that they have the skills to develop self-control and to avoid patterns of thinking and acting that lead to problems and negative outcomes.

Figure 1 on page 215 below and *Figure 2*, page 44 in *Workbook* provide the schematic for understanding how our thoughts are strengthened by behavioral outcomes. It shows that both good and bad outcomes strengthen or reinforce the thoughts that produced the behaviors leading to the outcomes.

The second part of this lesson explores how our actions or behaviors get reinforced or weakened when those actions lead to certain outcomes. Three rules that determine how behavior is learned and reinforced are discussed, particularly as to how these are related to DWI conduct. Attention is given to helping clients understand why Rule III - that a behavior that is punished should not occur again - doesn't always work. This provides a sound explanation as to why people continue to engage in behaviors that lead to bad outcomes.

Steps are outlined for changing thoughts and behaviors. Specific thought changing and behavioral changing tools and skills are taught and practiced within the framework of thoughts and behaviors that lead to DWI conduct.

PRESENTATION PROCESS AND GUIDELINES

The material is presented in a deliberate and slow-paced fashion. The concepts and ideas should be given in small segments and clients are asked to discuss these concepts as they are presented. The following process and presentation sequence is recommended for this lesson.

▶ Take about 10 minutes for processing what clients have learned thus far.

▶ Present how our thinking, attitudes and beliefs control our feelings and actions.

▶ Present the five rules of thinking. When presenting the rule related to "errors in thinking," do *Work Sheet 5*.

▶ Present the schemata for mapping the pathway for self-control and positive outcomes.

▶ Present the three rules of how behavior is learned and changed and have clients complete the exercises at the end of each rule presentation.

- Carefully review the schemata that explains the process of learning and change and how our thoughts, feelings, beliefs and behaviors are strengthened or reinforced.

- Discuss the skills for changing thinking and behavior and how these skills can lead to positive or good outcomes.

- **Exercise:** Have clients complete *Work Sheet 6*. Have one of the clients provide an example of something that happened recently that was frustrating or difficult. Walk the client through the automatic thinking and thought habits, feelings, underlying attitudes and beliefs, the behavioral choice and the outcome. Then, take the client back through the example, using the cognitive change skills to produce a desirable outcome.

- **Exercise:** Have clients share their work on Work Sheet 6. If there is time, have clients present other events, and using the CB Map, have them identify their automatic thoughts, underlying beliefs and emotional and behavioral outcomes. Have them practice changing thoughts to produce positive outcomes. Help clients label the different automatic thoughts: expectations, appraisals, attributions and decisions.

- Review any work that the clients have done with the work sheets that chart the AOD use thinking and action patterns (TAP).

LESSON CLOSURE

Take time for some discussion and questions. If there is a time period between this and the next lesson, give clients this homework.

- Keep track of bad outcomes that happen during the week and identify the thoughts that led to those outcomes.

- Keep track of good outcomes that happen during the week and identify the thoughts that led to those outcomes.

- Have clients take one thought management and change skill and practice it all week, e.g., self-talk, shifting the view.

Remind clients to do the TAP (Thinking and Action Patterns) Charting for the coming week.

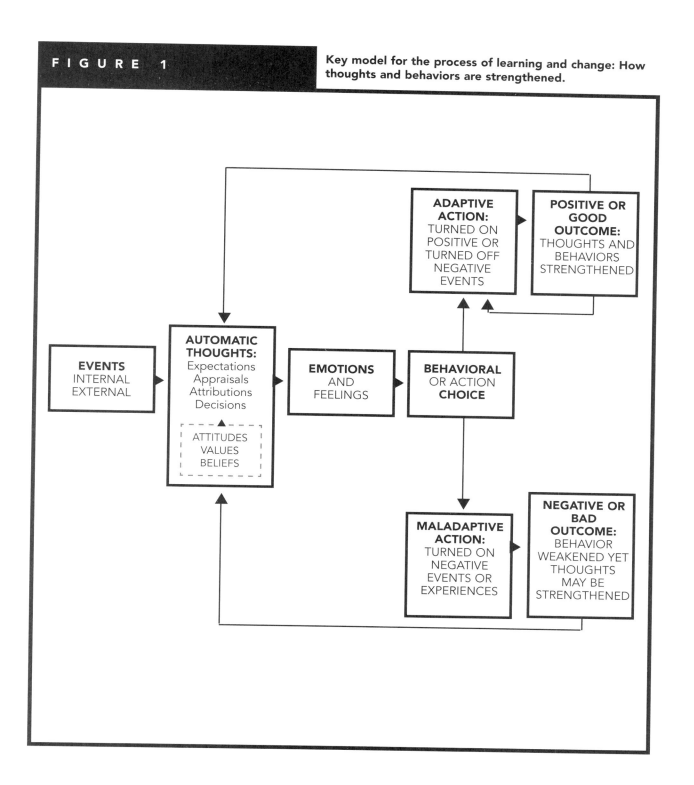

FIGURE 1

Key model for the process of learning and change: How thoughts and behaviors are strengthened.

LESSON 4: ALCOHOL AND OTHER DRUGS: HOW DO THE FACTS AND IDEAS ABOUT ALCOHOL AND OTHER DRUGS FIT YOU?

RATIONALE AND OVERVIEW OF LESSON

In order for clients to meet the challenge of preventing DWI behavior, it is important that they have basic knowledge about alcohol and other drugs. The purpose of this lesson is to provide this most basic knowledge in a relatively unbiased, and non-theoretical approach to AOD misuse. Of particular importance is a clear understanding of how blood alcohol concentration (BAC) is related to DWI conduct specifically and to cognitive and behavioral processes in general. A variety of sources were used to develop this lesson including: Ray and Ksir (2002); Wanberg, 1990; and Wanberg and Milkman, (1998, 2005.)

LESSON CONTENT

This *Lesson* presents some basic concepts around alcohol and other drugs. Two classifications of drugs are presented: *system enhancers* or drugs that stimulate the system; and *system suppressor*, drugs that sedate the system. The direct and indirect (withdrawal) effects of drugs in these two classifications are presented. The important idea to convey is that the direct effect of the system enhancers is the opposite of the direct effect of the system suppressors; and that both the direct and withdrawal effects of a drug are disruptive, particularly to driving behavior.

The concepts of *drug toxicity, tolerance, drug interactions,* and *drug withdrawal* (indirect effects) are discussed. Considerable time is devoted to discussing alcohol since it is the primary drug associated with impaired driving. The concepts of the amount of alcohol in different kinds of beverages, the meaning of blood alcohol concentration (BAC), different effects of different levels of BAC, and the measurement of BAC by time of drinking and weight of client and number of drinks are presented. The effect of alcohol on health and the body is discussed. Some discussion is devoted to cannabis, since this is often the most misunderstood drug that people use. General health risks related to drug use are discussed including AIDS and FAS. *The most important topic of this lesson is the effect of specific drugs on driving behavior.*

The work sheets in this *Lesson* are designed to maximize client interaction with the lesson content and to relate the material to the specific condition and situation of clients. These work sheets will take some time. *Work Sheet 10* is the most complicated, since this helps clients determine the number of drinks they had at the time of arrest based on number of hours drinking, weight and BAC.

Review any homework assigned. Provide time for discussion around the following questions: What is an alcohol problem? What is a drug problem? What is addiction? What causes alcohol and drug use problems? Then present the material in the following sequence.

▶ Discuss the concepts around the two kinds of drugs and the direct and indirect effect of drugs outlined in *Table 3* in the Workbook.

▶ Discuss the issues around alcohol, BAC, and the harmful effects of alcohol on the body.

▶ Present material on drug toxicity, tolerance and drug interaction.

▶ Take time to go over the material about alcohol, the amount of alcohol in certain drinks, and the mental and behavioral responses to certain BAC levels.

▶ Present the material on cannabis. Cannabis users often get defensive around this presentation. Don't argue or debate the issues. Present the information and roll with the resistance.

▶ Discuss the direct effects of drugs on driving behavior and have clients share how alcohol affected their driving.

▶ **Exercises:** The work sheets are designed to relate the material presented to the client's unique situation. The more resistive clients will have problems with some of these work sheets. Be matter-of-fact about the exercises. *Work Sheet 7* asks clients to list the drugs they have used, using *Table 3* in the *Participant's Workbook*. *Work Sheet 8* helps clients look at their personal BAC levels based on number of drinks and hours of drinking and *Work Sheet 9* provides an estimate of their levels of tolerance to certain drugs. *Work Sheet 10* is the most complicated and requires an understanding of *Tables 4 and 5*. Take time to complete this work sheet. *Work Sheets 11 and 12* provides further opportunity to have clients identify how certain kinds of drugs affect their mind and body and how AOD use is related to their DWI.

▶ Make the presentation interactive. Facilitate client sharing around personal experiences related to specific ideas discussed.

LESSON CLOSURE

Have clients share what they got out of this lesson. If there is a period of time between lessons, have them complete the TAP (Thinking and Action Patterns) Charting for the coming week, using the charts at the end of the Participant's Workbook. Provide some time for discussion at the end of the lesson.

LESSON 5: UNDERSTANDING ALCOHOL AND OTHER DRUG (AOD) USE AND PROBLEM OUTCOME PATTERNS: HOW DO THEY FIT YOU?

RATIONALE AND OVERVIEW OF LESSON

Many, if not most clients in *Level I Education* will have no identifiable AOD misuse problems other than impaired driving conduct. Yet, the rationale of this Lesson is based on the assumption that DWI conduct represents an AOD misuse pattern. This lesson focuses on the idea that if you have had a problem from drinking or other drug use, you have had, at least at one time, a drinking problem. This assumption justifies including content that deals with AOD misuse.

Another assumption of this lesson is that clients who have a legal DWI disposition also have an established pattern of alcohol or other drug use. Defensive clients will resist this idea (they will score high on *ASUDS* defensive). The provider should have some knowledge of the results of assessment instruments taken during the DWI evaluation process. Clients who have a low or even "0" score on alcohol use scales are extremely defensive. Most persons who use alcohol at even a rather low frequency and quantity level will have a raw score of two or three on these kinds of scales (Wanberg & Timken, 1998).

There will be a relatively high degree of defensiveness among *Level I* clients. When evaluated, they show an absence or minimal evidence of AOD problems beyond the DWI conduct. Thus, present the AOD misuse material in this lesson in a low profile manner. This lesson places emphasis on styles of AOD use and the presentation of the *Mental-Behavior Impaired Control Cycle* (ICC). Most clients will fit the first steps of this model and a few may fit the full impaired control cycle.

The *Impaired Control Cycle* (ICC), Figure 2 is presented as a basis for understanding how problem outcomes develop from the AOD use and for understanding the learned impaired control process. Information about how AOD abuse and dependence are defined a la the *DSM IV* (American Psychiatric Association, 1994, 2000) model is presented. The *ICC* model is appropriate for this clientele in that the use of alcohol or other drugs by clients has clearly led to one problematic outcome: DWI conduct and arrest. **All DWI clients will evidence some kind of impaired driving pattern. For most, it was not a one-time occurrence.**

The most important rationale for presenting this material is to prevent recidivism. Recognizing that the AOD use pattern of clients in this program led to DWI behavior, then there is a need to change that pattern to prevent further DWI behavior. Thus, the emphasis is on helping clients identify their patterns of use and misuse and their patterns of impaired driving so as to change these patterns and prevent recidivism.

Important: Clients should complete the work sheets in this lesson based on their AOD use patterns they were involved in **prior to their DWI arrest.**

LESSON CONTENT

The above outlined rationale summarizes the content of this Lesson. The first task in this lesson is to help clients identify their AOD use patterns that include:

▶ *Quantity-Frequency-Prediction* (QFP) pattern for both alcohol and other drugs;

▶ their *social use* (solo or gregarious or both) pattern; and

▶ the *benefits* they derive from use.

This allows clients to put a label on their unique alcohol or other drug use pattern. They are asked to write that down and discuss it in class. A client might describe himself as a *moderate, frequent, daily consistent drinker who drinks at bars with friends and to relax.* Some clients will resist doing this exercise. Use motivational enhancement skills to help clients be open and willing to self-disclose. The purpose of alcohol use style description is to give clients some idea of their risk for recidivism. *Work Sheet 13* provides guidelines to estimate this risk. The main objective of this task is for clients to identify their pattern of impaired driving. Their pattern will be tied in with their DWI pattern.

The **second task** of this lesson is to help clients understand the problem outcomes of AOD misuse. The concept of problem outcomes is much more appealing than the concept of addiction or disease. Most *Level I* clients have problem outcomes from AOD use but do not fit the addiction or disease model. *Table 7* in the *Participant's Workbook* provides the problem outcomes for seven drug categories. Clients are asked to see if any of those problem outcomes or symptoms fit them.

Rather than using the more traditional disease and addiction models, this lesson places emphasis on styles of AOD use and the presentation of the *Impaired Control Cycle* (ICC). Most clients will fit the first steps of this model and a few may fit the full addiction cycle.

Review the three learning rules presented in *Lesson 3*. They provide the basis for understanding the *Impaired Control Cycle* (ICC), *Figure 2* below (*Figure 4* in the *Participant's Workbook*). An interactive didactic format should be used to present the ICC. The assumption is that all clients will have at least gone as far as block D of this cycle.

Using the ICC model, four problem outcome patterns are defined:

▶ the drinking or AOD use problem;

▶ the problem user without abuse or dependence;

▶ the problem user with AOD abuse; and

▶ the problem user with AOD dependence.

The *DSM IV* criteria are introduced and clients are asked to evaluate themselves across these criteria. At the end of the lesson, they are asked to identify which of the four categories of misuse they fit. All clients will fit at least the first category, *history of a drinking problem.* Help each client see that they in fact fit at least the first category "having had a drinking/drug use problem."

Depending on the time available, it is suggested that the lesson start out with discussing at least one or two of the following questions.

▶ How would you describe your AOD use before you received your DWI arrest?

▶ What are the different kinds of alcoholic beverages or drugs you have used?

▶ How much did you drink each day? How much of other drugs did you use?

▶ Did you drink or use other drugs daily, periodic, on weekends?

▶ Did you drink alone, at home, with friends, at bars, at parties?

▶ Did you drink to relax, to feel less tense, more sociable?

▶ How are your use patterns related to your DWI pattern? Have some clients describe their DWI pattern.

Following a group discussion of these questions, present the material using the following guidelines.

▶ Present the *QFP, social and benefits patterns* and have clients use these variables to describe their AOD use pattern and then have them estimate their risk for engaging in future DWI behavior. Have clients do the "write in" exercises in the text, e.g., "Describe your alcohol or other drug use pattern."

▶ **Exercise:** Complete *Work Sheet 13* which identifies risk level for another DWI based on the *social and benefits patterns* they tend to fit. Then, have them write down their specific DWI pattern.

▶ Present the problem outcomes of various drugs as presented in *Table 7* of the *Participant's Workbook*. Have clients check the ones they have had.

▶ Go over the *Impaired Control Cycle, Figure 2* below. Using the *ICC*, have clients place themselves into one of the four problem outcome patterns.

▶ **Exercises:** *Work Sheets 14 and 15* provide clients with the opportunity to see whether they fit the *DSM IV Substance Abuse or Substance Dependence* diagnoses. *Work Sheet 16* asks clients to rate themselves as to whether they fit the four categories of AOD misuse and problem outcomes.

LESSON CLOSURE

Have clients share their perceptions of their AOD use and whether that use falls into a misuse pattern. Facilitate group discussion around how these patterns increase risk of future DWI behavior.

FIGURE 2

Mental-behavioral impaired control cycle (ICC).

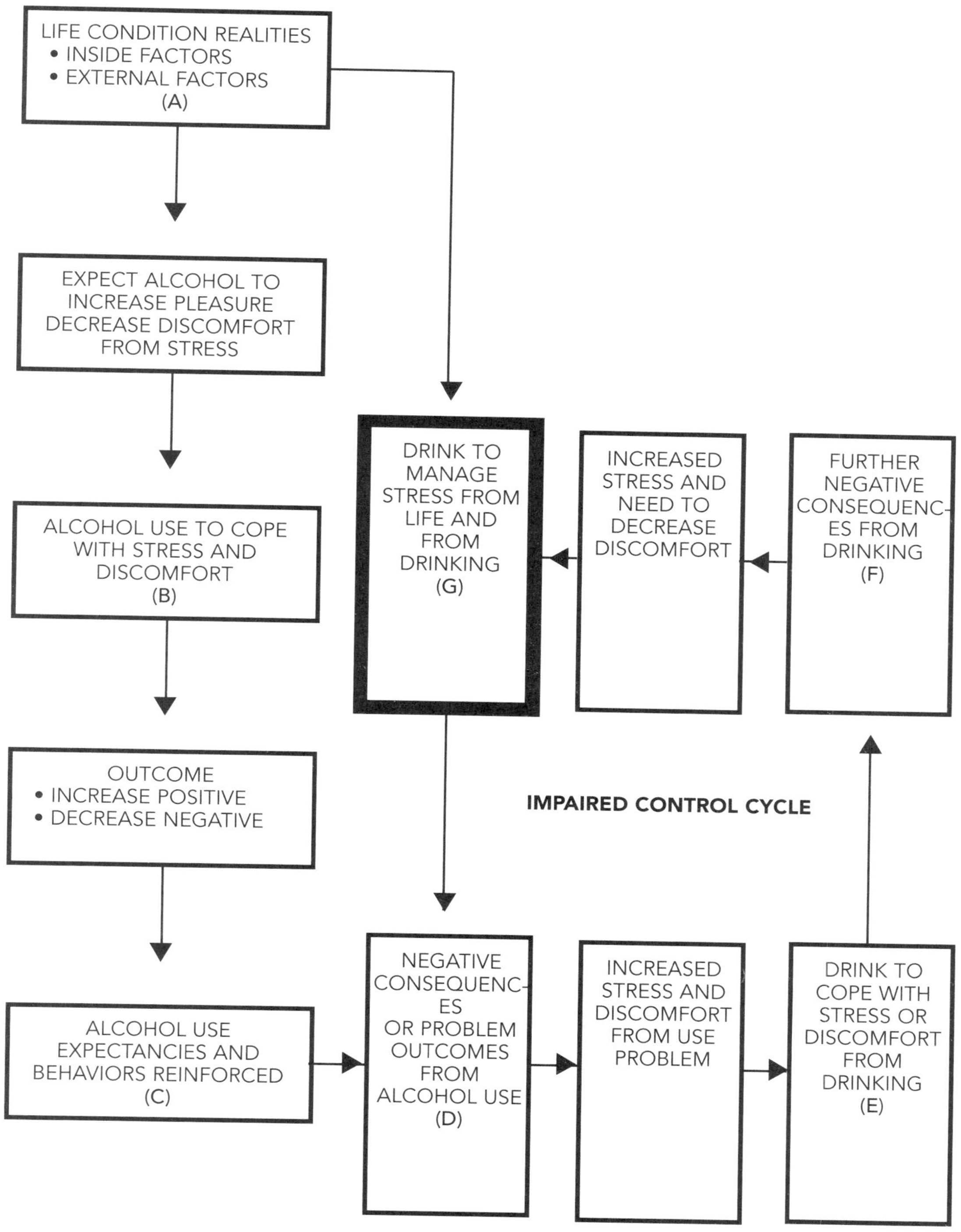

LIFE CONDITION REALITIES
• INSIDE FACTORS
• EXTERNAL FACTORS
(A)

EXPECT ALCOHOL TO INCREASE PLEASURE DECREASE DISCOMFORT FROM STRESS

ALCOHOL USE TO COPE WITH STRESS AND DISCOMFORT
(B)

OUTCOME
• INCREASE POSITIVE
• DECREASE NEGATIVE

ALCOHOL USE EXPECTANCIES AND BEHAVIORS REINFORCED
(C)

DRINK TO MANAGE STRESS FROM LIFE AND FROM DRINKING
(G)

INCREASED STRESS AND NEED TO DECREASE DISCOMFORT

FURTHER NEGATIVE CONSEQUENCES FROM DRINKING
(F)

IMPAIRED CONTROL CYCLE

NEGATIVE CONSEQUENCES OR PROBLEM OUTCOMES FROM ALCOHOL USE
(D)

INCREASED STRESS AND DISCOMFORT FROM USE PROBLEM

DRINK TO COPE WITH STRESS OR DISCOMFORT FROM DRINKING
(E)

(Adapted from Wanberg, 1971, 1990)

221

LESSON 6: PREVENTING RECIDIVISM AND RELAPSE

RATIONALE AND OVERVIEW OF LESSON

This is the last lesson in the *Level I Education* protocol. This program has challenged clients to look at their own AOD use and misuse patterns in relationship to their DWI behavior. Clients have been challenged to relate the lesson material to their own patterns of DWI behavior and AOD use, assess their risk for recidivism and relapse and to come to the point of making a commitment to goals and actions that will prevent recidivism. The challenge has been to get clients to become fully aware and to confront directly the bad outcomes of their thinking and behavior and the burden that their DWI arrest and disposition has placed on them, their families and their community. The assumption of this program and the rationale of this *lesson* is that self-confrontation and awareness are powerful influences in preventing recidivism - most likely more powerful than sanctions imposed on them by the courts and the *Motor Vehicle Division*.

It has been made clear that the goal of preventing legal recidivism is not their choice but the choice of society and the community - *to never operate a motor vehicle while exceeding the legal BAC limits or when under the influence of any mind-behavior altering drug*. Yet, clients have the option to choose the "zero tolerance-zero risk" recidivism prevention goal. We have challenged clients to commit themselves to this goal.

Even though returning to problem drinking and drug use increases the risk of DWI behavior, these two behavior patterns are independent to the extent that the choice of relapse prevention goals is personal and not society determined. We have spelled out the goal options for AOD use, one of which is to continue the pattern or use irrespective of whether that pattern is one that leads to AOD problems. Yet, we have challenged clients to choose one of two more realistic goals: *to prevent relapse into a pattern of use that leads to AOD problems and misuse; or to prevent relapse by maintaining abstinence from mind-behavior altering drugs*. This *Level I* program has taken no specific stand other than to make clear to the client that relapse into problematic AOD use increases the risk of legal recidivism.

Clients are asked to *make choices* as to what their goal of recidivism and relapse prevention will be. We have helped them see that recidivism and relapse are gradual erosion processes and that thoughts, beliefs and attitudes always underlie these processes. We have challenged clients to commit themselves to a recidivism and relapse prevention choice. Whatever the commitment choice, we want clients to clearly understand that high-risk thinking and high-risk situations increase the risk of relapse (as defined by the client) and legal recidivism as defined by the community and society. We also want clients to know that their choices are strongly influenced by their thought habits or automatic thoughts and the beliefs and attitudes underlying these thoughts. Thoughts, feelings, attitudes and beliefs are powerful influences in determining the behavior choices that lead to either good or bad outcomes.

LESSON CONTENT

The content of this lesson covers the most basic issues and concepts of recidivism and relapse prevention. Information is provided on the prevalence of DWI behavior in society, the impact of this behavior on the community as victim, and how BAC impacts on risk of accidents and fatalities. The typical DWIO is described and then clients are asked to summarize the cost and burden of their DWI. The definition and processes of recidivism are discussed with a focus on high-risk thinking and situations that lead to DWI behavior. Clients are asked to commit to the personal goal of "zero tolerance-zero risk" recidivism which goes beyond society's expectation of preventing recidivism as defined by the law.

> The definition and process of relapse is discussed and clients are asked to define what relapse means to them and then to select a relapse prevention goal. High-risk thinking and situations along with triggers for relapse are discussed. Preventing future problem drinking or abstinence are two choices clients are asked to consider. Abstinence is recommended for those whose AOD use problems indicate drug dependence.
>
> Skills in preventing relapse and recidivism are discussed. For those who will choose to drink, guidelines for responsible alcohol use are presented. Alternatives to drinking and driving are also presented. Clients are asked to develop both a recidivism and relapse prevention plan.

PRESENTATION PROCESS AND GUIDELINES

Start with giving clients opportunity to ask questions or to provide input as to their concerns. The presentation should then follow the following sequence.

- Presentation of the prevalence and impact of DWI behavior in the community and how the community is a victim of DWI conduct. Given the number of deaths from impaired driving, have clients discuss the idea that DWI conduct is a violent crime.

- Present data and information around the relationship of BAC to risk of death and accidents.

- **Exercises:** Using Work Sheets 17 through 20, have clients enumerate and calculate their DWI burden, financial costs, time costs and what each drink they took before being arrested cost them.

- Define recidivism, the process of recidivism and the high risk exposures, e.g., high risk thinking and situations associated with DWI behavior. Have clients do the "write in" exercises in the lesson text.

- Have clients understand that the legal recidivism choice is that of society, not theirs. Yet, challenge clients to commit themselves to the personal goal of zero-tolerance zero-risk recidivism prevention.

- Have clients define what relapse means to them, to understand the high risk thinking and situations associated with that definition and to get clients to commit to a relapse prevention goal.

- Recognizing that many clients will choose the goal of continuing to drink alcohol but to prevent relapse into problem drinking, discuss guidelines for CAREFUL and responsible drinking.

- **Exercise:** Have clients use *Work Sheet 21* to calculate their risk of getting another DWI. Have the group discuss their findings.

- Present the skills for relapse and recidivism prevention, discuss the refusal skills and discuss the alternatives to drinking and driving. Practice refusal skills by role playing different scenarios.

- **Exercise:** *Work Sheet 22* provides several problem solving scenarios around preventing driving after having ingested alcohol. Do the problem solving in the group.

- **Exercise:** Use *Work Sheet 23* to have clients develop a relapse prevention plan and *Work Sheet 24* to develop the recidivism prevention plan.

- Make it clear that this program in no way has indicated that it is OK to use illicit or illegal drugs, and that our expectation is that clients will abstain from all drugs that are illegal.

- Have clients complete all work sheets. Based on their community and personal relapse and recidivism prevention goals, help clients develop a recidivism and relapse prevention plan.

LESSON CLOSURE

Have each client share what was the most important thought or idea they learned in the program. Have each client complete the *Driving With CARE Inventory* as the post-test for the program and the CPR — Client Program Response Survey.

SUMMARY OF CURRICULUM GUIDE FOR LEVEL 1 EDUCATION

Before presenting the lessons of *Level I Education*, the provider will need to become thoroughly familiar with content of the *Participant's Workbook*. It is important that the introductory material of *Level I Education* of the *Provider's Guide* is studied carefully, and that the lesson guide, provided above, is studied before each lesson is presented.

Much of the content in the *Provider's Guide* above is repeated for comparable sessions in *DWC Level II Education* below. However, the rationale for comparable *Level II* lessons is often more enhanced and addresses the issues that are pertinent to *Level II* clients. The next section in this *Provider's Guide* will present guidelines for presenting *Level II Education*.

ALCOHOL, OTHER DRUGS AND DRIVING SAFETY EDUCATION

LEVEL II EDUCATION

_____

_____

_____

_____

_____

_____

OVERVIEW AND INTRODUCTION TO LEVEL 2 EDUCATION

This is a 24-hour education program for persons who have been convicted of driving while their blood alcohol level went beyond legal limits or while they were under the influence of a drug other than alcohol. More specifically, this program is designed for impaired driving offenders who have at least minimal indicators, at initial screening, of past problems associated with AOD use or misuse and/or whose arrest BAC was higher (e.g. .15 or higher).

For some clients, *Level II Education* may be the only DWI education-intervention service requirement that has to be met. However, many clients in this protocol will be required to continue DWI services into a treatment therapy protocol. Clients should complete *Level II Education* before entering *DWC Therapy.*

There are two main goals of DWC *Level II Education.* The first is to help clients prevent future driving while impaired by alcohol or other drugs - **to prevent recidivism.** The second goal is to help clients avoid a future pattern of alcohol or other drug use that has caused them problems and discomfort in the past and led to impaired driving - **to prevent relapse.**

Participants will take an active part in each of the 12 program lessons. Each lesson has exercises and work sheets that help clients apply the topics and material to their own situation. Clients are motivated to become an active part of their group through sharing what they learned in the exercises and work sheets.

This program is built on the approach that we make changes in our actions by changing how we think. We will give clients the knowledge and skills on how to change their thinking so that they can change their actions.

Level II Education will help clients understand how behaviors are learned and how those behaviors are strengthened. They will come to have a good understanding of their involvement in impaired driving and how their state laws apply to that involvement. Clients will be given opportunity to see how their own AOD use fits clinically identified patterns and cycles of AOD use and misuse. They will learn approaches and strategies that will prevent future problems of use and misuse and involvement in DWI behavior. Another objective is to help clients develop the understanding and skills to prevent relapse and recidivism by managing their stress and emotions, building healthy family and social relationships, and building attitudes and values that help them live in harmony with their community.

> Our overall goal is to help clients to be responsible to themselves, others and to their community. Thus, what this program is really about, is helping clients develop approaches and strategies for responsible living and change.

Compared with *Level I Education, Level II Education* places greater emphasis on the pathways to AOD problems and addiction. There is more emphasis on helping clients identify whether they fit the problem use, AOD abuse or AOD dependence classifications. For those who do fit these classifications, there is a stronger challenge to consider abstinence as one path for recidivism and relapse prevention.

We want participants to understand that *Driving With CARE* means caring about themselves and caring about others. We want CARE to be an important part of their driving and CARING to be an important part of their lives. Our overall goal is to help clients to be responsible to themselves, others and to their community. Thus, what this program is really about, is helping clients to develop approaches and *strategies for responsible living and change.*

Here are the program objectives.

SPECIFIC GOALS AND OBJECTIVES OF LEVEL II EDUCATION

The purpose of *Driving With CARE: Alcohol, Other Drugs and Driving Safety Education - Level II Education,* is to prevent the operation of a motor vehicle while under the influence of or impaired by alcohol or other drugs. We want clients to develop knowledge and learn skills that will help them to engage in CAREFUL and responsible thinking and behavior about alcohol or other drug (AOD) use and to prevent involvement in impaired driving.

- **Prevent recidivism** or returning to driving a motor vehicle while exceeding the legal BAC limits or while having ingested any other mind-altering drugs that impair driving behavior.

- **Prevent relapse** or returning to a pattern of alcohol or other drug use that is harmful and disruptive to normal living, including impaired driving.

- Increase clients' awareness of their past history of driving while impaired and to help them understand their current DWI charge and conviction.

- Teach clients how to change thinking, beliefs and attitudes that control actions and behavior and which lead to driving while involved in AOD use.

- Understand how AOD use and abuse affect and influence the mind, body, social behaviors, relationship with others, and responsibilities towards the community.

- Understand the impact of driving while under the influence of alcohol or other drugs on personal living and on the community.

- Understand the laws around impaired driving and help clients be clear about their obligations to the court and to the *Motor Vehicle Division.*

- Encourage clients to commit to a goal of "zero tolerance-zero risk" - never driving with alcohol or other mind-behavior altering drugs in the body.

- Challenge clients to commit to living an AOD problem free life.

- TO HAVE CLIENTS COMMIT TO DRIVING WITH CARE AND TO RESPONSIBLE BEHAVIOR IN THE COMMUNITY.

Two hours are needed to present each of the lessons in *Level II Education*. *Level II Education* may be presented in a closed group, presenting all 12 lessons in the sequence as they are found in the *Participant's Workbook*. For most agencies, this will not be a practical presentation structure. A **second option** is an open group method in which *Lesson 1* is used as an orientation session and then *Lessons 2 through 12* are presented in sequence. Clients may be admitted into the lesson series after they have finished *Lesson 1* orientation. For larger agencies, group intake and orientation sessions can be conducted on a once-a-month basis. All clients must receive Lesson 1 before proceeding into the program. The orientation, Lesson 1, can be done in an individual session.

When an open group is used, it is recommended that clients be introduced into the *Level II Education* lesson series at the following break points:

▶ at the beginning of *Lesson 2*;

▶ at the beginning of *Lesson 3*, but not at *Lesson 4* so that all clients receive *Lessons 3 and 4* in sequence;

▶ at the beginning of *Lesson 5*;

▶ at the beginning of *Lesson 6* but not at Lesson 7 so that all clients receive *Lessons 6 and 7* in sequence;

▶ at the beginning of *Lesson 8*; but not at *Lesson 9*, so that all clients receive *Lessons 8 and 9* in sequence.

▶ at the beginning of *Lesson 10*;

▶ at the beginning of *Lesson 11*;

▶ at the beginning of *Lesson 12*.

Even using this assigned protocol, the provider will discover that a particular lesson in the *Participant's Workbook* will refer to a lesson that some clients will have not yet received. In these cases, the provider will need to do a brief introduction to that material, which will be a review for clients having already received the lesson.

Providers are asked to adhere closely to the lesson content. All lesson content and material in *Level II Education* need to be presented to clients. This content is spelled out in detail in the *Participant's Workbook*. Most DWI education providers have developed their own materials, methods of presentation, specific handouts and exercises, and have strong opinions of what should be presented in these curricula. Providers should make sure that all material and content that are added to the DWC *Level I and II Education* curricula complement the essential content and concepts of DWC and not detract from the content, objectives and purpose of the lesson.

The legal issues and state laws related to DWI convictions change periodically. Thus, Lesson 2 provides a generic presentation of the laws that relate to DWI arrests and convictions. The provider will need to give the group a handout with the most current laws for the client's jurisdiction.

It is expected that clients be given the complete *Workbook* at intake into the *Level II Education* protocol. If that intake session is at a time different from the *Lesson 1: Program Orientation,* the client should be asked to review *Lesson 1* for the orientation session. Again, it cannot be emphasized enough that **for the client to develop a sense of ownership of the DWC program and curricula, the entire *Participant's Workbook* must be given to the client** at the beginning of the program. The provider should not assume that the client will read the lesson even if having time.

The following approaches have been found effective in delivering the DWC **Level II** curriculum.

▶ Present material in an interactive teaching format.

▶ Use overheads, media posters and charts for presentation.

▶ Have clients read portions of the material to the group.

▶ Create a balance across the tasks of: presenting the lesson content; having clients do the interactive work on the content; and facilitating group discussion around the exercises and work sheets.

PROVIDER SKILLS AND SERVICE STRATEGIES NEEDED FOR LEVEL II EDUCATION AND THERAPY

Significant proportions of the content of this protocol need to be presented within an interactive teaching format. The content should be presented so as to maximize the participants' interaction with the material, the provider and members of the group.

> For the client to develop ownership of the DWC program, the entire *Paticipant's Workbook* must be given to the client at the beginning of the program.

Level II Education providers should have basic skills in differential screening, and differential and in-depth assessment. At both the individual and group level, they should be skilled at: facilitating self-disclosure; using feedback clarification and therapeutic confrontation; and at reinforcing positive program involvement and positive changes. Providers should be able to enhance client participation and motivation to be open and accepting towards the program. They should be knowledgeable in patterns of AOD use and abuse, the assessment of such patterns, relapse and recidivism, and relapse and recidivism prevention protocols.

In addition to the above identified skills, providers will need to have: basic knowledge of cognitive-behavioral approaches to learning and change; understand and operationally integrate the correctional and the therapeutic approaches; knowledge of the community reinforcement model; referral resources in the community; and skills to make effective referral to aftercare services.

Even though this is still an educationally oriented curriculum, providers of *Level II Education* (compared with *Level I* providers) will need to be more proficient in counseling and therapeutic skills. This is for the following reasons:

▶ clients are in the program for a longer period of time and more clinical material will surface that needs to be handled;

▶ clients come to *Level II Education* with more AOD misuse and life-situation problems; and

▶ the curriculum material is more focused on social-emotional issues even though these issues are always related to preventing recidivism.

COMPLETION REQUIREMENTS AND EXPECTATIONS OF CLIENTS

The following are the comprehension and skill development expectations of clients.

▶ Understanding the facts and details of their DWI conviction.

▶ A basic understanding of the patterns of AOD use and abuse and how their use fits these patterns.

▶ A basic understanding of the cognitive-behavioral change principle that our *thoughts, attitudes and beliefs, not the events outside of ourselves, lead to our feelings and behaviors.*

▶ A basic understanding of the principles of relapse and recidivism and relapse and recidivism prevention.

▶ Know the difference between antisocial and prosocial attitudes and behaviors and demonstrate changes towards a more prosocial and caring approach towards the community and society.

▶ Explore and disclose social-emotional issues and relate these issues to DWI behavior.

▶ Develop a basic relapse and recidivism plan.

▶ Meet the following participation expectations.

- Complete all of the exercises and work sheets.

- Attend all sessions and be on time.

- Be involved in structured sharing exercises in the group.

- Complete homework assignments, including AOD thinking and action charting.

- Keep all information learned about group members in trust and confidence, and not discuss it with other people.

- Remain free from AOD use during the course of the program. As discussed in Section II, programs may vary with respect to this expectation.

- Be AOD free when attending all sessions.

INTAKE AND ASSESSMENT

The provider should meet individually with the client for the intake session. This would first involve completing the following basic intake procedures.

> ▶ Complete the Agency's personal data intake form.
>
> ▶ Client rights and responsibilities.
>
> ▶ Consent to treatment involvement.
>
> ▶ Consent for release of information to court, probation department or other agencies and persons as requested by the client or as required by the judicial district.
>
> ▶ Advisement of credentials and full disclosure statement.
>
> ▶ Confidentiality advisement.
>
> ▶ Fees and collection procedures.
>
> Samples of all of the above forms are found in *Appendix C* except for personal data intake form.
>
> Although an in-depth assessment is not necessary for *Level I* and *Level II Education* clients, the provider should review the referral information from the evaluator. This would include reviewing the results of any assessment instruments administered during the evaluation process. This will help the provider understand the level of defensiveness of the client as well as the levels of *AOD involvement and disruption* disclosed by the client.

DRIVING WITH CARE INVENTORY (DWCI)

The *Driving With Care Inventory* is administered to clients during the orientation session and then readministered in the last session that the client attends. The re-testing can take place before the client's last group or as part of the closure session with the client. The DWCI is found in the **Appendix B** of this *Provider's Guide along with an answer sheet and scoring guide.*

> In the initial administration of DWCI it is important to tell clients that they are not expected to know many of the answers to the test questions. They are asked to do their best.
>
> At re-testing, clients should be expected to get *at least 80 percent correct.* The results should be reviewed with each client, and wrong answers are discussed in light of the correct answer.

OUTLINE OF PROGRAM LESSONS

1. Program orientation: Developing a working relationship.

2. Alcohol and other drug impaired driving: The laws and beyond the law.

3. How thinking, attitudes and beliefs control our actions.

4. Understanding how behavior is learned and changed: Learning self-control and *Driving With CARE*.

5. Alcohol and other drugs: How do the facts and ideas about alcohol and other drug use fit you?

6. Alcohol and other drug use patterns: How do they fit you?

7. Problem outcomes of alcohol and other drug use: Patterns of misuse and abuse — how do they fit you?

8. Pathways to relapse and recidivism.

9. Process and steps to preventing relapse.

10. Preventing relapse and recidivism: Building personal values and prosocial attitudes and behaviors and driving with care.

11. Preventing relapse and recidivism: Managing stress and emotions.

12. Preventing relapse and recidivism: Building healthy family and social relationships.

> Present material in an interactive format.
>
> Use overheads, posters, charts for presentation.
>
> Create balance between lesson presentations, clients' interacting with content through work sheets and group discussions.
>
> Build trust and harmony in the group and with clients.

MEETING CLIENT THERAPEUTIC NEEDS DURING LEVEL II EDUCATION

Some Level II clients may have therapeutic needs that cannot be met in the Level II Education protocol. These needs may be detected at the time of intake or while they are in DWC Education. These needs may range from more urgent marital or relationship problems to mental health concerns. For clients who will proceed into *DWC Therapy*, these needs may be met in that protocol. However, the needs may be too urgent to wait for *DWC Therapy*. In these cases, providers will want to assist clients in accessing the necessary resources to address these needs, either within or outside the provider's agency.

LESSON 1: PROGRAM ORIENTATION: DEVELOPING A WORKING RELATIONSHIP

RATIONALE AND OVERVIEW OF LESSON

The rationale and mission of *Level II Education* take on different features because clients at this Level will have more extensive histories of AOD misuse, impaired driving and higher levels of arrest BAC. In the orientation session, the provider helps clients see that *Level II Education,* compared to *Level I,* is longer, more intense and expands its focus in life adjustment areas that affect self-control and responsibility to the community. This overview will give providers the basis for understanding and describing this difference.

Level II Education clients may be more open and motivated to take part in the DWC program. *Level II* clients will have a higher level of problem awareness than *Level I* clients. Yet, many will not perceive themselves as having an AOD use problem and some will not even see that getting a DWI is indicative of such a problem. There will be initial resistance and reluctance to openly share and participate in discussion.

Using *client-centered and motivational interviewing approaches* (Miller & Rollnick, 2002), the initial intake and orientation sessions for *Level II* clients will convey high expectations with respect to the clients' involvement in the program. They will not be expecting to take a passive role in the program. The DWC *Level II Education* curriculum presents a *greater challenge to relate the content to the client's personal and unique situation.* There is more concentration on the cognitive-behavioral approach for developing self-control and change. There is more in-depth presentation of AOD use and misuse styles and greater challenge to get clients to identify their own styles, particularly as these relate to DWI behavior.

An effort is made to maximize participation and interaction while not sacrificing teaching the essential concepts and content related to AOD use and misuse and recidivism and relapse prevention. The approach for *Level II* is also premised on a non-confrontational, motivation enhancing and client-centered facilitation model. Client resistance is not confronted but accepted and reflected. Motivating clients to change now becomes just as important as the motivation to interact and participate.

AOD education and driving safety education and recidivism prevention are still the primary focuses. Yet there is a more expanded focus on responsible living, self-control and enhancing psychosocial adjustment since these impact on DWI conduct and behavior. As with *Level I Education,* the mission of the *Level II* provider and the primary change focus is that of helping clients *alter their thinking and behavior patterns* so as to prevent future DWI behavior (recidivism). The enhanced focus on changing AOD use patterns is to the extent that this helps prevent recidivism, and to help clients see that they have had at least one problem related to AOD use: being arrested for DWI.

Level II Education moves more in the direction of getting clients to make major changes in their AOD use patterns, since this group will be more involved in AOD misuse. An important goal is to help clients clearly determine if they have an AOD addiction, abuse or dependence problems, since this group has higher risk of their AOD problems leading to recidivism.

In *Driving With CARE,* recidivism and relapse are the major themes. Yet, underlying these themes and the desired spinoff is still **responsible living and change.** *Driving With CARE,* not engaging in DWI conduct and behavior and changing life direction enough to avoid future AOD related problems represent a demonstration of responsible living.

The objectives and goals of *Lesson 1: Orientation,* are outlined in the *Participant's Workbook.* Essentially, the objectives are to convey to clients the purpose of the program, understand the meaning of *Driving With CARE* and responsible living, introduce clients to the concepts of recidivism and relapse, introduce clients to the concept of cognitive-behavioral approaches in preventing recidivism and relapse and outline the expectations of clients and program agreements and guidelines.

SUMMARY OF LESSON CONTENT

The essential material and content to be presented in all of the Level II lessons are spelled out in detail in the *Participant's Workbook.* Only the most salient components of this content are summarized.

There are *three important concepts* that are at the core of *Level II Education* which clients are asked to discuss and interact around: *recidivism; relapse;* and the *cognitive-behavioral* approach for developing self-control and change.

Preventing recidivism. This lesson provides clients with the basic concept of legal recidivism defined as returning to the behavior of driving with a blood alcohol concentration (BAC) at .05 or higher, or, for those under age 21, when the BAC is .02 or higher and to not drive under the influence of any mind-behavior altering drug. This is society's expectation of the client. This lesson also challenges clients to consider the recidivism prevention goal of *"zero tolerance-zero risk."*

Preventing relapse. The concept of relapse is defined and the relationship between recidivism and relapse is explored. Many clients have no intention to stop AOD use. However, the abstinence approach may be appropriate for some *Level II Education* clients. Thus, *Level II Education* does emphasize this relapse prevention alternative. Yet, the provider must balance the presentation between acknowledging that one can use alcohol and not go into recidivism - drinking and driving - while at the same time conveying the concept that alcohol use and misuse increase the risk of future DWI behavior. It is also important to convey that abstinence is the sure way to prevent recidivism and getting another DWI arrest as well as preventing further AOD problems.

Working definitions are provided for *relapse pattern, lapse and relapse*. A *relapse pattern* or pathway to relapse is defined as the process of thinking about AOD use or putting oneself in situations that could cause involvement in or return to a harmful pattern of alcohol or other drug use. A *lapse* is defined as any pattern of AOD use that **could lead to** harming self or others after having made a commitment to a non-harmful pattern of use or to no use at all. A *relapse* is developing further problems from alcohol or other drug (AOD) use, or the person **is now into** a harmful pattern of AOD - which may or may not involve DWI recidivism.

There are three important concepts that are at the core of Level II Education which clients are asked to discuss and interact around: recidivism; relapse; and the cognitive-behavioral approach for developing self-control and change.

Clients are asked to look at their choices around AOD use and preventing relapse. They are asked to look at their **legal and moral community commitment** which is the same as the legal community commitment around recidivism: *to not drive when the presence of alcohol in your body has gone beyond the legal BAC limits or to not drive when you are impaired by the presence of other drugs.*

The clients' **personal commitments or goals around AOD use** are explored helping them see that, beyond the legal commitment to the community with respect to AOD use and driving, there are clear choices around AOD use that can provide the basis for the client setting a relapse prevention goal.

▶ **To use alcohol or other drugs with no goal of preventing harm or disruption to self or others,** letting the "cards fall as they may." Help clients see the consequence of how this goal could be dangerous.

▶ **To not use alcohol or other drugs to the extent that they cause harmful effects to oneself, to others, or to the community.** Again, it is helpful to remind clients that they are in the program because they lost self-control and that use of alcohol or other drugs led to harmful or potentially harmful effects on others and the community.

▶ **To live an alcohol and drug-free life.** This means abstaining from the use of alcohol and all mind-behavior altering drugs unless prescribed by a medical specialist. This will not be an acceptable goal to clients who do not see themselves as having had significant problems related to AOD use.

The cognitive-behavioral approach to self-control and change is presented during this orientation lesson. This part of the orientation is extremely important, since this will introduce clients to the baseline concepts necessary to negotiate *Level II Education.* These are presented in the *Participant's Workbook* but will be reviewed here.

▶ Self-control and changes in our actions occur by changing how we think, what we believe about ourselves and the world and how we feel. Change and improvement begin first in our mind.

▶ It is our thoughts and our beliefs and our attitudes - not what happens around us or to us - that cause us to feel and act in a certain way or cause us to do certain things. It was the client's thinking - not the events outside the client - that led to DWI behavior.

- Changing our mental world gives us more control over our life and prevents repeating the behavior or action of driving while using alcohol or other drugs. This involves learning:

  - how thinking, attitudes and beliefs control our actions and behaviors, and

  - how actions or behaviors become habits or patterns that can result in a positive or negative outcomes.

- Learning and change through the cognitive-behavioral approach takes place through the development of three kinds of skills:

  - **mental restructuring or thought changing skills** to enhance self-control over actions and prevent future DWI conduct;

  - **social and relationship skills** that enhance self-control over our relationship with others and prevent driving and AOD use; and

  - **community responsibility skills** that increase reliable and responsible actions in the community.

- The cognitive - behavioral change model is introduced to the group (*Figure 1* in *Work Book*).

- **Exercise:** Present some examples as to how the change model works, using client experiences as the basis of the examples.

PRESENTATION PROCESS AND GUIDELINES

Facilitating group discussion and interaction around lesson topics and content is important. The basic individual and group counseling skills to use in this and subsequent lessons are encouraging individual and group sharing, reflecting back on what the group is saying, and reinforcing positive group and individual involvement and change. The following are some guidelines that are useful when working with DWI groups.

- Be non-confrontational and avoid argumentation.

- Get people to share and talk.

- Express empathy.

- Roll with the resistance.

- Reinforce positive involvement and sharing.

- Use the round-robin technique of asking everyone in the group to participate. Clients should be asked to make brief and crisp statements - usually no more than 10 to 20 seconds per person.

The following presentation process and sequence is recommended for Lesson 1: Orientation.

- ▶ Welcome the clients to the program, and clearly spell out the theme of the program: *Driving With CARE.*

- ▶ Define the program structure and group setup and format.

- ▶ Administer the DWCI.

- ▶ Introduce the concepts of recidivism and relapse and have clients define their initial goals in this area.

- ▶ Go over the objectives of the program.

- ▶ Present the partnership of caring triad: client, community and provider.

- ▶ Go over the CPR — Client Progress Report. Clients are asked to complete this at the end of their sixth lesson and 11th lesson. It is recommended that clients or the provider give the CPR to their judicial supervisor (probation worker).

- ▶ Spell out what the program expects and define the program agreements and guidelines.

- ▶ Introduce the group to the cognitive-behavioral (CB) approach to self-control and change.

- ▶ **Exercise:** Present examples how the CB change model works.

- ▶ **Exercise:** Have clients complete *Work Sheet 1* and read each question on the work sheet. Have clients briefly introduce themselves and share their DWI arrest and conviction story, using *Work Sheet 1* as a guide.

- ▶ **Exercise:** Introduce the *TAP — Thinking and Action Patterns Chart, Work Sheet 2,* spending time to be sure clients clearly understand how to complete the chart and that they are asked to do this each week.

LESSON CLOSURE

Ask each client to make one statement about what they would like to get out of the program and one statement of what they got out of the first lesson. This will provide a view of where clients are and the level of client resistance.

LESSON 2: ALCOHOL AND OTHER DRUG IMPAIRED DRIVING: THE LAWS AND BEYOND THE LAW

RATIONALE AND OVERVIEW OF LESSON

This lesson provides clients with generic legal information related to DWI penalties, sanctions (punishments), and loss and reinstatement of driving privileges. Clients take a look at their own DWI situation. A goal of this lesson is to have clients see the impact of their DWI on their own lives, on those who were impacted by their DWI behavior, some of whom are classified as victims. This is the responsibility to the community focus of this program. Help clients keep the major theme of this program continually in mind: Responsible living involves *Driving With CARE.*

In this lesson, *clients identify their current court and legal obligations and define whether they are fulfilling those obligations.* The rationale of this lesson is that the greater the personal identification with the laws and statutes and the more clients clarify their own involvement in DWI legal issues and obligations, the higher the probability of preventing recidivism. When this identification reaches affective levels, the impact may be even higher.

LESSON CONTENT AND PRESENTATION PROCESS AND GUIDELINES

The lesson begins with general legal information related to DWI laws. Clients are then given a handout addressing the current DWI laws specific to their jurisdiction or state.

- ▶ Categories of offenses.

- ▶ Outcomes of charges and convictions.

- ▶ Understanding that the county courts and the *Division of Motor Vehicle* in most states are two completely separate legal agencies or authorities that impose sanctions (punishments) and AOD education or treatment for charges related to DWI convictions; and understanding what the specific education and treatment and education requirements that each can impose.

- ▶ Understand how driver's licenses are revoked or suspended and how they are reinstated.

- ▶ Understand the specific laws and conditions related to DWI convictions including the *Expressed Consent Law, Habitual Offender Laws,* the *Persistent Drunk Driver Law,* ignition interlocks, and penalties for DWI offenses.

This lesson also focuses on *victim identification and awareness.* The rationale for this is empathy development, an area to be dealt with in more depth in *Level II Therapy.*

Getting the client to identify with and show interest in the lesson content are major challenges for the provider, particularly this lesson. When clients *apply the material to their own unique situation,* the material takes on a personal and even an emotional quality. For example, when presenting the three categories of offenses and the possible outcomes of these offenses, have clients identify which ones fit their DWI conviction. Have them determine the consequences of another DWI based on the laws presented in this lesson. Which sanctions and outcomes would apply to them? In essence, at every point in the presentation, continually ask the question, "how does this one apply to you?"

The provider will need to monitor the client's work in the *Participant's Workbook* to be sure that the various work sheets in the text or those at the end of the lesson are being done. The content of this lesson is presented in the following sequence.

▶ Present the DWI laws, convictions and penalties and make this presentation interactive with the group as described above. Have clients write in, at the bottom of Table 1, the education and therapy program they are required to take. Then, at the bottom of *Table 2*, have them write down their specific offense and penalties.

▶ Present the statistics and DWI impact data given in the lesson.

▶ **Exercise:** In the part of *Lesson 2* pertaining to the clients' unique situation, have them write down their offense and BAC level at arrest. Then have each client share something about their offense and the circumstances of their arrest. It might be the offense, the penalty, the BAC. Have them refer back to *Work Sheet 1* in *Lesson 1*.

▶ **Exercise:** Complete *Work Sheet 3*, the obligations and sanctions that clients have to meet.

▶ **Exercise:** Have clients mark in *Figure 2* in the *Participant's Workbook* all of the entities that were affected by their DWI and have them circle which of these were victims of their DWI. Do the *victim identification* work sheet in the text and have them note the responses of victims and how they were affected.

▶ **Exercise:** Review the *AOD Thinking and Action Patterns (TAP) Chart* that clients completed last week. Have a couple of group members share their results.

LESSON CLOSURE

Exercise: Have clients briefly share what they got out of the session. Give the group feedback as to how it did and reinforce positive group responding. Remind clients to complete Work Sheet 4, the TAP Charting for the coming week.

LESSON 3: HOW THINKING, ATTITUDES AND BELIEFS CONTROL OUR ACTIONS

RATIONALE AND OVERVIEW OF LESSON

Research findings support the efficacy of cognitive-behavioral (CB) approaches in developing self-control and change and in intervening in AOD misuse. The CB approach is the underlying strategy of the DWC curricula. It is important that clients have an understanding of the cognitive and behavioral processes that lead to both maladaptive and adaptive thinking and acting and to enhancing self-control and change. Miechenbaum (1977, 1985, 1993b), who has made major contributions to cognitive therapy, emphasizes the importance of providing the client with an early, clear and distinct framework for therapy. He suggests that this conceptualization and structure play an important role in helping the client to understand the change process and should precede any specific treatment interventions.

An important component of self-control and change is enhancing clients' belief that they have the skills and confidence to develop self-control and to avoid thinking and behaviors that cause problems and bad outcomes.

The main purpose of this lesson is to apply the principles of cognitive-behavior therapy to preventing DWI recidivism and AOD relapse. There are two pathways to developing self-control and positive and adaptive behaviors: through reinforcing thoughts that lead to positive outcomes and behavior; and by reinforcing the behaviors that produce positive outcomes or events. This lesson focuses on the first of these two pathways. Traditional behavioral therapy focuses on the idea that when behavior leads to favorable outcomes, that behavior is reinforced. The cognitive model adds a new link to that reinforcement path: that favorable and unfavorable outcomes often strengthen the thoughts that lead to the behaviors that produce them. This explains why behaviors from negative outcomes often do not become weakened or extinguished. Behaviors that produce unfavorable outcomes get reinforced if the outcome strengthens the thoughts that produce the behavior. This model is particularly relevant to DWI behavior and conduct.

> An important component of self-control and change is enhancing clients' belief that they have the skills and confidence to develop self-control and to avoid thinking and behaviors that cause problems and bad outcomes.

LESSON CONTENT AND PRESENTATION PROCESS AND GUIDELINES

The first part of this lesson explores how our thoughts, attitudes and beliefs lead to our actions and behaviors and to driving while impaired. **Six rules of thinking** are presented to help the client see how this happens. The first rule is that automatic thoughts or thought habits are responses to outside events and that these trigger feelings and actions. Underlying these thought habits are attitudes and beliefs. Other rules of thinking that are discussed are those of resisting change, that we have choices over how we think and what thoughts we have about what happens to us, that we develop thinking errors which lead to disturbed thoughts and emotions and to bad outcomes, that we can train ourselves to use the thought "what is best for me in the long-term" before responding to events that happen to us, and that outside events bring on thoughts based on our beliefs and attitudes. A map is provided for developing self-controlled thinking and different habit thoughts are presented that include expectations, appraisals, attributions and decisions. Steps and tools are presented for changing thoughts and for developing self-control.

Figure 3 below (*Figure 3* in the *Participant's Workbook*) provides the schematic for understanding how our thoughts are strengthened by behavioral outcomes. It shows that both good and bad outcomes strengthen or reinforce the thoughts that produced the behaviors leading to the outcomes.

The concepts and ideas in this lesson should be given in small segments and clients are asked to discuss these concepts as they are presented. The following provides the presentation sequence of this lesson.

▶ Take about 10 minutes for processing what clients have learned thus far and their questions and comments.

▶ Present how our thinking, attitudes and beliefs control our feelings and actions.

▶ Present the six rules of thinking and all the material associated with those rules. Do *Work Sheet 5* when presenting *Rule 4*.

▶ Help clients learn to map the pathway for self-control and positive outcomes. Carefully go over the schematic in *Figure 3* below that explains the process of learning and change and how our thoughts, feelings and beliefs are strengthened or reinforced. Demonstrate how this works by using an example. Be sure to teach that beliefs and attitudes underlie the automatic thoughts, and are not produced by the thoughts and feelings. Also indicate that this is the *cognitive* part of the cognitive-behavior model. The behavior part is discussed in *Lesson 4.*

▶ Discuss the steps and tools for changing thinking and how these skills can lead to positive or good outcomes.

▶ **Exercise:** Do *Work Sheet 6* in class. The focus is on the clients' DWI arrest event. Walk clients through the automatic thinking and thought habits, feelings, underlying attitudes and beliefs, the behavioral choice and the outcome related to the DWI arrest. Then go back to the event. Use the cognitive change skills to produce an outcome that is not a DWI arrest. If there is time, have clients pick another event other than their DWI arrest.

▶ Review last week's *TAP Chart*. Have some clients share their charting. Answer any questions around the charting. Remind clients to do the *TAP Chart* as homework for the coming week.

LESSON CLOSURE

Take time for some discussion and questions. Depending on where the group is, consider giving some mental homework. Here are some examples.

▶ Keep track of bad outcomes that happen during the week and then try to figure out the thoughts that led to these outcomes.

- Keep track of good outcomes that happen during the week and then try to figure out the thoughts that led to these outcomes.

- Have clients take one thought management and change skill and practice it all week. This could include the self-talk skills, shifting the view or relaxation exercises.

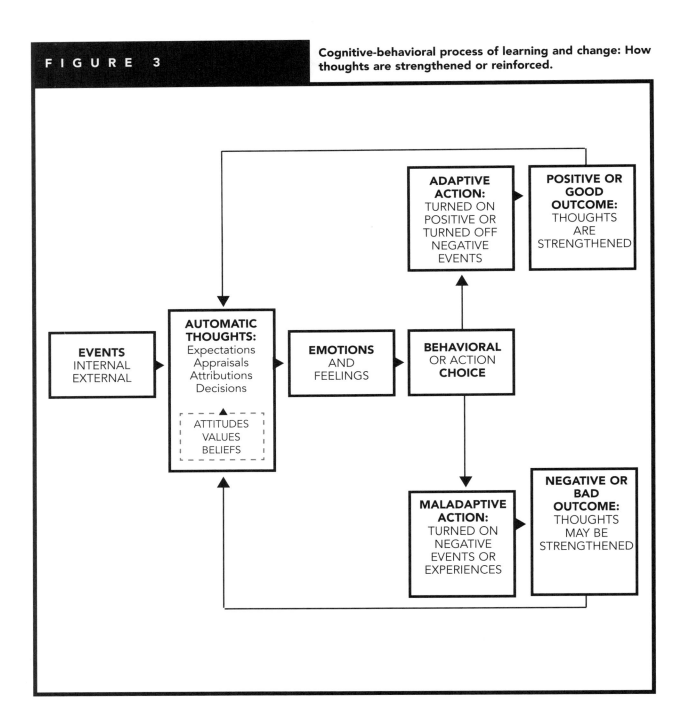

FIGURE 3   **Cognitive-behavioral process of learning and change: How thoughts are strengthened or reinforced.**

LESSON 4: HOW BEHAVIOR IS LEARNED AND CHANGED: LEARNING SELF-CONTROL AND DRIVING WITH CARE

RATIONALE AND OVERVIEW OF LESSON

For the open group structure, this lesson should be preceded by *Lesson 3* which provided the basic understanding of how our thoughts, attitudes and beliefs that lead to positive or negative behaviors get reinforced or strengthened. The current lesson focuses on how our actions or behaviors get reinforced or weakened when those actions lead to certain outcomes. The three rules that determine how behavior is learned and reinforced are discussed, particularly how these are related to DWI conduct. These rules are based on traditional models of operant conditioning. Attention is given to helping clients understand why Rule III doesn't always work: that a behavior that is punished often continues to persist and repeat itself. This provides an explanation as to why people continue to engage in behaviors that lead to bad outcomes. The lesson then shows how reinforcing thinking and reinforcing behavior are integrated into the overall cognitive-behavioral model of developing self-control and change.

SUMMARY OF LESSON CONTENT, PRESENTATION SEQUENCE AND GUIDELINES

Whereas **Lesson 3 focused** on **thought habits** (automatic thoughts), **this lesson focuses on** the concept of **action or behavior habits** or automatic behaviors. Action habits are developed and reinforced through the simple rules of operant conditioning: when a behavior produces a positive or good outcome it gets reinforced; when a behavior turns off a negative event, that behavior is strengthened (negative reinforcement model). The second of these two rules (negative reinforcement) is the most powerful in developing behaviors that are resistant to change. The third rule is that behavior that is sanctioned or punished will extinguish or drop out of the behavioral repertoire.

The last rule often confuses people. If that rule works, then why do we repeat behaviors that punish or lead to bad outcomes? Why do people get a second DWI? As discussed in the *Participant's Workbook,* the first two rules of learning are very powerful. Time should be taken to discuss this issue.

This lesson then puts together how our thinking and acting lead to the process of learning. *Figure 4* (and *Figure 4* in the *Participant's Workbook*) provides this integration and a careful explanation of how thinking and behavior are reinforced is provided in the *Participant's Workbook.*

Before presenting this lesson, review the essential ideas of *Lesson 3.* Then, the following presentation sequence is suggested.

 ▶ Interactively present the three learning rules by having clients present examples to illustrate the rules.

▶ Using *Figure 4* below (*Figure 4* in the *Participant's Workbook*), discuss how thinking and acting lead to learning thought habits and behaviors and how these are integrated in the cognitive-behavior model of learning self-control and change.

▶ **Exercise:** Do *Work Sheet 8.* Have clients use a recent event. Have a client volunteer to illustrate his/her situation for the group. Then, have each client complete the work sheet.

▶ Review last week's *TAP Chart.* Have some clients share their charting. Answer any questions around the charting. Assign TAP *Work Sheet 9* for homework.

LESSON CLOSURE

Exercise: Close the lesson by having each client talk about the number of times they drove while impaired prior to getting their DWI. Then, from what they have learned about themselves, have clients see if they can identify a belief they have held that might explain their DWI conduct. Remind clients to complete the AOD Thinking and Action Patterns Chart, Work Sheet 9 for the coming week and review the one they did for the past week.

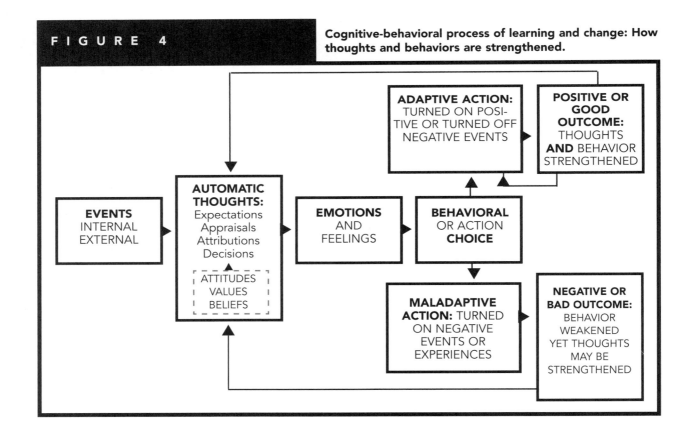

FIGURE 4   **Cognitive-behavioral process of learning and change: How thoughts and behaviors are strengthened.**

LESSON 5: ALCOHOL AND OTHER DRUGS: HOW DO THE FACTS AND IDEAS ABOUT ALCOHOL AND OTHER DRUGS FIT YOU?

RATIONALE AND OVERVIEW OF LESSON

This program challenges clients to change behaviors and patterns in AOD use and abuse. A part of this challenge is providing clients with sufficient knowledge about alcohol and other drugs and about abuse and addiction. The purpose of this lesson is to provide the client with the most basic knowledge about alcohol and other drugs. The approach of the DWC curriculum is to present this material in a factual and relatively unbiased, non-theoretical manner. Information for this lesson comes from a variety of sources, including Ray & Ksir (2002), Wanberg (1990) and Wanberg & Milkman (1998; 2005).

SUMMARY OF LESSON CONTENT, PRESENTATION SEQUENCE AND GUIDELINES

This lesson presents some basic concepts about alcohol and other drugs. Drugs are classified into two groups: *system enhancers* or drugs that stimulate the system; and *system suppressors,* or drugs that sedate the system. These are provided in *Table 3* of the *Participant's Workbook.* The direct and indirect (withdrawal) effects of these two classes of drugs are described along with the concept that the direct effect of the system enhancers is the opposite of the direct effect of the system suppressors. A point that this lesson emphasizes that is usually overlooked in the literature is that both the direct and withdrawal effects of a drug are disruptive, particularly to driving behavior. In *DWC Therapy,* we will look at the withdrawal effects as an important component of psychophysical addiction.

This lesson also discusses drug toxicity, tolerance, drug interactions, and drug withdrawal (indirect effects). Special focus is devoted to discussing alcohol since it is the primary drug associated with impaired driving. The concepts of the amount of alcohol in different kinds of beverage drinks, the meaning of blood alcohol concentration (BAC), different effects of different levels of BAC, and the measurement of BAC relative to drinking duration, weight and number of drinks are discussed. This discussion is assisted by *Tables 4 and 5* in the *Participant's Workbook.*

The effects of alcohol on health and the body and the effects of cannabis are also presented. General health risks related to drug use are discussed including AIDS and FAS. The most important topic of this lesson is the effect of specific drugs on driving behavior, *Table 6* in the *Participant's Workbook.*

The work sheets in this lesson are designed to maximize client interaction with the lesson content and to relate the specific condition and situation of clients to the material. These work sheets will take some time.

Review any homework assigned. Provide time for discussion around the following questions: What is an alcohol problem? What is a drug problem? What is addiction? What causes alcohol and drug use problems? Then present the material in the following sequence.

▶ Present the concepts of the two kinds of drugs and the direct and indirect effect of drugs and go over *Table 3* in the *Participant's Workbook*.

▶ Discuss toxicity, tolerance and drug interactions.

▶ Discuss the issues around alcohol and BAC. Use *Figure 5* in the *Participant's Workbook* to show how the amount of alcohol affects certain parts of the brain. Go over the BAC *Tables 4 and 5* in the *Participant's Workbook*.

▶ Present the effects of alcohol on the body, the material on cannabis and the health risks of AOD use.

▶ Discuss the direct effects of drugs on driving behavior and have clients share how alcohol affected their driving. Take time to go over *Table 6*.

▶ **Exercises:** *Work Sheets 10 through 15* should be done in class and will take some time to complete. These work sheets help clients apply the material of this lesson to their own drug use and DWI event. Go over each work sheet carefully. After explaining the work sheet, it might help to have clients work in pairs to do the work. *Work Sheet 13* is the most complicated, since this determines the number of drinks a client had at the time of arrest based on number of hours drinking, weight and BAC. There may be some defensiveness in completing *Work Sheet 13*. These exercises will clearly indicate to what degree clients are willing to openly self-disclose. Look for the more defensive clients and give them special support. Remember, our approach is to use therapeutic confrontation in dealing with defensiveness.

▶ Review *Work Sheet 9* that clients completed this past week, the *TAP Chart*. Remind them to do this for the coming week.

Make the presentation as interactive as possible, facilitating sharing of the clients' personal experiences related to specific concepts and ideas discussed.

LESSON CLOSURE

Have some clients share what they got out of this lesson. Have some of the clients share their *TAP Charts*.

LESSON 6: UNDERSTANDING ALCOHOL AND OTHER DRUG (AOD) USE PATTERNS: HOW DO THEY FIT YOU?

RATIONALE AND OVERVIEW OF LESSON

This Lesson is based on the assumption that clients who are arrested and have a DWI legal disposition also have an established pattern of alcohol or other drug use that was a key factor that led to DWI behavior. This lesson focuses on helping clients learn the different kinds of AOD use patterns and then to identify their own AOD use pattern or patterns. Defensive clients initially will have a hard time with this task and may even resist the idea that they have a unique AOD use pattern, let alone, seeing that this pattern was the basis of their DWI behavior. Such clients will score high on scales measuring defensiveness. It is important that the provider have the results of tests taken during the DWI evaluation process. Clients who have a low or "0" score on alcohol use scales are usually very defensive.

> Once clients identify their own AOD use pattern, they may see how that pattern is linked to their DWI behavior. If this link is established, then the door is open to help the client make the necessary changes to prevent further DWI behavior.

SUMMARY OF LESSON CONTENT, PRESENTATION SEQUENCE AND GUIDELINES

The first task in this lesson is to help clients identify their AOD use patterns which include:

▶ *Quantity-Frequency-Prediction* (QFP) pattern for both alcohol and other drugs;

▶ their *social use* (solo or gregarious or both) patterns; and

▶ the *benefits* they derive from use.

This allows clients to put a label on their unique alcohol or other drug use pattern. After clients write down their pattern of use, have them discuss it in class. A client might be described as a *moderate, frequent, daily consistent drinker* who drinks at bars with friends and to relax. Clients often resist doing this exercise. However, the provider has had opportunity to establish rapport with the group and clients may be more open and willing to self-disclose. The purpose of this drinking style description is to give clients some idea of their risk for recidivism. *Work Sheet 20* provides guidelines to estimate this risk.

Start this lesson having clients describe their alcohol or other drug use before they received their DWI. Here are some questions to help them.

▶ What are the different kinds of alcoholic beverages or drugs you have used? Review *Work Sheet 10* of *Lesson 5.*

▶ How much did you drink each day? Did you use any other drugs?

▶ Did you drink or use other drugs daily, periodically, on weekends?

▶ Did you drink alone, at home, with friends, at bars, at parties?

▶ Did you drink to relax, to feel less tense, more sociable?

▶ How are your use patterns related to your DWI?

Following some discussion around these questions, present the material in the sequence outlined below.

▶ Present the *QFP, social and benefits patterns* and have clients use these variables to describe their AOD use pattern.

▶ <u>Exercises:</u> Complete *Work Sheets 17, 18 and 19 and Profile 1* in order to help clients identify their AOD use patterns. Structure some discussion around their findings.

▶ <u>Exercise:</u> Have clients estimate their risk for engaging in future DWI behavior using *Work Sheet 20*.

▶ <u>Exercise:</u> Have clients read the description of one client's DWI pattern. Then, have them identify the *specific AOD use pattern* that led to their DWI. Are they defensive about this? How serious did clients take this exercise? Was it accurately presented by clients?

▶ Work on helping clients see how their thought habits, attitudes and beliefs are part of their AOD use and how they led to their DWI. <u>Exercise:</u> Complete *Work Sheet 21*, how thoughts, attitudes and beliefs are part of AOD use.

LESSON CLOSURE

Have clients share their perceptions of their own AOD use pattern in group. How do these patterns increase risk of future DWI behavior?

▶ **Exercise:** Have clients share what they got out of this lesson. Review their *AOD Thinking and Action Patterns Charts (Work Sheet 16)* from *Lesson 5*. Remind them to do this for homework for the coming week (*Work Sheet 22*).

▶ *Interpersonal interaction homework:* Have each client do a validity check on how they see their AOD use pattern (*QFP, social style, benefits*) by asking another person how that person sees the client's AOD use pattern.

LESSON 7: PROBLEM OUTCOMES OF ALCOHOL AND OTHER DRUG USE: PATTERNS OF MISUSE AND ABUSE - HOW DO THEY FIT YOU?

RATIONALE AND OVERVIEW OF LESSON

Two assumptions underlie this lesson: 1) There is considerable variability of AOD problem outcome patterns among DWC Level II clients (Wanberg & Timken, 2005a); and 2) All DWI clients will have had some problem due to AOD use, albeit the DWI arrest and conviction. *Lessons 5 and 6* provide a sound foundation for looking at AOD negative consequences and problem outcomes.

Even though many DWI clients have moderate AOD problems, and some even severe problems, we are assuming, that on the average, these clients will be *resistive and defensive* around seeing themselves as fitting the more traditional addiction or disease model. Thus, we are presenting a number of problem outcome patterns, based on social learning theory and cognitive-behavioral approaches to self-control and change. This provides clients with considerable flexibility in identifying their own problem outcome patterns.

In DWC, we use two models to describe the pathways to AOD problems: the mental-behavioral impaired control cycle (ICC) and the mental-physical impaired control cycle. In this lesson, we present the mental-behavioral ICC to describe different levels and patterns of problem outcomes. Most DWIO clients will identify with some aspects of this cycle, and some will identify with the full addiction and impaired control cycle. The premise of the ICC model is that if a person has had even one problem from AOD use, then that person fits the AOD problem category. To this extent, all DWIOs fit this category.

The ICC model is also used as a basis for presenting and describing AOD abuse and dependence a la the *DSM IV* (American Psychiatric Association, 1994) model. The mental-physical impaired control cycle is presented in depth in the *DWC Therapy* curriculum.

Defensive thinking and denial are addressed in this lesson. The position in this *Provider's Guide* is that if we use the concept of denial in a positive light, then it represents a step towards change rather than a resistance to change.

Defensiveness (denial) is a way of saying "I don't want to be that way." What we are being defensive (or denying) about gives a clue of how we "don't want to be" and what we might need to change if we "don't want to be that way." When we "deny" we are a certain way, it sets up **contrasting self-perceptions** as to how we see ourselves. "I do not have a drinking problem. I do not see myself in that way." This must mean the client also has the opposite perception of "having a drinking problem." The powerful need to defend the self results in "But, I see myself the opposite way," or "opposite" from having a drinking problem. "I don't have one." This sets the stage for change. The view of "not having a drinking problem" *is a perception that we want to actualize* - of not having a drinking problem.

Thus, the client's "denial" is in the exact direction that we want the client to move or exactly what we want the client to be. That is, not have a drinking problem. In this sense, "denial" is the first step to change. The goal is to get clients to see the contrasting view of the self, or the view **"I do have a drinking problem,"** or what it means to have a drinking problem. Once the client can "tolerate" that view, "maybe I do have a drinking problem, and here are some reasons why," the defensiveness is lowered, and the client moves in the direction of changing thoughts and actions so that they can be what they were initially defensive about - not have a drinking problem.

However, many clients are forthcoming with their view "I have a problem." They have worked through the defensiveness. The door is open to make the kind of changes to achieve, now in a realistic way, the initial defensive perception of the self "I do not have a drinking problem. I'm doing something about it."

The main purpose of this lesson is help clients see how their past AOD use fits the *Impaired Control Cycles* and how they classify their own problem outcomes with respect to the four AOD problem outcome categories described in this lesson.

SUMMARY OF LESSON CONTENT, PRESENTATION SEQUENCE AND GUIDELINES

As a foundation for understanding AOD problem outcomes, *Table 7* in the *Participant's Workbook* is presented and discussed. This provides problem outcomes for seven drug groups. Clients are asked to see if any of those problem outcomes or symptoms fit them. This discussion, along with a review of the three learning rules presented in *Lesson 3* sets the stage for presenting and understanding the **Mental-Behavioral Impaired Control Cycle** (ICC), *Figure 5 below* (*Figure 7* in the *Participant's Workbook*).

Use an interactive-teaching format when presenting the Mental-Behavioral (MB) ICC model. The assumption is that all clients will have at least gone as far as block D of this cycle. Through group discussion, have clients identify how far they have gone in this cycle.

Using the MB ICC model, different problem outcome patterns are defined. These outcomes include four categories: **the drinking problem; the problem user without abuse or dependence; the problem user with AOD abuse; and the problem user with AOD dependence.** *Work Sheet 23* provides the client with an opportunity to determine to what extent does the client fit the *AOD Disruption* or *AOD Problems* scale. *Profile 2* then helps clients get a more complete picture of their AOD use patterns. Together, they can see their *social style pattern* (gregarious or solo or both), their *use benefits pattern* and their *AOD disruption* or *problems pattern.*

The DSM IV (American Psychiatric Association, 1994) criteria are introduced and clients evaluate themselves across those criteria using *Work Sheets 24 and 25.* *Work Sheet 26* helps clients look at their risk for engaging in a criminal conduct pattern.

FIGURE 5

Mental-behavioral impaired control cycle (MB - ICC).

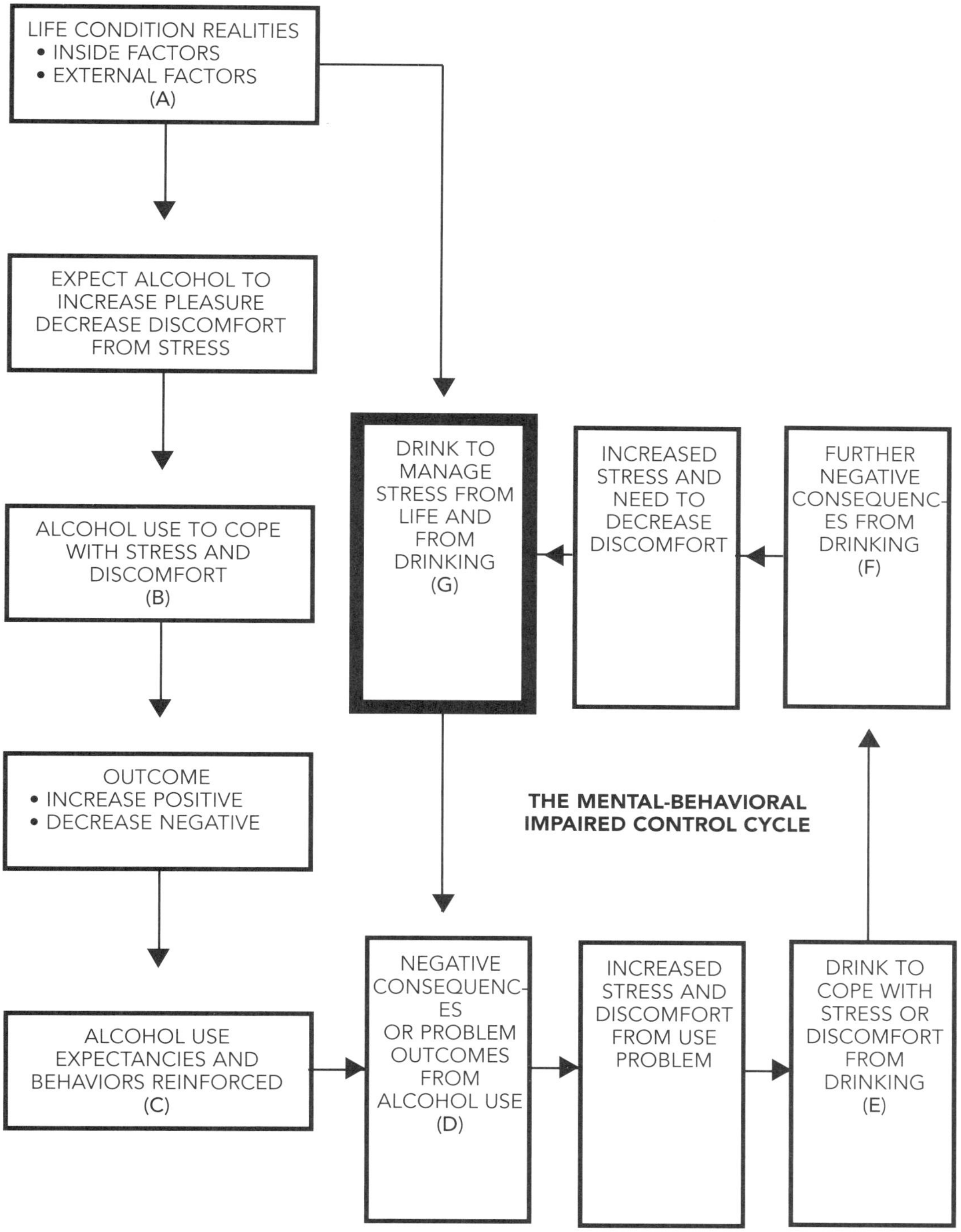

LIFE CONDITION REALITIES
- INSIDE FACTORS
- EXTERNAL FACTORS
(A)

EXPECT ALCOHOL TO INCREASE PLEASURE DECREASE DISCOMFORT FROM STRESS

ALCOHOL USE TO COPE WITH STRESS AND DISCOMFORT
(B)

OUTCOME
- INCREASE POSITIVE
- DECREASE NEGATIVE

ALCOHOL USE EXPECTANCIES AND BEHAVIORS REINFORCED
(C)

DRINK TO MANAGE STRESS FROM LIFE AND FROM DRINKING
(G)

INCREASED STRESS AND NEED TO DECREASE DISCOMFORT

FURTHER NEGATIVE CONSEQUENCES FROM DRINKING
(F)

THE MENTAL-BEHAVIORAL IMPAIRED CONTROL CYCLE

NEGATIVE CONSEQUENCES OR PROBLEM OUTCOMES FROM ALCOHOL USE
(D)

INCREASED STRESS AND DISCOMFORT FROM USE PROBLEM

DRINK TO COPE WITH STRESS OR DISCOMFORT FROM DRINKING
(E)

(Adapted from Wanberg, 1971, 1990)

FIGURE 6

Mental-behavioral impaired control cycle (ICC): Client work sheet.

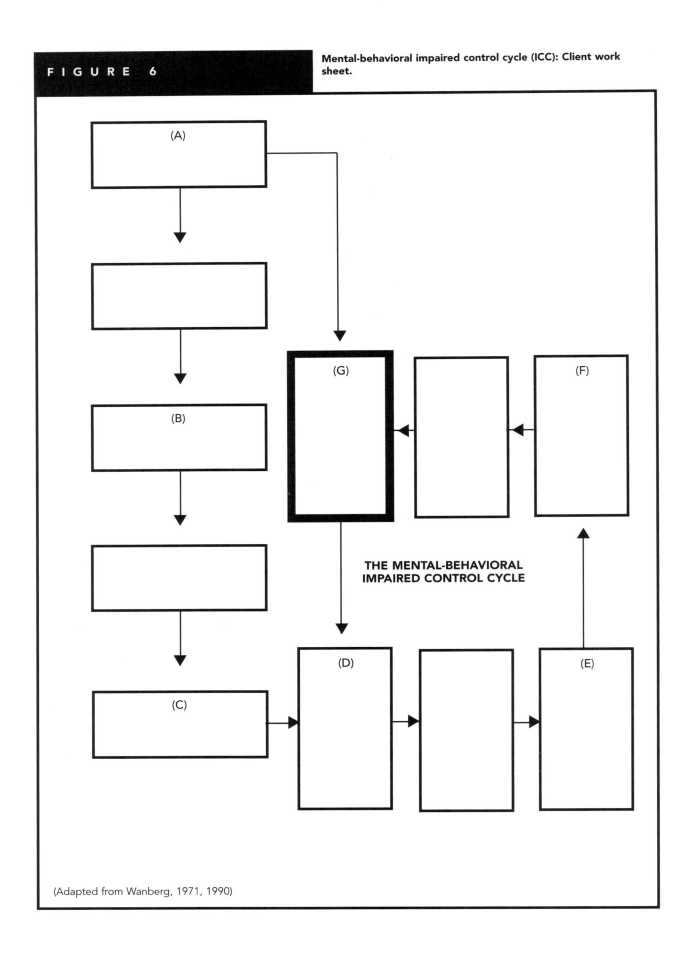

THE MENTAL-BEHAVIORAL
IMPAIRED CONTROL CYCLE

(Adapted from Wanberg, 1971, 1990)

Much of this lesson will be devoted to presenting the MB-ICC and then doing the work sheets around identifying how clients fit a particular AOD problem outcome pattern. The following presentation sequence is suggested.

▶ Present and discuss *Table 7*, problem outcomes of drugs.

▶ Review the three rules of learning in *Lesson 4*.

▶ Present the problem outcomes of AOD and the MB-ICC.

▶ **Exercise:** Complete *Work Sheet 23* and put the score on *Profile 2*. Then have clients put their scores on the Gregarious solo and Benefits scales from Profile 1, page 99 on Profile 2, page 118 of the Workbook. Have them discuss their profile on AOD use patterns and their AOD problem as compared with their peers.

▶ **Exercises:** Have clients complete *Work Sheets 24 and 25* to determine if they fit the DSM IV *Abuse or Dependence* diagnosis.

▶ Present the alcohol and other drug use and criminal conduct material. **Exercise:** Have clients complete *Work Sheet 26* on the risks of involvement in criminal conduct. Discuss their results in class.

▶ Discuss defensive thinking and denial.

Two assumptions underlie this lesson: 1) There is considerable variability of AOD problem outcome patterns among DWC Level II clients and 2) All DWI clients have had some problem due to AOD use, albeit the DWI arrest and conviction.

▶ **Exercise:** *Work Sheet 27* challenges clients' defensiveness and has them do more work on identifying who has been hurt by the problem outcomes of their AOD use.

▶ **Exercise:** Once again, have clients look at *Profile 2*. How does their profile relate to DWI behavior? Do *Work Sheet 28*. These two exercises help clients to "put it together" and gives them a good perspective of their AOD use and misuse patterns.

▶ Get clients to review their AOD personal commitment goals. For those clients who choose the goal to live an AOD **problem free life** but not stop drinking, go over the guidelines for CAREFUL and responsible drinking. Again, this is a good point to reiterate that clients who do fit the Dependence or *Abuse or Problem Drinker* pattern will want to choose abstinence as their personal commitment goal.

LESSON CLOSURE

Review *Work Sheet 22*, the *TAP Charting* that clients did this past week. If time permits, have clients share with the group how they now see their AOD patterns. Remind them to do their **TAP Charting**, *Work Sheet 29,* in the coming week.

LESSON 8: PATHWAYS TO RELAPSE AND RECIDIVISM

RATIONALE AND OVERVIEW OF LESSON

This is the first of two lessons that focus specifically on relapse and recidivism. Lesson 8 focuses on the pathways to relapse and recidivism (R&R), and Lesson 9 the Pathways to preventing R&R.

Clients have been challenged to look at their own AOD use and misuse patterns and relate them to their DWI behavior, to assess their risk for recidivism and relapse and to come to the point of making a commitment to goals and actions that will prevent recidivism. They have been challenged to become aware of and to confront directly the bad outcomes of their thinking and behaviors and the burden that their DWI has placed on them, their families and their community. The rationale of this Lesson is that self-confrontation and awareness are powerful influences in preventing recidivism - most likely more powerful than sanctions imposed on them by the courts and the Motor Vehicle Division.

Clients are informed that the goal of preventing legal recidivism is not only their goal and choice, but the goal and choice of society and the community - to never operate a motor vehicle while exceeding the legal BAC limits or when under the influence of any mind-behavior altering drug. Yet, they have the option to make the personal choice of a "zero tolerance-zero risk" recidivism prevention goal. The DWC program challenges clients to choose this as their goal. The rationale for this choice is clearly spelled out in Lesson 1. Review those with the group.

Even though returning to problem drinking and drug use increases the risk of DWI behavior, these two behavior patterns are independent to the extent that the choice of a relapse prevention goal is personal and not society determined. As well, they are independent to the extent that relapse does not necessarily mean recidivism. We have spelled out the goal options for AOD use, one of which is to continue their past pattern of use irrespective of whether that pattern leads to AOD problems. Yet, we have challenged clients to chose one of two more realistic goals: to prevent relapse into a pattern of use that leads to AOD problems and misuse; or to prevent relapse by maintaining abstinence from mind-behavior altering drugs.

We are asking clients to make choices as to what their goal of recidivism and relapse prevention will be. We have helped them see that recidivism and relapse are gradual erosion processes and that thoughts, beliefs and attitudes always underlie this process. We have challenged clients to commit themselves to a recidivism and relapse prevention choice. Whatever the commitment choice, we want clients to clearly understand that high exposures (e.g., high risk thinking and high risk situations) increase the risk of relapse (as defined by the client) and legal recidivism as defined by the community. We also want clients to know that their choices are strongly influenced by their thought habits and the underlying attitudes and beliefs. These are powerful influences in determining the behavior choices that lead to either good or bad outcomes.

The specific objectives of this lesson are in the *Participant's Workbook*. The main purpose of this lesson is for clients to have a clear understanding of the pathways to recidivism and relapse (R&R). The next lesson will cover the pathways to and skills necessary for preventing R&R.

SUMMARY OF LESSON CONTENT, PRESENTATION SEQUENCE AND GUIDELINES

This lesson begins with a review of the two main purposes of DWC: preventing recidivism and preventing relapse. Clients are given opportunity to ask questions and share concerns. It is recommended that the presentation follow the following sequence.

- Presentation of the impact of DWI conduct on the community, facts about the community as victim and the prevalence of DWI behavior in the community, e.g., one of the most frequently committed violent crimes.

- Present information around the relationship of BAC to risk of accidents/death. Have clients complete the exercises on determining what their risk was of having an accident or being involved in a single-car fatal accident based on their arrest BAC.

- Present the section on understanding and defining relapse. Have clients define what relapse means to them and go over the process of relapse. Go over the relapse example and see if clients identify with the client in the example. Then, define the high risk (HR) exposures that lead to AOD relapse. These exposures are HR situations, thoughts, feelings, attitudes and beliefs. Have clients identify their own HR exposures, completing the exercises within this section.

- Present the section on DWI recidivism. This follows the same format as the section on relapse. It defines recidivism, has clients define what recidivism means to them, and then defines the HRs for recidivism. Have clients do the exercises within this section that define their own HR episodes.

- Present the section on the risk for relapse into problem drinking, focusing on the common triggers for relapse. **Exercise:** Do Work Sheet 30, triggers for problem drinking and relapse.

- Present the section on the risk for recidivism. Have clients check how many of the specific features in the DWI profile they fit. Review the risk factors for recidivism. **Exercise:** Clients are asked to calculate their risk for recidivism by doing Work Sheet 31.

- The pathways to R&R are outlined in Figure 7 below (Figure 8 in the *Participant's Workbook*). **Exercise:** After reviewing the R&R pathways, have clients complete Work Sheet 32, which maps their high risk exposures and potential pathways to R&R.

LESSON CLOSURE

Have each client share the most important idea they have learned from the program. Have clients share their findings in *Work Sheet 32*. Remind them to complete their TAP charting for the coming week, *Work Sheet 33*.

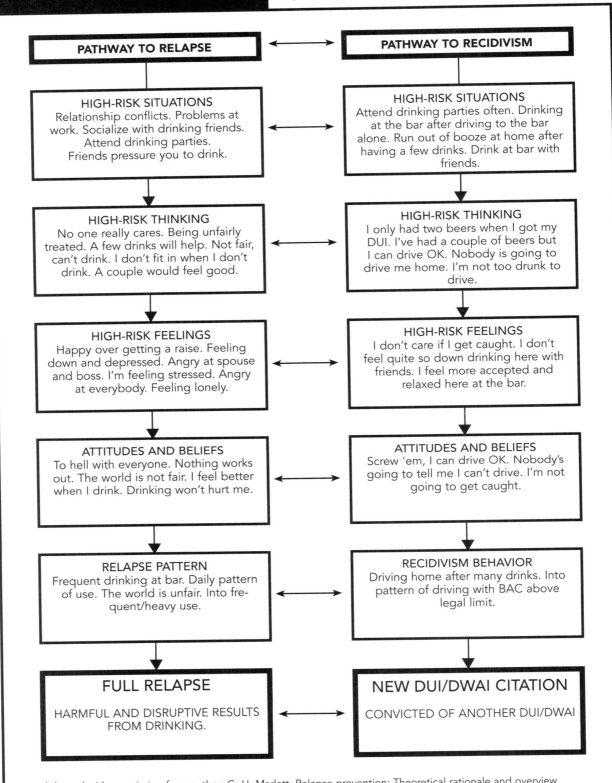

FIGURE 7

Cognitive-behavioral map for relapse and recidivism.

PATHWAY TO RELAPSE ↔ **PATHWAY TO RECIDIVISM**

HIGH-RISK SITUATIONS
Relationship conflicts. Problems at work. Socialize with drinking friends. Attend drinking parties. Friends pressure you to drink.
↔
HIGH-RISK SITUATIONS
Attend drinking parties often. Drinking at the bar after driving to the bar alone. Run out of booze at home after having a few drinks. Drink at bar with friends.

HIGH-RISK THINKING
No one really cares. Being unfairly treated. A few drinks will help. Not fair, can't drink. I don't fit in when I don't drink. A couple would feel good.
↔
HIGH-RISK THINKING
I only had two beers when I got my DUI. I've had a couple of beers but I can drive OK. Nobody is going to drive me home. I'm not too drunk to drive.

HIGH-RISK FEELINGS
Happy over getting a raise. Feeling down and depressed. Angry at spouse and boss. I'm feeling stressed. Angry at everybody. Feeling lonely.
↔
HIGH-RISK FEELINGS
I don't care if I get caught. I don't feel quite so down drinking here with friends. I feel more accepted and relaxed here at the bar.

ATTITUDES AND BELIEFS
To hell with everyone. Nothing works out. The world is not fair. I feel better when I drink. Drinking won't hurt me.
↔
ATTITUDES AND BELIEFS
Screw 'em, I can drive OK. Nobody's going to tell me I can't drive. I'm not going to get caught.

RELAPSE PATTERN
Frequent drinking at bar. Daily pattern of use. The world is unfair. Into frequent/heavy use.
↔
RECIDIVISM BEHAVIOR
Driving home after many drinks. Into pattern of driving with BAC above legal limit.

FULL RELAPSE
HARMFUL AND DISRUPTIVE RESULTS FROM DRINKING.
↔
NEW DUI/DWAI CITATION
CONVICTED OF ANOTHER DUI/DWAI

Adapted with permission from author, G. H. Marlatt, Relapse prevention: Theoretical rationale and overview. in G.A. Marlatt, & J.R. Gordon (Eds.), *Relapse prevention: Maintenance strategies in the treatment of addictive behaviors* (p. 38), Guilford Press.

LESSON 9: PROCESS AND STEPS TO PREVENTING RELAPSE AND RECIDIVISM

RATIONALE AND OVERVIEW

It is important that the provider reiterate that: the pathways to recidivism and relapse are gradual processes of erosion, and unless checked, will lead to relapse into AOD use problems, DWI conduct, and eventually, another DWI arrest. Clients should know that around 35 percent of first offenders get rearrested if they do not have a R&R prevention plan; the percent is greatly reduced if they follow the plans they develop in DWC.

> An important deterrent to recidivism is an awareness of the cost of a DWI arrest and conviction. This awareness is most apt to occur through self-disclosure in a caring, non-threatening, and trusting environment. For many clients, this awareness is very awakening. This process is part of a key mantra of this program: **Self-disclosure leads to self-awareness, and self-awareness leads to change.**

SUMMARY OF LESSON CONTENT, PRESENTATION SEQUENCE AND GUIDELINES

An important part of preventing R&R is understanding the stages that people go through when making change. This lesson introduces the client to the three stages of change: **Challenge, commitment and ownership.** After this material is presented, they are asked to rate themselves on what stage they might be in relative to changing their AOD use and impaired driving patterns.

> When making changes, clients need to be challenged. Exercises in this lesson on the burden and cost of clients' DWI arrest and conviction is an important part of this **challenge.** For many clients, it sets the stage for a **commitment** to change. The initial stages of commitment are enhanced when clients set their own goals for change. This session again has them restate their relapse and recidivism goals.
>
> The rest of the lesson is devoted to understanding how relapse and recidivism are related and learning R&R prevention skills. The pathways to R&R are reintroduced, but are coordinated with the steps and skills for R&R prevention. The most important component of this Lesson is introducing and practicing the skills of R&R prevention and understanding what skills are used for various HR exposures. Considerable time is devoted to refusal skills training. The lesson ends with clients developing their own R&R prevention plan.
>
> Clients are introduced to the modification of the Marlatt Relapse model, *Figure 11.6* in *Chapter 11* of this work. They are then presented with the map that describes both the pathways to R&R and the pathways to prevention, *Figure 11.7* in *Chapter 11*. These are Figures 9 and 10 in Lesson 9 in the *Participant's Workbook.* The provider will want to review the R&R concepts presented in *Chapter 11* and in Lesson 9 of the *Participant's Workbook.*

It is recommended the following sequence is used when presenting this lesson.

- ▶ Present the stages of change model used in DWC and have clients rate themselves as to what stage they are in relative to changing AOD use and DWI patterns.

- ▶ Have clients determine what their DWI arrest and conviction cost them. This represents a challenge to change. **Exercises:** Work Sheets 34 through 37.

- ▶ Have clients redefine their R&R prevention goals, which strengthen their **commitment** to change. Clients are asked to commit to the personal goal of **zero tolerance-zero risk** recidivism which goes beyond society's expectation of preventing legal recidivism. Have clients understand that legal recidivism is the expectation of the community and society. Encourage clients to commit to the personal goal of **zero-tolerance zero-risk** recidivism prevention.

- ▶ Present the section on preventing R&R which discusses how relapse and recidivism are related, similar and different.

- ▶ The Marlatt model is presented in some detail, Figure 9 in the Workbook.

- ▶ Then present the specific prevention skills that can be used to manage specific HR exposures, using Figure 10 as a guide. Refusal skills training is given a special focus.

- ▶ **Exercise:** Work Sheet 38 presents some problem solving situations where clients can apply various prevention skills.

- ▶ Explain the personal change plan for R&R and have clients use Work Sheets 39 and 40 to develop their own plan. This exercise and focus will help increase the commitment to change and preventing R&R. Clients are encouraged to use this as their maps for prevention, and to add to it from time to time as their knowledge and skills increase.

LESSON CLOSURE

Have each client share some aspect of their R&R prevention plan. Remind them to do their TAP charting, *Work Sheet 41.*

LESSON 10: PREVENTING RELAPSE AND RECIDIVISM: BUILDING PERSONAL VALUES AND PROSOCIAL ATTITUDES AND BEHAVIORS AND DRIVING WITH CARE

RATIONALE AND OVERVIEW

This lesson focuses on the third cognitive-behavior task of learning self-control - learning skills to enhance responsible attitudes and behaviors towards and within the community. This is the sociocentric emphasis of CB therapy and the DWC protocols. One underlying assumption of this program is that DWI conduct is not only irresponsible behavior in the community, it represents one dimension of antisocial behavior. Too often we have "walked softly" in being straightforward with our clients around our assessment of their psychological and behavior problems. Just as we want our physicians who care for our physical health to be open and direct about our medical condition, we should expect that our clients also want to know what we assess as being "wrong with them" from a psychological and behavioral standpoint. Certainly, discretion is needed with respect to how we share our assessment of clients. We need to do so within a therapeutic and supportive framework. Yet, clients need to know what they need to change - from a correctional as well as a therapeutic perspective.

Antisocial attitudes and behavior involve a pattern of disregarding and violating the rights of others, doing harm to others and going against the standards, morals, rules and laws of society. We are making the distinction between antisocial behaviors and attitudes and the Antisocial Personality Disorder as defined by the DSM IV (American Psychiatric Association, 1994, 2000) which is defined by a "pervasive pattern of disregard for, and violation of, the rights of others" (p. 645). To meet this diagnosis, one has to fit three or more of the following criteria:

> failure to conform to social norms by repeatedly performing acts that are grounds for arrest;

> repeated deceitfulness;

> impulsivity or failure to plan ahead;

> repeated irritability and aggressiveness;

> reckless disregard for safety of self or others;

> consistent irresponsibility;

> lack of remorse or being indifferent to or rationalizing having hurt, mistreated, or stolen from another.

Many of our clients do not fit this diagnosis. Yet, one can engage in antisocial behavior and attitudes and not fit the Antisocial Personality Disorder as identified by these criteria. The fact is that DWI behavior is antisocial. Individuals who frequently engage in impaired driving behavior fit two of the above DSM IV criteria: failure to conform to social norms by repeatedly performing acts that are grounds for arrest; and consistent irresponsibility. Certainly, some DWI clients have not repeatedly driven while impaired. However, many if not most of our clients have done just that, when we consider the statistics that the average DWI client has driven from 800 to 1,000 times or more before being arrested the first time for impaired driving. Thus, as we define antisocial behavior, impaired driving is antisocial conduct.

Our intent in this lesson is to help clients look at their behaviors and attitudes that go against the norms, laws and expectations of society and the rights of others **and** to see how these behaviors and attitudes play into DWI behavior. In essence, this lesson focuses on what we call moral responsibility and prosocial values - values that emphasize positive relationships with others, with our community and with society. We have defined moral values and responsibility as a set of ethical and principled thoughts, attitudes and behaviors directed at:

▶ respecting the rights of others;

▶ being accountable to the laws and rules of our community and society;

▶ having positive regard for and caring about the welfare and safety of others; and

▶ contributing to the ongoing good of the community.

In essence, it means engaging in responsible thinking and actions towards others and society.

Driving a motor vehicle is our most obvious metaphor for community responsibility. It is our most obvious interface with the community. Driving with CARE is responsible living. Yet we take driving too casually, as if it is a right and not a privilege. We seldom reflect on the dangers and risks of driving -even when driving. Various disasters such as tornados, floods, earthquakes, flying, lightning, and food poisoning account for less than 700 deaths in the United States each year. Yet, over 42,000 die on the highways each year. Driving is the cultural norm. It is like "second nature" to us. We just simply take for granted the skills and positive attitudes that are required to practice CAREFUL and SAFE driving.

> DWI behavior is antisocial. It goes against the norms, laws and expectations of society and the rights of others. Driving a motor vehicle is our most obvious metaphor for community responsibility. Driving with CARE demonstrates responsible living.

This lesson, then, looks at the skills and attitudes that underlie CAREFUL and responsible driving, the impact of AOD use on these skills, and helps clients assess their driving skills and habits so as to find areas in which these can be improved. The literature indicates that DWIOs tend to have a history of poor and unsafe driving habits. Thus, in an effort to enhance prosocial behaviors in DWIOs, it is appropriate for this lesson to also focus on driving skills and safety.

This lesson is only an introduction to the area of antisocial and characterological patterns that contribute to DWI conduct. In *DWC Therapy* we will look further at strengthening moral development and prosocial attitudes and behaviors.

The most difficult part of this lesson will be to get clients to reflect on the meaning of antisocial and prosocial behavior, to have them explore which of their behaviors and attitudes are antisocial, and to see how these behaviors and attitudes led to DWI conduct. The following presentation sequence is recommended.

▶ Since the purpose of this lesson is to help clients gain a better perspective of personal and prosocial values, **start the Lesson by clarifying the values upon which DWC Education is based:** self-control over thoughts, emotions and behavior; responsible living; and a positive relationship with others and the community.

▶ **Exercise:** Have an open discussion on the values of this program and then have clients identify some of their own personal values.

▶ Spend time defining prosocial and antisocial behavior. **Exercise:** Have clients identify at least one of their behaviors that is prosocial and one that is antisocial.

▶ **Exercise:** Complete *Work Sheet 42, Prosocial Questionnaire,* which is the Social Scale from the Adult Substance Use Survey (ASUS; Wanberg, 1991, 1997). This scale, however, is now scored in the direction of prosocial behavior. We are reverse scoring the items so that a high score now reflects prosocial attitudes and behaviors. A low score on this scale now reflects antisocial behaviors and attitudes. Carefully read the directions at the top of the scale and help the client score this test. Have clients put their raw score on Profile 3 and then facilitate some discussion around the meaning of their score and how they compare with other DWIOs. Scores in the low and low-medium range indicate the client may fit an antisocial pattern. A high-medium to high score would indicate fairly strong prosocial attitudes and behaviors. A very high score (maximum of 30) would indicate defensiveness, since one question measures "being charged with driving under the influence of drugs or alcohol" and all of our clients have had this happen to them. Thus, no client should have a raw score of 30.

▶ Present the topics of personal values and complete *Work Sheet 43* which has clients list their five most important personal **values.** Do *Work Sheet 44* which has clients list their five most important personal **morals.**

▶ Present the topics of community norms or standards and prosocial thoughts and behaviors. Have clients list five important norms or standards of conduct held by their community, using *Work Sheet 45.* Using *Work Sheet 46,* have clients list five important prosocial values that they think people should hold.

▶ Present and discuss the skills that lead to prosocial behaviors. Once again, study the list of thinking errors presented in Lesson 3, *Work Sheet 5* in the *Participant's Workbook.* **Exercise:** Do *Work Sheet 47* which focuses on thinking errors and social relationships that can lead to antisocial behaviors and outcomes and then replacing them with prosocial thoughts or prosocial relationships that lead to prosocial behavior.

▶ Present the section on community responsibility through driving with care. Introduce the lesson with the idea that driving a motor vehicle is the most dangerous activity we take part in and it provides us with the greatest opportunity to demonstrate moral responsibility towards our community. Discuss the factors that go into CAREFUL and safe driving: judgment; sensory-motor skills; decision making; and behavioral skills. Proper and healthy attitudes are major factors in SAFE and CAREFUL driving. Discuss what contributes to being a risk and road hazard.

Exercise: Have clients take the Driving Assessment Survey (Wanberg & Timken, 1991, 1997, 2005b) and put their scores on the DAS profile, Work Sheet 48. Discuss their findings in class and look at five driving risk factors: Power, Hazard, Impulse, Stress, and Relax. There are two non-driving factors that also increase driving risk: Rebelliousness and Convivial Drinking. Persons scoring high across all of these factors clearly increase their risk of injuring themselves or others and the risk of engaging in DWI behavior.

Exercise: Complete Work Sheet 49, Changing driving skills, attitudes and patterns.

▶ Review last week's AOD Use Thinking and Action Patterns Chart (Work Sheet 43).

LESSON CLOSURE

Have clients discuss their antisocial and prosocial patterns. Give opportunity for them to share the results on their *Prosocial Questionnaire*. Have clients share how they see their driving patterns and how they can change these to increase CAREFUL and safe driving and responsibility towards the community. If time permits, have clients again reflect on how personal morals and values relate to DWI behavior. Remind them to do their TAP charting for the week, *Work Sheet 50.*

LESSON 11: PREVENTING RELAPSE AND RECIDIVISM: MANAGING STRESS AND EMOTIONS

RATIONALE AND OVERVIEW OF LESSON

This session represents an introduction to the understanding and management of emotions and stress. More concentrated work will be done in the area of stress and emotions in *DWC Therapy.*

> The important cognitive-behavioral components of stress is that the perceived demand is the *appraisal* of the situation and the perceived ability to handle the demand is the *coping ability* of the person.

Emotional or psychological disturbances found among DWI offenders can be viewed as either primary or secondary (Wanberg & Milkman, 1998). A primary psychological disturbance or disorder exists relatively independent from, yet interacts with, substance abuse. Depression, anxiety or psychotic symptoms are underlying and primary. Although reports vary as to prevalence of primary mental disturbances among DWI offenders, a study by Wanberg and Timken (2005a) indicates that about 15 to 20 percent of DWIOs would indicate primary significant mood adjustment problems on self-report and that about five to ten percent would warrant referral for a mental health evaluation. With respect to all adult criminal justice offenders, including DWIOs, most studies (e.g., Guy et al., 1985; Hodgins & Cote, 1990; Teplin & Swartz, 1989; Daniel et al., 1988; Cloninger, 1970) indicate that the prevalence of severe mental disorders, such as schizophrenia or other psychotic expressions, ranges from one to ten percent. These same studies indicate that the prevalence rates of primary depression or other affective disorders range from one to 17 percent. The upshot of these findings suggests that primary emotional and psychological problems probably are found in less than five percent of the DWIO population.

Secondary emotional or psychological problems are probably more prevalent among DWIOs. These are problems that are interactive with or are consequences of involvement in DWI legal problems and other AOD problem outcomes. Guilt, self-blame, anger, depressive and anxious moods are common with persons recovering from a pattern of substance abuse and misuse. These psychological and mood disruptions are also found among many DWIOs. Often, they are contributing factors in DWI conduct.

The literature indicates that *emotional distress and anxiety are important factors* that lead to AOD use and abuse. The stress and emotional discomfort that people experience on a daily basis are often handled by AOD use. There are three major events that produce stress (e.g., Bloom 1985; D'Zurilla and Nezu, 2001).

▶ Major negative life events such as death of loved one, divorce, loss of job, major illness.

▶ Daily negative life events such as not getting work done, daily demands of family life and marriage.

- Major and minor positive events such as getting married, a new job, salary raise, having a baby.

One of the major triggers of AOD relapse identified in the literature is unpleasant emotions such as sadness, depression or anger (Wanberg & Milkman, 1998). Anger, guilt and depression should be considered high-risk feelings, for they may lead to relapse and a vicious cycle of repeated failures. These automatic thoughts related to these feelings need to be challenged since they are often part of recidivism and relapse.

Selye (1956, 1974, 1976), the famous stress researcher, defines stress as "the non-specific response of the body to any demand made upon it" (1974, p. 27). He states that it is more than merely nervous tension. He categorizes over 1,000 physiological responses that happen in stress and adaptation (Selye, 1974).

Fried (1993) sees it as an orienting response in which activity, especially breathing, is inhibited. This is followed by an excitatory increased metabolic demand for oxygen. Fried states that the body cannot sustain this intermittent orientation and sympathetic arousal for very long without relief. He uses the example that we are like quarter horses. We can run fast, but not for long. Thus, he concludes that the so called nonspecific response identified by Selye is "not so nonspecific after all; it is increased tissue air hunger, and all that this entails" (p. 302).

Bloom's (1985) definition is generally accepted by most clinicians: *that stress occurs when the coping responses fail to deal with stressful life events that present a person with strong demands for personal, social or biological readjustment.*

Most authorities in the field define stress from a transactional view (Meichenbaum, 1993a; Lazarus & Folkman, 1984). This model proposes that stress occurs when the perceived demands of a situation or event go beyond the perceived ability or resources of the system to meet those demands, especially when the security or well-being of the individual is threatened or challenged (Meichenbaum, 1993a, p. 382). The important cognitive-behavioral components of stress is that the perceived demand is the **appraisal** of the situation and the perceived ability to handle the demand is the **coping ability** of the person. The appraisal and coping abilities are both cognitive and behavioral. Thus, stress is characterized by the interaction or relationship between the environment and the person wherein the person perceives (appraisals) the adaptive demands as taxing or going beyond internal or external available coping resources (Miechenbaum, p. 382).

Where do depression, guilt and anger fit in with stress? Emotional stress refers to the immediate emotional response of a person to a stressful event, as modified or transformed by appraisals and coping processes (Lazarus, 1999, p. 220). Beck (1993) becomes more specific with respect to these emotions and identifies guilt, fear, anger and depression as stress syndromes (p. 348). He sees these as cognitive schemes with their own content and structure and which lead to behavioral outcomes.

It is also important to see stress as not only negative, e.g., depression or anger, but as also coming from and representing positive experiences such as hope, relief, exhilaration (D'Zurilla and Nezu, 2001, p. 220).

Stress, then, is the system's response to situations that exceed coping abilities and become manifested in specific syndromes of depression, anger and guilt. This understanding of stress fits in with the mental-behavioral ICC model described above where AOD use is one way of coping with stress and the emotional syndromes associated with stress. Since this coping works, AOD use is reinforced. There are a number of theories that have been used to explain the coping model including *Social Learning Theory* (Abrams & Niaura, 1987; Maisto, Carey & Bradizzo, 1999), *Expectancy Theory* (Goldman, Del Boca & Darkes, 1999; Goldman, Brown & Christiansen, 1987), *Opponent Process Theory* (Shipley, 1987), *Tension Reduction Theory* (Leonard & Blane, 1999; Cappell & Greeley, 1987), the *Self-awareness Model* (Hull, 1987; Sayette, 1999), and the *Stress Reduction Dampening* theory (Greeley & Oei, 1999; Sher, 1987).

Stress and its emotional syndromes, are powerful determinants of AOD use behavior and are related to negative outcomes such as DWI behavior. The rationale and purpose of this lesson are to help clients understand how stress and the emotions related to stress lead to AOD problems and to recidivism. Another purpose is to help clients learn skills to manage stress and emotions so as to prevent relapse and recidivism. The specific objectives of this lesson are enumerated in the *Participant's Workbook*.

SUMMARY OF LESSON CONTENT, PRESENTATION SEQUENCE AND GUIDELINES

Introduce this session with a review of the cognitive-behavioral approach to self-control and change and that stress and our emotions are triggers for relapse and recidivism. Clients will have a hard time identifying with this idea. Have a few clients share experiences where stress and emotions led to drinking and then to DWI behavior. Then present the lesson using the following sequence.

- Present the definition of stress, the idea of external and internal stressors and our mental responses - the automatic thoughts - to stress.

- Discuss the various responses we have to stress. They can be physical, mental, emotional or behavioral. Stressful events can occur inside of the person as well as outside the person, that stress is based on our response to those outside or inside events and that maladaptive responses to stressful events can lead to problem outcomes. These problem outcomes, or the stress syndromes can be depression, anxiety, guilt and anger.

- **Exercise:** Using *Figure 4*, page 244, above (*Figure 1* in the *Participant's Workbook*), discuss how stress relates to cognitive-behavioral self-control and change.

- **Exercise:** Using *Figure 5*, page 251, above (*Figure 7* in *Lesson 7*), have clients discuss how the ICC model fits into stress and stress management.

- **Exercise:** Do *Work Sheet 51*. Have clients list some negative stressful events that have happened in the past year and then have them identify their thoughts, emotions and behavioral responses to these events.

- Discuss the stress syndromes of anger, guilt and depression. Each of these syndromes are dealt with separately and their roles in leading to AOD use and DWI behavior are discussed. Spend some time dealing with aggression and violence. These topics will be further explored in *DWC Therapy.*

- Present the *guilt-anger cycle. (Figure 11 in Participant's Workbook.)* **Exercise:** Have some group members share how they fit the *guilt-anger cycle.*

- The last topic of this lesson is breaking the *guilt-anger cycle* and the steps and tools of handling stress. Complete *Work Sheet 52* by having participants list the skills they have learned to use to manage depression, guilt and anger. This work sheet is completed as each of these three stress syndromes are discussed. Completing this work sheet is a building process. The skills portion of this work sheet is completed at the end of the lesson after discussing the skills and methods to handle stress.

- **Exercise:** Have clients take the *Mood Assessment Survey* (MAS), *Work Sheet 53,* which is taken from the *ASUS* (Wanberg, 1997). The provider may want to spend some individual time with clients whose scores are 14, 15 or higher. The *MAS* may also spark concern in some clients as to their mood adjustment problems and they may want to talk with a counselor about this.

LESSON CLOSURE

Indicate to clients that more work will be done on handling stress and emotions in *DWC Therapy.* Spend a brief time reviewing the TAP Chart that clients did for this past week (*Work Sheet 50*). Remind them to complete this for the coming week (*Work Sheet 54*).

LESSON 12: PREVENTING RELAPSE AND RECIDIVISM: BUILDING HEALTHY FAMILY AND SOCIAL RELATIONSHIPS

RATIONALE AND OVERVIEW OF LESSON

Another major trigger for relapse and recidivism is conflict in our close relationships and with members of our family. DWI behavior often follows conflicts with parents, spouse, a significant other (SO) such as a girl/boyfriend or other family members. The bar can become a second (or even primary) home and drinking friends become family. A very common impaired driving offender pattern is that of drinking at bars and with friends away from home as a response to relationship conflicts. A basic human need is closeness, the need to belong and social support. When that need is lacking in our primary relationships, we seek to meet those needs in other places.

Another important trigger for relapse and recidivism is *loneliness.* A study of DWI clients (Wanberg & Timken, 2005a) indicated that about 75 percent were single, separated or divorced at the time of the arrest. Thus, a lack of close and intimate relationships or a sense of loneliness due to the absence of close relationships or relationship estrangement can also lead to DWI behavior. *The bar or pub can also become a second (or primary) home and drinking friends become family.* Individuals who mix driving with going to the bar to mitigate loneliness are high risks for DWI behavior.

As the material in this lesson is presented, the provider needs to keep in mind that many clients in the group will be unmarried or single. However, most of these clients are, have been or want to be in a close or intimate relationship, and the content and concepts of this lesson are just as applicable to them as to those in a marital or intimate partner relationship.

The role of social support in maintaining physical and mental health is well documented in psychological and behavioral literature. Following a DWI arrest, support from family may have lessened because of the disruptive nature of the event. Family members, intimate partners and girl/boyfriends are often angry. It often takes time for those relationships to be repaired. However, the support of family and significant others (SOs) is one of the most valuable resources the client may have (Kadden et al., 1992).

Just as the need for closeness and relationships is important, the need to be individual and separate, to be unique and different, to be ourselves is just as important. We seek activities to support our sense of self, our individuality and separateness. The very basis of many of our conflicts with people we are close to is the **need to be separate and individual** - to "do our own thing," to have freedom from the control of close relationships. AOD use is often the very way we cope with relationships that are controlling and dominating. It is one way of "breaking loose" this control.

These two needs, the *need for intimacy and closeness* and the *need for separateness and individuality* are often in conflict. Maslow (1954) identifies these conflicts in his hierarchy of needs. He sees self-esteem and self-actualization as higher levels of need than the need for relationships and closeness. Yet, the latter need is very powerful and can even lead us into problem behaviors. The need for friends, close associations, peer support and closeness will often override our sense of what is right or wrong, moral or immoral. For example, one of the most robust predictors of criminal conduct is criminal associates (Andrews & Bonta, 1994, 2003; Wanberg & Milkman, 1998).

The rationale for this lesson is based on the idea that AOD problems in general and DWI behavior in particular are often related to the conflicts we experience between the need for closeness and intimacy and the need for separateness. Often, individuals think that they are getting their separateness and individuality by "getting away" from the control of relationships with family or SOs by drinking with friends or at the bar. However, this often amounts to the proverbial "frying pan" dilemma.

The purpose of this lesson is to help clients address these relationship issues, see how they are related to DWI behavior, and to resolve these issues by learning skills to build and support healthy family, intimate partner and social relationships. It is recommended that clients bring family members, SOs or roommates to this lesson.

Although it is important to have SOs involved with the client, there is frequently a great deal of distrust and miscommunication in families where substance misuse and DWI behavior are involved. Thus, facilitation of interactions with family members and SOs and even skills training should initially be low-key, supportive, and avoid areas that are sensitive and conflictive (Cavaiola & Wuth, 2002; Monti, et al., 1989; Wanberg & Milkman, 1998). Working on basic communication skills is a good place to start with respect to structured activities. The goals, particularly in a single session, should be modest, hoping to encourage the beginning of honest and caring communication about concerns and problems that clients and their SOs are struggling with.

SUMMARY OF LESSON CONTENT, PRESENTATION SEQUENCE AND GUIDELINES

Some clients will not have significant others attend this lesson. When doing exercises, have those without a SO have in mind some significant relationship they have in their lives.

An important concept in presenting this lesson is Maslow's (1954) model of hierarchy of needs. The two that are pertinent to this lesson are: the *need for closeness;* and the *need for self-esteem and actualization - separateness.* Learning to balance these two needs in a healthy relationship is the major theme of this lesson. The *Relationship Balance Model* (Wanberg & Milkman, 1998) is the primary focus of this lesson.

There are many unhealthy ways that people try to resolve the conflict between these two needs. AOD use as one method is discussed. Communication skills are presented as one of the primary healthy methods in resolving the relationship-individuality need conflict and establishing a healthy balance in relationships. This lesson focuses on two kinds of communication skills:

▶ self-oriented communication which is achieved through

- self-disclosure, and

- receiving feedback;

▶ other-oriented communication which is achieved through

- inviting the other person to share, and

- giving feedback or reflective listening.

Developing good communication skills is an important component in this lesson. Some approaches in getting close to one's family or significant other are summarized. Evaluation questionnaires help clients to evaluate their family relations and relationship problems with others.

If family members and other significant others are invited to this lesson, some time should be devoted to introductions. The lesson agenda is very full and the provider will need to keep the pace moving. The following presentation sequence is recommended.

▶ Clearly describe the human dilemma of the conflict between the powerful need to be close and accepted and loved and the need to be separate and individual. Structure some discussion around this. Start out with asking the group which need is most stressed in our society.

▶ Present Maslow's five needs.

▶ Present the Balance Relationship Model (Figure 12, p. 209 in the *Participant's Workbook*). Describe the process of becoming enmeshed, establishing separateness and then integrating balance. Talk about how we seek support from other relationships, the bar and drinking friends when we experience relationship conflicts and try to establish separateness and individuality. **Exercise:** Do Work Sheet 55 and have clients and their significant others use the two overlapping circles to describe their relationship. This could be a relationship with spouse, parent, intimate partner, etc.

▶ One solution to developing a balance relationship with SOs or intimate partners is through the use of effective communication skills. Describe both kinds of communications that lead to healthy relationships. **Exercise:** Have clients and SOs practice using the "I" message and avoiding using the "you" message. For those without SOs in the group, have them pair with other clients and have one client role play of the other client's SO.

- Discuss how we can get closer to our family, and our significant other. **Exercise:** Do *Work Sheet 56* and have group members define their specific closeness and separateness needs.

- **Exercises:** Do *Work Sheets 57* and *58*, The Family Relationship Questionnaire and the Relationship Problems Questionnaire. Have group members share how these questionnaires describe their family relationships and their relationship problems.

LESSON CLOSURE

Have group members briefly share what they got out of the lesson. Briefly review the clients' TAP charting on their AOD use thinking and action patterns for the past week. Remind them to do this for the coming week (*Work Sheet 59*) unless this is their last Level II Education Lesson.

PROGRAM CLOSURE: CLOSING THE PROGRAM - REVIEW AND REFLECTION

PURPOSE OF CLOSING EXPERIENCE

This closure experience should provide clients with the opportunity to reflect on what was learned and review where they are at the time of closure. Keep the final focus on the strategies that the client learned for driving with CARE and responsible living and change. Give clients an opportunity to receive feedback from group members as to how others see their growth and change. Clients will be asked to complete the post-test. For those clients who are going into DWC Therapy, this will be an opportunity to complete the intake, evaluation and assessment process for that program.

HOW THE CLOSING EXPERIENCE IS STRUCTURED

▶ Closed groups can use the last part of Lesson 12 for closure.

▶ For open group structures, have clients do the following tasks.

- Clients will meet individually with the provider, complete the post-test, *Driving with Care Inventory - DWCI (Appendix B)*, and review what they learned and how they have changed.

- In the last group session they attend, ask clients to share with the group the following:

  1. Most important things learned.

  2. How have they changed?

  3. Share their goals of relapse and recidivism and how they see them-selves with respect to maintaining an AOD problem free life and a DWI free life.

▶ **Exercises: For those clients going into** *DWC Therapy,* after they complete the intake assessment and receive feedback from this assessment, have clients complete *Work Sheet 60,* their *Master Profile.* Then, have clients complete *Work Sheet 61,* their *Master Assessment Plan.* The provider also completes a *Master Profile* on each client and compares that profile to the offender's profile. It is recommended that this is done for each client who is not continuing into *DWC Therapy.* It is critical that the *Master Profile* and *Master Assessment Plan* be reviewed and discussed with clients regardless of whether or not they are continuing into *DWC Therapy.*

ALCOHOL, OTHER DRUGS AND IMPAIRED DRIVING OFFENDER TREATMENT

LEVEL II THERAPY

OVERVIEW AND INTRODUCTION TO LEVEL II THERAPY

DWC Therapy provides a core program of 21, two-hour, manual guided sessions, which is called Track A. Tracks B through D are designed for clients who are required to take additional therapy sessions. These tracks will be described below. *DWC Therapy* is designed for clients convicted of driving while their blood alcohol level went beyond legal limits or while they were under the influence of a drug other than alcohol. It is a sequel to the Driving With CARE: Alcohol, Other Drugs and Driving Safety Level II Education program. We will refer to this program in this Provider's Guide as *DWC Therapy*.

This treatment protocol is designed for individuals who, at minimum, show fairly clear pathognomonic signs of AOD misuse and problems and/or who had a high arrest BAC (e.g., .15 or higher). Referral is determined by the BAC level at arrest, prior DWI convictions, prior AOD education and treatment and other clinical indicators.

DWC Therapy is for clients with *higher levels of AOD disruption and psychosocial problems*. To prevent recidivism into DWI behavior and relapse into problematic patterns of AOD use, clients are in need of treatment interventions over longer periods of time that will produce change in thinking and action patterns. For such clients, a twelve week, twelve session program of AOD education and driving safety is not sufficient. Patterns of behaviors related to AOD use and psychosocial problems are more hardy with this category of clients.

The literature is clear that impaired driving and other criminal justice offenders who have significant levels of AOD use disruption need treatment programs that go beyond educational protocols. These programs address change in both AOD problems and psychosocial areas. Such programs are more protracted and therapeutically oriented with more intense change interventions in order to establish patterns of positive outcomes in the areas of self-control, interpersonal and social relationships and in responsibility to the community. A more in-depth focus on AOD misuse and problems, and on prevention of relapse and recidivism is needed.

DWC Education is a prerequisite to *DWC Therapy*. *It is an essential component for effective involvement in therapy and treatment.* *DWC Therapy* builds on the core concepts and ideas of *DWC Education*. These core concepts and ideas are reviewed and revisited throughout the *DWC Therapy* curriculum. The four categories of AOD misuse will be reviewed, and clients will again be asked to identify which of these patterns of misuse they now fit. For those who do fit the DSM diagnosis of *Abuse* or *Dependence*, there is a stronger challenge to consider abstinence as the path for recidivism and relapse prevention.

Even though *DWC Therapy* is more intensive and more therapeutically based, the sociocentric emphasis on community responsibility and the correctional approach is important. The treatment protocol intensifies the focus on the three areas of cognitive-behavioral learning and change.

> ▶ Developing strategies and skills to enhance cognitive self-control over feelings and emotions and behavior outcomes - the intrapersonal skill building focus.

> ▶ Developing strategies and skills to manage and improve family and interpersonal relationships - the social and interpersonal skills building focus.

> ▶ Developing strategies and skills to increase responsible behavior in the community.

Skill building in these three areas is a primary focus in *DWC Therapy*. In Orientation Session 2, clients are introduced to the *Master Skills List*, page 31 of the *Workbook*. This list helps clients monitor the skills they develop and their level of skill mastery.

GOALS AND OBJECTIVES OF THE LEVEL II TREATMENT PROTOCOL

DWC Therapy continues to focus on *Driving With CARE* and on the treatment and intervention of AOD problems and addiction. The primary objectives are preventing recidivism and relapse with the overarching goal of developing strategies for responsible living and change.

The following are specific objectives of *DWC Therapy*.

▶ **Prevent recidivism:** Explore in more depth the concept of *recidivism* - or returning to driving a motor vehicle while exceeding the legal BAC limits or while having ingested any other mind-altering drugs that impair driving behavior - and further challenge clients to accept the **zero tolerance-zero risk** goal as the basis of their *recidivism prevention plan*.

▶ **Prevent relapse:** Explore in more depth the concept of *relapse* -or returning to a pattern of thinking and to a pattern of alcohol and other drug use that is harmful and disruptive to normal living, including impaired driving, and do further work on the client's *recidivism prevention* plan.

▶ Do further work on the client's *recidivism* and *relapse prevention* plan using the lifestyle balance model.

▶ To skillfully apply the *cognitive-behavioral model* of changing thinking, beliefs and attitudes that control actions and behavior and which lead to more responsible living and change.

▶ Identify the patterns of and *pathways to AOD problems, addiction, abuse and dependence* and help clients understand how these pathways and patterns might fit them.

▶ Build and strengthen cognitive *self-control skills* to manage and change thoughts, emotions and beliefs in order to prevent negative outcomes including recidivism and relapse.

▶ Build and strengthen *interpersonal and social skills* to manage and change relationships in order to increase positive relationship outcomes and prevent negative relationship outcomes that lead to recidivism and relapse.

- Build and strengthen *community relationship* attitudes and skills in order to increase responsible social behavior and prevent negative relationships with the community such as DWI behavior and AOD abuse.

- Develop a *treatment plan* in partnership with the client that meets the client's individual and specific needs.

- Have clients develop a plan for *responsible living* and change that will lead to positive outcomes for themselves, for others and for the community.

INDIVIDUALIZED TREATMENT PLAN

All *DWC Therapy* clients should have an *individualized treatment plan* (ITP). This plan is developed during intake and orientation. As shown below, *Sessions 1 and 2* are structured to represent the orientation to *DWC Therapy*. *Session 2* is devoted primarily to helping clients develop their own treatment plan. The provider may also utilize this session to finalize the client's formal ITP.

The ITP will change over the course of treatment, depending on the emerging needs of clients. Initial ITPs should also project the needs of clients in *Tracks B* through D, since the sessions for these clients will exceed the *Track A* core curriculum of 21 sessions. Some adjustments may need to be made for some *Track A* clients who have individual treatment needs such as marital therapy, specialized anxiety-reduction treatment, etc. *Track A* clients are expected to complete all 21 core curriculum sessions. Thus, such clients may have to engage more than the required 42 hours of treatment in order to meet these needs.

TREATMENT PROTOCOL STRUCTURE

DWC Therapy is comprised of *four treatment* tracks. *Track A* is the core curriculum for the treatment protocol. Then, depending on the additional required treatment, clients are assigned to the *Extended Treatment Program, Tracks B through D*. The required additional treatment hours for a particular client may not fit exactly the number of therapy hours in the respective tracks. Thus it is recommended that clients be assigned to the track that best fits their required hours.

Track A Treatment is comprised of 21 two-hour curriculum-based therapy sessions. Each session will have around 90 minutes of *manual guided* therapy activities followed by a 30 minute process group focusing on the session topic and client concerns.

Track B treatment is comprised of the 21 two-hour *Track A* sessions and an additional 10 hours of therapy (group or individual). During those therapy sessions, *Track B* clients select **two manual guided** therapy projects to work on and present in their group.

Track C involves the 21 two-hour *Track A* sessions plus an additional 26 hours of therapy (group or individual). *Track C* clients select and present at least **four manual guided** therapy projects to their group.

Track D includes the 21 session *Track A* program plus an additional 44 hours of therapy. *Track D* clients select and present **eight manual guided** therapy projects to their group.

Tracks B through D clients may choose their projects from the 10 guided projects outlined in the *Level II Therapy Participant's Workbook*. However, a client may have the latitude of selecting other therapy project topics, if that client feels another topic has more relevance to his or her concerns and issues. Clients will present their therapy projects in the group to which they are assigned. From 10 to 15 minutes will be allotted for the presentation. Clients may use a method for presenting their therapy projects that is most comfortable for them. It is recognized that many clients will find it difficult to present in front of a group. The provider will need to work with clients to make it as comfortable and as meaningful as possible for individual clients.

PROGRAM SERVICE DELIVERY STRUCTURE OPTIONS

Service delivery options will first be discussed for the *Track A* core therapy curriculum. Then, the different options for *Tracks B through D* will be discussed.

Track A Core Curriculum

There are two possible models for presenting the *Track A* core curriculum: the **closed;** or **open** group. If the provider uses a closed group method, the same group of clients start and complete the program together, and no new clients are added in the course of the program. The *DWC Therapy* sessions are then presented in the order outlined in the *Participant's Workbook*.

For most agencies, the closed group approach is not practical. When an open group is used, the following method should be used.

▶ *Sessions 1 and 2* are used as the orientation to *DWC Therapy* and involve two, two-hour sessions. It is done in a closed group and conducted monthly, or as needed, depending on the rate and number of clients referred to therapy. During the orientation phase, and particularly in *Session 2*, the client and provider will develop the client's initial ITP.

▶ *Sessions 3 through 21* are conducted in an open group manner. The *21 core therapy* sessions are organized in five logical clusters.

- Pathways to addiction, reviewing the client's problem outcome symptoms, and managing cravings and urges - *Sessions 3 through 5*.

- Skills in developing cognitive self-control - *Sessions 6 through 9*.

- Relationship and social skills building - *Sessions 10 through 16*.

- Strengthening relapse and recidivism skills - *Sessions 17 and 18*.

- Developing community responsibility skills - *Sessions 19 through 21.*

▶ Even though the *Track A* core curriculum is divided into these five logical clusters, within these clusters, sessions are logically linked. It is best that a client waits until the end of these logical links before entering the open group. No more than two sessions are logically linked. Therefore, clients will not have to wait more than two weeks after completing their orientation session before entering the open core curriculum group. The following is a summary of the entry and no-entry points.

- Orientation *Sessions 1 and 2* are linked, there is no-entry at *Session 2.*

- *Sessions 3 and 4,* which focus on pathways to addiction and AOD problem outcomes, are linked, *Session 3* being a prerequisite for *Session 4.* There is no-entry at *Session 4.*

- *Sessions 6 and 7* are linked, and there is no-entry at *Session 7.*

- *Sessions 8 and 9* are linked, and there is no-entry at *Session 9.*

- *Sessions 10 and 11* are linked, and there is no-entry at *Session 11.*

- *Sessions 14 and 15* are linked, and there is no-entry at *Session 15.*

- *Sessions 17 and 18* are linked, and there is no-entry at *Session 18.*

Tracks B through D Clients

The following are two service delivery structures that providers can use for *DWC Therapy Tracks B through D*:

▶ **Structure One:** separate and open group for *Tracks B through D* clients that centers around an individualized treatment plan;

▶ **Structure Two:** clients have an individualized treatment plan that utilizes the resources of the *Track A* curriculum, other agency resources for treating DUI/DWAI and a *Peer Support Client* model. Each of these structures will be discussed.

Structure One: Separate and open group for *Tracks B through D* clients along with individualized treatment plan. This would be a group exclusively for these clients. The group is primarily a process therapy group, however, clients would present their therapy projects in this group. Providers who choose the exclusive *Tracks B through D* group approach would still develop an individualized treatment plan for clients, as discussed earlier. This individualized plan could use some of the resources described in **Option Two** below.

Structure Two: Individual treatment plan that utilizes all agency resources for treating **DWC Therapy** DWI clients when there is not a separate group for *Tracks B through D* clients. Agencies that do not have the resources to staff both a *Track A DWC Therapy* group and a *Tracks B through D* group will need to use this structure. There are several options for clients within this structure.

- **Option One:** *Individualized treatment plan* **and** involvement as *Peer Support Clients* in the 21 session *DWC Therapy* core curriculum. A client would repeat a certain number of *Track A* sessions, but would also help group members with classroom exercises and be supportive of clients in their involvement in the session. *Tracks B through D* clients would fulfill most of their required treatment hours in this kind of modality and present their therapy projects in the *Track A DWC Therapy* group. Based on the individual treatment plan, a client might fulfill some hours in other therapy modalities. Clients with many individual therapy needs should be placed in **Option Three** below. Some agencies may be limited as to the number of Peer Support Clients they can place in Track A (core) *DWC Therapy*. If group size is kept at 12 to 13, then any one *DWC Therapy* group may have only one or two slots available for *Peer Support Clients*. Thus, depending on the number of Tracks B through D clients at any one time, agencies may have to exercise options two and three along with option one.

- **Option Two:** *Individualized treatment plan* and involvement in a support group provided by the agency such as a support process group, relapse prevention group or a formal 12-step therapy group led by a certified or licensed addictions counselor. The clients would present their therapy projects in this group. In this option, a client may receive some special therapy, but if the ITP determines that there are many special needs, the client should be assigned to **Option Three.**

- **Option Three:** All *Tracks B through D* hours are assigned on the basis of specialized treatment needs as specified by their ITP. These specialized treatment approaches may include:

  - specialized treatment such as marital therapy, stress management, anger management, family therapy;

  - repeating specific *Level II Education* lessons or *DWC Therapy* sessions based on specific needs;

  - spending some of the hours as a *Peer Support Client* as described in **Option One;** or

  - utilization of the resources of other agencies or other therapists in order to meet the needs as outlined in the ITP.

  Option three is a very individualized and tailor-made approach to fulfilling *Tracks B through D* hours. Clients in this option would still present their required therapy projects in a group they are attending.

SESSION DELIVERY STRUCTURE

Each session in the *Participant's Workbook* is organized into the following sections:

- Overview and session objective;

- Session Content and focus;

- Session homework or activity; and

- Closure Process group.

The guidelines for the delivery of each session in the *Provider's Guide* are organized into the following sections:

▶ *Overview of session* which provides the rationale of the session and provider support material to enhance presentation skills and knowledge;

▶ *Session content, presentation sequence and process and presentation guidelines* which provides directions for effective presentation of the session; and

▶ *Guidelines* for the closure process group.

The provider presents the core concepts of the session and then guides clients though the session exercises and work sheets. Clients will complete most work sheets in the group guided by the provider. An unstructured process group will then be conducted in the last 20 to 30 minutes of the session which allows clients to share what they learned from the session and how they will apply what they have learned to enhance responsible living and quality of life.

Tracks B through D clients present *Manual Guided Therapy Projects* in the group they are attending. Ten projects are described in the *Extended Treatment Program* part of the *Participant's Workbook.* Clients will need to spend some time outside of class to prepare for their presentation in group. The organization of the manual guided therapy projects will be similar to the Core 21 sessions. There will be a brief introduction and overview of the therapy project, statement of objectives brief description of project content and work sheets. Clients complete the work sheets on their own and then present them to their group.

It is important that clients have the understanding that the primary objective of *DWC Therapy* is to *prevent recidivism and relapse.* However, we expand our goals and objectives to helping clients develop strategies to live in a CARING and responsible manner. We want CARE to be an important part of our clients' driving and responsible CARING to be an important part of their lives. Our overall goal is to help clients to be responsible to themselves, others and to their community. We continually keep in mind that this program is really about helping clients to develop approaches and strategies for responsible living and change.

STRATEGIES FOR SESSION CONTENT PRESENTATION

It is expected that clients be given the complete *Participant's Workbook* when entering *DWC Therapy.* The client is asked to review the two orientation sessions before attending the orientation to *DWC Therapy.* It is important for clients early on to develop a sense of ownership of the *Impaired Driver Treatment* program.

The following approaches have been found effective in delivering the *DWC Therapy* type of programs.

▶ Present material in an interactive format having clients share personal material around the session content.

▶ Use overheads, posters and charts when presenting the session material.

▶ Have clients review their *thinking reports* and *AOD Weekly Monitoring Chart* at the beginning of the session or during the group process and sharing portion.

> Try to keep the focus of the counselor-directed closure groups on the session content and topic. If a client shares material that diverges from the session topic, and is an emotional and unresolved issue, then the provider will utilize therapeutic skills to bring about some resolve with the client and group at the time the issue is revealed. The provider discerns if the client needs individual work. The provider will need to be therapeutically skilled in creating a balance between client and group resolution around individual therapeutic issues and fulfilling the objectives of each session. *Assessment as to whether individual work or more intensive group work is needed is an ongoing process.*

PROVIDER SERVICE DELIVERY SKILLS NEEDED FOR LEVEL II THERAPY

DWC Therapy is presented within the context of a therapeutic-interactive format. Materials are presented so as to maximize the participant's interaction with the material, the provider and members of the group. We have reviewed some of the core skills needed by providers for delivering the *DWC Education* and *Therapy* protocols. The provider is referred to this discussion in the *Level II Education* part of this section of the *Provider's Guide*. However, there are additional skills that will be need in delivering *DWC Therapy*.

> Differential and in-depth assessment.

> Use of the three types of group facilitation: facilitation **in** the group, **with** the group and **of** the group, with clear knowledge and skills around how to "treat" the group as a client with the goal that a healthy group produces healthy members. These group facilitation approaches were discussed in more depth in *Section II, Chapter 14* of this *Provider's Guide*.

> Use of therapeutic skills to handle psychological and emotional material that arise in group and to bring about temporary resolution of these issues as they arise.

> The provider is also skilled in making referrals for unresolved issues that arise in group.

These higher level skills are needed in *DWC Therapy* because more personal-emotional material will surface due to it's protracted nature. Clients will have *higher level AOD disruption and higher life-situation and psychosocial problem profiles.*

COMPLETION REQUIREMENTS AND EXPECTATIONS OF CLIENTS

The following are the comprehension and skill development expectations of clients.

> Develop an understanding of the *pathways to addictions* and an understanding of how the client's own patterns of use and misuse fit diagnostic descriptions.

> Have an applied understanding of the *cognitive-behavioral* change principle that our thoughts, attitudes and beliefs, not the events outside of ourselves, lead to our feelings and behaviors.

> Have a deeper understanding of the *principles of relapse and recidivism prevention* and enhance the plan that the client developed in *DWC Level II Education* utilizing the concepts of *life-style balance.*

- Know how to apply the skills of *cognitive self-control* in managing emotions and feelings.

- Know how to apply the skills of building and managing healthy *social and interpersonal relationships*.

- Develop skills that lead to a more *prosocial and caring* approach towards the community and society.

- Be willing to explore and *disclose social-emotional* issues and relate these issues to DWI behavior.

The following are the participation and completion expectations of clients for *DWC Therapy.*

- Complete all of the exercises and work sheets.

- Attend all sessions.

- Be involved in structured sharing exercises in the group.

- Complete homework assignments, including AOD thinking and action charting.

- Remain free from AOD use while in the program.

- Do not engage in recidivistic behavior — that is, the client will not drive while impaired or under the influence of other drugs.

- Present manual guided therapy projects, the number depending on the track to which the client is assigned.

- Will follow all of the terms of his or her probation and obey the law such as — will not drive with suspended license.

INTAKE AND ASSESSMENT

The provider will meet individually with the client for the intake session. This would first involve completing the following basic intake procedures.

- Completion of the Agency's personal data intake form.

- Complete all forms related to treatment consent and follow-up, release of information to court or other agencies and persons as requested by the client, confidentiality advisement, client rights and responsibilities, privacy notification, fees and collection procedures and advisement of credentials and full disclosure statement (see example forms in *Appendix C*).

- Review of all information received from the collaterals, including court services, motor vehicle and the results of psychometric testing.

◗ Complete an in-depth, differential assessment to include:

- interview information and psychosocial summary;

- completion of an approved self-report, psychometric differential instrument as discussed in *Chapters 7 and 13* of this *Provider's Guide;* and

- client completes the *Master Profile* and initial *Master Assessment Plan* with the assistance of the provider.

OUTLINE OF DWC THERAPY SESSIONS

There are 21 **Core Therapy Sessions** and 10 **Manual Guided Therapy** projects. These are summarized below:

Core Therapy Sessions:

1. *Program orientation I :* Understanding and engaging the change process.

2. *Program orientation II:* In-depth assessment and targets and tools for change.

3. *Pathways to AOD outcomes and addiction.*

4. *Reviewing your problem outcome symptoms and patterns.*

5. *Managing AOD cravings and urges.*

6. *Skills in cognitive self-control:* Recognizing and changing negative thinking.

7. *Skills in cognitive self-control:* Recognizing and changing errors in thinking.

8. *Skills in cognitive self-control:* Managing stress and emotions.

9. *Skills in cognitive self-control:* Recognizing and managing anger.

10. *Social and relationship building:* Learning communication skills.

11. *Social and relationship building:* Starting a conversation.

12. *Social and relationship building:* Giving and receiving positive reinforcement.

13. *Social and relationship building:* Learning problem solving skills.

14. *Social and relationship building:* Learning the art of being assertive.

15. *Social and relationship building:* Practicing refusal skills.

16. *Social and relationship building:* Developing and keeping intimate relationships.

17. *Strengthening recidivism and relapse prevention skills.*

18. *Relapse and recidivism prevention:* Your relapse and recidivism prevention plan and lifestyle balance.

19. *Community responsibility skills:* Strengthening character and prosocial values and behaviors.

20. *Community responsibility skills:* Understanding and practicing empathy.

21. *Community responsibility skills:* Learning the skills of conflict resolution.

Manual Guided Therapy Projects for Tracks B through D:

1. Healthy play and leisure time.

2. Does your work match your job?

3. Learning to search for a job.

4. Learning to relax: Your daily relaxation plan.

5. Preventing relapse: What is working best?

6. Preventing recidivism: What is working best?

7. Skills in time management and completing tasks.

8. Getting support from groups and others.

9. Giving support: Mentoring and role modeling.

10. Sharing your future biography.

SESSION 1: INTRODUCTION AND PROGRAM ORIENTATION I: UNDERSTANDING AND ENGAGING THE CHANGE PROCESS

RATIONALE AND OVERVIEW OF SESSION

This is the first of two orientation sessions for *DWC Therapy.* The purpose of the first orientation session is to introduce clients to the program by **using the introduction material in the** *Participant's Workbook* and then to carefully review the core concepts of the cognitive-behavioral approach to change as outlined in Session 1. The content in this session is essential because the underpinning of *DWC Therapy* is the cognitive-behavioral model for change. The most important goal of the orientation sessions is to begin to establish a working relationship with clients.

SESSION CONTENT AND PRESENTATION SEQUENCE, PROCESS AND GUIDELINES

Following is a summary of the content and the presentation sequence for the first orientation session of *DWC Therapy.*

▶ Start by introducing clients and providers. Then carefully go over the *Introduction* in the *Participant's Workbook.* This includes:

- Introducing the *Participant's Workbook;*

- who the program is for;

- how it is set up;

- its goals and objectives;

- expectations of clients and program agreements; and

- what is the approach of *DWC Therapy.*

▶ Using the material in *Session 1*, review the approach of *DWC Therapy* and then review the key concepts of *cognitive-behavioral learning and change.* The substance of this review is found in *Lessons 3 and 4* of the *DWC Level II Education Participant's Workbook.* Here is a summary of these concepts.

- The cognitive-behavioral model for learning and change and the three categories of self-control skills: cognitive restructuring, social and relationship skill building, and community responsibility skills.

- The six rules of thinking that lead to our actions and the three rules of learning that determine how our behaviors are strengthened are reviewed. **Exercise:** After reviewing the concepts of automatic thoughts, beliefs and attitudes, do *Work Sheet 1.* This has clients identify the automatic thoughts, attitudes and beliefs that led to their DWI behavior.

- Review the three rules of learning that reinforced behavior.

- Discuss why *Learning Rule 3* - When behaviors turn on a negative event, that behavior is weakened or extinguished - does not always work. This explains how reinforced thoughts continue to lead to negative or undesirable outcomes.

- Review the cognitive-behavior change map, *Figure 4, page 244,* above (*Figure 1,* Page 14 in the *Workbook*). **Exercise:** During the rest of this Provider's Guide we will refer to this as the **CB Map Exercise.** *Work Sheet 2* is the structure for this exercise. It is explained in the *Participant's Workbook,* Page 19. Providers may want to put this on a large poster board, since it will be used repeatedly during *DWC Therapy.* When doing this exercise, have clients give examples of events that lead to thoughts, feelings and actions. Have them go back through the process of changing thoughts that will lead to different outcomes.

- Review the skills and tools for changing thoughts and behaviors. Clients often insist that outside events are so powerful that they override the effects of our internal thoughts or cognitions. McMullin (2000) contends that, although external events are powerful, and they do incline people to act, they do not "make them act" (p. 24). McMullin concludes that the predisposition of early childhood, physical conditions, biochemistry or heredity can often be offset or mitigated by the client's change in thoughts, attitudes and beliefs (p. 24). He suggests that we point to examples where people have handled overpowering external events, such as Frankl's explanation of how people handled the Nazi death camp experiences (Frankl, 1959, 1980) or stories such as the *Diary of Anne Frank.*

- Go over the steps of how thoughts lead to actions, using *Figure 1,* page 14, in the *Participant's Workbook.* Again, an overhead or poster-board chart of *Figure 1* will aid in this process. Focus on the importance of changing beliefs. See if they can get in touch with their **core beliefs.** McMullin (2000) sees the core beliefs as the basis for all other beliefs we hold. They are so basic and fundamental that clients may not be aware that they have them.

- Go over the steps to changing those thoughts. Again, work on the underlying beliefs of the automatic thoughts.

- Clients are again asked to state their recidivism prevention goal. Have each client quickly share whether this goal has changed.

- Have clients do *Work Sheet 3, Defining the Problem Areas for the Master Profile and Master Assessment Plan,* in class and as homework. This is used in *Session 2: In-Depth Self-Assessment and Targets for Change.*

SESSION CLOSURE

Due to the amount of review material only 15 to 20 minutes may be available for the unstructured group. Have new group members introduce themselves and have clients share their expectations of the program. Remind them to do the AOD Weekly Monitoring Chart.

SESSION 2: PROGRAM ORIENTATION II: IN-DEPTH ASSESSMENT AND TARGETS AND TOOLS FOR CHANGE - YOUR MASTER PROFILE AND YOUR MASTER ASSESSMENT PLAN

RATIONALE AND OVERVIEW OF SESSION

One of the basic assumptions of *Driving With CARE* is that change occurs through a partnership between the client and the provider and the client and the group. In that partnership, the client has opportunity for self-disclosure. Self-disclosure is the first step to self-awareness. Self-awareness leads to change.

The first step of assessment is *self-disclosure*. It opens the door for a *feedback process* which enhances *self-awareness*. Self-disclosure and feedback are the two key communication channels for effective assessment. Effective assessment is able to tap more deeply into the self-disclosure channel of communication. The rationale for this session is that it provides clients a formal and informal process of self-disclosure through completing standardized **self-report** instruments.

An important part of the process of self-disclosure is self-evaluation and monitoring. The first task in this session is introducing the clients to the *Master Skills List* (MSL), *Table 2,* Page 31 of the *Workbook*. This is a guide for self-evaluation and monitoring of the cognitive-behavioral skills learned in *DWC Education and Therapy*. After most sessions, clients are asked to update the MSL and reevaluate themselves on the skills they have learned.

Clients entering *DWC Therapy* will most likely have completed a differential and in-depth self-report instrument. Several instrument options were outlined in the *Assessment Chapter* of *Section II* of this *Provider's Guide*. The client is asked to use the profiles derived from these assessments and *Work Sheet 3* that was completed in the first orientation session and complete the *Master Profile* (MP) in *Work Sheet 4* of this Session. The main purpose of this exercise is for the client to increase self-awareness through the self-disclosure process. At this point, clients are more likely to be open and less defensive, having completed *DWC Education* and the orientation session of *DWC Therapy*.

Assessment is also a process of receiving feedback. This is completed through **other-report** ratings completed by the provider. Having reviewed the screening and the intake instruments, the provider has a good view of the client and the client's major problem areas. The provider now is asked to rate the client across the scales and factors on the MP. It is recommended that the clients first rate themselves and then the provider rates the client using the client's MP. In this way, comparisons can be made between the client's self-report and the provider's other report on the same MP. The major areas of assessment are clearly outlined in the MP. They include:

- the area of alcohol and other drug use and abuse;

- assessment of impaired driving;

- assessment of thinking, feeling and attitude patterns;

- background and childhood development;

- current life situation problems in the areas of job, living situation, social and interpersonal relationships, marital and family, legal problems and physical health; and

- motivation and readiness for treatment.

Once the client and the provider have completed the MP, the client is asked to complete the *Master Assessment Plan* (MAP), Worksheet 5, which is the client's own individual treatment plan (ITP). The provider should utilize the information on the MAP when completing the ITP. The client's MAP and the provider's ITP provide the guidelines for the client's individualized treatment program.

Assessment also involves ongoing self-disclosure and feedback. In this session, clients are trained on writing their the *autobiography*, doing the *thinking report*, the *re-thinking report* and the *AOD weekly monitoring chart*. These tools continue to facilitate the *self-disclosure* and *feedback* process throughout the program.

SESSION CONTENT AND PRESENTATION SEQUENCE, PROCESS AND GUIDELINES

Following this session, the special needs of the client may be more defined. For *Tracks B through D* clients, the results of this session should provide a guide for selecting the therapy projects and look at which *Tracks B through D* option the client might choose. However, final decisions around these choices can be made towards the end of the *Core Track A* curriculum.

Here are some important guidelines in implementing this session.

- Start with introducing clients to the *Master Skills List* (MSL), Table 2, page 31; and how to add to and update the list.

- Carefully go over all of the assessment factors in the MP. Then have the client complete the MP. It is advised that the provider rate clients before the session and then give the ratings to clients so that they can put the provider's ratings on their own MP. The provider will have to work out the logistics in order to accomplish this task. It is suggested that a copy of the MP is made for each client and then given to the clients after *Work sheet* 4 is completed in class.

- Clients define the targets for change by completing the MAP. Take time to go over the MP and MAP in group.

- Make it clear that the MAP is the client's ITP and that the provider also has an ITP in the client's file. If the client consents, a copy of Worksheet 5 can be placed in the client's record and used as the ITP.

The first step of assessment is self-disclosure. It opens the door for a feedback process, which enhances self-awareness. Self-disclosure and feedback are the two key communication channels for effective assessment. The rationale for this session is that it provides clients a formal and informal process of self-disclosure through competing standardized self-report instruments.

▶ Explain the four tools clients will use in this program.

- **Autobiography:** Review the elements of the autobiography and make it clear that clients who have difficulty writing may have someone help them, or even do it with drawings and pictures. Remind clients that the autobiography includes the future biography. Give clients a time line for completion - four to six weeks. Have them share their findings in group. The provider will need to develop a schedule as to when clients are to complete their autobiographies.

- **Thinking Report:** Daley and Marlatt (1992) identify the use of inventories as an important relapse prevention strategy. These inventories have the goal of getting clients to monitor their lives so as to identify high-risk factors (including subjective warning signs and situational cues) that would contribute to a relapse. *The Thinking Report* is such an inventory. The specific elements of the *Thinking Report* are: the *event or situation; thoughts; feelings; attitudes and beliefs; and outcome.*

- The **Re-thinking Report** takes an event we experience and then changes the thoughts, beliefs and actions to produce positive outcomes. It is a map for change and our plan as to how we will handle similar future events. We change the thoughts and then hypothesize what underlying beliefs would have to change in order to produce those thoughts. Then, we hypothesize actions that could result from those changes and which lead to good outcomes.

- Another process inventory used in this program is the *AOD Weekly Monitoring Chart.* The work sheet forms for this are in the back of the *Participant's Workbook.*

▶ **Exercise:** Do the *CB Map Exercise.* This exercise uses the *CB Map, Figure 1* on p. 14 in the *Participant's Workbook* as a basic guide. It is illustrated in *Work Sheet 2* on page 21. Clients are asked to do this brief exercise almost every session. The basic process of the *CB Map Exercise* will remain the same from session to session, however, this exercise can vary from having the client identify the underlying beliefs and attitudes leading to the automatic thoughts to having the group help the client with this. Again, it is recommended that the provider have an enlarged copy of both *Figure 1* and *Work Sheet 1* in the *Participant's Workbook* and display that in the treatment room.

SESSION CLOSURE

Have clients do some sharing around their MP and MAP. Have them discuss how the provider's rating compares with their own rating. Do clients agree with any discrepancies between these two ratings? Have clients discuss how they feel about doing an autobiography.

SESSION 3: PATHWAYS TO ALCOHOL AND OTHER DRUG USE OUTCOMES AND ADDICTION

RATIONALE AND OVERVIEW OF SESSION

Some *DWC Therapy* clients will not fit an AOD problem outcome or addiction pattern. Others will but will resist accepting that they do. Others will have clear signs of fitting these patterns and openly accept it. The purpose of this session is to provide clients with knowledge of the patterns of AOD problem outcomes and impaired control and how they might fit these patterns. Such patterns can lead to problem use and to abuse and dependence. Remember, *Sessions 3 and 4* are in sequence.

This session will also discuss the *genetic factors* in alcoholism or drug abuse. Before summarizing the session content and guidelines for presentation, we will discuss some of the salient issues of the pathways to AOD problem outcomes and to addiction, giving literature backup to these concepts. We will also look at what is involved in cocaine addiction and some issues around genetics.

Pathways to impaired control and addiction: The main focus of this session is on the *two addiction pathways* which are clearly described in the *Participant's Workbook*. In the *Provider's Guide* we will review some of the key concepts of these two pathways to addiction.

Mental-Behavioral Impaired Control Cycle (MB-ICC): This cycle of AOD addiction and problem outcomes provides an understanding of how thinking and behavior get reinforced around alcohol or other drug use. It is built on the concepts of cognitive-behavior learning and change as illustrated in the CB map and on the learning rules of how behaviors are strengthened and reinforced. These learning rules are important in understanding the ICC model: if a behavior turns on a positive event, that behavior gets strengthened; if a behavior turns off a negative event, that behavior gets strengthened.

There are a number of theories that have been used to explain the MB-ICC model including *Social Learning Theory* (Bandura, 1969, 1977a; Abrams & Niaura, 1987; Collins, Blane & Leonard, 1999), *Expectancy Theory* (Collins, Blane & Leonard, 1999; Goldman, Brown & Christiansen, 1987; Goldman et al., 1999; Hull & Bond, 1986; Webb, Baer, Francis, & Caid, 1993), *Opponent Process Theory* (Shipley, 1987), *Tension Reduction Theory* (Cappell & Greeley, 1987), the *Self-Awareness Model* (Hull, 1987; Sayette, 1999), and the *Stress Reduction Dampening Theory* (Greeley & Oel, 1999; Sher, 1987). Expectancy and coping (stress and tension reduction) are the two key concepts of the ICC model. It can also be seen as an operant conditioning model.

Mental-physical Impaired-Control Cycle (MP-ICC): This pathway helps us understand how people get into an addiction cycle because of the physical and chemical changes in the nervous system. This pathway to addiction is based on the work of Gitlow (1970, 1982, 1988). It has been illustrated by Glenn and Hochman (1977), Glenn and Warner (1975), and Glenn, Warner, and Hockman (1977), has been further discussed by Peyser (1988) and Grilly (1989) and has been illustrated in detail by Wanberg (1990) and Wanberg and Milkman (1998). It has support in Fromme and D'Amico's descriptions of the neurobiological bases of the psychological effects of alcohol (1999). Also, Dr. Stanley Gitlow's son, Dr. Stuart Gitlow, has provided an excellent update on this model of addiction and impaired control (2001).

The mental-physical MP-ICC pathway to addiction is based on the *withdrawal effects* of drugs and the *neurochemical imbalances* resulting from the use of drugs. These withdrawal effects and neurochemical imbalances are mitigated or "cured" by the use of the substance causing withdrawal. This pathway to addiction can be explained, to some extent, by the theory of classical condition (see Collins, Blane & Leonard's discussion of classical conditioning and addiction, 1999). However, the essence of this theory of addiction is the *imbalance of the neurochemical system* resulting in a "rebound" from the use of a drug.

When the suppressor or sedative type drug such as alcohol begins to wear off, the system can experience a "rebound" or nerve-excitement effect (Fromme & D'Amico, 1999; Gitlow, 2001). This neurological stress or tension is explained by an increase of natural stimulant drugs in the system that get stored up and suppressed due to the effects of the sedative, e.g., alcohol. This is the withdrawal reaction from the use of a sedative drug. This rebound effect is what Gitlow (1970, 1982, 1988) and Peyser (1988) call the *asynchronous* relationship between the *short-term large-amplitude* sedative effect of alcohol and its *long-term agitating* (withdrawal) effect. Every alcohol dose has to work against the "rebound" effect of the drug (Gitlow, 2001). This is similar to what Ray and Ksir (2002) describe as the continuation of the body's response to compensate from the sedation of the body resulting from using a sedative or suppressor (alcohol) drug.

The work of Fromme and D'Amico (1999) supports this theory. They contend that *acute alcohol withdrawal* from chronic alcohol intake is associated with increased *norepinephrine* (also called noradrenaline) (NE) activity, which contributes to sympathetic arousal (i.e., increase blood pressure, heart rate) as well as the delirious features of withdrawal (i.e., hallucinations, delirium tremens). At the behavioral level, NE increases arousal and alertness. Whereas low doses of alcohol increase NE release, high doses of alcohol decrease NE release which contributes to the sedative-hypnotic effect of alcohol.

Gitlow contends that the rebound or withdrawal effect may continue for several weeks or even months following a longer period of alcohol use. The stimulation and agitation effects become less intense and less noticeable. However, the very presence of this agitation creates an ongoing level of stress. When this low level of stress is added to normal daily tension, stressful events are more difficult to handle. This may be a factor that contributes to relapse. *Thus, one may be more vulnerable to relapsing during the several weeks or months following quitting drinking.*

A person who has developed a pattern of daily, steady drinking may need to use the drug every one or two hours during non-sleep periods in order to avoid the agitation of withdrawal and "cure" the *rebound effect*. This describes the case of the "strung out" user. Thus, the rebound effect reduces the strength of each dose of alcohol.

This process explains one reason why people become addicted to a drug. For many people, it will take the person into the addiction cycle or the impaired control cycle where the drug is needed to manage the withdrawal effects of the drug (Gitlow, 2001). Peyser (1988) calls this the "autonomous self-perpetuating" factor of addiction. The body demands more of the drug to maintain the body balance (homeostasis) - the very drug that set off the state of nervous system imbalance. It is related to what the drug does to the nerve chemistry at the nerve endings themselves.

A steady use of the drug may be for only the purpose of "curing" the discomfort of the rebound or withdrawal phase of use. If the drug is discontinued after a period of use, minor symptoms such as inability to sleep, shakes or being irritable may occur within 24 hours. For the person who has been drinking steady for several days to several weeks, more serious symptoms will begin to occur within 72 hours (Ciraulo & Ciraulo, 1988; Hodding, et al., 1980). These symptoms may be very serious, depending on the strength and intensity of the rebound.

The effects of the rebound or withdrawal from a drug are the opposite of the direct or intoxicating effects of the drug (Grilly, 1989, p. 94). Thus, this psychophysical model can be applied to other drugs such as stimulants. The direct effects of a stimulant (amphetamines, cocaine) would be physical and mental excitability, stimulation or agitation. When the blood level of the stimulant drug drops, the rebound or withdrawal process begins resulting in depression, tiredness, and a "crashing" effect. Some of these symptoms could also include a decrease in vital signs (blood pressure, heart rate). Again, the most effective short term way to "cure" these reactions is to re-engage in the use of the drug. *Thus, the cocaine-addicted person begins to use cocaine to counteract the opposite or withdrawal effects of the cocaine.*

Cocaine Addiction and the Neurochemical Process: Because stimulants, particularly cocaine, are drugs used by some DWI clients, the provider may want to give the neurochemical explanation of cocaine addiction. As discussed, as the presence of cocaine or other stimulants in the system declines, a reaction opposite effect of euphoria, pleasure and stimulation occurs - neurological slowing and depression. This effect (both physically and psychologically) can be "treated" by using more cocaine. There is extensive evidence in the literature on the relationship between cocaine and brain chemistry and the direct and indirect (withdrawal) effects of cocaine (Blum et al., 1996; Milkman & Sunderwirth, 1987; Ray & Ksir, 2002; Roehrich, Dackis & Gold, 1987; Volkow et al., 1993).

The principal place where cocaine takes effect is the dopamine D2 receptor. Neuronal excitement can induce the flow of dopamine, a neurotransmitter that activates the brain pleasure centers (Roehrich, Dackis & Gold, 1987). Under normal conditions of dopamine flow, the excess is recycled into the dopamine releasing nerve cells and deactivated. When cocaine is used, the excess dopamine is prevented from being recycled and excessive pleasure or euphoria results. More dopamine stimulates other neurons to produce still more dopamine leading to increased euphoria or pleasure. In essence, cocaine prevents the dopamine releasing neurons from performing the normal reuptake process.

After prolonged use, cocaine leaves the system, there is a depletion of the D2 receptors, and an opposite effect of pleasure and euphoria is felt. Chronic administration of cocaine results in a decrease of D2 receptors, resulting in a craving for cocaine to achieve effects of pleasure and euphoria (Volkow et al., 1993).

Genetic Factors: A common concern of many clients is whether alcoholism or drug abuse is inherited. Thus, it is helpful for the provider to have a basic knowledge in this area. It is important that clients understand these four ideas.

▶ There appears to be no specific genetic pathway or gene for alcoholism or the abuse of other substances.

▶ However, there is a significant common genetic influence on the risk of developing alcoholism and substance abuse and that clients are at higher risk for developing AOD abuse or dependence problems if their family members, particularly biological parents, have AOD abuse and dependency problems.

▶ Biogenetic factors work together with psychological, social and environmental factors to increase the risk of developing AOD abuse and dependence patterns and problems.

▶ Psychological and social risk factors are very potent in the development of AOD abuse problems.

SESSION CONTENT AND PRESENTATION SEQUENCE, PROCESS AND GUIDELINES

The following session content and presentation sequence are recommended for this session.

▶ Briefly review the progress clients are making on their *autobiography* and update *Master Skills List (MSL)*.

▶ Briefly review the elements of the *Thinking Report* and go over the *AOD Weekly Monitoring Chart*.

▶ **Exercise:** Do the *CB Map Exercise* described above. This time, have a client choose an event where they were faced with the pressure from peers to drink.

▶ **Exercise:** Use Work Sheet 6, have clients do a thinking report.

▶ Present the content of the session using an interactive learning model.

▶ Update Master Skills List (MSL).

Much of this session's content will require the provider to summarize the MB-ICC and the *Mental-Physical Addiction Pathways* in an interactive-teaching format. Recognizing that the MB-ICC will be a review for most clients in the program, the provider can engage the clients in interacting around the ICC concepts.

The *MP-ICC and Rebound Model* may require a more formal didactic presentation. However, clients should be engaged with respect to how they might identify or fit the models. Most clients will benefit from a brief summary of the neurochemical process of cocaine addiction and the genetic factors as these are related to the *reward deficiency syndrome* (RDS) as described in Blum et al., 1996.

SESSION CLOSURE

The closing process group can be structured around how clients identify with the session material.

SESSION 4: REVIEWING YOUR PROBLEM OUTCOME SYMPTOMS AND PATTERNS

RATIONALE AND OVERVIEW OF SESSION

Lessons 5 through 7 of **DWC Level II Education** dealt extensively with facts and ideas about alcohol and other drugs and the patterns of use and abuse. Since clients in **DWC Therapy,** on the average, will have more extensive involvement in AOD use and problems, this session will review the AOD problem outcome symptoms and patterns. The main goal will be to have clients take a look at their problem outcome patterns and see if their perceptions of these patterns and their willingness to report AOD use problems have changed. If the clients are less defensive and more open, and by this time, this should be the case, then there will be an increase in the number of clients endorsing problem patterns.

The platform for reviewing the problem outcome symptoms and patterns will be the MB-ICC model and the *DSM IV Substance Abuse and Substance Dependence Diagnosis.* **Alert: Session 3 is a prerequisite to this session. This is a no-entry point for new clients.**

SESSION CONTENT AND PRESENTATION SEQUENCE, PROCESS AND GUIDELINES

Begin the session by having clients look at their self ratings on the *Master Profile* in the area of AOD use. From this review, clients are then asked to update their MAP and the provider is asked to review the client's ITP.

Clients are then asked to review the various symptoms and problem outcomes related to the use of different drugs and check those that they now see apply to them. The provider is asked to do this in group, going over each of the symptoms in *Work Sheet 7.*

Following the symptoms review, present the following four AOD problem outcome categories, using the MB-ICC as a platform for presentation.

▶ *Drinking (AOD) problem category:* the person had a past problem from AOD use, e.g., DWI.

▶ *Problem drinker or user category:* individual has had several problems from AOD use and these problems form a pattern.

▶ *Problem drinker (user) with symptoms of abuse:* via the DSM IV criteria for Abuse.

▶ *Problem drinker (user) with symptoms of dependence:* via the DSM IV criteria for Dependence.

Briefly review the *mental-physical ICC.* Have clients share if they now see themselves fitting this cycle.

Work Sheets 8 and 9 are directed at having the clients evaluate themselves on the *Abuse* and *Dependence* criteria. *Work Sheet 10* is used to have clients check whether they fit the four AOD problem outcome categories. Have clients review their *relapse prevention* (RP) goal. The provider is asked to review the two broad RP goals and then have clients write their goal in their workbook.

This is a good time to provide some guidelines as to who might consider choosing *Personal Commitment Goal II:* maintain abstinence from AOD use. Use the following steps in helping clients develop some guidelines for this kind of decision.

▶ Have clients review their work on the AOD symptom scale on *Work Sheet 23* in *Lesson 7* of the *Level II Education Participant's Workbook* (page 117). It might be helpful for clients to retake that test. This could be done by providing this as a handout for the clients. Have them plot their new score, or review their old score using *Profile 2* on page 118 of the *Level II Education Participant's Workbook*. Clients who have a raw score of above 21 or 22 have had definite AOD use problems. Clients who score above 43 should strongly consider abstinence as their RP goal. Clients who score higher than 48 to 50 are in the range of having had substance abuse or even dependence problems.

▶ Clients who see themselves falling in the *Substance Abuse* category should give the RP goal of abstinence strong consideration. Clients who see themselves fitting the *Substance Dependence* category should be encouraged to select *abstinence* as their RP goal.

Finally, the issue of the use of illegal or illicit drugs is discussed. The provider makes it **very clear** that use of illicit and illegal drugs is not acceptable and that the expected goal is abstinence from use of these drugs. This includes alcohol for clients under age 21. However, it is important that providers deal with this issue within the framework of therapeutic interaction and the use of therapeutic skills.

Have clients complete the *Thinking Report* on *Work Sheet 11* and review their work on the *AOD Weekly Monitoring Chart* they did for the past week. Have them update the *Master Skill List (MSL)*, page 31 in the *Workbook*.

SESSION CLOSURE

Have clients discuss where they see themselves now with respect to their AOD problem outcome pattern. Discuss the issue of the use of illegal and illicit drugs. Give clients opportunity to express their views even though those views may differ from those of the provider.

SESSION 5: MANAGING CRAVINGS AND URGES

RATIONALE AND OVERVIEW OF SESSION

Many clients in *DWC Therapy* will not experience cravings per se. However, clients who do not have cravings or urges for alcohol or other drugs may have desires or even strong impulses to continue to engage in a drinking lifestyle, such as stopping off at the bar after work. These desires can place the client at high-risk for recidivism.

Although there are mixed findings regarding urges and cravings in the literature, there is a strong corpus of literature that support these phenomena in drinkers and other drug users. Fisher and Harrison (2000) note "clients often report that the cravings and urges are so powerful that they lose focus on other aspects of relapse prevention" (p. 247). Marlatt (1985a) defines a **craving** as the *degree of desire* for the positive effects a person expects as a result of use and an *urge* as the *intention* to *engage* in use to satisfy the craving. Thus, a craving is the desire for the drug and an urge is the drug-seeking behavior to fulfill that desire.

The crucial issue has to do with individuals who seek alcohol or other drugs, e.g., have cravings and urges, in the absence of drug reinforcement (Boker, Cooney & Pomerleau, 1987). Thus, the alcohol-seeking behavior is strong even though the drug reinforcement properties are no longer there. That is, even though the individual no longer gains benefits from use, e.g., reduce tension, manage stress, relax, etc., the person still seeks alcohol. This explains why some clients will score high on *obsessive-compulsive* drinking and high on the *disruption scales* on the *Alcohol Use Inventory* (Horn, Wanberg & Foster, 1990), yet low on the *psychological* and *social benefits scale*. Their alcohol-seeking behavior or their urges and cravings are powerful even though no direct psychological or social reward is forthcoming.

Fromme and D'Amico (1999) attribute this to the shift in the prominence of the two neural systems of primary reinforcement and the information processing system as the use of alcohol proceeds to abuse and dependence (p. 445). "Tolerance to the reinforcing effects of alcohol is combined with impaired functioning of the information processing. As a consequence, the power of craving for alcohol overrides judgment, and drinking is continued despite significant negative consequences. This shift may contribute to alcohol-seeking behavior in the absence of significant reinforcement..." (p. 445).

Alcohol-seeking behavior or craving may also be attributed to levels of NE (norepinephrine). Borg, Czarnecka, Kvande, Mossberg & Sedvall (1983) found that cravings increase with decrease levels of NE metabolites. Thus, Borg et al., Fromme and D'Amico and others certainly see urges and cravings and alcohol-seeking behavior as strongly related to the neural and neurochemical system.

> The concept that cravings occur when the automatic thinking process is aborted and after an individual makes a conscious effort to stop has important implications for treatment. Cognitive therapy might, at least initially, increase cravings and urges. This is why continual proactive and application of thought restructuring is essential to give the individual cognitive control over drug-seeking behavior.

Whereas the literature typically links cravings and urges to neurochemical processes, physiological withdrawal or the desire for substances, others argue that they are more connected with *cognitive processes* (Tiffany, 1990). Tiffany contends that empirical support for these explanations for the physiological and neurochemical basis of cravings and urges are not strong. Findings that mitigate against these arguments are that drug urges often occur after withdrawal symptoms have remised and addicted persons often do not ascribe relapse to urges (Tiffany, 1990; Collins, et al., 1999).

Tiffany argues that *automatic processing* or quick processing is often the basis of drug use behavior and behavioral responses, and that there are low cognitive demands required for the behavior. Automatic processing (or in the scheme of this work, automatic thinking) leads to the behavior, and is hard to stop once it starts. Under this condition, cravings and urges may not be experienced because the automatic thinking and action occur quickly - it is effortless. If the automatic process is interrupted - such as the individual is unable to access alcohol - then the nonautomatic process takes over and the person may experience cravings. Another condition of the interrupting of the automatic process is when the individual makes a conscious effort to halt the process and stop drinking, e.g., when the client gets in touch with the automatic thoughts leading to drinking and makes a conscious effort to change the process. At this point, alcohol seeking thoughts and behaviors may be experienced as craving or urges.

The concept that cravings occur when the automatic thinking process is aborted, and after an individual makes a conscious effort to stop use has important implications for treatment. This may suggest that treatment in general and cognitive therapy in particular might, at least initially, increase cravings and urges (drug-seeking behavior) because treatment interrupts the automatic process which has allowed the person to go right to the drinking or drug using behavior without experiencing the drive for or urge to drink. Through enhancing the individual's cognitive awareness of the thoughts that lead to use, the automatic thinking process now is replaced by the nonautomatic process. This is why continual practice and application of thought restructuring (the nonautomatic process) is essential so as to give the individual cognitive control over the drug-seeking behavior.

The truth of cravings and urges most likely involves both the neurophysical and cognitive processes for some persons and for others, involves one or the other. In either case, there are cognitive-behavioral approaches that can be used to manage drug-seeking behavior and cravings and urges. This is the essential objective of this session.

SESSION CONTENT AND PRESENTATION SEQUENCE, PROCESS AND GUIDELINES

The following session content and presentation process is recommended for this session.

▶ Review the *Thinking Report* assigned last week as homework (an event that challenged the clients' *relapse prevention* plan) and the *AOD Weekly Monitoring chart.*

▶ **Exercise:** Do the *CB Map Exercise* structuring it around any topic.

- Present the content of the session starting with defining cravings and urges. Then the common situations that can trigger cravings and urges are presented (Kadden et al., 1992; Monti et al., 1989; Wanberg & Milkman, 1998). The skills and methods of coping with cravings and urges are then discussed (Kadden et al., 1992, Monti et al., 1989; Wanberg & Milkman, 1998). "Toughing it out" or "urge surfing" (Kadden, et al., 1992) is an important coping component.

- It is important to help clients associate their alcohol-seeking behaviors with their DWI. Although they may not have had a psychological craving or physical urge for alcohol or other drugs, they have been pulled towards drinking environments (bars, parties, etc.). Thus, thoughts and behaviors that seek alcohol-related environments are an integral part of their DWI conduct. An important cognitive model for helping clients manage alcohol-environment seeking thoughts and behaviors is to have them identify their most important pleasures and joys (*Work Sheet 12*) and then to have them decide if they would lose those joys and pleasures if they got another DWI.

Exercise: Worksheet 13 is important for even those who do not experience physical urges for alcohol or other drugs. It focuses on the "desire" to drink or to get drunk. For those clients who have chosen the relapse prevention plan of preventing problem drinking (rather than abstinence), the desire may be more than to drink but to get drunk - or to drink to excess. Worksheet 13 brings to bear the mental, social and physical skills that the client has learned to manage desires, cravings or urges to drink/use drugs.

Exercise: This sessions thinking report (Worksheet 14) focuses on an event related to desires, urges or cravings.

Remind clients to:

- Do their AOD Weekly Monitoring Chart;

- Update their MSL on page 31.

SESSION CLOSURE

Make alcohol-environment seeking behavior and cravings and urges an integral focus in the closure group. Have every client identify their thoughts and behaviors that led them to seek drinking environments if not substances themselves.

SESSION 6: SKILLS IN SELF-CONTROL: RECOGNIZING AND CHANGING NEGATIVE THOUGHTS AND NEGATIVE THINKING

RATIONALE AND OVERVIEW OF SESSION

When negative thinking becomes a way of life, it is as comfortable as the other distorted thoughts to which people may cling. Negative thoughts lead to negative emotions that are generally accompanied by tension from which we want to escape. The escape may take the form of drinking or spending time with friends at the bar. Negative thinking can set us up for taking part in DWI behavior. The results of this behavior will subsequently lead to negative feelings about oneself including reduced self-respect, anger and depression. This session identifies patterns of negative thinking and relates them to DWI conduct. This session is a prerequisite to Session 7.

> Another objective of this session is to give clients the cognitive restructuring skills to manage, stop or change negative thoughts and replace them with positive ones. These skills will be used in managing and dealing with many different thoughts and emotions. It will only be with repetition and practice that these techniques are learned. It will take participants time to notice a change, probably reflected in a more positive outlook on life.

SESSION CONTENT AND PRESENTATION SEQUENCE, PROCESS AND GUIDELINES

Use the following content and presentation sequence for this session.

- ▶ Review the *Thinking Report* assigned last week as homework - An event that made you think you wanted a drink.

- ▶ Review the mantra of this program: **It is what and the way we think that determines the way we feel and act.** People and events in your life can lead to bad results if you allow them to do so. You are in control of what you think or say to yourself. "People don't upset you; you allow them to upset you" (Monti et al., 1989, p. 112). As Cassias said about Caesar: Caesar's fate lies not in the stars, but within him."

- ▶ **Exercise:** Do the *CB Map Exercise*. Have the client who volunteers to do this exercise choose the event without structuring it around any topic.

- ▶ Have clients look at their MP and their MAP. How do their ratings on the *Assessment of Thinking, Feeling and Attitude Patterns* in the MP relate to negative or self-defeating behavior? High self-ratings across *Current Life Situation Problems* on the MP could indicate the client has a generally negative view of self and the world. Do clients need to update their MAP and the provider update the ITP based on this assessment?

▶ Discuss how clients see negative thinking as affecting their lives. Using the list of errors in thinking in *Session 7, Work Sheet 19,* page 77, see how these errors in thinking relate to negative thinking. Do *Work Sheet 15* which relates negative thoughts to errors in thinking.

Exercise: Apply the CB schema for learning and change (*Figure 1,* p. 14) to events that lead to negative thinking. Then discuss how negative thinking can lead to recidivism. Do *Work Sheet 16.*

▶ Review the steps and skills that can be used in changing negative thinking (McMullin, 1986, 2000; Monti, et al., 1989; Wanberg & Milkman, 1998). *Work Sheet 17* will help clients develop a list of positive thoughts they can arm themselves with and use in situations that can lead to negative and self-defeating thinking.

Exercise: Have group pick a situation that can lead directly to certain thoughts that are negative. For example, a wife is late getting home from work. The husband's automatic thought may be "she's running around" (appraisal). He is angry and accuses her of being out with another man (behavioral outcome). Now take the same situation and let the thought occur. Then intervene with THOUGHT STOPPING **and** PLANTING A POSITIVE THOUGHT.

Exercise: Have clients share an incident in which negative thoughts led to substance abuse or DWI conduct. What were their specific negative thoughts? Do they think their behavior was justified by the event or have they reached the point that they recognize the decision and responsibility for their actions is theirs alone? Do they think they would have behaved differently if they had stopped long enough to consider alternatives and consequences?

▶ Relate the steps and skills to changing negative thinking to the overall skill of self-talk. When we replace negative thoughts, we are doing *self-talk.* **Self-talk is powerful.**

▶ *Worksheet 18* is a Rethinking Report. Start with an event that led to negative thoughts. Have clients rethink the thoughts to get a better outcome.

▶ Have clients update their MSL, page 31.

SESSION CLOSURE

This session may open up some unresolved issues with clients. Take time to deal with these issues, but don't get caught up in resolving the issues of each client. Instead, help them to learn the skills to manage these issues. "Feed a man a fish and he can eat for a day. Teach him to fish, and he can eat for a lifetime."

SESSION 7: SKILLS IN SELF-CONTROL: RECOGNIZING AND CHANGING OUR ERRORS IN THINKING

RATIONALE AND OVERVIEW OF SESSION

Thinking errors or cognitive distortions have become a major focus in the treatment of clients with substance abuse problems and a history of criminal conduct. Given all of the emphasis of the prevention of impaired driving and the degree to which this gains attention in our society, it is a compelling argument that impaired driving involves an error in logic and thinking. It is just "illogical" to drive and drink. From this perspective, we also have to conclude that thinking errors are a very powerful determinant of behavior. It is for this reason that we have focused on thinking errors on several occasions in the *Driving With CARE* education and treatment protocols.

A cognitive distortion or error in thinking is automatic to the point that we continue to engage in the errors of thinking even though our experiences and the facts do not support the thinking error. *Errors in thinking are distortions or misrepresentations that we do as a matter of habit.* They become so automatic that we accept them even if we have no facts to support what we think (Bush & Bilodeau, 1993).

In relating thinking errors to criminal conduct, Yochelson and Samenow (1976) define thinking errors as the mental process required by the offender to live his or her kind of life. They feel that thinking errors are habitual and are patently obvious in day-to-day transactions of the criminal. This statement certainly applies to the Driving While Impaired Offender (DWIO). The fact that the average DWI offender drove from 800 to a 1,000 times or more before being arrested certainly validates automatic and habitual nature of thinking errors. Thus, addressing thinking errors is an essential component of impaired driving offender treatment.

The objective of this session is to help clients see the common thought patterns that lead to errors in thinking, identify what thinking errors they "habitually" use and then to explore one of the most powerful thinking errors - *entitlement and the entitlement trap.*

Alert: Session 6 is a pre-requisite to this session. This is a no-entry point for new clients.

SESSION CONTENT AND PRESENTATION SEQUENCE, PROCESS AND GUIDELINES

We will summarize the content focus and presentation sequence for this session.

> ▶ Review the clients' work on the *AOD Weekly Monitoring Chart.* Then have clients review their MP to see how they rated themselves on thinking errors. Have clients update their MAP and the provider update the ITP.

▶ Review the basic elements of the *CB Map* in the *Workbook* (Figure 1, p. 14) including the categories of automatic thoughts or thought habits: expectancies, appraisals, attributions and decisions. Have clients share what they now think some of their core beliefs are. Go over these concepts again and review the meaning of attitudes and beliefs.

- Our attitudes, beliefs and thinking patterns control how we react to people and situations in our everyday life.

- Our **attitudes** are our basic thoughts for or against persons, ideas and objects in our life. Our attitude is the position we take in relationship to the outside world. They are emotionally based.

- Our **beliefs** are values, ideas and principles we use to evaluate other people and ourselves. They bond us to the outside world.

▶ **Exercise:** Do the *CB Map* Exercise (using Worksheet 2, page 21 in the *Participant's Workbook*). For this session choose an event that led to a negative thought.

▶ Discuss the concept of *thinking error*. Have clients discuss the idea that DWI behavior is based on thinking errors - it is illogical to drive when impaired. Have them complete *Work Sheet 19*. This was compiled from a variety of sources (Beck, 1976; Burns, 1980, 1989; Wanberg & Milkman, 1998; Yochelson and Samenow, 1976). When doing *Work Sheet 19*, have clients check those thinking errors that they think contributed most to their DWI behavior.

▶ Present and discuss the common thought patterns or thought habits that lead us to errors in thinking and become barriers to change (Adapted from King, et al., 1994; Wanberg & Milkman, 1998).

Exercise: Practice *thought stopping* to deal with a thinking error. Have group members say out loud a thought that they know is an error in thinking. Then, have them say in a loud voice, "STOP." Have them visualize a stop sign before saying "STOP."

Exercise: Practice *shifting the view* to deal with a thinking error. Demonstrate with the thinking error "I feel I've been screwed." This is a basis of anger for many people. Shift the view. Have group members give a different view to this thinking error. "I've had some things go my way." "I know of several people who have helped me and not 'screwed' me." Then, have clients state out loud a thinking error. Then have them make a statement that "shifts the view."

▶ Introduce and discuss the **entitlement trap.** This is a broad error in logic and is supported by a number of thinking errors. The entitlement trap for the DWI offender is this: By some quirk of fate, the impaired driver has earned the right to drive while impaired. There is a strong entitlement to engaging in impaired driving behavior. Part of this has to do with the use of the error "victim stance." Have clients discuss these ideas.

Exercise: Do a round robin and have each client identify how the entitlement trap contributed to their impaired driving behavior. Clients will resist this. This is an abstract concept for some clients. Be patient and stick with them. Roll with the resistance.

An important reason people use the entitlement error is that they are unable to put themselves in the place of others.   We will deal with empathy in a later session, but this exercise may help prepare them for that session.

Exercise: Have clients identify a situation where they have a disagreement with another person.   Then do a role play with selected clients.   Have the client describe the situation and have another client play the role of the person they are disagreeing with.   Then reverse roles.   Have the client take the role of the person they are disagreeing with.   Have the group discuss whether the client could take the position of the other person.

Exercise: Do Work Sheet 20, page 78, Thinking Report on the "Entitlement Trap."

Exercise: Have clients update their MSL, page 31.

SESSION CLOSURE

The content of this session may increase client resistance, particularly when dealing with the idea that DWI behavior is based on errors in thinking.   Let clients express their views and resistance.

SESSION 8: SKILLS IN SELF-CONTROL: MANAGING STRESS AND EMOTIONS

RATIONALE AND OVERVIEW OF SESSION

Emotional **stress and anxiety** are important factors in AOD use and abuse. For the person who uses alcohol or other drugs, stress is a two-edged sword. First, stress is an important reason why people use alcohol or other drugs. We use drugs to reduce stress, to turn off unpleasant events to "not feel bad." That is only one edge of the sword. The other edge is that stress can result from the use of alcohol or other drugs. AOD related problem outcomes cause us stress and anxiety. Everyone in this program can vouch for this: a DWI arrest can be a major cause of stress. The body experiences stress following a period when we were sedated by alcohol. AOD use can produce stress.

Stress and anxiety, then, have a strong relationship to AOD use. **Stress and anxiety** and emotional discomfort can also be triggers for relapse to AOD use or into a harmful pattern of AOD use. Understanding and managing stress and its emotional syndromes of guilt, anger and depression are crucial in developing and maintaining cognitive-self control. Because of this, we will look more deeply into the issue of stress and look at how we can manage our stress responses. Here is what we want to accomplish in this session.

Lesson 11 of *DWC Level II Education* presents the basic concepts for the understanding and management of stress and emotions. This session builds on those ideas and skills. The research and literature support for this session is found in the *Level II Education* part of this *Provider's Guide* and will not be repeated. The provider is asked to review this material.

One of the main objectives of this session is to help clients understand the principles of stress management. As well, clients will look at the roots or sources of stress and evaluate themselves as to how many major stress events they have experienced.

Specific stress management coping methods are presented and practiced. In our previous sessions on developing cognitive self-control, we have had clients learn and practice *cognitive-restructuring* and *intrapersonal coping skills*. These self-control and coping skills are among the most important components of cognitive behavioral therapy in general and specifically in treating clients with AOD problems and a history of impaired driving (e.g., Dimeff & Marlatt, 1995; Freeman, et al., 1990; Goldfried, 1995; Kadden, 1999; Kaplan & Laygo, 2003; Linden, 1993; Monti et al., 1995; Monti et al, 1989; Wanberg & Milkman, 1998). This session will focus on these skills in the context of managing stress and anxiety.

Explanatory Note: In this work, stress and anxiety are used synonomously. However, stress can be viewed as a strain, pressure, force or burden that encumbers us whereas anxiety is more of an emotion or feeling of uneasiness, worry, fear, apprehension or concern we experience internally. The two words are most often used interchangeably.

▶ Start the session by having clients review their MP and see how they rated themselves on using drugs and alcohol to deal with emotional discomfort and psychological problems. *Sustained drinkers* may be more AOD dependent with respect to dealing with stress.

▶ Take five minutes and do the *CB Map Exercise*. This time, have a client choose an event that was stressful. Have the client identify the thoughts coming from the event.

▶ Then summarize the important concepts about stress and its related emotional syndromes described in *Lesson 11* of *Level II Education*. Review the four short-term cognitive structures - expectancies, appraisals, attributions and decisions and relate them to how they are used to manage stressful events. Discuss the concept of homeostasis.

▶ Next, have clients evaluate their past experiences to see if there are any significant roots or sources to their stress. *Work Sheet 21* will help in this self-evaluation. *Work Sheet 22, The Stress Ladder,* helps put clients' current stress in perspective with respect to the areas that are the most stressful for them and then decreasing down the ladder to less stressful situations in their life at this time.

▶ Next go over the steps in managing and coping with stress and anxiety. Again, the cognitive restructuring self-control skills are introduced and practiced. These skills are applied to all of the sessions that relate to self-control.

Exercise: *Work Sheet 23* gives clients an idea of the extent of stress symptoms they have experienced and will indicate if they need some individual work on stress management.

▶ Depression can be a trigger for R&R, but can also result from R&R. Help clients see that depression is one of the syndromes related to stress. *Work Sheet 24*, The *Depression Questionnaire* provides a tool for helping clients evaluate the extent of their depression.

▶ Have clients update their MSL, page 31.

SESSION CLOSURE

Keep the focus on the areas of stress and emotional discomfort. Some clients may feel the need for further work in this area. Help clients see the positive faces of anxiety, depression, anger and guilt. At the close of the session, do a round-robin exercise and have each client express a strength or skill that they feel they can use to manage stress in their lives. Remind clients to do their AOD Weekly Monitoring Chart.

SESSION 9: SKILLS IN SELF-CONTROL: RECOGNIZING AND MANAGING ANGER

RATIONALE AND OVERVIEW OF SESSION

Novaco (1978) wrote that anger is the most talked about emotion but it has been the least studied. O'Neill (1999), some 20 years later commented that "if it was studied, it was usually in conjunction with aggression or hostility rather than as an emotion in its own right" (p. 6). She then noted that this may be due to the fact that it has no formal clinical status of its own and does not have a formal diagnostic classification (e.g., in the DSM-IV, 1994), even though it is seen as a component of the post-traumatic stress disorder, borderline personality disorder and other DSM-IV disorders (O'Neill, 1999; Novaco, 1986). There is now a large group of contributors to the psychology and psychotherapy literature who point out that anger can be a major contributor to or direct cause of disturbances in emotions, thoughts and behavior and thus should have prominence in research and treatment (e.g., Beck, 1999; Eckhardt & Deffenbacher, 1995; McKay, Rogers & McKay, 1989; Novaco, 1978, 1994; O'Neill, 1999; Wanberg & Milkman, 1998; Wexler, 2000).

A robust finding in the literature is that negative emotions are major contributors to alcohol and other drug use and abuse and have been identified as primary triggers of relapse into AOD use patterns resulting in negative and harmful outcomes (Marlatt, 1985d). Cummings, Gordon, & Marlatt (1980) found that 75 percent of the relapses by alcohol and drug abuse and dependent clients were due to negative emotions, interpersonal conflict and social pressures. Anger is one of the most powerful emotions that can lead to harmful use of substances and relapse.

In our work on *Criminal Conduct and Substance Abuse Treatment* (Wanberg & Milkman, 1998, 2005), we said that criminal conduct is angry conduct and that anger drives much of the behavior of the substance abusing offender. We are taking the same position in this work. When a person's behavior hurts or potentially hurts another person, particularly when knowing this to be the case, then this is an angry act. Getting high or drunk often hurts others. This is an angry act. DWI conduct has the potential to hurt, and often does hurt others. Within this framework of thinking, impaired driving is an angry act. At first pass, most DWIOs will reject this statement. After working through their defensive posture and looking at the facts as to how much harm impaired driving does to others and the society, most DWIOs will agree with this statement.

The important issue here, however, is not that impaired driving is an angry act, but that *anger is a threat to self-control and is one of the major triggers to relapse and recidivism* (driving while impaired). Helping clients recognize and manage anger and hostility and to prevent aggressive and violent behavior stands as one of the most important parts of impaired driving treatment.

Alert: Session 8 is a prerequisite to this session. This is a no-entry for new clients.

An important part of this session is to help clients express anger in an appropriate and constructive manner - and in such a way that there is a *win-win* situation. When we talk about "expressing anger," we mean that it is communicated in such a manner that the person takes responsibility for the anger, does not blame the other person, and it is constructive. By "expressing" anger, we do not mean blowing up, "getting it off your chest" at the expense of others. The literature is relatively clear: that to get angry for the sake of getting angry and to "just feel better," is neither a short-term or long-term solution to the problems that are behind the anger. Just getting angry can actually feed anger. Our position is clearly cognitive: we identify the angry thoughts, generate self-control thinking around the anger, express the anger if it is done in a constructive and responsible way and then learn to replace angry thoughts with those that will lead to good outcomes. One may feel much better after expressing the anger in this way, but the goal is not "just to feel better." It is to resolve issues and problems and learn how to manage anger.

Here are the essential content and steps to take in implementing this Session.

▶ Have clients look at the MP to see if ratings are high on AOD use to cope with emotional discomfort, problems with the law and if there are behavioral disruptions from use. One important guideline is a high score on the *Loss of Behavioral Control* scale on the AUI (Horn, Wanberg & Foster, 1990). Then, see if anger management needs to be added to their MAP and to the client's ITP.

▶ Do the *CB Map Exercise*. Have a client choose an event.

▶ Interactively present the clues and signs of anger and look at the two kinds of external events that lead to angry thinking and that may be high-charged situations.

▶ Use an interactive approach to defining anger, hostility, aggression and violence (sources for these definitions are: Eckhardt & Deffenbacher, 1995; Novaco, 1994; O'Neill, 1999; Wanberg & Milkman, 1998).

▶ Talk about blaming, since this is seen by many experts as the basis or root of chronic anger (Perkinson, 1997).

▶ Go over the steps to managing and controlling anger, aggressive impulses and preventing violence. The main source for these steps is found in Wanberg & Milkman, 1998 (others include Donahue & Cavenagh, 2003; Eckhardt & Deffenbacher, 1995; Monti, et al., 1989; Novaco, 1978, 1994; O'Neill, 1999; Wexler, 2000).

  • First focus on enhancing anger-awareness. Begin with *Work Sheet 25* which helps clients assess what they are angry about and the thoughts related to what they are angry about.

  • Help clients understand the difference between feeling angry and the results of getting and being angry. Distinguish between destructive and constructive anger.

- Help clients learn anger and self-control techniques. Finish this part by constructing the *anger ladder* (Wexler, 2000), Worksheet 26. The purpose of the *anger ladder* is to help clients become desensitized to the high-charged anger situations or scenes and learn to use skills to manage these anger-provoking scenes. Be sure to have clients list specific skills they will use to manage those scenes. Review with clients the relaxation skills they have learned and in other sessions of this treatment protocol. Have clients engage in these relaxation exercises, such as generating a calm scene, and then have them focus on the lowest of the high-charged scene on the anger ladder. Have them then imagine a skill they will use in dealing with that scene. Move up the ladder until they addressed all of the scenes on the ladder. It is important that they discuss their response to this exercise in group and have them share whether they were successful in reducing anger and feeling confident in the skills they imagined using.

  In doing this exercise, identify clients who cannot show progress and success. For some clients, the best skill to manage a scene is to disengage or remove themselves from the scene and imagine getting calm and self-control. Ask clients if they need special help in dealing with any of their anger-scenes.

- Have clients study and reflect on their angry thoughts and make it clear that the goal is *problem solving,* which should begin when they feel the anger begin to build.

▶ **Exercise:** Go over Worksheet 27, Thinking Report on Self-Control.

▶ Have clients update their MSL, page 31.

Here are some additional exercises for this session or expanded anger management sessions.

▶ **Exercise:** What kind of things do you say to yourself when you are getting angry? What do you do to try and control what you say to yourself? Does it work? Make a list of the things people do that help themselves.

▶ **Exercise:** Have the group divide into dyads. Using examples of anger cited in the class discussion, have each group member role play a situation in which he or she demonstrates a constructive response to conflict.

▶ **Exercise:** Have clients in the group imagine a scene that arouses anger. Now lead them in practicing relaxation techniques. Have the group take slow, deep breaths. Use these words: "Take a deep breath. Hold your breath. Hold it, hold it, hold it. Now, let it go slowly through your mouth. Slowly blow out the air in your lungs. Clear your mind of your thoughts as you let go of the air. Now, tell yourself, 'I am relaxed, I feel calm, I feel relaxed.'" Repeat this three times with the group. Then, have clients do it on their own.

▶ **Caution:** When doing deep-breathing, make sure that clients do not take more than four or five deep breaths in one breathing exercise episode. Doing more than four or five in one episode could precipitate hyperventilation.

▶ **Exercise:** Have clients pick a scene that arouses anger in the client. Have them imagine the scene. Now have them practice these relaxation techniques.

- Relax by taking slow, deep breaths.

- Inhale slowly, hold your breath, count to five, and then release your breath.

- Repeat your deep breathing exercise, around four times, releasing your breath slowly.

- Now clear your mind of all thoughts, and if a thought interrupts, tell yourself, "I AM RELAXED." REPEAT THIS EXERCISE.

▶ **Exercise:** Now, have clients take another scene that brings up anger inside of them. This time, have them use self-talk to address the feelings of anger and to develop control over the anger. Use thought stopping to do this. Have clients use the other tools they have learned to manage their anger.

SESSION CLOSURE AND FURTHER ASSESSMENT

Use the unstructured portion of this session to have clients share the experiences in the session. Encourage clients to talk about their angry scenes on the *anger-ladder*. Identify clients who are still angry and feel that they still do not have self-control. These clients along with clients who have moderate to serious anger problems should be referred for more intensive anger management. Check to be sure all clients have neutralized their anger before leaving group. Be supportive.

The provider might consider utilizing an anger inventory such as *Spielberger's State Trait Anger Expression Inventory* (1988) for these clients. His two-factor anger model can be helpful in assessment. *State anger* is the existential and temporary state of emotions that comes from external events that are frustrating and that thwart one's needs and goals. *Trait anger* is more personality based, often tied into hostility and has internal etiologies.

When considering referral for further anger management, it is helpful to use some guidelines for determining appropriateness for further anger management work. O'Neill (1999) provides a list of suitability inclusion and exclusion criteria that can become a guide for referral decisions. The following are some of the criteria in her suitability inclusion list:

▶ Aggression to objects or others that is fed by anger;

▶ The person is upset about his or her anger because of loss of freedom, loss of objects or relationships;

▶ Gets easily upset by external events or triggers;

▶ Person is impatient and impulsive and this leads to reacting to triggers with anger;

▶ Low esteem; and

▶ Is motivated for help and wants treatment.

Other inclusion criteria should include (authors' list) the following:

▶ Person is impulsive and irrationally reacts to external frustrating events;

▶ There are repeated patterns of blow-ups;

▶ The person is aware that angry episodes are irrational;

▶ Inability to clearly recall the reasons or events that preceded past anger, but only remembers getting angry; and

▶ Much as the same with AOD problems and abuse, anger results in negative and harmful outcomes.

O'Neill (1999) suggests that persons who display the following may not be candidates for more concentrated anger management treatment:

▶ Show deliberate and planned, instrumental, rather than angry aggression;

▶ Do not want to change the anger pattern and in fact perceive benefits from getting angry;

▶ Involved in current and somewhat consistent or consistent use of drugs; and

▶ Have signs of psychosis, memory problems or language functioning that do not allow for self-instruction.

> Our position is clearly cognitive: we identify the angry thoughts, generate self-control thinking around the anger, express the anger if it is done in a constructive and responsible way and then learn to replace angry thoughts with those that will lead to good outcomes. The goal is not "just to feel better." It is to resolve issues and problems and learn how to manage anger.

SESSION 10: SOCIAL AND RELATIONSHIP SKILLS BUILDING: LEARNING COMMUNICATION TOOLS AND SKILLS

RATIONALE AND OVERVIEW OF SESSION

This is one of the most important of the seven sessions helping clients develop social and relationship skills. The purpose of this session is to enhance clients' self-efficacy through building the communication skills of *active sharing* and *active listening*. This session is a prerequisite to Session 11.

Many impaired driving offenders have not developed an awareness of their own and others' communication patterns and skills. They are often unable to effectively communicate to others how they feel or what they think. Or, they are unable to allow others to openly and effectively express their feelings and thoughts. They may take part in faulty automatic thinking that further allows them to ignore the problems in their personal lives and relationships.

People use alcohol or other drugs to overcome fear or anxiety that they experience when communicating with others. They may only share feelings and thoughts when "under the influence." Thus, talking about the self and sharing feelings and thoughts, will have to be learned under a new condition - being free of alcohol and other drugs or free from their comfortable drinking environment where they feel they can "communicate" with others, e.g., the bar.

Sharing thoughts and feelings and listening attentively are learned behaviors and the benefits of doing so are considerable. One way to build trust is through self-disclosure. It lets others know they are not alone in their emotions. Listening lets the other person know we are interested and helps us learn about others, the world, and ourselves.

Without adequate interpersonal skills, an individual's ability to communicate is restricted, leaving him/her without control or alternatives in certain situations. Frequently such deficits restrict the ability of the person to obtain social and emotional support from others.

SESSION CONTENT AND PRESENTATION SEQUENCE, PROCESS AND GUIDELINES

Start this session with the following exercises:

- Do the *CB Map Exercise* Work Sheet 2, page 21, having a client select an event that led to angry feelings. Also, review Work Sheet 27, this week's homework.

- Have clients review their MP to see how their high ratings might relate to problems in communicating with others. Have them update their MAP and provider update the clients' ITP. Now proceed with presenting the essential content of this session with a therapeutically interactive mode.

● **Verbal and non-verbal communication and opinions:** Present the two kinds of communications that humans engage in - *non-verbal and verbal.* The brief introduction to this topic does not do justice to the extensive literature on verbal and non-verbal communication epitomized in the seminal work of Knapp (1978) and the work of Dance (1982) who clearly distinguishes between verbal and non-verbal communication. Dealing with the topic of opinions is also important in this part of the session. It is helpful to present this material using the following exercises.

Exercise: Describe the following situation and have members discuss what they think is happening. A neighbor looks up the street and observes another neighbor holding a shovel over his head. The neighbor's wife is standing in front of him. He turns to the side, and slams the blade of the shovel on the ground. The wife puts her hands to her mouth as if to "gasp" and runs into the house. Five minutes later, a sheriff's car shows up. Give group members a few minutes to decide what they think was going on. Have them share their thoughts with the group.

After the sharing period, give the group this additional piece of information. The man was showing his wife how he had just tried to kill a rattlesnake in his backyard, but it got away. His wife called the sheriff for assistance.

This example shows how we interpret what is going on around us even if we can't hear what people are saying. Infants learn quickly to read their parents' attitudes and feelings by how they are handled when fed or diapered, by how long they are allowed to cry before someone checks to see what is the problem. No matter how we try, we cannot NOT communicate.

Exercise: Break the group into pairs. Have each in the pair take turns sharing something emotional that happened in the recent past. Have clients look for the nonverbal expressions and body language which also help tell that story: facial expressions; change in voice tone; body posture; and eye expressions. Then, when the story is completed, have the person who was listening give the other person feedback as to the nonverbal expressions that were observed.

Exercise: Have group members express the following emotions without words. Have them discuss the feelings and thoughts they had during the exercise.

ANGER   FEAR   SHAME   JOY   LOVE   SURPRISE

Exercise: Have clients identify their favorite music, food and sport. Look at how many different opinions there are.

Exercise: The same words may have different meanings. Have group members give different meaning to the words "fly" and "light." What are the different emotions associated with "fly"? With "light"?

Just as your opinions are determined by your experiences, so are the meanings of words. And if words can mean so many different things, what about the meanings of sentences and conversations? People often do not do a good job of communicating what they really want to say. It is important to try to discover what the person is thinking and feeling by watching body language and asking questions.

▶ **Present the two pathways to communication:** *Self-oriented* and *other-oriented communication*. These two paths of communication are the "bread and butter" of social and relationship skill building.

FIRST present ***self-oriented communication*** *which is active sharing involving self-disclosure and receiving feedback.* There is overwhelming evidence of the efficacy of reciprocity in self-disclosure. Based on Jourard's early hypothesis (Jourard, 1959) and continued research by him and his colleagues (e.g., Jourard & Friedman, 1970; Jourard & Resnick, 1970) and many other studies (see Cappella, 1985, p.409), self-disclosing to another person will facilitate self-disclosure in the other person. Further, partners tend to match the level of self-disclosure. Go over Figure 8, (page 106). Use these exercises to enhance the learning process.

Exercise: Have group members share a conflict they have had recently with another person. Have them describe that situation. Then, give them feedback as to how well they stuck with the *self-oriented communication*. Did they talk mostly about themselves or about the other person?

Exercise: Have each group member receive feedback from other members as to how they see him or her responding to the treatment program.

SECOND, present ***other oriented communication*** *or active listening*. Use these exercises to enhance learning both active sharing and active listening skills.

Exercise: Break the group into pairs. Then have members of each pair practice self-disclosure by talking about their thoughts and feelings. Have one member of the pair practice the skills of *active listening - open questions and reflections*. Then reverse roles. Monitor the activity. After 5 minutes, ask the partners to reverse roles for the next 5 minutes. Spend another 5 minutes discussing the experience in the group. When self-disclosing, did the person use "I" statements? Did they talk about themselves or the other person? When in the *active listening* role, did that person remain non-judgmental and not give his or her opinion? How did it feel to be the listener?

Exercise: Break up into groups of three. Again, have one share, one be the active listener and one observe. Have the observer give feedback on what he or she saw. PRACTICE...PRACTICE...PRACTICE...

- Inviting others to share with open questions and statements;
- Reflecting back what you heard them saying. It is parroting back; it is being a mirror.

▶ Go over *Work Sheets 28, 29 and 30,* homework for this coming week.

▶ Have clients update their MSL, page 31 of Workbook.

SESSION CLOSURE

Discuss the AOD Weekly Monitoring Chart. Because much of this session will be taken up with presenting the material and the exercises, take around 10 minutes for a closure rehash session.

SESSION 11: SOCIAL AND RELATIONSHIP SKILLS BUILDING: STARTING AND KEEPING A CONVERSATION GOING

RATIONALE AND OVERVIEW OF SESSION

This session builds on the foundation skills of *active listening* and *active sharing* and focuses on the skill of starting and maintaining a conversation. These are doors to communicating with those we know, to meeting new people, to buying a car, to getting a job. Sometimes people find themselves lonely and isolated because they lack confidence in developing meaningful interactions. Often, this is due to a reticence in initiating talk and interactions with others. For some, this becomes one of the reasons for using substances. Often, people who are highly anxious or who have negative feelings about themselves feel they cannot function in a social situation without a drink or a fix.

Most people can chit-chat or "shoot the breeze." However, starting and keeping a conservation going around a difficult and sensitive topic or issue may be hard. We avoid conflicts and dealing with sensitive issues. Sometimes, it is easier to approach difficult topics with a drink or two. It may not be difficult to talk with your spouse about going to the grocery store, but it may be more difficult to start a conversation about being upset that she got home late. This session is also about starting a conversation about a difficult and sensitive area.

Alert: Session 10 is a prerequisite to this session.

SESSION CONTENT AND PRESENTATION SEQUENCE, PROCESS AND GUIDELINES

The content for this session is briefly summarized along with the recommended presentation sequence and process.

▶ Start the session with: reviewing clients' *AOD Weekly Monitoring Chart;* and reviewing homework, Work Sheets 28, 29 and 30.

▶ Do the *CB Map Exercise.* Structure this exercise around an event where there was poor communication with another person.

▶ Review the basic pathways of communication: *active sharing* and *active listening.* THERE IS POWER IN COMMUNICATION. YOU FEEL THIS POWER WHEN YOU PUT THE SKILLS OF ACTIVE SHARING AND ACTIVE LISTENING TO WORK.

▶ Present the guidelines for starting and maintaining a conversation (Monti et al., 1989; Wanberg & Milkman, 1998): Emphasize that it is OK to talk about yourself. It is unselfish. Just as sharing your toys with your friends was unselfish as a child, sharing your experiences as an adult is also unselfish. Remind the group of the studies by Jourard and associates: self-disclosing facilitates self-disclosure by others.

Exercise: Have the group take turns role playing starting a conversation in these scenarios between two people:

- Two strangers at a party;

- Between two workers at coffee break, one of whom just came to work for the company; or

- Two people who see each other for the first time since high school.

Have the group discuss whether group members demonstrated the skills introduced above. Have group members practice these skills:

- Using "I" messages. Avoid using "you" messages;

- Receiving feedback from others;

- Using open-ended statements and questions; and

- Using statements to reflect back what others are saying.

Exercise: Break into pairs and have client practice starting a conversation.

▶ Present and discuss the skills and steps in starting a **difficult conversation** around a sensitive and difficult area. **Carefully go over these skills**. *Do Work Sheet 31.*

Exercise: In the whole group, have someone volunteer to role play starting a difficult conversation with someone close to him/her. Have another group member play the role of the other person. Use the role-reversal technique to have the client assume the role of the person with whom he or she wants to start the conversation. Afterwards, have the group evaluate whether the group member followed the steps of starting a conversation around a difficult or sensitive subject.

▶ Have the group discuss which step is most difficult to achieve when starting a conversation around a difficult or sensitive topic, e.g., the approach, setting the stage, sticking to the point, etc.

▶ Have clients update their MSL, page 31.

SESSION CLOSURE

First, have clients share their AOD monitoring they did this week. Then do an unstructured closure group. Let people share areas of concern whether they are related to the topic or not. This is giving them practice in starting a conversation. Remind group of the AOD Use Weekly Monitoring Chart for the coming week.

SESSION 12: SOCIAL AND RELATIONSHIP SKILLS BUILDING: GIVING AND RECEIVING POSITIVE REINFORCEMENT - PRAISE

RATIONALE AND OVERVIEW OF SESSION

Building on our communication skills platform, we will now learn and practice the social skill of *giving and receiving positive reinforcement or praise*. One specific way that we reinforce (strengthen) the positive features of other people is through giving and receiving compliments. Successful relationships depend on this reinforcement process - and more specifically, an atmosphere of give and take where positive experiences are shared and strengthened. Our chances of receiving in a relationship are increased when we give in that relationship. Our chances of giving in a relationship are increased when we receive something from that relationship. We call this the *quid pro quo* — something for something — of relationships. It is, therefore, important that people learn both to give and accept positive reinforcement. This is the purpose of this session.

Before proceeding with this session, it is helpful to keep in mind the three stages of skill development in cognitive behavior learning and change provided to us by Meichenbaum (1975, 1993a, 1993b) and which has been the main principle that has structured our sessions.

- Education stage or skill learning.

- Skill acquisition or rehearsal.

- Application.

Alert: Skills learned in this session are based on the skills of active listening and active sharing. Review these skills for the benefit of new clients.

SESSION CONTENT AND PRESENTATION SEQUENCE, PROCESS AND GUIDELINES

The material in this session is crisp and to the point. Yet time should be given to rehearsal and practice in giving and receiving compliments. An important discovery for clients will be that giving compliments is much easier than receiving them. Here are the content and guidelines for presenting this session.

- First review the clients' work on their *AOD Weekly Monitoring Chart.*

- Second, do the *CB Map Exercise.* Have the event be discussing a difficult or sensitive topic with another person.

▶ Have clients review their MP to see if any of their self-ratings are relevant to this session. For example, clients who rated themselves high on the scales of *Solo or Use by Yourself, Cope with Social Discomfort, Cope With Relationships, Loss of Self-Importance, and Social Relationship Problems* may be struggling with how to give and receive positive reinforcement.

▶ Review the skills of active listening and active sharing.

▶ Present the differences between positive reinforcement or praise and giving thanks or appreciation. Thanks focuses on what people have done for you; positive reinforcement focuses on the positive behavior of other people for which you have not necessarily received any benefits.

▶ Present the concepts related to giving praise and positive reinforcement. Go over Work Sheet 32, Practice giving compliments, homework for next week.

▶ Present the concepts related to receiving praise and positive reinforcement. Go over Work Sheet 33, Practice receiving compliments, homework for next week.

▶ Do the following exercises to give clients opportunity for skill acquisition and training.

Exercise: Using the round robin wagon wheel technique, have clients practice giving and receiving praise and compliments. Most members of the group will have at least a fair knowledge of each other. Have clients use this knowledge when practicing giving and receiving positive reinforcement. Have group members share whether it was more difficult to give or receive praise and positive reinforcement.

Exercise: Form groups of threes. Have two members of the small group practice giving and receiving positive reinforcement and praise and the third person observe. Give example situations such as between friends, within the family, or a companion at work. Have the observer give feedback. Have observer practice compliments if the pair did well. Rotate roles. Have them share how it felt receiving and giving compliments. Was it unnatural or easy? Did their responses agree with their reported feelings? Were the compliments sincere or insincere? What were the consequences?

▶ **Homework:** As homework, have clients complete *Work Sheet 34*, a *Thinking Report* around an opportunity to praise or compliment another person. If clients do not finish the homework, have them complete it in the next session.

▶ Have clients update their MSL, page 31.

SESSION CLOSURE

The group can be unstructured, however, as group members share issues and concerns, tie the concepts of giving and receiving positive reinforcement into the content and process of the group as much as possible. REMEMBER TO PRAISE THE GROUP FOR ITS GOOD WORK. Providers are the client's best role models.

SESSION 13: SOCIAL AND RELATIONSHIP SKILLS BUILDING: LEARNING PROBLEM SOLVING

RATIONALE AND OVERVIEW OF SESSION

We could conclude that impaired drivers are not good problem solvers. If they were, they would have solved the problem of placing themselves in a circumstance that led to impaired driving. One could argue that the impaired driver is too intoxicated to solve problems. For the very intoxicated person, that may be true. Yet, for every impaired driver, there was a time period **prior** to intoxication or impairment, and **prior** to being so AOD affected, that rational decision making and problem solving were possible. The fact is, the impaired driver did not find a solution to the problem of being in a circumstance that led to impaired driving.

Here is another fact. Although some people are better problem solvers than others, everyone has used the skills of problem solving at one time or another, since every day we are faced with problems that we have to solve. This is true with impaired drivers. They also have solved problems in their lives. They have used the basic skills of problem solving. Given this logic, then we conclude that involvement in impaired driving is more than just the failure to solve the problem of being in a circumstance that led to impaired driving. Whatever contributes to impaired driving, we want to be sure that it is not due to a lack of having or applying the skills of problem solving. The purpose of this session is to provide clients with the skills of problem solving and apply those skills to not only preventing recidivism, but in living a more responsible life.

A problem is a behavior, situation, or circumstance that presents uncertainty or causes difficulty. The difficulty might boil down to not getting your way in a situation, not being sure what is expected of you, rebelling against custom or the law, conflict with another person over how things should be done, a difference between your own goal and the goal of someone close to you or trying to find someone or something. Usually, there is a goal attached to our problem.

John Dewey became the father of the problem solving method when he proposed a series of steps in reflective thinking (1910). Since then, theorists have developed many refinements of that sequence. He came up with a six-stage protocol that came from his observations of how most people confront problems or questions of choice of solutions. We have modified these steps, using a variety of sources (King et al., 1994; Monti et al., 1989, 2001; Myers & Myers, 1980; Nezu, Nezu & Lombardo, 2003; Smith & Meyers, 1995; Wanberg & Milkman, 1998).

Very basic to being a good problem solver is being able to identify problems or situations that are going to cause us a problem (Ross, et al. 1986). In essence, good problem solvers know when they have a problem. This is often a major barrier for substance abusers. They often are unable to see or acknowledge that they have a problem.

Here are the steps in presenting this session. As with all of the sessions in this treatment protocol, the core learning material is in the Participant's Workbook.

▶ Start with the *CB Map Exercise* and have the event represent receiving a compliment or positive reinforcement.

▶ Review *Work Sheets 32 and 33* from Session 12. Even though clients might have done these in group, still review them. Talk about how giving and receiving compliments and positive reinforcement went during the past week.

▶ Review *Work Sheet 34, the Thinking Report* on a situation of giving praise or positive reinforcement.

▶ Go over the introductory material for this session in the *Participant's Workbook*. Then, using interactive methods, present the topic What is a Problem? to the group.

▶ Go over the five steps of problem solving and the problem solving cycle, page 127 of Workbook. Do *Work Sheet 35* and have one or two clients present their work.

▶ Present the topics of *Learning to Apply Different Choices* and *How Do We Know We Have A Problem?* Have clients learn to "think outside" the box.

▶ Finally, present and discuss how to make your problem solving solution focused, using Fisher and Ury's (1981) key steps.

▶ A problem may only be in our thinking. That is the best place where we can solve our problem. We solve it in our head before it takes place in our actions.

Exercise: Present the following problem having clients apply the steps of problem solving. John would like to go out with his friend Cliff. Cliff always drinks. This means that John will most likely drink. When he goes out and drinks with Cliff, he usually puts himself at risk of getting into trouble. John has committed himself to not drinking since he is now attending a DWI treatment program. **Note:** the last piece of information is intentionally left out of the Participant's Workbook. Introduce that piece of information only after the group has tried to solve the problem about John's dilemma. Have the group apply the problem solving steps. Can this can be solved at the thinking level? After the group has come up with a consensus solution, introduce the fact that John is in a DWI therapy program. How does that change the goals, the solution, the outcome?

Exercise: Have clients discuss how the model for *Cognitive Behavioral Change — Figure 1*, page 14, in *Participant's Workbook* — is related to the five steps of problem solving. Where do automatic thoughts or thought habits fit into the steps of problem solving?

Exercise: In the total group, have clients apply the steps of problem solving to these scenarios.

- **Scenario one:** You are working in your yard on your day off. You have had four beers. The school calls and informs you that your son has been injured in football practice and he needs to be taken to the doctor. Your wife is working across town and can't pick him up. What do you do? Identify all of the problems in this scenario. Have a client write all of the problems on a flip chart.

- **Scenario two:** You are preparing dinner for your husband's boss and his wife. You have had two glasses of wine. You are about to make the pies when you discover you have no sugar. There is no one at home to go to the store for you. Your husband thinks you have stopped drinking because you are still on probation for getting a DWI. You don't want him to know you have been drinking. What do you do? Spend time brainstorming solutions. Write them on a flip chart.

Exercise: Do Work Sheet 36, Thinking Report in a group. Take some problem and do a re-thinking report. Have clients identify the different thoughts that lead to a different outcome - solution - for the problem. Help clients look at the underlying beliefs that led to the thoughts that led to the outcomes. Remind clients of the mantra: **Self-control leads to good outcomes.**

▶ Spend time updating and reviewing the MSL.

SESSION CLOSURE

Make this an unstructured group around clients sharing past problems clients have had that were made worse because they did not apply good problem solving skills. If clients bring up some emotional and unresolved issues that are not related to the topic, use good therapeutic skills to address those issues. In addressing the client issues that arise in group, use the problem-focused and solution-focused therapy approach. Remind clients to do the *AOD Weekly Monitoring Chart*.

SESSION 14: SOCIAL AND RELATIONSHIP SKILLS BUILDING: ASSERTIVENESS SKILLS DEVELOPMENT

RATIONALE AND OVERVIEW OF SESSION

We channel a lot of energy into getting our needs met. But getting our needs met and still being responsible to others and our community requires certain skills. Remember, the major goal of the treatment of impaired driving offenders is to help clients to be responsible to others and the community. The sessions on giving and receiving positive reinforcement and problem solving are directed at building strategies for responsible living. This session takes a further step in that direction. Assertiveness skill building will help clients get their needs met within the framework of responsibility - of not being harmful but in fact, being helpful to others to get their needs met. We want to convey to clients that using appropriate assertive skills leads to responsible behavior towards others and the community. Session 14 is a prerequisite to Session 15.

Assertiveness training is a premier component of most AOD treatment programs. It is recognized as an important skill to form positive and productive relationships with others and to refuse involvement in behaviors that lead to bad outcomes. The seminal works in this field were done by Alberti and Emmons (1995) whose book *Your Perfect Right* provided the key principles of assertiveness behavior and Fisher and Ury (1981), *Getting to a Yes: Negotiating Agreement Without Giving In.* These and the work of Wanberg and Milkman (1998, 2005) provided the basic guidelines for this session.

This session contrasts three ways that people try to solve problems, deal with conflicts and get their needs met that often lead to bad outcomes: 1) avoidance (flight); 2) aggression (fight); 3) being passive-aggressive (fake). These approaches most often results in the outcome where neither party gets their needs met, or one gets their needs met at the expense of the other. The outcomes are either lose-lose or win-lose. These styles are contrasted with the assertive style which is a win-win approach to need fulfillment and problem solving and is basic to responsible living. This session will help clients to identify thoughts that lead to the three counterproductive ways to get their needs met. Tie the cognitive restructuring model into the session content.

SESSION CONTENT AND PRESENTATION SEQUENCE, PROCESS AND GUIDELINES

Start this session by having clients review their MP and MAP. Clients who rate themselves high on AOD use benefits or AOD use to cope with social and relationship discomforts will have high needs for improving on their assertiveness skills.

> ▶ **Exercise:** Do the *CB Map Exercise* and have the event represent a situation of having to solve an important problem.

- Present interactively the three ways of getting needs met that are counterproductive in building healthy relationships: flight, fight and fake.

- Discuss the healthy relationship choice - assertiveness or fair. Then, discuss the 10 ways of being assertive. Have clients check those that they do easily. Then use these exercises.

  Exercise: Have clients do the exercise in the *Participant's Workbook* of taking off Friday afternoon to attend your son's football game. Have group members play the role of the four ways to handle this problem - fight, fake, flight or fair. Have clients apply the 10 key ways of being assertive.

  Exercise: Have clients role play each of the four scenarios in the *Participant's Workbook.*

  - Boss promising you a bonus.

  - Store claims the bill you paid is delinquent.

  - An appliance you bought at full price is now half price.

  - A friend wants you to drive him home when you both have had too much to drink.

  Each time, use all four methods to solve the problem. When using the assertive role, point out the 10 key ways of being assertive. Have clients identify how effective each of the different methods were in resolving the problem.

  Exercise: Have clients choose a real situation to role play. Keep the focus on the assertive style. Have the group give feedback and suggestions regarding how the assertive character could have achieved the desired outcome.

- In class do *Work Sheets 37, a Thinking Report* on a situation where clients could have been assertive but were not and then *Work Sheet 38, a Re-Thinking Report* as to how that situation could have been approached in an assertive way.

- Clients update their MSL.

- Remind clients to do their AOD Weekly Monitoring Chart.

SESSION CLOSURE

Close this session with an unstructured format. Often, sessions on assertiveness tend to confront people with their failures. Clients should be made to feel that whatever mistakes they have made in the past, they have the opportunity for change and growth. Remind clients to do the AOD monitoring chart.

SESSION 15: SOCIAL AND RELATIONSHIP SKILLS BUILDING: LEARNING AND PRACTICING REFUSAL SKILLS

RATIONALE AND OVERVIEW OF SESSION

An important part of preventing relapse and recidivism is recognizing and managing high-risk exposures e.g., high-risk situations and high-risk thinking. One high-risk situation is the pressure from peers to drink, particularly in social settings or bars away from home - when driving is involved. When clients, who are committed to making changes in their AOD use to prevent relapse and recidivism, are confronted with pressure from peers to drink or be exposed to high-risk situations for recidivism, then both skills in changing thinking and in managing relationships are needed. Refusal skills are part of this social skill armament.

Learning to "just say no" to the pressure to use or the pressure to be exposed to situations that are high-risk for recidivism is usually not sufficient in the early stages of change. Along with a commitment to not engage in high-risk thinking and situations, the client must be assertive enough to act on that decision. *An important part of refusal is assertiveness.* Difficult situations will still arise, even if the client has been successful in avoiding old companions and the peer pressure they exert. When the bar has become the client's "second home," it makes refusal more difficult. People who are unaware of a person's problem may pressure the person into high-risk situations. Some who are aware could be thoughtless and even try to force the issue. Different situations will present different difficulties. Practice in how to refuse invitations to relapse will be part of this session in refusal skills (Monti et al., 1989; Kadden et al., 1992; Wanberg & Milkman, 1998).

It is important for the Provider to be sensitive to cultural differences in "saying no." Be cautious that eye contact and body language as well as type and degree of assertiveness may vary across cultural groups. It is suggested that the Provider re-read the chapter on *Understanding and Enhancing Cultural Competence.*

Alert: Session 14 is a prerequisite to this session.

SESSION CONTENT AND PRESENTATION SEQUENCE, PROCESS AND GUIDELINES

Here are the steps to follow in presenting the content of this session. Session 14 is a prerequisite to this session. It is no-entry for new clients.

- ▶ Review MP so clients can identify their risks in the area of peer pressure to engage in high-risks situations: high ratings on *convivial or gregarious drinking, or drinking for social benefits.* Have clients update their MAP.

- ▶ **Exercise:** Do the *CB Map Exercise* and have the event represent a situation where the outcome behavior of a client was aggressive but non-violent.

- Review the Thinking and Rethinking reports that were done last session, Work Sheets 37 and 38.

- Go over the introduction and objective of session.

- Review the concepts of *high-risk situations, high-risk thinking, relapse and recidivism.*

- Review the key points in being assertive that were covered in the last session. Have clients share what they remember about the last group. If necessary, do some more role playing around being assertive. ASSERTIVENESS IS THE KEY TO REFUSAL.

- Present the two sections on peer pressure. Peer pressure is a major part of DWI involvement.

- Carefully go over the nine points of how to practice refusal.

  Exercise: Do the exercise in the *Participant's Workbook* - practice the nine refusal skills in different situations that clients can identify where they are expected or pressured to drink where that situation is high-risk for relapse and a setup for recidivism.

- Do *Work Sheet 39* which involves identifying situations where it is difficult for the client to refuse AOD use or getting into a pattern of AOD problem outcomes and which are setups for DWI behavior.

  Exercise: Do *Work Sheet 40* which helps clients to identify situations and thoughts that led to saying yes to drinking or using drugs. Clients are then asked to merge the cognitive with the behavioral, and identify the **thought** that led to the "yes" and the actual statement of consent or acquiescence. Then, clients are asked to change their thoughts that would lead to a "no" response. This is a difficult work sheet and clients will need help in completing it.

- Have clients update their MSL, page 31.

- Have clients do their weekly AOD Monitoring Chart.

- Challenge clients to practice assertiveness skills this next week.

SESSION CLOSURE

The content in this session is crisp but the opportunities for interactive therapeutic involvement are enormous. Give clients a good 30 minutes of unstructured processing time. **Have clients invite their significant other or intimate partner to *Session 16*.**

SESSION 16: SOCIAL AND RELATIONSHIP SKILLS BUILDING: DEVELOPING AND KEEPING INTIMATE AND CLOSE RELATIONSHIPS

RATIONALE AND OVERVIEW OF SESSION

One of the most important factors that interact with AOD problem use is *conflict in close and intimate relationships.* This is also one of the major triggers for relapse (Marlatt, 1985b). Many persons who have had AOD problems report problems in relationships and intimacy. This session is based on the core ideas and concepts in *Lesson 12 of DWC Level II Education.* The goal of this session is to enhance the ability of clients to continue to develop and maintain healthy close and intimate relationships. Clients' significant others are invited to this session.

SESSION CONTENT AND PRESENTATION SEQUENCE, PROCESS AND GUIDELINES

This session will involve a review of concepts and ideas learned in previous lessons and sessions. This review is important because the intimate partners and guests need to have a working knowledge of these concepts in order to benefit from this session. In reviewing these ideas, use the interactive-teaching approach. Also, make the guests feel welcome. Help those who do not have guests to participate fully in the session.

> ▶ Start by reviewing last session's material around high-risk "difficult to refuse" situations and the refusal skills learned in that session. Have clients review their MP and those scales pertinent to this session, which include:
>
>   • **Convivial or Gregarious use;**
>
>   • **Benefits of AOD Use:** *Cope with Relationships;*
>
>   • **Negative Consequences from Use:** *Behavioral Disruption from Use and Social Irresponsibility;*
>
>   • **Thinking, Feelings and Attitude Patterns** that tend to prevent healthy **intimacy,** e.g., *Blame Others;* and
>
>   • **Adult Problems** such as *Marital-Family Problems, Social-Relationship Problems.*
>
> ▶ Do the *CB Map Exercise* and have one client present a situation where a client was faced with pressure to drink and where there was a high-risk of driving and drinking.
>
> ▶ Review the conflict between the *need for closeness* (intimacy) and the *need for separateness* (individuality).
>
> **Exercise:** Do a group round robin and have clients and their guests share a closeness activity that they enjoy; then repeat the round robin and have clients share a separateness activity.

- Present the introduction and session objectives.

- Review the core communication skills of active sharing and active listening.

  Exercise: Have veteran group members demonstrate these two skills. Point out that these are seasoned members of the group who know how to use these skills.

- Present the 10 tips for developing and keeping healthy intimacy. Spend time on each tip and ask clients and guests to share how they currently follow the idea, e.g., after presenting the concept of being proactive in relationships, have couples and clients share how they might do this or how they in fact do this in their relationship.

- Spend time on **Keeping the Balance** by briefly presenting the *stages of intimacy model:* relationship enmeshment, detachment and balance presented on page 150 of the *Workbook.*

  Exercise: Do *Work Sheet 41* which has clients and their guests use the overlapping circles to draw their relationship.

  Exercise: Do *Work Sheet 42, Looking at your Closeness and Separateness Needs.*

- **Practicing active sharing and active listening.**

  Exercise: Have clients pair off with their intimate partners or guests and have them practice these skills. Pair clients without guests with each other.

- Have clients update their MSL and their mastery levels.

SESSION CLOSURE

For the closing group, do the following exercise. After the exercise, re-form into the total group for a few minutes for a brief closing session. Remind clients to do their AOD Weekly Monitoring Chart.

Exercise: Spend most of the closing process group time in this exercise, also described in the *Participant's Workbook.* First, have each person in the group give feedback to one other person on ways that other person has made self-improvement and change. Then have the group break into pairs with their intimate partners and just take time to talk and share whatever comes to their mind. Pair clients who do not have a guest and have each client in that pair share with the other client as if that other client were his/her significant other. The provider should make sure that couples leave on a positive note. If serious conflicts are noted in couples, spend some individual time with them and discern if they may need additional counseling.

SESSION 17: STRENGTHENING RECIDIVISM AND RELAPSE PREVENTION SKILLS

RATIONALE AND OVERVIEW OF SESSION

Marlatt and Gordon's classic work on *relapse prevention* caused a major paradigm shift in the treatment of persons with alcohol and other substance use problems. Prior to the 1980s, treatment programs would not realistically address the issue of relapse. In many treatment programs, it was a "taboo" subject. If you talk about it, "it might happen." The reality was that it did happen. Research in the late 1960s and 1970s clearly indicated from 60 to 80 percent of the clients went back to do some drinking within one year of coming out of treatment programs (see Wanberg & Milkman, 1998, and *Chapter 8 of Section 1* for a summary of relapse findings). Many of those who went back to some drinking experienced *full relapse* - returning to the same or similar pre-treatment problem outcome patterns.

> Each day clients prevent relapse and recidivism they become stronger. The patterns of living AOD problem free and free from impaired driving behavior become reinforced. It is important that clients understand that relapse and recidivism prevention is based on the use of self-control and relationship skills.

Marlatt concluded from these "sobering" findings that relapse was a reality that needed to be addressed within a formal treatment model. His early work and investigations in the 1970s and early 1980s (e.g., Marlatt, 1978, 1979, 1982) set the stage for his and Gordon's seminal work that produced the shift in treatment to address relapse and build *relapse prevention* (RP) approaches using *social learning and cognitive-behavioral theory* as the platform for the RP model. Today, with variations and modifications, most RP programs are modeled after the Marlatt approach.

The same concerns regarding relapse and substance abuse also surfaced with offenders in the criminal justice system. Recidivism rates were similar to the relapse rates. About 65 to 70 percent of the offenders in the criminal justice system reoffended. Within the DWI population, it was around 35 to 40 percent. The seminal work of Andrews and Bonta (1994, 2003) makes it very clear that, whatever the role of punishment and sanctioning is in the society, they do not prevent recidivism, but actually, increase rates of recidivism. They concluded that the evidence suggests that clinically relevant interventions involving treatment services have the best promise for reducing recidivism rather than interventions based only on criminal sanctions (Andrews & Bonta, 1994, 2003).

A thorough search of the relapse and recidivism literature (Wanberg & Milkman, 1998, 2005) showed striking similarities between relapse and recidivism - the process, the outcome rates, the triggers related to high-risk thinking and situation. Thus, using the Marlatt (1985d) model, Wanberg and Milkman (1998) developed a model for recidivism based on the essential concepts of relapse and relapse prevention. This model was originally developed for non-DWI criminal justice clients and in the current work has been enhanced and modified to fit the driving while impaired offender (DWIO).

This model has become the basis of the *Driving With CARE* education and treatment protocols. *Figure 7*, page 256, above summarizes the relapse and recidivism (R&R) pathways. *Figure 8* below provides the provides R&R prevention pathway (*Figure 10, page 160,* in the *DWC Therapy Participant's Workbook*).

Any viable education and treatment protocol for the DWIO must address both *recidivism and relapse prevention.* The approaches for the DWIO in the *Driving With CARE* education and treatment protocols build on the Marlatt model and on the adaptations of those models by Wanberg & Milkman (1998) in their work *Criminal Conduct and Substance Abuse Treatment: Strategies for Self-Improvement and Change.* For the current work further adaptation and refinements have been made to fit the education and treatment needs of the DWIO. As shown in Chapter 11, it is important that the client understand that the *erosion process* begins with a *perceived inability to cope,* i.e., *decreased self-efficacy.* The probability of *relapse and recidivism* - through the pathway of *initial lapse and the rule violation effect* - is significantly increased. See *Chaper 11, Figures 11.4, 11.5, 11.6 and 11.7.*

This and the next session will focus specifically on relapse and recidivism (R&R) and R&R prevention (R&RP). When presenting R&R and R&RP to DWI clients, it must be kept clearly in mind that clients may choose a non-abstinent goal of relapse prevention or the goal of not relapsing back into a pattern of harmful and disruptive use. Providers should review Lesson 8 and 9 of *Level II Education* before presenting their session. Several key principles have guided our treatment of these two areas.

▶ There are two concepts of relapse that provide clients guidelines when setting their relapse prevention goal:

- To never allow alcohol or other drugs to cause another problem in the client's life or to prevent return to a pattern of harmful use to self or to others; or

- To remain abstinent from the use of alcohol or other drugs.

▶ The distinction is made between the process of relapse, a lapse and a full relapse.

- Clients are into **relapse** when they engage in *high-risk exposures - high-risk situations* or *high-risk thinking* that has led to past problems with AOD use or, if the goal is abstinence, has led to any AOD use.

- A **lapse** is defined as an episode of AOD use or an episode of use that caused another AOD related problem.

- **Full relapse** is when clients once again become involved in a pattern of harmful and disruptive AOD use.

▶ There are two fundamental concepts of recidivism that we have asked clients to consider as the basis of their recidivism prevention goal:

- To never drive with a BAC beyond legal limits or while under the influence of other drugs - which is society's recidivism prevention goal; or

- To adopt a zero tolerance-zero risk goal of never driving with any alcohol or other drugs in the system.

- We distinguish between *being into recidivism* and *full recidivism*. The person is into recidivism when engaging in high-risk situations or high-risk thinking that has led to impaired driving behavior in the past. Full recidivism is the actual involvement in impaired driving.

- Encourage the client to adopt the *zero tolerance-zero risk* goal.

- It is the clients' decision as to which goals they choose, however, the provider is committed to helping the client discover important information that will help make this decision, e.g., clients' level of *AOD use problem severity level*.

- Some clients are at greater risk for relapse into a severe pattern of AOD use and at greater risk for recidivism.

- Relapse and recidivism steps and processes are very similar and they have similar features, e.g., prevention for both represents managing high-risk thinking and high-risk situations, both are an erosion process and occur gradually.

- Even though similar, here are some differences. A person can relapse without engaging in DWI recidivism. Providers must take a *zero-tolerance* approach to legal recidivism but there can be tolerance to relapse.

- The most appropriate model for teaching relapse and recidivism is through the *cognitive-behavioral* model of learning and change.

- An education or treatment program protocol for DWIOs must have a well integrated relapse and recidivism prevention program, and the path of all lessons or sessions in the protocol must lead towards relapse and recidivism prevention.

Each day clients prevent relapse and recidivism they become stronger. The patterns of living AOD problem free and free from impaired driving behavior become reinforced. Yet, it is important that clients understand that R&RP is based on the use of *self-control and relationship skills*. Whether clients use these skills depend on whether they are in the *commitment stage of change*. These R&RP patterns become strengthened when clients take *ownership* of their change.

SESSION CONTENT AND PRESENTATION SEQUENCE, PROCESS AND GUIDELINES

Clients at this point will have met many relapse and recidivism (R&R) challenges and many opportunities to practice their relapse and recidivism prevention (R&RP) skills. The purpose of this session will be a review of the basic concepts of R&R and R&RP, review the R&R map (*Figure 9* in the *Participant's Workbook*) and the R&RP map (*Figure 10* in the *Participant's Workbook*). Much of the session should be devoted to having clients apply this map to their situation. We will work on helping clients identify high-risk thoughts and high-risk situations for R&R and identify thinking and action skills for R&RP. This session is presented in the following sequence.

▶ Review the AOD Weekly Monitoring Chart.

▶ **Exercise:** Do the *CB Map Exercise* and have the event represent a situation where a client wanted to get close to his/her intimate partner but felt pushed away.

▶ Have clients review their MP and MAP. High ratings on the *quantity/frequency* scales, the *gregarious drinking* pattern, and the *negative consequence* scales portend high risk for relapse and high ratings on the *impaired driving scales* of the MP portend high risk for recidivism.

▶ Review the key concept related to *recidivism* and have clients list their high risk thinking and high-risk situation for recidivism on *Work Sheet 43*.

▶ Review the key concept related to *relapse* and have clients list their high-risk thinking and high-risk situation for relapse on *Work Sheet 44*.

▶ Review the concept of *erosion* as it applies to both relapse and recidivism. The following metaphor is often helpful in explaining RR erosion.

  • RR erosion is much like soil erosion which is a gradual wearing away of the top soil that has the power to produce rich and healthy crops. It is often hidden and difficult to see. It takes place over a long period of time. The same is true in the process of relapse and recidivism. There is a gradual wearing away of the rich resources of the mind. It is gradual and may take place over long periods of time. Sometimes, it takes a year or two before this gradual wearing away leads to a full relapse of returning to harmful and destructive patterns of AOD use, or full recidivism, driving while impaired.

  • The farmer prevents erosion with proper care of the land. He builds terraces or rows of soil which are barriers to the water wearing away the top soil. Crops are planted around the hills so as to prevent rains from washing away the soil. There is the continual adding of soil food or fertilizer to refresh and build up the soil. The same is true with our lives. We need to build good mental and action defenses against high-risk situations and thinking to prevent the erosion process. These skills prevent us from placing ourselves in high-risk situations or becoming overcome with high-risk thinking. We refresh ourselves with healthy friends and positive activities.

▶ Go over the R&R warning signs, triggers or high-risk exposures. Here are some additional warning signs to share with clients.

  • *Changes in attitudes:* from positive to negative.

  • *Changes in thoughts:* from self-confidence to self-weakness.

  • *Changes in emotions and moods:* from an up and hopeful mood to depressed mood, from a calm to an anxious mood.

  • *Changes in actions:* from activities not involving alcohol or other drugs to activities that are AOD involved.

▶ **Exercise:** Do Work Sheet 45, situations that trigger relapse.

▶ Present the Pathways to R&R, Figure 9 of the Workbook, page 159.

- Present the process and skills of relapse and recidivism prevention, *Figure 10* in the *Workbook,* page 160 and *Figure 8* on page 332 below. The provider should review the session on relapse and recidivism prevention in Chapter 11, particularly Figures 11.4, 11.5, 11.6 and 11.7. Go over the concepts of:

  - expected outcomes or expectancy;

  - self-efficacy or self-mastery; and

  - the rule violation effect.

  Discussion: Use the **MAP** metaphor. Whereas we can all become lost, the map keeps us on course. The critical signs are high risk situations, feelings and thoughts, underlying attitudes and beliefs. *Figure 8* below is such a map.

  Exercise: Complete *Work Sheets 46 and 47* which involves making a list of R&RP thinking and action skills.

- Have clients do a Thinking Report on a high-risk situation for R&R, Work Sheet 48.

- Update the MSL.

- Remind clients to do their AOD Weekly Monitoring Chart.

SESSION CLOSURE

Because of the amount of material to cover, the closure session may have to be brief. Remind clients to do the AOD Weekly Chart. Do a round robin closure exercise by having clients share their relapse and recidivism goals and how they see themselves meeting that goal. Have clients identify how they fit the pathways to R&R and R&RP in *Figure 8* below.

We go beyond helping clients develop and apply the skills and strategies to manage high-risk thinking and situations. For long-term maintenance and ownership of change, we help clients to create a stable and on-going lifestyle balance. Clients need a generalized ability to deal with stress and cope with high-risk thoughts and situations.

FIGURE 8

Cognitive-behavioral map for relapse and recidivism PREVENTION.

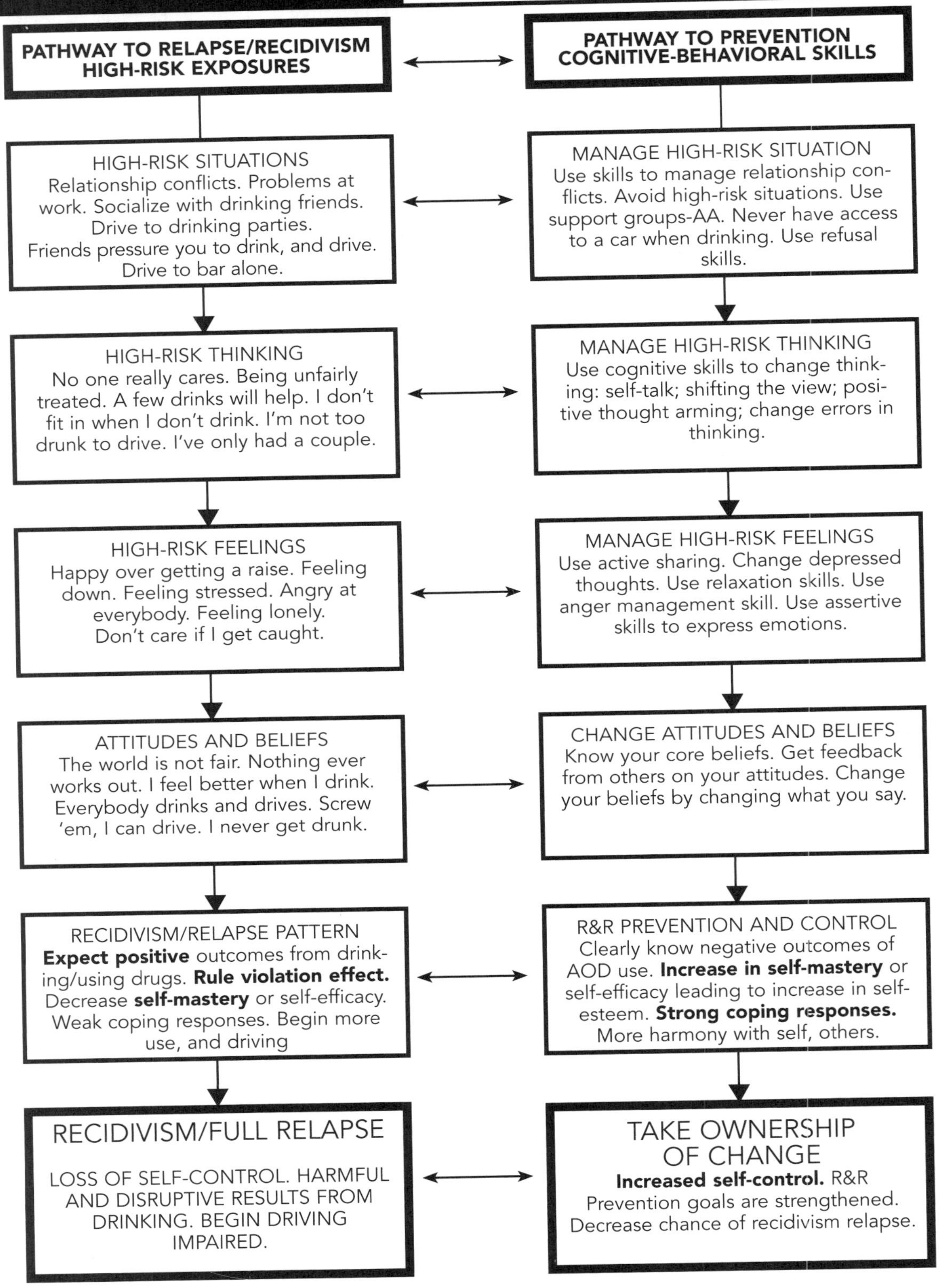

PATHWAY TO RELAPSE/RECIDIVISM HIGH-RISK EXPOSURES	⟷	PATHWAY TO PREVENTION COGNITIVE-BEHAVIORAL SKILLS
HIGH-RISK SITUATIONS Relationship conflicts. Problems at work. Socialize with drinking friends. Drive to drinking parties. Friends pressure you to drink, and drive. Drive to bar alone.	⟷	**MANAGE HIGH-RISK SITUATION** Use skills to manage relationship conflicts. Avoid high-risk situations. Use support groups-AA. Never have access to a car when drinking. Use refusal skills.
HIGH-RISK THINKING No one really cares. Being unfairly treated. A few drinks will help. I don't fit in when I don't drink. I'm not too drunk to drive. I've only had a couple.	⟷	**MANAGE HIGH-RISK THINKING** Use cognitive skills to change thinking: self-talk; shifting the view; positive thought arming; change errors in thinking.
HIGH-RISK FEELINGS Happy over getting a raise. Feeling down. Feeling stressed. Angry at everybody. Feeling lonely. Don't care if I get caught.	⟷	**MANAGE HIGH-RISK FEELINGS** Use active sharing. Change depressed thoughts. Use relaxation skills. Use anger management skill. Use assertive skills to express emotions.
ATTITUDES AND BELIEFS The world is not fair. Nothing ever works out. I feel better when I drink. Everybody drinks and drives. Screw 'em, I can drive. I never get drunk.	⟷	**CHANGE ATTITUDES AND BELIEFS** Know your core beliefs. Get feedback from others on your attitudes. Change your beliefs by changing what you say.
RECIDIVISM/RELAPSE PATTERN **Expect positive** outcomes from drinking/using drugs. **Rule violation effect.** Decrease **self-mastery** or self-efficacy. Weak coping responses. Begin more use, and driving	⟷	**R&R PREVENTION AND CONTROL** Clearly know negative outcomes of AOD use. **Increase in self-mastery** or self-efficacy leading to increase in self-esteem. **Strong coping responses.** More harmony with self, others.
RECIDIVISM/FULL RELAPSE LOSS OF SELF-CONTROL. HARMFUL AND DISRUPTIVE RESULTS FROM DRINKING. BEGIN DRIVING IMPAIRED.	⟷	**TAKE OWNERSHIP OF CHANGE** **Increased self-control.** R&R Prevention goals are strengthened. Decrease chance of recidivism relapse.

Adapted with permission from G.H. Marlatt, 1985, Relapse Prevention: Theoretical rationale and overview. In G.A. Marlatt, & J.R. Gordon (Eds.), Relapse Prevention: Maintenance Strategies in the treatment of addictive behaviors (p. 38), Guilford Press.

SESSION 18: RELAPSE AND RECIDIVISM: YOUR RELAPSE AND RECIDIVISM PREVENTION PLAN AND LIFESTYLE BALANCE

RATIONALE AND OVERVIEW OF SESSION

The main purpose of this session is to reinforce the progress clients have made in the R & RP area and to enhance the knowledge and skills to help clients take ownership of the changes they have made. This session will also review the three stages of change described by Wanberg and Milkman (1998). Session 17 is a prerequisite to this session. There is no-entry for new clients.

The primary focus of this session is to help clients integrate the R&RP *strategies of lifestyle balance* into the client's life. Lifestyle imbalance can lead to relapse and recidivism. An understanding of the how lifestyle imbalance relates to R & R and how lifestyle balance relates to R&RP, as described by Marlatt (1985a), is necessary in order for the provider to present that part of this session.

We have seen that high-risk exposure, e.g., high-risk thinking and high-risk situations are triggers that set into motion the R&R process. Often these thought-events or external situations create an internal desire to indulge in a behavior that "I deserve." With relapse, the payoff is quick. It can give immediate gratification. Individuals who are most vulnerable to what Marlatt (1985d) calls the relapse set-up are those whose lifestyles are out of balance. But the set-up is internal. At close look, the individual has made conscious choices that lead closer and closer (enhances the erosion process) to a full relapse (going back to a pattern of AOD problems) or recidivism (returning impaired driving). The individual would probably deny responsibility in the set-up process. But responsibility is clearly there. **Choices are clearly made.**

> The decision or choice process can present in a benign or unsuspecting manner and certain actions the individual chooses may seem irrelevant to the possibility of relapse. These choices may be referred to as *seemingly irrelevant decisions*.

The choices, however, not only rest in the relapse steps themselves but also in the *vulnerability of lifestyle imbalance* - based on choices that the individual also makes. Marlatt (1985d) suggests that the degree of lifestyle balance or imbalance impacts on the desire for indulgence or immediate gratification. They define balance as "the degree of equilibrium that exists in one's daily life between those activities perceived as external 'hassles' or demands (the 'shoulds'), and those perceived as pleasures or self-fulfillment (the 'wants')" (p. 47).

When the person is operating out of the imbalance of the "shoulds," that person begins to feel deprived. There is a corresponding desire for gratification that can come through returning to old patterns of use and styles of use (going to the bar every evening after work). The automatic thoughts are: "I deserve more than this," "I work hard and don't get nowhere," "They have more than I do. I deserve as much as they do," "I deserve a good time - a few drinks."

As the desire for indulgence increases, so does the need to "restore balance and equilibrium" (p. 48). This can lead to strong alcohol or other drug-seeking thoughts (cravings) and behaviors (urges). This sequence can lead to what Marlatt calls the *cognitive antecedents of relapse or returning to impaired drinking or impaired driving:* making an excuse to engage in a certain behavior; denial of any intent to use, drink or drive impaired; and decisions or choices associated with the R&R process. The individual becomes more vulnerable if he or she lacks the skills to deal with high risk exposures. This lack of skills - or self efficacy increases the risk of R&R.

The decision or choice process can present in a benign or unsuspecting manner and certain actions the individual chooses may seem even irrelevant to the possibility of relapse. Marlatt calls these choices **Seemingly Irrelevant Decisions** (SIDS). The individual becomes even more vulnerable if he or she engages in high-risk thinking ("I'll go down to the bar and chat with a couple of buddies") or high-risk situation (friend drops by with some dope). These decisions to engage in high-risk thoughts leads to the end gate of a high-risk situation and a high probability of relapsing into a pattern of problem AOD use or recidivism. This process is illustrated in the boxed components of *Figure 9* below *(Figure 11* in the *Participant's Workbook).*

Alert: Session 17 is a prerequisite to this session.

SESSION CONTENT AND PRESENTATION SEQUENCE, PROCESS AND GUIDELINES

The above discussion will help the provider prepare for presenting this session. When presenting this session, it is again important to remember that the relapse prevention model here presented is premised on either relapsing from abstinence or relapsing from a pattern of non-harmful or non-disruptive use. The following presentation sequence is recommended.

▶ Have clients again review their MP. From the last session, they may want to update their MAP. Also, have clients discuss their AOD weekly monitoring.

▶ **Exercise:** Very briefly do the *CB Map Exercise.* Have the event represent a situation where a client was in a high-risk situation to drink and drive. By now, clients should have considerable skill in doing this exercise.

▶ Summarize the **stages of change** upon which this program is based: *challenge to change, commitment to change and ownership of change.* Give clients a clear picture of these stages so that they can identify where they fit with respect to both relapse and recidivism. Do the following exercise.

Exercise: Have clients identify what stage of change they are in for relapse and recidivism. Do a round robin exercise. First take relapse; then do recidivism.

▶ **Review the R&RP map** and have clients do *Work Sheet 49.* This involves putting skills in each of the rectangles to handle the various triggers or warning signs, e.g., managing high-risk thinking.

▶ **Go over the decision window or matrix** (worksheet 50, page 174 in workbook) adapted from Marlatt (1985d, p. 58) though modified to fit the impaired driving offender. This deals with the *rationalization* and *defensive process* that clients develop around consequences of relapse and recidivism. *Worksheet 50* provides decision windows for *relapse* (upper window) and *recidivism* (lower window). Clients are to write in their *relapse prevention goal* and then to identify the immediate and long term positive benefits and outcomes of following that goal as well as the immediate and long-term negative outcomes of following that goal. Have clients do the same for recidivism, writing in their recidivism goal of either zero tolerance or meeting legal expectations. The window changes over time and clients can revise their decision window in such a manner so as to prevent R&R. Early on, clients might have included only minimal immediate and delayed positive outcomes of abstinence or a non-problematic pattern of AOD use. Now clients may see more positive benefits and outcomes from abstinence or a non-problematic use pattern. As clients revise their decision window, they may find that it is difficult for them to find positive benefits for continuing impaired driving or DWI behavior. However, for some clients, one positive consequence of continuing DWI behavior would be that they can continue to drive to the bar and drink with friends.

▶ **Developing a balanced lifestyle:** Now, we go beyond helping clients develop and apply the skills and strategies to manage high-risk thinking and situations. For long-term maintenance and ownership of change, we must help clients create a stable and on-going lifestyle balance. As Marlatt has noted, "simply teaching the client to respond mechanically to one high-risk situation after another is not enough" (p. 59). This is the "teaching to fish" metaphor. Providers cannot deal with each and every high-risk exposure their clients encounter. *Clients need broader and more global strategies and a generalized ability to deal with stress and cope with high-risk thoughts and situations.*

Figure 9 below (*Figure 11*, page 171 in *Workbook*) provides Marlatt's (1985d, p. 61) *Lifestyle Balance: Global Self-Control Strategies* diagram that clients can utilize to avoid high risk thinking and high- risk situations. These can be cognitive, behavioral or operational. For example, an operational strategy would be to never drive a car to the bar to drink with friends.

Figure 9 will require time for clients to understand. Read carefully the rationale and overview of this session before working with clients around *Figure 9*. Here is some additional material to be used in interpreting this diagram and helping clients apply it to their change process.

The boxed components of *Figure 9*, (*Figure 11* in *Workbook*) provide the process and antecedent conditions leading up to relapse or recidivism. The circled components provide the various intervention strategies that mitigate the boxed R&R antecedents. The circled intervention components will be briefly discussed.

Creating a balanced lifestyle and engaging in positive "involvements" are counters to the "shoulds" message of imbalance that will lead to feeling self-deprivation. The life- style daily balance is a process that is ongoing and stable. It involves built-in activities that are part of daily living and that give positive and meaningful gratification to the individual.

Substituting indulgences is also an intervention strategy. It is directed at countering the desire to indulge (indulgence could mean going beyond a non-harmful pattern of use). The substitute clearly is different from the normal indulging behavior of drinking or using drugs or a harmful pattern of AOD use. These are activities that provide immediate self-gratification (such as eating a nice meal, sexual activity, etc.).

Ways to cope or intervening in the cravings and urges antecedents involves countering the external cues that precipitate the cravings and urges (e.g., smell of alcohol; seeing people drink; noticing friends on the street; desire to join friends at the bar in the "usual" manner). Sometimes, as Marlatt notes, simply removing oneself from the external cues will do the job. *Detaching* from and *labeling* the cravings or urges are ways to "ride out" the urge. Just *not* going to the bar but going home and working on a hobby is enough. The client needs to know that the urge or craving - or the AOD seeking, or AOD environment seeking - will not last forever. It does go away. *Labeling* and *detaching* will often speed up the process of "going away."

Rationalization, Defensiveness, Seemingly Irrelevant Decisions (SIDS) and High-Risk Situations: A powerful component of the relapse process is rationalization - *defensiveness* (per our previous discussion of denial, we choose to use the term defensiveness) and SIDS. Clients can use several strategies to manage these antecedents to relapse and recidivism. First, *labeling SIDS* episodes will make them more relevant and increase awareness that these are danger signs. Second, revising the *decision matrix* or window, which was the exercise done in *Work Sheet 50* will help. Whereas the clients' decisions about being involved in a pattern of AOD use may have had more perceived positive outcomes at the beginning of treatment, now the client might look at how these expectations have changed. The decision now is that the positive benefits for not relapsing into that kind of pattern is that family and friends are not as upset with the client; long term positive outcome might be that the client has more time doing other activities rather than engaging in a harmful pattern of use.

▶ **Highway map for responsible living:** A helpful strategy is to visualize the R&R path and the R&RP path as a road map (*Figure 12* in the *Participant's Workbook*), adapted from Parks and Marlatt (1999) to address the issues of relapse and recidivism for impaired drivers. This "highway metaphor" is a way of illustrating the choices that clients have at the point leading to high-risk situations. When confronted with automatic thoughts or thought habits that lead to cravings, urges, desires for high risk drinking environments, the client has a choice of routes - *city of irresponsible living* - collapse and crash; or *city of responsible living and CARING*.

▶ Additional exercise for this session if time permits.

Exercise: Provider describes a typical high-risk situation for the impaired driver such as running into some old friends who pressure joining them at the bar. Clients are encouraged to describe two oppositional chains of events; 1) an effective coping response; 2) an ineffective coping response. After eliciting comments about what might constitute a coping response, clients are asked to elaborate on the likely chain of events that may occur in the case of an ineffective coping response.

Exercise: Have several clients share a brief *relapse or recidivism story*, explaining the progression from high-risk situation to high-risk thinking through decreased self-efficacy, positive outcome expectancies, initial drinking, if any, the rule violation effects and engagement in DWI behavior.

Have each member of the group share where they see themselves relative to the road map or the "highway metaphor." Review their AOD Weekly Monitoring Chart and remind clients to do this in the coming week.

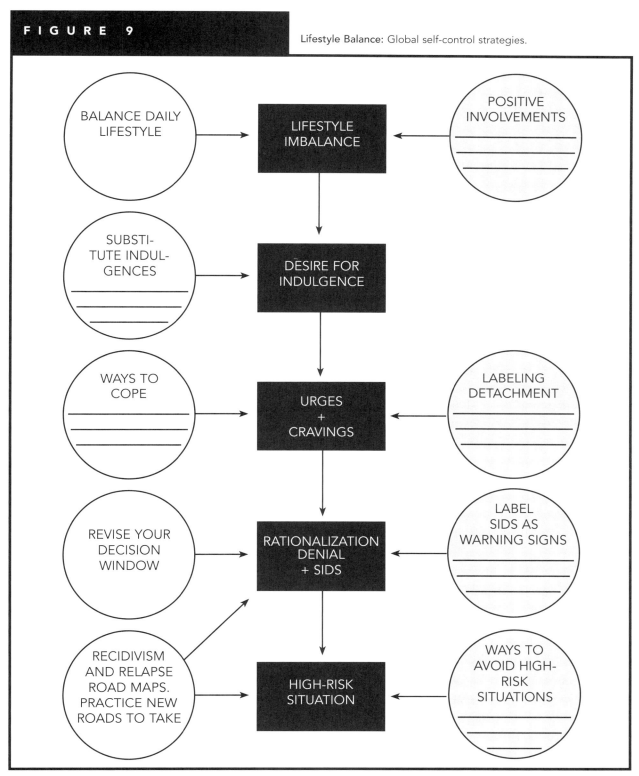

FIGURE 9

Lifestyle Balance: Global self-control strategies.

SESSION 19: COMMUNITY RESPONSIBILITY SKILLS: STRENGTHENING CHARACTER AND PROSOCIAL VALUES AND BEHAVIOR

RATIONALE AND OVERVIEW OF SESSION

In the Preface to this *Provider's Guide,* we talked about the need to include in DWI intervention and treatment a socio-centric emphasis that focuses on the dimensions of *moral and community responsibility.* We see moral responsibility as representing a set of ethical and principled thoughts, attitudes and behaviors directed at respecting the rights of others, being accountable to laws and rules of our community and society, having positive regard for and caring about the welfare and safety of others, and contributing to the ongoing good of our community. In essence, it means responding in a responsible way to others and to our community.

This is one of three sessions in **DWC Therapy** directed at providing information and developing skills that will enhance responsible attitudes and behaviors towards others and the community. This session is directed at *strengthening character and prosocial behavior.* Another session is directed at building the skills of empathy. The third session is directed at resolving conflicts with others so as to contribute to the benefit of oneself and others.

The psychotherapy literature has viewed antisocial patterns and characteristics as difficult if not impossible to treat (e.g., Sperry, 1999). As discussed earlier, this is in part due to the egocentric orientation of traditional psychotherapy. However, a sociocentric orientation and cognitive therapy approach can be effective in bringing about changes in antisocial patterns. As Beck et al. (2004) propose, this would involve helping the client with a history of antisocial behavior patterns to move from concrete thinking operations and self-determination towards more abstract thinking, interpersonal consideration and moral functioning (p. 169).

Beck et al. (2004) see the highest level of moral functioning and development involving a "...sense of responsibility or caring for others that includes a respect for the needs and wants of others or a commitment to laws as guiding principles for the good of society" (p.179). Whereas at the lower levels, the individual shows concern for others based on what he or she stands to gain or lose, at the higher levels, "... the person shows a greater ability to consider the needs of others or the needs of society in general" (p. 179).

DWC utilizes specific strategies to help individuals change antisocial thinking and behavior and to move towards a higher level of prosociality and moral responsibility. These include: using a provider-client collaborative approach; helping clients see their own antisocial features and patterns; structured treatment with clear expectations of the client; clear consequences for not complying with treatment structure and expectations; problem focused work; interpersonal and empathy skills development; identifying cognitive distortions and errors in thinking that lead to antisocial behavior; managing anger and impulsivity; self-monitoring and feedback through therapy exercises; using motivational enhancement skills; developing prosocial values and attitudes; and being a partner with judicial in sanctioning behaviors that violate the terms of the judicial sentence.

As discussed in the *Provider's Guide's* introduction to *Lesson 10* of *Level II Education,* one underlying assumption of this program is that DWI conduct is *anti-social behavior.* It is behavior that disregards and violates the rights of others, does harm to others and goes against the standards, morals, rules and laws of society. We are not saying that DWI clients necessarily fit the *Antisocial Personality Disorder* as defined by the DSM-IV (American Psychiatric Association, 1994) which is defined by a "pervasive pattern of disregard for, and violation of, the rights of others" (p. 645). We are saying that there is an antisocial dimension to persons who engage in driving while their BAC is beyond legal limits. Remember that the average DWI arrestee drove from 800 to 1,000 times before being cited. When we define anti-social patterns, whether it is vis-a-vis the DSM-IV criteria (see the introduction to *Lesson 10* in the *Provider's Guide*) or any abnormal psychology text, there are two criteria that certainly apply to most impaired driving offenders:

▶ failure to conform to social norms by repeatedly performing acts that are grounds for arrest; and

▶ reckless disregard for safety of self or others.

Clearly, one can engage in antisocial behavior and attitudes and not fit the *Antisocial Personality Disorder* as formally defined by the DSM-IV. We are all a bit antisocial from time to time in that we all endeavor to maintain our own individuality and uniqueness. In that process, sometimes we do come "up against" societal norms and rules.

This session utilizes and expands on the concepts and ideas in *Lesson 10* of *Level II Education.* We ask clients to assess themselves across a set of behaviors and attitudes that go against the norms, laws and expectations of society and the rights of others and to see how these behaviors and attitudes play into DWI behavior. We look at the definitions of *antisocial, prosocial and character.* Then we look at ways to strengthen our moral responsibility and prosocial attitudes and behavior towards our community. The **moral dilemma exercise** will be used which confronts clients on decisions around moral responsibility.

SESSION CONTENT AND PRESENTATION SEQUENCE, PROCESS AND GUIDELINES

We will outline the presentation process for this session's content. The provider should review the ideas and concepts of Lesson 10 of *DWC Education,* page 259. Following are the steps in therapy.

▶ **Have clients review their MP**. Here are the areas to have clients look for when assessing their risks of engaging in antisocial attitudes and behaviors: high scores on *Social Irresponsibility and Behavioral Disruption*; high scores across the scales of *Impaired Driving Assessment*; under *Assessment of Thinking, Feeling and Attitude Patterns*, scales measuring *Blame Others, Care-less, Irresponsible Thinking*, etc.; and *Problems With the Law* under *Areas of Adult Problems*.

▶ Do the CB Map exercise around an event that caused a craving.

▶ Review the homework of looking for high-risk exposures that lead to R&R.

- Discuss, "What guides us in responsible living?"

- Define **antisocial, prosocial** and the **concept of character.**

- **Exercise:** Using *Work Sheet 51,* have clients assess themselves across the *antisocial behavior* and *attitude* items. The Workbook provides some raw score cut off guidelines to interpret the findings of this scale. The more "sometimes" and "much of the time" responses clients have, the more antisocial they are and the higher the risk of violating the rights of others and engaging in DWI behavior.

- **Exercise:** have clients restate the questions on Work Sheet 51 to reflect a prosocial attitude and behavior.

- Have clients check one of the four statements on Page 177 of the *Participant's Workbook* regarding whether they see themselves as prosocial or antisocial.

- Present the 10 guidelines for *strengthening moral character* and *prosocial attitudes and values.* Have clients discuss the *10 guidelines.* One of the most important guidelines is to change our errors in thinking that can lead to antisocial actions.

  Exercise: Do *Work Sheet 52* which involves replacing the errors in thinking that can lead to antisocial actions with prosocial thoughts or prosocial relationships that lead to prosocial outcomes.

- Discuss the concept of the *moral dilemma* which puts a person in conflict with a value or moral that the person holds.

  Exercise: Have clients write down a moral dilemma they have faced in the past year.

  Exercise: Do the moral dilemma exercise in the Participant's Workbook involving the security guard and the nurse in the emergency room. Give clients time to share their views.

  Exercise: Have clients share how they might strengthen their moral character or moral strengths. Then, the provider gives feedback to each client, one specific area of character or moral strengths that he or she has shown.

- Have cleints relate their antisocial - prosocial view of themselves to their Master Profile.

- Update the MSL. Take some time to review this list. How are clients doing? Are they increasing mastery ratings?

SESSION CLOSURE

Keep the closing group focused around the topic of how clients see themselves with respect to being prosocial or antisocial. Some clients may be struggling with how antisocial-prosocial they are. Have clients share their moral dilemmas. Have clients do their *AOD Weekly Monitoring Chart.*

SESSION 20: COMMUNITY RESPONSIBILITY SKILLS: UNDERSTANDING AND PRACTICING EMPATHY

RATIONALE AND OVERVIEW OF SESSION

Self-control is an important part of responsible living and change. Gottfredson and Hirschi (1990) suggest that **low self-control** is a single construct that accounts for a significant amount of variance in explaining antisocial behavior including DWI conduct. An important component of the low self-control construct is lack of empathy, self-centeredness, indifference and insensitivity to the suffering and plight of others, and not identifying with or putting oneself in the place of others.

Values and morals differ across all peoples and nations. Yet, there are laws across all nations that have one thing in common: the safety and welfare of people. This is basic to most communities and cultures. Basic to this concern for others is what we call *empathy*.

The *Driving With CARE* education and treatment protocols consider self-control as underlying the values of change, freedom, positive relationship with others and community, and concern about others. The latter two values have to do with empathy. Empathy is one of the most important parts of moral character, prosocial behavior and responsibility towards the community. Responsible living is considering the attitudes, feelings and views of others - or to become more understanding towards and caring of others.

Individuals with a history of engaging in impaired driving have serious problems in identifying with the suffering of others, in placing themselves in the "shoes of another person," particularly their victims, and in being sensitive to and concerned about others and the community. Although some research would indicate that low empathy may not be a good predictor of recidivism (Andrews et al., 1985) there is a strong agreement in the field that empathy training should be an important component of offender treatment (e.g., Agee, 1979; Feshbach, 1984; Ross & Fabiano & Ross, 1986; Wanberg & Milkman, 1998).

Any discussion of empathy must include a discussion of the concept of *sympathy*. Sympathy is an emotional response that is aroused by a stimulus outside of ourselves. It is *feeling sorry for someone* and having a sense of or feeling the pain of others. The James-Lange theory of emotions (James, 1890) concludes that our subjective emotional experience is merely the awareness of our own bodily changes in the presence of outside emotionally arousing stimuli. Cannon (1927), however, concluded that this purely autonomic (sympathetic nervous system) arousal explanation was not enough. He felt that the emotional arousal is more than just an awareness of our visceral responses or sympathetic nervous system's discharge since we are able to differentiate different kinds of emotions.

Schachter and Singer (1962) took a step further and emphasized the role of *cognitive factors* or processes in the emotional response. We attribute meaning to our emotional responses; or we interpret our emotional responses based on our prior experiences and what we experience going on around us. This cognitive interpretation of emotion lays some ground work for the understanding of empathy.

Sympathy is an emotional response that certainly involves a cognitive attribution process. Feeling sorry for someone must involve more than just a visceral response; it involves understanding. Gordon Allport (1937), however, states neither ".... an 'instinct of sympathy' nor a theory of 'emotional contagion' will account for our understanding of others" (p. 529). Allport (1937) notes that Theodore Lipps was the first to discuss empathy in the psychological literature. Lipps saw empathy based on our capacity to imitate others. He saw knowledge as having three spheres: sensory perception; inner perception; and empathy (Lipps, 1907, as cited in Allport, 1937).

Empathy is not only the understanding of another person, but also involves *being able to put oneself in the place of the other person.* Allport (1937) states "....empathic knowledge achieves a unity through a welding of the objective and the subjective" (p. 533). Empathy is a deeper experience. It goes beyond the egocentric point of view. It assumes "...that the knowledge of others has complete priority over self-knowledge" (p. 533). Identification is emotional "and requires no specific mimicry" (page 533). Empathy does not require identification, although it can be part of empathy. We can develop empathy for someone who has no particular emotional significance to us (Allport, 1937).

Empathy involves imitation, mimicry and putting yourself in the place of the other person. The techniques of role reversal and doubling (Bischof, 1962) are powerful methods for enhancing the individual's understanding of the other person's position. It brings one beyond the ego (self). During role reversal, the individual takes the role of the other person. With the doubling technique, the double repeats back the words of the other person with the inferred meaning, emotional intonation and expression. There is the kinetic mimicking of the other person. An example is when the observer of another person makes the actual bodily movement similar to that of the other person. Allport uses the example of observers of a high jumper actually lifting their legs as they watch a person clearing the high jump bar.

Carl Rogers (1951), who stamped *empathic listening* into the psychotherapy process, concluded that "a high degree of empathy in a relationship is possibly the most potent factor in bringing about change and learning" (1980, p. 139). His formal definition focuses on "perceiving the internal frame of reference of another with accuracy and with the emotional components and meanings which pertain thereto as if one were the person, but without ever losing the 'as if' condition" (p. 140). It is "entering the private perceptual world of the other," it is "being sensitive," "it means sensing meanings," it means "temporarily living in the other persons' life," it is a process of "desiring to know" (pp. 142-144).

Both sympathy and empathy are important in developing prosocial attitudes and self-control. Ross (Ross et al., 1986) considers empathy to be one of the most important values people can learn when moving from antisocial conduct to prosocial living and responsible attitudes towards the community. Ross and associates teach that the person will have a greater chance to change his or her beliefs and thinking when he or she learns to consider the attitudes, feelings, and views of others - or to become more understanding towards and caring of others.

Start this session with a short open discussion about the last session on *Strengthening Character and Prosocial Behavior.* Then, use the following sequence.

Exercise: Begin with the *CB Map Exercise.*

▶ Distinguish between *sympathy* and *empathy.* Point out that: sympathy takes place after the fact — after we are aware of someone's hurt; and empathy takes place before the fact — before someone is in pain. Empathy is understanding pain some-one else **can** have. Have clients give their view of the two words. Have them give examples of sympathy and empathy. Define empathy and its process.

▶ Have clients practice having empathy or feeling empathic.

Exercise: Do *Work Sheet 53* by reading aloud each protocol and then have clients write down what they think the character in the story thought and felt.

Exercise: In small groups, have clients pick stories from newspapers and then practice making empathic statements about the main character in the story.

Exercise: In small groups, using the same newspapers, have each group try to find an article that illustrates the *moral dilemma.* Using *Work Sheet 54,* answer each of the questions regarding this story. Help them see that a reflective listening statement is an empathic-reflective statement.

▶ Help clients relate their MP ratings to the ideas of empathy.

Exercise: For either homework or in group, have clients complete the *Thinking Report* in *Work Sheet 55.* Work on helping clients identify the beliefs and attitudes underlying the thoughts and feelings.

Exercise: Following the guidelines in the Participant's Workbook, have clients write a letter to someone who was affected by their DWI behavior and arrest episode. This may cause emotional distress for some clients. These clients may need additional emotional support and/or intervention.

▶ Have clients update their MSL, page 31 of the *Workbook.*

SESSION CLOSURE

Keep the group unstructured but start off with a focused statement around what they got out of the session. Structure the closing session around how the clients see themselves with respect to having sympathy for others. Have them practice making empathetic - reflective statements over the next week. Remind clients to do their *AOD Weekly Monitoring Chart.*

SESSION 21: COMMUNITY RESPONSIBILITY SKILLS: RESOLVING CONFLICTS AND NEGOTIATION SKILL DEVELOPMENT

RATIONALE AND OVERVIEW OF SESSION

We could define conflict in terms of its synonyms - contention, controversy, rivalry, active opposition, friction, clash, competition, struggle, tussle, strife, etc. It is more helpful, however to define conflict as an interpersonal and intrapersonal process (Kelley, 1987). Peterson provides a process definition of conflict (1983): An interpersonal or social process that occurs whenever the actions and needs of one person interfere with the action and needs of another (p. 365). This definition presents the interpersonal dimension of conflict. Interference with the action of the other person also involves an intrapersonal process. The following example illustrates how the interpersonal interferences also create an intrapersonal interference.

A couple begins to argue following the wife's request that her husband help vacuum the house in preparation for the guests coming over for dinner that evening. Husband is in his study presuming to be reading a book, but really mulling over a problem he had with his boss on Friday. She begins to vacuum which annoys him and interferes with his musing over the problem. He jumps up, grabs the vacuum cleaner and starts to vacuum. She responds in anger and hurt, tells him that he can entertain the guests himself and leaves the house slamming the door behind her.

The conflict between the couple is defined by what Kelley (1987) calls the **interchain** (sequence of transactions between the couple) causing interference, and the interference in the **intrachain** organization of events (the thinking and pondering going on inside the husband). What is also important about Peterson's definition and the above illustration, is that feeling, thought and action (the three components of CB focus) interact in producing the *intrapersonal and interpersonal interference.* This provides the basis for the focus of conflict resolution: the interchain of feeling, thought and action in the interference process.

We can have conflicts with other people and with the community or society or what are called social or societal conflicts. DWI conduct is an example. The actions of one individual (impaired driver) interfered with the actions of others (the community). The interference is with and within the community. However, the actions of the community, or agencies within the community, e.g., law enforcement, the courts, also produces interferences within the impaired driving offender, much like the husband whose intrapersonal system is interfered with by the wife's vacuuming. The resolution of the DWI conflict is similar to the resolution of the husband-wife conflict. The first step to resolving this conflict is that the offender takes responsibility for his/her role in this conflict. The community takes responsibility in that it sets up structures, e.g., treatment program, court actions, to deal with the DWI behavior.

Kelley (1987) indicates that conflict has three aspects: *structure, content and process*. *Structure* is the situation and persons involved which are relatively stable factors that give rise to the conflict and represent the context of the conflict process - husband, wife, guests coming, vacuuming the house. *Content* is what the conflict is about - wife requesting husband to help vacuum, and husband resisting. *Process* is the *conflictual interaction* or the interpersonal and intrapersonal interference process - wife asks husband to help with house cleaning and vacuuming, husband resists because he is busy musing about a work situation, wife gets irritated and intentionally vacuums in his presence, husband gets angry and starts vacuuming, wife gets angry and leaves.

Although conflict resolution must include dealing with content, structure and process, we will focus mainly on process as we provide clients with a basis for resolving conflicts and engaging in negotiating as a method of conflict resolution.

Patton and Giffin (1981) define conflict as a process which has distinct elements.

▶ **Antecedent condition** and circumstances are the structures or characteristics of a situation that lead to conflict.

▶ **Conflict** - interference in the action of another person: perceived conflict; and felt conflict.

▶ **The resulting behaviors** - aggression, debate, argument.

▶ **Conflict ends** - either through resolution by agreement, or through suppression of one party by the other, or of both parties - win-win, win-lose, lose-lose.

▶ **Aftermath** or results of conflict: parties are alienated, brought closer together, neutralized.

Some people respond to or handle a potential or actual conflict by engaging in AOD use or even misuse or by engaging in antisocial conduct, e.g., get violent (Ross et al., 1986). The consequences of these responses are often escalation of the conflict, damage of the relationship or alienation of others. A person who drives while impaired and who gets a DWI may be actually fighting the community or society. There is a quality of rebellion to impaired driving behavior.

One way that we can approach the resolution of conflicts is through *negotiation*. Negotiation is working towards compromise and agreement between the parties that allow both to satisfy their needs. What is important to recognized is that "the act of engaging in communication is a process of negotiating our meanings with those of others" (Ruben, 1988, p. 105). When we communicate, what we really do is to negotiate meanings and understandings with other people. Thus, we practice the art of negotiation - because we engage in communication every day. When our meanings match well, we can say we are communicating - and we are in fact negotiating.

The DWIO is not communicating with the community and society. Impaired driving offenders are not negotiating meanings and understandings with the community. Their meanings and the community meanings are not matching.

It is important for the impaired driving offender to understand that compromise and negotiation is not defeat, but a way of achieving "no-lose" solutions to problems. Deciding to no longer drive while impaired is not a lose-win situation - the DWIO loses and the community wins. Nor does it mean that the DWIO is weak. Driving responsibly (when not impaired) is a **win-win** condition. As Ross and associates note, *negotiating is not a show of weakness, but requires social skill and courage to face the conflict in a constructive manner* (Ross et al., 1986). Several sources were used in generating the content for this session. These include Cummings, Long and Lewis (1983), Fisher and Ury (1981), Kelley (1987), King et al. (1994), Ross et al. (1986), Wanberg & Milkman (1998).

SESSION CONTENT AND PRESENTATION SEQUENCE, PROCESS AND GUIDELINES

Make it clear to clients that the concepts and skills of this session apply to our relationship with others and our relationship to the community and society. The following presentation sequence is recommended.

- ▶ Start the session with CB MAP update and review last week's Thinking Report, Work Sheet 55.

- ▶ **Discussion:** Have clients define conflict. Give the definition above: a conflict is an interpersonal or social process where the actions or needs of one person interfere with the actions or needs of another. Have clients share some of the conflicts that they have in their lives. If clients do not mention their DWI, pose this as a question: Did the DWI create a conflict with their community?

- ▶ Discuss the important parts of conflict and what to remember when trying to work out a conflict. The first step to conflict resolution is for clients to take responsibility for their role in the conflict. Have clients discuss whether they have taken full responsibility to resolve the conflict between them and the community.

- ▶ Review the counter productive ways of dealing with conflict: fight, fake, flight.

- ▶ Present the win-win solution approach and go over the nine skills to achieve such solutions. Review Fisher and Ury's work on conflict resolution and getting a win-win (1981).

- ▶ Go over the steps of negotiation. Focus on win-win solutions and the clients' role in responsible conflict resolution.

- ▶ **Exercise:** Do *Work Sheet 56*, having clients describe a recent conflict they were in. Analyze the conflict using the six points summarized from the session content. How might they have approached the conflict differently? Apply the nine ways to achieve a win-win in the conflict description.

- ▶ Have clients add to and update the MSL.

SESSION CLOSURE

Keep the focus of the process group on conflicts that clients currently have and how they see resolving those conflicts. Review the clients work on the *AOD Weekly Monitoring Chart*.

EXTENDED DWC THERAPY SESSIONS: REFLECTION AND REVIEW AND THE THERAPY PROJECTS

RATIONALE AND STRUCTURE FOR THE THERAPY PROJECTS

To meet the needs of clients who are required to take more than the 42 hours of the core 21 session *DWC Therapy* program, we have a developed an extended therapy protocol. This protocol includes various options for meeting the required therapy hours and includes self-guided therapy projects that clients present in their groups. There is considerable research support for the efficacy of self-guided projects in bringing about change in clients with AOD problems (Heather, Kissoon-Singh & Fenton, 1990; Miller & Munoz, 1982; Miller & Hester, 1986; Miller & Rollnick, 2002).

The ITP developed at the time of admission to *DWC Therapy* was modified and updated during the course of *DWC Therapy*. After the 21 *Core DWC Therapy sessions*, the ITP is reviewed with the client and used to developed the *extended therapy program*.

The structure for the extended *DWC Therapy* has been described in the first part of this section and will be briefly reviewed.

Structure one: Agencies may set up a separate and open group for extended therapy clients. The therapy projects are presented in that group and individualized treatment needs are addressed within the group or through specialized therapies. The 10 therapy projects can be used as 10 additional manual-guided therapy sessions for that group.

Structure two: The following options are for agencies that do not have a separate group for extended therapy clients:

▶ **Option one:** Individualized treatment plan and involvement as *Peer Support Clients* in the 21 session *DWC Therapy* core curriculum. The therapy projects are done in this group; the client may receive some specialized therapies.

▶ **Option two:** Individualized treatment plan and involvement in a counselor-directed therapy group provided by the agency such as a formal 12-step therapy group or relapse prevention group. The therapy projects are presented in this group and, based on the ITP; some specialized therapies may be offered.

▶ **Option Three:** All extended therapy hours are based on specialized treatment needs identified in ITP and are fulfilled through specialized therapies and repeating selected *DWC Therapy* sessions. This is a totally individualized and tailor-made approach.

During the time clients are in the extended therapy program, they are asked to:

▶ continue to update their master skills list (MSL);
▶ update their *Master Assessment Plan* (MAP); and
▶ continue their *AOD Weekly Monitoring Chart*.

REFLECTION AND REVIEW SESSION

Before starting the extended **Therapy** program, the provider will meet with the client for a reflection and review session and do the following:

▶ review the progress clients made in *DWC Therapy;*

▶ review the ITP and look at the clients' special needs;

▶ clients select their therapy projects; and

▶ decide the extended therapy structure and options clients will be assigned to.

During this reflection and review session the *stages of change* are reviewed with the client: **challenge to change, commitment to change and ownership of change.** Have clients identify what stage they see themselves as being in.

THE THERAPY PROJECTS

Ten self-guided therapy projects are described in the following pages. This may be one of the most difficult parts of the client's Therapy program. Clients do these self-guided projects on their own as homework. Providers may set up a special tutoring group to help clients prepare their projects. Time spent in this group should be counted as part of their Level II Therapy requirements if an agency staff, volunteer counselor or therapists lead the group.

Peer Support Clients may help clients prepare their therapy projects. This procedure should be approved and monitored by the agency.

Some clients may resist doing these projects, particularly since they will need to spend time on their own outside of group for which they would not receive therapy credit. However, most clients will cooperate in this endeavor.

Here are the guidelines for clients in preparing and presenting the therapy projects.

▶ Have client read the therapy project material and complete the exercises in the *Participant's Workbook.*

▶ Clients takes 10 to 15 minutes to present the therapy projects in the group to which they are assigned. If a client is very reticent about presenting, the group leader should take the lead in helping the client present.

▶ The provider should make an effort to briefly review the work that clients have done in the *Participant's Workbook* and to provide positive reinforcement for that work with particular attention and reinforcement given to clients after they finish their first project.

Each of the therapy projects will be briefly discussed. The content and work sheets for each therapy project topic are provided in the *Workbook.*

RATIONALE AND OVERVIEW OF PROJECT

The lifestyle of many impaired driving offender clients has been dominated with AOD use and related activities. Clients who are sincerely making major changes in this AOD use lifestyle are likely to experience a sense of loss and emptiness. They have most likely derived a considerable degree of pleasure from these activities. If they have not replaced that "empty time" with other healthy pleasurable activities, they may feel that life is an endless cycle of eating, sleeping and working. Unless the void is replaced with some pleasant activities, there is an increased probability some will experience loneliness, boredom and even depression. This is a setup for relapse or recidivism or both. If clients are to be successful in making change, they have to develop alternatives to this lifestyle. Healthy play and leisure time are among these alternatives.

Monti and his colleagues report "that the number of pleasant activities a person engages in is directly related to the occurrence of positive feelings" (1989, p. 87). People who spend all their time doing required activities, the things we consider "shoulds" and "have to's," may experience little reward in life. We addressed this issue in *Session 18* with respect to developing lifestyle balance. We saw that creating a balanced lifestyle and engaging in positive "addictions" are counters to the "shoulds" that contribute to the imbalance that leads to thoughts of self-deprivation.

The lifestyle daily balance is a *process that is ongoing and stable.* It involves built-in activities that are part of daily living and that give positive and meaningful gratification to the individual. Unless this happens, clients become vulnerable to relapse and recidivism. Unless an *alternative lifestyle* is developed which includes a balance of work and play, clients are likely to feel they deserve to reward themselves with drinking or the drinking environment such as the bar or parties. It is important that clients develop a balance in life by *devising a schedule of pleasant things that they want to do.*

An important concept in this project is healthy play. Although play is defined as moving freely in space, healthy play means setting limits on that movement in terms of cost, time and energy. It is of benefit to self and others, is wholesome, involves responsible action and results in feeling good about yourself and others.

THERAPY PROJECT IMPLEMENTATION

This self-guided therapy project may require some special tutoring by provider staff, volunteers or a *Peer Support Client.* A brief review of the client's work on this project should be made before the client presents it in group.

THERAPY PROJECT 2: DOES YOUR WORK MATCH YOUR JOB?

RATIONALE AND OVERVIEW OF PROJECT

Productive and meaningful work are essential pieces to relapse and recidivism prevention and maintaining a balanced lifestyle. They represent another primary alternative to AOD use patterns that lead to harmful outcomes. Research has shown (Wanberg & Milkman, 1998) that those individuals who are gainfully employed and who enjoy their job have much higher probability of preventing relapse and recidivism.

Even clients who are on disability, retired, or for other reasons, are unable to be gainfully employed, it is still important that they find outlets for being productive in their living. This productivity might be in doing volunteer work, maintaining the upkeep of their personal property or home, etc. It is also important that people feel that they have some kind of vocation or avocation with which to identify. This identity goes beyond just having a job. Thus, *we focus on helping clients see the difference between one's work and one's job.*

THERAPY PROJECT IMPLEMENTATION

The main objective of this project is to help clients learn what their work (versus their job) is, to learn skills to take part in rewarding work; and to look at their education and work goals for the next three years. Clients may need help in distinguishing between their work and their job beyond the material in the *Participant's Workbook.* Some clients may need special assistance in doing this project.

THERAPY PROJECT 3: LEARNING TO SEARCH FOR A JOB

RATIONALE AND OVERVIEW OF PROJECT

This therapy project explores the issues of being *gainfully employed and the skills of finding employment.* It is also relevant for clients who want to make job changes. It outlines the steps for looking for a job. Clients may be referred to another agency that is specialized in job and employment searching. The need for involvement in this therapy project should be identified in the client's MP and MAP and in the provider's ITP for the client.

THERAPY PROJECT IMPLEMENTATION

This project may require some special assistance by provider staff, volunteer counselors or a *Peer Support Client.* The intent of this project is not to help clients find a job, but to sharpen their skills in looking for employment.

THERAPY PROJECT 4: LEARNING TO RELAX: YOUR DAILY RELAXATION PLAN

RATIONALE AND OVERVIEW OF PROJECT

The education and therapy protocols for *Driving With CARE: Strategies for Responsible Living and Change* have provided clients opportunities to learn about and apply the skills to manage stress and its related emotional syndromes of guilt, anger and depression. The rationale for this therapy project rests on the research findings that *stress* and *intrapersonal conflicts* are major contributors to relapse and impaired driving recidivism. Clients with a history of anxiety problems, as identified in the ITP, may particularly benefit from this project. A variety of sources were reviewed when developing this therapy project (Barlow, 1988; Benson, 1975; Lacroix, 1998; Lehrer & Woolfolk, 1993; Linden, 1993; Maxwell-Hudson, 1996; Perkinson, 1997; Smith, 1999; Wanberg & Milkman, 1998, 2005).

THERAPY PROJECT IMPLEMENTATION

The provider may need to briefly introduce this therapy project to clients. If several clients choose this project, this introduction and briefing could be done in a small group. Again, using volunteer counseling staff or *Peer Support Clients* for this task should be considered. Most clients could benefit from the daily relaxation strategies, and the provider may find it to be helpful to include these in the *Stress Management Session* in the 21 core *DWC Therapy* protocol.

THERAPY PROJECT 5: PREVENTING RELAPSE - WHAT IS WORKING BEST?

RATIONALE AND OVERVIEW OF PROJECT

Relapse prevention is one of the core themes of the education and therapy *Driving with CARE* protocols. Evidence indicates that continual review and practice of the concepts and skills of *relapse prevention* improve treatment outcomes. When clients are introduced to this project, they should be asked to review their relapse prevention goal. Has that goal changed? Do they feel they need to change the goal, e.g., from preventing patterns of harmful use to abstinence? The main objective of this project is to *have clients identify which action and thinking skills are working best.*

THERAPY PROJECT IMPLEMENTATION

Clients are asked to review the work they have done in understanding relapse and building skills for relapse prevention in *Lesson 8* of *Level II Education* and *Session 17* of *DWC Therapy*. They are asked to restate their relapse prevention goal and list the thinking and action skills that have been working best for them in preventing relapse. A logical place for clients to present this therapy project would be in *Sessions 17 or 18* of *DWC Therapy*. This would complement these two sessions.

THERAPY PROJECT 6: PREVENTING RECIDIVISM: WHAT IS WORKING BEST?

RATIONALE AND OVERVIEW OF PROJECT

Recidivism prevention is one of the core themes of the *Driving with CARE* education and therapy protocols. This area needs constant work. Clients who choose the relapse prevention goal of avoiding harmful AOD use patterns are particularly vulnerable for engaging in future impaired driving behavior. The most vulnerable time for recidivism is two or three months after clients have their driving privileges returned. When clients are introduced to this project, they should be asked to *review their recidivism prevention goal.* Has that goal changed? Do they feel they need to change the goal, e.g., from preventing driving while exceeding legal BAC limits to the goal of *zero tolerance-zero risk?*

THERAPY PROJECT IMPLEMENTATION

Clients are asked to review the work they have done in understanding recidivism and building skills for recidivism prevention in *Lesson 8* of *Level II Education* and *Sessions 17 and 18* of *DWC Therapy.* They are asked to *restate their recidivism prevention goal and list the thinking and action skills that have been working best for them in preventing recidivism.* A logical place for clients to present this therapy project would be in *Sessions 17 or 18* of *DWC Therapy.*

THERAPY PROJECT 7: SKILLS IN TIME MANAGEMENT AND COMPLETING TASKS

RATIONALE AND OVERVIEW OF PROJECT

We have clearly identified that one factor contributing to relapse and recidivism is stress and its related emotional syndromes. A major contributor to stress is the daily pressures of completing tasks. An underlying cause of this stress is failure to properly manage time. Covey, Merrill and Merrill (1994) provide rather extensive methods and approaches to time management. This therapy project provides some very specific points and tips for time management. The two approaches of *time-framing* and *task-framing* are discussed.

THERAPY PROJECT IMPLEMENTATION

This self-guided therapy project provides the client with some very specific tools for *time management* and two exercises to practice these skills. This session could be offered as an extended therapy group for *DWC Therapy.* Again, it is important that providers maintain a high-profile on positive reinforcement, since clients are expected to work on these projects outside of group.

THERAPY PROJECT 8: GETTING SUPPORT FROM GROUPS AND OTHERS

RATIONALE AND OVERVIEW OF PROJECT

As discussed earlier in this *Provider's Guide,* community reinforcement approaches are effective in helping clients maintain the changes they have made and to sustain the *ownership phase of change* (Sisson & Azrin, 1989; Smith & Meyers, 1995). It is one way that clients receive positive reinforcement for these changes as well as receive support for their relapse and recidivism prevention goals in the community. This therapy project guides clients in the *direction of utilizing community support and self-help groups.* The utilization of these support groups is one way of enhancing responsible behaviors in the community and fits in with the community responsibility strategy of this program.

THERAPY PROJECT IMPLEMENTATION

Clients look at two kinds of community support resources: those that provide direct support such as AA; and those that provide indirect support such as healthy and prosocial involvement in hiking clubs, health spas, church, etc. Clients may need some guidance and literature support for doing this project, such as brochures giving AA meeting times, community recreation resources, lists of churches, etc. The *Yellow Pages* and the internet are excellent sources for this.

THERAPY PROJECT 9: GIVING SUPPORT - MENTORING AND ROLE MODELING

RATIONALE AND OVERVIEW OF PROJECT

Providing support to other persons with AOD use and DWI problems through 12-step work, mentoring and role modeling are powerful ways to reinforce clients in the *maintenance* and *ownership stages of change.* Even more important, this is another approach in fulfilling the *DWC Therapy* goal of helping clients learn the skills and attitudes of moral and community responsibility. This is another component of learning prosocial behavior and attitudes. This project should be done by clients who feel self-control and self-efficacy in maintaining and demonstrating their relapse and recidivism prevention goals.

THERAPY PROJECT IMPLEMENTATION

This project helps clients understand the two kinds of mentoring - formal and informal. The steps of engaging formal mentoring are outlined. An important ***caveat*** for clients in this project is not to over-extend themselves in mentoring and helping others. Boundary issues and problems that often are barriers to effective mentoring need to be discussed with the client. Clients are asked to identify their strong and weak areas, the latter being important in the area of not over-extending, boundaries and setting limits on the mentoring process.

THERAPY PROJECT 10: SHARING YOUR FUTURE BIOGRAPHY

RATIONALE AND OVERVIEW OF PROJECT

One component of the client's autobiography is that of writing about his or her projected future or *Future Biography*. This will help clients do some long range planning and building positive expectations and goals for taking ownership in responsible living and change.

THERAPY PROJECT IMPLEMENTATION

This therapy project provides guidelines for clients in constructing and sharing their *Future Biography*. It is important that the provider review this biography with clients once they have finished their autobiography. This is a very personal part of the *Driving With CARE Therapy* protocol.

REFERENCES

Abrams, D. B., & Niaura, R. S. (1987). Social learning theory. In H. T. Blane & K. W. Leonard (Eds.), *Psychological theories of drinking and alcoholism* (131-178). New York: Guilford.

Abramson, L. Y., Seligman, M. E., & Teasdale, J. (1978). Learned helplessness in humans: Critique and reformulation. *Journal of Abnormal Psychology, 87*, 32-48.

Addis, M., & Krasnow, A. (2000). A national survey of practicing psychologists' attitudes toward psychotherapy treatment manuals. *Journal of Consulting and Clinical Psychology, 68*, 331-339.

ADE, Inc. (1986). *Substance abuse life circumstances evaluation - SALCE.* Clarkston, MI: ADE, Inc.

Adebayo, A. (1991). Factors antecedent to impaired driving in a Canadian urban sample. *International Journal of the Addictions 26*, 897-909.

Agee, V. L. (1979). *Treatment of the violent incorrigible adolescent.* Lexington, MA: Lexington Books.

Agostinelli, G., & Miller, W. R. (1994). Drinking and thinking: How does personal drinking affect judgments of prevalence and risk? *Journal of Studies on Alcohol, 55*, 327-337.

Alberti, R. E., & Emmons, M. L. (1995). *Your perfect right: A guide to assertive living* (7th ed.). San Luis Obispo, CA: Impact Publishers.

Alcohol and Drug Abuse Division. (1998). *The Colorado DUI/DWAI alcohol education programs: Standardized curricula and format, (Revision III).* Denver, CO: Alcohol and Drug Abuse Division, Department of Human Services, State of Colorado.

Alcoholics Anonymous. (1976). *Alcoholics Anonymous: The story of how many thousands of men and women have recovered from alcoholism* (3rd ed.). New York: Alcoholics Anonymous World Series.

Alford, B., & Norcross, J. C. (1991). Cognitive therapy as an integrated therapy. *Journal of Psychotherapy Integration, 1*, 175-190.

Allen, J. P., & Columbus, M. (1995). *Assessing alcohol problems: A guide for clinicians and researchers.* Bethesda, MD: National Institute on Alcohol Abuse and Alcoholism, U.S. Department of Health and Human Services, Public Health Services, National Institutes of Health.

Allen, J. P., Sillanaukee, P., Strid, N.H., & Litten, R. Z. (2003). Biomarkers of heavy drinking. In J. P. Allen, V. B Wilson (Eds.), A*ssessing alcohol problems: A guide for clinicians and researchers (2nd edition),* (pp. 37-54). Bethesda, MD: U. S. Department of Health and Human Services, Public Health Service, National Institute on Alcohol Abuse and Alcoholism, NIH Publication No. 03-3745.

Allen, J. P., & Wilson, V. B. (2003). *Assessing alcohol problems: A guide for clinicians and researchers (2nd edition).* Bethesda, MD: U.S. Department of Health and Human Services, Public Health Service, National Institute on Alcohol Abuse and Alcoholism, NIH Publication No. 03-3745.

Allport, G. W. (1937). *Personality: A psychological interpretation.* New York: Henry Holt and Company.

Amaro, H., Hardy-Fanta, C. (1995). Gender relations in addiction and recovery. *Journal of Psychoactive Drugs, 27*, 325-337.

Ambtman, R. (1990). *Impaired Drivers' Program. Evaluation Report.* Winnipeg, Manitoba: Alcoholism Foundation of Manitoba, The Awareness and Information Directorate.

American Psychiatric Association. (1994). *Diagnostic and statistical manual of mental disorders* (4th ed.). Washington, DC: Author.

American Psychiatric Association. (2000). *Diagnostic and statistical manual of mental disorders* (4th ed., text revision). Washington, DC: Author.

American Society of Addiction Medicine (2001). *American Society of Addiction Medicine Patient Placement Criteria for the Treatment of Substance-Related Disorders-Revised* (ASAM PPC-2-R) (2nd edition). Chevy Chase, MD: Author.

Andrews, D.A. (1995). The psychology of criminal conduct and effective correctional treatment. In J. Mcguire (ed.), *What works: Reducing reoffending*, pp.35-61. New Jersey: Wiley.

Andrews, D. A., & Bonta, J. (1994). *The psychology of criminal conduct.* Cincinnati, OH: Anderson.

Andrews, D. A., & Bonta, J. (1998). *The psychology of criminal conduct (2nd Ed.).* Cincinnati, OH: Anderson.

Andrews, D. A., & Bonta, J. (2003). *The psychology of criminal conduct (3rd Ed.).* Cincinnati, OH: Anderson.

Andrews, D. A., Wormith, J. S., & Kiessling, J. J. (1985). *Self-reported criminal propensity and criminal behavior: Threats to the validity of assessment of personality* (Programs Branch User Report). Ottawa: Solicitor General Canada.

Andrews, D. A., Zinger, K. I., Hoge, R. D., Gendreau, P., & Cullen, F. T. (1990). Does correctional treatment work? A clinically-relevant and psychologically-informed meta-analysis. *Criminology, 28*, 369-404.

Annis, H. M., & Davis, C. S. (1988). *Situational Confidence Questionnaire (SCQ-39) User's Guide.* Toronto: Addiction Research Foundation.

Annis, H. M., Graham, J. M., & Davis, C. S. (1987). *Inventory of Drinking Situations (IDS) User Guide.* Toronto: Addiction Research Foundation.

Antony, M. M., & Roemer, L. (2003). Behavioral therapy. In A. S. Gurman, & S. B. Messer (Eds.), *Essential psychotherapies: Theory and practice* (2nd edition, pp. 183-223). New York: The Guilford Press.

Argeriou, M., & Manohar, V. (1977). Treating the problem drinking driver: Some notes on the time required to achieve impact. *British Journal of Addiction, 72*, 331-338.

Argeriou, M., McCarty, D., Blacker, E. (1986). Criminality among individuals arraigned for drinking and driving in Massachusetts. *Journal of Studies on Alcohol, 46:* 525-530.

Arkowitz, H. (1992). Integrative theories of therapy. In D. K. Freedheim (Ed.), *History of psychotherapy: A century of change* (pp. 261-304). Washington, DC: American Psychological Association.

Arnett, J. (1990). Drunk driving, sensation seeking, and egocentrism among adolescents. *Personality & Individual Differences, 11*,541-546.

Arnkoff, D. B., & Glass, C. R. (1982). Clinical cognitive constructs: Examination, evaluation, and elaboration. In P. Kendall (Ed.), *Advances in cognitive-behavioral research and therapy* (Vol. 1). New York: Academic Press.

Arnkoff, D. B., & Glass, C. R. (1992). Cognitive therapy and psychotherapy integration. In D. K. Freedheim (Ed.), *History of psychotherapy: A century of change* (pp. 657-694). Washington, DC: American Psychological Association.

Atkinson, D. R., Morten, G., & Sue, D. W. (1993). *Counseling American minorities: A cross-cultural perspective* (4th ed.). Dubuque, IA: Brown & Benchmark.

Attneave, C. L. (1985). Practical counseling with American Indian and Alaska Native clients. In P. Pedersen (Ed.), *Handbook of cross-cultural counseling and therapy* (pp. 135-140). Westport, CT: Greenwood Press.

Babor, T. F., Stephens, R. S., & Marlatt, G. A. (1987). Verbal report methods in clinical research on alcoholism: Response bias and its minimization. *Journal of Studies on Alcohol, 48*, 410-424.

Bachelor, A. (1991). Comparison and relationship to outcome of diverse dimensions of the helping alliance as seen by client and therapist. *Psychotherapy, 28*, 234-249.

Bachelor, K. A. (1995). Clients' perception of the therapeutic alliance: A qualitative analysis. *Journal of Counseling Psychology, 42*, 322-337.

REFERENCES

Bailey, S. L., Flewelling, R. L., & Rachal, J. V. (1992). The characteristics of inconsistencies in self-reports of alcohol and marijuana use in longitudinal study of adolescents. *Journal of Studies on Alcohol, 53,* 636-647.

Baker, E.A., & Beck, K.H. (1991). Ignition interlocks for DWI offenders a useful tool? *Alcohol Drugs and Driving 7*(2): 107-115.

Baker, L. H., Cooney, N. L., & Pomerleau, O. F. (1987). Craving for alcohol: Theoretical processes and treatment procedures. In W. M. Cox (Ed.), *Treatment and prevention of alcohol problems: A resource manual* (pp. 184-204). New York: Academic Press.

Bandura, A. (1969). *Principles of behavior modification.* New York: Holt, Rinehart & Winston.

Bandura, A. (1977a). *Social learning theory.* Englewood Cliffs, NJ: Prentice-Hall.

Bandura, A. (1977b) Self-efficacy: Towards a unifying theory of behavioral change. *Psychological Review, 84,* 191-215.

Bandura, A. (1978). The self-system in reciprocal determination. *American Psychologist, 33,* 344-358.

Bandura, A. (1981). Self-referent thought: A developmental analysis of self-efficacy. In J. H. Flavell & L. Ross (Eds.), *Social cognitive development: Frontiers and possible futures.* Cambridge: Cambridge University Press.

Bandura, A. (1982). Self efficacy mechanisms in human agency. *American Psychologist, 37,* 122-147.

Bandura, A. (Ed.) (1995). *Self-efficacy in changing societies.* New York: Cambridge University Press.

Banks, J. (1991). *Teaching Strategies for Ethnic Studies* (5th ed.). Boston: Allyn and Bacon.

Barber, J. P., Connolly, M. B., Crits-Christoph, P., Gladis, L., & Siqueland, L. (2001). Alliance predicts patients' outcome beyond in-treatment change in symptoms. *Journal of Consulting and Clinical Psychology*, 68, 1027-1032.

Barlow, D. H. (1988). *Anxiety and its disorders: The nature and treatment of anxiety and panic.* New York: The Guilford Press.

Barnes, G. M., & Welte, J.W. (1998). Predictor of driving while intoxicated among teenagers. *Journal of Drug Issues 18:* 367-384.

Bartol, C. R. (2002). *Criminal behavior: A psycho/social approach, 6th Edition.* Englewood Cliffs, NJ: Prentice-Hall.

Bateman, A., Brown, D., & Pedder, J. (2000). *Introduction to psychotherapy: An outline of psychodynamic principles and practice (3d ed.).* London: Routledge.

Baumer, T. L.,& Mendelsohn, R.I. (1992). Electronically monitored home confinement: Does it work? In: J. Petersilia, A.J. Lurigio & J.M. Byrne (Eds.), *Smart sentencing: The emergence of intermediate sanctions* (pp. 54-67). Newbury Park, CA: Sage Publications.

BBC Research & Consulting (2003). *Colorado persistent drunk driver social marketing research.* Denver, CO: LinhartMcClainFinlon Public Relations.

Beck, A. T. (1963). Thinking and depression. *Archives of General Psychiatry, 9,* 324-333.

Beck, A. T. (1964). Thinking and depression II: Theory and therapy. *Archives of General Psychiatry, 10,* 561-571.

Beck, A. T. (1970). The role of fantasies in psychotherapy and psychopathology. *Journal of Nervous and Mental Disease, 150,* 3 -17.

Beck, A. T. (1976). *Cognitive therapy and the emotional disorders.* New York: International Universities Press.

Beck, A. T. (1991). Cognitive as the integrative therapy. *Journal of Psychotherapy Integration, 1,* 191-198.

Beck, A. T. (1993). Cognitive approaches to stress. In P. M. Lehrer & R. L. Woolfolk (Eds). *Principles and practice of stress management* (2nd ed., pp. 333-372). New York: The Guilford Press.

Beck, A. T. (1996). Beyond belief: A theory of modes, personality, and psychopathology. In P. M. Salkovskis (Ed.), *Frontiers of cognitive therapy* (pp. 1-25). New York: Guilford.

Beck, A. T. (1999). *Prisoners of hate: The cognitive basis of anger, hostility, and violence.* New York: Harper Collins.

Beck, A. T., Freeman, A., Davis, D. D., & Associates. (2004). *Cognitive therapy of personality disorders.* New York: The Guilford Press.

Beck, A. T., Rush, A. J., Shaw, B. F., & Emery, G. (1978). *Cognitive therapy of depression: A treatment manual.* Philadelphia: Center for Cognitive Therapy.

Beck, A. T., Rush, A. J., Shaw, B. F., & Emery, G. (1979). *Cognitive therapy of depression.* New York: Guilford.

Beck, A. T., Wright, F. D., Newman, C. F., & Liese, B. S. (1993). *Cognitive therapy of substance abuse.* New York: Guilford.

Beck, C. K. (1981). Driving while under the influence of alcohol: Relationship to attitudes and beliefs in a college population. *American Journal of Drug and Alcohol Abuse, 8,* 377-388.

Beck, J. S. (1995). *Cognitive therapy: Basics and beyond.* New York: Guilford.

Bell, P., & Evans, J. (1981). *Counseling the black client: Alcohol use and abuse in black America.* Minneapolis, MN: Hazelden Foundation.

Bem, S. L. (1996). Transforming the debate on sexual inequality: From biological difference to institutionalized androcentrism. In J. C. Chrisler, C. Golden, & P. D. Rozee (Eds.), *Lectures on the psychology of women* (pp. 9-21). New York: McGraw-Hill.

Bennion, L., & Li, T. K. (1976). Alcohol metabolism in American Indians and whites. *New England Journal of Medicine, 284,* 9-13.

Benson, H. (1975). *The relaxation response.* New York: Morrow.

Berenson, B. G., & Carkhuff, R. R. (1967). *Sources of gain in counseling and psychotherapy.* New York: Holt, Rinehart & Winston.

Bernal, M., & Knight, G. P. (Eds.). (1995). *Ethnic identification.* Newbury Park, CA: Sage.

Bierness, D. (2004). Challenges to ignition interlock program implementation. In K. G. Stewart (Ed.), *Putting research into action: A symposium on the Implementation of Researched-based Impaired Driving Countermeasures.* Washington, DC: Transportation Research board.

Bischof, L. J. (1962). *Interpreting personality theories.* New York: Harper & Row.

Blackburn, I. M., & Twaddle, V. (1996). *Cognitive therapy in action.* London: Souvenir Press.

Blankenstein, K. R., & Segal, Z. V. (2001). Cognitive assessment: Issues and methods. In K. S. Dobson (Ed.). *Handbook of cognitive-behavioral therapies* (pp. 40-85). NY: The Guilford Press.

Bloom, B. L. (1985). *Stressful life event theory and research: Implications for primary prevention* (DHHS Publication No. AMD 85-1385). Rockville, MD: National Institute of Mental Health.

Bloomberg, R. O., Preusser, D. F., & Ulmer, R. O. (1978). Deterrent efforts of recidivism in DUIs. *Journal of Studies on Alcohol, 49,* 443-449.

Blum, K., Cull, J. G., Braverman, E. R., & Comings, D. E. (1996). Reward deficiency syndrome. *American Scientist, 84,* 132-145.

Blume, S. B. (1992). Alcohol and other drug problems in women. In J. H. Lowinson, P. Ruiz, R. B. Millman, & J. G. Langrod (Eds.), *Substance abuse: A comprehensive textbook* (pp. 794-807). Baltimore, MD: Williams & Wilkins.

Blume, S. B. (1997). Women: Clinical aspects. In J. H. Lowinson, P. Ruiz, R. B. Millman, & J. G. Langrod (Eds.), *Substance abuse: A comprehensive textbook* (3rd ed., pp. 645-653). Baltimore, MD: Williams & Wilkins.

Blume, S. B. (1998). Addictive disorders in women. In R. J. Francis, & S. I. Miller (Eds.), *Clinical textbook of addictive disorders* (2nd ed., pp. 413-429). New York: Guilford Press.

REFERENCES

Bohart, A. C. (2003). Person-centered psychotherapy and related experiential approaches. In *Essential psychotherapies: Theory and practice, 2nd edition* (pp. 107-148). New York: The Guilford Press.

Bordin, E. S. (1979). The generalizability of the psychoanalytic concept of the working alliance. *Psychotherapy: Theory, Research and Practice, 16*, 252-260.

Borg, S., Czarnecka, A., Knande, H., Mossberg, D., & Sedvail, G. (1983). Clinical conditions and concentrations of MOPEG in cerebrospinal fluid and urine of male alcoholic patients during withdrawal. *Alcoholism: Clinical and Experimental Research, 7*, 411-415.

Borkenstein, R. F., Crowther, R. F., Shumate, R. P., Zeil, W. B., & Zylman, R. (1964). *The role of the drinking driver in traffic accidents*. Indiana University: Department of Police Administration.

Botvin, G. J. (1983). *Prevention of adolescent substance abuse through the development of personal and social competence. Preventing adolescent drug abuse: Intervention strategies*. NIDA Research Monograph 47, Department of Health and Human Services, National Institute on Drug Abuse, 115 - 140.

Botvin, G. J. (1986). Prevention of adolescent substance abuse through the development of personal and social competence. In *Preventing adolescent drug abuse: Intervention strategies* (NIDA Research Monograph 47, pp. 115-140). Rockville, MD: Department of Health and Human Services, National Institute on Drug Abuse.

Botvin, G. J., & Griffin, K. W. (2001). Life skills training: Theory, methods, and effectiveness of a drug abuse prevention approach. In E. F. Wagner & H. B. Waldron (Eds.), *Innovations in adolescent substance abuse interventions*. Amsterdam, Netherlands: Pergamon/Elsevier Science Inc.

Boyd Andrew Chemical Dependency Care Center (1997). *Assessment Course Treatment (ACT)*. Helena, Montana: Boyd Andrew Chemical Dependency Care Center.

Boyle, J. M. (1995). *National survey of drinking and driving attitudes and behavior: 1993*. DOT HS 808 202. Washington, D.C.: U.S. Department of Transportation, National Highway Traffic Safety Administration.

Brecht, M. L., Anglin, M.D., & Wang, J.C. (1993). Treatment effectiveness for legally coerced versus voluntary methadone maintenance clients. *American Journal of Drug and Alcohol Abuse, 19:* 89-106.

Brenner, B., & Selzer, M.L. (1969). Risk of causing a fatal accident associated with alcoholism, psychopathology, and stress, further analysis of previous data. *Behavioral Science, 14,* pp. 180-192.

Brickman, P., Rabinowitz, V. C., Karuza, J., Coates, D., Cohn, E., & Kidder, L. (1982). Models of helping and coping. *American Psychologist, 37*, 368-384.

Brooker, R. G. (2002). *Evaluation of Alternatives to Incarceration for Repeat Drunken Driving, Phase I*: Database Search. Milwaukee, WI: The Dieringer Research Group.

Brown, S. A., Myers, M. G., Lippke, L., Tapert, S. F., Stewart, D. G., & Vik, P. W. (1998). Psychometric evaluation of the Customary Drinking and Drug Use Record (CDDR): A measure of adolescent alcohol and drug involvement. *Journal of Studies on Alcohol, 59*, 427-438.

Bruch, H. (1981). Teaching and learning of psychotherapy. *Canadian Journal of Psychiatry, 26*, 86-92.

Bry, B. H. (1983). Predictive drug abuse: Review and reformulation. *Journal of the Addictions, 18,* 223-233.

Bukstein, O. G. (1995). *Adolescent substance abuse: Assessment, prevention and treatment.* New York: Wiley.

Burnet, J. (1986, October 5). Amid rising concern, the drinking age is increased. *The New York Times*, p. E5.

Burns, D. D. (1980). *Feeling good: The new mood therapy*. New York: William Morrow.

Burns, D. D. (1989). *The feeling good handbook*. New York: William Morrow.

Bush, J. M., & Bilodeau, B. C. (1993). *Options: A cognitive change program* (Prepared by J. M. Bush and B. C. Bilodeau for the National Institute of Corrections and the U.S. Department of the Navy). Washington, DC: National Institute of Corrections.

Butcher, J. H. N., Dahlstrom, W. G., Graham, J. R., Tellegan, A. M., & Kaemmer, B. (1989). *MMPI-2: Manual for administration and scoring*. Minneapolis: University of Minnesota Press.

Butler, J. P. (1992). Of kindred minds: The ties that bind. In M. A. Orlandi, R. Weston, & L. G. Epstein (Eds.), *Cultural competence for evaluators: A guide for alcohol and other drug abuse prevention practitioners working with ethnic/racial communities* (pp. 23-54). Rockville, MD: U.S. Department of Health and Human Services.

Caddy, G. R. (1978). Towards a multivariate analysis of alcohol abuse. In P. E. Nathan, G. A. Marlatt, & T. Loberet (Eds.), *Alcoholism: New directions in behavioral research and treatment*. New York: Plenum.

Cameron, T. L. (1982). Drinking and driving among american youth: beliefs and behaviors. *Drug and Alcohol Dependence, 10*, 1-33.

Campbell, D. T., & Fiske, D. W. (1959). Convergent and discriminant validation by the multitrait-multimethod matrix. *Psychological Bulletin, 56*, 81-105.

Campbell, P. R. (1996). *Population projections for states by age, sex, race and Hispanic origin. 1995-2025*. Washington, DC: Bureau of the Census.

Cannon, W. B. (1927). The James-Lang theory of emotions: A critical examination and an alternative theory. *American Journal of Psychology, 39*, 106-124.

Cappell, H., & Greeley, J. (1987). Alcohol and tension reduction: An update on research and theory. In H. T. Blane & K. W. Leonard (Eds.), *Psychological theories of drinking and alcoholism* (pp. 15-54). New York: Guilford.

Cappella, J. N. (1985). The management of conversations. In M. L. Knapp & G. R. Miller (Eds.), *Handbook of interpersonal communication* (pp. 393-438). Beverly Hills, CA: Sage.

Carkhuff, R. R. (1969). *Helping in human relations* (Vols. 1 and 2). New York: Holt, Rinehart & Winston.

Carkhuff, R. R. (1971). *The development of human resources: Education, psychology and social change*. New York: Holt, Rinehart & Winston.

Carkhuff, R. R., & Berenson, B. G. (1977). *Beyond counseling and therapy* (2nd ed.). New York: Holt, Rinehart & Winston.

Carkhuff, R. R., & Truax, C. (1965). Training in counseling and psychotherapy: An evaluation of an integrated didactic and experimental approach. *Journal of Consulting Psychology, 29*, 333-336.

Cautela, J. (1966). Treatment of compulsive behavior by covert sensitization. *Psychological Record, 16*, 33-41.

Cautela, J. (1990). The shaping of behavior therapy: An historical perspective. *The Behavior Therapist, 13*, 211-212.

Cavaiola, A. A. (1984). Resistance issues in the treatment of the DWI offender. *Alcoholism Treatment Quarterly, 1*, 1-16.

Cavaiola, A. A., & Wuth, C. (2002). *Assessment and treatment of the DWI offender*. New York: The Haworth Press.

REFERENCES

Cavaiola, A. A., Wolf, J. M., & Lavender, N. J. (1999). *Comparison of DWI offenders with a non-DWI comparison group on the MMPI-2 and Michigan Alcoholism Screening Test.* Paper presented at the 34th Annual Symposium on Recent Development in the Use of the MMPI-2 and MMPI-A, April 18, 1999, Huntington Beach, CA.

C'de Baca, J., Lapham, S. C., Paine, S., Skipper, B. J. (2000). Victim impact panels: Who is sentenced to attend? Does attendance affect recidivism of first-time DWI offenders? *Alcoholism: Clinical and Experimental Research, 24, No. 9,* 1420-1426.

Centers for Disease Control and Prevention (CDC). (1996). Youth Risk Behavior Surveillance - United States, 1995. *Morbidity and Mortality Weekly Report* 45(SS-4), 1996.

Centre for Addiction and Mental Health (1999). *Back on Track Education Program.* Toronto, Canada: Centre for Addiction and Mental Health.

Century Council, The (2003). *The National Hardcore Drunk Driver Project. The National Agenda: A System to Fight Hardcore DWI.* Washington, DC: The Century Council.

Chang, I., & Lapham, S. C. (1996). Validity of self-report criminal offenses and traffic violations in screening of driving-while-intoxicated offenders. *Alcohol and Alcoholism, 31,* 583-590.

Chang, I., Lapham, S. C., & Wanberg, K. W. (2001). Alcohol Use Inventory: Screening and assessment of first-time driving-while-impaired offenders. I. Reliability and profiles. *Alcohol and Alcoholism, 36,* 112-121.

Cicourel, A. V. (1974). *Cognitive sociology.* New York: Free Press.

Ciraulo, D. A., & Ciraulo, A. M. (1988). Substance abuse. In J. P. Tupin, R. I. Shader, & D. S. Harnett (Eds.), *Handbook of clinical psychopharmacology* (pp. 121-158). Northvale, NJ: Jason Aronson.

Clark, D. A. (2004). *Cognitive-behavioral therapy for OCD.* New York: Guilford.

Clark, D. A., & Steer, R. A. (1996). Empirical status of the cognitive model of anxiety and depression. In P. M. Salkovskis (Ed.), *Frontiers of cognitive therapy* (pp. 75-96). New York: Guilford.

Clay, M. L. (1974). *Characteristics of high risk drivers, alcoholic and otherwise (Communication No. 304).* Ann Arbor: Health Research Institute, University of Michigan.

Clayton, R. R. (1992). Transitions in drug use: Risk and protective factors. In M. D. Glantz, & R. Pickens (Eds.), *Vulnerability to drug use* (pp. 15-51). Washington DC: American Psychological Association.

Cloninger, C. R., & Guze, S. B. (1970). Psychiatric illness and female criminality: The role of sociopathy and hysteria in the antisocial woman. *American Journal of Psychiatry, 127,* 79-87.

Coben, J. H., & Larkin, G. L. (1999). Effectiveness of ignition interlock devices in drunk driving recidivism. *American Journal of Preventive Medicine, 16,* 81-87.

Colby, A., & Kohlberg, L. (1987). *The measurement of moral judgement. Vol 1: Theoretical Foundations and Research Validation.* Cambridge: Cambridge University Press.

Collingwood, R. G. (1949). *The idea of nature.* London: Oxford University Press.

Collins, R. L., Blane, H.T., & Leonard, K. E. (1999). Psychological theories of etiology. In P. J. Ott, R. E. Tarter & R. T. Ammerman (Eds.), *Sourcebook on substance abuse: Etiology, epidemiology, assessment and treatment* (pp. 153-165). Boston: Allyn and Bacon.

Colorado Department of Human Services (1998). *Data Report.* Colorado Department of Human Services, Alcohol Drug Abuse Division (ADAD). Denver, CO: Author.

Colorado Department of Revenue. (2004). *The Colorado driver handbook.* Denver, CO: Author.

Commonwealth of Massachusetts (1996). *Driver Alcohol Education Program.* Lakeville, MA: Commonwealth of Massachusetts Office of Health and Human Services (1996).

Compton, R.P. (1986). Preliminary analysis of the effect of Tennessee's mandatory jail sanction on DWI recidivism. In: *Research Notes,* June. Washington DC. National Highway Traffic Safety Administration.

Compton, R.P. (1988). *Potential for application of ignition interlock devices to inhibit operation of motor vehicles by intoxicated individuals.* Report to Congress, May, 1988. Washington D.C. National Highway Traffic Safety Administration.

Connors, G. J., Carroll, K. M., DiClemente, C. C., Longabaugh, R., & Donovan, D. M. (1997). The therapeutic alliance and its relationship to alcoholism treatment participation and outcome. *Journal of Consulting and Clinical Psychology, 65,* 582-598.

Connors, G. J., Donovan, D. M., & DiClemente, C. C. (2001). *Substance abuse treatment and the stages of change.* New York: The Guilford Press.

Connors, G. J., & Volk, R. J. (2003). Self-report screening for alcohol problems among adults. In J. P. Allen, V. B Wilson, (Eds.), *Assessing alcohol problems: A guide for clinicians and researchers, second edition.* Bethesda, MD: U. S. Department of Health and Human Services, Public Health Service, National Institute on Alcohol Abuse and Alcoholism, NIH Publication No. 03-3745.

Costa, F. M., Jessor R., & Turbin, M. S. (1999). Transition into adolescent problem drinking: The role of psychosocial risk and protective factors. *Journal of Studies on Alcohol, 60*(4), 480-490.

Cottraux, J., & Blackburn, I. (2001). Cognitive therapy. In W. J. Livesley (Ed.), *Handbook of personality disorders* (pp. 377-399). New York: Guilford Publications, Inc.

Courtright, K. E., Berg, B. L., & Mutchnick, R. J. (1997). Effects of house arrest with electronic monitoring on DUI offenders. *Journal of Offender Rehabilitation, 24,* 35-51.

Covey, S. R., Merrill, A. R., & Merrill, R. R. (1994). *First things first: To live, to love, to learn, to leave a legacy.* New York: Simon & Schuster.

Crosby, I. B. (1995). *Portland's Asset Program: The Effectiveness of Vehicle Seizure in Reducing Rearrest Among "Problem" Drunk Drivers.* Portland, OR: Reed College Policy Workshop and the City of Portland Bureau of Police Asset Forfeiture Unit.

Cross, T. L., Bazron, B. J., Dennis, K. W., & Isaacs, M. R. (1989). *Towards a culturally competent system of care* (Monograph Vol. 1). Washington, DC: National Institutes of Mental Health.

CSAT-Center for Substance Abuse Treatment (1994). *Simple screening instrument for outreach for alcohol and other drug use and infectious diseases.* Department of Health and Human Services, Publication No. SMA 94-2094, Washington DC: U.S.Government Printing Office.

Cummings, H. W., Long, L. W., & Lewis, M. L. (1983). *Managing communication in organizations: An introduction.* Dubuque, IA: Gorsuch Scarisbrick Publishers.

Cummings, N. A., Gordon, J., & Marlatt, G. A. (1980). Relapse strategies of prevention and prediction. In W. R. Miller (Ed.), *The addictive behaviors.* Oxford, UK: Pergamon.

Curry, S. G., & Marlatt, G. A. (1987). Building self-confidence, self-efficacy and self control. In W. M. Cox (Ed.), *Treatment and prevention of alcohol problems: A resource manual* (pp. 117-138). New York: Academic Press.

REFERENCES

Daley, D. C., & Marlatt, G. A. (1992). Relapse prevention: Cognitive and behavioral interventions. In J. H. Lowinson, P. Ruiz, R. B. Millman, & J. G. Langrod (Eds.), *Substance abuse: A comprehensive textbook* (pp. 533-542). Baltimore, MD: Williams & Wilkins.

Dana, R. H. (1993). *Multicultural assessment perspectives for professional psychology*. Boston: Longwood.

Dana, R. H. (1998). *Understanding cultural identity in intervention and assessment*. Thousand Oaks, CA: Sage.

Dance, F.E.X (1982). A speech theory of human communication. In F.E.X. Dance (Ed.), *Human communication theory* (pp. 120-146). New York: Harper & Row.

Daniel, A. E., Robins, A. J., Reid, J. C., & Wifley, D. E. (1988). Lifetime and six month prevalence of psychiatric disorders among sentenced female offenders. *Bulletin of the American Academy of Psychiatry and the Law, 164*, 333-342.

Darbey, B. R. (1993). *Pre-trial Services Corporation Felony Driving While Intoxicated Diversion Program: An examination of program outcomes*. Rochester, New York. Report for the Pre-trial Services Corporation.

DeLeon, G. (1988). Legal pressure in therapeutic communities. *Journal of Drug Issues, 18*, 625-640.

Delia, J. G., O'Keefe, B. J., & O'Keefe, D. J. (1982). The constructivist approach to communication. In F. E. X. Dance (Ed.), *Human communication theory*. New York: Harper & Row.

DeMuro, S. A. (1997). *Development and validation of an instrument to measure DUI therapeutic educator style: Therapeutic educator countermeasures inventory*. Denver, CO: University of Denver Unpublished Doctoral Dissertation.

DeMuro, S. A., & Wanberg, K. W. (1998). *Therapeutic Educator Countermeasures Inventory (TECI)*. Denver, CO: Behavioral Health Services' Counselor Training Center.

Derogatis, L. R. (2001). *SCL-90 administration: Scoring and procedures manual*. Bloomington, MN: Pearson Assessments.

DeRubeis, R. J., Tang, T. Z., & Beck, A. T. (2001). Cognitive therapy. In K. S. Dobson (Ed.), *Handbook of cognitive-behavioral therapies* (2nd ed.). New York: Gilford.

Dewey, J. (1910). *How we think*. Washington, DC: Heath & Co.

Deyle, R. (1997). *The effectiveness of education and treatment in reducing recidivism among convicted drinking drivers*. Denver, CO: Alcohol and Drug Abuse Division of the Colorado Department of Human Services.

DeYoung, D. (1997). An evaluation of the effectiveness of alcohol treatment, driver license actions and jail terms in reducing drunk driving recidivism in California, *Addiction, 92*, 989-997.

DiClemente, C. C. (2003). *Addiction and change: How addictions develop and addicted people recover*. New York: Guilford.

DiClemente, C. C., & Valesquez, M. M. (2002). Motivational interviewing and the stages of change. In W. R. Miller, & S Rollnick (Eds.), *Motivational Interviewing: Preparing people for change, 2nd Edition* (pp. 201-216). New York: Guilford Press.

Dimeff, L. A., & Marlatt, G. A. (1995). Relapse prevention. In R. K. Hester & W. R. Miller (Eds.), *Handbook of alcoholism treatment approaches: Effective alternatives* (2nd ed., pp. 176-194). Boston: Allyn & Bacon.

Dobson, K. S., & Block, L. (1988). Historical and philosophical basis of the cognitive-behavioral therapies. In K. S. Dobson (Ed.), *Handbook of cognitive-behavioral therapies* (pp. 3-38). New York: Guilford.

Dobson, K. S., & Dozois, D. J. (2001). Historical and philosophical bases of cognitive-behavioral therapies. In K. S. Dobson (Ed.), *Handbook of cognitive-Behavioral Therapies* (2nd ed., pp. 3-40). New York: Guilford.

Donelson, A. C. (1985). *Alcohol and road accidents in Canada: Issues related to future strategies and priorities*. Ottawa: Ottawa Traffic Injury Research Foundation of Canada.

Donohue, B., & Cavenagh, N. (2003). Anger (negative impulse) management. In W. O'Donohue, J. E. Fisher, & S. C. Hayes (Eds.), *Cognitive behavior therapy: Applying empirically supported techniques in your practice* (pp. 10-15). Hoboken, NJ: John Wiley & Sons.

Donovan, D. M. (1980). *Drinking behavior, personality factors and high risk driving*. Unpublished doctoral dissertation, University of Washington, Seattle.

Donovan, D. M. (1999). Assessment strategies and measures in addictive behaviors. In B. S. McCrady & E. E. Epstein (Eds.), *Addictions: A comprehensive guidebook*. New York: Oxford University Press.

Donovan, D. M. (2003). Treatment planning: Assessment to aid in the treatment planning process. In J. P. Allen, V. B Wilson, (Eds.), *Assessing alcohol problems: A guide for clinicians and researchers, second edition* (pp. 125-188). Bethesda, MD: U. S. Department of Health and Human Services, Public Health Service, National Institute on Alcohol Abuse and Alcoholism, NIH Publication No. 03-3745.

Donovan, D. M., & Marlatt, G. A. (1982a). Reasons for drinking among DWI arrestees. *Addictive Behaviors, 7*, 423-426.

Donovan, D. M., & Marlatt, G. A. (1982b). Personality subtypes among driving-while-intoxicated offenders: Relationships to drinking behavior and driving risk. *Journal of Consulting and Clinical Psychology, 50*, 241-249.

Donovan, D. M., Marlatt, G. A., & Salzberg, P. M. (1983). Drinking behavior, personality factors and high-risk driving: A review and theoretical formulation. *Journal of Studies on Alcohol, 44*, pp.395-428.

Donovan, D. M., Queisser, H. R., Salzberg, P. M., Umlauf, R. L. (1985). Intoxicated and bad drivers: Subgroups within the same population of high risk men drivers. *Journal of Studies on Alcohol, 46(5)*: 375-382.

Donovan, D. M., Queisser, H. R., Umlauf, P. M., & Salzberg, P. M. (1986). Personality subtypes among driving-while-intoxicated offenders: Follow-up of subsequent driving records. *Journal of Consulting and Clinical Psychology, 54*, 563-565.

Donovan, D. M., Umlauf, R. L., & Salzberg, P. M. (1990). Bad drivers: Identification of a target group for alcohol-related prevention and early intervention. *Journal of Studies on Alcohol, 51*, 136-141.

Drummond, A. E., & Triggs, T. J. (1991). *Driving as skilled performance: A perspective for improving young driver safety*. Melbourne, Australia: Monash University, Accident Research Center.

Dryden, W., & Ellis, A. (2001). Rational emotive behavioral therapy. In K. S. Dobson (Ed.), *Handbook of cognitive-Behavioral Therapies* (2nd ed., pp. 295-348). New York: Guilford.

Dryden, W., & Mytton, J. (1999). *Four approaches to counseling and psychotherapy*. New York: Routledge.

Dunlap, K. (1932). *Habits: Their making and unmaking*. New York: Liveright.

Dvorak, J. A. (2002). Kansas launches racial profiling study. *The Kansas City Star*, 1, 11.

D'Zurilla, T. J., & Goldfried, M. R. (1971). Problem solving and behavior modification. *Journal of Abnormal Psychology, 78*, 107-126.

D'Zurilla, T. J., & Nezu, A. M. (2001). Problem-solving therapies. In K. S. Dobson (Ed). *Handbook of cognitive-behavioral therapies* (2nd ed., pp. 211-245). New York: The Guilford Press.

Eckhardt, C., & Deffenbacher, J. (1995). In H. Kassinove (Ed.), *Anger disorders: Definition, diagnosis and treatment.* Bristol: Taylor & Francis.

Edelbrook, C., Costello, A. J., Dulcan, M.K., & Kalas, R. (1986). Parent-child agreement on child psychiatric symptoms assessed via structured interview. *Journal of Child Psychology and Psychiatry, 27,* 181-190.

Edwards, G., Anderson, P., Babor T.F., Casswell, S., Ferrence, R., Giesbrecht, N., et al. (1994). *Alcohol policy and the public good.* Oxford: Oxford University Press.

Efran, J. S., & Clarfield, L. E. (1992). Constructionist therapy: Sense and nonsense. In S. McNamee & K. J. Gergen, *Therapy as Social Construction.* London: Sage.

Elkin, I. (1986). *NIMH treatment of depression collaborative research program.* Paper presented at the annual meeting of the Society for Psychotherapy Research, Wellesley, MA.

Ellickson, P. L., & Hays, R. D. (1991). Beliefs about resistance self-efficacy and drug prevalence: Do they really affect drug use? *International Journal of the Addictions, 25,* 1353-1378.

Ellinsgstad, V. S., & Springer, T. J. (1976). *Program level evaluation of ASAP diagnosis, referral and rehabilitation efforts. Volume III: Evaluation of rehabilitation effectiveness.* Contract No. DOT HS 191 3 759. Washington, DC: National Highway Traffic Safety Administration.

Elliott, D. S. (1987). Self-reported DWI and the risk of alcohol/drug related accidents. *Alcohol, Drugs and Driving, 3,* 31-44.

Ellis, A. (1962). *Reason and emotion in psychotherapy.* New York: Stuart.

Ellis, A. (1984). Rational-emotive therapy. In R. J. Corsini (Ed.), *Current psychotherapies* (3rd ed., pp. 196-238). Itasca, IL: Peacock.

Ellis, A. (1990). Live demonstration of rational-emotive therapy (Audio tape from *The Evolution of Psychotherapy: A conference*). Phoenix, AZ: The Milton H. Erickson Foundation.

Ellis, A., & Harper, R. A. (1961). *A guide to rational living.* Englewood Cliffs, NJ: Prentice-Hall.

Ellis, A., & Harper, R. A. (1975). *A new guide to rational living.* Englewood Cliffs, NJ: Prentice-Hall.

Empowerment Counseling Services, Inc. (1998). *Drug and Alcohol Education.* Lakewood, CO: Empowerment Counseling Services, Inc.

EMT Group (1990). *Evaluation of the California ignition interlock pilot program for DUI offenders* (Farr-Davis Driver Safety Act of 1986). Sacramento, CA: California Department of Alcohol and Drug Programs.

Epstein, J. A., Griffin, K. W., & Botvin, G. J. (2001). Risk taking and refusal assertiveness in a longitudinal model of alcohol use among inner-city adolescents. *Prevention Science, 2,* 193-200.

Erikson, E. H. (1959). *Childhood and society* (2nd ed.) NY: Norton.

Erikson, E. H. (1968). *Youth and crisis.* NY: Norton.

Erikson, E. H. (1975). *Life history and the historical moment.* NY: W. W. Norton

Eysenck, H. J. (1952). The effects of psychotherapy: An evaluation. *Journal of Consulting Psychology, 16,* 319-324.

Eysenck, H. J. (1960). *Behavior therapy and the neuroses.* London: Pergamon.

Falkowski, C.L. (1984). *The impact of two-day jail sentences for drunk drivers in Hennepin County, Minnesota.* DOT HS 806 839. Final report. Washington DC. National Highway Traffic Safety Administration.

Farris, J. J., & Jones, B. M. (1978). Ethanol metabolism in male American Indians and whites. *Alcohol and Clinical Experimental Research, 2,* 77-81.

Farrow, J. A. (1985). Drinking and driving behaviors of 16-19 year olds. *Studies on Alcohol 46,* 369-374.

Farrow, J. A. (1989). Evaluation of behavioral intervention to reduce DWI among adolescent drivers. International Symposium: The Social Psychology of Risky Driving (Santa Monica, California). *Alcohol, Drugs & Driving, 5,* 61-72.

Fazzalaro, J. J. (2001). *Office of Legislative Research Report: Drunk Driving Penalty Comparison.* Hartford, CT: Connecticut Office of Legislative Research.

Fell, J. C. (1993). Repeat DWI offenders: Their involvement in fatal crashes. In H. D. Utzelmann, G. Berhaus, & G. Kroj (Eds.), *Alcohol, drugs and traffic safety, 92,* (pp. 1044-1049). Cologne, Germany: Verlag TUV Rheinland GmbH.

Fell, J. C. (1994). Current trends: Drivers with repeat convictions or arrests for driving while impaired. *MMWR Weekly, 43,* 759-761.

Ferguson, S.A., Leaf, W.A., Williams, A.F., & Preusser, D.F. (1996). Differences in young driver crash involvement in states with varying licensure practices. *Accident Analysis and Prevention, 28,* 171-80.

Fergusson, D. M., Swain-Campbell, Nicola R., Horwood, L. John. 2002. Deviant peer affiliations, crime and substance use: A fixed effects regression analysis. *Journal of Abnormal Child Psychology, 30,* 419-430.

Feshbach, N. D. (1984). Empathy, empathy training and the regulation of aggression in elementary school children. In R. M. Kaplan, V. J. Konecni, & R. W. Novaco (Eds.), *Aggression in children and youth.* The Hague: Martinus Nijhoff.

Filkins, L. D., Mortimer, R. G., Post, D. V., & Chapman, M. W. (1973). *Field evaluation of court procedures for identifying problem drinkers: Final report.* Ann Arbor, MI: Highway Safety Research Institute, University of Michigan.

Fine, E. W., Scoles, P., & Mulligan, M. (1975). Under the influence: Characteristics and drinking practices of persons arrested for the first time for drunk driving, with treatment implications. *Public Health Reports, 90,* 424-429.

Finney, J. W. (2003). Assessing treatment and treatment processes. In J. P. Allen, V. B Wilson, (Eds.), *Assessing alcohol problems: A guide for clinicians and researchers, second edition* (pp. 37-54). Bethesda, MD: U. S. Department of Health and Human Services, Public Health Service, National Institute on Alcohol Abuse and Alcoholism, NIH Publication No. 03-3745.

Fischer, D. L., Dixon, D. J., & Maxwell, F. R. (1994). *Weekend Intervention Program - WIP.* Missouri State: Missouri Department of Mental Health, Division of Alcohol and Drug Abuse.

Fisher, G. L., & Harrison, T. C. (2000). *Substance abuse: Information for school counselors, social workers, therapists, and counselors.* Boston: Allyn and Bacon.

Fisher, H.R., Simpson, R. I., & Kapur, B.M. (1987). Calculation of blood alcohol concentration (BAC) by sex, weight, number of drinks and time. *Canadian Journal of Public Health, 78,* 300-304.

Fisher, R., & Ury, W. (1981). *Getting to YES: Negotiating agreement without giving in.* Boston: Houghton Mifflin.

Foldvary, L.A., & Lane, J.C. (1969). Car crash injuries by seating position and miles traveled. In *Proceeding of the 13th annual conference of the American Association for Automotive Medicine* (pp. 17-72). Minneapolis, MN.

Fors, S.W., & Rojek, D.G. (1999). The effect of victim impact panels on DUI/DWAI rearrest rates: A twelve-month follow-up. *Journal of Studies on Alcohol, 60,* 514-520.

Frank, J. D. (1963). *Persuasion and healing: A comparative study of psychotherapy.* New York: Schocken Books.

REFERENCES

Frank, J. D. (1971). Therapeutic factors in psychotherapy. *American Journal of Psychotherapy, 25*, 350-361.

Frank, J. D. (1974). Psychotherapy: Restoration of morale. *American Journal of Psychiatry, 131, 271-274.*

Frank, J. D. (1992). Historical development in research centers: The Johns Hopkins Psychotherapy Research Project. In D. K. Freedheim (Ed.), *History of psychotherapy: A century of change* (pp. 392-395). Washington, DC: American Psychological Association.

Frankl, V. E. (1959). *Man's search for meaning.* Boston: Beacon Press.

Frankl, V. E. (1980). *Man's search for meaning: An introduction to Logotherapy.* New York: Simon & Schuster.

Franks, C. M., & Barbrack, C. R. (1983). Behavior therapy with adults: An integrative perspective. In M. Hersen, A. E. Kazdin, & A. S. Bellack (Eds.), *Clinical psychology handbook* (pp. 507-524). New York: Pergamon.

Franks, C. M., & Wilson, G. T. (1973-1975). *Annual review of behavior therapy: Theory and practice* (Vols. 1-7). New York: Brunner/Mazel.

Freeman, A., Pretzer, J., Fleming, B., & Simon, K. M. (1990). *Clinical applications of cognitive therapy.* New York: Plenum.

Freud, S. (1893-1895). The psychotherapy of hysteria. *Studies on Hysteria.* In Standard edition, Vol. II. London: Hogarth Press.

Freud, S. (1913). *On beginning the treatment (Further Recommendations on the Technique of Psycho-Analysis I).* In Standard edition. London: Hograth Press.

Fried, R. 0. (1993). The role of respiration in stress and stress control: Toward a theory of stress as a hypoxic phenomenon. In P. M. Lehrer & R. L. Woolfolk (Eds.), *Principles and practice of stress management* (2nd ed., pp. 301-332). New York: Guilford.

Friedman, J., Harrington, C., Higgins, D. (1995). *Reconvicted drinking driver study.* AL 90-004. Albany, NY. New York State Governor's Traffic Safety Committee.

Fromme, K., & D'Amico, E. J. (1999). Neurobiological bases of alcohol's psychological effects. In K. E. Leonard & H. T. Blane (Eds.), *Psychological Theories of Drinking and Alcoholism* (2nd ed., pp. 442-455). New York: Guilford.

GAINS Center (1997). *Women's program compendium: A comprehensive guide to services for women with co-occurring disorders in the justice system.* Delmar, NY: The GAINS Center/Policy Research Associates, Inc.

Gardner, H. (1985). *The mind's new science: A history of the cognitive revolution.* NY: Basic Books.

Garfield, S. L. (1992). Major issues in psychotherapy research. In D. K. Freedheim (Ed.), *History of psychotherapy: A century of change* (pp. 335-359). Washington, DC: American Psychological Association.

Gaston, L. (1990). The concept of the alliance and its role in psychotherapy: Theoretical and empirical considerations. *Psychotherapy, 27,* 143-153.

George, R. L. (1990). *Counseling the chemically dependent: Theory and practice.* Englewood Cliffs, NJ: Prentice-Hall.

George, R. L., & Cristiani, T. S. (1981). *Theory, methods and processes of counseling and psychotherapy.* Englewood Cliffs, NJ: Prentice-Hall.

Gitlow, S. (2001). *Substance use disorders: A practical guide.* New York: Lippincott Williams & Wilkins.

Gitlow, S. F. (1970). The pharmacological approach to alcohol. *Maryland State Medical Journal, 19,* 93-96.

Gitlow, S. F. (1982). The clinical pharmacology and drug interaction of ethanol. In E. M. Pattison & F. Kaufman (Eds.), *Encyclopedic handbook of alcoholism* (pp. 1-18). New York: Gardner.

Gitlow, S. F. (1988). An overview. In S. E. Gitlow & H. S. Peyser (Eds.), *Alcoholism: A practical treatment guide* (2nd ed., pp. 1-18). Philadelphia: W. B. Saunders.

Glass, C. R., & Arnkoff, D. B. (1988). Common and specific factors in client descriptions of and explanations for change. *Journal of Integrative and Eclectic Psychotherapy, 7,* 427-440.

Glass, C. R., & Arnkoff, D. B. (1992). Behavior therapy. In D. K. Freedheim (Ed.), *History of psychotherapy: A century of change* (pp. 587-628). Washington, DC: American Psychological Association.

Glass, C. R., & Arnkoff, D. B. (1997). Questionnaire methods of cognitive self-statement assessment. *Journal of Consulting and Clinical Psychology, 65,* 911-927.

Glass, R. J., Chan, G., & Rentz, D. (2000). Cognitive impairment screening in second offense DUI programs. *Journal of Substance Abuse Treatment, 19,* 369-373.

Glassman, S. (1983). In, with, and of the group: A perspective on group psychotherapy. *Small Group Behavior, 14,* 96-106.

Glenn, H. S., & Hockman, R. H. (1977). *Substance abuse.* Unpublished manuscript, NDAC.

Glenn, H. S., & Warner, J. W. (1975). *Understanding substance dependence.* Unpublished manuscript, Social Systems, Inc.

Glenn, H. S., Warner, J. W., & Hockman, R. H. (1977). *Substance dependence.* Unpublished manuscript, NDAC.

Godley, S., White, W., Diamond, G., Passetti, L., & Titus, J. (2001). Therapist reactions to manual-guided therapies for the treatment of adolescent marijuana users. *Clinical Psychology: Science and Practice, 8,* 405-417.

Goldfried, M. R. (1995). *From cognitive-behavioral therapy to psychotherapy integration: An evolving view.* New York: Springer.

Goldfried, M. R., Decenteceo, E. T., & Weinberg, L. (1974). Systematic rational restructuring as a self-control technique. *Behavior Therapy, 5,* 247-254.

Goldiamond, I. (1965). Self-control procedures in personal behavior problems. *Psychological Reports, 17,* 851-868.

Goldman, M. S., Brown, S. A., & Christiansen, B. A. (1987). Expectancy theory: Thinking about drinking. In H. T. Blane & K. E. Leonard (Eds.), *Psychological theories of drinking and alcoholism* (pp. 181-226). New York: Guilford.

Goldman, M. S., Del Boca, F. K., & Darkes, J. (1999). In H. T. Blane & K. W. Leonard (Eds.), *Psychological theories of drinking and alcoholism* (2nd ed., pp. 203-246). New York: Guilford.

Goldstein, D. B. (1992). Pharmacokinetics of alcohol. In J. H. Mendelson & N.K. Mello (Eds.), *The medical diagnosis and treatment of alcoholism.* New York: McGraw-Hill.

Goldstein, L. G., & Mosel, J. N. (1958). A factor study of drivers' attitudes with further study on driver aggression. *Highway Research Board Bulletin, 172,* 9-29.

Gomberg, E. S. L. (1986). Women: Alcohol and other drugs. In B. Segal (Ed.), *Perspectives on drug use in the United States.* New York: Haworth.

Gomberg, E. S. L. (1999). Women: Alcohol and other drugs. In B. S. McCrady & D. E. Epstein (Eds.), *Addictions: A comprehensive guidebook* (pp. 527-541). New York: Oxford University Press.

Gottfredson, M. R., & Hirschi, T. (1990). *A general theory of crime.* Stanford, CA: Stanford University Press.

Gould, L.A., Gould, K.H. (1992). First-time and multiple-DWI offenders: A comparison of criminal history records and BAC levels. *Journal of Criminal Justice, 20:* 527-539.

Grant, B. (1998). The impact of family history of alcoholism on the relationship between age of onset of alcohol use and DSM-III alcohol dependence. *Alcohol Health & Research World, 22,* 144-147.

REFERENCES

Grant, B., & Dawson, D. A. (1999). Alcohol and drug use, abuse and dependence: Classification, prevalence, and comorbidity. In B. S. McCrady & D. E. Epstein (Eds.), *Addictions: A comprehensive guidebook* (pp. 9-29). New York: Oxford University Press.

Grant, B., Harford, T. C., Dawson, D. A., Chou, S. P., Dufour, M., & Pickering, R. P. (1994). Prevalence of DSM-IV alcohol abuse and dependence. *United States, Alcohol, Health and Research World, 18,* 243-247.

Greeley, J., & Oei, T. (1999). Alcohol and tension reduction. In H. T. Blane & K. W. Leonard (Eds.), *Psychological theories of drinking and alcoholism* (pp. 14-53). New York: Guilford.

Green, G. S., & Phillips, Z. H. (1990). An examination of an intensive probation for alcohol offenders: Five-year follow-up. *International Journal of Offender Therapy and Comparative Criminology, 34,* 34-41.

Greenberger, D., & Padesky, C. A. (1995). *Mind over mood: A cognitive therapy treatment manual for clients.* New York: Guilford.

Greenson, R. R. (1967). *Technique and practice of psychoanalysis.* New York: International University Press.

Griffin, K. W., Botvin, G. J., Epstein, J. A, Doyle, M. M. & Diaz, T. (2000). Psychosocial and behavioral factors in early adolescence as predictors of heavy drinking among high school seniors. *Journal of Studies on Alcohol, 61,* 603-606.

Griffin, K. W., Scheier, L. M., Botvin, G. J., & Dias, T. (2001). Protective role of personal competence skills in adolescent substance use: Psychological well-being as a mediating factor. *Psychology of Addictive Behaviors, 15,* 194-203.

Grilly, D. M. (1989). *Drugs and human behavior.* Boston: Allyn & Bacon.

Grube, J. W., Kearney, K.A. (1983). A "mandatory" jail sentence for drinking and driving. *Evaluation Review, 7,* 235-245.

Gruenewald, P. J., Steward, K., & Kiltzner, M. (1990). Alcohol use and the appearance of alcohol problems among first offender drunk drivers. *British Journal of Addiction, 85,* 107-177.

Guajardo-Lucero, Maria (2000). *The Spirit of Culture: Applying Cultural Competency to Strength-based Youth Development.* Denver: Assets for Colorado Youth.

Guidano, V. F. (1987). *Complexity of the self: A developmental approach to psychopathology and therapy.* New York: Guilford.

Guidano, V. F., & Liotti, G. (1983). *Cognitive processes and emotional disorders: A structural approach to psychotherapy.* New York: Guilford.

Gurman, A. S., & Messer, S. B. (2003). Contemporary issues in the theory and practice of psychotherapy. In *Essential psychotherapies: Theory and practice,* (2nd ed., pp. 1-24). New York: Guilford.

Gurnak, A. M. (1989). Rehabilitation outcomes for alcohol impaired drivers referred for assessment in two Wisconsin counties. *Journal of Alcohol and Drug Education, 35,* 45-59.

Guthrie, E. R. (1935). *The psychology of learning.* New York: Harper.

Guy, E., Platt, J. J., Zwerling, I., & Bullock, S. (1985). Mental health status of prisoners in an urban jail. *Criminal Justice and Behavior, 12,* 29-53.

Hagen, R.E. (1978). The efficacy of licensing controls as a countermeasure for multiple DUI offenders. *Journal of Safety Research 10,* 115-122.

Ham, H. (1957). *Lecture on the concepts of Kurt Lewin's theory of growth and learning.* Denver, CO: Iliff School of Theology.

Hanson, N. R. (1958). *Patterns of discovery.* Cambridge, UK: Cambridge University Press.

Harding, W. M., et al. (1989). *Assessment of multiple DWI offender restrictions.* National Highway Traffic Safety Administration Report No. HS 807 615. Springfield, VA: National Technical Information Service.

Hare, R. D. (1970). *Psychopathy: Theory and research.* NY: Wiley.

Hare, R. D. (1980). A research scale for the assessment of psychopathy in criminal populations. *Personality and Individual Differences, 1,* 111-119.

Hare, R. D. (1986). Twenty years experience with the Cleckley psychopath. In W. H. Reid, D. Door, J. I. Walker, & J. W. Bonner (Eds.), *Unmasking the psychopath.* New York: W. W. Norton.

Hare, R. D. (2003). *Hare Psychopathy Checklist-Revised.* Minneapolis, MN: Pearson Assessments.

Harper, F. D.(2003). Background: Concepts and History. In F. D. Harper & J. McFadden (Eds.), *Culture and counseling; New Approaches* (pp. 1-19). New York: Allyn and Bacon.

Harris, D. A. (1999). The stories, the statistics and the law: Why "Driving While Black" matters. *Minnesota Law Review, 84,* 265-326.

Harris, G. T., Rice, M. E., & Quinsey, V. L. (1992). *Psychopathy as ataxon: Evidence that psychopaths are a discrete class* (Research report 11(2), May). Penetanguishene, Ontario: Penetanguishene Mental Health Center.

Hart, L. (1991). *Training methods that work: A handbook for trainers.* Menlo Park, CA: Crisp Publication.

Hart, L. S., & Stueland, D. S. (1979). An application of the multidimensional model of alcoholism: Differentiation of alcoholics by mode analysis. *Journal of Studies on Alcohol, 40,* 283-290.

Hartley, D., & Strupp, H. (1983). The therapeutic alliance: Its relationship to outcome in brief psychotherapy. In J. Masling (Ed.), *Empirical studies of psychoanalytic theory* (Vol. 1, pp. 1-38). Hillsdale, NJ: Erlbaum.

Harwood, H., Fountain, D., Livermore, G., et al. (1998). *The economic costs of alcohol and drug abuse in the United States (Table 1.4).* NIH: National Institute on Drug Abuse and National Institute on Alcohol Abuse and Alcoholism.

Hawkins, J. D., Catalano, R. F., & Miller, J. Y (1992). Risk and protective factors for alcohol and other drug problems in adolescence and early adulthood: Implications for substance abuse prevention. *Psychological Bulletin, 112,* 64-105).

Hawkins, J. D., Lishner, D. M., & Catalano, R. F. (1985). Childhood predictors and the prevention of adolescent substance abuse. In C. L. Jones & R. J. Battjes (Eds.), *Etiology of drug abuse: Implications for prevention* (NIDA Research Monograph 56). Rockville, MD: National Institute on Drug Abuse.

Hays, R. D., & Ellickson, P. L. (1990). How generalizable are adolescents' beliefs about pro-drug pressures and resistance self-efficacy? *Journal of Applied Social Psychology, 20,* 321-340.

Heather, N., Kissoon-Singh, J., & Fenton, G. W. (1990). Assisted natural recovery from alcohol problems: Effects of self-help manual with and without supplementary telephone contact. *British Journal of Addictions, 85,* 1177-1185.

Hedlund, J., & McCartt, A. (2002). *Drunk driving: A roadmap for progress.* Lifesavers workshop, June 9, 2002. Preusser Research Group, Inc.

Heider, F. (1958). *The psychology of interpersonal relations.* New York: Wiley.

Hingson, R. (1996). Prevention of drinking and driving. *Alcohol Health and Research World, 20:* 219-229.

Hingson, R., Heeren, T., Jamanka, A., & Howland, J. (2000). Age of drinking onset and unintentional injury involvement. *JAMA: Journal of the American Medical Association, 284,* 1527-1533.

Hingson, R., Heeren, T., Levenson, S., et al., (2002). Age of drinking onset, driving after drinking and involvement in alcohol-related motor vehicle crases. *Accident Analysis and Prevention, 34,* 85-92.

REFERENCES

Hingson, R., Heeren, T., & Winter, M. (1996). Lowering state legal blood alcohol limits to 0.08%: The effect on fatal motor vehicle crashes. *American Journal of Public Health, 86*(9), 1297.1299.

Hingson, R., Heeren, T., & Winter, M. (1998). Effects of Maine's .05 percent legal blood alcohol level for drivers with DWI convictions. *Public Health Reports, 113*, 440-446.

Hingson, R., & Winter, M. (2003). Epidemiology and consequences of drinking and driving. *Alcohol Research & Health, 27*, 63-78.

Hodding, G. C., Jann, M., & Ackerman, I. P. (1980). Drug withdrawal syndromes: A literature review. *The Western Journal of Medicine, 133*, 383-391.

Hodgins, S., & Cote, G. (1990). Prevalence of mental disorders among penitentiary inmates in Quebec. *Canada's Mental Health, 38*, 1-4.

Hoffman, M. L. (1984). Moral development. In M. H. Bornstein & M. E. Lamb (Eds.), *Developmental psychology: An advanced textbook* (p. 279). Hillsdale, NJ: Lawrence Erlbaum.

Hoffman, M. L. (1987). The contribution of empathy to justice and moral judgment. In N. Eisenberg & J. Strayer (Eds.), *Empathy and its development* (p. 47). NY: Cambridge University Press.

Hollen, S., & Beck, A. T. (1986). Research on cognitive therapies. In S. L. Garfield & A. E. Bergin (Eds.), *Handbook of psychotherapy and behavior change*. (3rd ed., pp. 443-482). New York: Wiley.

Holubowycz, O.T., Koeden, C.N. & McLean, A.J. (1994). Age, sex and blood alcohol concentration of killed and injured drivers, riders, passengers. *Accident Analysis and Prevention 26*, 483-492.

Homel, R. (1981) Penalties and the drink-driver: A study of one thousand offenders. *Australia & New Zealand Journal of Criminology 14*, 225-241.

Homel, R. (1988). *Policing and punishing the drinking driver: A study of general and specific deterrence.* New York, Springer Verlag.

Horn, J. L., Skinner, H. A., Wanberg, K. W., & Foster, F. M. (1984). *Alcohol Use Questionnaire (AUQ).* Toronto, Canada: Addiction Research Foundation.

Horn, J. L., & Wanberg, K. W. (1969). Symptom patterns related to excessive use of alcohol. *Quarterly Journal of Studies on Alcohol, 30*, 35-58.

Horn, J. L., & Wanberg, K. W. (1973). Females are different: On the diagnosis of alcoholism in women. In N. Rosenberg (Ed.), *Contributions to an Understanding of alcoholism* (pp. 332-354). Rockville, Maryland: U. S. Department of Health, Education, Welfare.

Horn, J. L., Wanberg, K. W., & Foster, F. M. (1990). *Guide to the Alcohol Use Inventory (AUI).* Minneapolis, MN: National Computer Systems.

Horvath, A. O., & Symonds, B. B. (1991). Relation between working alliance and outcome in psychotherapy: A meta-analysis. *Journal of Counseling Psychology, 38*, 139-149.

Household Vehicles Energy Consumption (1994). Vehicle miles traveled, Chapter 3. *Household Energy Consumption.* Internet: www.eia.doe.gov/emeu/rtecs/chapter3.html.

Hull, C. L. (1943). *Principles of behavior.* New York: Appleton-Century-Crofts.

Hull, J. G. (1987). Self-awareness model. In H. T. Blane & K. W. Leonard (Eds.), *Psychological theories of drinking and alcoholism* (pp. 272-304). New York: Guilford.

Hull, J., & Bond, C. (1986). Social and behavioral consequences of alcohol consumption and expectancy: A meta-analysis. *Psychological Bulletin, 99*, 347-360.

Husserl, E. (1960). *Cartesian meditation*, D. Cairns (Ed.). The Hague: Nijhoff.

Hyman, M. M. (1976). Alcoholics 15 years later. *Annals of the New York Academy of Sciences, 273*, 613-623.

IIHS - Insurance Institute for Highway Safety. (1997). Alcohol impaired driving still a big problem. *Status Report, 32*(3), 1-2.

Inciardi, J. A. (1994). *Screening and assessment for alcohol and other drug abuse among adults in the criminal justice system: Treatment Improvement Protocol (TIP) Series.* Rockville, MD: U.S. Department of Health and Human Services, Public Health Services, Substance Abuse and Mental Health Services Administration, Center for Substance Abuse Treatment.

Inciardi, J. A. (1994). *Drug treatment and criminal justice.* Newbury Park, CA: Sage.

Institute of Medicine (1990). *Broadening the Base of Treatment for Alcohol Problems.* Washington, DC: National Academy Press.

International Council on Alcohol, Drugs & Traffic Safety (2001). Implications of low blood alcohol content for traffic safety: TRB Committee on Alcohol, Other Drugs and Traffic Safety Midyear Workshop - July, 2001. *ICADTS Reporter, 12*, No. 4. Woods Hole, MA.

Irgens-Jensen, O. (1975). The relationship between self-reported drunken driving, alcohol consumption, and personality variables among Norwegian students. In S. Israelstam, & S. Lambert (Eds.), *Alcohol, drugs and traffic safety* (pp. 159-168). Toronto, Ontario, Canada: Alcoholism and Drug Addiction Research Foundation.

Isaacs, M. R., & Benjamin, M. P. (1991). *Towards a culturally competent system of care* (Monograph Volume 2). Washington, DC: National Institutes of Mental Health.

Island Grove Community Counseling Center (1999a). *Impaired Driving Program - Level II Education.* Greeley, CO: Island Grove Community Counseling Center.

Island Grove Community Counseling Center (1999b). *Impaired Driving Program - Level II Therapy.* Greeley, CO: Island Grove Community Counseling Center.

Ivey, A. E., & Simek-Downing, L. (1980). *Counseling and psychotherapy: Skills, Theories, and Practice.* Englewood Cliffs, NJ: Prentice-Hall, Inc., 1980.

Izzo, R. L., Ross, R. R. (1990). Meta-analysis of rehabilitation programs for juvenile delinquents. *Criminal Justice and Behavior, 17*, 134-142.

Jacobs, J. B. (1990). Toward a jurisprudence of drunk driving recidivism. *Alcohol, Drugs and Driving 6*, 205-211.

Jacobson, E. (1938). *Progressive relaxation* (2nd ed.). Chicago: University of Chicago Press.

James, J., Etter, P., Moore, D., Lathem, G., Hamilton, W., Johnson, J., Grunenfelder, D., & Weber, R. (1998). *Alcohol and Other Drug Information School.* State of Washington: Department of Social and Health Services and Substance abuse.

James, W. (1890). *Principles of psychology.* New York: Henry Holt.

Jessor, R. (1984). Adolescent problem drinking: Psychosocial aspects and developmental outcomes. In L. H. Towle (Ed.), *Proceedings: NIAAA-WHO collaborating center designation meeting and alcohol research seminar* (pp. 104-43). Washington, DC: Public Health Service.

Jessor, R. (1987a). Problem behavior theory, psychosocial development and adolescent problem drinking. *British Journal of Addiction, 82*, 331-342.

Jessor, R. (1987b). Risky driving and adolescent problem behavior: An extension of problem behavior theory. *Alcohol, Drugs and Driving, 3*, 1-11.

Jessor, R. (1998). *New perspectives on adolescent risk behavior.* New York: Cambridge University Press.

Jessor, R., & Jessor, S. (1977). *Problem behavior and psychosocial development: A longitudinal study of youth.* New York: Academic Press.

Johnston, L. D., Bachman, J.G., & O'Malley, P.M. (2000). Monitoring the future study: A continuing study of the lifestyles and values of youth. Press release, *News and Information Services,* University of Michigan, Ann Arbor.

Johnston, L. D., O'Malley, P. M., & Bachman, J. G. (1997). *National survey results on drug use from the Monitoring the Future Study,* 1975-1995 (Vol. 2) NIH Publication No. 98-4140). Washington, DC: U.S. Government Printing Office.

Johnston, L. D., O'Malley, P. M., Bachman, J. G., & Schulberg, J. E. (2004). *Monitoring the future national results on adolescent drug use: Overview of key findings, 2003.* Bethesda, MD: National Institute on Drug Abuse Website: WWW.monitoringthe future.org.

Joksch, H. C. (1988). *The impact of severe penalties on drinking and driving.* Washington, DC. AAA Foundation for Traffic Safety.

Jonah, B. A. (1990). Psychosocial characteristics of impaired drivers: An integrated review in relation to problem behavior theory. In R. J. Wilson & R. E. Mann (Eds.), *Drinking and Driving: Advances in research and prevention* (pp. 13-41). New York: Guilford Press.

Jonah, B. A., & Wilson, R. J. (1986). *Impaired drivers who have never been caught: Are they different from convicted drivers. Technical Paper Series (No. 860195).* Warrendale, PA: Society of Automotive Engineers.

Jones, R. K., Joksch, H.C., Lacey, J.H., & Schmidt, H.J. (1988) Field evaluation of jail sanctions for DWI. *National Highway Traffic Safety Administration Report No. DOT HS 807 325.* Springfield, VA: National Technical Information Service, National Technical Information Service.

Jones, R. K., & Joscelyn, K. B. (1978). *Alcohol and highway safety 1978: A review of the state-of-knowledge.* Washington, DC: National Highway Traffic Safety Administration.

Jones, R. K., & Lacey, J.H. (1991). Review of the literature evaluating the effect of countermeasures to reduce alcohol impaired driving. *National Highway Traffic Safety Administration Report No. DOT HS 808 023.* Springfield, VA: National Technical Information Service.

Jones, R. K., & Lacey, J.H. (1998). Alcohol Highway Safety: Problem Update. Washington, DC. *Final Report for the National Highway Traffic Safety Administration.*

Jones, R. K., & Lacey J.H. (2000). *State of knowledge of alcohol-impaired driving: Research on repeat DWI offenders.* Grant No DTNH22-98-C-055109. National Highway Traffic Safety Administration, Washington, DC.

Jones, R. K., Lacey, J.H., Fell, J.C. (1996). Alternative sanctions for repeat DWI offenders. In: *49th Annual Proceedings of the Association for the Advancement of Automotive Medicine,* (pp.307-315). Des Plaines, IL. AAAM.

Jourard, S. M. (1959). Self-disclosure and other cathexis. *Journal of Abnormal and Social Psychology, 59,* 428-431.

Jourard, S. M., & Friedman, R. (1970). Experimenter-subject "distance" and self-disclosure. *Journal of Personality and Social Psychology, 15,* 278-282.

Jourard, S. M., & Resnick, J. L. (1970). The effect of high revealing subjects on self-disclosure of low revealing subjects. *Journal of Humanistic Psychology, 10,* 84-93.

Juhnke, G. A. (2002). *Substance abuse assessment and diagnosis: A comprehensive guide for counselors and helping professions.* New York: Brunner-Routledge.

Kadden, R. M. (1999). Cognitive behavior therapy. In P. J. Ott, R. E. Tarter & R. T. Ammerman (Eds.), *Sourcebook on substance abuse: Etiology, epidemiology, assessment and treatment* (pp. 272-292). Boston: Allyn and Bacon.

Kadden, R., Carroll, K., Donovan, D., Cooney, N., Monti, P., Abrams, D., Litt, M., & Hester, R. (1992). *Cognitive-behavioral coping skills therapy manual: A clinical research guide for therapists treating individuals with alcohol abuse and dependence* (Project MATCH Monograph Series, Vol. 3). Rockville, MD: National Institutes on Alcohol Abuse and Alcoholism, U.S. Department of Health and Human Services, National Institutes of Health.

Kandel, D. B., Kessler, R. C., & Margulies, R. Z. (1978). Antecedents of adolescent initiation into stages of drug use: A developmental analysis. In D. B. Kandel (Ed.), *Longitudinal research on drug use: Empirical findings and methodological issues* (pp. 73-99). Washington, DC: Hemisphere (Halstead-Wiley).

Kandel, D. B., Simcha-Fagan, O., & Davies, M. (1986). Risk factors for delinquency and illicit drug use from adolescence to youth adulthood. *Journal of Drug Issues, 16,* 67-90.

Kanfer, F. H. (1970). Self-regulation: Research, issues and speculations. In C. Neuringer & J. L. Michael (Eds.), *Behavior modification in clinical psychology* (pp. 178-220). New York: Appleton-Century-Crofts.

Kanfer, F. H. (1975). Self-management methods: In F. H. Kanfer & A. P. Goldstein (Eds.), *Helping people change.* New York: Pergamon.

Kanfer, F. H. (1986). Implications of a self-regulation model of therapy for treatment of addictive behaviors. In W. R. Miller & N. Heather (Eds.), *Treating addictive behaviors: Processes of change.* New York: Plenum.

Kaplan, A., & Laygo, R. (2003). Stress management. In W. O'Donohue, J. E. Fisher, & S. C. Hayes (Eds.), *Cognitive behavior therapy: Applying empirically supported techniques in your practice* (pp. 411-416). Hoboken, NJ: John Wiley & Sons.

Karenga, M. (1980). *Kawaida theory: An introduction.* Inglewood, CA: Kawaida Publications.

Kaufman, E. (1994). *Psychotherapy of Addicted Persons.* New York, Guilford.

Kazdin, A. E. (1978). Behavior therapy: Evolution and expansion. *The Counseling Psychologist, 7,* 34-37.

Kelleher, E. J. (1971). A diagnostic evaluation of 400 drinking drivers. *Journal of Safety Research, 3,* 52-55.

Kelley, H. H. (1971). Causal schemata and the attribution process. In E. E. Jones, D. E. Kanouse, H. H. Kelley, R. E. Nisbett, S. Valins, & B. Weiner (Eds.), *Attribution: Perceiving the causes of behavior.* Morristown, NJ: General Learning Press.

Kelley, H. H. (1987). Toward a taxonomy of interpersonal conflict process. In S. Oskamp & S. Spacapan (Eds.), *Interpersonal processes* (pp. 122-147). Beverly Hills, CA: Sage.

Kelly, G. A. (1955). *The psychology of personal constructs* (2 vols.). New York: Norton.

Kendall, P. C., & Bemis, K. M. (1983). Thought and action in psychotherapy: The cognitive-behavioral approaches. In M. Hersen, A. E. Kazdin, & A. S. Bellack (Eds.), *The clinical psychology handbook* (pp. 565-592). New York: Pergamon.

Kendall, P. C., & Hollon, S. D. (1979). Cognitive-behavioral interventions: Overview and current status. In P. C. Kendall & S. D. Hollon (Eds.), *Cognitive-behavioral interventions: Theory, research and procedures.* New York: Academic Press.

Kennedy, B. P., Isaac, N.E., and Graham, J.D. (1993). *Drinking Driver Literature Review.* Boston, MA: Harvard Injury Control Center, Harvard School of Public Health.

Kilpatrick, D. G., Schnurr, P. P., Aciereno, R., Saunders, B., Resnick, H. S., and Best, C.L. (2000). Risk factors for adolescent substance abuse and dependence: Data from a national sample. *Journal of Consulting and Clinical Psychology, 68,* 19-30.

REFERENCES

King, K., Rene, S., Schmidt, J., Stipetich, E., & Woldsweth, N. (1994). *Cognitive intervention program*. Madison, WI: Department of Corrections.

Klein, T. (1989). *Changes in alcohol-involved fatal crashes associated with tougher state alcohol legislation* (Contract No. DTNH 2288C07045). Washington, DC: National Highway Traffic Safety Administration.

Klepp, K., & Perry, C.L. (1990). Adolescents, Drinking and Driving: Who does it and why? In Wilson, R.J., & Mann, R.E. (eds), *Drinking and Driving: Advances in Research and Prevention* (pp. 42-67). New York, NY: The Guilford Press.

Knapp, M. L. (1978). *Nonverbal communication in human interaction*. New York: Hold, Rinehart and Winston.

Knowles, M. S. (1980). *The modern practice of adult education: From pedagogy to andragogy*. Chicago, IL: Follett Publishing Company.

Kohlberg, L. (1964). Development of moral character and moral ideology. In M. L. Hoffman and L. W. Hoffman (Eds.), *Review of child development research, Vol. I* (pp. 383-431). NY: Russell Sage Foundation.

Krupnick, J. L., Sotsky, S. M., Simmens, S., Moyer, J., Elkin, I., Watkins, J., & Pilkonis, P. A. (1996). The role of therapeutic alliance in psychotherapy and pharmacotherapy outcome: Findings in the National Institute of Mental Health Treatment of Depression Collaborative Research Program. *Journal of Consulting and Clinical Psychology, 64*, 532-539.

Kuhn, T. S. (1970). *The structure of scientific revolutions* (2nd ed.). Chicago: University of Chicago Press.

Lacey, J.H., Jones, R.K., & Stewart, R. (1991) Cost-benefit analysis of administrative license suspensions. *National Highway Traffic Safety Administration Report No. DOT HS 807 689*. Springfield, VA; National Technical Information Service.

Lacey, J. H., Jones, R. K., & Wiliszowski, C. H. (1997). *Validation of problem drinking screening instruments for DWI Offenders*. Washington, DC: U.S. Department of Transportation, National Highway Traffic Safety Administration.

Lacroix, N. (1998). *Relaxation: 101 essential tips*. New York: DK Publishing, Inc.

Lambert, M. J., & Bergin, A. E. (1992). Achievements and limitations of psychotherapy research. In D. K. Freedheim (Ed.), *History of psychotherapy: A century of change* (pp. 360-390). Washington, DC: American Psychological Association.

Lammers S. M. M., Mainzer, D. E. H, & Breteler, M.H.M. (1995). Do alcohol pharmacokinetics in women vary due to menstrual cycle? *Addiction, 90*, 23-30.

Landrum, J., Mile, S., Neff, R., Prichard,T., Roebuck, J., Wells-Parker, E., & Windham, G. (1982). *Mississippi DUI Probation Follow-Up Project: Final Report*. National Highway Traffic Safety Administration Report No. DOT-HS-806 274 (Springfield, VA: U.S. National Technical Information Service.

Lang, R. (1990). *Psychotherapy: A basic text*. Northvale, NJ: Jason Aronson Inc.

Lange, A. J., & Jakubowski, P. (1976). *Responsible assertive behavior*. Champaign, IL: Research Press.

Langenbucher, J., Sulesund, D., Chung, T., & Morgenstern, J. (1996). Illness severity and self-efficacy as course predictors of DSM-IV alcohol dependence in multisite clinical sample. *Addictive Behaviors, 214*, 543-553.

Lapham, S. C. (1999). *Randomized trial of sanctions to reduce drunk driving recidivism among repeat drunk driving offenders*. Federal Grant Application. Albuquerque, NM: Behavioral Health Research Center of the Southwest, Albuquerque, NM.

Lapham, S. C., Skipper, B. J., & Simpson, G. L. (1997). A prospective study of the utility of standardized instruments in predicting recidivism among first DWI offenders. *Journal of Studies on Alcohol, 58*, 524-530.

Lapham, S. C., Wanberg, K. W., Timken, D., & Barton, K. J. (1996). *A user's guide to the Lovelace Institutes Comprehensive Screen Instrument (LCSI) for evaluating DWI offenders*. Albuquerque, NM: Behavioral Health Research Center of the Southwest.

Latessa, E. J., and Travis, L.F (1988). The effects of intensive supervision with alcoholic probationers. *Journal of Offender Counseling, Services and Rehabilitation, 12*, 175-190.

Lazarus, A. A. (1971). *Behavior therapy and beyond*. New York: McGraw-Hill.

Lazarus, A. A., & Fay, A. (1982). Resistance or rationalization? A cognitive-behavioral perspective. In P. L. Wachtel (Ed.), *Resistance: Psychodynamic and Behavioral Approaches* (pp. 115-132). New York: Plenum.

Lazarus, R. S. (1999). *Stress and emotion: A new synthesis*. New York: Springer.

Lazarus, R. S., & Folkman, S. (1984). *Stress, appraisal and coping*. New York: Springer-Verlag.

Leahy, R. L., (1996). *Cognitive therapy: Basic principles and applications*. Northvale, NJ: Jason Aronson, Inc.

Leahy, R. L. (1997). Cognitive therapy interventions. In R. L. Leahy (Ed.), *Practicing cognitive therapy: A guide to Interventions* (pp. 3-20). Northvale, NJ: Jason Aronson Inc.

Leahy, R. L., & Doud, E. T. (2002). *Clinical advances in cognitive psychotherapy: Theory and application*. New York: Springer.

Lehrer, P. M., & Woolfolk, R. L. (1993). *Principles and practice of stress management* (2nd ed.). New York: Guilford.

Leonard, K. E., & Blane, H. T. (1999). Introduction. In H. T. Blane & K. W. Leonard (Eds.), *Psychological theories of drinking and alcoholism* (2nd ed., pp. 1-13). New York: Guilford.

Leukefield, C. G., & Tims, F. M. (1992). Directions for practice and research. In C. G. Leukefeld & F. M. Tims (Eds.), *Drug abuse treatment services in prisons and jails* (NIDA Monograph No. 118). Rockville, MD: National Institute on Drug Abuse.

Levy, P., Voas, R.B., Johnson, P., & Klein, T. (1977). Evaluation of the ASAPs. *Journal of Safety Research, 10*, 162-176.

Lewin, K. (1935). *A dynamic theory of personality*. New York: McGraw-Hill.

Lewin, K. (1936). *Principles of topological psychology*. New York: McGraw-Hill.

Lewin, K. (1951). *Field theory in social science: Selected theoretical papers* (D. Cartwright, Ed.). New York: Harper.

Lightsey, M. & Sweeney, M. (1985). Life problems experienced from drinking: Factors associated with level of problem drinking among youthful DWI offenders. *Journal of Alcohol and Drug Education, 30*, 65-82.

Lilly, J. R., Ball, R.A., Curry, G.D., & McMullen, J. (1993). Electronic monitoring of the drunk driver: A seven-year study of the home confinement alternative. *Crime & Delinquency, 39*(4), 462-484.

Lindeman, H. (1987). *Driver risk inventory (DRI)*. Phoenix, AZ: Behavior Data Systems, Inc.

Linden, W. (1993). The autogenic training method of J. H. Schultz. In P. M. Lehrer & R. L. Woolfolk (Eds.), *Principles and practice of stress management* (2nd ed., pp. 205-230). New York: Guilford.

Lipps, T. (1907). Das wissen von fremden ichen. *Psychol. Untersuchungen, 1*, 694-722.

Lipsey, M. W. (1989). *The efficacy of Intervention for Juvenile Delinquency: Results from 400 Studies*. Paper presented at the 41st annual meeting of the American Society of Criminology, Reno, NV.

REFERENCES

Lipsey, M. W. (1992). Juvenile delinquency treatment: A meta-analytic inquiry into the variability of effects. In T. D. Cook, H. Cooper, D. S. Cordray, H. Hartmann, L. V. Hedges, R. J. Light, T. A. Louis, & F. Mosteller (Eds.), *Meta-analysis for explanation* (pp. 83-127). New York: Russell Sage Foundation.

Lipsey, M. W., & Wilson, D. B. (1993). The efficacy of psychological, educational and behavioral treatment: Confirmation from meta-analysis. *American Psychologist, 48,* 1181-1209.

Lipton, D. S. (1994). The correctional opportunity: Pathways to drug treatment for offenders. *Journal of Drug Issues 24:* 331-348.

Little, R., & Clontz, K. (1994). Young drunk, dangerous and driving: Underage drinking and driving research findings. *Journal of Alcohol and Drug Education,* 37-49.

Liu, S., Siegel, P.Z., Brewer, R. D., Mokdad, A.H., Sleet, D.A., Surdual, M. (1997).Prevalence of alcohol-impaired driving: Results from a national self-reported survey of health behaviors. *Journal of the American Medical Association (JAMA) 277(2):* 122-125.

Lund, A. K., & Wolf, A.C. (1991). Changes in the incidence of alcohol-impaired driving in the United States, 1973-1986. *Journal of Studies on Alcohol, 52,* 293-301.

Lurie, N. O. (1971). The world's oldest on-going protest demonstration. *Pacific Historical Review, 40,* 311-332.

Lyddon, W. J., & Jones, J. V. (2001). Empirically supported treatments: An introduction. In W. J. Lyddon & J. V. Jones (Eds.), *Empirically supported cognitive therapies: Current and future applications* (pp. 1-12). New York: Springer.

Lyddon, W. J., & Weill, R. (2002). Cognitive psychotherapy and postmodernism: Emerging themes and challenges. In R. L. Leahy, & E. T. Dowd (Eds.), *Clinical advances in cognitive psychotherapy: Theory and Application* (199-210). New York: Springer.

MaGuire, K., & Flanagan, T. J. (1991). *Source book of criminal justice statistics 1990.* Washington, DC: U.S. Department of Justice, Bureau of Justice Statistics, U. S. Government Printing Office.

Mahoney, M. J. (1974). *Cognition and behavioral modification.* Cambridge, MA: Ballinger.

Mahoney, M. J. (1990). *Human change processes: Theoretical bases for psychotherapy.* New York: Basic Books.

Mahoney, M. J. (1993). Introduction to special section: Theoretical developments in cognitive psychotherapies. *Journal of Counseling and Clinical Psychology, 2,* 187-193).

Mahoney, M. J., & Arnkoff, D. B. (1978). Cognitive and self-control therapies. In S. L. Garfield & A. E. Bergin (Eds.), *Handbook of psychotherapy and behavior change* (2nd ed.). New York: Wiley.

Mahoney, M. J., & Lyddon, W. (1988). Recent developments in cognitive approaches to counseling and psychotherapy. *Counseling Psychology, 16,* 190-134.

Maisto, S. A., Carey, K. B., & Bradizza, C. M. (1999). Social learning theory. In H. T. Blane & K. W. Leonard (Eds.), *Psychological theories of drinking and alcoholism* (pp. 305-345). New York: Guilford.

Maisto, S. A., Connors, G. J., & Allen, J. P. (1995). Contrasting self-report screens for alcohol problems: A review. *Alcoholism: Clinical and Experimental Research, 19,* 1510-1516.

Mann, R. E., Smart, R. G., Stoduto, G., Beirness, D., & Vigilis, E. (2002). The early effects of Ontario's administrative driver's license suspension law on driver fatalities with a BAC > 80mg%. *Canadian Journal of Public Health, 9393,* 176-180.

Mann, R. E., Vingilis, E.R., Gavin, D., Adlaf, E., Anglin, L. (1991). Sentence severity and the drinking driver: Relationships with traffic safety outcome. *Accident Analysis and Prevention, 23,* 483-491.

Mann, R. E., Vingilis, E.R., Stewart, K. (1988). Programs to change individual behavior: Education and rehabilitation in the prevention of drinking and driving. In: M.D. Laurence, J.R. Snortum, & F.E. Zimring (eds.), *Social control of the drinking driver* (pp.248-269). Chicago, University of Chicago Press.

Mark, F. O. (1988). Does coercion work? The role of referral source in motivating alcoholics in treatment. *Alcoholism Treatment Quarterly, 5,* 5-22.

Marlatt, G. A. (1978). Craving for alcohol, loss of control, and relapse: A cognitive-behavioral analysis. In P. E. Nathan, G. A. Marlatt, & T. Loberg (Eds.), *Alcoholism: New directions in behavioral research and treatment.* New York: Plenum.

Marlatt, G. A. (1979). Alcohol use and problem drinking: A cognitive-behavioral analysis. In P. C. Kendall & S. D. Hollon (Eds.), *Cognitive-behavioral interventions: Theory, research, and procedures.* New York: Academic Press.

Marlatt, G. A. (1982). Relapse prevention: A self-control program for the treatment of addictive behaviors. In R. B. Stuart (Ed.) *Adherence, compliance, and generalization in behavioral medicine.* New York: Barunner/Mazel.

Marlatt, G. A. (1985a). Cognitive factors in the relapse process. In G. A. Marlatt & J. R. Gordon (Eds.), *Relapse prevention: Maintenance strategies in the treatment of addictive behaviors* (pp. 128-200). New York: Guilford.

Marlatt, G. A. (1985b). Situational determinants of relapse and skill training intervention. In G. A. Marlatt & J. R. Gordon (Eds.), *Relapse prevention: Maintenance strategies in the treatment of addictive behaviors* (pp. 71-124). New York: Guilford.

Marlatt, G. A. (1985c). Cognitive a assessment and intervention procedures for relapse prevention. In G. A. Marlatt & J. R. Gordon (Eds.), *Relapse prevention: Maintenance strategies in the treatment of addictive behaviors* (pp. 201-279). New York: Guilford.

Marlatt, G. A. (1985d). Relapse prevention: Theoretical rationale and overview of the model. In G. A. Marlatt & J. R. Gordon (Eds.), *Relapse prevention: Maintenance strategies in the treatment of addictive behaviors* (pp. 3-70). New York: Guilford.

Marlatt, G. A., Baer, J. S., & Quigley, L. A. (1995). Self-efficacy and addictive behavior. In A. Bandura (Ed.), *Self-efficacy in changing societies.* New York: Cambridge University Press.

Marlatt, G. A., & Barrett, K. B. (1994). Relapse prevention. In M. Galentern & H. Kleber (Eds.), *The textbook of substance abuse treatment.* New York: American Psychiatric Press.

Marlatt, G. A., & Gordon, J. R. (1985). *Relapse prevention: Maintenance strategies in the treatment of addictive behaviors.* New York: Guilford.

Marmor, J. (1975). Foreword. In B. Sloane, F. Staples, A. Cristol, N. J. Yorkston, & K. Whipple (Eds.), *Psychotherapy versus behavior therapy.* Cambridge, MA: Harvard University Press.

Marques, P. R., Tippetts, A. S., & Voas, R. B. (2003). The alcohol interlock: An underutilized resource for predicting and controlling drunk drivers. *Traffic Injury Prevention, 4,* 188-194.

Martin, D. J., Garske, J. P., & Davis, M. K. (2000). Relation of the therapeutic alliance with outcome and other variables: A meta-analytic review. *Journal of Consulting and Clinical Psychology,* 68, 438-450.

Martin, S. E., Annan, S., Forst B. (1993). The special deterrent effects of a jail sentence on first-time drunk drivers: a quasi-experimental study. *Accident Analysis and Prevention, 25,* 561-568.

REFERENCES

Maslow, A. H. (1954). *Motivation and personality.* New York: Harper.

Mauck, S. R., & Zagummy, M. J. (2000). Determinants of efforts in drunk-driving interventions: A path analysis. *Journal of Alcohol and Drug Education, 45(2),* 23-33.

Maxwell-Hudson, C. (1996). *Massage for stress relief.* New York: DK Publishing, Inc.

Mayfield, D., McLeod, G., & Hall, P. (1974). The CAGE questionnaire: Validation of a new alcoholism screening instrument. *American Journal of Psychiatry, 131,* 1121-1123

Mayhew, D.R., Donelson, A.C., Beirness, D.J., & Simpson, H.M. (1986). Youth, alcohol and relative risk of crash involvement. *Accident Analysis and Prevention 18,* 273-387,1986.

McCarty, D., & Argeriou, M. (1986). Rearrest following residential treatment for repeat offender drunken drivers. *Journal of Studies on Alcohol, 49,* 1-4.

McCaul, M. E., & Svikis, D. S. (1999). Intervention issues for women. In P. J. Ott, R. E. Tarter, & R. T. Ammerman (Eds.), *Sourcebook on substance abuse: Etiology, Epidemiology, Assessment, and Treatment.* London: Allyn and Bacon.

McClellan, A. T., Fureman, B., Parikh, G., Bragg, A. (1996). *Addiction Severity Index (ASI).* Philadelphia, PA: The University of Pennsylvania and Veterans Administration Center for Studies on Addiction.

McClellan, A. T., Luborsky, L., Cacciola, J., Griffith, J., Evans, F., Barr, H. L., & O'Brien, C. P. (1985). New data from the Addiction Severity Index: Reliability and validity in three centers. *Journal of Mental and Nervous Disease, 173,* 412-423.

McCord, J. (1984). Drunken drivers in longitudinal perspective. *Journal of Studies on Alcohol, 45,* 316-320.

McDermott, S. P., & Wright, F. D. (1992). Cognitive therapy: Long-term outlook for a short-term psychotherapy. In J. S. Ruttan (Ed.), *Psychotherapy for the 1990s* (pp. 61-99). New York: Guilford.

McGinn, L. K., & Young, J. E. (1996). Schema-focused therapy. In P. M. Salkovskis (Ed.), *Frontiers of cognitive therapy* (pp. 182-207). New York: Guilford.

McGuire, F. L. (1980). "Heavy" and "light" drinking drivers as separate target groups for treatment. *American Journal of Drug and Alcohol Abuse, 7,* 101-107.

McGuire, J., & Priestley, P. (1995). Reviewing "What works": Past, present and future. In J. McGuire (Ed.), *What works: Reducing reoffending* (pp. 3-34), New York: Wiley.

McKay, J. R., Maisto, S. A., & O'Farrell, T.J. (1993). End-of-treatment self-efficacy, after care, and drinking outcomes of alcoholic men. *Alcoholism: Clinical and Experimental Research, 17,* 1078-1083.

McKay, M., Rogers, P., & McKay J. (1989). *When anger hurts: quieting the storm within.* Oakland, CA: New Harbinger Press.

McKnight, A. J., Hyle, P., & Albricht, L. (1983, December). *Youth license control demonstration project* (Report No. DOT HS 806 616). Washington, DC: National Highway Traffic Safety Administration.

McMillan, D. L., Adam, M.S., Wells-Parker, E., Pang, M.G., & Anderson, B.J. (1992). Personality traits and behaviors of alcohol-impaired drivers: A comparison of first and multiple offenders. *Addictive Behaviors 17,* 407-414.

McMullin, R. E. (1986). *Handbook of cognitive therapy techniques.* New York: W. W. Norton.

McMullin, R. E. (2000). *The new handbook of cognitive therapy techniques.* New York: W. W. Norton.

Meichenbaum, D. (1975). A self-instructional approach to stress management: A proposal for stress inoculation training. In I. Sarason & C. D. Spielberger (Eds.), *Stress and anxiety* (Vol. 2). New York: Wiley.

Meichenbaum, D. (1977). *Cognitive-behavior modification: An integrative approach.* New York: Plenum.

Meichenbaum, D. (1985). *Stress inoculation training: A clinical guidebook.* Old Tappan, NJ: Allyan & Bacon.

Meichenbaum, D. (1993a). Stress inoculation training: A 20-year update. In P. M. Lehrer & R. L. Woolfolk (Eds). *Principles and practice of stress management, Second edition.* New York: The Guilford Press.

Meichenbaum, D. (1993b). Changing conceptions of cognitive behavior modification: Retrospect and prospect. *Journal of Consulting and Clinical Psychology, 61,* 292-304.

Mercer, G. W. (1986). *Frequency, types and patterns of traffic convictions and frequency and type of traffic accidents.* Counterattack Program, Ministry of Attorney General of British Columbia, Victoria, British Columbia, Canada.

Meyers, A., Heeren, T., & Hingson, R. (1987). Cops and drivers: Police discretion and the enforcement of Maine's 1981 OUI law. *Journal of Criminal Justice, 15,* 361-368.

Milkman, H. B., & Sunderwirth, S. G. (1987). *Craving for ecstasy: The consciousness and chemistry of escape.* Lexington, MA: D. C. Heath.

Milkman, H. B., & Sunderwirth, S. G. (1998). *Pathways to pleasure: The consciousness and chemistry of optimal experience.* Lexington, MA: Lexington Books.

Milkman, H. B., & Wanberg, K. W. (2005). *Criminal conduct and substance abuse treatment for adolescents: Pathways to self-discovery and change - The provider's guide.* Thousand Oaks, CA: Sage Publications.

Miller, B. A., & Windle, M. (1990). Alcoholism, problem drinking and driving while impaired. In R. J. Wilson & R. E. Mann (Eds.), *Drinking and Driving* (pp. 68-95. New York: Guilford Press.

Miller, G. A. (1994). *The Substance Abuse Subtle Screening Inventory Manual,* Bloomington, IN: SASSI Institute.

Miller, P. J., Ross, S. M., Emmerson, R. Y., & Todt, E. H. (1989). Self-efficacy in alcoholics: Clinical validation of the situational confidence questionnaire. *Addictive Behaviors, 14,* 217-224.

Miller, W. R. (1994). *SOCRATES: The stages of change readiness and treatment eagerness scale.* Albuquerque, NM: Department of Psychology, University of New Mexico.

Miller, W. R., & Hester, R. K. (1986). The effectiveness of alcoholism treatment: What research reveals. In W. R. Miller & N. Heather (Eds.), *Treating addictive behaviors: Processes of change.* New York: Plenum.

Miller, W. R., & Marlatt, G. A. (1984). *Manual for the Comprehensive Drinker Profile (CDP)* Odessa, FL: Psychological Assessment Resources.

Miller, W. R., & Munoz, R. F. (1982). *How to control your drinking* (rev. ed.). Albuquerque, NM: University of New Mexico Press.

Miller, W. R., & Rollnick, S. (1991). *Motivational Interviewing: Preparing people to change addictive behavior.* NY: Guilford.

Miller, W. R., & Rollnick, S. (2002). *Motivational Interviewing: Preparing people to change addictive behavior* (2nd ed.). NY: Guilford.

Miller, W. R., & Tonigan, J. S. (1996). Assessing drinker's motivation for change: The Stages of Change Readiness and Treatment Eagerness Scale (SOCRATES). *Psychology of Addictive Behaviors, 10,* 81-89.

Miller, W. R., Tonigan, J. S., & Longabaugh, R. (1994). *DrInC: An instrument for assessing adverse consequences of alcohol abuse. Test Manual.* NIAAA Project MATCH Monograph Series. Vol. 4. NIH Pub. No. 95-3911. Washington, DC: U.S. Government Printing Office.

Miller, W. R., Westerberg, V. S., & Waldron, H. B. (1995). Evaluating alcohol problems in adults and adolescents. In R. K. Hester & W. R. Miller (Eds.), *Handbook of alcoholism treatment approaches: Effective alternatives* (2nd ed., pp. 61-88). Boston: Allyn & Bacon.

Miller, W. R., Zweben, A. D., DiClemente, C. C., & Rychtarik, R. G. (1994). *Motivational enhancement therapy manual: A clinical research guide for therapists treating individuals with alcohol abuse and dependence* (Project MATCH Monograph Series, Vol. 2). Rockville, MD: National Institute on Alcohol Abuse and Alcoholism, U.S. Department of Health and Human Services, National Institutes of Health.

Millon, T. (1997). *Millon Clinical Multiaxial Inventory III - MCMI-III* (2nd ed.). Bloomington, MN: Pearson Assessments.

Minnesota Department of Corrections (2002). *Remote Electronic Alcohol Monitoring 2002 report.* St. Paul, MN: Minnesota Department of Corrections.

Missouri Division of Alcohol and Drug Abuse (1998). *Offender Education Program.* Jefferson City, MO: Missouri Department of Mental Health Division of Alcohol and Drug Abuse.

Monti, P. M., Abrams, D. B., Kadden, R. M., & Cooney, N. L. (1989). *Treating alcohol dependence: A coping skills training guide.* New York: Guilford.

Monti, P. M., Colby, S. M., & O'Leary, T. A. (2001). Introduction. In P. M. Monti, S. M. Colby, & T. A. O'Leary (Eds.), *Adolescents, alcohol, and substance abuse: Reaching teens through brief interventions* (pp. 1-16). NY: The Guilford Press.

Monti, P. M., Rohsenow, D. J., Colby, S. M., & Abrams, D. B. (1995). Coping and social skills training. In R. K. Hester & W. R. Miller (Eds.), *Handbook of alcoholism treatment approaches: Effective alternatives* (2nd. ed., pp. 221-241). Boston: Allyn & Bacon.

Moore, P. J., Turner, R., Park, C. L., & Adler, N. E. (1996). The impact of behavior and addiction on psychological models of cigarette and alcohol use during pregnancy. *Addictive Behaviors, 21,* 645-658.

Morse, B. J., & Elliott, D.S. (1992). Effects of ignition interlock devices on DUI recidivism: Findings from a longitudinal study in Hamilton County, Ohio. *Crime & Delinquency 38,* 131-157.

Mortimer, R. G., Filkins, L. D., Lower, J.S., et al. (1971). *Court procedures for identifying problem drinkers: Report on Phase I.* (DOT HS-800 630). Washington, DC: U. S. Department of Transportation.

Moskowitz, H., Walker, J., & Gomberg, C. (1979). Characteristics of DWIs, alcoholics and controls. In *Proceedings of the 1979 NCA Alcohol and Traffic Safety Session.* Washington, DC: national Highway Traffic Safety Administration, U. S. Department of Transportation.

Mowrer, O. H. (1947). On the dual nature of learning-a reinterpretation of "conditioning" and "problem-solving." *Harvard Educational Review, 17,* 102-148.

Mowrer, O. H. (1961). *Crisis in psychiatry and religion.* Princeton, NJ: D. Van Nostrand Company.

Mowrer, O. H. (1963). No guilt, no responsibility. In C. Rolo (Ed.), *Psychiatry in American Life.* Boston: Little, Brown and Company.

Mowrer, O. H. (1964). *The new group therapy.* Princeton, NJ: D. Van Nostrand Company, Inc.

Mowrer, O. H., & Mowrer, W. M. (1938). Enuresis: A method for its study and treatment. *American Journal of Orthopsychiatry, 8,* 436-459.

Mulligan, M. J., Steer, R. A., & Fine, W. W. (1978). Psychiatric disturbances in drunk driving offenders referred for treatment of alcoholism. *Alcoholism, Clinical and Experimental Research, 2,* 107-111.

Myers, G. E., & Myers, M. T. (1980). *The dynamics of human communication: A laboratory approach* (2nd ed.). New York: McGraw-Hill Book Company.

Najavits, L. M., Ghinassi, F., Van Horn, A., Weiss, R. D., Siqueland, L., Frank, A., Thase, M. E., & Loborsky, L. (2004). Therapist satisfaction with four manual-based treatments on a national multisite trial: An exploratory study. *Psychotherapy, Theory, Research, Practice, Training, 41,* 26-37.

Najavits, L. M., Weiss, R. D., Shaw, S. R., & Dierberger, A. E. (2000). Psychotherapists' views of treatment manuals. *Professional Psychology: Research and Practice, 31,* 404-408.

Nathan, P. E., & Gorman, J. M. (1998). *A guide to treatments that work.* New York: Oxford University Press.

Nathan, P. E., Gorman, J. M., & Salkind, N. J. (1999). *Treating mental disorders: A guide to what works.* New York: Oxford University Press.

National Center for Health Statistics (2000). *Summary Health Statistics for the U.S. Population: National Health Interview Survey 2000,* No. 214. Washington, DC: Center for Disease Control and Prevention, Department of Health and Human Services.

National Clearinghouse for Alcohol and Drug Information (1999). *Impaired Driving Among Youth.* The Department of Health and Human Services CHHS Publication No. (SMA)99-3364.

National Commission Against Drunk Driving (1999). *What the research says about treatment effectiveness and ways to apply this research.* <http://www.NCADD.com/tsra/abstract/treatment html>.

National Institute on Drug Abuse. (1983). *Data from the national drug and alcoholism treatment utilization survey (NDATUS), main finding for drug abuse treatment units* (Statistical series, Report F:10, DHHS Publication No. ADM 83-1284). Washington, DC: Government Printing Office.

National Transportation Safety Board. (2000). *Safety Report: Actions to Reduce Fatalities, Injuries and Crashes Involving the Hard Core Drinking Driver.* Washington, DC: National Transportation Safety Board.

Neenan, M., & Dryden, W. (2001). *Essential cognitive therapy.* London: Whurr Publishers.

Neimeyer, R. A. (1993). Constructivism and the cognitive psychotherapies: Some conceptual and strategic contrasts. *Journal of Cognitive Psychotherapy: An International Quarterly, 7,* 159-171.

Neimeyer, R. A., & Bridges, S. K. (2003). Postmodern approaches to psychotherapy. In *Essential psychotherapies: Theory and practice, 2nd edition* (pp. 272-316). New York: The Guilford Press.

Newcomb, M. D., & Bentler, P. M. (1989). Substance use and abuse among children and teenagers. *American Psychologist, 44,* 242-248.

Newcomb, M. D., Maddahian, E., & Bentler, P. M. (1986). Risk factors for drug use among adolescents: Concurrent and longitudinal analyses. *American Journal of Public Health, 76,* 525-531.

Nezu, A. M., Nezu, C. M., & Lombardo, E. (2003). Problem-solving therapy. In W. O'Donohue, J. E. Fisher, & S. C. Hayes (Eds.), *Cognitive behavior therapy: Applying empirically supported techniques in your practice* (pp. 301-307). Hoboken, NJ: John Wiley & Sons.

NHTSA - National Highway Traffic Safety Administration. (1972). *Alcohol Safety Action Programs: Evaluation of Operations, Vol. I, II.* Washington, DC: Author.

NHTSA - National Highway Traffic Safety Administration (1979). *Summary of national alcohol safety action projects.* Washington, DC: Author.

NHTSA - National Highway Traffic Safety Administration (1983). *A guide to self-sufficient funding of alcohol traffic safety programs.* (Contract HS 432). Washington, DC. Author.

NHTSA - National Highway Traffic Safety Administration (1986). *The Drunk Driver and the Jail Problem Vol 1.* National Highway Traffic Safety Administration Report No. DOT HS 806 761. Springfield, VA: National Technical Information Service.

NHTSA - National Highway Traffic Safety Administration (1989). *Improving Understanding of Alcohol Impairment and BAC Levels and Their Relationship to Highway Accidents.* Traffic Safety Administration Report No. DOT HS 807-433 806 761. Washington, DC: U.S. Government Printing Office.

NHTSA - National Highway Traffic Safety Administration (1993). *Police Time and Costs Associated with Administrative License Revocation.* National Highway Traffic Safety Administration Report No. DOT HS 808 064. Springfield, VA, National Technical Information Service.

NHTSA - National Highway Traffic Safety Administration (1996). *A guide to sentencing DUI offenders* (DOT HS 808-365), Washington, DC: U.S. Government Printing Office.

NHTSA - National Highway Traffic Safety Administration (1997a). *Driving While Intoxicated Tracking Systems.* Washington DC: U.S. Department of Transportation.

NHTSA - National Highway Traffic Safety Administration (1997b). *Traffic Safety facts*, 1996 - alcohol. Washington, DC: U.S. Department of Transportation.

NHTSA - National Highway Traffic Safety Administration (1998). *Youth Fatal Crash and Alcohol Facts.* Washington, DC: NHTSA, U.S. Department of Transportation.

NHTSA - National Highway Traffic Safety Administration (1999a). *Traffic Safety Facts, 1998: Alcohol,* DOT HS 808 950. Washington, D.C. Department of Transportation.

NHTSA - National Highway Traffic Safety Administration (1999b). *You Drink and Drive. You Lose. Driving Home the Facts-About Repeat Offenders.* Washington, DC: Author.

NHTSA - National Highway Traffic Safety Administration (2000). *State legislative fact sheet: January 2000.* Washington, DC: U. S. Department of Transportation.

NHTSA - National Highway Traffic Safety Administration (2001a). *Age of drinking onset, driving after drinking, and involvement in alcohol related motor vehicle crashes - Discussion.* Washington, D.C. Department of Transportation.

NHTSA - National Highway Traffic Safety Administration (2001b). *Blacks against drunk driving: A culture-based handbook to promote traffic safety.* Washington, D.C. Department of Transportation, Office of Communications and Outreach.

NHTSA - National Highway Traffic Safety Administration (2001c). *Hispanic Outreach "How To" Manual.* Washington, D.C. Department of Transportation, Office of Communications and Outreach.

NHTSA – National Highway Traffic Safety Administration (2003a). *Annual assessment of motor vehicle crashes.* Washington, DC: National Center for Statistical Analysis, U. S. Department of Transportation.

NHTSA - National Highway Traffic Safety Administration (2003b). *Traffic Safety Facts 2002: Alcohol.* Publication No. DOT HS-809. Washington, DC: U. S. Department of Transportation.

NHTSA - National Highway Traffic Safety Administration (2004). *Fatality analysis reporting system (FARS) web-based encyclopedia.* Washington, DC: National Center for Statistical Analysis, U. S. Department of Transportation.

NIAAA - National Institute on Alcohol Abuse and Alcoholism (1996). *Alcohol Alert No. 31: Drinking and Driving.* Rockville, MD: U.S. Department of Health and Human Services.

NIAAA - National Institute on Alcohol Abuse and Alcoholism (1997). *Alcohol Alert No. 37: Youth Drinking: Risk Factors and Consequences.* Rockville, MD: U.S. Department of Health and Human Services.

Nichols, J.L. (1990). Treatment vs. deterrence. *Alcohol Health & Research World, 14,* 44-51.

Nichols, J.L. & Ross, H.L. (1989). The effectiveness of legal sanctions in dealing with drinking drivers. In: *The Surgeon General's workshop of drunk driving: Background papers.* Rockville, MD. Office of the Surgeon General, U.S. Department of Health and Human Services.

Nichols, J.L., & Ross H.L. (1990). The effectiveness of legal sanctions in dealing with drinking drivers. *Alcohol, Drugs, and Driving 6,* 33-60.

Nichols, J. L., Weinstein, E. B., Ellingstad, V. S., & Struckman-Johnson, D. L. (1978). The specific deterrent effect of ASAP education and rehabilitation programs, *Journal of Safety Research, 10,* 177-187.

NIDA/NIAAA. (1993). National drug and alcoholism treatment unit survey (NDATUS): *1991 main findings report.* Rockville, MD: U. S. Government Printing Office.

Nochajski, T. H., Augustino, D. K., & Wieczorek, W. F. (1997). Treatment outcome and drinking driving recidivism. Paper presented at the Research Society on Alcoholism Annual Meeting, July, San Francisco, CA.

Nochajski, T. H., Leonard, K. E., Blane, H. T., & Wieczorek, W. F. (1991). *Comparison of problem-drinking young men with and without a DWI arrest.* Paper presented at Research Society on Alcoholism Conference, June, Maro Island, FL.

Nochajski, T. H., & Miller, B. A. (1995). *Training manual for the Research institute on Addictions Self Inventory (RIASI).* Buffalo, NY: Research Institute on Addictions.

Nochajski, T. H., Miller, B.A., & Parks, K.A. (1994). *Comparison of first-time and repeat DWI offenders.* Paper presented at the Annual Meeting of the Research Society on Alcoholism, Maui, Hawaii, June 18-23 1994. Buffalo, NY.: Research Institute on Addictions.

Nochajski, T. H., Miller, B. A., Wieczorek, W. F., & Whitney, R. (1993). The effects of a drinker-driver treatment program: Does criminal history make a difference? *Criminal Justice and Behavior, 20,* 174-189.

Nochajski, T. H., & Wieczorek, W. F. (1997). Study shows BAC not a reliable predictor of drinking and driving recidivism, new screen more comprehensive. In D. Foley (Ed.). *Impaired Driving Update, I,* No. 2, 19-32. Kingston, NJ: Civic Research Institute.

North Carolina Division of Mental Health (1995). *Alcohol and Drug Education Traffic Schools - ADETS.* Raleigh, North Carolina: North Carolina Division of Mental Health Developmental Disabilities and Substance Abuse Services

Novaco, R. W. (1978). Anger and coping with stress. In J. P. Foreyt & D. Rathjen (Eds.), *Cognitive behavior Therapy.* Lexington, MA: Heath.

Novaco, R. W. (1986). Anger as a clinical and social problem. In R. Blanchard, & C. Blanchard (Eds.), *Advances in the study of aggression, Volume 2.* New York: Academic Press.

Novaco, R. W. (1994). Clinical problems of anger and its assessment and regulation though a stress coping skills approach. In. W. O'Donohue & L. Krasner (Eds.), *Handbook of psychological skill training: Clinical techniques and applications.* Boston: Allyn & Bacon.

Oates, J. R., Jr. (1974). *Factors influencing arrests for alcohol-related traffic violations.* Washington, DC: National Highway Traffic Safety Administration.

Oetting, E. R., & Beauvalis, F. (1987). Peer cluster theory, socialization characteristics, and adolescent drug use: A path analysis. *Journal of Consulting Psychology, 34,* 205-213.

Office of Research and Traffic Records. (1998). *Volume II Methods Report - Racial and Ethnic Group Comparisons: National Surveys of Drinking and Driving: Attitudes and Behaviors - 1993, 1995 and 1997.* Washington, DC: U.S. Department of Transportation, National Highway Traffic Safety Administration (NHTSA).

O'Hara, M. (1997). Relational empathy: Beyond modernist egocentrism to postmodern holistic contextualism. In A. C. Bohart & L. S. Greenberg (Eds.). *Empathy reconsidered: New Directions in Psychotherapy* (pp. 295-320). Washington, DC: American Psychological Association.

O'Neill, H. (1999). *Managing anger.* London: Whurr Publishers.

Packard, M. A. (1987). DUI/DWAI offenders compared to clients seen in an outpatient alcohol-treatment facility. *Journal of Alcohol and Drug Education, 32,* 1-6.

Parks, G. A., & Marlatt, G. A. (1999). Relapse prevention therapy for substance-abusing offenders: A cognitive-behavioral approach. In E. Latessa (Ed.), *What works - strategic solutions: The International Community Corrections Association Examines Substance Abuse.* Maryland: American Correctional Association.

Parry, M. (1968). *Aggression on the road.* London: Tavistock Press.

Patterson, C. H. (1966). *Theories of counseling and psychotherapy.* New York: Harper and Row.

Patterson, C. H., & Hidore, S. C. (1997). *Successful psychotherapy: A caring, loving relationship.* Northvale, NJ: Jason Aronson Inc.

Pattison, E. M., & Kaufman, E. (1982). The alcoholism syndrome: Definitions and models. In E. M. Pattison & E. Kaufman, (Eds.), *Encyclopedic handbook of alcoholism* (pp. 3-30). New York: Gardner Press.

Pattison, E. M., Sobell, M. B., & Sobell, L. C. (1977). *Emerging concepts of alcohol dependence.* New York: Springer.

Patton, B. R., & Griffin, K. (1981). *Interpersonal communication in action: Basic text and readings.* New York: Harper & Row.

Paulsrude, S., & Klingberg, C. (1975). *License suspension: A paper tiger? Report No. 32.* Olympia, WA: Washington State Research and Technology Division, Department of Motor Vehicles.

Pavlov, I. P. (1927). *Conditioned reflexes: An investigation of the physiological activity of the cerebral cortex* (G. V. Anrep, Trans.). London: Oxford University Press.

Peck, R. C., Arstein-Kerslake, G.W., & Helander, C.J. (1994). Psychometric and biographical correlates of drunk driving recidivism and treatment program compliance. *Journal of Studies on Alcohol 55(6);667-678.*

Peck, R. C., Wilson, R.J., & Sutton, L. (July, 1994). *Driver license strategies for controlling the persistent DUI offender.* Background Paper. The Transportation Research Board Workshop on the Persistent Drinking Driver, Woods Hole, MA.

Peck, R. C., & Voas, R. B. (2002). Forfeiture programs in California: Why so few? *Journal of Safety Research, 33,* 245-258.

Perkinson, R.R. (1997). *Chemical dependency counseling: A practical guide.* Thousand Oaks, CA: Sage Publications.

Perrine, M. W. (1970). Identification of personality, attitudinal, and biographical characteristics of drinking drivers. *Behavioral Research and Highway Safety, 2,* 207-225.

Perrine, M. W. (1990). Who are the drinking drivers? *Alcohol Health & Research World, 14,* 26-35.

Perrine, M., Peck, R., & Fell, J. (1989). 1 Epidemiologic perspective on drunk driving. In: *Surgeon General's Workshop on Drunk Driving: Background Papers* (pp. 35-76). Rockville, MD: Department of Health and Human Services, Office of the Surgeon General.

Peters, K. D., Kochanek, K.D., Murphey, S.L. (1998). *Deaths: Final Data for 1996.* National Vital Statistics Reports, 47,26.

Peters, R. H., Greenbaum, P. E., Steinberg, M. L., Carter, C., Ortiz, M., Fry, F., & Valle, S. K. (2001). *Effectiveness of screening instruments in detecting substance use disorders among offenders.* University of South Florida.

Peterson, D. R. (1983). Conflict. In H. H. Kelley, E. Berscheid, A. Christensen, J. H. Harvey, T. L. Huston, G. Levinger, E. McClintock, L. A. Peplau, & D. R. Peterson (Eds.), *Close relationships.* New York: W. H. Freeman.

Peyser, H. S. (1988). Implications of the disease model for psychotherapy and counseling. In S. E. Gitlow & H. S. Peyser (Eds.), *Alcoholism: A practical treatment guide* (pp. 142-155). Philadelphia: W. B. Saunders.

Piaget, J. (1932). *The moral judgement of the child.* London: Routledge and Kegan Paul.

Piaget, J. (1954). *The construction of reality in the child.* New York: Basic Books.

Popkin, C. L., Li, L.K., Lacey, J.H., Stewart, J.R., & Waller, P.F. (1983). An initial evaluation of the North Carolina alcohol and drug education traffic schools. *Vol. I. Technical Report* T-92, Band 3: 1466-1470. Cologne, Germany, Verlag.

Popkin, C. L., Rudisill, L.C., Waller, P.F., & Geissinger, S.B. (1988). Female drinking and driving: Recent trends in North Carolina. *Accident Analysis and Prevention, 20,* 219-225.

Popkin, C. L., Stewart, J.R., Martell, C., & Birckmayer, J.D. (1992). *An evaluation of the effectiveness of the interlock in preventing recidivism in a population of multiple DWI offenders.* Raleigh, NC: Governor's Highway Safety Program.

Popkin, C. L., & Wells-Parker, E. (1994). A research agenda for the specific deterrence of DWI. *Journal of Traffic Medicine 22,* 10-14.

Powers, R., & Kutash, I. (1985). Stress and alcohol. *International Journal of the Addictions, 20,* 461-482.

Preusser, D. F., Ferguson, S.A., & Williams, A.F. (1998). The effect of teenage passengers on the fatal crash risk of teenage drivers. *Accident Analysis and Prevention.*

Preusser, D. F., & Preusser, C.W. (1992). *Obstacles to Enforcement of Youthful (Under 21) Impaired Driving.* Washington, DC: U.S. Department of Transportation.

Preusser, D. F., and Williams, A.F. (1992). Sales of alcohol to underage purchasers in three New York counties and Washington, D.C. *Journal of Public Health Policy 13,* 306-317.

Price, J. A. (1975). Applied analysis of North American Indian drinking patterns. *Human Organization, 34,* 17-26.

REFERENCES

Prochaska, J. O. (1999). Stages of change approach to treating addictions with special focus on driving while intoxicated (DWI) offenders. In P.M. Harris (Ed.), *Research to results: Effective community corrections*. Proceedings of the 1995 and 1996 Conferences of the Internal Community Corrections Association (ICCA). Lanham, MD: American Correction Association.

Prochaska, J. O., & DiClemente, C.C. (1986). Towards a comprehensive model of change. In W. R. Miller & N. Heather (Eds.). *Treating addictive behaviors: Processes of change* (pp. 3-27). New York: Plenum.

Prochaska, J. O., & DiClemente, C. C. (1992). Stages of change in the modification of problem behavior. In M. Hersen, R. Eisler, & P. M. Miller (Eds.), *Progress in behavior modification* (pp. 184-214). Sycamore, IL: Sycamore Publishing.

Prochaska, J. O., DiClemente, C. C., & Norcross, J. C. (1992). In search of how people change: Applications to addictive behaviors. *American Psychologist, 47,* 1102-1114.

Project MATCH Research Group (1993). Project MATCH: Rationale and methods for a multisite clinical trial matching patients to alcoholism treatment. *Alcoholism: Clinical and Experimental Research, 17,* 1130-1145.

Project MATCH Research Group. (1997). Matching alcoholism treatments to client heterogeneity: Project MATCH posttreatment drinking outcomes. *Journal of Studies on Alcohol, 58,* 7-29.

Ramirez, D., McDevitt, J., & Farrell, A. (2000). *A resource guide on racial profiling.* Washington, DC: U.S. Department of Justice.

Raue, P. J., & Goldfried, M. R. (1994). The therapeutic alliance in cognitive-behavior therapy. In. A. O. Horvath & L. S. Greenberg (Eds.), *The working alliance: Theory, research and practice* (pp. 131-152). New York: Wiley.

Raue, P. J., Goldfried, M. R., & Barkham, M. (1997). The therapeutic alliance in psychodynamic-interpersonal and cognitive-behavioral therapy. *Journal of Consulting and Clinical Psychology, 65,* 582-587.

Ray, O. S., & Ksir, C. (2002). *Drugs, society, and human behavior* (8th ed.). St. Louis, MO: C. V. Mosby.

Reinecke, M. A., Freeman, A. (2003). Cognitive therapy. In *Essential psychotherapies: Theory and practice,* (2nd ed., 224-271). New York: Guilford.

Reis, R.E. (1982). *The traffic safety effectiveness of education programs for first offense drunk drivers,* DOT Contract HS-6-01414, Washington: National Highway Traffic Safety Administration.

Research Triangle Institute (1991). *1990 Nationwide Personal Transportation Survey: User's guide for the public use tapes.* Washington, DC: U.S. Government Printing Office.

Responsible Driving, Inc. (1996). *Multiple Offender Program.* Author: Responsible Driving, Inc.

Robbins, L. N. (1988). *Driving under the influence of alcohol and drugs: The judge's role.* National Commission Against Drunk Driving Conference on Recidivism, A Summary of the Proceedings.

Roehrich, H., Dackis, C. A., & Gold, M. S. (1987). Bromocriptine. *Medical Research Review, 7,* 243-269.

Rogers, C. R. (1951). *Client-centered therapy: Its current practice, implications, and therapy.* Boston: Houghton Mifflin.

Rogers, C. R. (1957). The necessary and sufficient conditions of therapeutic personality change. *Journal of Consulting Psychology, 22,* 95-103.

Rogers, C. R. (1959). A theory of therapy, personality, and interpersonal relationships developed in the client-centered framework. In S. Koch (Ed.), *Psychology: A study of science: Vol. 3. Formulations of the person and the social context.* New York: McGraw-Hill.

Rogers, C. R. (1961). *On becoming a person: A therapist's view of psychotherapy.* Boston: Houghton Mifflin.

Rogers, C. R. (1980). *A way of being.* Boston: Houghton Mifflin Company.

Rogers, C. R., & Dymond, R. (1954). *Psychotherapy and personality change.* Chicago: University of Chicago Press.

Rogers, C. R., Gendlin, E. T., Kiesler, D., & Truax, C. B. (1967). *The therapeutic relationship and its impact: A study of psychotherapy with schizophrenics.* Madison: University of Wisconsin Press.

Rokke, P. D., & Rehm, L. P. (2001). In K. S. Dobson (Ed.), *Handbook of cognitive-behavioral therapies, Second edition.* New York: Guilford.

Rosen, A., & Proctor, E.K. (1981). Distinctions between treatment outcomes and their implications for treatment evaluation. *Journal of Consulting and Clinical Psychology, 49,* 418-425.

Rosen, H. (1988). The constructivist-development paradigm. In R. A. Dorfman (Ed.), *Paradigms of clinical social work* (pp. 317-355). New York: Brunner/Mazel.

Rosenhan, D. L., & Seligman, M. E. P. (1995). *Abnormal psychology* (3rd ed.). New York: W. W. Norton.

Ross, H. L. (1982) *Deterrence of the drinking driver: Legal policy and social control.* Lexington, MA: Lexington Books.

Ross, H. L. (1992). *Confronting drunk driving* New Haven, CT: Yale University Press.

Ross, H. L., & Gonzales, P. (1992). Effects of license revocation on drunk-driving offenders. *Accident Analysis and Prevention,* 20(5): 379-391.

Ross, H. L., Howard, J. M., Ganikos, M. L., & Taylor, E. D. (1991). Drunk driving among American Blacks and Hispanics. *Accident Analysis and Prevention, 23,* 1-11.

Ross, H. L., & Klette, H. (1995). Abandonment of mandatory jail for impaired drivers in Norway and Sweden. *Accident Analysis and Prevention* 27(2):151-157.

Ross, H. L., McCleary, R., & LaFree, G. (1990). Can mandatory jail laws deter drunk driving? The Arizona case. *Journal of Criminal Law and Criminology* 81(1): 156-170.

Ross, R. R., Fabiano, E. A., & Ross, R. D. (1986). *Reasoning and rehabilitation: A handbook for teaching cognitive skills.* Ottawa, Ontario: University of Ottawa.

Rotter, J. (1966). Generalized expectancies for internal versus external control of reinforcement. *Psychological Monographs, 80,* 1-\28.

Royal, D. (2000). Racial and ethnic group comparisons: National surveys of drinking and driving. *Attitudes and Behavior: 1993, 1995, and 1997. Volume 1: Findings; Volume 2: Methods.* Washington, DC: U.S. Department of Traffic Safety, National Highway Traffic Safety Administration.

Ruben, B. D. (1988). *Communication and human behavior.* New York: Macmillan.

Ruiz, P., & Langrod, J. G. (1992). Substance abuse among Hispanic Americans: Current issues and future perspectives. In J. H. Lowinson, P. Ruiz, R. B. Millman, & J. G. Langrod (Eds.), *Substance abuse: A comprehensive textbook* (2nd ed., pp. 868-874). Baltimore, MD: Williams & Wilkins.

Ruiz, P., & Langrod, J. G. (1997). Hispanic Americans. In J. H. Lowinson, P. Ruiz, R. B. Millman, & J. G. Langrod (Eds.), *Substance abuse: A comprehensive textbook* (3rd ed., pp. 705-711). Baltimore, MD: Williams & Wilkins.

Rychtarik, R. G., Koutsky, J. R., & Miller, W. R. (1998). Profiles of the Alcohol Use Inventory: A large sample cluster analysis conducted with split-sample replication rules. *Psychological Assessment, 10,* 107-119.

REFERENCES

Rychtarik, R. G., Koutsky, J. R., & Miller, W. R. (1999). Profiles of the Alcohol use Inventory: Correction to Rychtarik, Routsky, and Miller (1998). *Psychological Assessment, 11,* 396-402.

Rychtarik, R. G., Prue, D. M., Rapp, S. R., & King, A. C. (1992). Self-efficacy, aftercare and relapse in a treatment program for alcoholics. *Journal of Studies on Alcohol, 53,* 435-440.

Sacramento Department of Health and Human Services (2001). *Roadside Survey.* Sacramento, CA: Department of Health and Human Services.

Sadler, D. D., & Perrine, M. W. (1984). *An evaluation of the California drunk driving countermeasures system: Vol. II, The long-term traffic safety impact of a pilot alcohol abuse treatment as an alternative to license suspension.* Report No. 90, Sacramento, CA: Department of Motor Vehicle.

Safran, J. D. (1998). *Widening the scope of cognitive therapy: The therapeutic relationship, emotion, and the process of change.* Northvale, NJ: Jason Aronson Inc.

Salkovskis, P. M. (1996a). The cognitive approach to anxiety: Threat beliefs, safety-seeking behavior, and the special case of health anxiety and obsessions. In P. M. Salkovskis (Ed.), *Frontiers of cognitive therapy* (pp. 48-74). New York: Guilford.

Salkovskis, P. M. (1996b). *Frontiers of cognitive therapy.* New York: Guilford.

Salter, A. (1949). *Conditioned reflex therapy.* New York: Farrar, Straus.

Salzberg, P.M. & Paulsrude, S.P. (1984). An evaluation of Washington's driving while intoxicated law: Effect on drunk driving recidivism. *Journal of Safety Research, 15*(3): 117-124.

SAMHSA - Substance Abuse and Mental Health Services Administration. (1998). *Prevalence of Substance Use Among Racial and Ethnic Subgroups in the U.S.* Rockville, MD: Office of Applied Studies.

Sarason, I. G., & Sarason, B. R. (1995). *Abnormal psychology: The problem of maladaptive behavior.* Englewood Cliffs, NJ: Prentice-Hall.

Sayette, M. A. (1999). Cognitive theory and research. In H. T. Blane & K. W. Leonard (Eds.), *Psychological theories of drinking and alcoholism* (2nd ed., pp. 247-291). New York: Guilford.

Schachter, S., & Singer, J. (1962). Cognitive, social and physiological determinants of emotional state. *Psychological Review, 69,* 379-399.

Scheier, L. M., & Botvin, G. J. (1997). Expectancies as mediators of the effects of social influences and alcohol knowledge on adolescent alcohol use: A prospective analysis. *Psychology of Addictive Behaviors, 11*(1), 48-64.

Scheier, L. M., Botvin, G. J., & Griffin, K. W. (2000). Dynamic growth models of self-esteem and adolescent alcohol use. *Journal of Early Adolescence, Special Issue: Self-esteem in Early Adolescence, Part II. 20,* 178-209.

Schmidt, G., Klee, L., & Ames, G. (1990). Review and analysis of literature on indicators of women's drinking problems. *British Journal of Addiction, 85,* 179-192.

Schultz, A. (1967). *The phenomenology of the social world* (G. Walsh & F. Lehnert, Trans.). Evanston, IL: Northwestern University Press. (Original work published 1932).

Schuyler, D. (2003). *Cognitive therapy: A practical guide.* New York: W. W. Norton & Company.

Scott, N. E., & Bordovsky, L. G. (1990). Effective use of cultural role taking. *Professional Psychology: Research and Practice, 21,* 167-170.

Seligman, M. E. P., Walker, E. F., & Rosenhan, D. L. (2001). *Abnormal psychology* (4th ed.). New York: W. W. Norton & Company.

Selye, H. (1956). *The stress of life.* New York: McGraw-Hill.

Selye, H. (1974). *Stress without distress.* Philadelphia: J. B. Lippincott.

Selye, H. (1976). *The stress of Life, revised ed.,* New York: McGraw-Hill.

Selzer, M. L. (1971). The Michigan Alcoholism Screening Test: The quest for a new diagnostic instrument. *American Journal of Psychiatry, 127,* 1653-1658.

Selzer, M. L., & Barton, E. (1977). The drunken driver: A psychosocial study. *Drug and Alcohol Dependence, 2,* 239-253.

Selzer, M. L., Vinokur, A., & Wilson, T. D. (1977). A psychological comparison of drunken drivers and alcoholics. *Journal of Studies on Alcohol, 38,* 1294-1312.

Serenity Support Services, Inc. (1993). *Virginia Alcohol Safety Action Program.* Authors: Serenity Support Services, Inc and Virginia Alcohol Safety Action Program.

Shaffer, D., Fisher, P., & Dulcan, M. (1996). The NIMH Diagnostic Interview Schedule for Children (DISC 2,3): Description, acceptability, prevalences, and performance in the MECA study. *Journal of the American Academy of Child and Adolescent Psychiatry, 35,* 865-877.

Sheppard, M., & Stoveken, C. (1993). Convicted impaired drivers' knowledge about alcohol-relevance for program development. *Journal of Drug Education, 38,* 113-122.

Sher, K. J. (1987). Stress response dampening. In H. T. Blane & K. W. Leonard (Eds.), *Psychological theories of drinking and alcoholism* (pp. 227-271). New York: Guilford.

Shinar, D., & Compton, R. P. (1995). Victim impact panels: their impact on DWI recidivism. *Alcohol, Drugs and Driving, 11,* 73-87.

Shipley, T. E. (1987). Opponent process theory. In H. T. Blane & K. W. Leonard (Eds.), *Psychological theories of drinking and alcoholism* (pp. 346-387). New York: Guilford.

Shore, E. R., & Compton, K. L. (1998). Wadda ya mean, I can't drive?: Threat to competence as a factor in drunk driving intervention. *Journal of Prevention & Intervention in the Community, 17,* 45-53.

Shure, M., & Spivack, G. (1978). *Problem solving techniques in childrearing.* San Francisco: Jossey-Bass.

Siegal, H. (1987). Intervention: A successful technique for repeat offenders. In: P.C. Noordzij and R. Roszbach (eds.), *Alcohol, Drugs and Traffic Safety-T86.* Excerpta Medica. International Congress Series 721. Amsterdam: Elsevier.

Siegal, H. A., et al. (2000). The hardcore drunk driving offender. In: *Proceedings of the 15th International Conference on Alcohol, Drugs and Traffic Safety.* Stockholm, Sweden.

Simon, S. (2004). Vehicle sanctions for repeat DWI offenders: Factors that facilitate or impede their adoption or implementation. In K. G. Stewart (Ed.), *Putting research into action: A symposium on the Implementation of Researched-based Impaired Driving Countermeasures.* Washington, DC: Transportation Research board.

Simpson, H. M. (1995). Who is the persistent drinking driver? Part II: Canada and elsewhere. In: *Transportation Research Circular No. 437, Strategies for dealing with the persistent drinking driver.* Washington, D.C.: Transportation Research Board.

Simpson, H. M., and Mayhew, D.R. (1991). *The hard core drinking driver.* Ottawa, ON: Traffic Injury Research Foundation, 1991.

Simpson, H. M., Mayhew, D. R., & Beirness, D. J. (1996). *Dealing with hard core drinking driver.* Ontario, Canada: The Traffic Injury Research Foundation of Canada, Ottawa.

REFERENCES

Single, E., Kandel, D., & Johnson, B. D. (1975). The reliability and validity of drug use responses in a large scale longitudinal survey. *Journal of Drug Issues, 5*, 426-443.

Sisson, R., & Azrin, N. (1989). The community reinforcement approach. In R. K. Hester & W. R. Miller (Eds.), *Handbook of alcoholism treatment approaches* (pp. 242-258). New York: Pergamon.

Sitharthan, T., & Kavanagh, D. J. (1990). Role of self-efficacy in predicting outcomes from a program for controlled drinking. *Drug and Alcohol Dependence, 27*, 87-94.

Skinner, B. F. (1938). *The behavior of organisms: An experimental analysis*. New York: Appleton-Century-Crofts.

Skinner, B. F. (1953). *Science and human behavior*. New York: Macmillan.

Skinner, H. A. (1982). The Drug Abuse Screening Test. *Addictive Behaviors, 7*, 363-371.

Sloane, B., Staples, F., Cristol, A., Yorkston, N. J., & Whipple, K. (1975). *Psychotherapy versus behavior therapy*. Cambridge, MA: Harvard University Press.

Smith, E. M., & Cloninger, C. R. (1981). Alcoholic females: mortality at 12-year follow-up. *Focus on women, 2*, 1-13.

Smith, J. C. (1999). ABC Relaxation Training: A practical guide for health professionals. New York: Springer Publishing Company, Inc.

Smith, J. E., & Meyers, R. J. (1995). The community reinforcement approach. In R. K. Hester & W. R. Miller (Eds.), *Handbook of alcoholism treatment approaches: Effective alternatives* (2nd. ed., pp. 251-266). Boston: Allyn & Bacon.

Smith, M. L., Glass, G. V., & Miller, T. I.(1980). *The benefits of psychotherapy*. Baltimore, MD: Johns Hopkins University Press.

Snake, R., Hawkins, G., & La Boueff, S. (1977). *Report on alcohol and drug abuse Task Force Eleven: Alcohol and drug abuse* (Final report to the American Indian Policy Review Commission). Washington, DC: American Indian Policy Review Commission.

Snortum, J., & Berger, D. (1989). Drinking-driving compliance in the United States: Perceptions and behavior in 1983 and 1986. *Journal of Studies on Alcohol, 50*, 306-319.

Snow, R. W., & Cunningam O. (1985). Age, machismo, and the drinking locations of drunken drivers: A research note. *Deviant Behavior, 6*, 57-66.

Snow, R. W., et al. (1995). *Mississippi Alcohol Safety Education Program - MASEP: Group Intervention Approach, Education, Self-Assessment, and Referral*. Mississippi State, MS: Mississippi State University.

Snyder, H. N. (1997). *Juvenile court processing of alcohol-related cases*. Pittsburgh, PA: National Center for Juvenile Justice.

Sobell, L. C., & Sobell, M. B. (2000). Alcohol Timeline Followback (TLFB). In: *Handbook of psychiatric measures*. Washington, CC: American Psychiatric Association (pp. 477-479).

Sobell, L. C., & Sobell, M. B. (2003). Assessment of drinking behavior: Alcohol consumption measures. In J. P. Allen, V. B Wilson, (Eds.), *Assessing alcohol problems: A guide for clinicians and researchers, second edition* (pp. 75-100). Bethesda, MD: U. S. Department of Health and Human Services, Public Health Service, National Institute on Alcohol Abuse and Alcoholism, NIH Publication No. 03-3745.

Solomon, K. E., & Annis, H. M. (1990). Outcome and efficacy expectancy in the prediction of posttreatment drinking behavior. *British Journal of Addictions, 85*, 659-665.

Sovereign, R. G., & Miller, W. R. (1987). *Effects of therapist style on resilience and outcome among problem drinkers*. Paper presented at the Fourth International Conference on Treatment of Addictive Behaviors, Oslo/Bergen, Norway.

Sperry, L. (1999). *Cognitive behavioral therapy of DSM-IV personality disorders: Highly effective interventions for the most common personality disorders*. Philadelphia, PA: Brunner/Mazel.

Spielberger, C. (1988). *Manual for the State Trait Anger Expression Inventory*. Odesa, FL: Psychological Assessment Resources.

Spivack, G., & Shure, M. B. (1974). *Social adjustment of young children: A cognitive approach to solving real-life problems*. San Francisco: Jossey-Bass.

Stacy, A. L. Newcomb, M.D., & Bentler, P.M. (1991). Personality, problem drinking, and drunk driving: Mediating, moderating,, and direct-effect models. *Journal of Personality and Social Psychology* 60: 795-811.

Steer, R. A., Fine, E. W., & Scoles, P. E. (1979). Classification of men arrested for driving while intoxicated and treatment implications: A cluster analytic study. *Journal of Studies on Alcohol, 40*, 222-229.

Stein, L. A. R., & Lebeau-Craven, R. (2002). Motivational interviewing and relapse prevention for DWI: A pilot study. *Journal of Drug Issues, 32*, 1051-1070.

Stewart, E. I., Malfetti, J.L. (1970). *Rehabilitation of the drunken driver: A corrective course in Phoenix, Arizona for persons convicted of driving under the influence of alcohol*. New York, NY: Teachers College Press.

Stewart, K., & Ellingstad, V. S. (1989). Rehabilitative countermeasures for drinking drivers. In: *Surgeon General's Workshop on Drunk Driving: Background Papers* (pp. 234-246). Rockville, MD: Office of the Surgeon General, U. S. Department of Human Services.

Stewart, K., Gruenewald, P., Roth T. (1989). *An evaluation of administrative per se laws*. Final report on grant 86-IJ-CX-0081. Washington, DC. National Institute of Justice.

Stinchfield, R. D. (1997). Reliability of adolescent self-reported pretreatment alcohol and other drug use. *Substance Use and Misuse, 32*, 63-76.

Stitzer, M. L., & McCaul, M.E. (1987). Criminal justice interventions with drug and alcohol abusers. In: E.K. Morris & C.J. Braukmann (eds.) *Behavioral approaches to crime and delinquency: A handbook of application. Research and concepts*. New York, Plenum.

Stoduto, G., Vingilis, E., Kapur, B.M., Sheu, W.J., McLellan, B.A., & Liban, C.B. (1993), Alcohol and drug use among motor vehicle collision victims admitted to a regional trauma unit - demographic, injury and crash characteristics. *Accident Analysis and Prevention* 25(4): 411-420.

Straussner, S. L. A., & Zeulin, E. (1997). *Gender and Additions, Men and Women in Treatment*. Northvale, NJ: Jason Aronson.

Strom, J., & Barone, D. F. (1993). Self-deception, self-esteem, and control over drinking at different stages of alcohol involvement. *Journal of Drug Issues, 23*, 705-714.

Strupp, H. H., & Hadley, S. W. (1979). Specific versus nonspecific factors in psychotherapy. *Archives of General Psychiatry, 36*, 1125-1136.

Strupp, H. H., & Howard, K. I. (1992). A brief history of psychotherapy research. In D. K. Freedheim (Ed.), *History of psychotherapy: A century of change* (309-334). Washington, DC: American Psychological Association.

Sue, D. W. (1990). Culture-specific strategies in counseling: A conceptual framework. *Professional Psychology: Research and practice, 21*, 424-433.

Sue, D. W. (1997). Multicultural perspectives on multiple relationships. In B. Herlihy & G. Corey, *ACA ethical standards casebook* (5th ed., pp. 193-197). *Alexandria, VA: American Counseling Association*.

Sue, D. W., & Sue, D. (1999). *Counseling the culturally different* (3rd ed.). New York: Wiley.

Sutker, P. B., Brantley, P. J., & Allain, A. N. (1980). MMPI response patterns and alcohol consumption in DUI offenders. *Journal of Consulting and Clinical Psychology, 48,* 350-355.

Tashima, H. N., & Helander, C.J. (1995). *Annual report of the California DUI Management Information System.* CAL-DMV-RSS-95-145. Sacramento, CA: California Department of Motor Vehicles.

Tashima, H. N., & Peck, R.C. (1986). An evaluation of the specific deterrent effects of alternative sanctions for first and repeat DUI offenders. *Vol. III, An Evaluation of the California Drunk Driving Countermeasures System.* Sacramento, California: Department of Motor Vehicles.

Teplin, L. A., & Swartz, J. (1989). Screening for severe mental disorders in jails. *Law and Human Behavior, 13,* 1-18.

Tharp, V., Burns, M., & Moskowitz, H. (1981). *Development and field test of psychophysical tests for DWI arrest.* NHTSA Report No. DOT-HG-805-864, p. 88. Available from NTIS, Springfield, VA 22151.

Thorndike, E. L. (1931). *Human learning.* New York: Century.

Tiffany, S. T. (1990). A cognitive model of drug urges and drug use behavior: Role of automatic and nonautomatic processes. *Psychological Review, 97,* 147-168.

Timken, D.S. (1999). What works: Effective DWI interventions [Paper prepared for ICCA's 7th Annual Research Conference]

Timken, D. S. (2001a). *ADAD approved instrumentation for substance abusing adults.* Denver, CO: Alcohol and Drug Abuse Division of Colorado Department of Human Services.

Timken, D. S. (2001b). *The alcohol drug driving safety program placement criteria for substance abusing drivers-revised - ADDS-PC-R.* Boulder, CO: Timken & Associates.

Timken, D. S. (2002). What works: Effective DWI interventions. In H. Allen (Ed.), *What works - Risk reduction: Interventions for special needs offenders.* Lanham, MD: American Correctional Association.

Timken, D.S., Packard, M.A., Wells-Parker, E., & Bogue, B. (1995). Rehabilitation of the persistent drinking/drugging driver in *Transportation Research Board Strategies for Dealing with the Persistent Drinking Driver.* Transportation Research Circular No. 437. Washington, DC: National Research Council, pp. 64-69.

Timken, D. S., & Wanberg, K. W. (2001). *Alcohol and drug driving safety program: Screening and referral guidelines* (6th ed.). Denver, CO: Alcohol and Drug Abuse Division, Department of Human Services, State of Colorado

Tonigan, J. S. (2003). Outcome Evaluation: Applied issues in treatment outcome. In J. P. Allen, V. B Wilson, (Eds.), *Assessing alcohol problems: A guide for clinicians and researchers, second edition* (pp. 37-54). Bethesda, MD: U. S. Department of Health and Human Services, Public Health Service, National Institute on Alcohol Abuse and Alcoholism, NIH Publication No. 03-3745.

Toulmin, S. (1972). *Human understanding: Vol. 1. The collective use and evolution of concepts.* Princeton, NJ: Princeton University Press.

Townsend, T. N., Lane, J., Dewa, C.S., Brittingham, A.M. (1998). Driving after drug or alcohol use report. *Substance Abuse and Mental Health.* Services Administration, Rockville, MD.

Transportation Research Board (1995). *Strategies for dealing with the persistent drinking driver.* Transportation Research Circular 437. Washington, DC: National Research Council.

Truax, C. B. (1963). Effective ingredients in psychotherapy. *Journal of Consulting Psychology, 10,* 256-263.

Truax, C. B., & Carkhuff, R. R. (1967). *Toward effective counseling and psychotherapy.* Chicago: Aldine.

Truax, C. B., & Mitchell, K. M. (1971). Research on certain therapist interpersonal skills in relation to process and outcome. In A. E. Bergin & S. L. Garfield (Eds.), *Handbook of psychotherapy and behavioral change: An empirical analysis.* New York: John Wiley.

Trull, T. J., & Phares, E. J. (2001). *Clinical psychology: Concepts, methods and profession.* Belmont, CA: Wadsworth/Thompson Learning.

Turnbull, J. E. (1988). Primary and secondary alcoholic women. Social Casework: *The Journal of Contemporary Social Work,* 290-297.

U. S. Bureau of the Census. (1980). *Persons of Hispanic origin in the United States.* Washington, DC: Government Printing Office.

U. S. Bureau of the Census. (1990). *Statistical abstract of the United States.* Washington, DC: Government Printing Office.

U. S. Bureau of the Census. (1994). *Statistical abstract of the United States - 1994* (114th ed.) Washington, DC: Government Printing Office.

U. S. Bureau of the Census. (1996). *U. S. Census Bureau: The official statistics [Internet].* Table 2. Internet address: www.census.gov/population/socdemo/race/black.

U. S. Bureau of the Census. (2000). *United states population estimates by age, sex, race, and Hispanic origin and Asian origin.* Washington, DC: Government Printing Office.

U. S. Bureau of the Census. (2001a). *The Black Population in the United States, March, 2000* (UPDATE) (Report No. PPL-146). Washington, DC: Government Printing Office.

U. S. Bureau of the Census. (2001b). *The Hispanic population: Census brief* (C2KBR/01-3). Washington, DC: Government Printing Office.

U. S. Department of Health and Human Services, (2000). *Improving substance abuse treatment: The national treatment plan initiative.* Substance Abuse and Mental Health Services Administration, Center for Substance Abuse Treatment. DHHS Publication No. (SMA) 00-3480, NCADI Publication No. -BKD 383.

Vaillant, G. E. (1986). Cultural factors in the etiology of alcoholism: A prospective study. In T. F. Babor (Ed.), *Alcohol and culture: Comparative perspectives from Europe and America.* New York: New York Academy of Sciences.

VandenBos, G. R. (1986). Psychotherapy research: A special issue. *American Psychologist, 41,* 111-112.

Vannicelli, M. (1986). Treatment considerations. In *Women and alcohol health-related issues.* U. S. Department of Health and Human Services. Research monograph No. 16. Publication No. (ADM) 86=1139. Washington, DC: Department of Health and Human Services, 130-153.

Van Voorhis, P. (1987). Correctional effectiveness: The cost of ignoring success. *Federal Probation, 51,* 56-62.

Veneziano, C., Veneziano, L., & Fichter, M. (1994). Stress-related factors associated with driving while intoxicated. *Journal of Alcohol and Drug Education, 40,* 87-98.

Vingilis, E. R. (1983). Drinking drivers and alcoholics: Are they from the same population? In R. G. Smart, F. Glaser, Y. Israel, H. Kalant, R.E. Pophan and W. Schmidt (Eds), *Research advances in alcohol and drug problems* (Vol. 7) (pp. 299-342). New York: Plenum.

Vingilis, E. R., Stoduto, G., Macartney-Filgate, M. S., Liban, C. B., & McLellan, B. A. (1994). Psychosocial characteristics of alcohol-involved seriously injured drivers. *Accident analysis and prevention, 265,* 195-206.

Voas, R. B. (1982). *Drinking and driving: Scandinavian laws, tough penalties and United States alternatives.* (Final report on NHTSA Contract DTNH-22-82-)-05079). Washington, DC: NHTSA.

Voas, R. B. (1992). Assessment of impoundment and forfeiture laws for drivers convicted of DWI. *Phase I Report: Review of State Laws and Their Application.* National Highway Traffic Safety Administration Report No. DOT HS 807 870. Springfield, VA: National Technical Information Service.

Voas, R. B. (2001). Have the courts and the motor vehicle departments adequate power to control the hard-core drunk driver? *Addictions, 96,* 1701-1707.

Voas, R. B., & DeYoung, D. J. (2002). Vehicle action: Effective policy for controlling drunk and other high risk drivers? *Accident Analysis and Prevention, 34,* 263-270.

Voas, R. B., & Lacey, J.H. (1990). Drunk driving enforcement, adjudication, and sanctions in the United States, In Wilson, R.J. & Mann, R. E. (Eds.), *Drinking and driving: Advances in research and prevention.* New York, NY: The Guilford Press.

Voas, R. B., & Lacey, J.H. (1999). *Drunk driving enforcement adjudication and sanctions in the U.S.;* in The Addictions: A Comprehensive Guidebook; edited by McCrady and Epstein, New York, NY: Oxford University Press.

Voas, R. B., Tippetts, A.S. (1994). *Assessment of Impoundment and Forfeiture Laws for Drivers Convicted of DWI: Phase II Report.* Washington, D.C. National Highway Traffic Safety Administration.

Voas, R.B., Tippets, A.S., & Taylor, E. (1996). The effect of vehicle impoundment and immobilization on driving offenses of suspended and repeat DWI drivers. Presented at *40th Annual Proceedings of the Association for the Advancement of Automotive Medicine,* October 7-9, 1996. Vancouver, British Columbia.

Volkow, N. D., Fowler, J. S., Wang, G., Hitzemann, R., Logan, J., Schlyer, D., Dewey, S., & Wolf, A. P. (1993). Decreased dopamine D2 receptor availability is associated with reduced frontal metabolism in cocaine abusers. *Synapse, 14,* 169-177.

Wallace, B. C. (1991). *Crack cocaine: A practical treatment approach for the chemically dependent.* New York: Brunner/Mazel.

Wallace, W. A. (1986). *Theories of counseling and psychotherapy.* Boston: Allyn & Bacon.

Walsh, J., Kaplin, C., Carter, S., et al. (1999). *Kentucky Alcohol and Other Drugs Education Program.* State of Kentucky: Cabinet for Health Services, Department of Mental Health and Mental Retardation Services, Division of Substance Abuse.

Wampold, B. E. (2001). *The great psychotherapy debate: Models, methods and findings.* Mahwah, NJ: Erlbaum.

Wanberg, K. W. (1974). *Basic counseling skills manual.* Denver: Alcohol and Drug Abuse Division, Colorado Department of Health.

Wanberg, K. W. (1983). *Advanced counseling skills: The process and structure of therapeutic counseling, a client-oriented, therapist-directed model.* Denver: Alcohol and Drug Abuse Division, Colorado Department of Health.

Wanberg, K. W. (1990). *Basic counseling skills manual* (2nd. ed.). Denver: Alcohol and Drug Abuse Division, Colorado Department of Health.

Wanberg, K. W. (1992). *A user's guide for the Adolescent Self Assessment Profile.* Arvada, CO: Center for Addictions Research and Evaluation.

Wanberg, K. W. (1997). *The Adult Substance Use Survey (ASUS).* Arvada, CO: Center for Addictions Research and Evaluation.

Wanberg, K. W. (1998). *The Adult Clinical Assessment profile (ACAP): The Adult Self Assessment Profile (ADSAP) and Rating Adult Problems Scale (RAPS).* Arvada, CO: Center for Addictions Research and Evaluation.

Wanberg, K. W. (1999). *The Self Assessment Survey (SAS).* Arvada, CO: Center for Addictions Research and Evaluation.

Wanberg, K. W. (2000). *The Substance Use Survey (SUS).* Arvada, CO: Center for Addictions Research and Evaluation.

Wanberg, K. W. (2004). *Personal observations and experiences of the evolution and changes in psychotherapy.* Arvada, CO: Center for Addictions Research and Evaluation.

Wanberg, K. W., & Horn, J. L. (1970). Alcoholism symptom patterns of men and women: A comparative study. *Quarterly Journal of Studies on Alcohol, 31,* 40-61.

Wanberg, K. W., & Horn, J. L. (1983). Assessment of alcohol use with multidimensional concepts and measures. *American Psychologist, 38,* 1055-1069.

Wanberg, K. W., & Horn, J. L. (1987). The assessment of multiple conditions in persons with alcohol problems. In W. M. Cox (Ed.), *Treatment and prevention of alcohol problems* (27-56). New York: Academic Press.

Wanberg, K. W., & Horn, J. L. (1991). *The Drug Use Self Report: User's guide.* Arvada, CO: Center for Addictions Research and Evaluation.

Wanberg, K. W., & Horn, J. L. (2005): *User's Guide to the Alcohol and Drug Use Inventory (ADUI).* Arvada, CO: Center for Addictions Research and Evaluation (CARE).

Wanberg, K. W., Horn, J. L., & Foster, F. M. (1977). A differential assessment model for alcoholism: The scales of the Alcohol Use Inventory. *Journal of Studies on Alcohol, 38,* 512-534.

Wanberg, K. W., & Knapp, J. (1969). Differences in drinking symptoms and behavior of men and women. *British Journal of the Addictions, 64,* 1-9.

Wanberg, K. W., Lewis, R., & Foster, F. M. (1978). Alcoholism and ethnicity: A comparative study of alcohol use patterns across ethnic groups. *International Journal of the Addictions, 13,* 1245-1262.

Wanberg, K. W., & Milkman, H. B. (1993). *The Adult Self Assessment Questionnaire (AdSAQ).* Arvada, CO: Center for Addictions Research and Evaluation.

Wanberg, K. W., & Milkman, H.B. (1998). *Criminal conduct and substance abuse treatment: Strategies for self-improvement and change.* Thousand Oaks, CA. Sage Publications.

Wanberg, K. W., & Milkman, H. B. (2002) *The Adult Self Assessment Questionnaire (AdSAQ) - Updated norms.* Arvada, CO: Center for Addictions Research and Evaluation.

Wanberg, K. W., & Milkman, H.B. (2005). *Criminal conduct and substance abuse treatment: Strategies for self-improvement and change* (2nd ed.). Thousand Oaks, CA. Sage Publications.

Wanberg, K. W., & Timken, D. (1991). *The Driving Assessment Survey (DAS).* Arvada, CO: Center for Addictions Research and Evaluation.

Wanberg, K. W., & Timken, D. (1997). *User's Guide to the Driving Assessment Survey.* Arvada, CO: Center for Addictions Research and Evaluation.

Wanberg, K. W., & Timken, D. (1998). *The Adult Substance Use and Driving Survey.* Arvada, CO: Center for Addictions Research and Evaluation.

Wanberg, K. W., & Timken, D. (2001). *User's Guide to the Adult Substance use Survey (ASUDS).* Arvada, CO: Center for Addictions Research and Evaluation.

Wanberg, K. W., & Timken, D. (2004). *Comparison of Pre-sentenced with Post-sentenced Impaired Driving Offenders Using the Scales of the Adult Substance Use and Driving Survey (ASUDS).* Arvada, CO: Center for Addictions Research and Evaluation (CARE).

Wanberg, K. W., & Timken, D. (2005a). *Descriptive study of impaired driving offenders.* Arvada, CO: Center for Addictions Research and Evaluation.

Wanberg, K. W., & Timken, D. (2005b). *The Driving Assessment Survey (DAS) - Revised*. Arvada, CO: Center for Addictions Research and Evaluation.

Watson, C., Tilleskjor, C., Hoodecheck-Show, E., Purcel, J., & Jacobs, L. (1984). Do alcoholics give valid self-reports? *Journal of Studies on Alcohol,45*, 344-348.

Watson, J. B. (1913). Psychology as the behaviorist views it. *Psychological Review, 20*, 158-177.

Webb, J. A., Baer, P. E., Francis, D. J., & Caid, C. D. (1993). Relationship among social and intrapersonal risks, alcohol expectancies and alcohol usage among early adolescents, *Addictive Behaviors, 18*, 127-134.

Wechsler, H., Lee, J., Kuo, M., & Lee, H. (2000). College binge drinking in the 1990s: A continuing problem - Results of the Harvard School of Public Health 1999 College Alcohol Study. *Journal of American College Health, 48*, 199-210.

Weibel-Orlando, J. (1987). Culture-specific treatment modalities: Assessing client-treatment fit in Indian Alcoholism programs. In W. Cox (Ed.), *Treatment and prevention of alcohol problems: A resource manual* (pp. 261-281). New York: Academic Press.

Weibel-Orlando, J. (1989). Treatment and prevention of Native American alcoholism. In T. D. Watts & R. Wright (Eds.), *Alcoholism in minority populations* (pp. 121-139). Springfield, IL: Charles C Thomas.

Weinrath, M., & Gartrell, J. (2001). Specific deterrence and sentence length: The case of drunk drivers. *Journal of Contemporary Criminal Justice, 17*, 105-122.

Weishaar, M. E. (1996). Development in cognitive therapy. In W. Dryden (Ed.), *Developments in psychotherapy: Historical perspectives* (pp. 160-195). London: Sage Publications.

Weisner, T. S., Weibel-Orlando, J. C., & Long, J. (1984). Serious drinking, white man's drinking and teetotaling: Predictors of drinking level differences in an urban American Indian population. *Journal of Studies on Alcohol, 45*, 237-250.

Weissman, M. M., Wickramaratne, P., Warner, V., John, K., Prusoff, B. A., Merikangas, K. R., & Gammon, G. D. (1987). Assessing psychiatric disorders in children: Discrepancies between mother's and children's reports. *Archives of General Psychiatry, 44*, 747-753.

Wells-Parker, E. (1994). Mandated treatment. *Alcohol Health & Research World 18*(4): 302-306.

Wells-Parker, E., Bangert-Drowns, R., McMillen, D.L., Williams, M. (1995). Final results from a meta-analysis of remedial interventions with drink/drive offenders. *Addiction 90:* 907-926.

Wells-Parker, E., Kenne, D. R., Spratke, K. L., & Williams, M. T. (2000). Self-efficacy and motivation for controlling drinking and drinking/driving: An investigation of changes across a driving under the influence (DUI) intervention program and of recidivism prediction. *Addictive Behaviors, 25*, 229-238.

Werner, H. (1957). The concept of development from a comparative and organismic point of view. In D. B. Harris (Ed.), *The concept of development*. Minneapolis: University of Minnesota Press.

Westermeyer, J. (1992). Cultural perspectives: Native Americans, Asians, and new immigrants. In J. H. Lowinson, P. Ruiz, R. B. Millman, & J. G. Langrod (Eds.), *Substance abuse: A comprehensive textbook* (pp. 890-896). Baltimore, MD: Williams & Wilkins.

Westermeyer, J. (1997). Special populations: Native Americans, Asians, and New Immigrants. In J. H. Lowinson, P. Ruiz, R. B. Millman, & J. G. Langrod (Eds.), *Substance abuse: A comprehensive texbook.* (3rd ed., pp. 712-715). Baltimore, MD: Williams & Wilkins.

Westermeyer, J. (1997). Historical and social context of psychoactive substance disorders. In R. Francis, & S. Miller (Eds.), *Clinical textbook of addictive disorders* (2nd ed., pp. 14-32). New York: Guilford.

Wexler, D. B. (2000). *Domestic violence 2000: An integrated skills program for men.* New York: W. W. Norton & Company.

Wexler, H. K., Falkin, G. P., & Lipton, D. S. (1990). Outcome evaluation of a prison therapeutic community for substance abuse treatment. *Criminal Justice and Behavior, 17*, 71-92.

White, A. M. (2003). Substance use and adolescent brain development: An overview of recent findings with a focus on alcohol. *Youth Studies Australia, 22*, 39-45.

Widmark, E. M. P. (1932). *Die theoretischen grundlagen und die praktsch verwendbarkeit der gerichlich-medizinischen alkoholbetimmungg.* Berlin: Urban und Schwarzenberg.

Wieczorek, W. F. (1993). The role of treatment in reducing alcohol-related accidents involving DWI offenders. In R. R. Watson (Ed.), *Alcohol, cocaine, and accidents* (pp. 105-130). Totowa, NJ: Humana Press.

Wieczorek, W. F., Miller, B. A., & Nochajski, T. H. (1989). DSM-III and DSM-III-R alcohol diagnoses for problem drinking drivers. Paper presented at the American Psychological Association Convention, New Orleans, LA.

Wieczorek, W. F., Miller, B. A., & Nochajski, T. H. (1990). Alcohol diagnoses among DWI offenders. *The Problem-Drinker Project Research Note, 90-6*, Research Institute on Addictions: Buffalo, NY, August: 1-2.

Wieczorek, W. F., Miller, B. A., & Nochajski, T. H. (1992). The limited utility of BAC for identifying alcohol-related problems among DWI offenders. *Journal of Studies on Alcohol, 53*, 415-419.

Williams, A. F., Lund, A.K., & Preusser, D.F. (1986). Drinking and driving among high school students. *International Journal of Addictions 21*, 643-655.

Williams, A. F., Weinberg, K., & Fields, M. (1991). The effectiveness of administrative license suspension laws. *Alcohol, Drugs and Driving 7* (1), 55-62.

Williams, D. (1989). Togetherness is watchword for fighting drunk driving. *Nation's Cities Weekly*, 2, 7-11.

Williams, G. D., & Debakey, S. F. (1992). Changes in level of alcohol consumption: United States 1983-1988. *Addiction, 87*, 643-643.

Williams, G. D., Grant, B. F., Harford, T. C., & Noble, J. (1989). Population projections using DSM-III criteria, alcohol abuse and dependence, 1990-2000. *Alcohol Research World, 13*, 366-470.

Wilsnack, R. W., & Cheloha, R. (1987). Womens' roles and problem drinking across the life span. *Social Problems, 34*, 21-248.

Wilsnack. S. C., & Wilsnack, R. W. (1991). Epidemiology of women's drinking. *Alcohol Health and Research World 18*(3): 173-181.

Wilson, G. T., & O'Leary, K. D. (1980). *Principles of behavioral therapy.* Englewood Cliffs, NJ: Prentice-Hall, Inc.

Wilson, J. Q. (1998). Never too early. In R. Loeber & D. P. Farrington (Eds.), *Serious & violent juvenile offenders: Risk factors and successful interventions.* Thousand Oaks, CA: Sage Publications.

Wilson, R. J. (1991). Subtypes of DWIs and high risk drivers: Implications for differential intervention. *Alcohol, Drugs and Driving, 7*, 1-12.

Wilson, R. J. (1992). Convicted impaired drivers and high-risk drivers: How similar are they? *Journal of Studies on Alcohol, 53*, 335-344.

Wilson, R. J., & Jonah, B. A. (1985). Identifying impaired drivers among the general driving population. *Journal of Studies on Alcohol, 46*, 531-537.

Winters, K. C. (1995). *Personal Experience Inventory for Adults (PEI-A)*. Los Angeles: Western Psychological Services, Inc.

Winters, K. C. (1999). *Screening and assessing adolescents for substance use disorders*. Rockville, MD: U.S. Department of Health and Human Services, Public Health Service, Substance Abuse and Mental Health Services Administration, Center for Substance Abuse Treatment.

Winters, K. C. (2001). Assessing adolescent substance use problems and other areas of functioning: State of the art. In P. M. Monti, S. M. Colby & T. A. O'Leary (Eds.), *Adolescents, alcohol, & Substance abuse: Reaching teens through brief Interventions* (pp. 80-108). New York: Guilford Press.

Winters, K. C., Anderson, N., Bengston, P., Stinchfield, R.D., & Latimer, W. W. (2000). Development of a parent questionnaire for use in assessing adolescent drug abuse. *Journal of Psychoactive Drugs, 32*, 3-13.

Winters, K. C., Stinchfield, R. D., Henly, G. A., & Schwartz, R. H. (1991). Validity of adolescent self-report of alcohol and other drug involvement. *International Journal of Addictions, 25*, 1379-1395.

Winters, K. C., & Zenilman, J. M. (1994). *Simple screening instruments for outreach for alcohol and other drug abuse and infectious diseases*. Treatment Improvement protocol (TIP) Series. Rockville, MD: U.S. Department of Health and Human Services, Center for Substance Abuse Treatment.

Wolfe, A. (2001). The final freedom. *The New York Times Magazine*, March 18, 48-51.

Wolpe, J. (1958). *Psychotherapy by reciprocal inhibition*. Stanford, CA: Stanford University Press.

Woodall, W. G., Delaney, H., Rogers, E., & Wheeler, D. (2000). *A randomized trial of victim impact panels' DWI deterrence effectiveness*. Poster session presented at the 23rd Annual Scientific Meeting of the Research Society on Alcoholism, Denver, Colorado.

Yochelson, S., & Samenow, S. E. (1976). *The criminal personality: Vol. I. A profile for change*. New York: Jason Aronson.

Yoder, R. D. (1975). Prearrest behavior of persons convicted of driving while intoxicated. *Journal of Studies on Alcohol, 36*, 1573-1577.

Yoder, R. D., & Moore, R. A. (1973). Characteristics of convicted drunken drivers. *Quarterly Journal of Studies on Alcohol, 34*, 927-936.

Yost, J., & Michaels, R. (1985). Stress and alcoholism. In T. Bratter & G. Forrest, (eds.) *Alcohol and Substance Abuse: Strategies for Clinical Intervention*. New York: The Free Press.

Young, J. E. (1994). *Cognitive therapy for personality disorders: A schema-focused approach* (Rev. ed.). Sarasota, FL: Professional Resource Press.

Young, R. M., Oei, T. P. S., & Crook, G. M. (1991). Development of drinking self-efficacy questionnaire. *Journal of Psychopathology and Behavioral Assessment, 13*, 1-15.

Yu, J., & Williford, W. R. (1991). Calculating DWI/DWAI recidivism with limited data: Using state driver license files for drinking and driving research. *Journal of Drug Education, 21*, 285-292.

Zador, P.L. (1991). Alcohol-related relative risk of fatal driver injuries in relation to driver age and sex. *Journal of Studies on Alcohol 52*, 302-310.

Zeiner, A. R., Paredes, A., & Cowden, I. (1976). Physiologic responses to ethanol among the Tarahumara Indians. *Annals of the New York Academy of Science, 273*, 151-158.

Zelhart, P. F. Jr., Schurr, B. C., & Brown, P. A. (1975). The drinking driver: Identification of high risk alcoholics. In S. Israelstam, & S. Lambert (Eds.), *Alcohol, drugs and traffic safety* (pp. 159-168). Toronto, Ontario, Canada: Alcoholism and Drug Addiction Research Foundation.

Zinberg, N. (1990). Prologue. In H. Milkman & L. Sederer (Eds.), *Treatment choices for alcoholism and substance abuse*. New York: Lexington Books.

Zuckerman, M. (1990). *The psychophysiology of sensation seeking. Journal of Personality, 58*, 313-345.

Zuckerman, M. (2000). Are you a risk taker. *Psychology Today*, November-December, pp. 54-56,84-86.

Zuroff, D. C., et al. (2000). Relation of therapeutic alliance and perfectionism to outcome in brief outpatient treatment of depression. *Journal of Consulting and Clinical Psychology, 68*, 114-124.

INDEX

Abstinence, 5, 146, 223, 253, 254, 295
  outcomes goal, 2
  relapse and, 206
  relapse prevention goal, 2
Abstinence syndromes, treating, 5
Abstinence violation effect, 146
Abuse patterns, 275
Acculturation:
  linear view, 108
  3-dimensional view, 108
Action habits, 243
Action patterns, 270
Action skills, 352
Active listening, 311, 313, 314, 317, 326
  skills, 313
Active sharing, 311, 313, 314, 317, 326
Acute alcohol withdrawal, 291
Addiction:
  pathways, 277, 281
  patterns, 275
Addictions Severity Index (ASI), 56, 58, 174
Administrative license revocation (ALR), 10, 66. *See also* License revocation
Adolescent impaired drivers, 7
  at-risk, 29
  characteristics, 33-34
  compared with older drivers, 34
  personality, 32
  working with, 38
  See also Adolescent impaired driving
Adolescent impaired driving:
  cognitive errors/deficits, 33, 212, 213
  cultural factors/norms, 32
  drag racing, 33
  early drinking onset, 32
  predictive factors, 32-33
  prevention/reduction approaches, 34-38
  risk/causative factors, 32-33
  road rage, 33
  scope of problem, 29-30
  speeding, 33
  See also Adolescent impaired drivers; Adolescent impaired driving, measures to mediate; Problem Behavior Theory (PBT)
Adolescent impaired driving, measures to mediate, 34-38
  coordinated, 37-38
  intensified enforcement, 35
  psychosocial, 35
  stronger educational, 34
  See also Age 21 laws; Graduated licensing laws; Zero-tolerance laws/ approaches
Adolescent substance use and abuse, risk and causative factors of, 30-31
Adult Clinical Assessment Profile (ACAP), 56, 58, 63, 174, 175, 176
Adult Self-Assessment Profile (ADSAP), 174, 175
Adult Self-Assessment Questionnaire (ASAQ), 62, 63
Adult Substance Use and Driving Survey (ASUDS), 26, 33, 41, 48, 55, 58, 166-169, 170, 173, 174, 175, 182, 203, 231

Alcohol Involvement scale, 167, 218, 247
  Antisocial scale, 167
  Defensive scale, 169, 218, 247
  Disruption1 scale, 167
  Disruption2 scale, 169
  Driving Risk scale, 167
  Global Disruption scale, 169
  Involvement1 scale, 167
  Involvement2 scale, 169
  Mood Disruption scale, 169
  Motivation scale, 169
  Six Months scale, 169
  Spanish version, 113
Adult Substance Use Survey (ASUS), 55, 266
  Social Scale, 261
African Americans, 99, 102, 124
  BAC at arrest, 102, 111
  black value system, 111
  criminal justice system and, 110
  double-consciousness model, 111
  DWI conduct, 21, 101-102
  DWI intervention/treatment issues, 111
  DWI self-report, 101, 111
  Ebonics, 107
  group identity, 111-112
  impaired judgment, 110-111
  mood adjustment problems, 102
  substance use, 109-110
  treatment considerations, 109-112
  U.S. population, 109
Age:
  impaired driving and, 21, 22, 23, 102
  of drinking onset, 17, 20
Age 21 laws, 35-36
Aggression, 23-25, 266, 321
  driving-related, 25
  DWI offender, 23, 24, 25
  hard-core impaired drivers, 39
AIDS, drug use and, 216, 245
Alcohol and Drug Education Traffic Schools (ADETS), 81
Alcohol and Drug Evaluator (ADE), 167, 169
Alcohol and Other Drug Information School, 81
Alcohol and other drugs (AOD)
  adolescent/teen use, 30
  disruption, 116
  differential assessment of problem patterns, 57-58, 219
  involvement, 116
  treatment, 1, 70-71
  general treatment goal, 71
  pathways to outcomes and addiction, 290-293
Alcohol Drug Driving Safety (ADDS) Program Placement Criteria—Revised (PPC-R), 170
Alcoholic beverages, advertising of, 100
Alcoholics Anonymous (AA), 73, 138, 352
Alcohol Safety Action Projects (ASAPs), 12-13, 70, 82
  first-time offenders, 13
  repeat offenders, 13
  treatment-judicial partnership, 13
  See also Power Motivation Therapy (PMT)

Alcohol Timeline Followback (TLFB), 58
Alcohol Use Inventory (AUI), 57, 62, 115, 174, 307
American Civil Liberties Union (ACLU), 110
American Psychological Association, 96
American Society of Addiction Medicine Patient Placement Criteria 2—Revised (ASAM PPC-2-R), 170
Amphetamines, effects of on driving ability, 8
Andragogy:
  versus pedagogy, 128, 136
Anger, 197, 263, 264, 265, 266, 304, 305, 306, 351
  appropriate expression of, 307
  constructive, 307
  destructive, 307
  feeling versus being, 307
  managing, 306-310
  recognizing, 306-310
  stress and, 19
  See also State anger; Trait anger
Anger-awareness, 307
Anger ladder, 308, 309
Anglo-white Americans, 21, 99, 102
  AOD involvement, 102
  criminal justice system and, 116
  cultural differences among, 116
  DWI conduct, 101
  DWIOs versus other ethnic group DWIOs, 116
  mood adjustment problems, 102
  recidivism risk, 111
  treatment considerations, 116-117
Angry act, impaired driving as, 306
Antabuse, 5, 166
Antisocial, defining, 338
Antisocial behavior, xv, 1, 25, 28, 98, 230, 259, 260, 261, 338, 341, 345
  adolescents, 34
  assessment of DWIOs, 58
  DWI offenders and, 338-339, 341
  impaired driving as, 1, 250
  See also Adult Substance Use and Driving Survey (ASUDS); Antisocial personality pattern
Antisocial Personality Disorder, 259, 338-339
Antisocial personality pattern, 60, 98, 262
Anxiety, 263, 265, 304, 305, 311, 351
  management, 84
  traffic accidents and, 17
  See also Stress
AOD Weekly Monitoring Chart, 280, 286, 288, 289, 293, 295, 297, 298, 301, 305, 313, 314, 315, 316, 320, 322, 324, 330, 331, 336, 340, 341, 346, 347
Appraisals, 92, 140, 144, 213, 241, 242, 244, 264, 302, 305
Arrest for impaired driving, odds of, 65
Asian Americans, 99, 124
  culture of counseling and, 106
Assertiveness skills development, 321-322
Assertiveness training, 321
Assessment, 287-288
  major areas, 287-288
  See also Assessment, DWI offender
Assessment, DWI offender, 7, 43, 192

APPENDIX A

TABLE A.1 SIMPLE SCREENING INSTRUMENTS APPROPRIATE FOR DWI OFFENDERS

TABLE A.2 DIFFERENTIAL SCREENING INSTRUMENTS APPROPRIATE FOR DWI OFFENDERS

TABLE A.1 DIFFERENTIAL, IN-DEPTH ASSESSMENT INSTRUMENTS

INSTRUMENT NAME	AUTHORS	SOURCE
ADS: Alcohol Dependance Scale - Alcohol Use Questionnaire (AUQ)	Horn, Skinner, Wanberg & Foster, 1984	Center for Addictions and Mental Health, 33 Russell Street, Toronto, Ontario Canada M5S 2S1
CAGE (Cutting down, annoyed, guilty, eye-opener)	Mayfield, McLeod, & Hall, 1974	Center for Alcohol Studies, UNC School of Medicine, CB # 7140, Chapel Hill, NC 27599
DAST-20: Drug Abuse Screening Test	Skinner, 1982	Center for Addictions and Mental Health, 33 Russell Street, Toronto, Ontario Canada M5S 2S1
MAST: Michigan Alcoholism Screening Test	Selzer, 1971	Melvin L. Selzer 6967 Paseo Laredo La Jolla, CA 92037
M-F: Mortimer-Filkins	Mortimer & Filkins, 1971	Timken & Associates, Inc. 3153 Fern Place Boulder, CO 80304
RIASI: Research Institute on Addictions Self Inventory	Nochajski & Miller, 1995	Research Institute on Addictions 1021 Main Street Buffalo, NY 14203
SALCE: Substance Abuse Life Circumstances Evaluation	ADE, Inc., 1986	ADE, Inc. 20 West Washington St. Suite 12B Clarkston, MI 48016
SSI: Simple Screening Inventory	Center for Substance Abuse Treatment, 1994	Timken & Associates, Inc. 3153 Fern Place Boulder, CO 80304

T A B L E A . 2	Differntial Screening Instruments Appropriate for DWI Offenders*	
INSTRUMENT NAME	**AUTHORS**	**SOURCE**
Adult Substance Use Survey - ASUS	Wanberg, 1997	Center for Addictions Research and Evaluation 5460 Ward Road, Suite 140 Arvada, CO 80002
ASUDS: Adult Substance Use and Driving Survey	Wanberg & Timken, 1998	Center for Addictions Research and Evaluation 5460 Ward Road, Suite 140, Arvada, CO 80002
DrInC: The Drinker Inventory of Consequences	Miller, Tonigan & Longabaugh, 1994	National Clearinghouse for Alcohol and Drug Information 1-800-729-6686
DRI: Driving Risk Inventory	Lindeman, 1987	Behavioral Data Systems, Ltd. P.O. Box 32938 Phoenix, AZ 85064
LCI: Lovelace Comprehensive Screening Instrument	Lapham, Wanberg, Timken & Barton	Behavioral Health Research Center of the Southwest 6624 Gulton Court, NE Albuquerque, NM 87109
SASSI: Substance Abuse Subtle Screening Inventory	Miller, 1994	The SASSI Institute Rt. 2, Box 134 Springfield, IN 47462
SAS: Self-Assessment Survey	Wanberg, 1999	Center for Addictions Research and Evaluation - CARE 5460 Ward Road, Suite 140 Arvada, CO 80002

Differential, In-Depth Assessment Instruments

INSTRUMENT NAME	AUTHORS	SOURCE
ASI: Addiction Severity Index	McClellan, et al., 1985; McClellan, et al., 1996	Treatment Research Institute 600 Public Ledger Building 150 S. Independence Mall W Philadelphia, PA 19106
ACAP: Adult Clinical Assessment Profile (Adult Self Assessment profile - ADSAP and Rating Adult Problems Scale-RAPS)	Wanberg, 1998	Center for Addictions Research and Evaluation - CARE. 5460 Ward Road Suite 140 Arvada, CO 80002
AUI: Alcohol Use Inventory	Horn, Wanberg & Foster, 1990	Pearson Assessments P. O. Box 1416 Minneapolis, MN 55440
CDP: Comprehensive Drinker Profile	Miller & Marlatt, 1984	Wm. R. Miller Department of Psychology University of New Mexico Albuquerque, NM 87131
DUSR: Drug Use Self-Report	Wanberg & Horn, 1991	Center for Addictions Research and Evaluation - CARE. 5460 Ward Road Suite 140 Arvada, CO 80002
PEI-A: Personal Experience Inventory for Adults	Winters, 1995	Western Psychological Services, Inc. 12031 Wilshire Boulevard Los Angeles, CA 90025

* Reference for each instrument is found in the Provider's Guide list of REFERENCES.

APPENDIX B

DRIVING ASSESSMENT SURVEY - DAS

METHODS FOR SCORING THE DRIVING ASSESSMENT SURVEY

DRIVING WITH CARE INVENTORY - DWCI (PRE-POST TEST)

DRIVING WITH CARE INVENTORY ANSWER SHEET

DRIVING WITH CARE INVENTORY SCORING KEY

THERAPEUTIC EDUCATOR COUNTERMEASURES INVENTORY - TECI

DRIVING ASSESSMENT SURVEY (DAS)

Kenneth W. Wanberg and David Timken
Authors

PART I: PERSONAL DATA
(To be Completed by Test Taker)

NAME:	DATE:	PROGRAM:

GENDER: [ ] Female [ ] Male	AGE	YEARS OF SCHOOLING COMPLETED

MARITAL STATUS: [ ] Never Married [ ] Married [ ] Remarried [ ] Separated
[ ] Divorced [ ] Widowed

EMPLOYMENT STATUS: [ ] Full Time [ ] Part Time [ ] Student [ ] Housespouse
[ ] Retired [ ] Disabled [ ] Unemployed [ ] Other_____

USUAL OCCUPATION: [ ] Skilled Laborer [ ] Clerical and Office Worker
[ ] Skilled Craftsperson [ ] Manager [ ] Professional
[ ] Salesperson [ ] Other_____

ETHNICITY: [ ] African American [ ] Anglo American [ ] Asian American
[ ] Hispanic American [ ] Native American [ ] Other _____

PART II: INFORMATION AND INSTRUCTIONS ON THE USE OF THIS SURVEY

This survey contains a number of statements that describe the various approaches that people take, and the attitudes that people have, towards driving a motor vehicle. You are asked to read each question carefully and then choose the answer that best describes how the statement applies to you. You are asked to be as accurate in your answers as you can - that is, choose the answer that best fits you. In this way, the results of this survey can be used to provide you with information most helpful to you. Once you have chosen the answer of your choice, circle the letter corresponding to your choice. IN ORDER FOR YOUR RESULTS TO BE VALID, YOU ARE ASKED TO ANSWER ALL QUESTIONS.

Your responses will be kept strictly confidential, and any information release about your responses must be only upon your written consent.

You may now begin to complete this survey by beginning with question one below.

PART III: DRIVING ASSESSMENT SURVEY QUESTIONS

1. I like driving in heavy traffic.
   a. Never
   b. Seldom
   c. Often
   d. Very often

2. When driving at high speeds I feel powerful.
   a. Never
   b. Seldom
   c. Often
   d. Very often

3. I have owned vehicles with high horsepower engines.
   a. Never
   b. Seldom
   c. Often
   c. Very often

4. I have chased drivers who annoy me.
   a. Never
   b. Seldom
   c. Often
   d. Very often

5. I feel powerful behind the wheel.
   a. Never
   b. Seldom
   c. Often
   d. Very often

6. I have participated in sports such as auto racing, or hang gliding or sky driving.
   a. Never
   b. A few times
   c. Often
   d. Very often

7. High speed driving gives me a sense of power.
   a. Never
   b. Sometimes
   c. Often
   d. Very often

8. I have driven motor-cycles at high speed.
   a. Never
   b. Sometimes
   c. Often
   d. Very often

9. Beating other drivers away from intersections is fun.
   a. Never
   b. Sometimes
   c. Often
   d. Very often

1

Please go to the next page

10. I am a driver who likes to stay ahead of or out in front of traffic.
    a. Not true
    b. Somewhat true
    c. Usually true
    d. Always true

11. I exceed the speed limit if road conditions are safe.
    a. Not true
    b. Sometimes true
    c. Usually true
    d. Always true

12. I have tried to beat a red light.
    a. Never
    b. Seldom
    c. Often
    d. Very often.

13. When other drivers do stupid things, I lose my temper.
    a. Never
    b. Seldom
    c. Often
    d. Very often

14. I am easily provoked by other drivers when I am driving.
    a. Never
    b. Seldom
    c. Often
    d. Very often

15. I give the finger to other drivers.
    a. Never
    b. Seldom
    c. Often
    d. Very often

16. I have received a traffic ticket when I have been emotionally upset.
    a. Never
    b. Once
    c. Twice
    d. Three or more times

17. I have a hard time thinking about my driving when I am upset.
    a. Never
    b. Once in a while
    c. Quite often
    d. All the time

18. I have tried to beat trains at crossings.
    a. Never
    b. Seldom
    c. Often
    d. Very often

19. I drive fast and take my chances on getting caught.
    a. Never
    b. Sometimes
    c. Often
    d. Very Often

20. I dodge and weave through traffic.
    a. Never
    b. Seldom
    c. Often
    d. Very often

21. There are times when I have felt that I could easily kill another driver.
    a. Never
    b. Seldom
    c. Often
    d. Very often

22. I swear out loud or cuss under my breath at other drivers.
    a. Never
    b. Seldom
    c. Often
    d. Very often

23. It is hard to control my temper when driving.
    a. Never
    b. Seldom
    c. Often
    d. Very often

24. It annoys me when the light turns red just as I get to the intersection.
    a. Never
    b. Sometimes
    c. Often
    d. Very often

25. I find myself in a hurry when I drive.
    a. Never
    b. Seldom
    c. Often
    d. Very often

26. I pass other drivers when not in a hurry.
    a. Never
    b. Seldom
    c. Often
    d. Very often

27. I have taken a risk when driving just for the sake of it.
    a. Never
    b. Seldom
    c. Often
    d. Very often

28. I have outrun other drivers.
    a. Never
    b. Seldom
    c. Often
    d. Very often

2

29. I retaliate if the driver behind me has his bright lights in my rear view mirror.
    a. Never
    b. Seldom
    c. Often
    d. Very often

30. When angry, I have flashed my lights at drivers.
    a. Never
    b. Seldom
    c. Often
    d. Very often

31. I honk the horn when I am angry.
    a. Never
    b. Sometimes
    c. Often
    d. Very often

3

32. I have had accidents or received tickets when under stress.
    a. Never
    b. Once
    c. Two to three times
    d. More than three times

33. I tend to pay less attention when driving while I am angry.
    a. Incorrect
    b. Partly correct
    c. Usually correct
    d. Always correct

Please go to the next page

34. When I have had a bad day, I will drive to unwind.
    a. Never
    b. Seldom
    c. Often
    d. Very often

35. When I have problems such as marriage, job, finances, I find myself taking a drive.
    a. Never
    b. Seldom
    c. Often
    d. Very often

36. I have passed on a double yellow line.
    a. Never
    b. A few times
    c. Quite often
    d. Often

37. How many traffic citations have you received in your lifetime?
    a. Only one
    b. Two to three
    c. Four to five
    d. More than five

38. Driver's training should be required in order to get a drivers license.
    a. Do not agree
    b. Somewhat agree
    c. Mostly agree
    d. Completely agree

39. Driving skills are important when it comes to safety.
    a. Do not agree
    b. Somewhat agree
    c. Mostly agree
    d. Completely agree

40. Better driving training and skills would reduce accidents.
    a. Do not agree
    b. Somewhat agree
    c. Mostly agree
    d. Completely agree

41. I could benefit from a driving skills and safety class.
    a. No, not at all
    b. Maybe a little bit
    c. Yes, most likely
    d. Yes, definitely

42. When I am upset, I am less cautious when driving.
    a. Never
    b. Sometimes
    c. Often
    d. Very often

43. I have found myself driving fast without realizing it.
    a. Never
    b. Seldom
    c. Often
    d. Very often

44. It calms me down if I am able to drive when I am upset.
    a. Never
    b. Seldom
    c. Often
    d. Very often

45. I am able to relax and reduce tension while driving.
    a. Never
    b. Sometimes
    c. Often
    d. Very often

46. I leave extra early for work or other destinations when the roads are bad.
    a. Hardly ever
    b. Sometimes
    c. Usually I do
    d. I always do

47. I keep a safe distance from cars in front of me.
    a. Some of the time
    b. Much of the time
    c. Almost always
    d. Always

48. I use my turn signal.
    a. Sometimes
    b. Quite often
    c. Almost always
    d. Every time I turn

49. I rebel against authority.
    a. Never
    b. Once in awhile
    c. Quite often
    d. Often

50. When mad while driving, I am less cautious.
    a. Never
    b. Sometimes
    c. Often
    d. Very often

    [   ] 4

51. I forget about pressures when I am driving.
    a. Never
    b. Seldom
    c. Often
    d. Very often

52. I have driven to "blow off steam" after having an argument.
    a. Never
    b. Sometimes
    c. Often
    d. Very often

53. I go driving when I feel depressed.
    a. Never
    b. Sometimes
    c. Often
    d. Very often

    [   ] 5

54. When driving long distances, I take breaks for safety reasons.
    a. I usually do not
    b. Sometimes
    c. Quite often
    d. Routinely

55. I come to a complete stop at stop signs.
    a. Sometimes I do
    b. Usually I do
    c. I almost always do
    d. I always do

56. I use seat belts.
    a. Hardly ever
    b. Sometimes
    c. Usually I do
    d. Every time I drive or ride

57. I don't follow rules which I think are silly or don't make sense.
    a. No, not at all
    b. Yes, sometimes
    c. Yes, quite often
    d. Yes, often

Please go to the next page

58. At school or at work I break the rules in order to finish quicker.
    a. Never
    b. Sometimes
    c. Often
    d. Very often

59. I don't like police officers.
    a. Not true
    b. Somewhat true
    c. Usually true
    d. Always true

60. I have driven after drinking if I really had to get home.
    a. Never
    b. Sometimes
    c. Often
    d. Very often

61. I drink at bars.
    a. Never
    b. Sometimes
    c. Often
    d. Very often

62. When it comes to parties, I really like to live it up.
    a. No, not at all
    b. Yes, at times
    c. Usually
    d. Almost always

63. When it comes to the bottom line, nobody tells me what to do.
    a. Not true
    b. Somewhat true
    c. Usually true
    d. Always true

64. I have been in fights or brawls.
    a. Never
    b. Once or twice
    c. Several times
    d. Many times

65. After participating in sports, I will drink beer with my friends.
    a. Never
    b. Sometimes
    c. Often
    d. Very often

66. I enjoy going to parties where no one makes a big deal about heavy drinking.
    a. Never
    b. Sometimes
    c. Often
    d. Very often

67. I have had trouble because I don't follow rules.
    a. Never
    b. Seldom
    c. Often
    d. Very often

68. I have been tattooed.
    a. Never
    b. Once
    c. Twice
    d. Three or more times

    [ ] 6

69. I stay out all night and drink.
    a. Never
    b. Seldom
    c. Often
    d. Very often

70. I have been going to parties such as keggers on weekends.
    a. No, never
    b. Less than one weekend a month
    c. One to two weekends a month
    d. Three or more weekends a month

    [ ] [ ]
    7   G

PART IV: PROFILE

SCALE NAME	RAW SCORE	Low			Low-medium		DECILE RANK		High-medium				High			NUMBER IN NORM SAMPLE
		1	2	3	4	5	6	7	8	9	10					
1. POWER			0		1		2		3	4	5	6 7 8 9 19				392
2. HAZARD		0	1	2	3	4	5	6	7	8 9 10 11 13 21						393
3. IMPULSE		0	1	2	3	4		5	6	7 8 9 10 18						393
4. STRESS		0	1	2	3	4		5	6	7 8 9 11 15						395
5. RELAX		0	1	2	3	4	5		6 7	8 9 10 15						395
6. REBEL		0		1	2		3		4	5 6 7 8 17						393
7. CONVIVIAL		0 1 2	3	4	5		6	7	8	9 10 11 12 22						395
G. GENRISK		0 1 2 3 4 5	6 7	8 9	10 11	12 13 14 15	16 17 18 19 21 22 23 27 42									385
		0	10	20	30	40	50	60	70	80	90	100				
						PERCENTILE										

Authors: K. W. Wanberg and D. Timken

0195

Copyright (c) 1991, 2005   K. W. Wanberg and D. Timken

DRIVING ASSESSMENT SURVEY - DAS
SCORING PROCEDURES

1. General Scoring Scheme:

    a=0, b=1, c=2, d=3.

2. Scoring procedure for scales:

    Scale 1: Power - Items: 1 - 8.

    Scale 2: Hazard - Items: 10-12, 18-20 and 26-28.

    Scale 3: Impulse - Items: 13-14, 21-23, 29-31.

    Scale 4: Stress - Items: 24-25, 32-33, 42, 50.

    Scale 5: Relax - Items: 43-45, 51-53.

    Scale 6: Rebel - Items 58-59, 63-64, 67-68.

    Scale 7: Convivial - Items: 60-62, 65-66, 69-70.

    Genrisk: Items: Those items highlighted on the instrument - 2, 5, 7, 9, 10, 11, 12, 13, 14, 15, 19, 20, 22, 24, 26, 27, 28, 43, 62

POWER:
measures the extent to which the respondent reports feeling power when driving a motor vehicle.

HAZARD:
indicates the degree to which an individual takes part in hazardous or high-risk driving behavior.

IMPULSE:
indicates impulsive and temperamental driving behaviors and attitudes.

STRESS:
indicates the person feels irritability, stress and anger when driving.

RELAX:
indicates that driving is used as a means to relax and calm down.

REBEL:
measures rebellion toward authority and rules.

CONVIVIAL:
measures convivial and gregarious drinking.

GENRISK:
is a general and overall measure of driving risk and hazard.

The normative reference group is a sample of 395 alcohol and other drug related driving offenders being evaluated for treatment services. There are several different normative samples available for the DAS. The Driving Assessment Survey is copyrighted. The instrument and user's guide are distributed by the Center for Addictions Research and Evaluation (CARE), 5640 Ward Road, Suite 140, Arvada, Colorado 80002, (303) 421-1261.

DRIVING WITH CARE INVENTORY (DWCI)

Level I and Level Ii Education

DWCI - Part I

Questions 1 through 20 relate to facts about alcohol and other drug use and driving. Using the answer sheet provided, circle only one answer for each question.

1. **The broad goal(s) of DWI Education is/are:**
    a. to prevent relapse.
    b. to make you a safer driver.
    c. to prevent recidivism.
    d. a & c.

2. **Many DWI offenders have never learned to:**
    a. develop self-control over their thinking and actions.
    b. develop and maintain responsible thoughts and attitudes towards the community.
    c. hold their liquor.
    d. a & b.

3. **The National BAC level for DWI is:**
    a. .05
    b. .08
    c. .10
    d. .02.

4. **A problem drinker is one who:**
    a. receives a DWI.
    b. drinks too much.
    c. has developed a pattern of problems from drinking.
    d. doesn't stop after the first drink.

5. **Behavior is reinforced when:**
    a. our actions have negative consequences.
    b. our actions have positive consequences.
    c. it makes people mad at us.
    d. we get no reward from it.

6. **Drivers with two DWI convictions are considered to be:**
    a. very unlucky.
    b. nonproblem drinkers.
    c. potential problem drinkers.
    d. problem drinkers with high risk for recidivism.

7. **A driver who refuses to take a breathalyzer test and who has had no previous trouble with drinking and driving will:**
    a. have no action taken.
    b. have a warning placed on his/her record.
    c. be jailed for 90 days.
    d. generally lose his/her license.

8. **A person required to complete the Level II Treatment program must, as a prerequisite:**
    a. complete a defensive driving course.
    b. complete residential treatment.
    c. undergo acupuncture.
    d. complete Level II Education.

9. **Our thoughts, attitudes and beliefs:**
    a. control whether we drive after drinking.
    b. control things that happen to us.
    c. determine what people say to us.
    d. do not affect our actions.

10. **When we are faced with change, we**
   a. have few choices as to how we change.
   b. have mixed feelings about change.
   c. just go along with it.
   d. always resist it.

11. **The first step in changing thoughts is:**
   a. change the other person.
   b. change your beliefs.
   c. recognize that thoughts lead to problem behavior.
   d. change what you do.

12. **People who have been drinking several years and who have six or seven drinks may not appear drunk. This is called:**
   a. behavioral tolerance.
   b. dispositional tolerance.
   c. polyneuropathy.
   d. vertical nystagmis.

13. **System suppressing drugs or drugs that depress the body include:**
   a. alcohol, sedatives.
   b. cocaine.
   c. speed.
   d. ecstasy.

14. **System enhancing drugs or those that speed up the system include:**
   a. alcohol.
   b. heroin.
   c. amphetamines.
   d. valium.

15. **Which of the following is not a skill for preventing recidivism and relapse?**
   a. change your thinking.
   b. using good relationship skills.
   c. avoid high risk situations.
   d. changing what people think about you.

16. **The pattern of drinking at highest risk for DWI behavior is:**
   a. abstinence.
   b. gregarious, convivial and party drinking.
   c. less than once a month.
   d. drinking only at home.

17. **Recidivism is:**
   a. strictly a repeat conviction for DWI.
   b. something that only involves your choice.
   c. going back to the patterns of thinking and behavior that led to your DWI.
   d. the same as relapse.

18. **When a driver is stopped for suspected drunk driving, (s)he may be asked to:**
   a. take a driving test.
   b. call a lawyer.
   c. take a breathalyzer test.
   d. go to treatment as quickly as possible.

19. **Which of the following is most apt to affect your Blood Alcohol Concentration (BAC)?**
   a. amount of food in stomach.
   b. weight.
   c. gender.
   d. amount of alcohol you drink.

20. **Which of the following is one of the most important parts of DWI Education?**
   a. paying all fines and fees before completing the program.
   b. learning attitudes and skills to be responsible to the community and society.
   c. understanding the laws and regulations.
   d. learning defensive driving skills.

DRIVING WITH CARE INVENTORY (DWCI)

Part II

Questions 21-40 relate to drinking and driving behavior. Using the answer sheet provided, circle the letter A or D to indicate whether you agree or disagree with the statement.

		AGREE	DISAGREE
21.	Two drinks do not affect your ability to drive.	A	D
22.	Experienced drivers can drive safely after a few drinks.	A	D
23.	I would not feel safe riding with a driver who had many drinks.	A	D
24.	Drinking before driving poses little risk.	A	D
25.	The law should limit the amount of alcohol served to a person who drives away from a bar.	A	D
26.	I would feel safe riding with a driver who had successfully completed Level II Education and Treatment.	A	D
27.	We, as citizens should be obligated to report drunk drivers.	A	D
28.	Driving after drinking is wrong.	A	D
29.	One drink can be relaxing and can improve driving.	A	D
30.	What you hear about the relationship between alcohol and driving tends to exaggerate the effects of alcohol.	A	D
31.	Some people can drive safely after drinking.	A	D
32.	You shouldn't drive after many drinks, but it is OK to drive after a few.	A	D
33.	Drinking helps some people handle driving emergencies better.	A	D
34.	License revocation should be automatic for a person convicted of driving while intoxicated.	A	D
35.	Suspected drunk drivers should be required to take a test to determine the BAC.	A	D
36.	Some people can drive just as well after four drinks as they can when they have had nothing to drink, though some drive worse.	A	D
37.	Too many people drive drunk without getting caught.	A	D
38.	Convicted drunk drivers should have to pay a stiff fine.	A	D
39.	After drinking, most people drive with extra care.	A	D
40.	The amount of alcoholic beverages served to driving guests should be limited by party givers.	A	D

DRIVING WITH CARE INVENTORY (DWCI)

Answer Sheet

NAME: _____DATE: _____

      Last   MI   First

PART I: Questions 1 through 20 relate to facts about drinking and driving. Circle the letter identifying the most correct answer. Circle only one answer for each question.

1.	a b c d	6.	a b c d	11.	a b c d	16.	a b c d
2.	a b c d	7.	a b c d	12.	a b c d	17.	a b c d
3.	a b c d	8.	a b c d	13.	a b c d	18.	a b c d
4.	a b c d	9.	a b c d	14.	a b c d	19.	a b c d
5.	a b c d	10.	a b c d	15.	a b c d	20.	a b c d

PART II: Questions 21 through 40 relate to drinking and driving behavior. Circle the letter A or D to indicate whether you agree or disagree with the statement.

	Agree	Disagree			Agree	Disagree
21.	A	D		31.	A	D
22.	A	D		32.	A	D
23.	A	D		33.	A	D
24.	A	D		34.	A	D
25.	A	D		35.	A	D
26.	A	D		36.	A	D
27.	A	D		37.	A	D
28.	A	D		38.	A	D
29.	A	D		39.	A	D
30.	A	D		40.	A	D

DRIVING WITH CARE INVENTORY (DWCI)
Scoring Key

PART I: Knowledge Test scores may range from zero to 100. Add five points for each item correctly answered. Do not count items for which more than one option has been selected. A passing score for the Post Test is 80 (80%). The answer key for the twenty items is as follows:

1.	d	6.	d	11.	c	16.	b
2.	d	7.	d	12.	a	17.	c
3.	b	8.	d	13.	a	18.	c
4.	c	9.	a	14.	c	19.	d
5.	b	10.	b	15.	d	20.	b

PART II: The attitudinal survey is a measure of attitude towards the practice of driving after drinking. Use the scoring wieghts for each item below. For example, an answer of "A" to item 21 results in a score of "1," an answer of "D" to item 22 results in a score of "0," etc. Add across all 20 items. The highest score for Part II is 20 and the lowest score is zero. Higher scores indicate the client's attitude is one that favors driving after drinking and lower scores oppose driving after drinking. Higher scores could indicate higher risks of recidivism. Review the results with clients.

21.	A=1, D=0		31.	A=1, D=0
22.	A=1, D=0		32.	A=1, D=0
23.	A=0, D=1		33.	A=1, D=0
24.	A=1, D=0		34.	A=0, D=1
25.	A=0, D=1		35.	A=0, D=1
26.	A=0, D=1		36.	A=1, D=0
27.	A=0, D=1		37.	A=0, D=1
28.	A=0, D=1		38.	A=0, D=1
29.	A=1, D=0		39.	A=0, D=1
30.	A=1, D=0		40.	A=0, D=1

Therapeutic Educator Countermeasures Inventory - TECI
Authors: Scott A. DeMuro and Kenneth W. Wanberg

This inventory is designed for therapeutic educators providing services to AOD driving offenders. DUI educators differ as to how they view and provide Therapeutic Education to DUI offenders. Rate yourself on the following statements by circling the letter under the response that best reflects how you see yourself.

Section # 1

	Strongly Disagree	Disagree	Slightly Disagree	Slightly Agree	Agree	Strongly Agree
1. A DUI educator should stress probation requirements to participants.	a	b	c	d	e	f
2. It is important for therapeutic educators to report the clients' cooperation to the court.	a	b	c	d	e	f
3. The court mandate is the primary reason DUI clients cooperate in DUI Education.	a	b	c	d	e	f
4. DUI clients should comply with their probation requirements.	a	b	c	d	e	f
5. It is important that class rules be clarified as often as necessary.	a	b	c	d	e	f

	Never	Very Rarely	Rarely	Occasionally	Frequently	Always
6. I make sure DUI clients know the name of their probation officer.	a	b	c	d	e	f
7. I use the court mandate as leverage to get the best results.	a	b	c	d	e	f
8. I have close working relationships with probation officers.	a	b	c	d	e	f
9. To get DUI clients to cooperate, I refer to probation revocation.	a	b	c	d	e	f
10. Getting clients to stop drinking is one of my main goals.	a	b	c	d	e	
11. I use the term DUI offender to remind clients that they are under court order.	a	b	c	d	e	f
12. I required DUI clients to attend AA meetings.	a	b	c	d	e	f
13. I remind DUI participants of their probation requirements.	a	b	c	d	e	f
14. I require antabuse monitoring for DUI clients.	a	b	c	d	e	f ____

#1 [_____]

Section # 2

	Strongly Disagree	Disagree	Slightly Disagree	Slightly Agree	Agree	Strongly Agree
15. Genetics play the primary role in alcoholism.	a	b	c	d	e	f
16. The medical model of alcoholism is an important part of DUI therapeutic education.	a	b	c	d	e	f
17. It is important that DUI clients understand that alcoholics are different from other people.	a	b	c	d	e	f
18. Most DUI offenders are alcoholic.	a	b	c	d	e	f
19. Alcoholism is a disease.	a	b	c	d	e	f
20. The disease of alcoholism should be addressed in most DUI session.	a	b	c	d	e	f

	Never	Very Rarely	Rarely	Occasionally	Frequently	Always
21. A DUI educator should emphasize abstinence.	a	b	c	d	e	f
22. I present alcoholism as a progressive illness.	a	b	c	d	e	f ____

#2 [_____]

Go to page 2

Section # 3

	Strongly Disagree a	Disagree b	Slightly Disagree c	Slightly Agree d	Agree e	Strongly Agree f
23. Presenting the entire class agenda is important in every session.	a	b	c	d	e	f
24. Guest speakers are an important part of DUI clients' learning.	a	b	c	d	e	f

	Never a	Very Rarely b	Rarely c	Occasionally d	Frequently e	Always f
25. As the DUI educator, I decide (rather than students) which classroom activities are appropriate.	a	b	c	d	e	f
26. I require each client to be involved in structured class exercises.	a	b	c	d	e	f
27. I begin each session with a clear plan of what material is to be covered.	a	b	c	d	e	f
28. I distribute educational handouts in class.	a	b	c	d	e	f
29. I maintain a controlled environment in my DUI classes.	a	b	c	d	e	f
30. I assess and evaluate each participant's progress on a weekly basis.	a	b	c	d	e	f
31. I assign reading or other homework.	a	b	c	d	e	f
32. I present all elements of the DUI lesson plan each session.	a	b	c	d	e	f
33. I divide the class into smaller groups for discussion and exercises.	a	b	c	d	e	f
34. I closely follow the preplanned DUI therapeutic education curriculum.	a	b	c	d	e	f

#3 [_____]

Section # 4

	Strongly Disagree a	Disagree b	Slightly Disagree c	Slightly Agree d	Agree e	Strongly Agree f
35. A therapeutic educator should primarily focus on the participant's treatment needs.	a	b	c	d	e	f
36. The relationship between clients and the educator is a primary consideration in DUI Education.	a	b	c	d	e	f
37. DUI educators must believe in the basic goodness of each participant.	a	b	c	d	e	f
38. DUI educators should help clients resolve their personal issues.	a	b	c	d	e	f
39. An empathic client-centered approach should be used with DUI clients.	a	b	c	d	e	f
40. A DUI educator's acceptance of clients is a critical component in facilitating their change.	a	b	c	d	e	f

	Never a	Very Rarely b	Rarely c	Occasionally d	Frequently e	Always f
41. My focus deals with the feelings and attitudes of the DUI participants.	a	b	c	d	e	f
42. I consider the DUI client's individual needs when formulating course material.	a	b	c	d	e	f
43. I focus on the DUI clients' personal issues.	a	b	c	d	e	f
44. I make individual time available for each DUI client.	a	b	c	d	e	f
45. I use self disclosure to get clients to share personal material.	a	b	c	d	e	f
46. I strive to be a significant person to each of the DUI participants.	a	b	c	d	e	f

#4 [_____]

Go to page 3

414

Section # 5

	Strongly Disagree a	Disagree b	Slightly Disagree c	Slightly Agree d	Agree e	Strongly Agree f
47. DUI client generated content is more beneficial than the educator's scheduled content.						
48. DUI clients benefit most from class discussion.	a	b	c	d	e	f
49. DUI clients must have the opportunity to evaluate their own progress.	a	b	c	d	e	f
50. The primary responsibility of the DUI educator is to facilitate rather than direct DUI learning activities.	a	b	c	d	e	f
51. Group brainstorming is essential to DUI Level II education.	a	b	c	d	e	f
52. Reflective listening is a necessary therapeutic educator skill.	a	b	c	d	e	f
53. Group discussion is more important than providing DUI clients with information.	a	b	c	d	e	f
54. DUI clients should evaluate and critique the DUI curriculum.	a	b	c	d	e	f
55. Reflecting the client's personal information back to him or her is important.	a	b	c	d	e	f
56. Group process is an important element in personal change for DUI clients.	a	b	c	d	e	f

	Never a	Very Rarely b	Rarely c	Occasionally d	Frequently e	Always f
57. I begin sessions by inviting clients to share personal information.						
58. I rely on group dynamics to help me facilitate therapeutic education.	a	b	c	d	e	f
59. I use class discussion.	a	b	c	d	e	f

#5 [＿＿＿]

Section # 6

	Strongly Disagree a	Disagree b	Slightly Disagree c	Slightly Agree d	Agree e	Strongly Agree f
60. It is the client's responsibility to learn and utilize the material that is presented.	a	b	c	d	e	f

	Never a	Very Rarely b	Rarely c	Occasionally d	Frequently e	Always f
61. My job is to help DUI participants become more aware of themselves.						
62. I use supportive attitudes when working with DUI clients.	a	b	c	d	e	f
63. I help DUI participants strive to become self responsible.	a	b	c	d	e	f
64. I explore ways for clients to influence each other.	a	b	c	d	e	f
65. I encourage clients to examine and develop their own values.	a	b	c	d	e	f
66. I use open-ended questions to get clients to talk.	a	b	c	d	e	f
67. I convey theoretical and practical material to DUI clients.	a	b	c	d	e	f
68. I show positive and empathic attitudes during DUI classes.	a	b	c	d	e	f
69. I praise and reinforce the clients' efforts to change.	a	b	c	d	e	f
70. I encourage clients to take responsibility for their own learning.	a	b	c	d	e	f
71. I encourage DUI clients to evaluate their own learning.	a	b	c	d	e	f
72. I use a caring and understanding approach with DUI clients.	a	b	c	d	e	f

#6 [＿＿＿]

Go to page 4

415

T / S - 2ND ORDER	Strongly Disagree	Disagree	Slightly Disagree	Slightly Agree	Agree
73. Educators' evaluation of the client's learning should be immediate.	a	b	c	d	e
74. A DUI educator should always maintain a professional manner.	a	b	c	d	e

P / R - 2ND ORDER	Never	Very Rarely	Rarely	Occasionally	Frequer
75. I give DUI clients plenty of room to express themselves.	a	b	c	d	e
					P /

TECI - SCORING PROCEDURE

Put your score for each question to the right (margin) of each question.

If your answer was : a = 0,   b = 1,   c = 2,   d = 3,   e = 4,   f = 5

Total the question scores within each section and put that total in the line [____] following the last question in that

Sections: 1 - Court   2 - Disease   3 - Formal   4 - Participant   5 - Informal   6 - Empathic Resp

_____   _____   _____   _____

2nd ORDER scale scores

    Task/Structure (T/S) _____ (Total Questions #1, 2, 6, 7, 9, 10, 11, 12, 13, 14, 21, 26, 31, 34, 73, 74)

    Process/Relationship (P/R) _____ (Total Questions # 36, 37, 38, 40, 41, 42, 43, 48, 49, 50, 51, 52, 56, 57, 58, 61,

To complete the Therapeutic Educator Styles Profile, transfer your section and 2nd order scores (above) to the corresponding "ra each section (below). Then put a line through that approximate number point on the scale profile bar adjacent to the respective s percentile and decile ranking compared to the normative group of Therapeutic Educators (Normed on 320 DWI Therapeutic Ed

DUI Therapeutic Educator Styles Profile

Name:_____   Age:_____   Gender:_____   Date:_____

SCALE NAME	RAW SCORE	Low			Low-medium			DECILE RANK	High-medium				High		
		1	2	3	4	5	6	7	8	9	10				
1. COURT		9 23 29¦30 31 34¦35 36 37¦ 38 39 ¦40 41 42¦43 44 ¦45 46 47¦48 49 50¦51 52 53¦54 57 64													
2. DISEASE		2 11 13¦14 16 17¦18 19 ¦20 21 ¦ 22 23 ¦ 24 25¦ 26 ¦ 27 28 ¦ 29 30¦31 32 40													
3. FORMAL		15 30 31¦32 35 36¦ 37 38 ¦ 39 40¦ 41 ¦ 42 ¦43 44 ¦ 45 46 ¦ 47 48 ¦49 51 57													
4. PARTICIPANT		13 25 28¦29 31 33¦ 34 35 ¦ 36 37 ¦ 38 39¦ 40 ¦41 42 ¦43 44 45¦ 46 47¦48 50 58													
5. INFORMAL		21 34 36¦37 39 40¦41 42 43¦ 44 45¦ 46 ¦ 47 ¦48 49 50¦ 51 52 ¦ 53 54 ¦55 58 63													
6. EMPATHY		40 46 48¦ 49 50 ¦ 51 52¦ 53 ¦ 54 ¦ 55 ¦ 56 57 ¦ 58 59 ¦ 60 61¦62 63 65													
A. TASK		14 28 33¦34 36 37¦38 40 42¦43 44 45¦ 46 47 ¦48 49 50¦51 52 53¦54 55 56¦57 58 60¦61 64 73													
B. PROCESS		32 49 51¦52 55 57¦ 58 59 ¦60 62 63¦ 64 65 ¦ 66 67 ¦ 68 69 ¦70 71 72¦73 75 76¦77 81 88													
		1	10	20	30	40	50	60	70	80	90	99			
					PERCENTILE										

APPENDIX C

CLIENT EVALUATION SUMMARY

CLIENT RIGHTS STATEMENT - SAMPLE

CONSENT FOR PROGRAM INVOLVEMENT - SAMPLE

CONSENT FOR RELEASE OF CONFIDENTIAL INFORMATION - SAMPLE

FULL DISCLOSURE STATEMENT - SAMPLE

NOTICE OF FEDERAL REQUIREMENTS REGARDING CONFIDENTIALITY

PROVIDER EVALUATION SUMMARY

CLIENT EVALUATION SUMMARY (CES)

CLIENT NAME_____ DATE _____ DWC Program_____

Rate the Driving With CARE (DWC) program using the following questions. Please feel free to make any comments or notes regarding this program.

1. Overall, did you understand the ideas and material presented in DWC?

    ❏ No, not at all.
    ❏ Yes, somewhat.
    ❏ Yes, most of the ideas and material.
    ❏ All of the ideas and material.

2. Will you be able to apply what you learned in DWC to your daily living?

    ❏ No, not at all.
    ❏ Yes, somewhat.
    ❏ Most of what I learned.
    ❏ All of what I learned.

3. Will DWC be helpful to you in avoiding problems with alcohol or other drug use?

    ❏ No, probably not.
    ❏ Somewhat helpful.
    ❏ Yes, helpful.
    ❏ Yes, very helpful.

4. Will DWC be helpful in preventing you from becoming involved in further impaired driving behavior?

    ❏ No, probably not.
    ❏ Somewhat helpful.
    ❏ Yes, helpful.
    ❏ Yes, very helpful.

5. Now, rate your group leader on the following:

Started sessions on time:	❏ No	❏ Sometimes	❏ All the time
Was prepared for sessions:	❏ No	❏ Sometimes	❏ All the time
Used examples to get ideas across:	❏ No	❏ Sometimes	❏ All the time
Used exercises in sessions:	❏ No	❏ Sometimes	❏ All the time
Made material easy to understand:	❏ No	❏ Sometimes	❏ All the time
Helped group to talk and share	❏ No	❏ Sometimes	❏ All the time
Listened to group members:	❏ No	❏ Sometimes	❏ All the time
Showed respect to group members:	❏ No	❏ Sometimes	❏ All the time
Expects group members to change:	❏ No	❏ Sometimes	❏ All the time

6. Comments and notes:

_____

_____

_____

_____

CLIENT RIGHTS STATEMENT - SAMPLE

As a client in Driving With CARE (DWC): Strategies for Responsible Living and Change, you have certain rights. First, you need to know that a qualified provider may consult with other experts on treatment issues. You are encouraged to discuss your progress in this program at any time with your provider. If you are court ordered to attend this program, you may not be able to end this program without permission of the Probation Department that made the referral.

You are entitled to receive information about the methods and approaches of the program. You will be an active participant in the development of your treatment service plan. You may also seek consultation from another expert regarding the appropriateness of this program for you.

You need to know that the information you give during this program is legally confidential except as required by law. This confidentiality is regulated by state law, and for individuals in substance abuse programs, also by Federal law. Information about your treatment and your case can only be release upon your written request. It may be that you have been ordered to attend this program and it may be a condition of probation, parole or community corrections placement. If this the case, and if there is a condition that a progress report must be sent to your court supervisor (e.g., probation officer) then you still must sign a written consent for such information to be released. Your provider will provide a consent form for you.

There are also exceptions to the law of confidentiality. These exceptions are as follows: if there is a "threat of harm to self or others," the person is of imminent danger to self or others, there is a suspicion of child abuse or if an individual is considered to be gravely mentally disabled. In these cases, a provider, by professional ethics and State Statutes, is obligated to protect the individual or others. In any situation where child abuse is suspected by a provider or other professional person, that suspicion must be reported to the Department of Social Services in the county where the abuse is suspected.

Sexual contact between a client and provider is not a part of any recognized therapy or rehabilitation and is never seen as acceptable under any circumstance or condition. Sexual intimacy between client and provider is illegal and should be reported to the appropriate grievance or professional licensing authority.

I have been informed of my provider's professional credentials, training and experience. I have also read the above information and understand my rights as a client.

_____   _____
Client Signature   Date

_____   _____
Provider Name   Date

CONSENT FOR PROGRAM INVOLVEMENT - SAMPLE

I agree to take part in the Driving With CARE (DWC): Strategies for Responsible Living and Change program. I understand that this program can range from six weeks (for Level I Education, one two-hour session per week) to 13 months (for DWC Education and Treatment) in length.

I understand that all programs of this type are not exact sciences, and that not everyone is helped by these programs. It is known that programs set up to help people with substance abuse problems and impaired driving history have a greater chance of being successful when the client is willing to fully take part in the program.

I have been fully informed about my right to confidentiality and the exceptions to that right. I have also been informed of the ground rules and guidelines of this program and I have gone over these with my provider. My signature below is my seal for consent to be part of this program.

_____   _____
Client Signature   Date

_____   _____
Providers Signature   Date

_____
Program Name

CONSENT FOR RELEASE OF CONFIDENTIAL INFORMATION - SAMPLE

I,_____ hereby consent to communication between
(Name of Client)

_____and
(Name of agency providing Driving With CARE program)

_____
(court, probation, parole, and/or other agency)

Under this consent for release of confidential information, the above client agrees that the following information may be release to the above named agency or agencies:

information about my assessment, my attendance and progress in the program, my cooperation with the program, any violation of the terms of my probation or court requirements, if I drive without a valid driver's license, and if I attend the program while under the influence of alcohol or other drugs.

I also consent to release the following information to the above agency or agencies:

_____

_____

_____

I understand that this consent will remain in effect and cannot be revoked by me until:

_____There has been a formal and effective termination or revocation of my release from confinement, probation, or parole, or other proceedings under which I was referred into the program, or

_____ Consent is revoked and/or when it expires on the following date_____.

I also understand that any disclosure made is bound by Part 2 of Title 42 of the Code of Federal Regulations governing confidentiality of alcohol and drug abuse records and that recipients of this information may redisclose if only in connection with their official duties. I also release the agency disclosing this information from any and all liability with respect to the release of this information. My signature below provides the authority to release such information.

Name of Client_____

Address of Client_____

Client Signature_____ Date_____

Witness Signature_____ Date_____

FULL DISCLOSURE STATEMENT - SAMPLE

PHIL JONES, M.A.
CERTIFIED ADDICTIONS COUNSELOR III

Mr. Smith is an addictions counselor with ABX Treatment Center in Denver, Colorado. He has a Bachelor's Degree in Criminal Justice from the University of Maine and a Master's Degree in Counseling from Northern Colorado University. He has worked in the field of addictions for 17 years. His major fields of interest are impaired driving offender treatment and psychosocial problems of impaired driving offenders.

Mr. Smith takes a client centered and cognitive behavioral orientation in counseling. He sees alcoholism and drug addiction as having many causes, including social, psychological and physical. He also holds that social and biological genetics are important factors in the development of a substance abuse problem. He sees the importance of assuming the roles of therapist and correctional specialist in working with impaired driving offenders.

Mr. Smith has special training in the areas of stress management, relaxation therapy, treatment of depression, education and treatment of the impaired driving offender, substance abuse problems, cognitive behavioral approaches and motivational interviewing. He also has specialized training and experience in working with juvenile justice clients.

He is a member of the association of Substance Abuse Counselors of Texas, the American Corrections Association and the National Association of Alcoholism and Drug Abuse Counselors.

Client Name:_____

Client Signature_____ Date_____

Provider Name:_____

Provider Signature_____ Date_____

NOTICE OF FEDERAL REQUIREMENTS REGARDING CONFIDENTIALITY OF ALCOHOL AND DRUG ABUSE PATIENT RECORDS

The confidentiality of alcohol and drug abuse patient records maintained by this program is protected by Federal Law and Regulations. Generally, the program may not say to a person outside the program that a client attends the program, or disclose any information identifying a client as an alcohol or drug abuser unless:

- The client consents in writing;

- The disclosure is allowed by a court order, or;

- The disclosure is made to medical personnel in a medical emergency or to qualified personnel for research, audit or program evaluation.

Violation of the federal law and regulations by a program is a crime. Suspected violations may be reported to appropriate authorities in accordance with federal regulations.

Federal law and regulations do not protect any information about a crime committed by a client either at the program or against any person who works for the program or about any threat to commit such a crime.

Federal laws and regulations do not protect any information about suspected child abuse or neglect from being reported under State law to appropriate State or local authorities (See 42 U.S.C. 290dd-3 and 42 U.S.C 290ee-3 for Federal laws and 42 CFR Part 2 for Federal regulations).

Client Name_____

Client Address_____

Client Signature_____ Date_____

Witness Signature_____ Date_____

PROVIDER EVALUATION SUMMARY (PES)

PROVIDER NAME_____ DATE _____ DWC PROGRAM_____

Rate your presentation of Driving With CARE (DWC) using the following questions.

1. Overall, did clients understand the ideas and material presented in DWC.

   ❏ No, not at all.
   ❏ Yes, somewhat.
   ❏ Yes, most of the ideas and material.
   ❏ All of the ideas and material.

2. Will clients be able to apply what they learned in DWC to prevent impaired driving recidivism?

   ❏ No, not at all.
   ❏ Yes, somewhat.
   ❏ Most of what they learned.
   ❏ All of what they learned.

3. Now, rate yourself on the following:

Started sessions on time:	❏ No	❏ Sometimes	❏ All the time
Was prepared for sessions:	❏ No	❏ Sometimes	❏ All the time
Used examples to get ideas across:	❏ No	❏ Sometimes	❏ All the time
Used exercises in sessions:	❏ No	❏ Sometimes	❏ All the time
Made material easy to understand:	❏ No	❏ Sometimes	❏ All the time
Helped group to talk and share:	❏ No	❏ Sometimes	❏ All the time
Listened to group members:	❏ No	❏ Sometimes	❏ All the time
Showed respect to group members:	❏ No	❏ Sometimes	❏ All the time
Expects group members to change:	❏ No	❏ Sometimes	❏ All the time
Satisfied with your performance:	❏ No	❏ Sometimes	❏ All the time

4. Now, rate the group's response to the session:

Group was attentive:	❏ No	❏ Sometimes	❏ All the time
Group showing good interaction:	❏ No	❏ Sometimes	❏ All the time
Most members participated:	❏ No	❏ Sometimes	❏ All the time
Members had a positive attitude:	❏ No	❏ Sometimes	❏ All the time
Satisfied with your performance:	❏ No	❏ Sometimes	❏ All the time
Materials appropriate for group:	❏ No	❏ Sometimes	❏ All the time

5. Now, rate the DWC sessions as to how difficult versus how easy they are to present.
   ❏ Very difficult ❏ Somewhat difficult ❏ Somewhat easy ❏ Very easy

6. Overall, what has been the clients' response to the DWC programs?
   ❏ Very poor ❏ Poor ❏ Fair ❏ Good ❏ Very good